(b) leads to a result which is manifestly absurd or unreasonable.

The preparatory works, or travaux préparatoires, include but are not limited to records of negotiations and discussions as well as earlier drafts providing insight into the process of creating a treaty.[26] Circumstances, however, are historic developments and contemporary conditions that influenced its conclusion.[27] Article 32 VCLT entails no exhaustive list of supplementary materials that can be used for interpretation (hence the wording '*including*'). Instead, all documents and facts that give insights into a treaty's intended meaning can be means of interpretation pursuant to Article 32 VCLT[28] such as declarations, unilateral behaviour, and all other instruments of information that are related to the treaty.[29] Even though supplementary means of interpretation are deemed less indicative of the final agreement than the primary rules under Article 31 VCLT, they can be an essential factor in treaty interpretation. Pursuant to Article 32 VCLT, supplementary means can be employed to determine the meaning of a treaty provision if the norm would otherwise be ambiguous[30] or to confirm the meaning found by methods mentioned in Article 31 VCLT.[31] Therefore, after applying the latter, historical documents and other supplementary materials can be examined and used in the interpretation process in any case. If these means do not question the previous interpretation result, they are still used for confirming the true meaning of the law and reinforcing the interpretation result that has already been deemed correct.[32] If the supplementary materials that are originally consulted merely for confirmation imply a different interpretation than what was found by applying Article 31 VCLT, the previously upheld meaning of the law becomes ambiguous. It now depends on the weighing of different interpretation methods, including the historical method, to determine a reasonable meaning. As a consequence, the means of interpretation in Article 32 VCLT can always be included in the process of doing so. If they are in accordance with the other methods, they merely confirm the interpretation result, however, by suggesting another reading of the law, they can lead to new conclusions in every legal interpretation.[33]

---

26. Chang-fa Lo, *Treaty Interpretation under the Vienna Convention on the Law of Treaties* 229 (Springer Singapore 1st ed. 2017).
27. Humphrey Waldock, *Third Report on the Law of Treaties*, Yearbook of the International Law Commission 59 (Document A/CN.4/167 and Add.1-3 ed. 1964).
28. Oliver Dörr, *Art 32. Supplementary Means of Interpretation, in Vienna Convention on the Law of Treaties* 627 (Oliver Dörr & Kirsten Schmalenbach eds, Springer Berlin Heidelberg 2018).
29. *Ibid. See also* Mark E. Villiger, *Commentary on the 1969 Vienna Convention on the Law of Treaties* 445 et seq. (Martinus Nijhoff Publishers 2009). This is also true for the OECD or UN Commentary if they are not already part of the travaux préparatoires or to be considered under Art. 31 VCLT; cf. Petrus Johann Hattingh, *The Interpretation of Bilateral Tax Treaties: Changing Tax Law – Unchanging Treaty Obligations?* 214 et seq. (University of Cambridge 2021).
30. *See* WTO case WT/DS285/AB/R, para. 195; Dörr, *Art 31. General Rule of Interpretation, in Vienna Convention on the Law of Treaties*, *supra* n. 18, at 631.
31. Makane Moïse Mbengue, *Rules of Interpretation (Article 32 of the Vienna Convention on the Law of Treaties)*, 31 ICSID Review 406 (2016) https://doi.org/10.1093/icsidreview/siw004.
32. For example, *LaGrand (Germany v. United States of America)* ICJ Rep (2001) 466, para. 77.
33. Dörr, *Art 31. General Rule of Interpretation, in Vienna Convention on the Law of Treaties*, *supra* n. 18, at 629.

What further demonstrates that the drafters of the VCLT were in no way opposed to using historical documents for interpretation is the fact that the role of such documents was the only part of the interpretation rules on which there was a substantial debate at the Vienna Conference in 1969.[34] Hence, the relation between Articles 31 and 32 VCLT is not as hierarchical as it might initially seem. By reading the two provisions together, it becomes apparent that the VCLT does not impose a strict process of interpretation that would prevent a diligent practitioner from coming to the most reasonable conclusion via standard interpretation methods. Rather, it promotes the idea of interpretation constituting a single combined operation. In a practical case, the relevance of supplementary means will depend on their quality, accessibility, clarity, and consistency with other means of interpretation.[35] The interpretation rules introduce the interpretation methods in a general manner and allow for their simultaneous application without forcing a certain order or hierarchy.

3 A COMPARISON TO THE INTERPRETATION METHODS OF THE CJEU

As Article 31 and Article 32 VCLT encompass all methods that are typically used for interpretation and offer significant flexibility in their application, the question arises of how interpretation could be regulated differently. In the realm of international, respectively supranational law, it is most prominently the Court of Justice of the European Union (CJEU) that interprets law autonomously without reference to the VCLT.[36] It must be stated that the CJEU's interpretation methods are subject to ongoing and extensive debate with a history of more than sixty years.[37] For the purposes of this chapter, which is to compare and contrast the CJEU interpretation of European Union (EU) primary law[38] with Articles 31 and 32 VCLT, only the main points of this debate will be featured.

Even though the EU and, before that, the European Community, was founded on international treaties between sovereign states, the CJEU views Union law as a legal order sui generis and does not see a need to reference the VCLT for interpreting it.

34. Richard K. Gardiner, *Treaty Interpretation* 348 et seq. (Oxford University Press 2d ed. 2015).
35. Dörr, *Art 32. Supplementary Means of Interpretation, in Vienna Convention on the Law of Treaties, supra* n. 28, at 624.
36. Werner Schroeder, *Die Auslegung des EU-Rechts*, 44 Juristische Schulung 181 (2004).
37. *See* already *Zehn Jahre Rechtsprechung des Gerichtshofs der Europäischen Union. Europäische Arbeitstagung Köln vom 24. Bis 26. April 1963* 177-200 (Karl Carstens & Bodo Börner eds, Carl Heymanns Verlag 1965). *See also* Stefan Vogenauer, *Die Auslegung von Gesetzen in England und auf dem Kontinent: Eine Vergleichende Untersuchung der Rechtsprechung und ihrer Historischen Grundlagen* (Mohr Siebeck 2001); Schroeder, *supra* n. 36; Walter Georg Leisner, *Die Subjektiv-Historische Auslegung des Gemeinschaftsrechts. Der 'Wille des Gesetzgebers' in der Judikatur des EuGH*, 42 EuR (2007) Rudolf Streinz, *Interpretation and Development of EU Primary Law, in European Legal Methodology* (Karl Riesenhuber & Fritz Thyssen-Stiftung eds, Intersentia 2017).
38. As EU primary law is based on international treaties, it is more comparable to the scope of the VCLT than secondary law that the CJEU interprets, in part, differently from primary law. *See* Karl Riesenhuber, *Interpretation of EU Secondary Law, in European Legal Methodology* (Karl Riesenhuber & Fritz Thyssen-Stiftung eds, Intersentia 2017).

Rather, the European treaties create a foundation for a new legal community.[39] From there, the CJEU monopolizes interpreting Union law. This is also relevant with respect to other international institutions as the CJEU is not willing to share its authority to interpret EU law with other courts.[40] Most prominently, the CJEU rejects the accession of the EU to the European Convention on Human Rights (ECHR) for this reason.[41]

Now that the autonomous and exclusive interpretation of Union law by the CJEU is established, it remains to be examined what methods the CJEU exactly uses for doing so. In its landmark decision in *Van Gend en Loos*, the CJEU states the following: 'To ascertain whether the provisions of an international treaty extend so far in their effects it is necessary to consider the spirit, the general scheme and the wording of those provisions.'[42] Later, it reaches the conclusion: 'It follows from the foregoing considerations that, according to the spirit, the general scheme and the wording of the Treaty, Article 12 must be interpreted as producing direct effects and creating individual rights which national courts must protect.'[43] Although not exhaustive for later case law, this decision can function as an apt exemplification of the interpretation methods employed by the CJEU. Therein, three major interpretative methods are mentioned: the spirit of the law relating to teleological interpretation; the general scheme translatable to the systematic interpretation; and the wording, i.e., grammatical interpretation.

Unsurprisingly, the grammatical interpretation serves as the point of departure for interpretation in many cases and also for the CJEU. There are decisions, however, in which the grammatical interpretation is not a major factor at all but is overshadowed entirely by teleological interpretation.[44] For example, the CJEU decided in favour of the admissibility of actions for annulment by the European Parliament even at the time when Article 230 EC did not include any indication of that in its wording.[45] The wording is certainly not the outer boundary of interpretation for the CJEU as it subsumes legal reasoning that could be considered judicial development under its definition of interpretation[46] akin to the French legal tradition.[47]

Similarly, the systematic interpretation of the law as determining the meaning of one term or provision in the context of one article or the entire legal system can be a deciding factor in some cases but can also be pushed into the background. For example,

39. Most prominently, CJEU 5.2.1963, Van Gend en Loos, C-26/62, ECLI:EU:C:1963:1; and more explicitly in establishing a separate legal order, CJEU 15.7.1964, Costa/E.N.E.L., C-6/64, ECLI:EU:C:1964:66.
40. For more details on the relation between the CJEU and other international court systems, *see*, for example, Francisco de Abreu Duarte, *'But the Last Word Is Ours': The Monopoly of Jurisdiction of the Court of Justice of the European Union in Light of the Investment Court System*, 1 Jean Monnet Working Paper (2018); Steffen Hindelang, *Circumventing Primacy of EU Law and the CJEUs Judicial Monopoly by Resorting to Dispute Resolution Mechanisms Provided for in Inter-Se Treaties? The Case of Intra-EU Investment Arbitration*, 39 LEIE (2012) https://doi.org/10.54648/leie2012012.
41. CJEU 18.12.2014, Opinion 2/13, ECLI:EU:C:2014:2454.
42. *Supra* n. 37, CJEU 5.2.1963, *Van Gend en Loos*, C-26/62, ECLI:EU:C:1963:1, 11.
43. *Supra* n. 37, CJEU 5.2.1963, *Van Gend en Loos*, C-26/62, ECLI:EU:C:1963:1, 13.
44. Schroeder, *supra* n. 36, at 182.
45. CJEU 23.4.1986, *Les Verts*, 294/83, ECLI:EU:C:1986:166.
46. Schroeder, *supra* n. 36, at 184.
47. For the German concept of 'Wortlautgrenze', however, *see* Matthias Klatt, *Making the Law Explicit: The Normativity of Legal Argumentation* (Hart Pub 2008).

the CJEU views a directive to be directly applicable to the benefit of the individual if the Member State did not implement it in time even though the system of two main types of European law – regulations and directives – would indicate that the failure to comply with the goals of the directive only effectuates legal consequences between the Member State and the EU.[48] Systematic interpretation is vital in other areas, however. For example, the general system of EU law is cited by the CJEU to establish EU competences.[49] A difference between CJEU interpretation and the context pursuant to Article 31 VCLT concerns the relevance of subsequent agreements and practices. According to Article 31(3) lit. a and lit. b VCLT, subsequent agreements and subsequent practices of the states are to be taken into account together with the context for interpreting a treaty.[50] The CJEU, however, does not grant the Member States the power of authentic interpretation as it controls their compliance with the treaties on which they have agreed. In this matter, no influence is granted by the CJEU to the parties of European treaties by subsequently agreeing on a preferred interpretation.[51] This is not to say that the context after the VCLT is incomparable to the systematic interpretation by the CJEU as a whole. Rather, the CJEU has adjusted the context as it sees appropriate for the special requirements of Union law. As shall be seen, this can also be done in the case of tax treaty interpretation.

Crucially, the teleological interpretation serves as the basis for many CJEU decisions.[52] The prevalence of EU law over national law, for instance, is derived from the spirit of the law and is deemed necessary for the object and purpose of the EC treaty.[53] It is conspicuous that the CJEU cites the spirit of the law before the scheme and the wording of provisions in the abovementioned quote regarding *Van Gend en Loos*, indicating an emphasis on teleological interpretation. Even though the order of enumeration does not necessarily equate to the relative importance of the terms, it is notable that this is the exact opposite of the wording in Article 31(1) VCLT. There, the ordinary meaning is mentioned before the context, and the object and purpose are only mentioned at the end of the sentence.

One reason for the prevalence of teleological interpretation in CJEU case law is the formulation of goals of the EU in Article 2 Treaty of the European Union (TEU) that tie the actions of the EU to a political and economic program and reveal the overarching spirit of Union law. The CJEU confirms this by stating that every provision must be placed in its context and interpreted in light of the Community (now Union) law as a whole with regard to the objectives thereof.[54] Singular provisions are not an end in itself but a means to the end of the *ius commune*.[55] The importance of teleological interpretation becomes even more apparent when considering the dynamism of the

48. CJEU 4.12.1974, *Yvonne van Duyn*, 41-74, ECLI:EU:C:1974:133. *See also* Schroeder, *supra* n. 36, at 183.
49. CJEU 31.3.1971, *Commission v. Council*, C-22/70, ECLI:EU:C:1971:32, at 12; *see also* Streinz, *supra* n. 37, at 161.
50. For more details, *see* s. 5 of this chapter.
51. Schroeder, *supra* n. 36, at 181.
52. *Ibid.*, at 182.
53. *Supra* n. 35, CJEU 15.7.1964, *Costa/E.N.E.L.*, C-6/64, ECLI:EU:C:1964:66.
54. CJEU 6.10.1982, *CILFIT*, C-283/81, ECLI:EU:C:1982:335, at 20.
55. CJEU, 14.12.1991, Opinion 1/91, ECLI:EU:C:1991:490, at 17 et seq.

objectives of the Union as Article 1 TEU declares the aim of 'creating an ever closer union among the peoples of Europe'.[56] Teleological interpretation further takes the form of the principle of effectiveness, also referred to as *ut res magis valeat quam pereat,* which is pivotal in the CJEU's methodology.[57] Norms are to be interpreted in a way that their *effet utile* is ensured. Arguments of effectiveness are thus central for advancing the object and purpose of EU law.[58] While not a unique feature of the interpretation of EU law, the principle of effectiveness certainly takes on a much more prominent role than in public international law where it is regarded as a concept related to the object and purpose of Article 31 VCLT.[59]

Attention is drawn to the absence of the historical interpretation method in the programmatic dictum of the CJEU in *Van Gend en Loos.*[60] Indeed, the examination of the legislator's intention by reference to preparatory works, explanatory statements, and other historical documents has little tradition in community law. The critical reason for this used to be the practical impossibility as many preparatory documents for EU law were classified.[61] However, missing opportunities alone could not warrant a categorical exclusion of the subjective-historical method.[62] In any case, ever since the drafting of the Treaty of Lisbon, the lack of documents is no longer an issue.[63] Even though the CJEU does not recognize the importance of the historical method in a programmatic statement, it is used on several occasions.[64] Still, as the CJEU calls for a dynamic interpretation of the law, a reference to the historical will of the legislature is less appealing than a teleological enquiry with the principle of effectiveness in mind.[65]

While several interpretative specifications can be observed in CJEU case law, the methods used are generally the same as those introduced in Articles 31 and 32 VCLT.[66] The differences can be attributed to the CJEU nuancing generally accepted interpretation rules to the needs of the specific use case, specifically primary Union law. As mentioned previously, the interpretative methods as conceived in the VCLT place more emphasis on the intention of the parties than the CJEU which does not view the Member States as competent for authentic interpretation. The VCLT, however, provides possibilities for the states to form agreements in connection with the conclusion of the treaty (Article 31(2) VCLT) and even subsequent agreements and practices

56. Streinz, *supra* n. 37, at 163.
57. Walter Georg Leisner, *Die Subjektiv-Historische Auslegung des Gemeinschaftsrechts. Der 'Wille des Gesetzgebers' in der Judikatur des EuGH,* EuR 694 (2007).
58. *See,* for example, CJEU 19.1.1982, *Becker,* C-8/81, ECLI:EU:C:1982:7, at 23; CJEU 19.11.1991, *Francovich,* C-6/90 and C-9/90, ECLI:EU:C:1991:428, at 33; CJEU 22.11.2005, *Mangold,* C-144/04, ECLI:EU:C:2005:709.
59. *See* Dörr, *Art 31. General Rule of Interpretation, in Vienna Convention on the Law of Treaties, supra* n. 18, at 578 et seq.
60. *Supra* n. 35, CJEU 5.2.1963, *Van Gend en Loos,* C-26/62, ECLI:EU:C:1963:1, 11.
61. Manfred Zuleeg, *Die Auslegung des Europäischen Gemeinschaftsrechts,* 4 EuR 101 (1969).
62. Cf. in this respect Georg Leisner, *supra* n. 37, at 686 et seq.
63. Streinz, *supra* n. 37, at 163 et seq.
64. CJEU 27.11.2012, *Pringle,* C-370/12, ECLI:EU:C:2012:756, at 135-37; CJEU 3.10.2013, Inuit Tapiriit Kanatami, C-583/11, ECLI:EU:C:2013:625, at 59 et seq.
65. *See* already Zuleeg, *supra* n. 61, at 108; *See also* Streinz, *supra* n. 37, at 162-164.
66. The CJEU additionally uses comparative law as a separate interpretative method, especially for the autonomous development of general legal principles of Union law pursuant to Art. 6(3) TEU, *see* Streinz, *supra* n. 37, at 164 et seq.

(Article 31(3) VCLT).[67] Furthermore, even though no explicit ranking exists in the CJEU's methods,[68] the historical method tends to bear less weight for the interpretative result. This is reminiscent of the formulation in Article 32 VCLT described as 'supplementary means of interpretation'. However, the reasons for this treatment vary. While the dynamism and the emphasis on effectiveness as well as the former unavailability of historical documents in EU law prompted the CJEU to rely on other methods, the supplementary means of Article 32 VCLT were simply regarded as less reliable for determining the consensus between the contracting parties.[69] In contrast, the CJEU gives more weight to the teleological interpretation in order to advance EU objectives. Thus, it is the objective- and integration-driven conception of the EU that primarily causes the CJEU interpretation to adjust the rules stipulated in the VCLT. Other than that, however, the CJEU's interpretative practice is largely in accordance with the VCLT rules. This is not surprising as the VCLT rules were meant to codify the generally accepted interpretation methods. Even though the CJEU does not refer to the VCLT for interpretation, the rules are flexible enough such that the CJEU interpretation of Union law could be regarded as a special application of them. After all, the VCLT does not dictate a certain weighing of methods or their linear application which gives courts the discretion to apply them in the most beneficial way for elucidating the meaning of the norm.

4 THE APPLICABILITY OF VCLT INTERPRETATION RULES TO DTCs

The VCLT as a multilateral treaty possesses the same legal authority as other international treaties, including double tax conventions (DTCs). While Article 1 VCLT states that the VCLT shall apply to all international treaties between states, it does not legally stand above bilateral or multilateral tax treaties.[70] This is a consequence of the largely non-existent normative hierarchy in international law resulting in an equal rank of all international law treaties but the provisions constituting *jus cogens* owed to the international community as a whole (obligations *erga omnes*)[71] that are irrelevant for the purposes of tax treaty law and interpretation rules. It is therefore conceivable that two parties choose not to apply the VCLT interpretation rules by agreeing to different ones. The parties to the treaty could achieve this by explicitly excluding the application

67. *See also* s. 5 of this chapter.
68. Streinz, *supra* n. 37, at 165.
69. Gustavo Weiss de Resende, *Supplementary Means of Interpretation (Article 32 VCLT) and Tax Treaty Interpretation*, Chapter 8 in this book.
70. Lang, *Can Law Regulate Its Own Interpretation? Relevance and Meaning of Articles 31-33 of the Vienna Convention of the Law of Treaties (VCLT) and Article 3 para. 2 of the Model Convention of the Organisation of Economic Co-Operation and Development (OECD MC) for the Interpretation of Double-Taxation Conventions, in Research Handbook on International Taxation, supra* n. 8, at 176.
71. Cf. Alexander Orakhelashvili, *Peremptory Norms in International Law* (Oxford University Press 2006); *See also Barcelona Traction*, ICJ Reports (1970) 3, 32. *See also* ILC, *Draft Conclusions on Identification and Legal Consequences of Peremptory Norms of General International Law (jus cogens)* (2022).

of Articles 31 and 32 VCLT for the purpose of the treaty. However, such treaties have – to the best of the authors' knowledge – never been discussed in tax literature or in case law and hence are not practically relevant to international tax law.[72] Alternatively, the parties can exclude the rules by introducing different ones in the DTC that prove to be incompatible with Article 31 and Article 32 VCLT without referring to them.[73] Most notably, applying the VCLT rules of interpretation can even be prevented or modified implicitly without introducing new interpretation rules if the special nature of the subject matter so requires.[74] The lack of hierarchy in international law affords the possibility of freely choosing suitable interpretative rules for any international treaty. This means that subjects of international law can decide for every treaty they agree on if and in how far the VCLT interpretation rules shall be taken for reference. As the treaty parties do not always do so explicitly, it is the interpreter's obligation to determine the relevant interpretation rules.

The lack of normative hierarchy in international law also applies to the CIL. Even though treaties are regularly drafted to replace it,[75] it is also acknowledged that treaty law may exist simultaneously with it on the same subject matter.[76] Indeed, it is recognized that, though not true for all provisions of the VCLT, Article 31 and Article 32 VCLT constitute CIL as they are generally accepted rules for interpretation.[77] Since a common state practice and the belief of subjects of international law to be obligated to the rules (*opinion iuris*) are necessary for a norm to be recognized as CIL, it shows the wide proliferation of the interpretation rules formulated in the VCLT.[78] Hence, they can also be relevant between states that have not ratified the VCLT as a treaty as long as they are not persistent objectors to the interpretation rules having openly opposed

72. Lang, *Can Law Regulate Its Own Interpretation? Relevance and Meaning of Articles 31-33 of the Vienna Convention of the Law of Treaties (VCLT) and Article 3 Para. 2 of the Model Convention of the Organisation of Economic Co-Operation and Development (OECD MC) for the Interpretation of Double-Taxation Conventions, in Research Handbook on International Taxation, supra* n. 8, at 177.
73. With respect to Art. 3(2) OECD MC as *lex specialis, see* Franciscus Antonius Engelen, *Interpretation of Tax Treaties under International Law* 549 (IBFD 2004); Edwin van der Bruggen, *Unless the Vienna Convention Otherwise Requires: Notes on the Relationship Between Article 3(2) of the OECD Model Tax Convention and Articles 31 and 32 of the Vienna Convention on the Law of Treaties*, 43 E.T. 147 (2003).
74. Lang, *Can Law Regulate Its Own Interpretation? Relevance and Meaning of Articles 31-33 of the Vienna Convention of the Law of Treaties (VCLT) and Article 3 Para. 2 of the Model Convention of the Organisation of Economic Co-Operation and Development (OECD MC) for the Interpretation of Double-Taxation Conventions, in Research Handbook on International Taxation, supra* n. 8, at 177.
75. R.R. Baxter, *Multilateral Treaties as Evidence of Customary International Law*, 41 British Yearbook of International Law 275 (1965).
76. *Nicaragua v. US*, ICJ Reports (1986) 14, 95.
77. *Inter alia*, ICJ Arbitral Award (*Guinea-Bissau v. Senegal*) ICJ Rep (1991) 53, para. 48; ICJ Territorial Dispute (*Libya v. Chad*) ICJ Rep (1994) 6, para. 41; *see also* Santiago Torres Bernárdez, *Interpretation of Treaties by the International Court of Justice Following the Adoption of the 1969 Vienna Convention on the Law of Treaties, in Festschrift Seidl-Hohenveldern* 721 et seq. (Gerhard Hafner ed., Kluwer 1998).
78. For more details on the CIL as a source of international law, *see* Malcolm Shaw, *International Law* 58-78 (Cambridge University Press 9th ed. 2021).

them from the ignition of the custom.[79] DTCs, like all international treaties, are not subsidiary to the CIL either, Articles 31 and 32 VCLT have equal priority as provisions in DTCs just as any other VCLT rule.[80] Nothing prevents states from therefore using other interpretation rules than those codified in the VCLT in their bilateral (or multilateral) tax treaties.

CIL as a source of international law also allows for the existence of other interpretation principles that are not given positive expression in the VCLT or any other international treaty. The principle of *in dubio mitius* was previously considered a contender and was cited in international law to favour the sovereignty of states by strictly interpreting state obligations in international treaties.[81] However, since the drafting of the VCLT interpretation rules, the focus lies much more on the effective interpretation of international treaties but on a restrictive understanding of obligations.[82] The principle is therefore seldom cited in international cases and is not granted the status of CIL.[83] Furthermore, *contra preferentem* is a widespread rule to interpret a norm against the interest of the drafting party provided that unclear wording is causing ambiguity. The doctrine is used when two parties have opposing interests and one of them is responsible for formulating the contested norm.[84] The *contra preferentem* rule is codified in some international documents, especially regarding international private law, such as in Article 5:103 in the Principles of European Contract Law. However, the rule cannot be considered CIL as the drafting of a treaty or of singular norms is usually the responsibility of all participating states.[85] Moreover, as DTCs regularly have symmetric legal effects on the taxing rights of both states, *contra preferentem* is not apt to serve as an interpretation rule for tax treaties. Additionally, the disputed rule of restrictive interpretation of exceptions is occasionally mentioned as an independent means of interpretation.[86] The rule has been contested because the somewhat arbitrary formulation of a rule as an exception alone cannot determine how frequently it shall be applied.[87] Last, the principle of effectiveness (*ut res magis valeat quam pereat*) is frequently used in public international law as a means of interpretation.[88] It is aimed at facilitating the purpose of the law to the highest degree in its context and leaving no part of the norm without meaning. Therefore, the principle of effectiveness is cohesively related to the object and purpose as an interpretation method under Article 31

79. For the origin of the persistent objector rules, *see Anglo-Norwegian Fisheries*, ICJ Reports (1951), at 116; 18 ILR, at 86.
80. Antonius Engelen, *supra* n. 73, at 47.
81. *See*, for example, *Free Zones of Upper Savoy and the District of Gex* PCIJ Ser A/B No. 46 (1932), 167; WTO Appellate Body *EC–Hormones* WT/DS26 and DS48/AB/R (1998), para. 165.
82. ICJ *Dispute Regarding Navigational and Related Rights* ICJ Rep (2009) 213, para. 48.
83. Dörr, *Art 31. General Rule of Interpretation, in Vienna Convention on the Law of Treaties, supra* n. 18, at 578.
84. *Ibid.*, at 579.
85. Hersch Lauterpacht, *Restrictive Interpretation and the Principle of Effectiveness in the Interpretation of Treaties, in British Year Book of International Law* 64 (1949).
86. *See*, for example, ECtHR *Litwa v. Poland* App No. 26629/95, ECHR 2000-III, para. 59.
87. Michael Lang, *Tax Treaty Interpretation and Art 3 (2) OECD Model Convention, in Tax Treaty Interpretation in Light of the Vienna Convention on the Law of Treaties*, s. III. 3 (Robert Danon et al. eds, IBFD), forthcoming.
88. *Inter alia*, ICJ *Fisheries Jurisdiction (Spain v. Canada)* ICJ Rep (1998) 432, para. 52.

VCLT and is an important but not independent factor in the interpretation of treaties.[89] Interpretation might finally also show that a specific provision has just clarifying or signalling effects.[90] Even rules of the VCLT, like its Article 26, might turn out to be redundant.[91]

It remains to be said that, in international law, the principles of *lex posterior* and *lex specialis* are employed to determine the priority of two conflicting rules in cases of doubt. The lex posterior rule is codified in Article 30(3) VCLT itself: '3. When all the parties to the earlier treaty are parties also to the later treaty but the earlier treaty is not terminated or suspended in operation under article 59, the earlier treaty applies only to the extent that its provisions are compatible with those of the later treaty.'

The principle of *lex specialis derogat legi generali,* however, states that the rule whose scope is a subset of a more general rule is given priority.[92] It then needs further analysis to determine whether the *lex posterior* should derogate the older, more special provision or if the newer rule was created for general cases, and the older *lex specialis* should still be applied as an exception to the later norm.[93] However, these rules of doubt are not needed to determine whether the VCLT provisions are applicable to a specific tax treaty or not. In case of a conflict, *lex specialis* and *lex posterior* are not an automatism that leads to the applicable rule as it can be dubious which norm is the more special one in which instance and if the later provision was meant to be in conflict with an earlier rule. Rather, the general interpretative methods must be applied to ascertain the meaning of the provisions in the DTC; as stated before, interpretation can never be a mechanistic process but must consider all relevant circumstances.[94] Moreover, it has already been established that, due to the lack of hierarchy of international law, the interpretation of each international treaty can be regulated separately without reference to the VCLT. It is therefore a question of interpretation if and in how far the parties to a DTC wanted the VCLT interpretation rules to be applicable for the specific treaty which cannot be solved solely by referring to a conflict rule.

89. Dörr, *Art 31. General Rule of Interpretation, in Vienna Convention on the Law of Treaties, supra* n. 18, at 578 et seq.
90. *See* Michael Lang, *The Signalling Function of Article 29(9) of the OECD Model: The 'Principal Purpose Test'*, 74 Bulletin for International Taxation (2020) https://doi.org/10.59403/3ndvejx.
91. Michael Lang, *Treaty Override und Gemeinschaftsrecht, in Reden zum Andenken an Klaus Vogel* (Moris Lehner ed., Beck 2010).
92. Michael Lang, *Normenkonflikte zwischen den Vorschriften des nationalen Steuerrechts und der Doppelbesteuerungsabkommen, in Festschrift für Jürgen Lüdicke* 439 (Dietmar Gosch et al. eds, C.H.Beck 2019).
93. *See* Bydlinski, *supra* n. 23, at 572-574 for a theoretical analysis. In favour of *lex posterior* Joost Pauwelyn, *Conflict of Norms in Public International Law: How WTO Law Relates to Other Rules of International Law* 405-409 (Cambridge University Press 2003). In favour of *lex specialis* Jan Neumann, *Die Koordination des WTO-Rechts mit anderen völkerrechtlichen Ordnungen: Konflikte des materiellen Rechts und Konkurrenzen der Streitbeilegung* 90 (Duncker & Humblot 2002); Hans Aufricht, *Supersession of Treaties in International Law,* 37 Cornell L. Rev (1952); with some caveats Michael Reiertsen, *Governing Conflicts of Law: Lex Posterior, Lex Specialis and the Swordfish Case,* 10 Zeitschrift für europarechtliche Studien 405-406 (2007).
94. Lang, *supra* n. 92, at 439-444.

5 THE ADEQUACY OF THE VCLT RULES FOR THE INTERPRETATION OF DTCs IN CONSIDERATION OF ARTICLE 3(2) OECD MC

As every treaty regulates its interpretation - explicitly or implicitly - on its own, thereby accepting, modifying, or even rejecting the VCLT rules, the question arises of whether the VCLT rules are typically adequate for DTCs. Does the special nature of DTCs require interpretation different from the methods conceived by the VCLT? In particular, DTCs modelled after the Model Convention of the Organisation for Economic Co-operation and Development (OECD MC) feature an explicit interpretation rule in Article 3(2) OECD MC that could be regarded as a deviation from the VCLT rules. It reads as follows:

> 2. As regards the application of the Convention at any time by a Contracting State, any term not defined therein shall, unless the context otherwise requires or the competent authorities agree to a different meaning pursuant to the provisions of Article 25, have the meaning that it has at that time under the law of that State for the purposes of the taxes to which the Convention applies, any meaning under the applicable tax laws of that State prevailing over a meaning given to the term under other laws of that State.

As the VCLT rules do not provide a recourse to domestic law by default for interpreting international treaties, Article 3(2) OECD MC initially appears to be incompatible with the VCLT. However, to confirm the conflict between these regulations, Article 3(2) OECD MC needs further analysis; it must be interpreted itself to find it consistent or inconsistent with the VCLT. For the preliminary matter of determining the meaning of Article 3(2) OECD MC, the interpretation methods codified in the VCLT can be employed as the standard for international law. Incompatibility with the DTC cannot be assumed from the outset.

It is clear from the beginning that Article 3(2) OECD MC does not derogate from the VCLT rules for the entirety of the DTC. The provision is only relevant for terms in the DTC not defined therein.[95] For all other interpretational issues, using the VCLT rules is not jeopardized in any case.[96] When interpreting non-defined terms, however, the meaning of Article 3(2) OECD MC is heavily disputed among tax scholars. Crucially, the interpretation depends on the understanding of the phrase ‘unless the context otherwise requires’ which has given rise to vastly different theories revolving around it.[97]

---

95. Lang, *Tax Treaty Interpretation and Art 3 (2) OECD Model Convention, in Tax Treaty Interpretation in Light of the Vienna Convention on the Law of Treaties, supra* n. 87, s. III. 4 forthcoming. In contrast, *see* John F. Avery Jones, *The Interpretation of Tax Treaties With Particular Reference to Article 3(2) Of The OECD Model: I*, 28 B.T.R. at 21 (1982), who argues that domestic law can be employed when non-exhaustive definitions are used in the DTC in order to fully develop the meaning of the term.
96. Michael Lang, *Art. 3 Abs. 2 OECD-MA und die Auslegung von Doppelbesteuerungsabkommen*, 16 IWB at 287 (2011).
97. For a detailed analysis, refer to Michael Lang & Benjamin Beer, *The Relation Between Article 3(2) OECD MC and the Interpretation Rules of the Vienna Convention on the Law of Treaties*, Chapter 11 in this book.

In order to determine the consequences of Article 3(2) OECD MC, the meaning of 'context' as used in the provision must be established first. It has been suggested that considering the wording, it could be identified as the context featured as an interpretation method in Article 31 VCLT.[98] The context pursuant to Article 31(1) VCLT shall therefore be examined more closely. It naturally entails systematic considerations[99] but is extended in Article 31(2) VCLT:

> 2. The context for the purpose of the interpretation of a treaty shall comprise, in addition to the text, including its preamble and annexes:
>
> (a) any agreement relating to the treaty which was made between all the parties in connection with the conclusion of the treaty;
> (b) any instrument which was made by one or more parties in connection with the conclusion of the treaty and accepted by the other parties as an instrument related to the treaty.

Thus, the context of a treaty provision not only refers to the intra-legal system but also contains agreements between the parties that were made in connection to the treaty. Article 31(2) lit. a and lit. b require an agreement loosely in the temporal vicinity of the conclusion of the treaty and a nexus in substance.[100] For tax treaties, this could mean, for example, that the contracting states agree on the interpretation of a term used in the DTC at the time of its conclusion. According to the VCLT, such an agreement is to be considered context. It is important to distinguish the general relevance of interpretation from any binding force for the judiciary or other interpreters. As context, such agreements are only taken into account when juxtaposed with other interpretative methods and can be outweighed. To mandate interpretation, the parties cannot disregard the constitutional requirements of ratification by concluding informal agreements in connection with the treaty. For illustration, the version of the Organisation for Economic Co-operation and Development (OECD) Commentaries that existed at the time of the treaty's conclusion is already sometimes subsumed under Article 31(2) lit. a VCLT in tax literature. This would require a mutual understanding that the Commentaries or a part thereof shall serve as an authentic interpretation for a DTC. It is reasonable to assume that this requirement is met if the parties to it used the exact formulation proposed in the model convention. If the model convention is not followed verbatim, however, it cannot be readily assumed without further evidence that the parties agreed on the meaning stipulated in the Commentaries.[101]

If context as used in Article 3(2) OECD MC was equated with the context in the VCLT, subsequent practices and agreements as evidenced by Article 31(3) VCLT could also be included as they shall be considered together with the context:

---

98. Bernhard Gröhs & Christopher Herbst, *Die Interpretation von Doppelbesteuerungsabkommen als Problem der Auslegung von Völkerrechtlichen Verträgen im Nationalen Recht*, 11 Z.f.V. at 24 (1986).
99. Dörr, *Art 31. General Rule of Interpretation, in Vienna Convention on the Law of Treaties, supra* n. 18, at 582 et seq.
100. *Ibid.*, at 590 et seq.
101. In more detail, *see* Rita Szudoczky & Iris Tschatsch, *The Interpretation of Tax Treaty Terms in Its Context (Article 31 paragraphs 1 and 2 VCLT)*, Chapter 4 in this book.

3. There shall be taken into account, together with the context:

(a) any subsequent agreement between the parties regarding the interpretation of the treaty or the application of its provisions;
(b) any subsequent practice in the application of the treaty which establishes the agreement of the parties regarding its interpretation;
(c) any relevant rules of international law applicable in the relations between the parties.

According to Article 31(3) lit. a VCLT, it initially seems to be possible for the contracting states to influence the interpretation of the DTC by forming a new agreement after concluding the binding treaty. Agreements under Article 31(3) lit. a VCLT do not need to take the form of official amendments of the treaty including the constitutional procedure that comes with it. Rather, a potentially informal agreement between the states suffices.[102] However, these can only be relevant as they indicate the meaning of a treaty provision that it had already from the beginning. Article 31(3) lit. a VCLT does not grant permission to modify the treaty. It is part of the general rule of interpretation.[103]

Furthermore, Article 31(3) lit. b VCLT affirms the relevance of common, subsequent state practices for treaty interpretation.[104] In general, the same standards that have been mentioned in the context of subsequent agreements are also relevant for subsequent practices.[105] In light of the VCLT, subsequent agreements and practices shall be considered together with the context since they are regarded as authentic interpretation rules by the contractors even though they are not issued together with the treaty. In this respect, they are closer to the parties' genuine intentions and are more indicative of the true meaning of the provision than supplementary means of interpretation pursuant to Article 32 VCLT that are deemed less authentic as they were not unambiguously agreed upon.[106]

The relevance of subsequent information for interpretation does not necessarily imply dynamic interpretation. If a static interpretation is embraced, the consideration of subsequent actions of the legislators can only go as far as being informative about the intention of the contracting parties *ab initio*.[107] However, concerns may still arise against the applicability of subsequent agreements and practices in international tax law:

- As a principle, the legal relevance for *ex post* actions of treaty parties for interpretation is not easily warranted. This is especially true for tax treaty law

102. Dörr, *Art 31. General Rule of Interpretation, in Vienna Convention on the Law of Treaties, supra* n. 18, *supra* n. 18, at 593 et seq.
103. *See also* Dominic Krenn & Daniel W. Blum, *Subsequent Agreements and Tax Treaty Interpretation (Art. 31 para. 3 subpara. a VCLT)*, Chapter 6 in this book.
104. *See* United Nations, *Report of the International Law Commission, Seventieth Session A/73/10* 37 (2018).
105. For details, *see* Michael Lang & Eric Coenen, *Subsequent Practices and Tax Treaty Interpretation (Art. 31 para. 3 subpara. b VCLT)*, Chapter 7 in this book.
106. Dörr, *Art 31. General Rule of Interpretation, in Vienna Convention on the Law of Treaties, supra* n. 18, at 593 et seq.
107. *Ibid.*, at 574. *See also* ICJ *Kasikili/Sedudu Island* ICJ Rep (1999) 1045, para. 20.

as international law impacting the rights and obligations of private taxable persons and not only the parties to the treaty themselves.[108] As a consequence, subsequent practices are not allowed to transgress the boundaries of interpretation and step into modification of the law, which is naturally an obscure line.[109] States cannot change the rights and obligations of taxable persons by reinterpreting existing legal contracts after the fact thereby circumventing the due lawmaking process. At the very least, just as agreements in connection with the treaty, subsequent practices and agreements cannot prevail over other means of interpretation but are to be read by the interpreters alongside the entire canon of interpretation methods stipulated in Article 31 and Article 32 VCLT.[110] Any other interpretation of Article 31(3) lit. a and lit. b would allow the administration to dictate the meaning of tax rules to the tax courts.
- From a practical standpoint, there are even more reasons to be cautious with subsequent practices and agreements in tax treaty law. The public authorities applying tax treaty law are, as a general rule, mainly the local tax offices and responsible appellate bodies in each state. They apply tax treaty law as part of the domestic law independently from each other. Due to tax secrecy, it will be very difficult to provide evidence about a consistent practice. Furthermore, if the tax administration's decisions are successfully appealed, a state practice can no longer be regarded as uncontested. Therefore, the concept of subsequent practices seems to have very limited value in tax law.[111]

As has been demonstrated, the context pursuant to Article 31 VCLT is an important aspect of interpretation featuring systematic considerations and agreements in relation to the treaty. However, there is a broad consensus in literature that the term 'context' in Article 3(2) OECD MC must be differentiated from the term used in the VCLT. To begin with, there is no reference to the VCLT rules by the OECD MC which would be unlikely if the context in the OECD MC was supposed to be understood synonymously.[112] More importantly, the secluded application of the context pursuant to Article 31 VCLT would lead to an exclusion of all other means of interpretation from the decision of whether an undefined term requires autonomous interpretation. As a consequence, even the object and purpose of the DTC could not be factored into the decision. Every means of interpretation apart from the context, including principles

108. Michael Lang, *Doppelbesteuerungsabkommen und Innerstaatliches Recht: Die Einordnung von Doppelbesteuerungsabkommen in Die Österreichische Rechtsordnung* 86 et seq. (Orac 1992).
109. Gerhard Hafner, *Subsequent Agreements and Practice: Between Interpretation, Informal Modification, and Formal Amendment, in Treaties and Subsequent Practice* 114 et seq. (Georg Nolte ed., Oxford Univ. Press 2013).
110. Lang, *Can Law Regulate Its Own Interpretation? Relevance and Meaning of Articles 31-33 of the Vienna Convention of the Law of Treaties (VCLT) and Article 3 para. 2 of the Model Convention of the Organisation of Economic Co-Operation and Development (OECD MC) for the Interpretation of Double-Taxation Conventions, in Research handbook on international taxation, supra* n. 8, at 183.
111. *Ibid.*, at 182.
112. *See also* Christian Gloria, *Die Doppelbesteuerungsabkommen der Bundesrepublik Deutschland und die Bedeutung der Lex-Fori-Klausel für ihre Auslegung: Ein Plädoyer für die Auslegung der Doppelbesteuerungsabkommen nach den Regeln Der WVK.*, 31 R.I.W. 976 (1986).

like good faith, would be regarded as contracted out of the DTC by the parties. This, of course, could lead to absurd interpretation results.[113] The VCLT interpretation rules are not meant to be applied separately to reach a conclusion;[114] they only serve the aim of interpretation when read together. Instead, the context in Article 3(2) OECD MC must be seen as a wide-ranging term encompassing all interpretation methods mentioned in Articles 31 and 32 VCLT, including Article 33 VCLT for treaties authenticated in more than one language. This broad understanding ensures that Article 3(2) OECD MC is not a barrier to eliminating double taxation which is the object and purpose of the treaty.[115] However, there is a limitation: Given that tax law, as an exercise of the right to intervene, significantly impacts the legal sphere of those subject to it, caution is necessary when considering subsequent agreements and practices mentioned pursuant to Article 31(3) VCLT. As stated previously, these should be applied restrictively in the interpretation of tax treaties and should therefore be of minor relevance in the context of Article 3(2) OECD MC.[116] In fact, the use of 'context' in Article 3(2) OECD MC can even be regarded as an argument for the restrictive use of subsequent agreements and practices in its own right. It is exactly the context of tax treaties that makes the limited consideration necessary.

With a broad understanding of context in mind, the content of Article 3(2) OECD MC must still be determined. Generally speaking, there are three major approaches in literature that result in different conclusions regarding the compatibility with the VCLT interpretation rules. Briefly, one line of interpretation maintains that the requirement of the context as a threshold to apply domestic law shall be interpreted narrowly such that an autonomous interpretation is almost never deemed necessary. This is extrapolated from the common law basis of the provision.[117] Additionally, proponents of a narrow interpretation have noted that references to domestic law simplify the practical handling of cases by domestic offices and courts since they are generally only familiarized with their own domestic law.[118] This reliance on domestic law, however, creates qualification conflicts that have negative effects on the efficacy of the DTC. This is contrary to the object and purpose of a DTC which is part of the context pursuant to Article 3(2) OECD MC. A large part of this risk can be averted if the domestic courts

113. Bruggen, *supra* n. 73, at 144 et seq.
114. John F. Avery Jones, *The Interpretation of Tax Treaties with Particular Reference to Article 3(2) of the OECD Model: II*, 28 B.T.R. 104 (1982).
115. *See* Bruggen, *supra* n. 73; Michael Lang, *Tax Treaty Interpretation: A Response to John Avery Jones*, 74 Bulletin for International Taxation at 667 (2020) https://doi.org/10.59403/826m30; Klaus Vogel & Rainer Prokisch, *Generalbericht/General Report/Rapport Général/Ponencia General, in Interpretation of Double Taxation Conventions* 50 (IFA ed., 1993).
116. *See, e.g.*, Michael Lang, *Aussagen des VfGH Zur Auslegung von Doppelbesteuerungsabkommen*, 25 SWI 569 (2015).
117. Avery Jones, *supra* n. 114, at 106.
118. Helmut Loukota, *Über das Verhältnis zwischen Internationalem und Nationalem Recht*, 15 Finanzjournal 107 (1976); Helmut Loukota, *Der Ministerialentwurf für ein DBA-Durchführungsgesetz*, 7 Steuer und Wirtschaft International (1997).

interpret the DTC autonomously and thereby more concertedly than a recourse on familiar domestic law would allow.[119]

Another interpretation of the phrase 'unless the context otherwise requires' is based on the emphasis of the word *'require'*. It is claimed that not all contextual reasons should be sufficient to effectuate an autonomous interpretation but only strong arguments that not only indicate but also *'require'* a deviation from domestic law.[120] While being more sympathetic to an autonomous interpretation than the narrow understanding of the phrase depicted above, it still regularly encounters the same problems as before: The two contract states would both frequently have recourse to their own domestic law which leads to qualification conflicts and prevents the national courts from developing a common interpretation of a DTC inevitably resulting in its uneven application.[121]

These major issues can be mitigated by interpreting Article 3(2) OECD MC as endorsing the prevailing relevance of the context for determining the meaning of undefined terms. Above all, this understanding facilitates the object and purpose of a DTC which is to avoid double taxation. Only in the rare instances that the interpretation in light of the context, encompassing systematic as well as teleological and historical considerations, does not lead to a convincing autonomous conclusion would direct referral to the domestic law be preferable.[122] The purpose of Article 3(2) OECD MC can also be inferred by examining Articles 6(2) and 10(3) OECD MC that explicitly refer to the law of the source state.[123] This would hardly be necessary if this procedure was the general case of the application of Article 3(2) OECD MC.[124] Additionally, a preliminary autonomous interpretation is unavoidable even if giving precedence to domestic law.

119. Lang, *Tax Treaty Interpretation and Art 3 (2) OECD Model Convention, in Tax Treaty Interpretation in Light of the Vienna Convention on the Law of Treaties, supra* n. 87, s. III. 1, forthcoming; Lang, *Art. 3 Abs. 2 OECD-MA und die Auslegung von Doppelbesteuerungsabkommen, supra* n. 96, at 288.
120. Klaus Vogel, *Doppelbesteuerungsabkommen und ihre Auslegung (II)*, 59 StuW (1982); Vogel & Prokisch, *supra* n. 115, at 81.
121. *See also* Lang, *Tax Treaty Interpretation and Art 3 (2) OECD Model Convention, supra* n. 87, s. III. 3, forthcoming.
122. *See, inter alia,* Helmut Debatin, *System und Auslegung der Doppelbesteuerungsabkommen*, 38 Der Betrieb Beilage Nr. 23/85 1 (1985); Gloria, *supra* n. 112, at 978; Lang, *Art. 3 Abs. 2 OECD-MA und die Auslegung von Doppelbesteuerungsabkommen, supra* n. 96, at 287; Michael Lang, *Die Bedeutung des Originär Innerstaatlichen Rechts für die Auslegung von Doppelbesteuerungsabkommen (Art. 3 Abs. 2 OECD-MA), in Aussensteuerrecht Doppelbesteuerungsabkommen und EU-Recht im Spannungsverhältnis: Festschrift für Helmut Debatin zum 70. Geburtstag* 285 et seq. (Gabriele Burmester & Dieter Endres eds, C.H. Beck 1997); Lang, *Tax Treaty Interpretation and Art 3 (2) OECD Model Convention, supra* n. 87, s. III. 2, forthcoming; Lang & Beer, *supra* n. 97, Chapter 11 in this book.
123. *See* Michael Lang & Guglielmo Maisto, *The Relation between Tax Treaty Law and National Law in the Definition of Immovable Property under Article 6(2) of the OECD Model, in Immovable Property under Domestic Law, EU Law and Tax Treaties*, s. 5.3 (IBFD 2015).
124. Lang, *Art. 3 Abs. 2 OECD-MA und die Auslegung von Doppelbesteuerungsabkommen, supra* n. 96, at 289; Michael Lang & Wolfgang Gassner, *Double Non-taxation of a Belgian Tax Law Professor Lecturing in Vienna, in Liber Amicorum Luc Hinnekens* 227 (Bruylant Emile ed., S.A. 2002); Daniel Dürrschmidt, *OECD-MA 2017 Art. 3,* Doppelbesteuerungsabkommen der Bundesrepublik Deutschland auf dem Gebiet der Steuern vom Einkommen und Vermögen: Kommentar auf der Grundlage der Musterabkommen 1.40 (Klaus Vogel et al. eds, C.H. Beck 7th ed. 2021).

An undefined term can only be interpreted with its help if a similar concept also exists in the domestic system. Such a comparison can only be drawn if the meaning of the term in the DTC is somewhat clear to the interpreter.[125] Autonomous interpretation is therefore always a precondition for treaty interpretation. This is especially true for countries in which the domestic law is written neither in English nor French, the authentic languages of the OECD and thus of the MC and the Commentaries, and the DTC is not authenticated in the domestic language either. In this case, no terms can possibly exist in the domestic language that are immediately recognizable as equivalent concepts to terms used in the DTC.[126] Rather, an autonomous interpretation of the DTC is necessary before terms therein can be compared to concepts in domestic law with terminology in another language.[127] The broad interpretation of context and its priority over domestic law does not mean that domestic law can only seldom be a factor in tax treaty interpretation. Rather, it is the aim of DTCs to restrict the taxing rights that stem from domestic law in the first place.[128] The relevance of domestic law is not borrowed from the interpretation regulation in Article 3(2) OECD MC but is due to the context requiring it. As the DTC rules relate to the taxing rights of states, it is clear that the domestic tax provisions must be considered part of the context and can be taken into account under the VCLT rules.[129]

As has been shown, the compatibility of Article 3(2) OECD MC with the VCLT rules depends heavily on the interpretation of Article 3(2) OECD MC. While a narrow interpretation of the phrase 'unless the context otherwise requires' would cause Article 3(2) to conflict with the VCLT rules,[130] a broad interpretation leaves them applicable to the interpretation of undefined terms in the DTC. Considering the object and purpose of the treaty, Article 3(2) OECD MC should be interpreted as a confirmation of VCLT rules that emphasize the importance of the context of the tax treaty and not as a deviation from general international interpretative rules.[131]

125. Lang, *Tax Treaty Interpretation: A Response to John Avery Jones*, *supra* n. 115, at 669.
126. John F. Avery Jones, *Treaty Interpretation: Global Tax Treaty Commentaries*, s. 4.3.2.1 (IBFD 2021).
127. Lang, *Tax Treaty Interpretation and Art 3 (2) OECD Model Convention*, *supra* n. 87, s. III. 2; Lang, *Tax Treaty Interpretation: A Response to John Avery Jones*, *supra* n. 115, at 661 et seq.
128. Lang, *Die Bedeutung des Originär Innerstaatlichen Rechts für die Auslegung von Doppelbesteuerungsabkommen (Art. 3 Abs. 2 OECD-MA)*, *in Aussensteuerrecht Doppelbesteuerungsabkommen und EU-Recht im Spannungsverhältnis: Festschrift für Helmut Debatin zum 70. Geburtstag*, *supra* n. 122, at 296 et seq.
129. Lang, *Doppelbesteuerungsabkommen und Innerstaatliches Recht: Die Einordnung von Doppelbesteuerungsabkommen in Die Österreichische Rechtsordnung*, *supra* n. 108, at 111 et seq.
130. This is argued for in Vogel, *Doppelbesteuerungsabkommen und Ihre Auslegung (II)*, *supra* n. 120, at 295; Richard Xenophon Resch, *Tax Treaty Interpretation: A Response to Michael Lang*, 67 B.T.R. 612 et seq. (2021); Gröhs & Herbst, *Die Interpretation von Doppelbesteuerungsabkommen als Problem der Auslegung von Völkerrechtlichen Verträgen im Nationalen Recht*, *supra* n. 98, at 22.
131. Lang, *Tax Treaty Interpretation: A Response to John Avery Jones*, *supra* n. 115, at 668; for more details to Art. 3(2) OECD MC, *see* Lang & Beer, *supra* n. 97, Chapter 11 in this book.

6 CONCLUDING REMARKS

In conclusion, the interpretation rules of the VCLT provide a flexible framework that allows for adequate treatment of the most common interpretational issues in tax treaty law. This is not surprising as they were intended to provide a framework for a wide array of international treaty law and are therefore general and broadly applicable by design. Apart from a restrictive use of subsequent agreements and practices due to practical reasons and the consequences of tax treaty law for rights and obligations of individuals, DTCs do not implicitly call for excluding the VCLT interpretation rules and employing different means of interpretation. Furthermore, the object and purpose of DTCs, among other things, demand that Article 3(2) OECD MC, in contention to be in conflict with the general VCLT rules, is to be regarded as a confirmation of the importance of context and hence in accordance with the VCLT rules. However, to infer that using Articles 31 and 32 VCLT automatically leads to one correct interpretation of DTCs is erroneous. Rather, the VCLT interpretation rules are generally adequate for purposes of DTC interpretation not because they reveal the interpretation result but because they are usually sufficient for allowing for adequate legal deliberation in their framework. Eventually, the process of interpretation must primarily remain true to its purpose of finding the meaning of the law by utilizing all tools that are expedient for doing so. Hence, the VCLT interpretation rules are best viewed as a flexible tool demonstrating the methods that usually contribute to determining the 'true' meaning of the law and not as a legal obligation that could not be adapted if interpretation so requires. The unequivocal application of the VCLT rules would not erase interpretational controversies in tax literature because, even then, more than one solution remains conceivable when accounting for the ordinary meaning, the context, the object and purpose as well as supplementary means. Uncontested interpretation results must be deemed wishful thinking in any case as interpretation can never follow linear instructions. Instead, all interpretational means must be weighed and balanced on a case-by-case basis to uncover a result close to the meaning of the norm.[132] This does not only follow from VCLT rules or any other interpretation canon but also from the objective of interpretation itself. It therefore seems likely that, even in the absence of the VCLT, methods of interpretation used for tax treaty law would be rather similar just as they were before the VCLT was drafted. Nonetheless, the VCLT provides an interpretational framework that can be referenced in the tax literature and contributes to transparent legal arguments. It can hold practitioners accountable to thoroughly explain their interpretation process by explaining why their weighing of interpretation methods in a particular case furthers the aim of interpretation to illuminate the meaning of the law.

132. *See also* Larenz & Canaris, *supra* n. 7, at 166.

CHAPTER 2

The 'Ordinary Meaning', the 'Special Meaning', and Tax Treaty Interpretation

Georg Kofler & Bence Péter Komár

1 Introduction: The Application of Article 31 VCLT to Double Tax Conventions
2 The 'Ordinary Meaning' of a Treaty's Terms (Article 31(1) VCLT)
  2.1 The 'Ordinary Meaning' Standard: Means of interpretation to Establish the 'Ordinary Meaning' of a Treaty's Terms
    2.1.1 The 'Textual Approach' to Treaty Interpretation
    2.1.2 The Principle of Integration: 'Crucible'
3 The Role of Article 32 VCLT in Treaty Interpretation
4 The 'Special Meaning' of a Treaty's Terms (Article 31(4) VCLT)
5 'Ordinary' and 'Special Meaning' in Tax Treaty Interpretation
  5.1 Fitting the OECD MC and Its Commentaries into the VCLT Pattern
  5.2 'Ordinary Meaning' in Light of the OECD MC and Its Commentaries
  5.3 'Special Meaning' in Light of the OECD MC and Its Commentaries
    5.3.1 Article 31(4) VCLT: A Bridge Between Article 31(1) and Article 32 VCLT?
    5.3.2 Can the OECD MC and Its Commentaries Still Constitute a 'Special Meaning' Pursuant to Article 31(4) VCLT?
6 Conclusion

1 INTRODUCTION: THE APPLICATION OF ARTICLE 31 VCLT TO DOUBLE TAX CONVENTIONS

In public international law, interpretation principles have been codified in Articles 31 et seq. of the Vienna Convention on the Law of Treaties (VCLT).[1] Pursuant to its Article 1, the VCLT applies to treaties between states. Double tax conventions (DTCs) are treaties between states subject to public international law at the level of the contracting states. Therefore, the interpretative rules of the VCLT are applicable to DTC interpretation[2] and are also often considered customary international law (CIL).[3] For this reason, the rules might still be relevant for interpreting DTCs between states that have not ratified the VCLT.[4] However, just as with DTCs, the VCLT itself is an international convention and has the same hierarchical rank in public international law as any DTC.[5] That is also true for the CIL.[6] Thus the interpretation and application of DTCs is governed by the VCLT (being of a general nature) only insofar as the DTC itself (being of a specific nature) does not contain provisions in this regard.[7] Consequently, it should

1. Michael Lang, *Introduction to the Law of Double Taxation Conventions* 13 (Linde/IBFD 3rd ed. 2021); August Reinisch, *Österreichisches Handbuch des Völkerrechts* 76 (Manz 6th ed. 2021); Malcolm N. Shaw, *International Law* 813 (Cambridge University Press 9th ed. 2021); James Crawford, *Brownlie's Principles of Public International Law* 380 (Oxford Public International Law 9th ed. 2019); Alfred Verdross & Bruno Simma, *Universelles Völkerrecht* 490 (Duncker & Humblot 3d ed. 1984); Christoph Grabenwarter et al., *Völkerrecht*, para. 52 (Vahlen 3rd ed. 23 June 2021), Chapter 3.
2. Juan Angel Becerra, *Chapter 5: Tax Treaty Interpretation, in Interpretation and Application of Tax Treaties in North America* (IBFD Revised 2d ed. 2013); Brian J. Arnold, *The Interpretation of Tax Treaties: Myth and Reality*, Bulletin for International Taxation 2 (2010) https://doi.org/10.59403/3gjyvnr; Klaus Vogel, *Transnationale Auslegung von Doppelbesteuerungsabkommen*, IStR 525 (2003); Hugh J. Ault, *The Role of the OECD Commentaries in the Interpretation of Tax Treaties*, Intertax 144 (1994) https://doi.org/10.54648/taxi1994023.
3. Lang, *Introduction to the Law of Double Taxation Conventions, supra* n. 1, at 13; Shaw, *supra* n. 1, at 707; Crawford, *supra* n. 1, at 380; *Dispute regarding Navigational and Related Rights (Costa Rica v. Nicaragua), Judgment, I.C.J. Reports 2009*, p. 213, I.C.J. Reports 2009; *LaGrand (Germany v. United States of America), Judgment, I.C.J. Reports 2001*, p. 466, I.C.J. Reports 2001; *Kasikili/Sedudu Island (Botswana/Namibia), Judgment, I.C.J. Reports 1999*, p. 1045, I.C.J. Reports 1999; Grabenwarter et al., *supra* n. 1, para. 54, Chapter 3.
4. Lang, *Introduction to the Law of Double Taxation Conventions, supra* n. 1, at 13; Michael Lang, *Can Law Regulate Its Own Interpretation? Relevance and Meaning of Articles 31-33 of the Vienna Convention on the Law of Treaties (VCLT) and Article 3 para. 2 of the Model Convention of the Organisation of Economic Co-operation and Development (OECD) for the Interpretation of Double-Tax Conventions*, in Yariv Brauner, Research Handbook on International Taxation 174 (177) (2020).
5. Lang, *Introduction to the Law of Double Taxation Conventions, supra* n. 1, at 13; Lang, *Can Law Regulate Its own interpretation? Relevance and Meaning of Articles 31.33 of the Vienna Convention on the Law of Treaties (VCLT) and Article 3 para. 2 of the Model Convention of the Organisation of Economic Co-operation and Development (OECD) for the Interpretation of Double-Tax Conventions*, in Yariv Brauner, Research Handbook on International Taxation 2020 174 (177).
6. Lang, *Introduction to the Law of Double Taxation Conventions, supra* n. 1, at 13; Lang, *Can Law Regulate Its own interpretation? Relevance and Meaning of Articles 31.33 of the Vienna Convention on the Law of Treaties (VCLT) and Article 3 para. 2 of the Model Convention of the Organisation of Economic Co-operation and Development (OECD) for the Interpretation of Double-Tax Conventions*, in Yariv Brauner, Research Handbook on International Taxation 2020 174 (177).
7. G. Kofler, *Vor Art. 1, II. Auslegung von Doppelbesteuerungsabkommen*, in Dietmar Aigner et al., *DBA*, para. 80 (Linde 2d ed. 2019); to that effect Ekkehart Reimer, *Interpretation of Tax Treaties*, European Taxation 463 (1999); VwGH 87/16/0071.

first be considered that DTCs generally contain explicit references to the meaning of a term under the domestic law of a state (e.g., Article 2(4), Article 4(1), and Article 6(2) Model Convention of the Organisation for Economic Co-operation and Development (OECD MC)).[8] However, numerous terms are defined in a DTC itself (Article 3(1) OECD MC) with the qualification that those definitions are decisive 'unless the context otherwise requires'. If the DTC definition is indeed decisive, it must be interpreted according to the VCLT's interpretative rules. In addition, DTCs typically contain a general rule of interpretation (Article 3(2) OECD MC) for terms not defined therein:[9]

> As regards the application of the Convention at any time by a Contracting State, any term not defined therein shall, unless the context otherwise requires or the competent authorities agree to a different meaning pursuant to the provisions of Article 25, have the meaning that it has at that time under the law of that State for the purposes of the taxes to which the Convention applies, any meaning under the applicable tax laws of that State prevailing over a meaning given to the term under other laws of that State.

To conclude, when interpreting DTCs, it must first be examined whether the respective treaty itself provides rules for its own interpretation and application. Insofar as this is not the case, DTCs are treaties between states, thus, they are to be interpreted based on section 3 VCLT, *inter alia*, Article 31 VCLT.

While the VCLT has a complex and comprehensive set of rules concerning interpreting international treaties, the authors only seek to examine specific aspects of those rules and their relation to other means of interpretation within the VCLT. The first part of this chapter primarily focuses on the general rule of interpretation. Article 31(1) VCLT stipulates that a 'treaty shall be interpreted in good faith in accordance with the ordinary meaning to be given to the terms of the treaty in their context and in the light of its object and purpose'. Within that rule, the 'ordinary meaning' standard is of particular interest:

> Paragraph 1 [Article 31(1) VCLT] contains three separate principles. The first – interpretation in good faith – flows directly from the rule *pacta sunt servanda.* The second principle is the very essence of the textual approach: the parties are to be presumed to have that intention which appears from the ordinary meaning of the terms used by them. The third principle is one both of common sense and good faith; the ordinary meaning of a term is not to be determined in the abstract but in the context of the treaty and in the light of its object and purpose.[10]

To elucidate its content, the authors conduct a general positive analysis of the 'ordinary meaning' standard with reference to scholars' opinions and case law. This is followed by examining the role of Article 32 VCLT in treaty interpretation in relation to the general rule. In the subsequent section, the authors discuss the 'special meaning' standard provided by Article 31(4) VCLT: 'A special meaning shall be given to a term

8. W. Haslehner, *Introduction*, in Ekkehart Reimer & Alexander Rust, *Klaus Vogel on Double Tax Conventions*, para. 113 (Wolters Kluwer 5th ed. 2021); Kofler, *supra* n. 7, para. 80; Vogel, *Transnationale Auslegung von Doppelbesteuerungsabkommen*, *supra* n. 2, at 524.
9. Kofler, *supra* n. 7, para. 81.
10. *Yearbook of the International Law Commission 1966 Volume II*, 221.

if it is established that the parties so intended.' Again, the authors conduct a positive analysis of Article 31 (4) VCLT without regard to particular types of treaties. At last, the authors turn to tax treaty interpretation to examine its particularities when applying the VCLT. The main points of discussion are the relevance of the OECD MC and its Commentaries to establish the 'ordinary' or the 'special meaning'. The final section provides a summary of the authors' research findings.

2 THE 'ORDINARY MEANING' OF A TREATY'S TERMS (ARTICLE 31(1) VCLT)

2.1 The 'Ordinary Meaning' Standard: Means of interpretation to Establish the 'Ordinary Meaning' of a Treaty's Terms

2.1.1 The 'Textual Approach' to Treaty Interpretation

The general rule of interpreting treaties between states is specified in Article 31 VCLT. Its paragraph 1 stipulates that a treaty shall be interpreted in good faith in accordance with the 'ordinary meaning' to be given to the terms of the treaty in their context and in light of the treaty's object and purpose. In the 1960s, when the VCLT was drafted, interpreters differed to some extent in their basic approach to treaty interpretation. Some gave relatively more argumentative weight to the actual intentions of the parties and admitted recourse to elements extrinsic to the text (subjective approach).[11] Others gave significant weight to the object and apparent or 'emergent' purpose of the treaty and would admit teleological interpretations of the texts. Those interpretations would partly go beyond or even diverge from the original intentions of the parties (teleological approach).[12] However, the majority of interpreters at that time emphasized the primacy of the text as the basis for interpreting a treaty (textual approach).[13] This approach places the emphasis on the treaty's actual words and does not ask: 'What did the parties mean?' It rather questions: 'What did the parties say?'[14]

Like the subjective approach, the textual approach finds the aim of treaty interpretation in giving effect to the parties' intention.[15] The opposite of bringing about something that is not within the parties' intention would not be a proper outcome of interpretation.[16] The difference between those approaches lies in the methodology.[17]

11. Reinisch, *supra* n. 1, at 76; Shaw, *supra* n. 1, at 813; Grabenwarter et al., *supra* n. 1, para. 54, Chapter 3.
12. Shaw, *supra* n. 1, at 813; Martin Dixon, *Textbook on International Law* 74 (Oxford University Press 7th ed. 2013).
13. Reinisch, *supra* n. 1, at 76; Shaw, *supra* n. 1, at 813; Dixon, *supra* n. 12, at 73; Verdross & Simma, *supra* n. 1, at 492.
14. Francis G. Jacobs, *Varieties of Approach to Treaty Interpretation: With Special Reference to the Draft Convention on the Law of Treaties Before the Vienna Diplomatic Conference*, 18 319 (1969); *YBILC 1966-II, supra* n. 10, p. 218.
15. Reinisch, *supra* n. 1, at 76; Gerald Fitzmaurice, *The Law and Procedure of the International Court of Justice 1951-4: Treaty Interpretation and Other Treaty Points* 204 (1957).
16. Fitzmaurice, *The Law and Procedure of the International Court of Justice 1951-4: Treaty Interpretation and Other Treaty Points, supra* n. 15, at 204.

How is the desired end to be achieved? Where can the authentic intention of the parties be evidenced? According to the subjective approach, the true intention of the parties prevails over the treaty text if the latter contradicts their intention.[18] The textual approach adheres to a different logic. Based on the fact that a treaty is drafted to give expression to the parties' intentions, they must be sought there. Truly, the text must be the parties' authentic expression as their rights and obligations derive from the text. Therefore, this is what they must have intended when concluding the treaty. According to the textual approach, interpretation begins with careful consideration of the text and, if it is unclear, recourse must be had to extraneous sources. Nevertheless, to ascertain the parties' true intentions, first, what the text means must be determined.[19]

From the genesis of the VCLT, it has been clear that the majority of its drafters were proponents of this textual approach. The Institute of International Law (IIL) had already adopted it in Article 1(1) of a resolution in 1956: 'L'accord des parties s'étant réalisé sur le texte du traité, il y a lieu de prendre le sens naturel et ordinaire des termes de ce texte comme base d'interprétation.'[20] In this connection, it is significant that the later proposals of the special rapporteur on the Law of Treaties, Sir Humphrey Waldock, to the International Law Commission (ILC) on the means of interpretation were primarily based on that resolution and on Sir Gerald Fitzmaurice's article on the International Court of Justice's (ICJ's) law and procedure.[21] Sir Gerald Fitzmaurice demonstrates in that article that the textual approach to treaty interpretation was indeed adopted by the ICJ at that time. He describes the textual approach as follows:[22]

> The thought of the majority could be summed up by saying that in their view the intentions of the framers of a treaty, as they emerged from the discussions or negotiations preceding its conclusion, must be presumed to have been expressed in the treaty itself, and are therefore to be sought primarily in the actual text, and not in any extraneous source. Furthermore, treaties must be interpreted as they stand, and subject to the limitations inherent in the fact that they only contain so many articles, phrases and words. The intentions or presumed intentions of the framers cannot be invoked to fill in gaps, or import into the treaty something which is not there, or to correct or alter words or phrases the meaning of which is apparently plain, or to give them a sense different from that which they possess according to their normal and natural meaning. In short, the attitude of the Court to a text is not, primarily, to ask itself what was this text intended to mean (still less of course what ought it to mean, or to be made to mean), but what does it in fact mean on its actual wording?

17. *Ibid.*
18. Grabenwarter et al., *supra* n. 1, para. 54, Chapter 3.
19. Reinisch, *supra* n. 1, at 76; Crawford, *supra* n. 1, at 379; Fitzmaurice, *The Law and Procedure of the International Court of Justice 1951-4: Treaty Interpretation and Other Treaty Points, supra* n. 15, at 204-207; *Yearbook of the International Law Commission 1964 Volume II*, 55.
20. *Annuiare de l'Institut de Droit International, Volume 46 (1956)*, p. 359.
21. Jacobs, *supra* n. 14, at 326.
22. Gerald Fitzmaurice, *The Law and Procedure of the International Court of Justice* 48 (Grotius 1986).

This view, e.g., is expressed by the ICJ in the *Iranian Oil*[23] case. In it, the ICJ stated that Iran's declaration of accepting the compulsory jurisdiction of the former international court respective certain categories of treaties must be interpreted as it stands having regard to the words actually used. The ICJ also indicated on multiple occasions that the function of interpretation was not to revise treaties or to read into them what they do not expressly or by implication contain.[24]

At the sixteenth session of the ILC then Special Rapporteur Sir Humphrey Waldock took up the questions of interpretation of treaties and submitted a corresponding report to the ILC.[25] His draft on the general rule of interpretation – Article 70 – states:[26] 'The terms of a treaty shall be interpreted in good faith in accordance with the natural and ordinary meaning to be given to each term – (a) in its context in the treaty and in the context of the treaty as a whole; and (b) in the context of the rules of international law in force at the time of the conclusion of the treaty.' This article corresponds to the above-cited Article 1 of the IIL and to the following major principles of Sir Gerald Fitzmaurice:[27]

> I. Principle of actuality (or textuality). Treaties are to be interpreted primarily as they stand, and on the basis of their actual texts.
>
> ...
>
> III. Principle of integration. Treaties are to be interpreted as a whole, and particular parts, chapters or sections also as a whole.
>
> ...
>
> VI. Principle of contemporaneity. The terms of a treaty must be interpreted according to the meaning which they possessed, or which would have been attributed to them, and in the light of current linguistic usage, at the time when the treaty was originally concluded.

Furthermore, the Commentary on Article 70 of Sir Humphrey Waldock's original draft reveals that the article in its entirety 'takes as the basic rule of treaty interpretation the primacy of the text as evidence of the intention of the parties'.[28] Sir Humphrey Waldock indeed considered 'the actual text the dominant factor in the interpretation of the treaty' and accepted 'the view that the text must be presumed to be the authentic expression of the intentions of the parties; and that, in consequence, the starting point and purpose of interpretation is to elucidate the meaning of the text, not to investigate *ab initio* the intentions of the parties'.[29]

23. *Anglo-Iranian Oil Co. case (jurisdiction), Judgement of 22 July 1952, I.C.J. Reports 1952*, I.C.J. Reports 1952 93, 105.
24. *Rights of nationals of the United States of America in Morocco case, Judgement of 22 August 1952, I.C.J. Reports 1950*, 196 and 199; *Interpretation of Peace Treaties (second phase), Advisory Opinion, I.C.J. Reports 1950*, 229.
25. *Yearbook of the International Law Commission 1964 Volume II, supra* n. 19, at 6; *Yearbook of the International Law Commission 1966 Volume II, supra* n. 10, at 175.
26. *YBILC 1964-II, supra* n. 19, at 52.
27. Fitzmaurice, *The Law and Procedure of the International Court of Justice 1951-4: Treaty Interpretation and Other Treaty Points, supra* n. 15, at 212 et seq.; *YBILC 1964-II, supra* n. 19, at 55–56.
28. *YBILC 1964-II, supra* n. 19, at 56.
29. *Ibid.*

At its 18th session, the ILC had adopted the final text of its draft articles on the law of treaties. In it, the general rule of interpretation was placed in Article 27 and its paragraph 1 stipulated: 'A treaty shall be interpreted in good faith in accordance with the ordinary meaning to be given to the terms of the treaty in their context and in the light of its object and purpose.' Article 27(1) of the 1966 draft fully corresponds with Article 31(1) VCLT. The Commentary to Article 27 reaffirms that the commencement of an interpretation is the elucidation of the meaning of the text.[30]

In conclusion, under Article 31(1) VCLT, it is assumed that parties to a treaty used all of the words of the treaty text according to their 'ordinary meaning' and that these express the intention of the parties. Consequently, interpretation must begin by examining the text, and not the intentions of the parties. Yet, the text is not the only evidence of the parties' intentions:[31] 'the ordinary meaning of a term is not to be determined in the abstract but in the context of the treaty and in the light of its object and purpose'. Stated otherwise, to determine the 'ordinary meaning', interpretative elements other than the text itself must also be taken into consideration.

This view seems to be in accordance with the jurisprudence of the ICJ and the former Permanent Court of International Justice (PCIJ). In its Advisory Opinion on the Competence of the General Assembly for the Admission of a State to the United Nations, the ICJ stated:[32]

> The Court considers it necessary to say that the first duty of a tribunal which is called upon to interpret and apply the provisions of a treaty, is to endeavour to give effect to them in their natural and ordinary meaning in the context in which they occur. If the relevant words in their natural and ordinary meaning make sense in their context, that is an end of the matter.

Before that, the PCIJ stressed in an advisory opinion that the context is not merely the article or section of the treaty in which a term occurs but the treaty as a whole:[33] 'In considering the question before the Court upon the language of the Treaty, it is obvious that the Treaty must be read as a whole, and that its meaning is not to be determined merely upon particular phrases which, if detached from the context, may be interpreted in more than one sense.'

2.1.2 The Principle of Integration: 'Crucible'

In this context, there are three deductions that can be made from the general rule of interpretation. The first is that the VCLT states that the 'ordinary meaning' is 'to be given' to a term. In the *Agean Sea* case, the ICJ itself uses the formula 'effect [...] ought to be given to the words'. Furthermore, the ILC sees the 'ordinary meaning' as a point

30. *YBILC 1966-II, supra* n. 10, at 221.
31. *Ibid.*
32. *Competence of Assembly regarding admission to the United Nations, Advisory Opinion: I.C.J. 1950.*
33. *Competence of the International Labour Organization in Regard to International Regulation of the Conditions of Labour of Persons Employed in Agriculture, Advisory Opinion.*

at which the interpreter should arrive.[34] This position is also supported by the wording of Article 27(1) of the 1966 Draft:[35] 'the ordinary meaning to be given to the terms'. As demonstrated above, Article 31(1) VCLT is identical in this respect to Article 27(1) of the 1966 Draft. From the foregoing, it can be deduced that the 'ordinary meaning' is not just the starting point of interpretation. It is a meaning that the interpreter arrives at as the result of the interpretative process.

The second deduction that can be made based on the general rule is that the 'ordinary meaning' of the terms is not solely their literal, grammatical, natural, dictionary, or intrinsic meaning but instead a qualified one. International courts and tribunals have often reached the conclusion that the 'ordinary meaning' principle does not mean that the terms of a treaty must necessarily be interpreted in a literal manner.[36] On the contrary, interpreters must often choose among multiple possible meanings of a term on the basis of their context as well as the treaty's object and purpose.[37] Sir Humphrey Waldock, speaking in his capacity as an expert consultant to the United Nations Conference on the Law of Treaties (UNCLT) expressed at that conference's first session in 1968 that 'nothing could have been further from the ILC's intention than to suggest that words had a dictionary or intrinsic meaning'.[38]

In the *South West Africa* case, the ICJ states that the rule of interpretation based on the natural and ordinary meaning of the words employed is not an absolute one since when such a method of interpretation results in a meaning incompatible with the spirit, purpose, and context of the clause or instrument in which the words are contained, no reliance can be validly placed on it.[39] Although the actual treaty text is the starting point of the interpretative process, it does not have absolute prominence. Much rather, interpreters should weigh all elements provided by the general rule and

34. *YBILC 1966-II, supra* n. 10, p. 221.
35. *Ibid.*, p. 181.
36. *Anglo-Iranian Oil Co. case (jurisdiction), Judgement of 22 July 1952, I.C.J. Reports 1952*, I.C.J. Reports 1952 93, 104.
37. *Competence of the International Labour Organization in Regard to International Regulation of the Conditions of Labour of Persons Employed in Agriculture, Advisory Opinion* at 23: '*In considering the question before the Court upon the language of the Treaty, it is obvious that the Treaty must be read as a whole, and that its meaning is not to be determined merely upon particular phrases which, if detached from the context, may be interpreted in more than one sense.*'; *Temple of Preah Vihear* case *(Cambodia v. Thailand), Preliminary Objections, Judgement of 26 May 1961: I.C.J. Reports 1961*, I.C.J. Reports 1961 17, 31-33; *International Centre of Settlement of Investment Disputes, 21 October 2005, Aguas del Tunari v. Republic of Bolivia*, No. ICSD Case No. ARB/02/03, slip op., para. 91 (International Centre for Settlement of Investment Disputes 2005); *Arbitral Award of 31 July 1989, Judgement, I.C.J. Reports 1991*, I.C.J Reports 1991 53, para. 48; Paolo Arginelli, *Chapter 6: Positive Analysis of Articles 31 and 32 of the VCLT and Their Contribution to the Author's Normative Analysis and Legal Theory on Treaty Interpretation, in Multilingual Tax Treaties: Interpretation, Semantic Analysis and Legal Theory* (IBFD 2015); *Land, Island and Maritime Frontier Dispute (El Salvador v. Honduras), Judgement*, para. 190 separate opinion of Judge Torres Bernández; Georg Schwarzenberger, *Myths and Realities of Treaty Interpretations: Articles 27-29 of the Vienna Draft Convention on the Law of Treaties*, 9 Va. J. Int'l L. 13 (1968).
38. *United Nations Conference on the Law of Treaties, First Session, Vienna, 26 March-24 May 1968* 184 (1968); John F. Avery Jones & Johann Hattingh, *Treaty Interpretations: Global Tax Treaty Commentaries* (Global Topics IBFD).
39. *South West Africa* case *(Ethiopia v. South Africa; Liberia v. South Africa), Preliminary Objections, Judgement of 21 December 1962: I.C.J. Reports 1962*, 336.

consider all items of evidence.[40] An interpretation of a term that does not emerge from the text is indeed not acceptable.[41] Nevertheless, based only on the text, different possible interpretations might emerge.[42] These must be examined under all means of interpretation, otherwise, the result could be an erroneous conclusion.[43] In this respect, the VCLT seems to be influenced by the IIL's 1956 resolution and the principles of interpretation formulated by Sir Gerald Fitzmaurice. Both not only point to the text as a start but also highlight that the treaty is to be interpreted as a whole taking into account its object and purpose.[44]

The third deduction that can be made based on the general rule is that the result of interpretation, i.e., 'ordinary meaning', should be reached using a holistic approach. Concerning the interpretative methods stipulated in the general rule, the ILC has expressed that Article 27 of the 1966 draft does not specify a legal hierarchy of the interpretative methods stipulated therein.[45] The order of appearance of the means of interpretation provided by Article 27 (Article 31 VCLT) is purely based on logic. All of them are of an obligatory character and cannot be considered to be norms of interpretation in any way inferior to those that precede them.[46]

Interpretation is therefore not a step-by-step operation but a single combined process.[47] All of the relevant elements are thrown into a crucible, and their interaction results in the legally relevant interpretation.[48] This view is further supported by the fact that Article 27 of the 1966 draft and Article 31 VCLT are entitled to a 'general rule of interpretation' in the singular and not 'rules' in the plural. The ILC desired to emphasize that the interpretative process is a unity and that the provision of the article forms a single, closely integrated rule.[49]

40. Michael Lang, in Franz Wassermeyer, *Vor Art. 1*, in *Doppelbesteuerung*, Vol. I, para. 6 (94th ed. 2023); Alexander Rust, in Gerrit Frotscher, *Internationales Steuerrecht*, para. 281 (5., völlig überarbeitete Auflage, Studium und Praxis, C.H. Beck 2020); Arginelli, *supra* n. 37; Shaw, *supra* n. 1; Dixon, *supra* n. 12, 75.
41. *Yearbook of the International Law Commission 1966 Volume II, supra* n. 10. pp. 220-221; *Rights of nationals of the United States of America in Morocco case, Judgement of 22 August 1952, I.C.J. Reports 1950*, 196 and 199.
42. *Aguas del Tunari v. Bolivia*, No. ICSD Case No. ARB/02/03, slip op., para. 91; Schwarzenberger, *supra* n. 37, at 13.
43. Arginelli, *supra* n. 37.
44. Fitzmaurice, *The Law and Procedure of the International Court of Justice 1951-4: Treaty Interpretation and Other Treaty Points, supra* n. 15, at 220; *Yearbook of the International Law Commission 1964 Volume II, supra* n. 19, pp. 55-56; *Rights of nationals of the United States of America in Morocco case, Judgement of 22 August 1952, I.C.J. Reports 1950*, 209; *Ambatielos case (jurisdiction), Judgement of 1 July 1952: I.C.J. Reports 1952*, 30.
45. Arnold, *supra* n. 2, at 6; *YBILC 1966-II, supra* n. 10, p. 220.
46. *YBILC 1966-II, supra* n. 10, p. 220; *Rights of nationals of the United States of America in Morocco case, Judgement of 22 August 1952, I.C.J. Reports 1950* with reference to 'context' at 183-184, with reference to 'purpose' at 197-198 and with reference to 'preparatory work' at 198.
47. Lang, in Wassermeyer, *supra* n. 40, para. 6; Michael Lang, *Doppelbesteuerungsabkommen und innerstaatliches Recht: die Einordnung von Doppelbesteuerungsabkommen in die österreichische Rechtsordnung* 95 (Wirtschaftsverl. Orac 1992); *Yearbook of the International Law Commission 2018 Volume II*, p. 29; *YBILC 1966-II, supra* n. 10, p. 219; Schwarzenberger, *supra* n. 37, at 4.
48. Arginelli, *supra* n. 37; *YBILC 1966-II, supra* n. 10, p. 220; Frank Engelen, *Chapter 6: The General Rule of Interpretation, in Interpretation of Tax Treaties under International Law.*
49. *YBILC 1966-II, supra* n. 10, pp. 219-220; *YBILC 2018-II., supra* n. 47, p. 26; to that effect, Lang, in Wassermeyer, *supra* n. 40, para. 6.

On balance, the approach implemented in the VCLT cannot be reduced to a textual interpretation approach. An accurate reading of Article 31 VCLT, the ILC's commentaries, and an analysis of their application by courts and tribunals clearly demonstrate that elements typical of the different approaches coexist therein and interact with one another.

3 THE ROLE OF ARTICLE 32 VCLT IN TREATY INTERPRETATION

Article 32 VCLT stipulates:

> Recourse may be had to supplementary means of interpretation, including the preparatory work of the treaty and the circumstances of its conclusion, in order to confirm the meaning resulting from the application of article 31, or to determine the meaning when the interpretation according to article 31: (a) leaves the meaning ambiguous or obscure; or (b) leads to a result which is manifestly absurd or unreasonable.

In general, recourse to supplementary means of interpretation is viewed from very different angles. This is probably due to the fact that there are two very strong interpretation schools in doctrinal controversies with one favouring the parties' intentions (subjective approach)[50] as the basis for interpretation and another favouring a textual approach.[51]

Regarding the question of whether the few general principles to be included in the draft convention on the law of treaties had to be organized in some hierarchical order, the solution adopted by the ILC and then implemented in the VCLT is two-sided. On the one hand, there is indeed a hierarchical distinction between the means of interpretation provided in Article 31(1) VCLT that 'all relate to the agreement between the parties at the time when or after it received authentic expression in the text'[52] and those provided in Article 32 VCLT where that is not necessarily[53] the case. Supplementary means, particularly preparatory work, do not have the same 'authentic character' as means of interpretation under Article 31 VCLT even though they may sometimes be valuable for interpreting an expression used in the treaty text.[54] Therefore, the distinction between authentic and supplementary means of interpretation is both justified and desirable.

Notwithstanding Article 32 VCLT's subordinate nature,[55] there is no rigid demarcation between Article 32 and Article 31 VCLT.[56] For example, the former can be used to confirm the result reached by using the latter. In practice, international tribunals

50. Both the subjective and the textual approaches seek to determine the parties' true intentions. The textual approach suggests that this should be sought in the treaty text whereas the subjective approach permits all types of evidence (e.g., *traveaux préparatoires*) to ascertain this.
51. Juan Angel Becerra, *Chapter 4: Treaty Interpretation, in Interpretation and Application of Tax Treaties in North America* (IBFD Revised 2d ed. 2013); Verdross & Simma, *supra* n. 1, at 492.
52. *YBILC 1966-II, supra* n. 10, p. 220.
53. This is based on a hypothesis made by the ILC, cf., *ibid.*, p. 220: 'Ex hypothesi this is not the case with preparatory work which does not in consequence, have the same authentic character as an element of interpretation.'
54. Arginelli, *supra* n. 37; *YBILC 1966-II, supra* n. 10, p. 220.
55. Verdross & Simma, *supra* n. 1, at 492 et seq.
56. *YBILC 1966-II, supra* n. 10, p. 220.

indeed have recourse to subsidiary means of interpretation to confirm the 'ordinary meaning' that appears to result from such an interpretation (Article 31 VCLT).[57] Therefore, a distinction must be made between the interpretative weight of the elements of interpretation and the chronological place. Concerning the interpretative weight, it has been established that Article 31 VCLT carries more weight, and Article 32 VCLT is secondary.[58]

On the other hand, concerning the chronological aspect, it appears from case law and the above-demonstrated view of scholars[59] (cf., section 2.1.2) that the analysis of all of the potentially relevant means of interpretation, including those that are supplementary, constitutes a single intellectual process.[60] Under this approach, the position is rejected whereby the process of discovering the appropriate meaning of a term should be carried out without any investigation of, for example, the *travaux préparatoires* or the circumstances of the treaty's conclusion. It also denies that such means had to be resorted to only in a second, logically distinct moment for the purpose of confirming such a meaning or determining the appropriate one when the first part of the process did not lead to a satisfactory result.[61]

Moreover, based on the view that interpretation is a single unitary exercise, some contend that the circumscription of using supplementary means in Article 32 VCLT does not mean that their use as an aid becomes optional. Their use is encouraged as a check on the meaning established under Article 31 VCLT.[62] The ILC itself indicated in its Commentaries on the Draft Articles on the Law of Treaties that the process of treaty interpretation is intended to be a unity even though consisting of various elements. Again, there is no 'rigid line' between Articles 31 and 32 VCLT, and the elements stipulated in the VCLT were not intended to be exhaustive of the principles and maxims used in practice when interpreting treaties.[63] On the contrary, all relevant material that is beneficial for achieving a sensible interpretation should be taken into account.[64]

The following example shall demonstrate that using Article 32 VCLT is not only optional, but it is also necessary for a correct interpretation under Article 31 VCLT. To confirm the 'ordinary meaning' under it, the interpreter has recourse to supplementary means pursuant to Article 32 VCLT that do not confirm the meaning resulting from Article 31 VCLT. This may show the existence of another possible meaning under Article 31 VCLT that can be confirmed by the supplementary means. Furthermore,

57. [PRETITLE], *Payment of Various Serbian Loans Issued in France* case [LOCATOR] [JURIS-TAIL] p. 30; [PRETITLE], *Payment in Gold of Brazilian Federal Loans Contracted in France* case [LOCATOR] [JURIS-TAIL] pp. 119-120; [PRETITLE], *Interpretation of the Convention of 1919 Concerning Employment of Women During the Night* [LOCATOR] [JURIS-TAIL] p. 380; *YBILC 1966-II, supra* n. 10, p. 223.
58. Arginelli, *supra* n. 37.
59. Lang, in Wassermeyer, *supra* n. 40, para. 6; Lang, *Doppelbesteuerungsabkommen und innerstaatliches Recht: die Einordnung von Doppelbesteuerungsabkommen in die österreichische Rechtsordnung, supra* n. 47, at 95; *Yearbook of the International Law Commission 2018 Volume II, supra* n. 47 p. 29; *YBILC 1966-II, supra* n. 10, p. 219; Schwarzenberger, *supra* n. 37, at 4.
60. *YBILC 2018-II, supra* n. 47, p. 29.
61. Arginelli, *supra* n. 37; *YBILC 2018-II, supra* n. 47, p. 26.
62. Avery Jones & Hattingh, *supra* n. 38.
63. *Ibid.*
64. Ault, *supra* n. 2, at 145.

using Article 32 VCLT may disclose an ambiguity that had not previously been seen that could then be resolved by the supplementary means.[65]

In conclusion, with reference to its chronological place, Article 32 VCLT should be used during the interpretative process simultaneously with Article 31 VCLT.[66]

4 THE 'SPECIAL MEANING' OF A TREATY'S TERMS (ARTICLE 31(4) VCLT)

Under Article 31(4) VCLT, a 'special meaning' shall be given to a term if it is established that the parties so intended. The main issue that the ILC and scholars have debated regarding Article 31(4) VCLT concerns the means of interpretation that the interpreter should use in order to establish and argue for the 'special meaning' that the parties intended to attach to the relevant treaty term.[67] For instance, during the ILC's eighteenth session, the ILC members did not agree on whether recourse to supplementary means of interpretation was allowed for this.[68] In the course of the UNCLT, some comments proposed by the delegations focused on the relation between the parties' intention to attach a 'special meaning' to a treaty term (Article 31(4) VCLT) and the *travaux préparatoires* (Article 32 VCLT).[69]
The United States delegation stated concerning Article 31(4) (then Article 27(4)):

> The purpose of the United States amendment (A/CONF.39/C.1/L.156) was to eliminate the rigidities, restrictions and hierarchical distinctions in draft Articles 27 and 28. The text of a treaty and the common public meanings of words would be made the point of departure of interpretation, but not the end of the inquiry. The text would be treated as one important index among many of the common intent of the parties. No fixed hierarchy would be established among the elements of interpretation; the amendment sought to make accessible to interpreters whatever elements might be significant in a particular set of circumstances, including ordinary meaning, subsequent practice and preparatory work, but not excluding others that might be also relevant.[70]

The Vietnamese delegation was of a similar opinion: 'In his delegation's opinion, however, preparatory work and the circumstances in which the treaty had been concluded often represented means of interpretation as valid, if not as essential, as the context, particularly when they were concerned with ascertaining the intention of the parties.'[71]

65. Avery Jones & Hattingh, *supra* n. 38.
66. Arginelli, *supra* n. 37.
67. *Ibid.*
68. Arginelli, *supra* n. 37, Books IBFD (accessed 18 November 2022).
69. Cf., written statement of the International Bank for Reconstruction and Development *UN Doc. A/Conf.39/7/Add. 1* pp. 14-15; *UNCLT-I* (1968) the comments of the US delegation p. 168, paras 47 et seq., Vietnamese delegation p. 168, para. 51, Ghanian delegation p. 171, para. 70 and the Austrian delegation p. 178, para. 14.
70. *UNCLT-I, supra* n. 69 cf., the comments of the US delegation p. 168, para. 49.
71. *Ibid.*, cf., the comments of the Vietnamese delegation p. 168, para. 51.

The Austrian delegation noted:

> The problem [the role of preparatory work] also arose in paragraph 4 of Article 27, which provided that a special meaning should be given to a term if it was established that the parties so intended. With the exception of the cases where, according to the commentary, the technical or special use of a term appeared from the context, the intention of the parties could only be ascertained by recourse to the preparatory work; and yet, according to the Commission's wording of Article 28, the preparatory work would not be considered in such a case, because it met none of the requirements stipulated in that Article. First, the search was evidently not intended to confirm the meaning resulting from the application of Article 27, because the intention of the parties to use the term in its technical sense might not be apparent before the preparatory work was examined. Secondly, the interpretation according to Article 27 would neither leave the meaning ambiguous or obscure nor lead to a result which was manifestly absurd or unreasonable. On the other hand, if the ordinary meaning of the term, instead of its technical meaning, were used for interpretation, the results might not correspond to the true intention of the parties.[72]

In this respect, Sir Humphrey Waldock, in his capacity as an expert consultant, replied to such comments:

> He [Sir Humphrey Waldock] could not agree with the Austrian representative's remark that in such cases the special meaning could only be arrived at by reference to the preparatory work. That type of case was comparatively rare; but those which had occurred did not support the Austrian representative's view. For example, in the 'Legal Status of Eastern Greenland' case, the Permanent Court of International Justice had considered whether the word 'Greenland', used in certain treaties between the parties to the case, meant the whole island, or had been used in the special meaning of Eastern Greenland; that question had been discussed in the Court by reference to the context and not to the preparatory work. The fact that the Commission had considered doing away with paragraph 4 of Article 27 clearly illustrated its wish to associate in the strongest possible way the 'ordinary meaning' with the context; the Commission had, moreover, stated in paragraph 3 an expanded concept of 'context' to cover the relevant elements of authentic interpretation.[73]

To answer the question as to what means of interpretation should be used to establish the 'special meaning', it must first be defined how the expression 'special meaning' itself is to be understood. It is a 'particular' meaning that differs from the more common meaning or meanings.[74] The official French version of Article 31(4) VCLT refers to 'un sens particulier' which means a 'particular meaning'. This indicates that the English 'special' should be interpreted as a concrete, precise, or a particular one in contrast to a common one.

That view also seems to adhere to the ILC approach according to which the application of each interpretative element depends on the interpreter's conviction and

72. *Ibid.*, p. 19, para. 14.
73. *Ibid.*, p. 184, para. 71.
74. Richard Gardiner, *Treaty Interpretation* 291 (Oxford Public International Law 1st ed.). Article 31(4) of the VCLT is mainly apt to cover cases of 'a particular meaning given by someone using a term that differs from the more common meaning or meanings'; Avery Jones & Hattingh, *supra* n. 38.

on the particular circumstances of the case.[75] The VCLT does not dictate how much weight must be given to the elements listed in the general rule.[76] Therefore, more than one 'ordinary meaning' can be attributed to a term depending on how much qualitative weight is given to each element of interpretation under Article 31(1) VCLT. Hence, the 'special meaning' can be considered the result of a particular 'weighting' of those elements.

Moreover, the Commentaries on the Draft Articles suggest that the 'special meaning' is to be understood as a technical meaning:[77]

> [Article 31(4) VCLT] provides for the somewhat exceptional case where, notwithstanding the apparent meaning of a term in its context, it is established that the parties intended it to have a special meaning. Some members doubted the need to include a special provision on this point, although they recognized that parties to a treaty not infrequently employ a term with a technical or other special meaning. They pointed out that technical or special use of the term normally appears from the context and the technical or special meaning becomes, as it were, the ordinary meaning in the particular context.

It is apparent that the ILC members agreed that such a technical meaning might often appear already from the context – it then becomes the 'ordinary meaning'. The utility of Article 31(4) VCLT was thought to be to emphasize that the burden of proof lies on the party invoking the 'special meaning' of the term:[78] 'Other members, while not disputing that the technical or special meaning of the term may often appear from the context, considered that there was a certain utility in laying down a specific rule on the point, if only to emphasize that the burden of proof lies on the party invoking the special meaning of the term.' This again supports the view that the 'special meaning' is to be perceived as the result of one specific weighting of those elements and therefore as one particular 'ordinary meaning'.

Since the 'special meaning' is to be understood as one of the many possible 'ordinary meanings' and the rule concerning terms having a 'special meaning' forms an integral part of the general rule of interpretation stipulated in Article 31 VCLT, the same rules of interpretation should apply to establish the 'special meaning' as those that apply to establish the 'ordinary meaning'. In consequence, the 'special meaning' should be determined by reference to the context as defined in paragraph 2, the object and purpose of the treaty, and the subsequent agreements and practices that, according to paragraph 3, should also be thrown into the 'crucible' together with the context.

Furthermore, the abovementioned considerations as to the hierarchy between Article 31 and Article 32 VCLT remain applicable in the case of the 'special meaning'. Reliance on supplementary means of interpretation is therefore only permissible in the cases specifically provided in Article 32 VCLT;[79] precisely, such recourse is only

75. *Yearbook of the International Law Commission 1964 Volume II, supra* n. 19, p. 52; *Yearbook of the International Law Commission 1966 Volume II, supra* n. 10, p. 218.
76. Arnold, *supra* n. 2, at 6.
77. *YBILC 1966-II, supra* n. 10, p. 222.
78. *Ibid.*, p. 222; some scholars therefore argue that Art. 31, para. 4 VCLT is only of a procedural nature, cf., Arginelli, *supra* n. 37; Avery Jones & Hattingh, *supra* n. 38; Engelen, *supra* n. 48.
79. Arginelli, *supra* n. 37.

permissible as far as it is permissible in establishing the 'ordinary meaning'. The VCLT's structure – *in concreto* the fact that Article 31(4) VCLT is part of the general rule – also supports the view that supplementary means alone cannot be used to establish the 'special meaning'. Based on the ILC's Commentaries to the Draft Articles, establishing a 'special meaning' is not one of the purposes for which Article 32 VCLT admits recourse to supplementary means of interpretation.[80] However, similar to the case of the 'ordinary meaning', Article 32 VCLT can also be used the confirm the 'special meaning'.[81]

To conclude, the general rule of interpretation embodied in Article 31 VCLT provides that the terms of a treaty should be given the meaning that emerges from the context of the treaty considering its object and purpose. The utility of Article 31(4) VCLT is to emphasize that the burden of proof lies on the party invoking that 'special meaning' of a term.

5 'ORDINARY' AND 'SPECIAL MEANING' IN TAX TREATY INTERPRETATION

5.1 Fitting the OECD MC and Its Commentaries into the VCLT Pattern

As DTCs are treaties between states, the VCLT's interpretative rules are applicable when interpreting them (Article 1 VCLT).[82] This means, when interpreting a DTC, the 'ordinary meaning' must be given to the treaty's terms in their context and in light of the treaty's object and purpose (Article 31(1) VCLT). Recourse may be had to supplementary means of interpretation to confirm the meaning resulting from using Article 31 VCLT or with restrictions to determine the meaning of a treaty's term (Article 32 VCLT). The VCLT constitutes a normative framework for whether and to what extent extrinsic instruments are relevant for DTC interpretation.

Although a single, worldwide harmonized tax system might seem utopian, many tax treaties are based on modelized tax rules, and the OECD MC is the most influential.[83] It is moreover accompanied by extensive commentaries.[84] Scholars opine differently on how to subsume the OECD MC and its Commentaries within the VCLT.[85] In the following chapters, the authors focus on DTCs that are based on the OECD MC and examine whether and how it and its Commentaries may be relevant for establishing the 'ordinary meaning' and – in the next section – the 'special meaning' of terms in DTCs.

80. *YBILC 1966-II*, *supra* n. 10, p. 223; Engelen, *supra* n. 48.
81. Avery Jones & Hattingh, *supra* n. 38; Engelen, *supra* n. 48.
82. Rust, in Frotscher, *supra* n. 40, para. 272.
83. Friedl Weiss, *Interpretation of Tax Treaties in Accordance with the Commentaries on the OECD Model Tax Convention under the Vienna Convention on the Law of Treaties*, in *The Legal Status of the OECD Commentaries* (IBFD 2008).
84. David A. Ward, *The Role of the Commentaries in the OECD Model in the Tax Treaty Interpretation Process*, Bulletin – Tax Treaty Monitor 97 (2006).
85. *Ibid.*, at 98; Vogel, *Transnationale Auslegung von Doppelbesteuerungsabkommen*, *supra* n. 2, at 527.

The authors deliberately restrict their research to the significance or non-significance of the OECD MC and its Commentaries in finding the 'ordinary' or the 'special meaning' pursuant to Article 31(1) and (4) VCLT. The broader question of whether the OECD MC and its Commentaries are relevant for tax treaty interpretation at all might not be as relevant as it would initially appear. Considering the ILC Commentary on the Draft Articles of the VCLT, the ILC never intended the rules stipulated in Articles 31 and 32 VCLT to be exhaustive: 'Any attempt to codify the conditions of the application of those principles of interpretation whose appropriateness in any given case depends on the particular context and on a subjective appreciation of the varying circumstances would clearly be inadvisable.'[86] It is also clear that no interpreter would or should deliberately disregard any material that can usefully serve as a guide towards establishing the meaning of a text.[87] There is even a view in literature according to which Articles 31 and 32 VCLT are only a limited factor in applying the OECD Commentaries.[88]

Indeed, the VCLT does not provide an exhaustive set of interpretative methods[89] and, therefore, the authors agree with the view that there is no absolute need for an express provision in the VCLT to use the OECD MC and its Commentaries in treaty interpretation in general. However, the VCLT does cover some specific rules – methods, principles, maxims – of interpretation with two of them being the 'ordinary' and the 'special meaning' standards. When applying those methods, the interpreter must adhere to the rules of the VCLT and, thus, the question remains as to whether Article 31(1) and (4) VCLT allow using the OECD MC and its Commentaries to establish the 'ordinary' or the 'special meaning' of a DTC's term.

5.2 'Ordinary Meaning' in Light of the OECD MC and Its Commentaries

Concerning Article 31 VCLT, some argue that the OECD MC and its Commentaries constitute the 'ordinary meaning' or the context in general under Article 31, paragraph 1 VCLT[90] while others posit that they are relevant for determining the 'special meaning' pursuant to Article 31(4) VCLT.[91] Scholars, courts, and tax administrations have also

86. *Yearbook of the International Law Commission 1966 Volume II, supra* n. 10, pp. 218-219; cf., Avery Jones & Hattingh, *supra* n. 38; Arnold, *supra* n. 2, at 6; Ward, *supra* n. 84, at 98.
87. Ian Sinclair, *The Viennat Convention on the Law of Treaties* 117 (Manchester University Press Second, revised and enlarged edition ed. 1984).
88. Ward, *supra* n. 84, 98.
89. *YBILC 1966-II, supra* n. 10, p. 218.
90. Lehner, in Klaus Vogel & Moris Lehner, *Grundlagen des Abkommensrechts,* Doppelbesteuerungsabkommen, para. 126 (7th ed. 2021); Michael Lang, *Rechtsquellen und Prinzipien des Internationalen Steuerrechts,* in *Internationales Steuerrecht* vol. DStJG Band 36, 19 (M. Achatz ed., Veröffentlichungen der Deutschan Steuerjuristischen Gesellschaft e.V., Dr. Otto Schmidt 2013).
91. Lehner, in Vogel & Lehner, *supra* n. 90, para. 126a; Lang, *Rechtsquellen und Prinzipien des Internationalen Steuerrechts, supra* n. 90, at 19; Michael Lang, *Art. 3 Abs. 2 OECD-MA Und Die Auslegung von Doppelbesteuerungsabkommen,* IWB 285 (2011); Michael Lang, *Wer Hat Das Sagen Im Steuerrecht?,* ÖStZ 206 (2006); Klaus Vogel, *Problems of the Interpretation of Tax Treaties,* SWI 108-109 (2000); Heinz Jirousek, *Critical Comments on the Interpretation of Tax Treaties,* SWI 115 (1998).

attempted to subsume the OECD MC and its Commentaries into virtually every other interpretative provision of the VCLT[92], however, the focus shall be on Article 31 (1) and (4) VCLT.

Although there are different views under which exact part of Article 31 VCLT the OECD MC and its Commentaries can be appropriately included, among many scholars and courts, there seems to be an agreement that both of them are important sources of interpretation for the purposes of Article 31 VCLT.[93] The authors would like to recall what was discussed in section 2.1.2. The 'ordinary meaning' is not only the starting point of interpretation in the context of a textual approach but it is also the result of the interpretative process during which the interpreter examines the context, the object, and the purpose of the treaty in question. Therefore, if the OECD MC and its Commentaries can be subsumed under just one of these concepts, they will be a significant factor in ascertaining the 'ordinary meaning' of a DTC's term.

The OECD MC and its Commentaries contain *the* tax treaty language that has been commonly used by tax treaty negotiators around the world over the last fifty years.[94] Many scholars and courts seem to share this view and argue that, under the OECD MC and its Commentaries, a specialized (tax) terminology has been developed into a 'tax language' that can constitute the 'ordinary meaning' pursuant to Article 31 (1) VCLT.[95] The OECD Council itself recommends to the governments of the member countries 'when concluding new bilateral conventions or revising existing bilateral conventions, to conform to the Model Tax Convention, as interpreted by the Commentaries thereon'.[96]

In the sense of the textual approach, parties are assumed to have used all of the words of a treaty according to their 'ordinary meaning'. At the same time, parties are also assumed to have employed the OECD MC and its Commentaries when drafting their tax treaties.[97] Therefore, and based on the OECD Council's recommendation, the

92. Cf., e.g., Heinz Jirousek, *Critical Comments on the Interpretation of Tax Treaties*, SWI 113 (1998) for Art. 31, para. 2 lit. a VCLT; dBMF 19 April 2023, Bedeutung des OECD-Musterkommentars für die Auslegung von Abkommen zur Vermeidung der Doppelbesteuerung; Urteil des BFH vom 11. Juli 2018 – I R 44/16, IV B 2 -S 1301/22/10002:004, 2022/1218103 for Art. 31 para. 3 lit. b VCLT; *Canada v. MIL (Investments) S.A.*, August 2006, Tax Court of Canada, Case No. 2006 TCC 460 for Art. 31 para. 3 lit. c; DE: BFH [Federal Tax Court], 22 June 2011, I R 103/10; DE: BFH [Federal Tax Court], 25 May 2011, I R 95/10; DE: Bundesfinanzhof, 23 September 2008, I R 57/07 for Art. 32 VCLT.

93. Ault, *supra* n. 2, at 144; Brian J. Arnold, *The Interpretation of Tax Treaties: Looking to the Future*, Bulletin for International Taxation 665 (666) (2021).

94. Becerra, *Chapter 5: Tax Treaty Interpretation, in Interpretation and Application of Tax Treaties in North America, supra* n. 2.

95. To that effect: Lehner, in Klaus Vogel & Moris Lehner, *Grundlagen des Abkommensrechts*, Doppelbesteuerungsabkommen, para. 108 (7th ed. 2021); Rainer Prokisch, *Fragen Der Auslegung von Doppelbesteuerungsabkommen*, SWI 54 (1994); *House of Lords v. 16.7.1959, Rs. Ostime v. Australian Mutual Provident Society, (1960) A. C. 459 (480): DBA Großbritannien/Australien; High Court of Australia v. 22.8.1990, Rs. Thiel v. FCT, 171 C. L. R. 338 (349): DBA Australien/Schweiz*; Klaus Vogel, *Transnationale Auslegung von Doppelbesteuerungsabkommen*, IStR 523 (2003); *House of Lords, Ostime v. Australian Mutual Provident Society, Tax Cases 38 (1956-1960) 492*, at 517 [AC 459, at 480].

96. Recommendation of the OECD Council C(97)195/FINAL.

97. Klaus Vogel, *The Influence of the OECD Commentaries on Tax Treaty Interpretation*, 54 Bulletin for International Taxation 614 (1 December 2000); Ault, *supra* n. 2, at 145.

following presumption seems to be appropriate: If the contracting parties incorporate the text of the OECD MC into a DTC, the content of the corresponding provision of the OECD MC is generally to be attributed to the individual provision of the bilateral agreement.[98] This means that, even if a term is not defined in the concrete DTC, it can be presumed that the parties attributed a meaning to that term that can be derived from a definition in the Commentaries.[99]

It is also possible to see the OECD Commentaries in general as part of the context under Article 31(1) VCLT. In this case, they have a similar significance to legislative materials under national law: they must be taken into account in the interpretation process and provide indications of the view of the historical legislature but are not the only aspect to be considered in the interpretation process. The authors stress that this is only true to that version of the Commentaries that existed concurrently with the treaty negotiations and its conclusion. An amendment to the OECD Commentaries at a later time cannot retroactively establish the 'ordinary meaning' of a treaty's terms at the time they were drawn up.[100] The question, for example, of whether the OECD Commentaries can be considered subsequent practice in the application of the treaty that establishes the agreement of the parties regarding its interpretation (Article 31(3)(b) VCLT)[101] will be discussed by Michael Lang and Eric Coenen in this volume.

In conclusion, the OECD MC and its Commentaries are a significant source of interpretation to find the 'ordinary meaning' of a DTC's terms.

5.3 'Special Meaning' in Light of the OECD MC and Its Commentaries

5.3.1 Article 31(4) VCLT: A Bridge Between Article 31(1) and Article 32 VCLT?

As has already been described in section 3, it is accepted that recourse to supplementary material under Article 32 VCLT can be made even if the meaning under Article 31(1) VCLT is clear. In that case, recourse is made to confirm the meaning arrived at under Article 31(1) VCLT. It is then possible that such recourse to supplementary

98. VwGH 31.7.1996, 92/13/0172, ÖStZB 1997, 235; Michael Lang, *Grundsatzerkenntnis Des VwGH zur DBA-Auslegung*, SWI 427 et seq. (1996); Michael Lang, *Article. 3 Abs. 2 OECD-MA und Die Auslegung von Doppelbesteuerungsabkommen*, IWB 285 (2011); Ward, *supra* n. 84, at 99; Juan Angel Becerra, *Chapter 5: Tax Treaty Interpretation in Interpretation and Application of Tax Treaties in North America* (IBFD Revised 2d ed. 2013), Books IBFD (accessed 18 November 2022);dBMF 19 April 2023, Bedeutung des OECD-Musterkommentars für die Auslegung von Abkommen zur Vermeidung der Doppelbesteuerung; Urteil des BFH vom 11. Juli 2018 – I R 44/16, IV B 2 -S 1301/22/10002:004, 2022/1218103.
99. Kofler, *supra* n. 7, para. 70.
100. K. Vogel, *The Influence of the OECD Commentaries on Tax Treaty Interpretation*, 54 Bulletin for International Taxation 12, 615 (1 December 2000); Lang, *Rechtsquellen Und Prinzipien Des Internationalen Steuerrechts, in Internationales Steuerrecht, supra* n. 90, at 18.
101. dBMF 19 April 2023, Bedeutung des OECD-Musterkommentars für die Auslegung von Abkommen zur Vermeidung der Doppelbesteuerung; Urteil des BFH vom 11. Juli 2018 – I R 44/16, IV B 2 -S 1301/22/10002:004, 2022/1218103. For a critical assessment *see, e.g.*, Michael Lang, *Die Auffassung Des BMF Zur Bedeutung Des OECD-Kommentars Für Die Auslegung von DBA*, IStR 555 (2023).

material would indicate that the 'ordinary meaning' resulting from the exclusive use of Article 31(1) VCLT is erroneous. As some authors[102] point out, this may indicate the existence of another possible meaning under Article 31 VCLT. As a meaning under it can also be a 'special meaning' pursuant to its paragraph 4, the supplementary means could show the existence of a 'special meaning'. Based on the same hypothesis, Ault suggests that Article 31(4) VCLT should be interpreted as allowing supplementary material (e.g., the OECD Commentaries) to be used to establish the intent of the parties to use a term in a 'special' manner despite the seeming lack of ambiguity based on the other Article 31 VCLT material. As a matter of fact, Ault makes two suggestions with the first one being that the OECD Commentaries are supplementary material pursuant to Article 32 VCLT. The second suggestion is that Article 31(4) provides for the use of supplementary material pursuant to Article 32 VCLT to establish the 'special meaning'.

Concerning Ault's second suggestion, the authors opine that the 'special meaning' standard under Article 31(4) VCLT is not to be understood as a gateway to using supplementary materials provided in Article 32 VCLT. First, based on the wording of Articles 31 and 32 VCLT, it is clear that the VCLT differentiates between the interpretative weight of the means provided in Article 31(1) from those of Article 32. The title of Article 31 VCLT is 'General rule of interpretation' in the singular which suggests that all of the elements stipulated in that provision together form one unitary rule of interpretation. However, Article 32 VCLT provides 'supplementary means of interpretation'. From the term supplementary, it can clearly be derived that the VCLT intends to provide some hierarchy between the elements of Article 31 VCLT and those of Article 32 VCLT. The notion that Article 31(4) VCLT allows supplementary material to be used to establish without restriction a meaning under Article 31 VCLT – in concrete, the 'special meaning' – would render this hierarchy obsolete.

Second, the authors highlighted in section 2 that the 'textual approach' had a significant influence on the VCLT's formation. Under that approach, the parties' intentions are determined based on the treaty text. Additionally, the ICJ stressed that it is not the function of interpretation to read into treaties what they do not expressly or by implication contain.[103] It would contradict the textual approach to give supplementary material the same interpretative weight as the means of interpretation under Article 31 VCLT are given.

Third, as the authors expressed in section 4, the 'special meaning' is to be understood as a particular meaning; to be precise, as a particular 'ordinary meaning'. This view is supported by the French version of Article 31(4) VCLT: 'un sens particulier'. The ILC Commentaries on the Draft Articles also suggest that the 'special meaning' is not to be understood as the opposite of the 'ordinary meaning'. Rather, it is one meaning that can become the 'ordinary meaning':

> Some members doubted the need to include a special provision on this point, although they recognized that parties to a treaty not infrequently employ a term with a technical or other special meaning. They pointed out that technical or

102. Avery Jones & Hattingh, *supra* n. 38.
103. *Rights of nationals of the United States of America in Morocco case, Judgement of 22 August 1952, I.C.J. Reports 1950.*

> special use of the term normally appears from the context and the technical or special meaning becomes, as it were, the ordinary meaning in the particular context.[104]

With reference to the *Greenland* case,[105] ILC members stated that the utility of Article 31(4) VCLT is to emphasize that the burden of proof lies on the party invoking the 'special meaning'.[106] Stated differently, if wanting to give a particular meaning to a treaty term as its 'ordinary meaning', there is a burden of proof that such a meaning was intended by the parties.

5.3.2 *Can the OECD MC and Its Commentaries Still Constitute a 'Special Meaning' Pursuant to Article 31(4) VCLT?*

With a view to Ault's first suggestion, the authors refer to the previous chapter and point out that subsuming the OECD MC and its Commentaries under Article 32 VCLT would automatically allocate a subsidiary role to them and allocate a relatively low interpretative weight to them.

However, as Ault correctly points out and as has been described in section 5.2, most DTCs are based on the OECD MC, and its Commentaries form the background against which the specific provisions of a DTC are tailored.[107] Therefore, it is logical to assume that the intent of the drafters was to adopt an interpretation of a term borrowed from the OECD MC that is in accordance with the OECD Commentaries' interpretation. Thus, the OECD MC and its Commentaries can be used to establish the 'special meaning' directly without 'diversions' via Article 32 VCLT. This approach would also fulfil the main purpose (Article 31(1) VCLT) of DTCs which is to avoid double taxation.[108]

Now, this is the same reasoning as that used to support the view that the OECD MC and its Commentaries can be used to establish the 'ordinary meaning' under Article 31(1) VCLT. Although this approach might initially seem odd, it is actually in line with the view expressed by the authors in section 4 and with that of most scholars: Article 31(4) VCLT does not provide any alternative interpretative methods to Article 31(1) VCLT. The utility of Article 31(4) VCLT is merely to emphasize that the burden of proof lies on the party invoking the 'special meaning' of the term.

6 CONCLUSION

At the beginning of this chapter, the authors highlighted that the VCLT's interpretative rules are relevant when interpreting bilateral tax treaties as they are treaties between states and, thus, they are encompassed within the VCLT's scope of application. However, those interpretative rules are only applicable insofar as the particular DTC

104. *YBILC 1966-II, supra* n. 10, p. 222.
105. [PRETITLE], *Legal Status of Eastern Greenland* [LOCATOR] [JURIS-TAIL].
106. *YBILC 1966-II, supra* n. 10, p. 222.
107. Ault, *supra* n. 2, at 146.
108. *Ibid.* at 147.

itself - being the object of interpretation - does not provide rules for its own interpretation. Under this *provisio*, the authors first analysed the 'ordinary' and 'special meaning' standards stipulated in Article 31 VCLT in general without regard to tax treaties.

Concerning the 'ordinary meaning' standard, it can be maintained that the standard was strongly influenced by the 'textual approach' of treaty interpretation that was the dominant school of thought at the time of the genesis of the VCLT. Under the 'textual approach', the primal purpose of interpretation is to find the meaning of the words used in the treaty text rather than finding the subjective intention of the parties to a treaty. Nevertheless, the VCLT does not provide an utter textual interpretation. On the contrary, it requires the consideration of the treaty's context, its object, and its purpose. Therefore, in the authors' opinion, the 'ordinary meaning' of a treaty term is not to be understood merely as the grammatical meaning of it. It must be understood as a meaning that is attached to a term after careful consideration of all of the relevant means of interpretation. The 'ordinary meaning' is the result of the interpretative process. Moreover, based on the ILC's Commentaries on the Draft Articles of the VCLT, the authors maintain the view that the interpretative elements of Article 31 VCLT are not exclusive. Consequently, interpreters should bear in mind all maxims or principles of interpretation.

Regarding the hierarchy between the general rule of interpretation (Article 31 VCLT) and supplementary means (Article 32), the authors differentiate between the chronological place and the interpretative weight of the means of interpretation under those rules. Since it is a single combined operation, interpreters should take a holistic approach to it and simultaneously use all of the interpretative elements. However, the interpretative weight of Article 31 VCLT is higher than that of Article 32 VCLT. Notwithstanding that, within Article 31 VCLT, there is no hierarchy between the interpretative rules. It is at the discretion of the interpreter, under the given circumstances, how much qualitative weight is given to the different elements. Consequently, there can be multiple 'ordinary meanings' to a term based on the qualitative weighting of the interpretative elements of Article 31 VCLT.

With that said, the 'special meaning' of a term pursuant to Article 31(4) VCLT is not to be understood as an opposite to 'ordinary' but as one particular 'ordinary meaning'. Article 31(4) VCLT is a procedural norm of which the purpose is to emphasize that the burden of proof lies with the person invoking the 'special meaning'. Since this is to be understood as one particular 'ordinary meaning', interpreters must adhere to the same interpretative principles as those applicable when establishing the 'ordinary meaning' under Article 31(1) VCLT.

Regarding the 'ordinary meaning' standard in connection with tax treaty interpretation, the authors concluded that both the OECD MC and its Commentaries offer an international tax language that can constitute the 'ordinary meaning' of a tax treaty's term. The same interpretative principle applies when establishing the 'special meaning'. Hence, the OECD MC and its Commentaries have the same relevance in establishing the 'special meaning' of a term as they have in establishing the 'ordinary meaning'.

CHAPTER 3

Good Faith and Tax Treaty Interpretation

Giuseppe Moramarco & Karoline Spies

1 Introduction
2 The Foundations of the Principle of Good Faith
  2.1 Concept of Good Faith
  2.2 Relationship Between Treaty Interpretation and Performance
3 Good Faith and Treaty Interpretation: Article 31, Paragraph 1 VCLT
  3.1 International Public Law
  3.2 International Tax Law
4 Relation to Other Means of Interpretation under and Beyond the VCLT
  4.1 International Public Law
  4.2 International Tax Law
5 Relation with Legitimate Expectations, Estoppel, Acquiescence
  5.1 International Public Law
  5.2 International Tax Law
6 Abuse of Rights
  6.1 International Public Law
  6.2 International Tax Law
7 Conclusion

1 INTRODUCTION

The principle of good faith is considered to be a fundamental aspect of treaty law. This is confirmed, *inter alia*, by Article 31(1) Vienna Convention on the Law of Treaties

(VCLT)[1] according to which treaties must be interpreted in good faith. This chapter explores the role of good faith in treaty interpretation in an attempt to draw a parallel and scrutinize the implications of this principle in international public law on the one hand and international tax law on the other. The overall objective of the chapter lies in identifying – and also questioning – the potential meaning and obligations stemming from good faith when interpreting (tax) treaty provisions.

After a general overview of the foundations of the principle of good faith (section 2) and the rule in Article 31 VCLT (section 3), the analysis will be divided into three subsections with each of them dealing with a specific manifestation that scholars and/or jurisprudence are attributing to it. Section 4 will discuss the function of good faith as a potential aid in selecting one interpretative method or material over another. Section 5 will address whether and under what circumstances good faith may lead to legitimate expectations, estoppel, and acquiescence thereby establishing a specific interpretation of a treaty. Finally, section 6 will focus on the principle as a tool to resolutely contend with the abuse of rights by states in the interpretation process. Each pillar will be addressed from both the perspective of international public law and subsequently focus on potential specificities of tax law. A summary of the results is presented at the end of the chapter.

2 THE FOUNDATIONS OF THE PRINCIPLE OF GOOD FAITH

2.1 Concept of Good Faith

Good faith or bona fides was a key element in ancient Roman law, appeared again in the medieval mercantile law, and was an important component of the natural law concept and the early modern classics of public international law.[2] According to prevailing opinion, it can be considered[3] a general principle of law within the meaning of Article 38(1)(c) of the Statute of the International Court of Justice (ICJ).[4] Some scholars also qualify the principle of good faith as a principle of customary international law.[5] Its importance is also confirmed by international jurisprudence; for example, the ICJ held in the famous *Nuclear Tests* case of 1974 that good faith is 'one

1. Vienna Convention on the Law of Treaties, opened for signature 23 May 1969, entered into force 27 January 1980 (VCLT).
2. Markus Kotzur, *Good Faith (Bona fide)*, in *Max Planck Encyclopedia of Public International Law*, ss 1 et seq. (Anne Peters & Rüdiger Wolfrum eds, 2009) https://doi.org/10.1093/law:epil/9780199231690/e1412; Talya Uçaryılmaz, *The Principle of Good Faith in Public International Law*, 68 Estudios de Deusto 43-59 (2020) https://doi.org/10.18543/ed-68(1)-2020pp43-59.
3. Ian Brownlie, *Principles of Public International Law* 19 (Oxford University Press 7th ed. 2008); Andreas R. Ziegler & Jorun Baumgartner, *Good Faith as a General Principle of (International) Law, in Good Faith and International Economic Law* 10 (Oxford University Press 2015).
4. Article 38(1)(c) of the Statute of the ICJ refers to the application of 'the general principles of law recognized by civilized nations'. These principles serve as a source of international law, alleviating deficiencies when treaties or customary international law may be silent. *See* Brownlie *supra* n. 3.
5. Andrew Mitchell, *Good Faith in WTO Dispute Settlement*, 7 Melbourne Journal of International Law 339 et seq. (2006) https://doi.org/10.2139/ssrn.3157444.

of the basic principles governing the creation and performance of legal obligations, whatever their source'.[6]

Despite the general acceptance as an important 'principle', the normative value of good faith is disputed in academic writing. Whereas some hold that good faith has 'no normative quality',[7] others argue that it has a certain normative effect, although usually being applied in conjunction with other norms and principles.[8] The ICJ[9] and the Appellate Body of the World Trade Organization (WTO)[10] have ruled that the principle of good faith does not intrinsically create legal obligations.[11] Despite this, courts have referred to it when applying other norms of the VCLT (*see* sections 3 and 4) which supports that the principle might have some normative value - although not on a stand-alone basis.[12] In this context, scholars, e.g., Schwarzenberger, noted that good faith can be considered to function as a measuring rod for (other) existing legal obligations.[13] Similarly, Kolb argues that the principle primarily operates through a network of other intermediate principles and norms.[14] As it hence seems to require other norms in order to be operable, scholars have already found its function in practice to be 'negligible'.[15]

The normative qualification of the principle of good faith does not help in identifying its precise content. Scholars generally argue that its legal concept remains an abstract and value-driven principle because it integrates moral aspects such as trust,

6. *Nuclear Tests (Australia v. France)*, Judgment, I.C.J. Reports 1974, para. 46.
7. Mark E. Villiger, *Commentary on the 1969 Vienna Convention on the Law of Treaties* 425 (Martinus Nijhoff Publishers 2009).
8. Robert Kolb, *Good Faith in International Law* 29-31 (Oxford: Hart Publishing 2017); Ziegler & Baumgartner, *supra* n. 3, at 14.
9. In the cases of *Nicaragua v. Honduras* and *Cameroon v. Nigeria* (preliminary objections), the ICJ addressed disputes involving territorial boundaries. In both decisions, it emphasized that, while good faith is a fundamental principle in international relations, it does not itself constitute a standalone legal obligation. For the court, 'The principle of good faith is [...] one of the basic principles governing the creation and performance of legal obligations [...] it is not in itself a source of obligation where none would otherwise exist.' *See Border and Transborder Armed Actions (Nicar. v. Hond.)*, Jurisdiction and Admissibility 1988 I.C.J. 105 (20 December). *Land and Maritime Boundary Between Cameroon and Nigeria (Cameroon v. Nigeria)*, Preliminary Objections 1998 I.C.J. 275 (11 June).
10. Panel Report, European Communities – Anti-Dumping Duties on Imports of Cotton-Type Bed Linen from India – Recourse to Art. 21.5 DSU by India, WTO Doc WT/DS141/RW (adopted 24 April 2003) paras 6.89-6.91.
11. Investment tribunals do not appear to ever have explicitly discussed the question of a possible normative autonomy of the principle of good faith as have the ICJ and the WTOs (*see* Ziegler & Baumgartner, *supra* n. 3, at 16-17).
12. Kolb, *Good Faith in International Law, supra* n. 8.
13. Georg Schwarzenberger, *The Fundamental Principles of International Law* 300 et seq. (The Hague Academy Collected Courses Online/Recueil des cours de l'Académie de La Haye en ligne, Brill|Nijhoff, 1955).
14. Kolb, *Good Faith in International Law, supra* n. 8, at 31. Along the same lines, Michel Virally, *Notes and Comments: Review Essay – Good Faith in Public International Law,* 77 AJIL 130-133 (1983) https://doi.org/10.1017/s0002930000205071.
15. Ziegler & Baumgartner, *supra* n. 3, at 15; Helge Elisabeth Zeitler, *Good Faith in the WTO Jurisprudence: Necessary Balancing Element or an Open Door to Judicial Activism?*, 8 Journal of International Economic Law 721-758 (2005) https://doi.org/10.1093/jiel/jgi043.

honesty, fairness, loyalty, and reasonableness.[16] Analysing these elements in each individual case is not straightforward. Indeed, the risk for interpreters to rely on a subjective concept has been highlighted in literature.[17]

The principle of good faith finds manifestation in different international treaties in various ways.[18] Some of its most important expressions are codified in the VCLT even though the latter does not include a specific definition of the term 'good faith' itself:

- The preamble of the VCLT confirms that the principles of good faith and the *pacta sunt servanda* rule are 'universally recognized'.
- Article 26 VCLT provides that a treaty must be performed in good faith.
- Article 31 VCLT, on the general rule of interpretation, provides that good faith also applies when interpreting a treaty.
- Article 46(2) VCLT specifies that a state can only claim a treaty is invalid due to a manifest violation of its internal law if the violation is obvious to any state acting normally and in good faith.
- Article 69(2)(b) VCLT, on the consequences of the invalidity of a treaty, provides that any act performed in good faith before the invalidity was invoked is not rendered unlawful by reason only of the treaty's invalidity.

In addition, as this study will explain further, in treaty law, the principle of good faith also finds manifestation in related principles or concepts such as legitimate expectations, estoppel, acquiescence, and the abuse doctrine. Its meaning in treaty interpretation will be further elaborated in section 3 following an explanation of its relationship with the *pacta sunt servanda* rule.

2.2 Relationship Between Treaty Interpretation and Performance

The most important manifestation of the principle of good faith in the VCLT is the rule of *pacta sunt servanda* in Article 26 VCLT. According to prevailing opinion, this rule is one of the fundamental principles of international treaty relations[19] and is recognized as customary international law.[20] According to Article 26 VCLT: 'Every treaty in force

16. Kotzur, *supra* n. 2, at paras 22-26; Robert Kolb, *La Bonne Foi en Droit International Public* 82-85 (Presses Universitaires de France 2000); Richard K. Gardiner, *Treaty Interpretation* 164 et seq. (Oxford Univ. Press 2d ed. 2015).
17. Kotzur, *supra* n. 2, at para. 26; Zeitler *supra* n. 15, at 721-753.
18. The duty to fulfil one's obligations in good faith is, for example, most prominently found in Art. 2(2) of *the Charter of the United Nations*. The duty to settle disputes in good faith can be found in its Art. 33 as well as in para. 5 of the 1982 *Manila Declaration on the Peaceful Settlement of International Disputes*.
19. Christina Binder, *The Pacta Sunt Servanda Rule in the Vienna Convention on the Law of Treaties: A Pillar and Its Safeguards*, in *International Law between Universalism and Fragmentation: Festschrift in Honour of Professor Gerhard Hafner* 317 et seq. (Isabelle Buffard, James Crawford, Alain Pellet & Stephan Wittich eds, Brill 2008).
20. Marion Panizzon, *Good Faith in the Jurisprudence of the WTO: The Protection of Legitimate Expectations, Good Faith Interpretation and Fair Dispute Settlement* 27 (Hart Publishing 2006); Mitchell, *supra* n. 5, at 346. *See also* the explicit recognition in the third preambular paragraph

is binding upon the parties to it and must be performed by them in good faith.' The importance of the *pacta sunt servanda* rule is also emphasized in international tax law. For example, based on the Organisation for Economic Co-operation and Development (OECD) Report on Treaty Overrides, it shall be recognized as a 'fundamental, universally recognized principle' in the law of the treaties.[21]

As explained in literature, interpreting a treaty is closely linked to its performance, i.e., there can be no treaty performance without prior interpretation of its provisions. Stated otherwise, interpreting a treaty is always a first step towards its performance.[22] The question of the content and meaning of the rights and obligations enshrined in a treaty is, in fact, essentially one of interpretation.[23] An early draft of the *pacta sunt servanda rule* directly included a reference to treaty interpretation which explains that acknowledging good faith in a treaty interpretation follows directly from the rule *pacta sunt servanda*.[24] This also explains why it is sometimes difficult to find a clear distinction in court decisions between Article 26 and Article 31 VCLT. For example, the ICJ referred to Article 26 VCLT (rather than Article 31(1) VCLT) in the case *Gabčíkovo-Nagymaros* when arguing that the purpose of the treaty and the parties' intentions in concluding it should prevail over its literal application.[25] This overlap is also evidenced in the decisions of some tax courts.[26]

In this context, the reference to good faith in Article 31(1) VCLT, as discussed in the sub-sequent sections in more detail, may be classified as a mere clarification of its role as already embedded in Article 26 VCLT but for the more specific area of

of the VCLT ('Noting that the principles of free consent and of good faith and the pacta sunt servanda rule are universally recognized').

21. 'The obligation "pacta sunt servanda" is one of the fundamental, universally recognised principles of the law of treaties, which has been codified in the preamble and in Article 26 of the Vienna Convention' (OECD, *Tax Treaty Override*, Report of the Committee on Fiscal Affairs, 29 June 1989, para. 9).
22. Gardiner, *supra* n. 16; Ian Sinclair, *The Vienna Convention on the Law of Treaties* 119 (Manchester Univ. Press 2d ed. 1984).
23. Christina Binder & Jane A. Hofbauer, *The Pacta Sunt Servanda Principle or the Limits of Interpretation: The Gabčíkovo-Nagymaros Case Revisited*, in *The Gabčíkovo-Nagymaros Judgment and its Contribution to the Development of International Law* 58-77 (Serena Forlati, Makane Moïse Mbengue & Brian McGarry eds, Brill Nijhoff 2020); Kirsten Schmalenbach, *Vienna Convention on the Law of Treaties: A Commentary*, Art. 26 (Oliver Dörr & Kirsten Schmalenbach eds, Springer 2d ed. 2018).
24. 'A treaty is binding upon the parties and must be applied by them in good faith in accordance with its terms and in the light of the general rules of international law governing interpretation of treaties' (International Law Commission (ILC), Third report on the law of treaties by Sir Humphrey Waldock, Special Rapporteur, draft Art. 55(1), UN Doc A/CN.4/167 and Add.1-3, Yearbook of the International Law Commission 1964, Vol. II). *See also* Commentary to Art. 27 of the 1966 Draft Convention, YBILC 1966-II, p. 219, para. 5.
25. *Gabčíkovo-Nagymaros Project (Hungary/Slovakia)*, Judgment, I.C.J. Reports 1997, p. 7, para. 142.
26. For example, the Switzerland Supreme Court referred to the principle of good faith contained in both Arts 26 and 31 VCLT in a landmark case on beneficial ownership. *See* ATF 141 II 447, para. 4.3.2, reported in 18 ITLR 138. Sjoerd Douma & Craig Elliffe, *Good Faith in Domestic and International Tax Law*, in *Cahiers de Droit Fiscal International vol. 107B* 751 (International Fiscal Association, 2023).

interpretation.[27] Arguably, in relation to this, the concept of good faith in Article 31(1) VCLT does not have a constitutive meaning in itself.

3 GOOD FAITH AND TREATY INTERPRETATION: ARTICLE 31, PARAGRAPH 1 VCLT

3.1 International Public Law

An interpretation in international law must ensure that it reflects the expressed will of the parties as articulated in the terms that are used.[28] In the context of interpretation, the principle of good faith is regarded as a component of customary law due to its manifestation in various provisions of the VCLT that are deemed to have attained that status of customary law.[29] Indeed, Article 31(1) of the VCLT which incorporates the general rule of interpretation dictates that a 'treaty shall be interpreted in good faith in accordance with the ordinary meaning to be given to the terms of the treaty in their context and in the light of its object and purpose'.

The wording of this provision suggests that interpreting a treaty must adhere to the principles of good faith. However, scholars struggle to give a coherent definition of the concept of good faith for interpretation purposes.[30] As described, for example, by Kolb, there are different and contrasting opinions in the literature regarding the specific weight of good faith in the interpretative process.[31] De Brabandere and Van Damme argue that considering the obvious definitional difficulties of the principle, clarifying what constitutes a good faith interpretation appears more feasible by delineating what it is not: an interpretation that is arbitrary, abusive, unreasonable, dishonest, and so forth.[32]

When aiming at grouping the potential tasks of the principle of good faith in the interpretation process as discussed in academic writing, the following manifestations may be identified:

27. *See* for a detailed explanation, Gardiner, *supra* n. 16, who highlights how the drafters of the VCLT wanted to include a broad view of good faith, but this concept was also linked from the beginning to other elements of the general rule such as the role of object and purpose.
28. Oliver Dörr, *Vienna Convention on the Law of Treaties: A Commentary*, Art. 31, 560 (Oliver Dörr & Kirsten Schmalenbach eds, Springer 2d ed. 2018).
29. Eric De Brabandere & Isabelle Van Damme, *Good Faith in Treaty Interpretation in Good Faith and International Economic Law* 40 (Andrew D. Mitchell, M. Sornarajah & Tania Voon eds, Oxford University Press, 2015).
30. Dörr, *supra* n. 28, at 587-588.
31. Some scholars perceive the concept of good faith as the most important and definitive rule of interpretation wherein all other detailed rules are regarded as merely specifications of it. In contrast, an opposing perspective posits that it does not contribute any distinctive elements to the interpretative process due to its perceived lack of material legal significance or its restriction to mandating the fulfilment of owed obligations. *See* Kolb, *Good Faith in International Law*, *supra* n. 8, at 62 et seq.
32. De Brabandere & Van Damme, *supra* n. 29, at 39.

- Assisting in choosing one hermeneutic criterion, interpretation method, and relevant material rather than another (*see* section 4).[33]
- Helping in the search for a 'reasonable' interpretation, specifically what a fair and rational party could reasonably have comprehended regarding the text and subsequent behaviours of the parties (legitimate expectations, *see* section 5).[34]
- Supporting the priority of the treaty's spirit compared to an excessive attachment to the specific wording of the text (*see*, in this respect, the abuse of rights doctrine in section 6).[35]

From the above, it seems that good faith is a flexible principle that can be called into action in different ways. However, despite the explicit reference to good faith in Article 31 VCLT, international courts do not seem to have used this principle to a great extent. Indeed, scholars emphasize that the ICJ has not yet interpreted a treaty based solely on good faith.[36] Rather, good faith is usually applied by international courts in conjunction with other interpretative principles and the substantive treaty provisions that have allegedly been breached (*see* section 4). Therefore, as will also be explained in the following sections, despite claims found in the literature, its role in treaty interpretation can be considered marginal in practice.[37] Moreover, the interpretation that is done in good faith is also limited by the prohibition against generating new rights or obligations (based on it) not supported by the treaty's text or the signatories' intent.[38]

3.2 International Tax Law

As with all international agreements, tax treaties are subject to the principle of good faith, and the rules of interpretation codified in Articles 31-33 VCLT apply to them.[39] The OECD itself recognizes the obligation to interpret tax treaties in good faith when

33. De Brabandere & Van Damme, *supra* n. 29, at 42 et seq.; Villiger, *supra* n. 7, at 425; Gardiner, *supra* n. 16.
34. Dörr, *supra* n. 28, at 587-588; Kolb, *Good Faith in International Law, supra* n. 8, at 62 et seq.
35. Kolb, *Good Faith in International Law, supra* n. 8, at 62 et seq.; Villiger, *supra* n. 7, at 426.
36. Gardiner, *supra* n. 16, at 164 et seq.; Stephan Reinhold, *Good Faith in International Law*, UCL Journal of Law and Jurisprudence 40-63 (2013) https://doi.org/10.14324/111.2052-1871.002. Hugh Thirlway, *The Law and Procedure of the ICJ 1960-1989: Part Three*, 62 British Y.B. Int'l L. 17 (1991) https://doi.org/10.1093/bybil/62.1.1.
37. Ziegler & Baumgartner, *supra* n. 3, at 15.
38. *See* the discussion in s. 2 concerning the degree of normativity of good faith.
39. Klaus Vogel et al., *Klaus Vogel on Double Taxation Conventions* 35, margin No. 68 (Kluwer Law International 1997): 'Therefore, the rules of the Vienna Convention are used in case law on the interpretation of double taxation treaties today as a basis even with regard to states which have not yet ratified the Vienna Convention.' *See also* Guglielmo Maisto, *Domestic Anti-abuse Rules and Bilateral Tax Conventions in the Light of Public International Law*, in *Essays on Tax Treaties: A Tribute to David A. Ward* 332-333 (Guglielmo Maisto, Angelo Nikolakakis & Jefferson VanderWolk eds, IBFD 2012): 'International tax scholars commonly accept that tax treaties are to be interpreted according to the rules of interpretation found in articles 31 et seq. of the VCLT [...].' Michael Lang, *Introduction to the Law of Double Taxation Conventions* 13 et seq. (IBFD/Linde 2021).

addressing the improper use of a treaty by taxpayers in the Commentary on Article 1 Model Convention of the Organisation for Economic Co-operation and Development (OECD MC) (2017).[40]

Thus far, academic discussions on interpretation in good faith in tax treaty law primarily focus on the following: (i) using the OECD Commentary (discussed in this section); (ii) and the (limitation of) reference to domestic law, particularly based on Article 3(2) OECD MC (discussed in section 4); which also indirectly includes (iii) the abuse of treaties by contracting states (discussed in section 6). While these aspects initially appear to be specific issues of tax treaty law, they also share similarities with related questions in public international law.

Some scholars have brought forward that the principle of good faith in Article 31(1) VCLT requires that the OECD MC and the Commentary are consulted in the interpretation process if it can be established by reference to the text of the treaty that a double taxation convention is based on the OECD MC. Here, the main argument is that the principle of good faith that requires trust in reasonable interpretations of the text implies that, if contracting states adopt the OECD MC wording in a provision, they likely intend to give it the meaning as defined by the OECD MC and its Commentary available at the time of negotiation.[41] Although agreeable in its conclusions, this position remains uncertain as to whether the application of 'good faith' is actually necessary to achieve this result.

First, there is an ongoing debate in academic literature on which (more specific) provision of the VCLT the relevance of the Commentary for interpretation purposes should or could be based. The discussion often revolves around Article 31(1), (2), or (4) or Article 32 VCLT with 'good faith' being only a very minor factor.[42] Second, the

40. OECD Model Tax Convention on Income and on Capital: Commentary on Art. 1, para. 59 (21 November 2017): 'Other States prefer to view some abuses as being abuses of the convention itself, as opposed to abuses of domestic law. These States, however, then consider that a proper construction of tax conventions allows them to disregard abusive transactions, such as those entered into with the view to obtaining unintended benefits under the provisions of these conventions. This interpretation results from the object and purpose of tax conventions as well as the obligation to interpret them in good faith (see Article 31 of the Vienna Convention on the Law of Treaties).'
41. Michael Lang & Florian Brugger, *The Role of the OECD Commentary in Tax Treaty Interpretation*, 23 Australian Tax Forum 99-100 (2008).
42. Werner Haslehner, *Introduction to Klaus Vogel on Double Taxation Conventions* 45 et seq. (Ekkehart Reimert & Alexander Rust eds, Kluwer Law International 5th ed. 2022). Aitor Navarro, *International Tax Soft Law Instruments: The Futility of the Static v. Dynamic Interpretation Debate*, 48(10) Intertax 848-860 (2020) https://doi.org/10.54648/taxi2020086; Klaus Vogel & Rainer Prokisch, *General Report*, in *Interpretation of double taxation conventions* (IFA ed., 1993); Hugh J. Ault, *The Role of the OECD Commentaries in the Interpretation of Tax Treaties*, 22(4) Intertax 144 (1994) https://doi.org/10.54648/taxi1994023; Ekkehart Reimer, *Interpretation of Tax Treaties*, 39(12) Eur. Tax. 458, 467 (1999); Eric van der Bruggen, *The Power of Persuasion: Notes on the Sources of International Law and the OECD Commentary*, 31(8/9) Intertax 259 (2003) https://doi.org/10.54648/taxi2003053; Hans Pijl, *Beyond Legal Bindingness*, in *The Legal Status of the OECD Commentaries*, 1 Conflict of Norms in International Tax Law Series s. 1 (S. Douma & F. Engelen eds, IBFD 2008) https://doi.org/10.59403/2r4mb2q006; Daniël Broekhuijsen & Kirsten van der Velde, *The Retroactive Effect of Changes to the Commentaries on the OECD Model*, 69(11) Bull. Int'l Tax. 623, 626 (2015) https://doi.org/10.59403/1qyhz95; Allison Christians, *BEPS and the New International Tax Order*, BYU. L. Rev. 1603, 1616-1617 (2016); Jacques Sasseville, *Influence of the OECD Commentary on Court Decisions*, *in Courts and*

same authors who emphasize the relevance of using the Commentary balance their position in accordance with the VCLT rules. They first acknowledge that the OECD MC and Commentary do not carry the same weight as the treaty text itself as they are not part of the treaty. Second, they recognize that the interpretation rules in the VCLT do not establish a strict hierarchy among interpretative elements thereby necessitating careful consideration of all relevant aspects in each case.[43] Indeed, as Lang pointed out:

> in addition to the OECD Model and the Commentary, other historical, teleological and systematic aspects, as well as the wording of the convention itself, have to be taken into account. Which arguments are more convincing is to be evaluated on a case-by-case basis. Art. 31 VCTL does not provide for a rule under which one interpretation method takes precedence over another.[44]

Third, it is generally not possible to argue that the Commentary is binding in international law based on good faith.[45] Besides the lack of a clear definition, the principle cannot create legal obligations where none exist.[46] Thus, since tax treaties, as a general rule,[47] do not provide for any obligation regarding using the Commentary, it cannot be assumed that it can arise from good faith.

For the same reasons above, the principle of good faith cannot serve as a deciding argument regarding the question of whether amendments to the OECD MC and to the Commentary made after the conclusion of the respective treaty have to be taken into account for interpreting a treaty predating their publication, i.e., this principle cannot support that later versions of the Commentary should always or never be relevant. This assessment will depend on the individual case and the substantive provision as well as its relevant context and historical background. It may particularly become a factor of whether the new Commentary only clarifies or codifies existing practice or definitions that could already be deduced from the (earlier) version of the OECD MC and Commentary existing at the time of the conclusion of the relevant treaty or – in comparison to earlier versions – lead to a material change.[48]

In conclusion, the underlying reasoning that if a treaty follows the OECD Model text, it is reasonable to refer to the Commentary at the time of the treaty's conclusion, is convincing. However, the authors disagree that good faith should be the legal basis. If the contracting parties use the same wording as that contained in the OECD Model,

---

Tax Treaty Law, 3 EC and International Tax Law Series 194 (Guglielmo Maisto ed., IBFD 2007); Friedl Weiss, *Interpretation of Tax Treaties in Accordance with the Commentaries on the OECD Model Tax Convention under the Vienna Convention on the Law of Treaties*, in *The Legal Status of the OECD Commentaries*, 1 Conflict of Norms in International Tax Law Series s. 2.1 (S. Douma & F. Engelen eds, IBFD 2008).

43. Lang & Brugger, *supra* n. 41, at 100.
44. Lang, *supra* n. 39, at 19 et seq.
45. David Ward, *The Role of the Commentaries on the OECD Model in the Tax Treaty Interpretation Process*, 60 Bull. Int'l Tax'n 3, 99 (2006); Jan Bossuyt, *The Legal Status of Extrinsic Instruments for the Interpretation of Tax Treaties* 968 et seq. (IBFD 2022).
46. *See* s. 2.
47. However, some states include a reference to the OECD Commentary in a protocol to the tax treaty which could arguably lead to the result that the Commentary becomes part of the treaty itself (*see* Chapter 4).
48. Lang, *supra* n. 39, at 22 et seq.

other interpretative elements, i.e., wording, context, object, and purpose, in a holistic approach, will be relevant in supporting that the explanations stipulated in the OECD Commentary are taken into account in order to establish the ordinary meaning of treaty terms. Good faith might merely corroborate this view without providing any additional normative value.

4 RELATION TO OTHER MEANS OF INTERPRETATION UNDER AND BEYOND THE VCLT

4.1 International Public Law

According to the prevailing opinion, the principle of good faith must be used during the entire interpretation process.[49] Indeed, since all of the elements in Articles 31 to 33 VCLT are to be viewed as one holistic rule, they should all be subject to the good faith principle.[50] More specifically, it is argued that it can help to justify choices for applying one hermeneutic criterion rather than another.[51] For example, the ICJ explicitly held in *Gabčíkovo-Nagymaros Project* that the obligation to perform a treaty in good faith suggests that it must be applied – and therefore also interpreted (*see* section 2) – in a reasonable manner by placing more emphasis on the spirit of the treaty than on the text.[52] Other choices that might be influenced by the principle of good faith could be: the acceptance of subparagraph 2(b) of Article 31 VCLT (agreements and instruments related to the context of the treaties); assessing subsequent practice under paragraph 3(b) (practice establishing agreement of the parties regarding the interpretation of the treaty); the recourse to Article 32 VCLT (supplementary means of interpretation such as preparatory work and circumstances of conclusion); or selecting or using supplementary means of interpretation not explicitly mentioned in Article 32 VCLT.[53]

Scholars and courts thereby seem to assume that focusing on one element of interpretation or material is more reasonable than another. This assumption, however, often seems to lack reasoning. For example, in the very few ICJ cases that mention the concept of good faith, there is a lack of any attempt at definition and explanation just as there is a lack of explanation of the decision to use one hermeneutic criterion rather than another based on good faith.[54] In many judgments, the ICJ merely referred to the

49. Dörr, *supra* n. 28, at 587; Villiger, *supra* n. 7, at 426.
50. Chang-fa Lo, *Treaty Interpretation under the Vienna Convention on the Law of Treaties* 292 et seq. (Springer Singapore 1st ed. 2017). Ulf Linderfalk, *What Are the Functions of the General Principles? Good Faith and International Legal Pragmatics*, 78 Zeitschrift für ausländisches öffentliches Recht und Völkerrecht: Heidelberg Journal of International Law, 5 et seq. (2018) https://doi.org/10.2139/ssrn.2955648.
51. De Brabandere & Van Damme, *supra* n. 29, at 42.
52. *See Gabčíkovo-Nagymaros Project (Hungary/Slovakia)*, Judgment, 1997 I.C.J., para. 142: 'It is the purpose of the Treaty, and the intentions of the parties in concluding it, which should prevail over its literal application. The principle of good faith obliges the Parties to apply it in a reasonable way and in such a manner that its purpose can be realized.'
53. Villiger, *supra* n. 7, at 426; De Brabandere & Van Damme, *supra* n. 29, at 42.
54. *See, e.g., Border and Transborder Armed Actions (Nicaragua v. Honduras)*, Judgment, 1988 I.C.J.; *Land and Maritime Boundary Between Cameroon and Nigeria (Cameroon v. Nigeria)*,

principle of good faith as part of its frequent reiteration of Article 31(1) VCLT as customary law applicable to treaty interpretation without explaining or discussing the concept of good faith as such.[55]

Outside the abovementioned ICJ approach, the situation does not seem to be different. In the very limited cases cited in literature[56] in which good faith is mentioned as a basis for selecting a hermeneutic criterion, it seems that the same result could have been achieved simply by making direct reference to the criterion chosen without resorting to the invocation of good faith. For example, the Permanent Court of Arbitration in *HICEE BV v. Slovakia* used supplementary means of interpretation, specifically explanatory notes from the Dutch Minister of Foreign Affairs during the BIT ratification process, to decide the case. The tribunal justified this choice on the need to interpret treaties in good faith, noting that disregarding such documents would defy 'logic and good sense'.[57] It is questionable whether the reference to good faith adds any reliable value to this choice and approach. The interpretation given in this decision could have been reached by relying directly on historical means of interpretation or on Article 32 VCLT without even making reference to good faith.

In addition to the above, the principle of good faith is also viewed as a meta-norm.[58] In this context, this principle acts as a valid foundation for recognizing additional tools, principles, or values even when they are not explicitly mentioned in the VCLT. Most importantly, the principle of good faith is used to justify reliance on what is commonly referred to as the 'principle of effectiveness'. As explained by Gardiner, the principle of effectiveness is a particular application of the principle of

Preliminary Objections, Judgment, 1998 I.C.J.; *Corfu Channel* case *(United Kingdom v. Albania)*, Judgment, 1949 I.C.J.; *Territorial Dispute (Libyan Arab Jamahiriya v. Chad)*, Judgment, 1994 I.C.J.; *Free Zones of Upper Savoy and the District of Gex (France v. Switzerland)*, Judgment, 1929 P.C.I.J. (ser. A) No. 22; *Anglo-Iranian Oil Co.* case *(United Kingdom v. Iran)*, Judgment, 1952 I.C.J.; *Constitution of the Maritime Safety Committee*, Advisory Opinion, 1960 I.C.J.; *LaGrand* case *(Germany v. United States of America)*, Judgment, 2001 I.C.J.; *Temple of Preah Vihear (Cambodia v. Thailand)*, Judgment, 1962 I.C.J.; *Fisheries* case *(United Kingdom v. Norway)*, Judgment, 1951 I.C.J.; *Land, Island and Maritime Frontier Dispute (El Salvador v. Honduras: Nicaragua Intervening)*, Judgment, 1992 I.C.J.

55. Gardiner, *supra* n. 16, at 164 et seq.; Thirlway, *supra* n. 36, at 17.
56. De Brabandere & Van Damme, *supra* n. 29; Gardiner, *supra* n. 16; Dörr, *supra* n. 28; Villiger, *supra* n. 7; Kotzur *supra* n. 2; Mitchell *supra* n. 5; Ziegler & Baumgartner, *supra* n. 3; Kolb, *Good Faith in International Law, supra* n. 8 and Kolb, *La Bonne Foi en Droit International Public, supra* n. 16; Panizzon, *supra* n. 20; Binder & Hofbauer, *supra* n. 23; Lo, *supra* n. 50; Linderfalk *supra* n. 50.
57. *See HICEE BV v. Slovak Republic (Partial Award)*, Case No. 2009-11, paras 122-147 (UNCITRAL, Perm. Ct. Arb. 23 May 2011). The claimant and respondent had put forward opposing interpretations of the phrase 'directly or through an investor of a third State' in Art. 1(a) of the Netherlands–Czechoslovakia bilateral investment treaty. The tribunal relied on supplementary means of interpretation, specifically explanatory notes submitted by the Dutch Minister of Foreign Affairs to the Dutch Parliament during the treaty ratification process. These documents were used to conclude that the phrase 'directly or through an investor of a third State' in Art. 1(a) of the Netherlands–Czechoslovakia BIT did not cover investments made by wholly-owned subsidiaries in the Slovak Republic. The tribunal justified relying on these documents to ensure a good faith interpretation of the treaty, stating that disregarding them would be illogical and inconsistent with the principle of good faith interpretation.
58. De Brabandere & Van Damme, *supra* n. 29, at 43.

good faith to the interpretation of treaties and includes two distinguishable rules.[59] The first is that good faith requires that all of the terms and expressions included in a treaty are to be given a meaning and that an interpretation of the treaty or a particular provision that attributes a meaning to all the terms is to be preferred to an interpretation that does not attribute any meaning to certain terms or expressions. The second is that an interpretation of the treaty that is more in accordance with the object and purpose thereof is to be preferred to one that is less so.[60] However, again, the limits of the concept of good faith seem evident also in this context. The principle of effectiveness as an interpretative tool is not an isolated concept based on good faith but may also be more concretely qualified as a specific application of the object and purpose requirement of treaty interpretation.[61] This also seems to emerge from reading the decisions by the ICJ in the *Anglo-Iranian Oil* case, in the *Constitution of the Maritime Safety Committee* in the *Fisheries Jurisdiction (Spain v. Canada)*, and in *LaGrand* where the principle of effectiveness was used in relation to the object and purpose of the treaty.[62]

To conclude, various approaches of treaty interpretation may be considered rooted in the application of logic and common sense and therefore be considered specific manifestations of the principle of good faith. Nevertheless, it is challenging to find precisely what unique contributions it makes to treaty interpretation beyond the other elements outlined in Articles 31 et seq. VCLT. The academic discourse and case law in this area lack clarity as what is considered an application of good faith might be viewed merely as a standard interpretive principle by others. In the authors' opinion, its role in justifying the selection of one hermeneutical criterion over another is debatable. Given that good faith is not significantly different from other interpretive criteria and lacks concrete significance, using it to justify certain interpretative choices does not meaningfully enhance the interpretive process.

4.2 International Tax Law

The conclusions reached above are equally applicable in the context of tax treaties. The unique contribution of good faith to tax treaty interpretation with respect to other means remains debatable and limited. Academic literature[63] shows that the issue of

59. Gardiner, *supra* n. 16.
60. *Gardiner, supra* n. 16.
61. Dörr, *supra* n. 28, at 578-579.
62. *See, e.g., Anglo-Iranian Oil Co.* case *(United Kingdom v. Iran)*, Judgment, (1952) I.C.J. Rep. 93, 105; *Constitution of the Maritime Safety Committee*, Advisory Opinion, (1960) I.C.J. Rep. 150, 160; *LaGrand* case *(Germany v. United States of America)*, Judgment, (2001) I.C.J. Rep. 466, para. 102; *Fisheries Jurisdiction* case *(Spain v. Canada)*, Judgment, (1998) I.C.J. Rep. 432.
63. Edwin van der Bruggen, *Good Faith in the Application and Interpretation of Double Taxation Conventions*, 1 British Tax Review, 167 et seq. (2003); Angelo Nikolakakis, *Current Tax Treaty Issues: Part Two – Treaty Definitions: Chapter 9 – Interpretation vs Qualification* 319 et seq. (IBFD 2020); John F. Avery Jones & Peter J. Hattingh, *Treaty Interpretation: Global Tax Treaty Commentaries*, Global Topics IBFD at para. 4.6. (accessed 21 June 2024).
    Engelen points out how 'the principle of good faith puts a limit on the reference to domestic law for the purpose of the interpretation and application of a tax treaty and prevents a

good faith in tax treaty interpretation is dominated by the debate surrounding the scope and limits of the referral to domestic law in Article 3(2) OECD MC and other sections of tax treaties.[64] As Article 3(2) OECD MC might be seen as a tax-treaty-specific rule of interpretation, this debate is included in this section on the relation of good faith to other means of interpretation.[65]

Avery Jones suggested that the issue of the relevance of a subsequent change of domestic law for treaty interpretation is a matter of good faith. In particular, with reference to Article 3(2) OECD MC, the latter author considers that: 'If the change to domestic law was made in good faith, for example, to clarify a borderline, the change should apply for treaty purposes. But if the change was made in order for the state to enlarge its taxing jurisdiction, it should not be used for treaty purposes.'[66] Thereby, there is a rather obvious significant amount of emphasis placed on the intention or the effect of the domestic legislation.

The Netherlands Supreme Court uses the good faith principle primarily in line with the above approach when assessing the impact of subsequent domestic law on tax treaty interpretation. This can be seen, for instance, in a decision of 2003 which concerned pension commutations that were exclusively taxable in the residence state under the 1971 tax treaty concluded by the Netherlands and Singapore (based on Article 19 of the OECD Model).[67] In 1994, Dutch legislation reclassified the above pension commutations for non-residents as 'employment income' sourced from the Netherlands which (potentially) could have led to the application of the allocation rule for employment income giving the taxing right to the Netherlands. The court ruled that interpreting these pension commutation amounts as employment income under the 1971 tax treaty would violate the principle of good faith as outlined in Article 31(1) VCLT. This was because the 1995 law effectively undermined and bypassed Singapore's taxing rights over its residents' pensions as originally agreed in the treaty. The court emphasized that good faith necessitates a holistic view, taking into account the impact of subsequent domestic legislation on the positions of both contracting states and the taxpayer. This approach requires comparing the situation at the time of the treaty's signing in 1971 with the circumstances following the legislative changes.[68]

---

contracting State from eroding or evading its obligations under the treaty by subsequently amending in its domestic law the scope of terms not defined in the treaty, either by means of legal definition or otherwise'. *See* Frank Engelen, *Interpretation of Tax Treaties Under International Law*, Doctoral Series Vol. 7, Ch. 6 (IBFD 2004).

64. The OECD Model also refers to domestic tax law in Arts 2(4), 4(1), 6(2) & 10(3) OECD MC.
65. In more detail on the relationship of Art. 3(2) OECD MC and the VCLT, *see* Chapter 11.
66. Avery Jones & Hattingh, *supra* n. 63, s. 4.6.
67. Netherlands Supreme Court, 5 September 2003, case number 37657, LJN: AE8403, BNB 2003/380.
68. *See also* with a similar approach, Netherlands Supreme Court, 19 June 2009, case numbers 43978, 08/02288 and 07/13267, LJN: BC5201, BI8566 and B18563, BNB 2009/263, BNB 2009/266 and BNB 2009/265 Netherlands Supreme Court, 20 February 2009, case numbers 43760, LJN: BD5481, BNB 2009/261; 07/12314, LJN: BD5468, BNB 2009/262; 42701, LJN: AZ2232, BNB 2009/260; 42699, LJN: AZ2230 and 42702, LJN AZ2238. For a comment *see* Petrus J. Hattingh, *The Interpretation of Bilateral Tax Treaties: Changing Tax Law: Unchanging Treaty Obligations?* 131 et seq. (Doctoral dissertation, University of Cambridge, 2021).

In a comparable case handed down in 2003, the Belgian Supreme Court ruled that legal fictions designed to undermine the allocation of taxing powers violated both the treaty and the principle of good faith. The court examined whether a domestic fiction – whereby a pension payment made after emigration was deemed to have occurred the day before emigration – contravened the Belgium-France Income Tax Treaty of 1964 that assigned exclusive taxing rights on pensions to the state of residence.[69] The Supreme Court upheld the Court of Appeal's decision, asserting that such fictions that erode the allocation of powers breach the treaty and the principle of good faith.

Additionally, outside European borders, there are courts that use good faith to test the reference to domestic law. In 2013, the High Court of Andhra Pradesh, Hyderabad, decided that the capital gains from the sale of shares in a French holding company were not taxable in India under Article 14 of the India-France tax treaty, rejecting the Indian tax authorities' reliance on domestic law definitions. The court pointed out that the treaty did not contain any textual, grammatical, or syntactic ambiguity warranting an interpretive recourse to national law, meaning that recourse to Article 3(2) OECD MC would violate the principle of good faith interpretation.[70]

Concluding from Belgian and Dutch jurisprudence, De Broe noted that, when changes in domestic law significantly disrupt the balance and primary objective of the treaty, the exception in Article 3(2) OECD MC ('unless the context otherwise requires') as well as the principle of good faith in Article 31 VCLT would prevent a contracting state from effectively applying its new domestic law definitions or fictions for interpreting undefined terms.[71]

As this analysis already suggests, the principle of good faith (again) is arguably not used on a stand-alone basis but together with other interpretative means (here, the 'context' as stipulated in Article 3(2) OECD MC).[72] In general, it is extremely complicated and risky to refer to an intrinsically subjective element linked to 'moral' qualities like good or bad faith (of a legislator) to deal with changes in domestic law (thereby implicitly aiming at attempting to effectively address treaty abuse by the contracting states; *see also* section 6).[73] The concept of good faith does not seem to provide a robust legal basis for the above outcomes. This study has shown in the public law part how good faith is not a solid concept on which to base interpretative choices between various hermeneutic criteria. Indeed, it is possible also in the tax area to demonstrate that the same interpretative outcome reached by the abovementioned courts may be achieved by interpreting Article 3(2) OECD MC and the term 'context' of the treaty without invoking or using ambiguous concepts like good faith. Stated otherwise, the authors opine that it is all a matter of a 'correct' interpretation of Article 3(2) OECD Model. For a detailed analysis in this regard, *see* Chapter 11.

---

69. Belgian Supreme Court, 5 December 2003, F.02.0042.F. *See* Luc De Broe, *International Tax Planning and Prevention of Abuse*, s. 2.2.1.1.4 (IBFD 2008).
70. Lang, *supra* n. 39, at 28, m.no 119.
71. De Broe, *supra* n. 69.
72. On the broad meaning of 'context' in Art. 3(2) OECD MC *see* Chapter 11.
73. Nikolakakis, *supra* n. 63: 'restoring good faith does give rise to considerable uncertainty, in that a judgement call will have to be made with reference to every subsequent change of domestic law, without very much by way of guidance in this regard'.

5 RELATION WITH LEGITIMATE EXPECTATIONS, ESTOPPEL, ACQUIESCENCE

5.1 International Public Law

According to some scholars, the principle of legitimate expectations is one of the expressions of good faith in international law.[74] The doctrine of legitimate expectations protects the fair and reasonable interests of a party that had every reason to believe that the treaty must be interpreted and applied in a particular way based on the actions or inactions of another party.[75] According to Kolb, each party must be able to rely on the *usus loquendi*, i.e., on what it could and should have been reasonably understood by the terms used in context.[76] The tool of reasonable interpretation is particularly important when a text gives each party a certain leeway of appreciation or discretionary. In this regard, any interpretation that leads to absurd results of the object and purpose of the treaty is 'legally wrong'.[77]

International courts refer to the principle of good faith when discussing legitimate expectations. For example, in the *Nuclear Tests* case, the ICJ referred to it and held that unilateral declarations made by states, when intended to be legally binding, create legitimate expectations for other states.[78] In the *Fisheries Jurisdiction* case, the ICJ also references the principles of good faith and legitimate expectations. The Court discusses these principles in the context of interpreting the 1961 Exchange of Notes between Iceland and the United Kingdom wherein the United Kingdom undertook to recognize an exclusive Icelandic fishery zone up to a limit of 12 miles and to withdraw its fishing vessels from that zone over a period of three years. The court emphasizes that the parties had legitimate expectations regarding the durability and stability of the above arrangements.[79] To challenge these decisions within the realm of contemporary international law, it might be questioned whether the existing legal framework,

74. Kolb, *Good Faith in International Law, supra* n. 8, at 62 et seq.
75. Thomas Cottier & Krista Nadakavukaren Schefer, *Good Faith and the Protection of Legitimate Expectations in the WTO*, in *New Directions in International Economic Law: Essays in Honour of John H. Jackson* 47-68 (Marco Bronckers & Reinhard Quick eds, Kluwer Law International 2000); Eirik Bjorge, *Legitimate Expectations* (Max Planck Encyclopedia of Public International Law (MPEPIL), May 2023).
76. Kolb, *Good Faith in International Law, supra* n. 8, at 62 et seq.
77. Scholars pointed out that this is also the understanding in which the concept of good faith is at least hinted at in the rules of interpretation themselves, albeit only as an obligation of result. What is to be avoided by applying the principle of good faith is stipulated in Art. 32 lit. b), i.e., that a treaty interpretation should lead to a result that is manifestly absurd or unreasonable. Thus, the ordinary meaning, if established in its context, must always be submitted to the test of reasonableness. *See* Gardiner, *supra* n. 16 at 164 et seq.; Dörr, *supra* n. 28 at 560; Villiger, *supra* n. 7, at 425.
78. In the *Nuclear Tests* case, the ICJ ruled that assurances given unilaterally by France about ceasing atmospheric nuclear tests established a legal obligation. *See Nuclear Tests* case *(Austl. v. Fr.)*, Judgment, 1974 I.C.J. 253, para. 46.
79. According to the court, 'In consequence, the exercise of jurisdiction by the Court to entertain the present application would fall within the terms of the compromissory clause and correspond exactly to the intentions and expectations of both parties when they discussed and consented to that clause.' *See Fisheries Jurisdiction (U.K. v. Ice.)*, Judgment, 1973 I.C.J., paras 21 et seq.

particularly Article 31(3) of the VCLT, already offers adequate mechanisms to account for the subsequent behaviours and practices of states.[80] Consequently, it could be argued that relying on the principles of good faith and legitimate expectations, which are not as clearly defined, might be perceived as unnecessary.

In the context of the WTO, the Appellate Body has not accepted the protection of legitimate expectations as a principle of good faith interpretation.[81] For example, in *India-Patents,* the Appellate Body found that 'the legitimate expectations of the parties to a treaty are reflected in the language of the treaty itself'. In its view, recognizing the protection of legitimate expectations as a stand-alone principle conflicts with the VCLT because 'these principles of interpretation neither require nor condone the imputation into a treaty of words that are not there or the importation into a treaty of concepts that were not intended'.[82] Additionally, in investment law, it is debated whether the legitimate expectations of the foreign investor constitute a key element of the fair and equitable treatment standard.[83]

Overall, there does not seem to be a consistent approach from international courts regarding legitimate expectations in treaty interpretation. In this regard, the question arises whether taking into account a parties' actions or inactions for the purposes of interpretation requires a reference to good faith and legitimate expectations or whether it would not be better to use Article 31(3) VCLT as a legal basis.

The principle of good faith is furthermore also considered being reflected in the principle of estoppel and acquiescence which are both closely linked to legitimate expectations. Estoppel is a principle for which a state can be bound by its actions or representations if another state has reasonably relied on them.[84] This can occur if a state has accepted a particular interpretation during negotiations or if that interpretation is later applied routinely when implementing a treaty. Similar to estoppel, acquiescence is also grounded in the principle of protecting legitimate expectations and thus good faith. To provide more detail, when a state does not contest certain actions or claims by another state within a reasonable period, it may be deemed to have

80. *See* in more detail on this provision Chapter 7.
81. De Brabandere & Van Damme, *supra* n. 29, at 49.
82. *India – Patent Protection for Pharmaceutical and Agricultural Chemical Products,* WTO Doc. WT/DS50/AB/R para. 45 (16 January 1998).
83. The 'Fair and Equitable Treatment' (FET) clause in BITs is a crucial standard of international investment law. It mandates that host states provide foreign investors with fair and equitable treatment which essentially means treatment that is just, even-handed, and fosters the promotion of foreign investment. This standard is generally interpreted to include principles such as respecting an investor's legitimate expectations, acting in a non-arbitrary and non-discriminatory manner, and adhering to principles of transparency, consistency, good faith, due process, and proportionality. For a discussion, *see* Martins Paparinskis, *Good Faith and Fair and Equitable Treatment in International Investment Law,* in *Good Faith and International Economic Law* (Andrew D. Mitchell, M Sornarajah & Tania Voon eds, Oxford Univ. Press 2015) https://doi.org/10.1093/acprof:oso/9780198739791.003.0007; Andrew Newcombe & Lluís Paradell, *Law and Practice of Investment Treaties: Standards of Treatment* 279 (Kluwer Law Int'l 2009).
84. Scholars qualify estoppel as *lex specialis* to the principle of protection of legitimate expectations (Thomas Cottier & Johannes P. Müller, *Estoppel* (Encyclopedia of Public International Law 2021)).

acquiesced to those actions or claims, thereby affecting its legal rights and obligations.[85] Both estoppel and acquiescence can lead to a situation in which a state is precluded from unilaterally changing a specific legal status. Estoppel pertains to a change in conduct compared to previous representation or behaviours whereas acquiescence involves a state's passivity concerning the rights of another state.[86]

The ICJ has only explicitly based its decision on estoppel (and acquiescence) in one case.[87] In the *Temple of Preah Vihear* case, which relates to a boundary dispute between Cambodia and Thailand, the ICJ held that Thailand was bound by a map[88] that was drafted by experts from French Indochina (i.e., Cambodia) and sent to Thailand – or Siam, the predecessor of Thailand. The map showed the Preah Vihear Temple and a large surrounding area falling within the territory of Cambodia. Siam raised no objection to this. Furthermore, there was a visit to the Preah Vihear Temple made in 1930 by Prince Damrong in his capacity as President of the Royal Institute of Siam. Upon arriving at the Preah Vihear Temple, Prince Damrong was received by the French authorities who acted in a sovereign capacity there. Once again, Siam did not oppose the occupation of the Preah Vihear Temple by France. For the court, this meant that Cambodia had jurisdiction over the Temple of Preah Vihear even if it was proven that Thailand did not explicitly recognize it. The court, however, considered that Thailand did accept the Annex 1 map as representing the outcome of the work of delimitation in 1908-1909 and hence recognized the line on that map as being the frontier line of which the effect is to situate Preah Vihear in Cambodian territory. The court considered further that, looked at as a whole, Thailand's subsequent conduct confirms and bears out its original acceptance. Both parties' conduct demonstrated that they recognized the line and thereby essentially agreed to regard it as being the frontier line.[89]

It has to be noted in this respect that the *Temple of Preah Vihear* case was issued prior to the conclusion of the VCLT. Currently, within the scope of the VCLT, the issue discussed in the *Temple of Preah Vihear* case may also exemplify subsequent practice under Article 31(3)(b) VCLT.[90] In fact, this article could be considered a more solid foundation when wanting to challenge these principles as it gives them a more precise scope and definition, thus contributing to legal certainty.[91] Both the notification of the

85. Nuno Sérgio Marques Antunes, *Acquiescence* (Encyclopedia of Public International Law 2006) https://doi.org/10.1093/law:epil/9780199231690/e1373.
86. Despite the close connection between estoppel and acquiescence, scholars emphasize a distinction between the two. *See, e.g.*, Ziegler & Baumgartner, *supra* n. 3, at 20 et seq.
87. The ICJ has been more open in recognizing the existence of acquiescence rather than estoppel, however, both concepts have only been used in boundary cases. *Fisheries* case (*United Kingdom v. Norway*), [1951] I.C.J. Rep. 116; *Land, Island and Maritime Frontier Dispute* (*El Salvador v. Honduras: Nicaragua intervening*) (Merits), [1992] I.C.J. Rep. 351, 408-409. *See* Ziegler & Baumgartner, *supra* n. 3, at 20 et seq.
88. The map was drawn up in 1907 by a joint commission to fix the border between the two countries.
89. ICJ, *Temple of Preah Vihear* case *(Cambodia v. Thailand)*, Judgment of 15 June 1962, I.C.J. Reports 1962, pp. 32 et seq.
90. Georg Nolte, *Second Report on Subsequent Agreements and Subsequent Practice in Relation to Treaty Interpretation*, UN Doc. A/CN.4/671 paras 61-62 (2014).
91. Irina Buga, *Modification of Treaties by Subsequent Practice* 2.3.5 et seq. (Oxford Univ. Press 2018) https://doi.org/10.1093/oso/9780198787822.001.0001.

1908 map and the exercise of sovereign powers by France in the disputed area are elements that could amount to a later practice developed pursuant to the 1904 Franco-Siamese Treaty which Thailand recognized as legitimate through its own prolonged silence. The ICJ decision also seems to lean towards such an approach.[92] Finally – and this only adds to the confusion over these principles – it is also disputed in literature whether the court in *Temple Preah Vihe*ar considered the result of the subsequent practice by estoppel and acquiescence as leading to a potential treaty amendment rather than treaty interpretation.[93]

While multiple attempts have been made to promote the principle of estoppel in WTO disputes, none have been successful. The WTO Appellate Body has been hesitant to adopt this principle likely for reasons similar to its rejection of a standalone normative obligation of good faith.[94] In investment law, parties to investment claims have also pleaded the principle of estoppel several times with the aim of arguing that the other party was estopped from specific procedural steps or representations not made earlier. However, like WTO tribunals, investment arbitral tribunals also seem to be reluctant to use the estoppel principle.[95] The doctrine of acquiescence has not resulted in any notable pronouncements in WTO law.[96] Similarly, acquiescence is not a prominent factor in investment arbitration.[97]

In conclusion, whereas, as mentioned above, for legitimate expectations, international courts seem to give minimal weight (albeit with contrasting approaches), estoppel and acquiescence is a rarely used concept for a good faith interpretation and seems to have little relevance in general (unless for cases concerning borders). Instead, when the subject of interpretation is the behaviours or silence of states, reference should be made – when requirements are met – to Article 31(3)(b) VCLT that may establish a relevant practice between the parties that has to be considered during the interpretation process (*see* Chapter 7).

92. 'It has been contended on behalf of Thailand that th[e] communication of the maps by the French authorities was, so to speak, ex parte, and that no formal acknowledgment of it was either requested of, or given by, Thailand. [...] [I]t is clear [however] that the circumstances were such as called for some reaction, within a reasonable period, on the part of the Siamese authorities, if they wished to disagree with the map or had any serious question to raise in regard to it. They did not do so, either then or for many years, and thereby must be held to have acquiesced'; ICJ, *Temple of Preah Vihear* case *(Cambodia v. Thailand)*, Judgment of 15 June 1962, I.C.J. Reports 1962, at 23.
93. Buga, *supra* n. 91, at 251 et seq. *See*, in more detail on the discussion about the difference between interpretation and modification, Chapter 7.
94. Ziegler & Baumgartner, *supra* n. 3, at 20 et seq.; Mitchell, *supra* n. 5, at 360-361; *see also* Panizzon, *supra* n. 20, at 26.
95. Ziegler & Baumgartner, *supra* n. 3, at 20 et seq.; *See also* Andreas Kulick, *Estoppel in the Jurisprudence of International Investment Arbitration Tribunals*, 27 Eur. J. Int'l L. 107-128 (2016).
96. Ziegler & Baumgartner, *supra* n. 3, at 20 et seq.; Panizzon, *supra* n. 20, at 26.
97. Ziegler & Baumgartner, *supra* n. 3, at 20 et seq.

5.2 International Tax Law

There is little debate in the academic tax literature about using legitimate expectations as a basis for interpretation[98] while more attention has been given to estoppel and acquiescence. The principle of estoppel has been discussed in international tax law, particularly by Engelen, who contended that the Commentary should be treated as a legally binding interpretative tool for OECD member countries under the principle of estoppel and acquiescence. Engelen links this to the ICJ decision in the *Temple of Preah Vihear* case (*see* above) in which a non-binding document (a map showing the borders) attained binding status through the application of good faith as manifested in the principle of estoppel and acquiescence.[99] Engelen bases his argument on the following two assumptions, i.e., that: (i) the Commentary is part of the negotiation; and (ii) despite the clearly expressed non-binding character of the Commentary, contracting states are under an obligation to make observations or interpretational declarations on which part of the Commentary they are noncompliant.[100] Engelen also argues that the Commentary is binding because of acquiescence. According to him, the parties must be considered to have acquiesced in the interpretation set out in the latest version of the Commentaries which amounts to a tacit agreement regarding the interpretation of the treaty.[101]

As demonstrated by many scholars,[102] Engelen's position can be criticized for various reasons.

First of all, he does not take into account the fact that the *Temple of Preah Vihear* case is a boundary case with a completely different context than the Commentary.[103] Second, his position would require that, after signing a tax treaty, a state would follow the interpretation within the Commentary in a strict sense in all circumstances. However, the latter seems implausible as the practice in many jurisdictions deviates from the interpretative solutions within the Commentary. Moreover, states could agree

98. van der Bruggen, *supra* n. 42 argued that tax treaties involve a significant degree of standardization and, thus, they create legitimate expectations between the contracting states. According to this author, disregarding a widely recognized and accepted interpretation of a treaty as understood by the international community may constitute a breach of good faith. However, when a treaty incorporates domestic provisions of a state, it becomes questionable whether the international community's prevailing practice should dominate.
99. Engelen, *Interpretation of Tax Treaties Under International Law, supra* n. 63; Frank Engelen, *Some Observations on the Legal Status of the Commentaries on the OECD Model*, 60(3) Bull. Int'l Tax'n 105 (2006); Frank Engelen, *How 'Acquiescence' and 'Estoppel' Can Operate to the Effect That the States Parties to a Tax Treaty Are Legally Bound to Interpret the Treaty in Accordance with the Commentaries on the OECD Model Tax Convention*, in *The Legal Status of the OECD Commentaries, Conflict of Norms in International Tax Law Series*, Vol. 1 (S. Douma & F. Engelen eds, IBFD 2008) https://doi.org/10.59403/2r4mb2q004.
100. Engelen, *Interpretation of Tax Treaties Under International Law, supra* n. 63, at 466 et seq.
101. Engelen, *Interpretation of Tax Treaties Under International Law, supra* n. 63, at 468.
102. *See, inter alia*, David A. Ward et al., *The Interpretation of Income Tax Treaties with Particular Reference to the Commentaries on the OECD Model* 48-53 (IBFD 2005); Hans Pijl, *The OECD Commentary as a Source of International Law and the Role of the Judiciary*, 46 Eur. Tax., 216 et seq. (2006); Bossuyt, *supra* n. 45, at 894 et seq.
103. *See* ss 5, 5.1) above for a comment. *See also* Pijl, *supra* n. 102.

that the interpretation according to the Commentary should be determinant.[104] By not doing so, it implies that the member countries also do not want to be bound by it indirectly via general principles of law.[105] The definitive approval of the final text of the Commentary occurs in the OECD Council as a recommendation, i.e., as a non-binding document.[106] The fact that states decide not to upgrade the status of the Commentaries to the category of binding rules implies that they assume their non-binding nature and, therefore, estoppel and acquiescence find a major obstacle in this.[107] Ultimately, no decisions have been published in which a tax court has referred to these principles of acquiescence and estoppel to justify recourse to the Commentaries.

In conclusion, the principles of legitimate expectations, estoppel, and acquiescence have thus far been of minor importance from an interpretative perspective in tax treaty law. In this context and the specific facts of the *Temple of Preah Vihear* case, Hongler argues that its potential relevance might be limited to tax disputes that are actually a border dispute.[108] As these cases could (currently) also be solved by assessing the existence of 'subsequent practice' according to Article 31(3)(b) VCLT providing a more specific legal basis, however, the scope of application of these manifestations of good faith in the interpretation process seems to be even more limited.

6 ABUSE OF RIGHTS

6.1 International Public Law

An additional important particularization of the principle of good faith brought forward in academic writing is the abuse of rights doctrine.[109] Abuse of rights is understood as the exploitation of an individual right injuriously affecting the interest of others (e.g.,

104. And some states actually do so in a protocol to a treaty (*see, e.g.*, the new tax treaty and protocol between the Netherlands and Belgium signed on 21 June 2023).
105. Peter Hongler, *Justice in International Tax Law: A Normative Review of the International Tax Regime* 202 et seq. (IBFD 2019).
106. Pijl, *supra* n. 102; Niels Blokker, *Skating on Thin Ice? on the Law of International Organizations and the Legal Nature of the Commentaries on the OECD Model Tax Convention*, in *The Legal Status of the OECD Commentaries, Conflict of Norms in International Tax Law Series*, Vol. 1, s. 2 (S. Douma & F. Engelen eds, IBFD 2008) https://doi.org/10.59403/2r4mb2q002; Felix Alberto Vega Borrego, *The Legal Status and Effects of Reservations, Observations and Positions to the OECD Model in Departures from the OECD Model and Commentaries: Reservations, Observations and Positions in EU Law and Tax Treaties*, s. 2.2.1 (Guglielmo Maisto ed., IBFD 2014).
107. Aitor Navarro, *International Tax Soft Law Instruments: The Futility of the Static v. Dynamic Interpretation Debate*, 48 Intertax 848-860 (2020) https://doi.org/10.54648/taxi2020086.
108. The taxation of offshore oil platforms or of oil pipelines, for instance, could also be referred to as these are areas in which border conflicts might arise. *See* Hongler, *supra* n. 105, at 204.
109. Ziegler & Baumgartner, *supra* n. 3, at 30; Villiger, *supra* n. 7, at 426, para. 7; Michael Byers, *Abuse of Rights: An Old Principle, A New Age*, 47 McGill L.J. 411 (2002): 'It is also possible to argue that abuse of rights is redundant because it is itself only a more specific expression of a broader principle, namely that of good faith.'; Gardiner, *supra* n. 16, at 164 et seq.; van der Bruggen, *supra* n. 42, at 173.

community).[110] In its more specific manifestation in international (treaty) law, this generally refers to a state exercising a right either in a way that hinders the enjoyment by other states of their own rights or for an end different from that for which the right was created to the injury of another state.[111]

The question of whether the prohibition of the abuse of rights by states is recognized as a general principle of (international) law is debated by scholars. The majority view seems to accept the abuse of rights as a general principle of law.[112] The main arguments supporting the existence of the abuse of rights as a general principle of international law are:

- The prohibition in many jurisdictions of abuse of rights so that it could be argued that it is widely recognized as a general principle.[113]
- Article 26 VCLT requires states to perform obligations that they assumed by concluding treaties in good faith which supports that an abuse-of-rights principle is recognized in international law.[114]
- The explicit inclusion of the principle of the abuse of rights in some international treaties and conventions.[115]

According to another (seemingly minority) view, the principle of abuse of rights is not part of international law. One relevant argument in this regard is that, thus far, there is no uniform concept of 'abuse'.[116] However, even supporters of the abuse doctrine caution against its overuse, warning that it could grant interpreters too much discretionary power. This doctrine should be applied sparingly to prevent the abuse of

110. *See, e.g.*, Byers, *supra* n. 109, at 100.
111. Kolb, *La Bonne Foi en Droit International Public, supra* n. 16, at 468 et seq.; Alexandre Kiss, *Abuse of Rights*, in *Max Planck Encyclopedia of Public International Law*, para. 1 (Max Planck Institute, Heidelberg and Oxford University Press 2012); Panizzon, *supra* n. 20, at 30.
112. *See, e.g.*, Ziegler & Baumgartner, *supra* n. 3, at 31; and Byers, *supra* n. 109, at 404 for further reference.
113. Kiss, *supra* n. 111; Hersch Lauterpacht, *The Function of Law in the International Community* 294 et seq. (Oxford University Press 2011); Byers, *supra* n. 109 at 397.
114. Panizzon, *supra* n. 20, at 30; Kolb, *La Bonne Foi en Droit International Public, supra* n. 16, at 463; Lauterpacht, *supra* n. 113 at 298; Byers, *supra* n. 109 at 397.
115. For example, according to Art. 33 of the *Convention on the Conservation and Management of Highly Migratory Fish Stocks in the Western and Central Pacific Ocean*: 'The obligations assumed under this Convention shall be fulfilled in good faith and the rights recognized in this Convention shall be exercised in a manner which would not constitute an abuse of right.' The concept of abuse of rights is also referenced in Art. 2(2)(c) of the *Helsinki Convention on the Protection and Use of Transboundary Watercourses and International Lakes* (17 March 1992). *See Convention on the Conservation and Management of Highly Migratory Fish Stocks in the Western and Central Pacific Ocean*, Art. 33, 5 September 2000, 2275 U.N.T.S.; *Convention on the Protection and Use of Transboundary Watercourses and International Lakes*, Art. 2(2)(c), 17 March 1992, 1936 U.N.T.S.
116. Brownlie, *supra* n. 3, at 444: 'In conclusion, it may be said that the doctrine is a useful agent in the progressive development of the law, but that, as a general principle, it does not exist in positive law'; *See also* Kiss, *supra* n. 111, at para. 34: 'The idea that a subject of rights and competences can misuse them seems to be inherent to legal thinking and to have roots in all legal systems and leads to the establishment of controls on the use of recognized rights. The prohibition of abuse of rights in international law is, however, problematic because of differences in the content of the concept itself [...].' *See also* Byers, *supra* n. 109, at 412-413 with further references.

rights principle from being abused. Against these risks, scholars emphasize the subsidiary nature of the abuse of rights doctrine.[117]

With reference to the context of this study, it is particularly brought forward that an abuse of rights by contracting states via interpretation may exist if a contracting state focuses on a literal interpretation of a treaty provision that leads to a benefit for this particular contracting party to the detriment of the other. The principle of good faith as enshrined in Article 31(1) VCLT would be a tool to combat such cases. For example, Kotzur has phrased this function of good faith accordingly: 'Each party shall finally refrain from taking unfair advantage due to a literal interpretation, if the mere focus on the wording would fall short of respecting the objects, purposes, and spirit of the agreement.'[118] The principle of good faith seems, thus, to be a supporting argument to take into account for a contextual and teleological interpretation as opposed to an excessively textual interpretation.

International courts have referred to the concept of abuse by states that are party to a treaty.[119] However, international courts have never considered the conditions for its application to be fulfilled.[120] For example, in the *Certain German Interests* case, the Permanent Court of International Justice (PCIJ) concluded that 'such misuse has not taken place in the present case. The act in question does not overstep the limits of the normal administration of public property and was not designed to procure for one of the interested Parties an illicit advantage and to deprive the other of an advantage to which he was entitled'.[121] In particular, the PCIJ highlighted that an abuse cannot be easily presumed,[122] showing the international tribunals' awareness of the gravity of accusing a state of abuse of rights. In some areas of international law, the recourse to this doctrine is more frequent, e.g., in WTO law[123] or in international investment

117. Byers, *supra* n. 109, at 421 et seq.; Panizzon, *supra* n. 20, at 34.
118. Kotzur, *supra* n. 2, at para. 20.
119. *See, e.g., Oscar Chinn* case *(United Kingdom v. Belgium)* (Judgment) [1934] PCIJ (ser. A/B) No. 63, 86; *Free Zones of Upper Savoy and District of Gex (France v. Switzerland)* (Judgment) [1932] PCIJ (ser. A/B) No. 46, 167; *Certain German Interests in Polish Upper Silesia (Germany v. Poland)* (Judgment) [1926] PCIJ (ser. A) No. 7, 30; *Trail Smelter Arbitration (United States v. Canada) (Award II)* (1941) 3 UNRIAA 1905, 1965; *Avena and Other Mexican Nationals (Mexico v. United States) (Judgment)* [2004] ICJ Rep 12, 37-38.
120. Ziegler & Baumgartner, *supra* n. 3, at 30 et seq.; Kiss, *supra* n. 111, para. 12: 'The principle has been mentioned in several cases as a possible basis for a condemnation for violation of international law, but without having been actually used for that purpose.'
121. *Certain German Interests, supra* n. 119, at 37-38. The case involved a dispute over the interpretation of the Geneva Convention concerning the rights and property of German nationals in Upper Silesia that had been transferred to Poland. The PCIJ ruled that Germany's rights were protected under the convention but that Poland had sovereignty over the territory.
122. *Free Zones, supra* n. 119, at 167; *Certain German Interests, supra* n. 119, at 30.
123. *See, e.g.,* Appellate Body Report, *US – Shrimp*, WTO Doc WT/DS58/AB/R (adopted 6 November 1998); Appellate Body Report, *United States – Transitional Safeguard Measure on Combed Cotton Yarn from Pakistan*, WTO Doc WT/DS192/AB/R (adopted 5 November 2001); Appellate Body Report, *United States – Measures Affecting the Cross-Border Supply of Gambling and Betting Services*, WTO Doc WT/DS285/AB/R (adopted 20 April 2005). The Appellate Body found in *US-Shrimp* that one expression of the principle of good faith is the prohibition of *abus de droit*. Recognizing that the function of the abuse of rights doctrine is to prevent the 'abusive exercise by a Member of its own treaty right thus [resulting] in a breach of the treaty rights of the other Members and, as well, a violation of the treaty obligation of the Member so acting' (Appellate Body Report, *US – Shrimp*, para. 158). However, the Appellate Body has once again

law.[124] However, once again, these courts have been very cautious and overall reluctant to assume an abuse too lightly.[125] This is partly due to the requirement that establishing an abuse of rights necessitates a demonstration of violation of good faith, a challenging feature concerning states.[126]

6.2 International Tax Law

In tax literature, abuse of rights by taxpayers is much more discussed than that by states. Nevertheless, potential abuse by states has recently gained more attention in academic literature.[127] Indeed, if assuming that a concept of abuse as a separate principle of international law exists,[128] then this principle should be applied to taxpayers and states.[129] Contracting states can circumvent tax treaty obligations by designing legislation in accordance with the wording of the treaties aiming to avoid undesirable treaty consequences or creating convenient situations for them. States may, for example, aim at increasing tax revenues or fostering certain economic undertakings for their benefit (tax competition). This phenomenon is categorized in academic tax literature as 'treaty dodging'[130] but might also be described more generally as treaty avoidance by states.[131] To avoid the disadvantages of a direct treaty override or when such an option is not available within the national system because of the limits of the constitution, states can employ a treaty-dodging mechanism. There are

---

been very cautious not to apply the abuse of rights doctrine (as an expression of the principle of good faith) autonomously but rather to attach it to a substantial rule. *See* Mitchell, *supra* n. 5, at 368; Panizzon, *supra* n. 20, at 32-33.

124. *See Pac Rim Cayman v. El Salvador*, ICSID Case No. ARB/09/12, para. 2.99; *Tidewater v. Venezuela*, ICSID Case No. ARB/10/5, para. 193; *Lao Holdings v. Lao*, ICSID Case No. ARB(AF)/12/6, para. 76.
125. Ziegler & Baumgartner, *supra* n. 3, at 30 et seq.
126. *Certain German Interests, supra* n. 119; Virally, *supra* n. 14, at 132.
127. Vanessa Arruda Ferreira, *The Improper Use of Tax Treaties by Contracting States: Tax Treaty Dodging* (IBFD 2021).
128. Similar to international public law, there is also an intense discussion by tax scholars in international tax law whether the abuse of rights doctrine is a general principle (*see, inter alia,* De Broe, *supra* n. 69). In order to bring clarity, some scholars even suggest including a specific anti-abuse rule (e.g., a principle purpose test) for states in the OECD MC (Robert Danon, *The Principal Purposes Test (PPT) in Post BEPS Tax Treaty Law, It Is a GAAR but just a GAAR!*, 74 Bull. Int'l Tax'n 4-5 (2020) https://doi.org/10.59403/136hxah) or the UN-MC (Francisco A. Garcia Prats, *Abuse of Tax Law: Prospects and Analysis*, in *Essays in International and European Tax Law* 75 (G. Bizioli ed., Jovene 2010)).
129. Michael Lang, *Abusive Application of International Tax Agreements*, in *IFA* 68 (Kluwer 2001).
130. *See, inter alia,* Haslehner, *supra* n. 42, paras 161 et seq. The distinction between treaty dodging and treaty overriding or abuse of the treaty is not always very clear in the literature. The term 'treaty dodging' was first used by Klaus Vogel in an article published in 1985 (Klaus Vogel, *Steuerumgehung nach Innerstaatlichem Recht und nach Abkommensrecht*, 62 Steuer und Wirtschaft 4, 369-381 (1985)). For a deep analysis *see* Arruda Ferreira, *supra* n. 127; Luisa Scarcella, *IFA Research Report: Cancun Congress 2022 Good Faith in Domestic and International Tax Law*, in *Cahiers de Droit Fiscal International: Studies on International Fiscal Law*, Vol. 107B (IFA 75th Congress, Cancun 2023); Sjoerd Douma & Craig Elliffe eds, *Cahiers de Droit Fiscal International: Studies on International Fiscal Law*, Vol. 107B (IFA 75th Congress, Cancun 2023).
131. Douma & Elliffe, *Cahiers de Droit Fiscal International: Studies on International Fiscal Law*, *supra* n. 130, at 47.

a number of court decisions for which domestic tax courts have used the good faith principle in treaty dodging cases, although without explicitly using the terms 'abuse of rights'.[132]

Tax treaty dodging may take different forms.[133] One of the most discussed and practically relevant case is using a definition in domestic law for purposes of treaty interpretation, in particular by relying on Article 3(2) OECD MC[134] or on a more specific reference to domestic law (e.g., Article 6(2) OECD MC).[135] Through a change in its domestic law ('redefining a undefined treaty term'),[136] a contracting state could, for example, be able to broaden the scope of circumstances that it is allowed to tax under a given treaty.[137] Scholars have brought forward that such a practice might lead to an abuse of rights by the specific contracting state under specific circumstances which is prohibited by the principle of good faith.[138] For example, Engelen states that attempts by contracting states to render the treaty partially inoperative by later amending in their legislation the scope of terms not defined in the treaty 'would clearly constitute an abuse of right' and that 'the principle of good faith and the doctrine of abuse of right distinctively and directly related there to, sets a limit with respect to the references to domestic laws of the contracting state for purposes of interpretation'.[139] According to this view, the principle of good faith may hence be seen as an implicit general anti-avoidance rule (GAAR) for states inherent to any treaty.

This abuse of rights scenario does not occur in international public law in a similar manner as it is specifically caused by the rule in Article 3(2) OECD MC (or a more specific reference to domestic law in the OECD MC). Examples of such scenarios have already been mentioned in section 4. In particular, the jurisprudence of the Dutch Supreme Court has received attention from scholars. It ruled in a number of cases that a potential shift in the allocation of taxation rights as a consequence of a deeming provision in Dutch tax law (e.g., a fictitious wage concept) represents a violation of the principle of good faith and, hence, the context of Article 3(2) OECD MC would require disregarding the domestic deeming provision.[140] Even though there seems to be no explicit reference to the abuse of rights in these judgments, scholars are discussing

132. *See* examples in cases law in the IFA General Report, Douma & Elliffe, *Cahiers de Droit Fiscal International: Studies on International Fiscal Law, supra* n. 130, at 48-51.
133. *See, inter alia,* Arruda Ferreira, *supra* n. 127, at s. 3.3.; and Danon, *supra* n. 128, at 261 et seq.
134. *See, inter alia,* Haslehner, *supra* n. 42, para. 161; Arruda Ferreira, *supra* n. 127, at s. 3.3.1.2.; van der Bruggen, *supra* n. 42, at 173.
135. Arruda Ferreira, *supra* n. 127, at s. 3.3.1.2.
136. Arruda Ferreira, *supra* n. 127, at s. 3.3.1.2.
137. Haslehner, *supra* n. 42, para. 161; Danon, *supra* n. 128, at 261 et seq.
138. Ekkehart Reimert, *Klaus Vogel on Double Taxation Conventions*, Art. 6, para. 95 (Ekkehart Reimert & Alexander Rust eds, Kluwer Law International 5th ed. 2022); Arruda Ferreira, *supra* n. 127, at s. 4.2.1-4.2.3.
139. Engelen, *Interpretation of Tax Treaties Under International Law, supra* n. 63, at 490 and 494.
140. In more detail, Frank Pötgens, *The Relationship Between Preservative Tax Assessments and Netherlands Tax Treaties: Not Always Pacta Sunt Servanda?,* 50 Eur. Taxn. 183 et seq. (2010) https://doi.org/10.59403/213kv94; Frank Pötgens, Norbert Vis & Elena Kool, *IFA National Report-Good faith in Domestic and International Tax Law,* presented at the IFA Congress (2023).

them under the heading of treaty dodging.[141] Regarding domestic deeming provisions linked to treaty provisions other than Article 3(2) OECD MC, states could, for example, define certain things as 'immovable property' in their domestic law (e.g., gambling machines)[142] based on Article 6(2) OECD MC in order to expand their taxing rights as the situs state.[143]

Another discussed cause of abuse of rights in tax treaty law is the design of a domestic tax in a way that falls outside the scope of a tax treaty (tension with the substantive scope of Article 2 OECD MC).[144] The most recent examples are the introduction of digital service taxes by various states around the world that are commonly characterized as 'side-stepping' tax treaties,[145] but similar questions might also arise for other taxes. Some domestic courts have referred to good faith when assessing whether new taxes are covered by a tax treaty. For example, the Greek Supreme Court has ruled that excluding a special social security contribution under Greek law that was meant to be applicable for a limited time only from the scope of covered taxes due to its temporary character only would allow easy circumvention of the treaty.[146] Similar to the Dutch courts, the Greek court has not explicitly referred to 'abuse of rights', however, the argument on circumventing the treaty can easily be linked to this doctrine.

Although several courts and scholars refer to the principle of good faith and/or its manifestation in the abuse of rights doctrine to counter such treaty dodging practices by states, it remains debatable whether such reliance is necessary and recommendable. Most of these treaty dodging practices may only be successful if significant weight is placed on the wording of a treaty. Although the treaty text is considered to be an important element in the process of interpretation, an undeniable fact is that the principles of treaty interpretation in international law as expressed in the VCLT also take other factors into account (in particular, the context and the object and purpose of the treaty), thus leaving very limited opportunity for a pure literal application of international agreements when this is contrary to the spirit of the treaty. This is an important aspect for the purpose of this study since the more literal an interpretation is, the more exposed tax treaties become to tax treaty dodging practices. As indicated by

141. Arruda Ferreira, *supra* n. 127, at ss 4.2.1 and 3.3.1.2.6; Douma & Elliffe, *Cahiers de Droit Fiscal International: Studies on International Fiscal Law, supra* n. 130.
142. For example, the Austrian authorities had negotiated a treaty provision with Belarus that was similar to the one in Art. 6(2) of the OECD MC (2017), i.e., granting taxing rights and the right to define the term 'immovable property' to the source country. However, the Austrian authorities were taken aback when Belarus later included 'gambling machines' in its domestic definition of 'immovable property'. This inclusion occurred at a time when there was an Austrian company with gambling machines in Belarus. By broadening the definition of 'immovable property' to include gambling machines, Belarus shifted the related income from the scope of the business profit article (which granted taxing rights to Austria) to that of the immovable property article which allowed taxation in Belarus.
143. Arruda Ferreira, *supra* n. 127, at s. 3.3.1.2.3.
144. Danon, *supra* n. 128, at 262.
145. Douma & Elliffe, *Cahiers de Droit Fiscal International: Studies on International Fiscal Law, supra* n. 130, at 48.
146. Katerina Perrou, *IFA National Report-Good Faith in Domestic and International Tax Law*, presented at the IFA Congress (2023).

Vogel, the stronger relevance of the literal meaning within the concept of the ordinary meaning in the process of interpretation makes tax treaties more vulnerable to structures aiming at circumventing the agreement by either taxpayers or contracting states. Therefore, any element reducing the weight of a literal interpretation of the treaty consequently limits the scope of tax treaty dodging practice. In this sense, by incorporating other elements such as the context and the object and purpose of treaties into the process of interpretation - as stipulated by Article 31(1) VCLT anyway - the general principle of interpretation balances the relevance of the ordinary meaning of terms and consequently reduces the chances of treaty abuse under a purely textual interpretation.[147] As Article 31 VCLT includes and promotes a holistic approach to interpretation taking into account all of these elements,[148] a referral to good faith, read as requiring taking into account the object and purpose of the rules, does not seem to add anything new.[149]

In essence, all criticism that has been raised for general-anti-abuse rules on a domestic and European Union (EU) level and the principle-purpose test (PPT) on an international level also apply to the application of the abuse doctrine to states.[150] Even if taking for granted that an abuse doctrine exists as a general principle of international law, its scope and conditions are unclear and difficult to put into practice. In particular, determining whether a contracting state's action is exercised in good or bad faith requires an assessment based on the moral values at the core of this principle such as honesty, fairness, and reasonableness. These elements inherently cannot be precisely defined or specified in more detail as very much depends on the specific circumstances of the case. Therefore, it is challenging to derive a clear, objective, and precise line of demarcation from the principle of good faith between treaty avoidance and the legitimate exercise of rights by the contracting states. In this context, even proponents of the abuse doctrine (as well as international courts) caution against its excessive use due to the risk of granting too much discretionary power to the interpreter. Indeed, the analysis of public law in the section above highlights the subsidiary nature of the abuse of rights doctrine. Whether a result is 'reasonable' or 'fair' in light of a tax treaty and thereby in line with good faith can only be assessed by taking into account the context, history, object, and purpose of the specific provision of the treaty in question. The concept of good faith itself on a stand-alone basis does not help in identifying what is a reasonable interpretation of a specific rule.

Finally and probably most importantly, it should also be considered that qualifying an act as illegitimate based on the principle of good faith may depend on the role of the subjective element. The issue is whether the condemnable abusive acts pertain

147. Klaus Vogel, *Steuerumgehung nach Innerstaatlichem Recht und nach Abkommensrecht*, 62 Steuer und Wirtschaft 4, 372-373 (1985).
148. *See* s. 3 and Chapter 1.
149. Similar Michael Lang, *Chapter 5: The Relation Between Tax Treaty Law and National Law in the Definition of Immovable Property under Article 6(2) of the OECD Model*, in *Immovable Property under Domestic Law, EU Law and Tax Treaties* 57 et seq. (G. Maisto ed., IBFD 2015).
150. *See, e.g.*, Michael Lang, *BEPS Action 6: Introducing an Anti-abuse Rule in Tax Treaties*, 74 Tax Notes Int'l 655 et seq. (2014) https://doi.org/10.2139/ssrn.2500827; Lang, *Introduction to the Law of Double Taxation Conventions*, *supra* n. 39, at 35 et seq.

only to the intentional actions (or omissions) or if they also include unintentional actions (or omissions) considering their consequences (thus focusing more on the effect rather than the intention). Some scholars deem the role of intention as not really relevant[151] while others might view intention as a necessary condition for characterizing an act as illegitimate under the principle of good faith.[152] For example, Arruda holds that the threshold provided is built on 'very subjective pillars'.[153] In the authors' opinion, it is not possible to establish with certainty whether or not the changes to domestic law have the sole or main purpose of circumventing the treaty or whether they are an unintended side effect of changes caused by other reasons.[154]

Instead of referring to the concept of abuse of rights and good faith (as an implicit anti-abuse rule), potential treaty dodging cases should be assessed by interpreting the material rules of the treaty (e.g., Article 2 or Article 3(2) OECD MC) by taking into account the wording, context, and object and purpose of the specific rule. For example, whether a tax is covered by a specific tax treaty is a question of interpretation of the substantive scope in the respective tax treaty. According to Article 2 OECD MC, treaties cover 'taxes on income and capital' (as defined in Article 2(3) OECD MC), list the taxes that are covered in a separate paragraph (Article 2(2) OECD MC), and then extend their scope to 'identical or substantially similar taxes' that are imposed after the date of signature of the convention (Article 2(4) OECD MC). Good faith is of no help when conducting such an assessment as this would require taking into account the (subjective) intention (bad faith) of the legislator of one of the contracting states which is very difficult to assess (particularly for courts of the other contracting state).[155] Whether a specific tax (introduced at a later point) is covered by the tax treaty should depend on a comprehensive comparison of the respective taxes' constituent elements (e.g., tax object and calculation of the tax base).[156] The assessment might also be influenced by the taxes listed in a specific tax treaty and their characteristics and might also take into account the tax system of the contracting state as a whole, e.g., the interaction of various single taxes (macro-approach).[157] Scholars have brought forward that certain digital services taxes show features of income taxes which might justify qualifying them as covered taxes.[158] Although it might be tempting as an 'easy' solution, the

151. Jan Wouters & Matthias Vidal, *The International Law Perspective*, in *Tax Treaties and Domestic Law* 16 et seq. (G. Maisto ed., IBFD 2006).
152. De Broe, *supra* n. 69; van der Bruggen, *supra* n. 42, at 167 et seq.
153. Arruda Ferreira, *supra* n. 127, at s. 4.2.3.
154. As Haslehner has stated it, whether the result is the purpose of a legislative change or whether it is an unintended side-effect of changes occasioned by other reasons cannot always be determined (*see* Haslehner, *supra* n. 42, paras 161 et seq.); similar Lang, *Chapter 5: The Relation between Tax Treaty Law and National Law in the Definition of Immovable Property under Article 6(2) of the OECD Model, supra* n. 149, s. 5.3.3.
155. Roland Ismer & Christoph Jescheck, *Taxes on Digital Services and the Substantive Scope of the Application of Tax Treaties: Pushing the Boundaries of Article 2 of the OECD Model?*, 46 Intertax 575 (2018) https://doi.org/10.54648/taxi2018059.
156. Roland Ismer & Alexander Blank, in *Klaus Vogel on Double Taxation Conventions*, Art. 2 para. 70 (Ekkehart Reimert & Alexander Rust eds, Kluwer Law International 5th ed. 2022).
157. Ismer & Blank, *supra* n. 156.
158. Ismer & Jescheck *supra* n. 155, at 573 et seq.; Pasquale Pistone & Andreas Ullmann, *Digital Taxes and Article 2 OECD Model Convention 2017*, in *Taxes Covered under Article 2 of the OECD Model* 167-199 (Georg Kofler et al. eds, IBFD 2021).

authors posit that the principle of good faith as an abstract and vague concept should not be used to achieve results when the treaty is extended to taxes that do not fulfil the criteria of covered taxes in a specific case.

Similar arguments apply, *inter alia*, to deeming provisions under national law. As already established in section 4, these cases should be solved based on an interpretation of Article 3(2) OECD MC and the context of the treaty, leading to an autonomous interpretation of treaty terms in many cases. According to the authors, the context of the treaty should also set certain outer limits when using definitions in domestic law for treaty interpretation that are based on special rules explicitly referring to the domestic law (e.g., Article 6(2) OECD MC). Based on the context and purpose of the rules, contracting states should, for example, not be totally at liberty to define whatever they want as an 'immovable property' for purposes of Article 6(2) OECD MC.[159] Following the general doctrine that a treaty-autonomous interpretation is to be preferred, next to the term 'immovable property' itself, the positive and negative list in Article 6(2) OECD MC may provide a guideline on the core concept of an 'immovable property' which could serve as a basis to establish outer limits for the discretion of contracting states.[160] The intention and motives of the domestic legislator as well as good faith in general should not be a decisive factor in this assessment. As the positive list in Article 6(2) OECD MC provides a rather diverse set of items including, for example, livestock (i.e., animals), any object ('property accessory to immovable property') and rights linked to land, the discretion is arguably rather broad.[161] A similar approach has been developed by the Court of Justice of the European Union (CJEU) when interpreting provisions in the VAT Directive that make a (comparable) explicit reference to a definition by the EU Member States.[162] When assessing (and in fact limiting) EU Member States' discretion, the CJEU relied on a grammatical, contextual, and teleological interpretation of the directive provision. It held that Member States defining terms provided by the directive are prohibited from 'undermining the very terms' of it (grammatical and contextual interpretation)[163] and 'may not prejudice the objectives pursued by the [Directive]'

159. Similarly, *see* Lang (*see* Lang, *BEPS Action 6: Introducing an Anti-abuse Rule in Tax Treaties, supra* n. 150, at s. 5.3.1 and 5.5) who derives a limit from the systematic context (relationship to other articles of the OECD MC) and the term 'property' used in Art. 6 OECD MC, according to which, *inter alia*, 'persons' cannot be deemed to be immovable property; referring to the principle of good faith for this purpose Reimert, *supra* n. 138.

160. Similarly (but with broad discretion for contracting states), Lang, *Chapter 5: The Relation Between Tax Treaty Law and National Law in the Definition of Immovable Property under Article 6(2) of the OECD Model, supra* n. 149, at 64.

161. The exclusion of ships and aircraft as well as the fact that other tangible items mentioned need to have some link to land ('accessory', 'used in agriculture', 'landed property'), however, seems to suggest that some connection to land is a general prerequisite. It might hence be questioned whether a state can legitimately define, for example, a right on a movable item (i.e., right to use a vehicle) or an animal, e.g., a cat (not used in agriculture), to be 'immovable property'. In this context, defining gambling machines (and buildings) that are usually meant and designed to be located at a certain place for a longer period of time as 'immovable property' within domestic law could still be within the discretion of contracting states.

162. *See*, for example, the exemption for 'the management of special investment funds as defined by Member States' (Art. 135(1)(g) EU VAT Directive).

163. CJEU, *Wheels Common Investment Fund Trustees Ltd v. Commissioners for Her Majesty's Revenue and Customs*, Case C-424/11, [2013] ECLI:EU:C:2013:144, para. 17.

(teleological interpretation).[164] Even if EU law is a different legal order than international tax treaty law and, therefore, principles developed under one legal order cannot automatically be transferred to the other,[165] this approach might nevertheless be used as inspiration for an alternative means in potential treaty dodging cases rather than invoking good faith or the abuse of rights doctrine.

7 CONCLUSION

This analysis has demonstrated that, from an international public law perspective, the principle of good faith, despite being often emphasized as a fundamental element of treaty interpretation according to Article 31(1) VCLT, is a limited factor in the actual interpretation process of international treaties. Good faith is more of a morally-oriented rule rather than a concrete legal one thereby making its role in treaty interpretation somewhat residual and contributing little compared to other hermeneutical criteria. In the context of international tax law, good faith is primarily invoked to justify using the Commentary and to limit the reference to domestic law based on Article 3(2) of the OECD MC for interpretation purposes. Both references to good faith in these contexts do not appear to be pertinent. Even in the realm of tax treaties, indeed, such a vague and subjective concept as good faith does not seem to enhance the process of reasoning and interpretation. Using and accepting it as a decisive interpretative element carries the risk that courts and other interpreters do not elaborate properly and intensively on the wording, context and object, and purpose of the treaty and thereby (intentionally or unintentionally) 'hide' the actual reasons for their decision. Considering these inherent risks and the way in which good faith is handled by some courts (and scholars), the question remains whether the removal of this reference from the text of Article 31(1) VCLT would change anything and/or might even lead to less confusion and better interpretative results.

164. CJEU, *JP Morgan Chase Bank NA v. Finanzamt Essen-Süd*, Case C-363/05, [2007] E.C.R. I-6619, para. 22.
165. *See* Chapter 1.

CHAPTER 4

The Interpretation of Tax Treaty Terms in Its Context

Rita Szudoczky & Iris Tschatsch

1 Introduction
2 Methods and Issues of Legal Interpretation
 2.1 The Necessity of Rules for Legal Interpretation and Its Relevance to Different Legal Texts
 2.2 Possible Meanings and Uses of the Vienna Convention Rules
 2.3 Additional Aspects of the Interpretation of Tax Treaties
3 'Context' in the Vienna Convention
 3.1 Nature of Article 31(1) VCLT
 3.2 The Non-exhaustive List of 'Context' According to Article 31(2) VCLT
 3.3 Forms of Context According to Article 31(2) VCLT
  3.3.1 Definition of the Term Treaty
  3.3.2 Integral Part of the Treaty
   3.3.2.1 Syntactic Context of the Specific Provision
   3.3.2.2 Ordinary Meaning in Context
    3.3.2.2.1 Internal Context of the Provision: Title and Headings
    3.3.2.2.2 Internal Context of the Treaty: Other Provisions, Preamble and Annexes

3.3.3 Extrinsic Part of the Treaty: Cross-Treaty Context
3.3.3.1 Conditions to Become Extrinsic Context of a Treaty
3.3.3.2 Understanding of the Term 'Any Agreement'
3.3.3.3 Understanding of the Term 'Any Instrument'
3.4 Relationship of Article 31(2) VCLT to Other Interpretive Provisions of the VCLT
4 Context Outside the List of Article 31(2) VCLT
4.1 Analogues Wording of Other Agreements and Practices Among a Subgroup of Parties
4.2 Analogues Wording of Other Sources
5 Consideration of 'Context' in Tax Treaties
5.1 Integral Part of Tax Treaties: The Preamble
5.2 Extrinsic Part of Tax Treaties: OECD Materials as 'Context'
5.2.1 Preamble of the 2017 OECD-MC
5.2.2 OECD Commentaries
5.2.2.1 Practical Relevance of the Commentaries as a Result of International Consensus
5.2.2.2 In General: Not Context in the Narrow Sense of Article 31(2) VCLT
5.2.2.3 Conditions That the Commentary Becomes Context in the Narrow Sense of Article 31(2) VCLT
5.2.3 OECD Subsequent Commentaries as Context Outside the List of Article 31(2) VCLT
6 Conclusions

1 INTRODUCTION

The meaning of words depends on their context as sentences are never drafted in isolation.[1] The Oxford English Dictionary defines 'context' as 'the whole structure of a connected passage regarded in its bearing on any of the parts which constitute it: the parts which immediately precede or follow any particular passage or "text" and

1. Mark E. Villiger, *The Rules on Interpretation: Misgivings, Misunderstandings, Miscarriage? The 'Crucible' Intended by the International Law, in The Law of Treaties Beyond the Vienna Convention [Essays in Honour of Professor Giorgio Gaja]* 105, 109 (Enzo Cannizzaro & Mahnoush H. Arsanjani eds, Oxford Univ. Press 2011).

determine its meaning'.[2] This is a syntactic understanding of context. However, context can also be understood as the entire set of assumptions about the world in general that a reader – through decoding, interference, direct perception, or using his memory – has access to when reading a text.[3]

Can it be so easy to consider everything as context? According to Gardiner, 'context' has two main roles.[4] The first is as an immediate qualifier of the ordinary meaning of terms used in a treaty, i.e., as an aid for selecting the ordinary meaning and a modifier of any over-literal approach to interpretation.[5] This would imply that everything could be considered context. However, the second role is identifying the material that is to be considered forming context.[6] When looking at Article 31(1) and (2) Vienna Convention on the Law of Treaties (VCLT), it appears that the drafters had certain elements in mind to consider as context of which a list is contained in Article 31(2) VCLT. In particular, context comprises the integral part of the treaty, specifically the text, preamble, and annexes as well as the extrinsic part of the treaty, i.e., any agreement relating to it that was made between all of the parties in connection with the treaty's conclusion (lit a) and any instrument that was made by one or more parties associated with the treaty's conclusion and accepted by the other parties as an instrument related to the treaty (lit b). Accordingly, context in the meaning of Article 31(2) VCLT would be limited.

The purpose of this chapter is to first answer the question of what context is for the purpose of legal interpretation of international agreements and more specifically tax treaties. Which materials are to be used or could be used when interpreting them in their context? In this respect, one of the key questions is whether the definition of context in Article 31(2) VCLT is exhaustive. Although the VCLT is silent on the question of 'how', this chapter will, second, address the problem of how the sources of context that have been identified under the previous question are to be used.

This contribution commences with the analysis of Article 31(2) VCLT considering the case law in international law and subsequently attempts to apply the conclusions from it to the interpretation of tax treaties.

Therefore, section 2 addresses the topic with a methodological approach when it first analyses why rules of interpretation in general are necessary and specifically why rules on 'context' are required. Second, the possible meanings and uses of the VCLT with respect to context will be discussed. Third, on the basis of the assumptions gathered for international law, it will highlight what additional aspects need to be considered when interpreting tax treaties.

Section 3 analyses 'context' in the meaning of Article 31(1) and (2) VCLT. It will be discussed whether the list in Article 31(2) VCLT can be exhaustive or not and how the different forms of context according to this list can be used for interpretation purposes. This section concludes with an analysis of the relationship between Article

2. Oxford English Dictionary, *Context (Noun)*, para. 1577 (22 July 2024). https://www.oed.com/dictionary/context_n?tab=meaning_and_use#8442522.
3. Ulf Linderfalk, *On the Interpretation of Treaties* 35 (2007).
4. Richard K. Gardiner, *Treaty Interpretation* 197 (2015).
5. *Ibid.*
6. *Ibid.*

31(2) VCLT and the other means of interpretation. Section 4 analyses what other sources of context could be considered in the contextual approach. In section 5, the observations drawn from international law are transferred to selected aspects of tax treaties. Special attention will be paid to the role of the preamble in tax treaties in general, the preamble of the Organisation for Economic Co-operation and Development (OECD) Model Convention in particular, the consideration of OECD materials as context, and context outside the list of Article 31(2) VCLT. In this framework, it will be examined to what extent that specific time period can be taken into account (the 'spirit of the time') as context in the interpretation process and what the latter would mean for using OECD materials that were issued later than a treaty's conclusion in such a process. The contribution ends with a conclusion in section 6.

2 METHODS AND ISSUES OF LEGAL INTERPRETATION

2.1 The Necessity of Rules for Legal Interpretation and Its Relevance to Different Legal Texts

The question is whether rules of interpretation are generally needed and, if so, whether the same rules apply to all types of legal texts. These questions aim to find the relevance of context for interpretation.

Interpretation is a term that permeates various fields including literature, theology, law, arts, history, and everyday conversation.[7] It is an intuitive human activity that occurs whenever words are read or encountered.[8] There can never be *a* timeless and correct meaning of words since it is inherent in language that it is imprecise.[9] Words before and after another word or phrases affect its meaning as well as the overall context in which words are written or spoken. As there is often the possibility of multiple purposes (respectively understandings), the interpreter must choose the one that best elucidates and justifies the text in question (process of justification of a particular interpretation).[10]

The aim of interpretation is to gain a better understanding of the normative text in relation to a specific case or group of cases, i.e., to find the true meaning of words.[11] The question is whether the interpreter should aim for an appropriate interpretation

7. Werner Haslehner, *Introduction, in Klaus Vogel on Double Taxation Conventions,* para. 90 (Ekkehart Reimert & Alexander Rust eds, Wolters Kluwer 2022); Kent Greenawalt, *Comparative Legal Interpretation* 154 (2011).
8. Brian J. Arnold, *The Interpretation of Tax Treaties: Myth and Reality,* 64 Bull. Intl. Taxn. 2, 9, n. 1 (2010) https://doi.org/10.59403/3gjyvnr.
9. According to the adage 'in claris not fit interpretation', a legal text must not be interpreted if it is clear and unambiguous. However, this impression can be deceptive. It could also be stated that a text is clear and unambiguous when the work of interpretation is no longer noticed. Franz Reimer, *Juristische Methodenlehre,* para. 237 (2020).
10. Jörg Kammerhofer, *Taking the Rules of Interpretation Seriously, but Not Literally? A Theoretical Reconstruction of Orthodox Dogma,* 86 Nordic Journal of International Law 125, 130-131, n. 2 (2017) https://doi.org/10.1163/15718107-08602005; with critical comments, *see* Georg Graf, *Recht als Interpretation, in Beiträge zur juristischen Hermeneutik* 115, 118-119 (Helmuth Vetter & Michael Potacs eds, Literas-Universitätsverl. 1990).
11. Reimer, *Juristische Methodenlehre, supra* n. 9, para. 246.

(objective interpretation) or one that is in accordance with the will of the respective legislator (subjective interpretation). This overlaps with the question at which point in time is relevant in each case, i.e., that of the enactment or that of the application of the norm? Depending on which interpretation is followed, one of the four classic interpretation maxims (starting points for interpretation) becomes more significant than the others. The four main different interpretations are:[12] the interpretation of the wording,[13] the systematic interpretation, the historical and generic interpretation,[14] and the teleological interpretation.[15] The systematic interpretation is based on the context of the law, i.e., its structure and organization. It draws conclusions from headings, preceding provisions, or the provision's position. However, the boundaries from the systematic interpretation towards the interpretation of the wording are fluid, and the maxims of interpretation (and other means of interpretation) are also subject to interpretation. This leads to the insight that interpretation is a flexible endeavour.

There is the position that interpretation is unconscious or creative, leading to the concept that it is more an art than a science and therefore unavoidably subjective.[16] Following that, it cannot adhere to strict formal rules and should be left to the skill of the interpreter.[17] It is important to challenge this view. On the one hand, it is true that interpretation rules themselves are subject to interpretation. A rule-guided or rigid approach would therefore misunderstand the intent of interpretation and would lead to nothing more than another answer in need of interpretation.[18] Other commentators argue that 'interpretation cannot meaningfully be subjected to rules'[19] due to the unique nature of each case and the inherent novelty of applying the law.[20]

On the other hand, a methodological approach shall limit judicial discretion and prevent arbitrariness. It serves as a source of objectivity and provides a framework for

---

12. Klaus Röhl & Christian Röhl, *Allgemeine Rechtslehre* 613-625 (2008).
13. The interpretation of the wording (or grammatical interpretation) focuses on the clarification of the text itself and prioritizes the ordinary meaning of the words and phrases used.
14. The historical interpretation, in the narrower sense, is the interpretation that enquires *the status quo ante*, and the genetic interpretation is the interpretation that enquires into the history of origin and partly also into the history of development, Reimer, *Juristische Methodenlehre, supra* n. 9, paras 347-356.
15. The teleological interpretation is the interpretation according to the télos of the norm, i.e., its purpose.
16. Robert Y. Jennings, *General Course on Principles of International Law*, 121 Recueil des Cours 323, 544 (1967). *See also* 'There has, however, been a great deal of discussion in the legal literature on the question of the method of interpretation; the most delicate problem being to distinguish between what, in interpretation, can be the subject of precise rules and what, being the subject of individual cases, could only be the subject of an art rather than a science and, as such, should be left to the skill of the interpreter' (unofficial translation) of Paul Reuter, *Introduction au droit des traités* 140-143 (Graduate Institute Publications 1985).
17. Haslehner, *supra* n. 7, para. 90; Dirk M. Broekhuijsen, *A Modern Understanding of Article 31(3)(c) of the Vienna Convention (1969): A New Haunt for the Commentaries to the OECD Model?*, 67 Bull. Int'l Tax'n Chapter 3.1, n. 9 (2013) https://doi.org/10.59403/2chwwce.
18. Arnold, *The Interpretation of Tax Treaties: Myth and Reality, supra* n. 8, 2, 7.
19. Jan Klabbers, *Virtuous Interpretation, in Treaty Interpretation and the Vienna Convention on the Law of Treaties: 30 Years on* 20 (Malgosia Fitzmaurice, Olufemi Elias & Panos Merkouris eds, Martinus Nijhoff 2010).
20. Kammerhofer, *supra* n. 10, 125, 149.

making more informed choices.[21] This can be supported by the observation that different jurisdictions have various but generally not different types of rules of interpretation.[22] This allows for a more objective assessment of different interpretations and helps to prevent subjective biases from influencing the process and reinventing the law. Rules of legal interpretation should therefore be taken seriously but can never be taken literally because they themselves must be interpreted.[23] The rules of interpretation have more of a character of guidelines.[24] They provide a factual convergence of acts of application.[25] Formalizing and prescribing the method or decision-making process can establish a starting point for consistent interpretation.[26]

The question is whether the same rules of interpretation should be applied to different legal texts, specifically whether the interpretation framework for domestic law aligns with that for private contracts between parties or international treaties between sovereign states. Interpretation aims to ascertain the parties' intent from the text[27] thereby necessitating a clear definition of how and where this intent is expressed with an emphasis on identifying its most direct expression.[28]

In domestic law, this task appears straightforward due to the presence of a single legislator and a unified will. However, it might be questioned what constitutes this 'unified will'; whether it refers to the average parliamentary member who voted in favour of the law and their respective expectations regarding its regulation. This requires examining the abstract body and its intention.

The complexity escalates when multiple parliaments or legislative powers are involved as in the case of international treaties, including tax treaties. For such treaties to be effective, it is crucial – and more challenging than in domestic legislation – that they are interpreted and applied uniformly in both contracting states.[29] This necessity arises from different legal backgrounds, cultural aspects, and different views on the separation of powers.

2.2 Possible Meanings and Uses of the Vienna Convention Rules

To optimally achieve this uniformity, the drafters of the VCLT agreed on general rules for interpreting international agreements. Although the approach and the interpretation maxims considered may not differ significantly from those used for domestic legislation, Article 31(1) VCLT can be understood as a common denominator. This

21. *Ibid.*, 131; Broekhuijsen, *supra* n. 17, Chapter 3.1.
22. Haslehner, *supra* n. 7, paras 88-92; Klaus Vogel & Rainer Prokisch, *General Report, in International Fiscal Association 1993 Florence Congress* 55, 57 (Kluwer Law and Taxation 1993).
23. Kammerhofer, *supra* n. 10.
24. Humphrey Waldock, *Sixth Report on the Law of Treaties, in Yearbook of the International Law Commission (Document A/CN.4/186 and Add.1,2/Rev.1, 3-7)* 94 (United Nations 1966).
25. Kammerhofer, *supra* n. 10, 149; Catharine Titi, *The Arbitrator as a Lawmaker: Jurisgenerative Processes in Investment Arbitration*, 14 Journal of World Investment & Trade 829, 831, n. 5 (2013) https://doi.org/10.1163/22129000-01405003.
26. Kammerhofer, *supra* n. 10, 149.
27. Reuter, *supra* n. 16, 141.
28. *Ibid.*, 143.
29. Vogel & Prokisch, *supra* n. 22, 61.

should ensure consistency and prevent conflicting interpretations that could undermine the purpose of such agreements. These rules provide guidance and establish a framework for interpreting treaties, nevertheless, it is important to note that they cannot legally determine the meaning of treaties themselves.[30] Instead, they serve as tools to assist in the process of justification of a particular interpretation while respecting the specific context and intentions of the parties involved.

The International Law Commission's (ILC's) Commentaries on Draft Articles on the Law of Treaties (hereinafter 'ILC's Commentaries') recognize that these principles largely consist of logical and sensible guidelines rather than rigid rules.[31] Nonetheless, the ILC made efforts to codify a limited number of general principles that could serve as overarching rules for treaty interpretation. This endeavour aimed to equally balance the different interpretation maxims acknowledging the tension between an interpretation as both an art and an exercise constrained by certain rules.[32]

The ILC's Commentaries reflect a clear stance on the role of the text in treaty interpretation.[33] While it is recognized as paramount, they emphasize that the ordinary meaning of treaty words should not be determined in isolation but rather in its context and in light of its object and purpose. This approach ensures that the interpretation encompasses the intentions of the parties even if not explicitly reflected in the treaty's wording but in any instruments or agreements in connection with the treaty.

It is important to note that applying these rules does not necessarily lead to a uniform interpretation by contracting states.[34] The rules are worded in general terms and allow considerable latitude for interpretation, however, the VCLT identifies the most important elements of interpretation and relates them to each other,[35] thus helping to choose the purpose that best illuminates and justifies the object in question.

2.3 Additional Aspects of the Interpretation of Tax Treaties

The provisions of the VCLT apply to all treaties, including tax treaties, and are binding on all nations because they constitute a codification of the rules of customary international law.[36] Arnold summarizes that 'the interpretative provisions are "largely meaningless" and do not provide meaningful guidance for judges in interpretating tax treaties'.[37] He based this conclusion also on the fact that, in most tax treaty cases, the VCLT is not mentioned and, if it is, it does not appear to have decision-making relevance.[38] While it is true that the VCLT is not as prominently mentioned in the tax court decisions as, for example, in International Court of Justice (ICJ) cases, various

30. Kammerhofer, *supra* n. 10, 149.
31. International Law Commission, *Draft Articles on the Law of Treaties with commentaries, in Yearbook of the International Law Commission* 218-219 (United Nations Vol. II 1966).
32. *Ibid.*; Arnold, *The Interpretation of Tax Treaties: Myth and Reality, supra* n. 8, 7.
33. International Law Commission, *supra* n. 31, 218.
34. Vogel & Prokisch, *supra* n. 22, 67.
35. *Ibid.*
36. *Ibid.*, 66-67; Arnold, *The Interpretation of Tax Treaties: Myth and Reality, supra* n. 8, 5.
37. Brian J. Arnold, *The Interpretation of Tax Treaties: Looking to the Future,* 75 Bull. Intl. Taxn. 665-672, 666, n. 11/12 (2021) https://doi.org/10.59403/3acrt4x.
38. *Ibid.*, 665-666.

domestic courts, including the Canadian Supreme Court and the German Federal Fiscal Court, have applied the principles outlined in Articles 31 and 32 VCLT. These provisions provide a structured framework for treaty interpretation that can guide judges in their deliberations. As they summarize the most commonly used interpretation maxims, they are inherently also used for interpreting tax treaties. While the interpretative provisions are not frequently cited in tax treaty cases, their underlying principles can still be a crucial factor in ensuring a consistent and uniform interpretation of treaties which is essential for maintaining the integrity and effectiveness of international agreements.

Although tax treaties can be considered unique in the sense that - similarly to human rights treaties - individuals are their de facto beneficiaries, they do not demand a different set of rules of interpretation but a reasonable understanding of the object and purpose of the respective treaty when applying the general rule stipulated in Article 31 VCLT.[39] Thus, as Bossuyt concludes, tax treaties are not different from other international agreements, so the same interpretive rules should be applied to them.[40]

Tax treaties aim to allocate taxing rights by imposing mutual restrictions on the exercise of taxing rights by the contracting states. To achieve this goal, contracting states must strive for a uniform application of treaty provisions thereby ensuring a common interpretation by both parties.[41] This uniformity promotes consistency and reduces potential conflicts or discrepancies when interpreting and applying tax treaties.

A unique characteristic of tax treaties is that they are applied not only by the contracting states but also by taxpayers. Given the intrusive nature of tax laws - obligating taxpayers to financially contribute to government expenses and thus interfering with their right to private property - the interpretation process must be predictable as it is crucial for ensuring legal certainty for taxpayers. While interpretation cannot be entirely governed by rigid rules, it underscores the necessity for international interpretation principles as provided by Articles 31-33 VCLT. These must be taken seriously to achieve consistency and predictability in treaty interpretation.

When considering the relevance of context in the interpretation of international tax law rules, it is essential to address the role of documents issued by the OECD. Although these materials are not subject to the ratification/acceptance procedure by the parliaments of the contracting states, contracting states and other stakeholders, including courts, tax administrations, and taxpayers, frequently rely on them. The substantial volume of OECD materials has a significant impact on legislative activities and the interpretation of tax treaty provisions. This undeniable influence cannot be dismissed and warrants a thorough analysis.

39. Jasper Bossuyt, *The Legal Status of Extrinsic Instruments for the Interpretation of Tax Treaties*, 8.1.1 (2022); Oliver Dörr, *Article 31, in Vienna Convention on the Law of Treaties* 557, 575 (Oliver Dörr & Kirsten Schmalenbach eds, Springer Berlin Heidelberg 2018).
40. Bossuyt, *supra* n. 39, 8.1.1.
41. Vogel & Prokisch, *supra* n. 22, 62.

3 'CONTEXT' IN THE VIENNA CONVENTION

3.1 Nature of Article 31(1) VCLT

Article 31 VCLT contains the general rule of interpretation for international treaties. Article 31(1) states 'A treaty shall be interpreted in good faith in accordance with the ordinary meaning to be given to the terms of the treaty in their context and in the light of its object and purpose.' This general rule is neither innovative nor unusual[42] but describes a general rule of interpretation. The closely integrated single rule of Article 31(1) embraces various principles of 'how' to interpret and contains various means of interpretation, specifically the ordinary meaning of words (texts), context, and object and purpose.[43] The provision does not provide clear guidance on the weight to be given to each of the three elements[44] nor does it establish a chronological or hierarchical order in which they should be applied.[45] The singular form of the word 'rule' in the title of Article 31 ('General rule of interpretation') underscores that the various means are all to be employed and are all equally important:[46]

> The Commission, by heading the article 'General rule of interpretation' in the singular and by underlining the connexion between paragraphs 1 and 2 and again between paragraph 3 and the two previous paragraphs, intended to indicate that the application of the means of interpretation in the article would be a single combined operation. All the various elements, as they were present in any given case, would be thrown into the crucible, and their interaction would give the legally relevant interpretation. Thus, article 27 [now 31] is entitled 'General rule of interpretation' in the singular, not 'General rules' in the plural, because the Commission desired to emphasize that the process of interpretation is a unity and that the provisions of the article form a single, closely integrated rule.

The question that follows is whether Article 31 (together with Article 32) addresses the idea of acceptable and unacceptable means of interpretation for international treaties. Although there is contention,[47] this does not appear to be the proper approach to understanding the provision. The general rule is not intended to be

42. Arnold, *The Interpretation of Tax Treaties: Myth and Reality, supra* n. 8, 5; Jean-Marc Déry & David A. Ward, *Interpretation of Double Taxation Conventions: Canada, in Vol. 78a; Interpretation of Double Taxation Conventions* 269 (International Fiscal Association 1993).
43. Luc de Broe, *Role of the Preamble for the Interpretation of Old and New Tax Treaties and on the Policy of the Prevention of Treaty Abuse*, 74 Bull. Int'l Tax'n 163, 163, n. 4/5 (2020) https://doi.org/10.59403/3ceqp6z; Mark E. Villiger, *Commentary on the 1969 Vienna Convention on the Law of Treaties* 435-438 (2009). As Sinclair puts it 'the Convention rules on interpretation reflect an attempt to assess the relative value and weight of the elements to be taken into account in the process of interpretation rather than to describe the process of interpretation itself'. *See* Ian Sinclair, *The Vienna Convention on the Law of Treaties* 117 (1984).
44. Arnold, *The Interpretation of Tax Treaties: Myth and Reality, supra* n. 8, 6.
45. de Broe, *supra* n. 43, 163; Villiger, *Commentary on the 1969 Vienna Convention on the Law of Treaties, supra* n. 43, 436.
46. International Law Commission, *supra* n. 31, 219, 220.
47. Ulf Linderfalk, *On the Interpretation of Treaties: the Modern International Law as Expressed in the 1969 Vienna Convention on the Law of Treaties* 48 (2007).

comprehensive or exclusive.[48] Other interpretive principles or approaches such as regional rules, the historical approach or consequential analysis that consider the consequences of alternative interpretations are not precluded by the rule.[49] Determining the ordinary meaning of a treaty term is a holistic process.[50] There may be more relevant or less relevant means – as long as they are used within the field of legal interpretation. The broadly worded provision supports any type of interpretative approach from a narrow literal one to a broad purposive one.[51] It serves as a common denominator containing the most relevant means in most cases, which *must* be considered,[52] but not every means necessarily leads to a result when interpreting a treaty term.[53] It is therefore always necessary to consider and accept further interpretations based on the individual case.

The text is the authentic expression of the parties' intention and the starting point for interpretation since the latter is based on the meaning and scope of the written words.[54] The meaning of words used in treaties should not be inferred in isolation but should be determined by considering the context in which the words are used.[55] The objective of this is to avoid inconsistencies of the individual term with its surroundings and the ordinary meaning.[56] Article 31(1) mentions context as a general means of interpretation so, on the basis of this provision, it could have a very broad meaning. It could include not only the internal context of the treaty but also the external context, e.g., historical facts, economic, social, and other factual information and the state of the law at the time the law was enacted; documents that may elucidate the mischief or defect that the law was intended to remedy, and any relevant international treaties from which the law was derived.[57] However, Article 31(2) then arrives which defines and apparently limits the meaning of context for the purposes of interpreting international treaties. According to Engelen, both the description of 'context' in paragraph 2 and the words 'together with the context' in paragraph 3 are intended to incorporate the various elements of interpretation listed in them into paragraph 1.[58] The elements are to be read into Article 31(1) in order to determine the ordinary meaning of the terms

48. Dörr, *supra* n. 39, 560. *See* for further details on the discussion whether other interpretation rules or principles would also be considered, e.g., regional rules, *see* Frank A. Engelen, *Interpretation of Tax Treaties under International Law*, Chapter 6.8.4.2 (2004).
49. *Ibid.*
50. de Broe, *supra* n. 43, 163.
51. Brian J. Arnold, *The Interpretation of Tax Treaties: Looking to the Future*, 75 Bull. Intl. Taxn. 665, 665, n. 11/12 (2021) https://doi.org/10.59403/3acrt4x.
52. Donald H. Regan, *Understanding What the Vienna Convention Says about Identifying and Using 'Sources for Treaty Interpretation', in The Oxford Handbook of the Sources of International Law* 1047, 1049 (Jean d'Aspremont & Samantha Besson eds, Oxfords Handbooks 2017).
53. Villiger, *The Rules on Interpretation: Misgivings, Misunderstandings, Miscarriage? The 'Crucible' Intended by the International Law, in The Law of Treaties Beyond the Vienna Convention [Essays in Honour of Professor Giorgio Gaja]*, *supra* n. 1, 114.
54. Villiger, *Commentary on the 1969 Vienna Convention on the Law of Treaties*, *supra* n. 43, 436; Déry & Ward, *supra* n. 42, 261.
55. Arnold, *The Interpretation of Tax Treaties: Myth and Reality*, *supra* n. 8, 5; Engelen, *supra* n. 48; Déry & Ward, *supra* n. 42, 269.
56. International Law Commission, *supra* n. 31, 221, para. 12.
57. Déry & Ward, *supra* n. 42, 270.
58. Engelen, *supra* n. 48, Chapter 6.2.3.

of the treaty.[59] This raises the question of whether the sources of context listed in paragraph 2 are all of the accepted sources of context or whether additional sources of context not mentioned (e.g., historical, economic, social, and other factual information) could also be considered.

3.2 The Non-exhaustive List of 'Context' According to Article 31(2) VCLT

Article 31(2) VCLT specifies that:

> [t]he context for the purpose of the interpretation of a treaty shall comprise, in addition to the text, including its preamble and annexes:
>
> (a) any agreement relating to the treaty which was made between all the parties in with the conclusion of the treaty;
> (b) any instrument which was made by one or more parties in connection with the conclusion of the treaty and accepted by the other parties as an instrument related to the treaty.

The ILC's Commentary on the predecessor of Article 31 VCLT states that 'context' in paragraph 2 'is designed to link all the elements of interpretation mentioned in this paragraph to the word "context" in the first paragraph and thereby incorporate them in the provision contained in that paragraph.'[60] Further, the commentary states that 'for purposes of interpreting the treaty, these categories of documents should not be treated as mere evidence to which recourse may be had for the purpose of resolving an ambiguity or obscurity, but as part of the context for the purpose of arriving at the ordinary meaning of the terms of the treaty.'[61] This reaffirms the intention of the drafters of the VCLT to avoid an over-literal approach for interpretation purposes. It could also be read that the sources mentioned in paragraph 2 are to be understood as a parenthetical addition and not as a conclusive definition. Therefore, the first question regarding Article 31(2) VCLT that needs to be clarified is whether the list in paragraph 2 is an exhaustive or a non-exhaustive list.

The use of the word 'shall' indicates that it is mandatory to use the sources listed. The word 'comprise' could indicate that the list is exhaustive. Otherwise, the word 'includes' could have been used to make it clear that the list is not exhaustive. Thus, an overly textual interpretation could itself lead to Article 31(2) VCLT being seen as exhaustive.[62] This would reduce the role of 'context', however, to avoid an overly literal approach. An exhaustive nature of the list would be too narrow as an interpretation rule needs to be flexible to fulfil its purpose of finding the meaning of the treaty provisions. Some authors argue that the exhaustive interpretation of Article 31(2) VCLT is overly prescriptive and narrow.[63] They advocate for applying 'contextuality' to

59. *Ibid.*, Chapter 6.7.1.
60. International Law Commission, *supra* n. 31, 219, para. 8.
61. *Ibid.*, 221, para. 13.
62. *Ibid.*, 223, para. 18.
63. Myres S. McDougal, Harold D. Lasswell & James C. Miller, *The Interpretation of International Agreements and World Public Order: Principles of Content and Procedure* (1994).

encompass anything relevant to the realization of the shared expectations and values considering ongoing communication and cooperation between the parties.[64] This view could lead to an overly broad understanding and clash with the understanding that rules of interpretation are necessary precisely to limit judicial discretion and prevent arbitrariness. It only means that the list in Article 31(2) VCLT does not encompass all possible forms of 'context'[65] so that other sources cannot be excluded per se but, according to the authors, not every source of context can have the same relevance. The list likely covers the most pertinent or commonly used ones – depending on the current facts.

After clarifying the nature of the list, it is necessary to explore the structure of paragraph 2 in order to answer the question of what sources of context can be considered. The context comprises, first and foremost, the text of the treaty including its preamble and annexes. This follows from the introductory sentence of Article 31(2) VCLT.[66] These elements form an integral part of the treaty.[67] After the introductory sentence, it follows with 'any agreement relating to the treaty …' and 'any instrument […] in connection with the conclusion of the treaty …'. Both elements in Article 31(2) VCLT share a common feature: They refer to acts connected to the treaty's conclusion[68] and form part of the extrinsic component of it.[69]

Article 31(2) directs attention to 'what' should be considered rather than specifying 'how' the material should be utilized.[70] To summarize, context comprises the integral part of the treaty, the text, preamble and annexes, as well as the extrinsic part of the treaty that means any agreement and instrument that has a relationship to the treaty. In addition, other sources could also become relevant depending on the individual case.

3.3 Forms of Context According to Article 31(2) VCLT

3.3.1 Definition of the Term Treaty

Whereas it may be clear that the treaty comprises the text, its preamble, and annexes, the question of whether certain agreements and instruments related to the treaty can also be brought within the term 'treaty' is more difficult.[71] According to Article 2(1)(a) VCLT a 'treaty means an international agreement concluded between States in written form and governed by international law, whether embodied in a single instrument or in two or more related instruments and whatever its particular designation'. There was a longer, historical debate about whether context definition should also be placed in

64. *Ibid.*
65. Villiger, *Commentary on the 1969 Vienna Convention on the Law of Treaties, supra* n. 43, 439.
66. Engelen, *supra* n. 48, Chapter 6.7.2.1.
67. *See* s. 3.3.2 for further details.
68. Duncan B. Hollis, *The Oxford Guide to Treaties* 466 (2020).
69. *See* s. 3.3.3 for further details.
70. Hollis, *supra* n. 68, 466.
71. Engelen, *supra* n. 48, Chapter 6.7.2.1.

Article 2.[72] The drafters of the VCLT ultimately decided to include 'context' in the general rule of interpretation to make it more precise that it serves as a means of interpretation. Accordingly, the term treaty used in this respect necessarily follows the definition of Article 2(1)(a) VCLT but should not be regarded as too narrow since it is placed in the context of an interpretation rule.

3.3.2 *Integral Part of the Treaty*

3.3.2.1 *Syntactic Context of the Specific Provision*

When interpreting international treaties, it is crucial to analyse the syntactical context of the words or parts of the provisions being interpreted. This involves examining the words immediately surrounding the word or phrase in question to understand its meaning. The position of a particular word within a group of words or a sentence or a phrase within a paragraph and its place within the entire structure or scheme of the treaty should also be taken into account.[73] This is illustrated by the following ICJ decisions.

In the case, *Maritime delimitation and territorial questions*, between Qatar and Bahrain,[74] the dispute centred on the interpretation of the Arabic term 'al-tarafan' in the second sentence of the original Arabic text of paragraph 2 of the 1990 Doha Minutes ('the Minutes'): 'Once that period has elapsed, "al-tarafan" may submit the matter to the International Court of Justice.' The term 'al-tarafan' translated as 'the parties' by Qatar and 'the two parties' by Bahrain was analysed for its alternative or cumulative meaning. An alternative meaning would leave each of the parties with the option of acting unilaterally whereas a cumulative meaning would imply that the question to be submitted to the court would require the parties acting in concert. The ICJ first analysed the syntactical context and suggested that the most natural interpretation of 'may' allows a possibility.[75] This was reinforced both by the form of words and by the logical implications of the expression 'once that period has elapsed'.[76] The court noted that any other interpretation than a unilateral option or right would deprive the phrase of its effect and could lead to an unreasonable result.[77] This conclusion was confirmed in a second step when considering the context of the meaning of the provision and the treaty. Hence, paragraph 2 allowed the unilateral seisin of the court.[78]

The *Land, island maritime frontier Dispute between El Salvador and Honduras* involves the delimitation of the frontier line in sectors not previously delimited by the 1980 General Treaty of Peace, the determination of the legal situation of the islands in

72. *See* for details *ibid.*, Chapter 6.7.2.2.
73. Dörr, *supra* n. 39, 44.
74. ICJ Maritime Delimitation and Territorial Questions (*Qatar v. Bahrain*) [1995].
75. *Ibid.*, para. 35.
76. *Ibid.*
77. *Ibid.*
78. *Ibid.*, 40.

the Gulf of Fonseca, and the maritime spaces within and outside it.[79] The parties requested the ICJ to clarify the meaning of Article 2, paragraph 2 specifically 'to determine the legal situation of the islands and maritime spaces'. El Salvador claims that the waters are subject to a condominium in favour of the three coastal states of the gulf and that delimitation would therefore be inappropriate; Honduras argues that, within the gulf there, is a community of interests that both permits and necessitates a judicial delimitation.[80] In applying the 'normal rules of treaty interpretation'[81] the chamber ascertains whether the text is to be read as entailing such a delimitation.[82] According to it, 'it is difficult to see how one can equate "delimitation" with "determination of a legal situation ...". No doubt the word "determine" in English [...] can be used to convey the idea of setting limits, so that, if applied directly to the "maritime spaces" its "ordinary meaning" might be taken to include the delimitation of those spaces. However, the word must be read in its context; the object of the verb "determine" is not the maritime spaces themselves but their legal situation. No indication of a common intention to obtain a delimitation by the chamber can therefore be derived from this text as it stands.'[83] After analysing the immediate context of the word 'determine', the chamber also considered its wider context, first of the special agreement as a whole and then of the 1980 General Treaty of Peace to which the special agreement refers. It concluded that it is difficult to accept that the same wording 'to determine the legal situation' used for both the islands and the maritime spaces would have 'a completely different meaning' regarding the islands and the maritime spaces.[84]

The syntactical context also includes a grammatical interpretation. The relevance of using a comma was raised in the *Aegean Sea Continental Shelf* case[85] in which Greece and Turkey disputed over the Aegean Sea continental shelf. Greece asked the ICJ to declare that the Greek islands in the area are entitled to their rightful share of the continental shelf and to delimit the respective parts of the shelf belonging to Greece and Turkey. The relevant text reads as follows: 'Sont exclus des procédures décrites par l'Acte général, sans en excepter celle de conciliation visée à son chapitre 1: [...] b) les différends portant sur des questions que le droit international laisse à la compétence exclusive des Etats et, notamment, les différends ayant trait au statut territorial de la Grèce, [...]'.[86] The Greek Government maintained that reservation (b) does not cover all disputes relating to the territorial status of Greece but only such as both relate to its territorial status and, at the same time, concern 'questions which by international law

79. Nicaragua intervened in the case, but the chamber decided that Nicaragua had not shown such an interest that it might be affected by any decision concerning the delimitation of those waters or the legal situation of the islands and maritime spaces.
80. ICJ Land, Island and Maritime Frontier Dispute (*El Salvador v. Honduras*) [1992], para. 372.
81. *Ibid.*
82. *Ibid.*
83. *Ibid.*
84. *Ibid.*
85. ICJ Aegean Sea Continental Shelf (*Greece v. Turkey*) [1978].
86. Translation: 'The following disputes are excluded from the procedures described in the General Act, including the procedure of conciliation referred to in Chapter I: [...] b) disputes concerning questions which by international law are solely within the domestic jurisdiction of States, and in particular disputes relating to the territorial status of Greece, [...].'

are solely within the domestic jurisdiction of states'. The ICJ focused on the use of the phrase 'et, notamment, [...]' ('and in particular') which precede the reference to 'les différends ayant trait au statu territorial de la Grèce' (disputes relating to the territorial status of Greece). The ICJ noted that one possible purpose of these commas might have been to make it clear that the word 'et' in the phrase is intended to be a true conjunctive introducing a category of 'différends' additional to those already specified.[87] However, the question of whether the expression 'et, notamment' in the present instance has the meaning attributed to it by Greece thus depends on the context in which those words were used in Greece's instrument of accession and is not a matter simply of their preponderant linguistic use.[88] The ICJ questioned whether a purely grammatical interpretation affords the possibility that the phrase used was intended to specify an autonomous category of disputes additional to those concerning matters of domestic jurisdiction.[89] It recalls that, in any event, 'the Court cannot base itself on a purely grammatical interpretation of the text'.[90] It concluded that a number of considerations point decisively to the conclusion that reservation (b) contained two separate and autonomous reservations.[91]

This textual logic is a crucial factor in establishing the ordinary meaning of the provisions.[92] The ICJ has emphasized the importance of a proposed reading that allows the entire sentence in a treaty provision to be coherent as this guides the interpretative process and helps determine the meaning of the provision.[93]

3.3.2.2 Ordinary Meaning in Context

3.3.2.2.1 Internal Context of the Provision: Title and Headings

The title of a treaty or a specific heading within a legal text can provide important contextual information about the document's overall purpose and subject matter. It sets the tone for the subsequent provisions and can offer valuable insights into the intentions of the parties involved. By examining the title or headings, interpreters can gain a clearer understanding of the broader context in which specific terms or provisions are used. They function as signposts, directing the reader's attention to the key topics, organizing the content and providing a framework for the interpretation process.

The *Oil Platforms*[94] case serves as an example of how titles and headings can be an important factor when interpreting legal terms in international treaties. In this case, the ICJ was tasked with determining the meaning of the term 'commerce' in a bilateral treaty between Iran and the United States. The paragraph reads as follows: 'Between

87. ICJ Aegean Sea Continental Shelf (*Greece v. Turkey*) [1978], para. 53.
88. *Ibid.*, para. 54.
89. *Ibid.*
90. ICJ Anglo-Iranian Oil Co (*United Kingdom v. Iran*) [1952].
91. ICJ Aegean Sea Continental Shelf (*Greece v. Turkey*) [1978], para. 55.
92. Dörr, *supra* n. 39, 50.
93. *Ibid.*
94. ICJ Oil Platforms (*Islamic Republic of Iran v. United States of America*) [1996].

the territories of the two High Contracting parties there shall be freedom of commerce and navigation.' Iran argued that the provision does not contemplate only maritime commerce but only commerce in general.[95] The United States argued for a more restrictive interpretation that 'commerce' refers to maritime commerce.[96] The ICJ considered that, after this paragraph in which the word 'commerce' appears, the rest of the article clearly deals with maritime commerce.[97] However, in view of the court, this factor is not sufficient to restrict the scope of the word to maritime commerce when considering other indications in the treaty of the parties' intention to deal with trade and commerce in general. The court turned to the actual title of the treaty that broadly referred to 'economic relations'.[98] This choice of title suggested a wider reading of the term 'commerce'.[99] Thus the title and headings in general can provide relevant context about the meaning of specific provisions.

3.3.2.2.2 Internal Context of the Treaty: Other Provisions, Preamble and Annexes

Additionally, the possibility of giving a treaty provision an *a contrario* reading is also influenced by the contextual analysis, particularly if only one possible reading of the provision is reconcilable with the terms of other provisions.[100] The syntactical structure of provisions is closely associated with the interpretation of phrases and contributes to determining the ordinary meaning of terms in their contextual framework.[101]

It is imperative to consider the text of the treaty as a cohesive whole rather than isolating specific provisions or phrases.[102] A comprehensive understanding of the treaty is achieved by examining the interrelationship between its various provisions and identifying any necessary consequences or implications that may elucidate the disputed term. The treaty is also taken into account when it is established that other provisions of the same treaty have a certain reading of the disputed term as a necessary consequence or implication.[103] The ICJ pointed out that the text 'must be interpreted in a manner which is in harmony with the "natural and reasonable" way of reading the text, having due regard to the intention of the declarant'.[104] Therefore, the ICJ takes into account the context in which the term in question is used in other provisions in order to arrive at an understanding.[105]

95. *Ibid.*, para. 39.
96. *Ibid.*, para. 40.
97. *Ibid.*, para. 41.
98. *Ibid.*, para. 47.
99. *Ibid.*
100. ICJ Question of Delimitation of the Continental Shelf between Nicaragua and Colombia (*Nicaragua v. Colombia*) [2016], paras 35-38.
101. Gardiner, *supra* n. 4, 200.
102. Dörr, *supra* n. 39; Sinclair, *supra* n. 43, 127.
103. Dörr, *supra* n. 39, 48.
104. ICJ Fisheries Jurisdiction case (*Spain v. Canada*) [1998], para. 76.
105. ICJ Application of the International Convention for the suppression of the financing of terrorism and of the international convention on the elimination of all forms of racial discrimination (*Ukraine v. Russian Federation*) [2024], para. 49.

The treaty's preamble typically serves the purpose of stating its aims and objectives.[106] It is composed of a series of recitals that commonly outline the motivations, goals, and considerations of the contracting parties as well as affirm the shared values that have influenced the treaty's conclusion.[107] The preamble does not have a normative character, however, by articulating the aims and objectives of a treaty, it holds contextual and teleological significance.[108] As an integral part of the context, the preamble falls within the primary interpretative means of Article 31: '[t]he context for the purpose of the interpretation of a treaty shall comprise, in addition to the text, including its preamble and annexes ...'. It can contribute to clarifying the ordinary meaning of a term and may justify a broader or narrower interpretation (depending on the preamble and the term to be interpreted) than that which would result from considering the treaty's object and purpose alone.[109]

The last item that forms part of the internal context of the treaty is the annexes that might contain more details and circumstances in support of the treaty provisions.[110] They can be a smaller piece of the document to supplement the provisions in the main text, or they are designed to interpret, define, or illustrate the terms, e.g., maps or valuation methods.

3.3.3 *Extrinsic Part of the Treaty: Cross-Treaty Context*

3.3.3.1 *Conditions to Become Extrinsic Context of a Treaty*

Paragraph 2 of Article 31 designates two categories of documents that are considered part of the 'context' within the meaning of paragraph 1.[111] These documents are extrinsic to the treaty itself and are not integral parts of it.[112]

Agreements reached between the parties contemporaneously with the treaty are deemed to be part of the context of the treaty.[113] A unilateral document, by itself, cannot be considered to be part of the context. It requires some form of acceptance or recognition by the other parties to attain that status.[114] The status of a document created in relation to a treaty's conclusion as an actual part of that treaty depends on the parties' intention in each specific case.[115] If a document is part of the treaty consensus itself, it is regarded as an object rather than an interpretative instrument within the context.[116] However, paragraph 2 of Article 31 elevates documents that are not part of the treaty consensus but are related to its development as fully-fledged

106. de Broe, *supra* n. 43, 164; Dörr, *supra* n. 39, 49.
107. de Broe, *supra* n. 43, 163.
108. Dörr, *supra* n. 39, 49.
109. de Broe, *supra* n. 43, 164.
110. Bossuyt, *supra* n. 39, 707.
111. Dörr, *supra* n. 39, 61.
112. *Ibid.*, 62. Klicken oder tippen Sie hier, um Text einzugeben.
113. Arnold, *The Interpretation of Tax Treaties: Myth and Reality*, *supra* n. 8, 7-8.
114. Dörr, *supra* n. 39, 61.
115. *Ibid.*, 62.
116. *Ibid.*

interpretative instruments.[117] The documents listed become more relevant sources of context as the parties take the opportunity to agree on interpretative instruments related to the treaty thus determining its interpretation through means extrinsic to the treaty itself.[118] As Dörr puts it, the material accepted as related to the treaty's conclusion can help determine which of the various ordinary meanings of its terms should prevail.[119]

The case of *Sovereignty over Pulau Ligitan and Pulau Sipadan* was a territorial dispute between Indonesia and Malaysia over two islands located in the Celebes Sea off the south eastern coast of the Malaysian state of Sabah. The parties' disagreement was regarding the interpretation to be given to Article IV of the 1891 Convention between Great Britain and the Netherlands. 'From 4°10' north latitude on the east coast the boundary-line shall be continued eastward along that parallel, across the Island of Sebittik …'. A map accompanied the explanatory memorandum annexed by the latter to the draft law submitted to the Netherlands States-General with a view to ratifying the convention. This map shows a red line continuing out to sea along the 4°10' north parallel.[120] However, the explanatory memorandum and map were never transmitted by the Dutch Government to the British Government but forwarded to the latter by the British Minister at the Hague. He 'sent an official dispatch back to the Foreign Office … with which he sent two copies of the map: and he drew specific attention to it'.[121] There was no reaction from the foreign office. Indonesia maintains that this interaction, in terms of Article 31(2)(b), 'establishes an agreement between the two governments regarding the seaward course of the Anglo-Dutch boundary east of Sebatik'. It further indicates that the map was, within the meaning of Article 31(2)(b), an instrument made by the Dutch Government in connection with the conclusion of the 1891 convention and was accepted by the British Government as an instrument related to the treaty.[122] Indonesia states, *inter alia,* that '[the map] was officially prepared by the Dutch Government immediately after the conclusion of the 1891 Convention and in connection with its approval by the Netherlands States-General as specifically required by the Article VIII of the Convention', that 'it was publicly and officially available at the time', and that 'the British Government, in the face of its official knowledge of the map, remained silent'.[123]

In Malaysia's view, the map cannot be regarded as context as it was prepared exclusively for internal purposes, it was never promulgated by the Dutch authorities, and neither the government nor the parliament of the Netherlands sought to incorporate it into the convention. Further, the map in question was never officially communicated by the Dutch Government to the British Government.[124]

117. *Ibid.*
118. *Ibid.*, 64.
119. *Ibid.*
120. ICJ Sovereignty over Pulau Ligitan and Pulau Sipadan (*Indonesia v. Malaysia*) [2002], para. 44.
121. *Ibid.*
122. *Ibid.*
123. *Ibid.*
124. *Ibid.*, para. 45.

The ICJ did not accept Indonesia's argument regarding the legal value of the map as the explanatory memorandum and map were simply forwarded by a diplomatic agent.[125] The agent specified that the map had been published in the Official Journal of the Netherlands and formed part of a report presented to the Second Chamber of the States-General. He added that 'the map seems to be the only interesting feature of a document which does not otherwise call for special comment'. However, he did not draw the attention of his authorities to the red line drawn on the map among other lines. Due to the lack of reaction by the British Government to the line, the ICJ concluded that the map appended to the memorandum cannot be deemed to constitute acquiescence. Further, the ICJ decided that a map can neither be considered an agreement within the meaning of Article 31, paragraph 2(a) nor as an instrument within the meaning of Article 31, paragraph 2(b).[126]

According to *Dörr*, the following conditions can be identified that must be met in order for a document to be considered extrinsic context in treaty interpretation:[127]

1) General Consensus

The document in question must either be drawn up by all parties together or, if drafted by one or several parties, accepted by the other parties. It is essential that there is a general consensus among all parties regarding the document's status as extrinsic context.[128]

2) Parties

The consensus mentioned above must be shared by all 'parties' to the treaty as defined in Article 1(1)(g) VCLT according to which parties refer only to those states that have consented to be bound by the treaty and for which the treaty is in force. Therefore, acts, views, and instruments of states that participated in the negotiations but are ultimately not party to the treaty should not be considered extrinsic context.

3) Relate to the Substance of the Treaty

The material in question must have a substantive relation to the content of the treaty. This can include specifying or clarifying certain concepts used in it or limiting its scope of application. The relation must be both substantial and encompassed by the consensus of the parties.

4) Temporal Proximity

The temporal proximity is the fourth element and results from the requirement 'in connection with the conclusion of the treaty' (Article 31(2) VCLT). The term 'conclusion' is ambiguous as it may refer to a specific moment when the treaty is established as definitive or to the period of drafting a treaty, i.e., from the initiation of negotiations

125. *Ibid.*
126. *Ibid.*
127. Dörr, *supra* n. 39, 65.
128. Villiger, *Commentary on the 1969 Vienna Convention on the Law of Treaties*, *supra* n. 43, 430.

to the treaty's entry into force (or the moment that the treaty is signed and adopted).[129] Many authors[130] assume the former to apply, however, as *Bossuyt* correctly pointed out, without providing any justifications.[131] The term 'subsequent' in Article 31(3)(a) VCLT must be read together with 'in connection' whereas 'subsequent' is opposed to 'in connection with'.[132] According to *Bossuyt*, 'subsequent' encompasses a temporal component and, therefore, it only seems logical that 'in connection' also has the same.[133] The ordinary meaning of 'in connection' allows agreements and instruments concluded before and at the time of the treaty's conclusion to be taken into account, however, it does not require 'at the same time', but it needs some distance from the 'subsequent' element of Article 31(3)(a) VCLT.[134]

Statements made during a diplomatic conference, for example, may not carry significant weight as it is uncertain whether the treaty will indeed be concluded and which states will ultimately become parties to it.[135]

To be considered part of the treaty's context, an agreement or instrument must meet certain conditions. The provision does not specify the exact moment in time when the consensus, whether in the form of an agreement or acceptance, must have been established. In the event of an agreement, Article 31(2)(a) VCLT requires that it be made 'in connection with' the treaty's conclusion which implies a nexus in purpose and substance rather than a strict temporal coincidence.[136] Article 31(2)(b) VCLT does not provide any indication of a temporal requirement for acceptance. The structure of Article 31 VCLT suggests that the terms 'agreement' and 'acceptance' in paragraph 2 encompass a consensus that is established in a certain temporal proximity to the process of treaty conclusion. This implication arises from the fact that paragraph 3 of Article 31 VCLT specifically addresses acts and agreements subsequent to that. In practice, agreements of this nature are typically reached when the treaty text is adopted thus coinciding with the conclusion process. Individual parties may present unilateral documents at the time of signing or ratifying the treaty that may require a response from the other parties at a later date.

3.3.3.2 Understanding of the Term 'Any Agreement'

The term 'agreement' is broader than the concept of a treaty and encompasses any contractual instrument, including those not in written form.[137] In common treaty practice, these 'agreements' often take the form of final acts, protocols of signature,

129. Bossuyt, *supra* n. 39, Chapter 8.1.2.4.2, para. 722.
130. *See* for details Linderfalk, *On the Interpretation of Treaties: the Modern International Law as Expressed in the 1969 Vienna Convention on the Law of Treaties, supra* n. 47, 209-211.
131. Bossuyt, *supra* n. 39, Chapter 8.1.2.4.2, para. 722.
132. *Ibid.*
133. *Ibid.*
134. *Ibid.*
135. Villiger, *Commentary on the 1969 Vienna Convention on the Law of Treaties, supra* n. 43, 430.
136. For this and the following Dörr, *supra* n. 39, 65.
137. Dörr, *supra* n. 39, 66.

understandings, commentaries, or explanatory reports.[138] They are agreed upon by the governmental experts involved in drafting the treaty text and adopted simultaneously with it.[139]

According to the VCLT's drafters' explanation, the principle underlying this provision is that a unilateral document cannot be considered part of the context unless it was made in connection with the conclusion of the treaty and its relation to it was accepted by the other parties.[140] However, it should be noted that recognizing these two types of documents in paragraph 2 as forming part of the 'context' does not necessarily imply that they are integral parts of the treaty. Whether they are considered as such depends on the intention of the parties in each specific case.[141]

In practice, there may be differences in how these principles are applied.[142] For example, it is generally clear that a protocol of signature or a specific protocol on interpretation falls within the scope of Article 31(2)(a) VCLT.[143] However, classifying a 'memorandum of understanding', whether accompanying a treaty or standing alone, may be more challenging as it does not provide a conclusive indication of the legally binding nature of the agreement.[144]

A noteworthy example of material falling within the scope of Article 31(2) VCLT can be found in the declarations adopted by European Union (EU) Member States as part of the final act drawn up during Member State conferences amending the basic treaties of the EU, such as the Final Act attached to the Treaty of Lisbon.[145]

3.3.3.3 Understanding of the Term 'Any Instrument'

In relation to a treaty's conclusion, unilateral instruments or instruments that do not reflect the agreement of all parties often involve interpretative declarations.[146] These can include agreements inter se between certain parties or unilateral statements such as interpretative declarations made upon ratification or accession.[147]

Unilateral or plurilateral instruments are considered 'any instrument' in the meaning of Article 31(2)(b) VCLT when they are accepted by all of the other parties.[148] Statements made by individual parties before a treaty's conclusion or accompanying their expression of consent to be bound can also be unilateral interpretative declarations.[149] These declarations are presented by a state at the time of agreeing to the treaty and often share similarities with reservations to the treaty.[150] However, unlike a

138. *Ibid.*
139. *Ibid.*
140. International Law Commission, *supra* n. 31, 221.
141. *Ibid.*
142. Hollis, *supra* n. 68, 467.
143. *Ibid.*
144. *Ibid.*
145. Dörr, *supra* n. 39, 63.
146. Hollis, *supra* n. 68, 467.
147. Villiger, *Commentary on the 1969 Vienna Convention on the Law of Treaties*, *supra* n. 43, 430.
148. Dörr, *supra* n. 39, 67.
149. *Ibid.*
150. *Ibid.*

reservation, an interpretative declaration simply states that the declarant understands or interprets a specific provision without seeking to modify or exclude its application.[151] By making such a declaration, a state aims to influence the subsequent interpretation of the treaty, and the extent of this influence depends on the reaction of the other parties to the declaration.[152]

There is no formal requirement for acceptance by other parties, and it can be given informally or tacitly.[153] However, the wording states 'accepted by the other parties as an instrument related to the treaty'. Therefore, a certain interpretation based on extrinsic context must always demonstrate that the other parties actually accepted the proposed interpretation.[154] If the wording of an accompanying document refers to another treaty, it is necessary to consider the express link and, as appropriate, ensure a concordant interpretation between the two instruments. This is based on the express reference 'accepted by'.[155]

3.4 Relationship of Article 31(2) VCLT to Other Interpretive Provisions of the VCLT

It should be noted at this point that the boundaries between the means of interpretation according to Article 31 VCLT are fluid, and a strict categorization of sources for interpretation may not be appropriate. Nevertheless, some comments can be made on the relationship between Article 31(2) and the other provisions of Articles 31 and 32.

Article 31(2) VCLT must be interpreted in accordance with Article 31(1) VCLT. This demonstrates that the 'context' per se is considered 'one' means of interpretation, but all means of Article 31(1) VCLT must be taken into account. The documents mentioned in Article 31(3) lack the temporal proximity required under Article 31(2) as they are 'subsequent'.

Further, the documents mentioned in Article 31(2) should be distinguished from mere preparatory materials of the treaty, are to be considered part of the treaty's context, and are treated as an element of the general rule of interpretation. Bossuyt refers to it as 'the authentic means of interpretation' as 'the treaty text reflect the authentic expression of the parties' intention, and deciphering the text thus equates to deciphering the common intentions of the treaty partners'.[156] They are not considered supplementary means according to Article 32 VCLT which have a role in the interpretation process that is hierarchically lower than the means under Article 31.[157] However, it remains unclear how a distinction between extrinsic context (Article 31(2) VCLT) and a treaty's preparatory works (Article 32 VCLT) can be drawn in a given case.[158] One proposal suggests that the distinction lies in the phrase 'in connection with the

151. *Ibid.*
152. *Ibid.*, 68
153. *Ibid.*
154. *Ibid.*
155. Gardiner, *supra* n. 4, 200.
156. Bossuyt, *supra* n. 39, Chapter 8.1.1, paras 680, 682.
157. Dörr, *supra* n. 39, 63.
158. *Ibid.*, 61.

conclusion of the treaty' found in both alternatives of paragraph 2 of Article 31.[159] Documents connected with the act of concluding the treaty, rather than with the treaty itself, go beyond the preparatory stage and relate to the actual existence of the consensus on the treaty. To differentiate between preparation and conclusion, objective factors (such as the time taken to prepare the document) and the intention of the actors should be taken into account.[160] Treaty-related material that does not meet the conditions of 'context' under Article 31(2) VCLT may still be considered preparatory works within the meaning of Article 32 VCLT.[161]

4 CONTEXT OUTSIDE THE LIST OF ARTICLE 31(2) VCLT

4.1 Analogues Wording of Other Agreements and Practices Among a Subgroup of Parties

One of the conclusions drawn in section 3 was that the list in Article 31(2) VCLT is not exhaustive. The question that arises is what else might be considered relevant material. The documents referred to in paragraph 2 lit. a and lit. b have in common that they are related to the treaty in question. Agreements and practices among a subgroup of parties fall outside paragraph 2.[162] The question is whether an analogous wording of another treaty between the same parties or in a treaty to which only one of them is a party can also be considered in order to identify the context of meaning.

The ICJ referred in *Oil Platforms* to the most similar treaties concluded by the United States at that time, such as the treaty of 1956 between the United States and Nicaragua, not referring to 'commerce' but more broadly to economic relations.[163] The reference was made to identify the ordinary meaning of a specific word in context.

This conclusion by analogy seems obvious and appropriate in cases when the parties have a certain understanding of a term or provision and regard it as so self-evident that they do not discuss it further. However, it will be necessary to examine on a case-by-case basis whether that understanding actually reflects an appropriate interpretation or one in accordance with the will of the respective legislator. This subsequently leads to the conclusion that the elements listed in paragraph 2 must be examined first, and the context mentioned here forms part of the less relevant material for establishing the context in the course of interpretation.

4.2 Analogues Wording of Other Sources

The question is whether other sources could become relevant context for determining the meaning of certain provisions. This could include expert opinions reflecting the

159. *Ibid.*
160. *Ibid.*, 63.
161. *Ibid.*
162. Villiger, *Commentary on the 1969 Vienna Convention on the Law of Treaties*, *supra* n. 43, 36.
163. ICJ Oil Platforms (*Islamic Republic of Iran v. United States of America*) [1996], para. 47.

common understanding of certain words or circumstances relevant at the time of a treaty's conclusion or at the time of its application.

In *Kasikili/Sedudu Island*, Namibia and Botswana request the ICJ to determine the boundary around Kasikili/Sedudu Island and its legal status. The island is referred to in Namibia as 'Kasikili' and in Botswana as 'Sedudu' and is located in a river. The ICJ states that 'in order to illuminate the meaning of words agreed upon in the 1890 treaty, there is nothing that prevents the Court from taking into account the present-day state of scientific knowledge'.[164] The relevant provision locates the dividing line between the parties' spheres of influence in the 'main channel' of the river. However, there is no provision in the treaty setting out criteria for identifying the 'main channel'.[165] The court also notes that the English version refers to the 'centre' of the main channel, while the German version uses the term 'thalweg' of that channel (Thalweg des Hauptlaufes). Botswana claims that the thalweg of the river means its main channel, and the words 'des Hauptlaufes' add nothing to the text.[166] Namibia claims that the search must first be for the 'hauptlauf' and then, once it has been found, to search for the 'thalweg'.[167] The ICJ notes that different definitions of the term 'thalweg' are found in treaties delimiting boundaries and that the concepts of the thalweg of a watercourse and the centre of a watercourse are not equivalent.[168] The word 'thalweg' has variously been taken to mean 'the most suitable channel for navigation' on the river, the line 'determined by the line of deepest soundings', or 'the median line of the main channel followed by boatmen travelling downstream'.[169]

At the time of the conclusion of the treaty in question, it may be that the terms 'centre of the main channel' and 'Thalweg' des Hauptlaufes were used interchangeably. However, the ICJ noted that approximately three years before the conclusion of the treaty in question, the Institute of International Law[170] stated the following in Article 3, paragraph 2, of the 'Draft concerning the international regulation of fluvial navigation', adopted at Heidelberg on 9 September 1887: 'The boundary of States separated by a river is indicated by the thalweg, that is to say, the median line of the channel'.[171] On the basis of this expert's opinion, the ICJ concludes that the parties used the words 'centre of the main channel' as having the same meaning as the words 'Thalweg des Hauptlaufes'.[172] According to the ICJ, this understanding was confirmed by the travaux preparatoires of a related treaty between the parties.

164. ICJ Kasikili/Sedudu Island (*Botswana v. Namibia*) [1999], para. 20.
165. *Ibid.*, para. 21.
166. *Ibid.*, para. 22.
167. *Ibid.*, para. 23.
168. *Ibid.*, para. 24.
169. *Ibid.*
170. The Institut de droit international was founded in Belgium on 8 September 1873. Eleven international lawyers decided to create an institution independent of any governmental influence that would be able to contribute to developing international law and act to ensure its implementation. Institut de Droit International, *About the Institute*, https://www.idi-iil.org/en/a-propos/.
171. Institut de Droit International, *Annuaire 1887/1888*, https://www.idi-iil.org/app/uploads/2017/04/4025-9-OCR-min-TBU.pdf (accessed 26 June 2024), 182.
172. ICJ Kasikili/Sedudu Island (*Botswana v. Namibia*) [1999], para. 25.

This decision shows that the context can also be derived from other sources such as expert opinions that elucidate the understanding of words or circumstances at the time the treaty was drafted. However, as mentioned in section 4.1, it is crucial to verify the result with other means of interpretation in order to discuss the actual intention of the parties. It is therefore possible to conclude that this type of context does become a factor, but it is a subordinate one.

5 CONSIDERATION OF 'CONTEXT' IN TAX TREATIES

5.1 Integral Part of Tax Treaties: The Preamble

The precedent in international law has shown that the preamble serves as a valuable guide to the object and purpose of a treaty. However, it is crucial to note that Article 31(1) VCLT emphasizes the need to consider the entire text to determine the object and purpose, indicating that the preamble is only one aspect of the entire treaty. Another result of the international law section was that the preamble cannot be used to counter clear substantive provisions. The question is whether this can also be applied to tax treaties.

The case *Bayfine UK v. Commissioners for HMRC* concerned the double taxation relief pursuant to the US/UK tax treaty in the context of 'hybrid' entities.[173] The transactions were based on a complex self-cancelling scheme designed to create a loss for UK tax purposes without a corresponding UK taxable profit in another part of the group. Another UK resident company, BUK, realized a taxable profit on a forward contract governed by US law. As a result of BUK being disregarded for US tax purposes on the basis of the 'check the box' election, this profit was taxed in the United States as part of BUK's US tax resident parent company. BUK sought credit for this US tax under the terms of the US/UK tax treaty. With respect to the question of whether the United Kingdom is bound to give relief to BUK under the provision of the US/UK tax treaty, the judgment referred, *inter alia,* to the preamble.

The preamble to the US/UK tax treaty is brief and states that the parties are 'desiring to conclude a new Convention for the *avoidance of double taxation* and the *prevention of fiscal evasion* with respect to taxes on income and capital gains'[174] (emphasis added). Lady Justice Arden noted in *Bayfine UK v. Commissioners for HMRC*:

> These words, however, make it clear that the primary purposes of the Treaty are, on the one hand, to eliminate double taxation and, on the other hand, to prevent the avoidance of taxation. In seeking a purposive interpretation, both these principles have to be borne in mind. Moreover, the latter principle, in my judgment, means that the Treaty should be interpreted to avoid the grant of double relief as well as to confer relief against double taxation.[175]

173. *Bayfine UK v. Commissioners for H M Revenue and Customs* Court of Appeal (2011).
174. US-UK Tax Treaty, 24 July 2001, p. 1.
175. *Bayfine UK v. Commissioners for H M Revenue and Customs*, 17.

According to her judgment, the preamble includes the purpose of the treaty to prevent double taxation and double non-taxation. It must be added that, in the present case, the facts initially appear to be abusive/artificial in order to obtain double relief. It is therefore necessary to consider her judgment in the overall context of the facts of the case. That means that the judgment should be read in a way that the purpose of the treaty is to prevent double non-taxation when it is the result of tax avoidance. Another reading of the judgment would imply that tax treaties are aimed at preventing double non-taxation in general, including unintended double non-taxation, which is not the case even after implementing the changes to the preamble of the OECD Model proposed by BEPS Action 6.[176] Overall, it is interesting that LJ Arden already addressed the issues of 'double taxation' and 'double non-taxation' as well as 'preventing tax evasion' and 'preventing tax avoidance' given that the 2011 decision predates the launch of the BEPS initiative by two years and the heightened discourse on these very issues.

LJ Arden also noted that even if the wording of the preamble only refers to 'prevention of fiscal evasion', it would also include the purpose to prevent avoiding taxation. She added at a later point in the decision that 'the purposes [of art 23 and in the preamble to the treaty] are, therefore, to eliminate double taxation and to prevent fiscal evasion, which would include the avoidance of taxation'.[177] Understanding the term 'tax avoidance' as a subset of 'tax evasion' is rather a broad interpretation as the two terms refer to different phenomena. In the context of tax evasion, the taxpayer engages in illegal activities whereas tax avoidance describes the circumvention of a (treaty) provision whereby the taxpayer remains within the limits of the wording of the applicable law but contravenes its object and purpose. Admittedly, the idea of viewing the two terms as equally undesirable is increasingly reflected in the measures taken by the OECD within the BEPS Project and at the EU level and thus also in literature. The consolidated expression 'tax avoidance and tax evasion' became an established term in international taxation.

It could be argued that the reference to the preamble at this point is not helpful. Whether a provision is protected against its own circumvention does not depend on the general objective of the agreement but on the factual requirements for the application of the relevant provisions and their legal consequences.[178] It is true that the preamble cannot be used to counter clear substantive provisions. This is also supported by the analysis of international law. The preamble can, however, provide valuable context and background information, stating the parties' objectives and intentions – which become relevant when the substantive provisions are unclear and subject to interpretation. While the substantive provisions dictate the legal obligations for tax treaties specifically to restrict the taxing rights of one jurisdiction, the preamble can (only) serve as a guide to understanding the treaty's broader purpose and finding the true meaning of the substantive provisions. This is exactly LJ Arden's approach when she

176. BEPS Final Report Action 6.
177. *Bayfine UK v. Commissioners for H M Revenue and Customs*, 40.
178. Michael Lang, *DBA Malta: Wechsel von der Freistellungs- zur Anrechnungsmethode auf Grundlage einer EAS-Rechtsauskunft des BMF?*, SWI 10, 17 (2024).

read into the preamble the intention of the parties to prevent tax avoidance. The supporting role of the preamble is emphasized by the fact that she refers to the treaty article in question and the preamble. As it is only supportive, it can therefore be argued that the reference is obsolete and that the object and purpose of the provisions can also be found outside the preamble. This is true and could also be supported by the observation that fewer tax cases refer to the preamble of tax treaties than it is the case in international law with other international agreements.

5.2 Extrinsic Part of Tax Treaties: OECD Materials as 'Context'

5.2.1 Preamble of the 2017 OECD-MC

Action 6 of the OECD/G20 BEPS Project provided a minimum standard to prevent the abuse of tax treaties. The minimum standard consists of two elements. The first is the inclusion of a statement in the preamble of tax treaties expressing the common 'intention of the parties to a tax treaty ... to eliminate double taxation without creating opportunities for tax evasion and avoidance, in particular through treaty shopping arrangements'.[179] The pre-2017 Model Convention of the Organisation for Economic Co-operation and Development (OECD MC) contained the following guidance on the title and preamble of tax treaties: 'States wishing to do so may follow the widespread practice of including in the title a reference to either the avoidance of double taxation or to both the avoidance of double taxation and the prevention of fiscal evasion'; 'the preamble of the Convention shall be drafted in accordance with the constitutional procedure of both Contracting States'.

The second is implementing this intention by including a general anti-avoidance rule (GAAR) known as the principal purpose test (PPT) and/or a limitation on benefits (LoB) provision.[180] The 2017 OECD MC reflects these changes through modifications to its title and preamble. It states:

> State A and State B, Desiring to further develop their economic relationship and to enhance their cooperation in tax matters, Intending to conclude a Convention for the elimination of double taxation with respect to taxes on income and on capital without creating opportunities for non-taxation or reduced taxation through tax evasion or avoidance (including through treaty-shopping arrangements aimed at obtaining reliefs provided in this Convention for the indirect benefit of residents of third States) ... .

The primary significance of the preamble during interpretation could be seen in its relevance to Article 29 OECD MC which addresses the entitlement to benefits clause. The Commentary on Article 1(1) and Article 29 OECD MC states that this clause reflects

179. BEPS Final Report Action 6, p. 10.
180. de Broe, *supra* n. 43, 171.

'the intention of the Contracting States, incorporated in the preamble of the Convention'.[181]

There are two questions that should be addressed here regarding introducing the new preamble into the 2017 OECD MC in connection with its potential status as context in the meaning of Article 31(2) VCLT. The first question is what type of effect the new preamble has on interpreting a tax treaty in general. The second question is what is the role of the preamble to the 2017 OECD MC if it is not included in a concrete treaty? More specifically, the question asks whether something can be read into the preamble of a treaty that is not there, i.e., preventing tax avoidance when it is stipulated in the preamble of the model on which the treaty is based. This depends on whether the preamble of a model treaty can be regarded as context for interpreting a concrete treaty even if it was added to the model later than the treaty's conclusion.

Regarding the first question, according to *De Broe*, the mere inclusion of a new title and preamble in the model convention will not significantly impact the interpretation of its substantive provisions.[182] He argues that any effect that arises is because the objective of combatting treaty abuse is materialized in Article 29 OECD MC, and the tax treaties must incorporate a PPT rule and/or an LoB clause or both.[183] That means actual legal consequences can only be drawn from the concrete provisions of Article 29 OECD MC; thus, if these provisions are not included in a treaty, the preamble referring to the purpose of preventing tax avoidance would not change anything in interpreting and applying the treaty.

The inclusion of a PPT and/or LoB in tax treaties is a minimum standard of BEPS; a treaty without such provisions is therefore not very likely to be encountered. Nevertheless, the question is worth examining in order to properly understand the preamble's role when interpreting tax treaties. The present authors are not entirely convinced by De Broe's argument. First, both the context (which encompasses the preamble) and the object and purpose are authentic means of interpretation pursuant to Article 31(1) VCLT. The explicit expression in the preamble of the purpose of 'not creating opportunities for tax avoidance' might change the interpretation of a treaty's various provisions compared to their interpretation in the absence of this statement in the preamble. This follows from the method of contextual interpretation. The legal interpreter first examines the provision to be interpreted. Therefore, the syntactic context and then the context of meaning must be analysed via the other paragraphs of the article, the heading, the other articles as well as the preamble and the annexes. This means the approach is from the inside out in order to understand the context. This also makes sense in view of the fact that the preamble and the annexes provide a treaty's visual framework. Their significance radiates throughout the treaty (the annexes that refer explicitly to individual provisions might be an exception). The legal interpreter attempts to obtain insights from them that will help determine the actual meaning of

181. Robert J. Danon & Wolfgang Schön, *Foreword: Tax Treaty Interpretation after BEPS*, 74 Bull. Intl. Taxn. 159, 160, 4/5 (2020) https://doi.org/10.59403/3nvsvhd. Further references to the preamble are in Art. 1, para. 54 and Art. 29, paras 1, 173, 182.
182. de Broe, *supra* n. 43, 171.
183. *Ibid.*

the provision to be interpreted. It would not do justice to the means of contextual interpretation to use the preamble as a basis for determining the effect of certain provisions, i.e., to look selectively from the outside in.

This is demonstrated by the decision *Bayfine UK v. Commissioners for HMRC* in which LJ Arden specifically relied on the object of the treaty expressed in the preamble to deny the application of Article 23 of the treaty to the effect of granting double relief. Admittedly, she read into the treaty's preamble something that was not there insofar as she understood tax avoidance being covered by the term 'fiscal evasion'. This expansive understanding of the treaty's purpose leads us to the second question identified above.

Regarding the role of the preamble to the 2017 OECD MC if it is not included in a concrete treaty, it must be reiterated that the updated preamble is part of the minimum standards of BEPS Action 6 and, therefore, not many tax treaties will lack it. Nevertheless, the theoretical aspect of the question deserves attention as it may have broader implications for treaty interpretation. If the preamble text of the 2017 OECD MC is not incorporated into the actual treaty, it is not part of the context in the narrow sense of Article 31(2) VCLT. However, it can form part of the 'broader context', i.e., outside the list of Article 31(2) VCLT.

The OECD MC's updated preamble reflects the spirit of time, specifically that tax treaties are intended to eliminate double taxation without creating opportunities for tax evasion and avoidance, particularly through treaty shopping arrangements. Stated otherwise, an international consensus exists that using tax treaties for obtaining treaty benefits through artificial arrangements that comply with the letter of the law but defeat its object and purpose is undesirable and should be prevented. The importance of this update is emphasized by the fact that the preamble has become a minimum standard of the BEPS Project.

Does this mean that anything could become part of this wider context, for example, academic writings or representations in the media that are supposed to reflect the spirit of times when a treaty is applied? This is evidently not the case. There has to be an objective manifestation of the spirit of the time that reflects a broad consensus of nations. With regard to the BEPS Project, such a consensus definitely emerged in the course of its progression. The G20 leaders launched it in 2009 as a result of the financial crisis and the view that aggressive tax planning by multinational companies resulted in an annual revenue loss of USD 100-240 billion.[184] Various academic contributions on the subject, media coverage, and court rulings of the following years show that artificial arrangements were subjected to stricter scrutiny and were denied tax benefits when they defeated the purpose of the law. These discussions in various international fora and stakeholder groups (and even outside the tax field) led to the drafting of the updated wording of the preamble to the OECD MC. The precondition for considering the spirit of the times as a broader sense of context under Article 31(2) VCLT is that it is used to articulate an idea, a view, or a perception on which there is a broadly held consensus. Such a consensus emerged by the time of the initiation of the BEPS Project

184. OECD, *Background*, p. 9.

due to the necessity of countering tax treaty abuse which gained expression in the updated preamble to the OECD MC.

Referring to *Bayfine UK v. Commissioners for HMRC,* LJ Arden interpreted 'fiscal evasion' expansively to include tax avoidance in accordance with the spirit of the times. However, at the time of the judgment in 2011, there was not yet an objective manifestation of the changed perception of tax avoidance reflecting the spirit of times – as there is now in the form of the preamble to the 2017 OECD MC – her expansive interpretation may still be questioned from a methodological perspective.

5.2.2 OECD Commentaries

5.2.2.1 Practical Relevance of the Commentaries as a Result of International Consensus

In view of the abundance of contributions on the significance of the OECD Commentaries, it seems necessary to address the question of the extent to which they are applicable in the context of Article 31(2) VCLT. The OECD MC and the OECD Commentaries are adopted by the OECD Council in the form of a recommendation. That 'adoption' reflects the international consensus which is key to understanding the impact of the commentaries.

The following should, however, be mentioned in advance: In classifying the OECD Commentaries, it is important to first note that they are not legally binding (as recommendations of this type from international organizations never are). However, this does not make them legally irrelevant as they are often an important factor in practice. References to the commentaries are regularly made by several courts worldwide.[185] It can also be seen in the specific terminology commonly used to discuss certain tax issues in the media, government publications, court decisions, and academic writing.[186]

The second aspect to consider is the extent to which the OECD Commentaries can be used as an aid to interpretation. They can never counter existing provisions or define new ones. An example could be the changes made in the commentaries on Article 17(2) of the 1992 OECD MC regarding its scope. The commentaries introduced a new language and partly deviated from a mere interpretation. However, as in all other cases, the meaning of a particular provision is never to be found in a single source of interpretation and 'shall be interpreted in good faith in accordance with the ordinary

185. Niels Blokker, *Skating on Thin Ice? On the Law of International Organizations and the Legal Nature of the Commentaries on the OECD Model Tax Convention, in The legal status of the OECD commentaries* 13, §2 (Sjoerd Douma & F.A. Engelen eds, IBFD 2008); Katia Cejie, *The Commentaries on the OECD Model as a Mechanism for Interpretation with Reference to the Swedish Perspective,* 71 Bull. Intl. Taxn. 663, 666, n. 12 (2017) https://doi.org/10.59403/1xctetr; Maarten J. Ellis, *The Influence of the OECD Commentaries on Treaty Interpretation: Response to Prof. Dr Klaus Vogel,* Bull. Intl. Taxn. 617, 618 (2000).

186. Johannes M. Lammers, *The Spirit of International Tax Law: From Fiscal Virtue to Mission-Oriented Moon-Shot* 175 (2023).

meaning to be given to the terms of the treaty in their context and in the light of its object and purpose'.[187]

5.2.2.2 *In General: Not Context in the Narrow Sense of Article 31(2) VCLT*

Scholars have made attempts to classify the OECD Commentaries into the various paragraphs of Articles 31 and 32 VCLT.[188] As Bossuyt points out, 'It appears that authors already accept from the outset that "the" Commentaries should apply so that designating the applicable paragraph of articles 31 and 32 of the VCLT would only be a formality.'[189] These attempts have resulted in different viewpoints and perspectives, demonstrating that it is difficult or potentially impossible to arrive at a common view on how using the OECD Commentaries can be justified on the basis of the VCLT.[190] Some scholars therefore adopt a more relaxed stance suggesting that the efforts to forcefully subsume the commentaries within the various paragraphs of the general rule of interpretation or within the supplementary means of interpretation are misguided.[191] The question is therefore not whether the current version of the OECD Commentary at the time of the tax treaty ratification can or should be taken into account under this or that VCLT provision but whether the commentary must be taken into account in the course of interpretation.[192]

Since this contribution is about Article 31(2) VCLT, the question is first whether the current version of the OECD Commentary must be taken into account according to Article 31(2) VLCT, i.e., to determine what weight they have in the course of interpretation. The second question, which will be addressed in the following chapter, is whether subsequent commentaries need to be taken into account.

Whether the OECD Commentary can fall under Article 31(2) VCLT depends on whether it is considered to be part of the context of a particular tax treaty. According to Arnold, it is unlikely that the commentary fulfils this criterion[193] as it does not form an extrinsic part of the specific tax treaty for the following reasons:

> To become an extrinsic part of the treaty, there must first be a general consensus that the source is accepted by all parties. This could be achieved by an explicit statement by the parties. If this is not available, the question is whether there can be some sort of implicit general consensus. If both parties are OECD members, it could be assumed that both agree to use the commentary as an aid to interpretation. However, just because the parties agree on something in a large circle does not mean that they agree on something in a small, bilateral circle. The OECD itself states 'Although the Commentaries are not designed to be annexed in any manner

187. Article 31(1) VCLT.
188. Cejie, *supra* n. 185, 664.
189. Bossuyt, *supra* n. 39, 680.
190. Cejie, *supra* n. 185, 664.
191. *See* for an overview of these different standpoints and also the evolution of these standpoints at Bossuyt, *supra* n. 39, 680. Further details, *see* Déry and Ward eds, *Vol. 78a. Interpretation of Double Taxation Conventions: Canada*, §3.
192. Helmut Loukota, *Die rechtliche Relevanz von BEPS im Lichte der Wiener Vertragsrechtskonvention*, SWI 436, 440, n. 9 (2016); Blokker, *supra* n. 185, §3.
193. Arnold, *The Interpretation of Tax Treaties: Myth and Reality*, *supra* n. 8, 8-9.

> to the conventions signed by member countries, which unlike the Model are legally binding international instruments, they can nevertheless be of great assistance in the application and interpretation of the conventions and, in particular, in the settlement of any disputes.'[194] Tax treaties take into account the economic and political relationship between the contracting states. The intention and willingness to cooperate are therefore different from the circumstances in which the wording of the commentary was agreed. The allocation of taxing rights is still a political issue driven primarily by the self-interest of both contracting states.[195] In addition, observations or reservations by the executives of the contracting state to the relevant commentary would diminish its importance. If one or both of them were not members of the OECD and did not express a position, it would also be clear that there is no general consensus. An implicit general consensus would not be applicable for these reasons which is also in accordance with ICJ jurisprudence that has required an explicit consensus in order for a source to be considered context within the meaning of Article 31(2) VCLT.
>
> Second, the parties must be identical. The commentaries are drafted and agreed upon by government representatives of OECD members or third-party countries. In contrast, tax treaties are negotiated and concluded by possibly the same people between two contracting states. Can the fact that the commentaries were 'agreed upon' by a much broader scope of countries mean that it is not between the same parties? Probably not, if the contracting states are also OECD members. This means that the condition of 'the same parties' could be met.
>
> Third, there needs to be an explicit reference from the tax treaty to the commentary. This means that it needs to be 'intimately related to the text'.[196] *Bossuyt* concludes, 'A mere relationship between the substance of the agreement and the text of the treaty is therefore not necessarily sufficient (although presumably a strong factor in practice), but it must depend on the intentions of the parties whether a particular agreement may be considered to "relate to the treaty".'[197]

The commentaries are inherently related to the OECD MC and not to a specific treaty's text.[198] It could be different if the parties explicitly share their intention that they are intimately related to the text. In most cases, this is not the case,[199] as is the situation with the general consensus.

The temporal proximity is the fourth element and results from the requirement 'in connection with the conclusion of the treaty' (Article 31(2) VCLT). The ordinary meaning of 'in connection' allows agreements and instruments concluded before and at the time of the treaty's conclusion to be taken into account. This element could, in principle, be fulfilled (if the commentary is published before and at the time of the treaty's conclusion), but this would not be decisive for the question of whether the current commentary must be taken into account according to Article 31(2) VLCT.

This means that the commentary is generally not part of the context (under Article 31(2) VCLT) as not all of the above criteria – especially the general consensus – are necessarily met. However, it can be considered part of the context if: (a) the treaty

194. OECD, *Model Tax Convention on Income and on Capital* (2017), I-11, para. 29.
195. Lammers, *supra* n. 186, 175.
196. International Law Commission, *supra* n. 31, 220, para. 9.
197. Bossuyt, *supra* n. 39, 720.
198. *Ibid.*
199. Ekkehart Reimer, *Tax Treaty Interpretation in Germany, in Tax Treaty Interpretation* 119, 135 (Michael Lang ed., Wolters Kluwer 2001).

that has been concluded and ratified by a parliament does not deviate from the OECD Model; *and* (b) it has been made clear to a parliament that the OECD views have been followed.[200] Further, it can be considered part of 'legal context' which means, according to Ward, the legal background or the external background but not the textual context in the meaning of Article 31(2) VCLT.[201]

With respect to the relevance of the BEPS materials under Article 31(2) VCLT, the same conclusions could be drawn for the commentary. The BEPS Reports, developed in the context of the OECD/G20 BEPS Project, focus on providing recommendations, new minimum standards, common approaches, and guidance on best practices to attempt to effectively address tax avoidance, improve the coherence of international tax rules, ensure a more transparent tax environment, and address the tax challenges arising from the digitalization of the economy. It can be doubted whether there is a difference (in terms of substance) between the BEPS Reports dealing with tax treaty-related measures and the commentaries that were included in the 2017 update of the OECD Commentaries on the new measures.

Hattingh explores the relevance of BEPS materials for tax treaty interpretation and recognizes that the impact of BEPS on the framework of tax treaty interpretation differs depending on whether one is a tax advisor or a national court.[202] The consideration of BEPS materials has expanded the factors that tax advisors consider when assessing the relevance of such materials, extending beyond purely legal considerations. For national courts, treaty interpretation based on BEPS materials may lead to divergent outcomes in cases involving BEPS issues. Changes to the OECD Commentaries have been a factor in these divergent outcomes. In cases when significant changes or updates to the commentaries do not align with amendments to the text of the OECD MC and bilateral tax treaties, uniform tax treaty interpretation may be hindered.[203] Danon and Schön therefore concluded that the landscape for tax treaty interpretation in the post-BEPS era has become more diverse and multifaceted.[204]

It should first be noted that the BEPS materials (as well as the commentary) do not form part of the extrinsic part of the treaty because there is generally no consensus of the parties to consider these as agreements or instruments, and there is no substantive relation to the specific treaty. However, that does not mean that the commentary or the BEPS material should be ignored at all. They could be of relevance under the other provisions of Article 31 or 32 VCLT, or it could be argued that the boundaries between the provisions are so fluid that it is more a matter of principle. What can be stated with regard to the BEPS materials is that they will make the world of tax treaty interpretation more diverse. Admittedly, it has never been black and

200. Peter J. Wattel & Otto Marres, *The Legal Status of the OECD Commentary and Static or Ambulatory Interpretation of Tax Treaties*, 43 European taxation 222, 227, 7/8 (2003).
201. David A. Ward, *Is There an Obligation in International Law of OECD Member Countries to Follow the Commentaries on the Model?, in The legal Status of the OECD Commentaries*, Chapter 12 (Sjoerd Douma & Frank A. Engelen eds, IBFD Amsterdam 2008).
202. Johann Hattingh, *The Relevance of BEPS Materials for Tax Treaty Interpretation*, 74 Bull. Intl. Taxn. 179, 4/5 (2020) https://doi.org/10.59403/1fq7h0g.
203. Danon & Schön, *supra* n. 181, 161.
204. *Ibid.*

white. All that has been added are further potential sources of interpretation that can concretize a specific situation requiring interpretation.

The German Federal Fiscal Court highlighted in a recent decision that the OECD Commentaries can be considered in the course of interpreting a tax treaty. However, the relevance is (only) comparable to preparatory materials in the legislative process.[205] That means the commentaries would have no relevance under Article 31(2) VCLT (or any other means of the general rule of interpretation according to Article 31 VCLT) but under Article 32 VCLT as supplementary means of interpretation. The court also made it clear that the more the treaty deviates in its wording from the OECD Model, the less meaningful the explanations in the commentary are.[206]

5.2.2.3 *Conditions That the Commentary Becomes Context in the Narrow Sense of Article 31(2) VCLT*

The Dutch Supreme Court has considered the OECD Commentary to be of significant importance when the contracting states have clearly expressed their intention to adhere to the OECD Model and the provision to be interpreted is identical or virtually identical to the corresponding provision in it.[207] The court views the OECD Commentary as an agreement reached between the contracting states provided that two cumulative conditions are fulfilled: (1) the treaty provision being interpreted closely aligns with the OECD Model; and (2) the contracting states intended to adhere to the OECD Model as closely as possible. This intention can be inferred from circumstances such as both parties referring to their adherence to the OECD Model in explanatory notes to their respective parliaments. In the case at hand,[208] the Dutch Court of Appeals had not examined whether an Irish executive had notified the Irish Parliament of its intention to follow the 1963 OECD Model as it only rules on points of law. However, the court seems satisfied with the fulfilment of the second condition, particularly since many other provisions in the treaty closely accord with the OECD MC. Considering that both the model and commentary are drafted and adopted by the same bodies – the OECD Committee on Fiscal Affairs and the OECD Council – and published as a single document, it can be assumed that the commentary reflects the intentions of the model.[209]

An example is when the commentary could even become an 'integral' part of the treaty (as it is part of the text) is the 2023 tax treaty between Belgium and the Netherlands. The treaty states in its Protocol I, which is an integral part of the convention, that:

> it is understood that the provisions of this Convention which are identical or in substance similar to the provisions of the OECD Model Tax Convention on Income and on Capital shall be interpreted in accordance with the OECD Commentary

205. BFH 5.12.2023, I R 42/20, para. 40.
206. *Ibid.*
207. Wattel & Marres, *supra* n. 200, 227.
208. Hoge Raad, 2.9.1992, BNB 1992/379.
209. Wattel & Marres, *supra* n. 200, 227.

> thereon at the moment of the application of this Convention, insofar as the Contracting States have not made an observation on the relevant OECD Commentary to the effect that the Contracting States do not agree with the principles concerned and insofar as the Contracting States have not agreed on a different interpretation on the basis of the arrangement for mutual agreement under Article 24.[210]

5.2.3 *OECD Subsequent Commentaries as Context Outside the List of Article 31(2) VCLT*

The question raised at the beginning of this contribution was how the materials identified under Article 31(2) VCLT should be used. The VCLT is silent in this respect. One of the most important questions relating to interpreting a legal rule arises as part of the discussion on the static or dynamic approach to doing so.

The static approach seeks to determine the meaning of the treaty provision and to take into account the circumstances prevailing at the time the treaty was concluded – the principle of contemporaneity. The dynamic approach (evolutionary interpretation), on the other hand, seeks to determine the meaning of a treaty at the time of its interpretation.[211]

The dynamic approach is best demonstrated by a decision of the Swiss Supreme Court from 2015 that decided that the beneficial owner requirement was implicit in an old tax treaty concluded in 1972, i.e., well before the beneficial ownership requirement was introduced to the OECD MC, that did not expressly contain such a requirement for tax rate reduction at source.[212] The Swiss Supreme Court opined that, over time, the beneficial owner requirement has hardened into an unwritten rule that must be implied in all bilateral tax treaties.[213] It noted that:

> The common understanding in the two countries concerned here is also in line with what can be described as the (lowest) common denominator in the international arena for the assessment criterion of effective utilization rights: The relevant problems here have been discussed since the middle of the last century at the latest. From the outset, the various states realized that it was not in keeping with the purpose of double taxation agreements to also grant their benefits to persons or companies that, for example, had a merely formal relationship with the state of residence and were therefore only a pretext or intermediary for claiming these benefits. In the early years, fiduciary relationships or similar constructs that were common at the time (according to Anglo-Saxon terminology: nominees, agents, trustees) were discussed as examples of such an advance, and not the complex instruments of the international financial markets that only emerged later. When the discussions were then extended to such instruments and were now conducted from the point of view of the effective authorization to use them, it remained clear that this was not about the introduction of a different or stricter assessment

210. Article 1(1) of the Protocol I (2023) of the Double Taxation Treaty between Belgium and the Netherlands.
211. Dörr, *supra* n. 39, 22.
212. Swiss Tribunal federale, 2C_364/2012 and 2C_377/2012.
213. Hattingh, *supra* n. 202, 3.2.

> criterion. Rather, it was a matter of clarifying and, if necessary, refining the already implicit requirement that a merely formal right of use could not be categorized as sufficient, even in international matters.[214]

Article 31 VCLT does not explicitly deal with the question of static or dynamic interpretation. The question is whether the commentaries 'merely' reflect the spirit of the times which changes the interpretation so that the reality at the time of the treaty's interpretation is taken into account. Then, it is not a question of whether the commentaries (for example) per se must be taken into account but a general question of whether the static or the dynamic approach under Article 31(2) VCLT could be followed.

The extent to which later versions of the commentaries should be used for interpretation is hotly debated in the literature. Versions of them that post-date the conclusion of the treaty are not considered part of its context under Article 31(2) VCLT as, in addition to the explicit consensus, the temporal proximity is lacking – as the subsequent commentaries are not published before and at the time of the treaty's conclusion.[215] However, as the list of Article 31(2) VCLT is non-exhaustive, can the subsequent commentaries become part of the context in the broader sense?

As already noted above, tax treaties aim to allocate taxing rights between the contracting states by imposing mutual restrictions on their exercise of taxing rights in order to relieve international double taxation. To achieve this goal, they must strive for a uniform application of treaty provisions, ensuring a common interpretation by both parties.[216] This uniformity promotes consistency and reduces potential conflicts or discrepancies in interpreting and applying tax treaties. Using subsequent commentaries would undermine this objective in the context of legal certainty and the rule of law. The parties would then also have to agree on which version is to be used. Would it be the most up-to-date version at the time of application of the contract? Or could a version in between that is most favourable to at least one party (the party entitled to the tax treaty or the tax administration of one contracting state) also become relevant? While these considerations are highly important, it is necessary to acknowledge that a purely static interpretation that takes into account only the commentaries existing at the time of the treaty's conclusion may freeze the treaty and may make it incapable of being applied to contemporary facts and giving answers to current questions of the prevailing times.

The commentaries' periodical updates are an objective expression of the spirit of the times at which international consensus has been achieved. This can be seen, first, through the fact that the OECD MC has led to the development of an international tax language.[217] Lammers concludes that the OECD's work 'means that, more and more, a common legal language and shared taxonomy in international profit taxation emerge,

214. Swiss Tribunal federale, 2C_364/2012 and 2C_377/2012, 4.4.3.
215. Wattel & Marres, *supra* n. 200, 227.
216. Vogel & Prokisch, *supra* n. 22, 62.
217. Reimer, *Tax Treaty Interpretation in Germany, in Tax Treaty Interpretation, supra* n. 199, 135.

which are widely implemented in national legislation. Such dissemination of meta-language also ensures a more consistent legal interpretation across borders'.[218] This meta-language (the common denominator) is anchored accordingly in the OECD's work. The Commentaries could therefore be seen as dictionaries that could help to identify the syntactical context or, as the ICJ concluded, to find the 'most natural understanding' of words and terms. Ekkehart, however, comes to the conclusion that Article 31 (1) VCLT seems to focus on some sort of every meaning of the words used in a treaty.[219] However, the OECD work influences this 'every meaning of the word' as it developed into a meta-language and therefore became inherent to every meaning. The second aspect in which this objectification becomes clear is the instruments and projects that are initiated, discussed, and adopted by the OECD. Here, too, it is clear that these topics are characterized by the current spirit of the times because they are prioritized accordingly on international level.

This does not mean that everything in the Commentaries should be taken literally, however, the explanations show a certain development of the general understanding. It can rightly be argued that this meta-language is defined only from one perspective of the actors in international tax law, specifically representatives of the executive branch. Courts should therefore be wary of relying too heavily on this perspective as it always involves a degree of self-calculation. The general understanding that has the potential to express the spirit of the times should also be reflected in academic literature, legislation, or jurisprudence.

Dörr identified that the ICJ follows a static approach as a basic rule and a dynamic approach for interpreting generic terms; terms whose content is expected to change through time.[220] He concluded that the ICJ cases show that dynamic means of interpretation can also be used for applying the static approach, i.e., to establish the meaning of treaty provisions at the time of their conclusion.[221] Disregarding the changes in social, economic, political and moral circumstances would not be expedient, especially in view of the fact that international tax treaties are concluded over a very long period of time. This view was also recently expressed by Advocate General Capete: 'In parallel with the changes in the real world, it is necessary to adopt or (re)interpret the laws that already exist in order to govern the new relationships that emerge with such change.'[222]

Nevertheless, there are grave risks in allowing interpretation based on the spirit of the times, thus, it cannot be a purely subjective assessment of what the spirit of the times dictates but has to have an objective manifestation. A precondition is that a broad consensus of nations exists on it. This can be seen not only in the individual definitions of terms in the OECD Commentaries but also in the directives and laws enacted at an EU or domestic level as a result of the OECD recommendations. For an objective view, it is therefore necessary to look at different perspectives to find indications of a change

218. Lammers, *supra* n. 186, 174.
219. Reimer, *Tax Treaty Interpretation in Germany, in Tax Treaty Interpretation, supra* n. 199, 135.
220. Dörr, *supra* n. 39, 27.
221. *See* ICJ Kasikili/Sedudu Island (*Botswana v. Namibia*) [1999].
222. Opinion of AG Cápeta in Case C-60/23, *Skatteverket v. Digital Solutions GmbH*, 25 April 2024, para. 2.

in the spirit of the times. The authors posit that this is considered to be context in the wider meaning of Article 31(2) VCLT, the interpretation must also be in accordance with the other means of interpretation according to Article 31(1) VCLT, especially the object and purpose of the treaty. Taking the spirit of the times into account when interpreting words and terms does not mean allowing it to identify the will of the legislator. It means taking into account the reality that prevails at the time of interpretation in order to find the true meaning and the most natural interpretation. It also means that the meaning of the spirit of the times must always respect the limits of the treaty's object and purpose. This follows also from the fact that this is only part of the broader context, i.e., context not listed in Article 31(2) VCLT. Therefore, its weight in the interpretation process is lower than context as defined in Article 31(2) VCLT and object and purpose as these are all authentic means of interpretation according to the main rule of Article 31(1) VCLT. Overall, the spirit of the times cannot supersede the object and purpose of the treaty.

6 CONCLUSIONS

The VCLT considers 'context' as one of the means of interpretation of international treaties. In common parlance, context has a narrow meaning and essentially refers to the syntactic context. If reading Article 31(2) VCLT, it becomes clear that the VCLT has a broader understanding of the term and understands context to mean everything related to the text of the treaty.

The materials listed in Article 31(2) VCLT are to be used in the contextual interpretation, specifically the text, the preamble, and the annexes as well as the agreements and instruments related to the treaty. The text, preamble, and annexes form an integral part of the treaty while the text provides the syntactic context of the specific provision. The ICJ's jurisprudence suggests that, when interpreting a term, the most natural interpretation should be followed that adheres to the analysis of the immediate context. The syntactic context also includes a grammatical interpretation. It follows the interpretation of the ordinary meaning in context which means that the paragraphs of the specific article including the title and headings and the overall context of the treaty including the preamble and annexes must be considered. This indicates that the approach to interpretation follows an inside-out logic.

After the integral part, the extrinsic part of the treaty must be considered as context. Here, it was shown that four conditions are required to become extrinsic context in the meaning of Article 31(2) VCLT. These are the general consensus (either drawn up by all of the parties or, if it is done by one or more parties, accepted by the other parties), the identical parties, the relationship to the content of the treaty, and the temporal proximity, i.e., after the treaty's conclusion.

However, as it was argued, the list in Article 31(2) VCLT cannot be exhaustive as an interpretative rule can never be precise enough to identify and categorize specific elements. It helps to not only identify the most relevant sources of context but also leaves room for a less relevant one. The integral and extrinsic parts (the listed items) have more weight than the non-listed elements of context in the interpretation process.

However, those other elements or sources must be considered in some cases to correctly establish the parties' intent as expressed in the text, for example, other agreements where the parties are not identical. The wording of other sources, such as expert opinions, may also play a role in determining the 'most natural understanding' of terms.

It was shown that these observations can also be used for tax treaty purposes. Additionally, for these purposes, the preamble is only one aspect of the interpretation, and it cannot be used to counter clear substantive provisions. Measured against the wealth of decisions in which the ICJ, for example, refers to the preamble, the courts are comparatively reticent in tax law.

The preamble is prima facie part of the context and needs to be considered for the interpretation of all provisions. The statements in the preamble to the latest version of the OECD MC reflect the spirit of the times prevailing at the time of applying the treaty and are an objective expression of the latter on which international consensus has been achieved. Therefore, they can be a factor when interpreting a treaty in which the preamble to the 2017 OECD MC was not included. That means that the preamble can be taken into account as part of the context in the broader sense that exceeds the parameters of the list of Article 31(2) VCLT.

The OECD Commentary at the time of the treaty's conclusion is not necessarily part of the context (under Article 31(2) VCLT) as not all of the above criteria to become extrinsic context are met. However, it can be considered part of the context if: (a) the treaty that has been concluded and ratified by the parliament does not deviate from the OECD model; *and* (b) it has been made clear to the parliament that the OECD views have been followed.[223] The OECD Commentary can even be an integral part of the treaty if the treaty text (including its protocols) provides that it is to be interpreted in accordance with the commentary.

Moreover, the fact that the commentary does not generally fall under Article 31(2) VCLT does not mean that the commentary should not be taken into account at all. It could have relevance under the other provisions of Articles 31 and 32 VCLT. It could also be argued that the boundaries between the provisions are so fluid that an attempt to categorize it within the provisions of the VCLT is a theoretical exercise that is not very helpful for facilitating the interpretation of tax treaties.

Versions of the Commentaries that post-date the treaty's conclusion should not be considered part of the treaty context under Article 31(2) VCLT because, in addition to the absence of explicit consensus, there is a lack of temporal proximity. However, the list in Article 31(2) VCLT is not exhaustive so a broader understanding of the context would also be applicable under Article 31(1) VCLT. The Commentaries encompass a meta-language (the common denominator) that reflect the spirit of times in the international tax field. They could therefore be seen as dictionaries to identify, as the ICJ concluded, the 'most natural understanding' of words and terms. It was argued that the spirit of times can be considered in the course of interpretation by applying the means of 'context'. Undoubtedly, there are significant risks in doing so, thus it cannot

223. Wattel & Marres, *supra* n. 200, 227.

be a purely subjective assessment of what the spirit of the times dictates. Such an interpretation has to have strict limits and must be based on objective factors. A precondition is that a broad consensus of nations exists on the views and perceptions that are considered the expressions of the spirit of the times that must always respect the limits of the treaty's object and purpose. The spirit of the times cannot supersede it.

CHAPTER 5

Object and Purpose and Tax Treaty Interpretation

Alexander Rust & Juliane Beverungen

1 Introduction
2 Significance for International Law Interpretation
  2.1 Historical Background
  2.2 Concept
    2.2.1 Terminology
    2.2.2 Relationship with the Other Means of Interpretation
  2.3 Methodology
3 Significance for Tax Treaty Interpretation
  3.1 Object and Purpose of Tax Treaties
  3.2 Relevance for the PPT
  3.3 Differences Between the OECD and UN Model Conventions
4 Final Remarks

1 INTRODUCTION

According to linguistics, all language is indeterminate. No word has a single, true, absolute, and objective meaning. Any word used in speech or in writing requires interpretation to determine its content and intent. The major sources for the indeterminacy of words are ambiguity and vagueness. Both phenomena cannot be resolved based on the ordinary meaning of the words because it is (often) unclear. It can, however, be determined by referencing the context of the words used which in turn includes the object and purpose for which the words are used.[1] This principle applies not only to everyday language but also to the legal language. As a result, these elements have long been among the most important elements of interpretation.

The Vienna Convention on the Law of Treaties (VCLT) is a codification of existing international law principles and contains a set of rules in Articles 31 to 33 VCLT for interpreting treaties. It hands interpretation guidelines to contracting states, authorities, and courts that are in charge of this task. What is known as the general rule of Article 31(1) VCLT contains separate elements and combines them into one rule: the interpretation in good faith, the recourse to the ordinary meaning and the consideration of the context, and the object and purpose. These were perceived by the drafters of the VCLT as the most important aspects for the often quite versatile goals of treaty interpretation. The elements reflect, on the one hand, the existing principles of logic and good sense after which legal experts had based their treaty interpretation prior to the introduction of the VCLT and, on the other hand, reflect the interpretation methods often used in domestic law.

While object and purpose have sometimes been a legally decisive element in treaty-related decision-making in recent years, it is politically controversial because it is still very much unclear what exactly the object and purpose of a treaty is supposed to be, if and how it can be objectively determined, and how much influence it can and should hold in the interpretative process.[2] This chapter is therefore attempting to elucidate the concept of object and purpose. First, its international law implications are illuminated with the historical background behind its introduction into the VCLT, the concept itself, and the methodology. The insights gained are then transferred to tax treaty interpretation. There, the chapter discusses the object and purpose of tax treaties, its relevance for the principal purpose test (PPT) and the differences between the object and purpose of the Organisation for Economic Co-operation and Development (OECD) and United Nations (UN) Model Conventions.

2 SIGNIFICANCE FOR INTERNATIONAL LAW INTERPRETATION

2.1 Historical Background

While the introduction of the object and purpose element of Article 31(1) VCLT can be traced back to the component's crucial function in the French version of the International Court of Justice (ICJ) Advisory Opinion on Reservations to the Genocide Convention,[3] that is not the first time that the concept is used for treaty interpretation. It is apparent that the concept slowly emerged as a guiding principle of interpretation

1. Friedrich Müller & Ralph Christensen, *Juristische Methodik: 2: Europarecht* 383 (Duncker & Humblot 2d ed. 2007).
2. Isabelle Buffard & Karl Zemanek, *The 'Object and Purpose' of a Treaty: An Enigma?*, 3 Austrian Review of International & European Law 1 (Kluwer 1998) https://doi.org/10.1163/157365198x00177.
3. *Reservations to the Convention on the Prevention and Punishment of the Crime of Genocide*, ICJ Reports 1951, 15–30.

culminating in its introduction into the VCLT.[4] The idea seems to be mentioned for the first time in a Permanent Court of International Justice (PCIJ) opinion in 1926 in the form of *l'objet et la portée* (translated as *the aim and the scope)*[5] of a treaty. In later opinions, the terms *le but et l'objet* (translated as *the aim and the scope*), *l'objet et le but* (translated as *the subject and aim*) or *le sens et l'esprit des traités* (translated as *meaning and spirit of the treaties*) can be found. The difficulty of adhering to a coherent wording, both in French and in English, must be emphasized.[6] Thus, although the concept was used, it was never the deciding factor until the ICJ Advisory Opinion.

The General Assembly of the UN requested this opinion in 1950 in order to settle a dispute that had arisen between the UN and the Soviet Union. The UN required, in continuation of a practice introduced by the League of Nations, unanimous consent of all parties to a multilateral treaty for a reservation to become effective which was contested by the Soviet Union. In its opinion, the court therefore ruled on the admissibility of reservations and referenced *l'objet et le but* of the treaty. It then attempted to ascertain the aforementioned object and purpose[7] of the Genocide Convention and stated:

> The origins and character of that Convention, the objects pursued by the General Assembly and the contracting parties, the relations which exists between the provisions of the Convention, inter se, and between those provisions and these objects, furnish elements of interpretation of the will of the General Assembly and the parties.[8]

It proceeds to state that the object and purpose of the Genocide Convention seems to be the condemnation and punishment of genocide as a crime under international law.[9] Although these observations seem to be the result of an interpretation of the text, they appear as intuitive assumptions in the Advisory Opinion which, even though they seem self-evident, are too ambiguous to be beneficial for understanding the rationale of the process by which they were obtained. This view is supported by one of two dissenting opinions to the Advisory Opinion. It stated: '[...] [W]e have difficulty in seeing how the new rule can work. When a new rule is proposed for the solution of disputes, it should be easy to apply and calculated to produce final and consistent results.'[10]

While the four judges expressed their doubts concerning the objectivity of the object and purpose as an interpretation method, they did not seem to dismiss the idea altogether, and another opinion that was given also generally supported this idea. It

4. Buffard & Zemanek, *supra* n. 2, at 315.
5. *Competence of the International Labour Organization to Regulate, Incidentally, The Personal Work of the Employer*, PCIJ Series B No. 13 1926, 18.
6. *Rights of nationals of the United States of America in Morocco* case, 176, 176-213; *Certain Norwegian Loans* case *(France v. Norway)*, 9, 9-28; *Application of the Convention of 1902 Governing the Guardianship of Infants* case *(Netherlands v. Sweden)*, 55, 55-73.
7. Many scholars doubt that *l'objet et le but* has been translated correctly into object and purpose. This will be discussed in more detail below.
8. *Reservations to the Convention on the Prevention and Punishment of the Crime of Genocide*, ICJ Reports 1951, 12.
9. *Ibid.*
10. *Ibid.*, 24.

can even be considered a clear defence of the interpreters' need to have recourse to the object and purpose of a treaty:

> I do not see how it is possible to say that an article of a convention is clear until the subject and aim of the convention have been ascertained, for the article only assumes its true import in this convention and in relations thereto. Only when it is known what the Contracting Parties intended to do and the aim they had in view is it possible to say either that the natural meaning of terms used in a particular article corresponds with the real intention of the Parties, or that the natural meaning of the terms used falls short of or goes further than such intention.[11]

It can be concluded that, even though the ICJ judges generally agreed on using the object and purpose to interpret a treaty, their view on its objectivity varied. The wording itself also differed throughout the opinion as the order was sometimes reversed (*le but et l'objet*), and only one of the elements was used (only *l'objet* or only *le but*) at other times.[12] There are also times that the expression was used in its plural form while it was used other times only in the singular form.

This shows:

> that the idea that the intentions of the parties in drawing up their agreement should play a pivotal role in interpreting the text and in limiting the freedom of the parties in its implementation, although generally accepted, had not yet ripened into a settled concept, and no firm notion for expressing it existed at the time.[13]

Nonetheless, when preparing the draft articles for the VCLT, Sir Humphrey Waldock included a reference to the objects and purposes in the draft of Article 70(2), subparagraph (a) that dealt with cases in which the natural and ordinary meaning of the terms led to an absurd or unreasonable interpretation or the meaning of the terms was not clear.[14] However, the objects and purposes were not expressly mentioned as a primary element of treaty interpretation in Article 70(1) of the draft that only listed the natural and ordinary meaning of the terms and its context. Their placement in Article 70(2) of the draft was criticized by other members of the International Law Commission (ILC) as they preferred to include it as an element in the general rule of treaty interpretation as stipulated in Article 70(1) of the draft. It was stressed that the objects and purposes were an integral part of the treaty and should be taken into account before turning to external circumstances in the interpretation process.[15] Sir Waldock, in return, explained that the reference to the context of a treaty also included its objects and purposes. However, as a reference to it only in Article 70(2)(a) could convey the impression that the element could only be considered in the cases for which the ordinary meaning of the words would be ambiguous and in no other case, he therefore included a reference to the objects and purposes into Article 70(1) of the draft. It is

11. *Interpretation of the Convention of 1919 Concerning Employment of Women During the Night*, PCIJ Series A/B No. 50 1932, 22.
12. Buffard & Zemanek, *supra* n. 2, at 314 et seq.
13. *Ibid.*, at 315.
14. Frank Engelen, *Interpretation of Tax Treaties under International Law*, Chapter 6.6.2.1 (IBFD October 2004).
15. International Law Commission, *Yearbook of the International Law Commission*, 1, 281 (1964).

interesting to note that, while the reference was made in the plural form in this draft, when it became Article 30(1) VCLT the object and purpose was only referenced in the singular. After the VCLT's ratification, the expression of object and purpose is used rather consistently by the courts, especially after the *Nicaragua* case.[16]

2.2 Concept

2.2.1 Terminology

While it has been shown that the expression and the associated concept of object and purpose are extensively used by the PCIJ, the ICJ, and even the World Trade Organization (WTO) Appellate Body,[17] the concept itself is still unclear and disputed. At first, the terminology of object and purpose incites the question of whether there is a distinction to be made between them.

English dictionaries define 'object' not only as a 'goal, purpose, or aim; the end to which effort is directed; the thing sought, aimed at, or striven for' but also as 'a material thing that can be seen and touched'[18] while 'purpose' is defined as 'that which a person sets out to do or attain; an object in view; a determined intention or aim'.[19] These definitions show multiple things. First of all, one word cannot be explained without the other which makes it difficult to distinguish between the two terms and makes it seem as though both words are inextricable linked.[20] Second, it is difficult to understand why two words are used if only one word would suffice. The same problem occurs in the Spanish and Chinese versions of the VCLT.

Given the apparent French source for the expression and its equal authenticity in the VCLT, the French version could provide insights on how to consider the terminology in English and more specifically why Sir Waldock would use the words object and purpose if both are so similar.[21] French public law has developed a distinction between *l'objet* and *le but* for legal acts or legal instruments. The former refers to creating a particular set of rights and obligations through a legal act while the latter refers to the reason for establishing *l'objet*.[22] Therefore, the object indicates the substantial content of a norm or a provision, i.e., the instrument for achieving the treaty's purpose. The purpose, in turn, is the result that the parties want to achieve.[23] However, the term

16. *Military and Paramilitary Activities In And Against Nicaragua* case *(Nicaragua v. United States of America)*, 14, 14 et seqq.; Buffard & Zemanek, *supra* n. 2, at 315.
17. Isabelle Van Damme, *Treaty Interpretation by the WTO Appellate Body*, 21 European Journal of International Law 605 et seqq. (8 January 2010) https://doi.org/10.1093/ejil/chq049.
18. Oxford English Dictionary, *Object*, https://www.oed.com/dictionary/object_n (last visited 21 June 2024).
19. Oxford English Dictionary, *Purpose*, https://www.oed.com/dictionary/purpose_n (last visited 21 June 2024).
20. Richard Gardiner, *Part II Interpretation Applying the Vienna Convention on the Law of Treaties, A The General Rule, 5 The General Rule: (1) The Treaty, Its Terms, and Their Ordinary Meaning, in Treaty Interpretation* 38 (2d ed. 2015).
21. *Ibid.*
22. *Ibid.*
23. Buffard & Zemanek, *supra* n. 2, at 316.

l'objet in French can also mean *l'objective, l'intention,* or *le but.*[24] As a result, the French version does not give a clear indication either if there is a distinction between object and purpose or whether both terms are used synonymously. That leaves the Russian version of the VCLT which seems to be the only language where there is a clear difference between both terms with object only referring to what the object (= content) of the treaty is while purpose refers to what the treaty wants to achieve. As all versions are authentic and only one yields a clear result, that would mean that there must be a distinction made between object and purpose. This would also be supported by the wording of the VCLT which uses two words. However, looking at case law, it seems that the distinction is difficult to make[25] and therefore only a theoretical discussion.[26]

Another question that is still unclear is whether there can only be one single object and purpose for the treaty as a whole or if there can be multiple ones. Right from the beginning, it should be noted that the VCLT refers to object and purpose in their singular form. This signals the intention of the drafters that there can only be one object and purpose for the treaty as a whole so as to fall back on a single overarching notion for interpreting treaties. Some contend that, if there could be multiple objects and purposes throughout a treaty, then the whole point of this interpretation method would be lost as one possible interpretation may be in accordance with one object and purpose but not compatible with another one.[27] It can be otherwise argued that, since Sir Waldock used only the plural form, i.e., objects and purposes, in the VCLT's draft, he intended that a treaty could have a multiplicity of them. While the ILC never explicitly states that their use of the element in its singular form was to avoid an interpretation using multiple objects and purposes, there are arguments to support this claim: individual treaty provisions may serve different goals, but not necessarily a different object and purpose than another provision. If the general rule of Article 31(1) VCLT would refer to a plural notion, then treaty interpretation could become very difficult as the different goals of different provisions could be diametrically opposed. This would make the very notion redundant.[28]

While these arguments made in literature seem convincing, the ICJ and various WTO bodies have not been as consistent. There are various examples of cases that refer to the notion of object and purpose interchangeably in the singular and plural while sometimes applying it to the entire treaty and sometimes only to individual provisions.[29] Some authors also argue that it is unrealistic that the general rule of Article

---

24. Le Robert, *L'objet*, https://dictionnaire.lerobert.com/definition/objet (last visited 21 June 2024).
25. *Border and Transborder Armed Actions* case *(Nicaragua v. Honduras)*, 69, 24; *Oil Platforms (Islamic Republic of Iran v. United States of America)*, 803; *Asylum* case *(Colombia/Peru)*, 266.
26. Jan Klabbers, *Max Planck Encyclopedias of International Law: Treaties, Object and Purpose*, paras 6 et seq. (Oxford Public International Law 2006).
27. The same is valid for other references to the object and purpose in the VCLT, specifically Art. 19 VCLT. If a state could only make reservations to treaties that are compatible with its object and purpose, then there could be reservations only in line with one of the objects and purposes but not with others. This would make the entire reference in Art. 19 VCLT obsolete; Klabbers, *supra* n. 26.
28. Klabbers, *supra* n. 26.
29. *Ibid.*

31(1) VCLT only refers to one object and purpose of a treaty interpretation especially as it perhaps will not be identifiable in every case.[30] This view is supported by the Appellate Body of the WTO:

> most treaties have no single undiluted object and purpose but rather a variety of different, and possibly conflicting, objects and purposes. This is certainly true of the *WTO Agreement*. Thus, while the first clause of the preamble to the *WTO Agreement* calls for the expansion of trade in goods and services, this same clause also recognizes that international trade and economic relations under the *WTO Agreement* should allow for 'optimal use of the world's resources in accordance with the objective of sustainable development', and should seek 'to protect and preserve the environment'. The Panel in effect took a one-sided view of the object and purpose of the *WTO Agreement* when it fashioned a new test not found in the text of the Agreement.[31]

Regardless of the various voices who support the element of object and purpose as a singular notion, the argument towards multiple ones should prevail. First of all, it seems nearly impossible to limit a treaty to only one object and purpose. Most treaties pursue multiple ones that do not necessarily have to be opposed and hinder the interpretation process. It also seems that limiting interpreters to only one object and purpose could lead to arbitrary results as a lot in terms of the drafters' content or intentions must be excluded. Second, there is a significant amount of material by Sir Waldock that refers to the objects and purposes of a treaty. While there is no explanation of any sort as to why it was changed from plural in the draft to singular in the VCLT, it seems that he intended that there could be multiple goals that the drafters wanted to achieve with a treaty. As a result, the object and purpose element should be regarded in the plural form.

2.2.2 *Relationship with the Other Means of Interpretation*

It is often discussed in academic research what the relationship is between the object and purpose and the other means of interpretation in the VCLT, specifically within the general rule of Article 31(1) VCLT. While a holistic approach, so the simultaneous consideration of all interpretation elements, can be agreed upon,[32] it is still unclear whether the object and purpose element is an indicator of a general approach to be used for treaty interpretation or if it rather functions as a means to elucidate the ordinary meaning of the treaty terms.[33] In general, as already explained in the chapter by Kofler/Komár of this book, the ordinary meaning of the treaty terms cannot be established in the abstract but is determined in the context of the treaty and in light of its object and purpose. This view is supported by the wording of Article 31(1) VCLT. The rule does not require an extensive interpretation of a treaty but rather to establish

30. Gardiner, *supra* n. 20, at 41.
31. *United States – Import Prohibition of Certain Shrimp and Shrimp Products*, No. WT/DS58/AB/R, para. 17 (Appellate Body 12 October 1998).
32. Michael Lang, *DBA Malta: Wechsel von der Freistellungs- zur Anrechnungsmethode auf Grundlage einer EAS-Rechtsauskunft des BMF?*, SWI 16 (2024).
33. Gardiner, *supra* n. 20, at 38.

its context, including its object and purpose and then reconciling these elements in the ordinary meaning of the words. Therefore, an interpretation of a treaty in regard to its object and purpose is always limited in the text, so the VCLT can be considered prohibiting analogy. Article 31(1) VCLT prohibits interpretations that go beyond the wording of a treaty term. This view is supported by the Appellate Body of the WTO:

> A treaty interpreter must begin with, and focus upon, the text of the particular provision to be interpreted. It is in the words constituting that provision, read in their context, that the object and purpose of the states parties to the treaty must first be sought. Where the meaning imparted by the text itself is equivocal or inconclusive, or where confirmation of the correctness of the reading of the text itself is desired, light form the object and purpose of the treaty as a whole may usefully be sought.[34]

In this regard, the Iran-US Claims Tribunal also pointed out:

> Even when one is dealing with the object and purpose of a treaty, which is the most important part of the treaty's context, the object and purpose does not constitute an element independent of that context. The object and purpose is not to be considered in isolation from the terms of the treaty; it is intrinsic to its text. It follows that, under Article 31 of the Vienna Convention, a treaty's object and purpose is to be used only to clarify the text, not to provide independent sources of meaning that contradict the clear text.[35]

2.3 Methodology

The question of methodology is especially important for everyone interpreting and applying a treaty, i.e., the question of where the object and purpose of a treaty can be found. While many courts fall back on the preamble and the title of a treaty, others only look at the specific treaty provisions while still other courts seem to determine the object and purpose without falling back on the treaty text at all. This incites the question if the concept may be self-evident.[36]

First of all, it must be established that the general rule of Article 31(1) VCLT seems to refer to the text of the entire treaty. This would explain why not all courts, as is later shown, can explicitly state how they came to their conclusion of a treaty's object and purpose. It can be assumed that they 'simply' read the whole text and deduced it. However, this observation alone is not really enough to determine the methodology behind the concept of object and purpose. In order to achieve this, the following section examines different treaties and jurisprudence in which they were discussed or even the deciding factor.

The most obvious example of how a treaty's object and purpose can be determined is if it is explicitly stated in its text. Article 1 of the UN Charter serves as a

34. *United States – Import Prohibition of Certain Shrimp and Shrimp Products*, No. WT/DS58/AB/R, para. 114.
35. *Iran-US Claims Tribunals Case No. IUSCT Case No. A28 (19.12.2000)*, p. 1, para. 58.
36. Buffard & Zemanek, *supra* n. 2, at 318.

good example.[37] While this approach initially appears to be fairly easy, it raises the question of whether the rest of the text can then be disregarded when there is an object and purpose already stated.

There are some cases, for example, the *Certain Norwegian Loans* case,[38] where a court found the object and purpose of a treaty expressed in its title. In other cases, the ICJ relied heavily on the preamble to determine them, for example, in the *United States Nationals in Morocco* case[39] when interpreting the Convention of Madrid and the Act of Algeciras and in the *Territorial Dispute* case.[40] In the *Oil Platforms* case, the court was confronted with an Iranian claim that the US breached the object and purpose of a treaty. To make its point, Iran contrasted friendship treaties with the US-Iranian Treaty of Amity, Economic Relations, and Consular Rights. The ICJ denied the claim with the explanation that the treaty's object and purpose according to the preamble was not just friendship between two countries but rather encouraging mutually beneficial trade and investments and closer economic intercourse generally. It proceeded to state that the treaty type can also provide information as to its object and purpose.[41] The idea that they can naturally be found in the preamble was already supported by Sir Gerald Fitzmaurice, an ICJ judge:

> Although the objects of a treaty may be gathered from its operative clauses taken as a whole, the preamble is the natural place in which to embody, and the natural place to look for, any express or explicit statement of the treaty's objects and purposes. Where these are stated in the preamble, the latter will, to that extent, govern the whole treaty.[42]

In contrast to this, there are other ICJ cases such as the *Application of the Convention of 1902 Governing the Guardianship of Infants* case[43] and the *Military and Paramilitary Activities in and Against Nicaragua* case[44] in which it is not clearly stated where exactly in the text the court determined the object and purpose. It seems that the entirety of the treaty text is used to ascertain them in these cases.

The case law shows that especially the preamble can act as a starting point for determining the object and purpose with a further reference to the full treaty text where a further formulation of the notion can subsequently be found of significance for interpretation.[45] However, some authors, like Lang, advise caution when using the

37. Due to the dispute of whether there can only be one object and purpose of a treaty or several, it is questionable whether the UN Charter has four purposes or whether they must be combined into one overall object and purpose. However, as this subchapter is concerned with the methodology to determine these, this discussion will be excluded.
38. *Certain Norwegian Loans* case *(France v. Norway)*, 9.
39. *Rights of nationals of the United States of America in Morocco* case, 176.
40. *Territorial Dispute (Libyan Arab Jamahiriya/Chad)*, 6.
41. *Oil Platforms (Islamic Republic of Iran v. United States of America)*, 803, 14 et seq.
42. Sir Gerald Fitzmaurice, *The Law and Procedure of the International Court of Justice*, Vol. 1, 60 (Grotius Publications Limited 1996).
43. *Application of the Convention of 1902 Governing the Guardianship of Infants* case *(Netherlands v. Sweden)*, 55.
44. *Military and Paramilitary Activities in and Against Nicaragua* case *(Nicaragua v. United States of America)*, 14.
45. Gardiner, *supra* n. 20, at 41.

preamble to determine object and purpose due to various reasons. First, preambles are not always carefully drafted and may therefore need interpretation in itself as opposed to being clear enough to help with interpreting the remainder of the treaty.[46] Second, he argues that the preamble has no independent normative significance.[47]

Overall, the idea that the title of a treaty, its type, and, most importantly, the preamble are a starting point that should be supported but, as Buffard and Zemanek argue, it is a two-step procedure:

> In a first stage, a prima facie assumption of the object and purpose of a treaty must be formed by having recourse to the title, preamble and, if available, programmatic articles of the treaty. This assumption must then be tested in a second stage against the text of the treaty and all other available material and, if necessary, adjusted in the light of that test. The result of that process can then be used as a guideline in the interpretation of other treaty provisions or for assessing compliance with them.[48]

3 SIGNIFICANCE FOR TAX TREATY INTERPRETATION

3.1 Object and Purpose of Tax Treaties

As previously stated, there are two steps to consider when identifying the object and purpose of a treaty. In a first step, assumptions should be made by taking recourse to the title and the preamble of the tax treaty. Both of these for the Model Convention of the Organisation for Economic Co-operation and Development (OECD MC) have been changed multiple times since its first draft in 1963.[49] In the beginning, the purpose of tax treaties seemed to be to foster international trade and investment by eliminating international double taxation. The Commentary to the 1977 OECD MC then added that tax treaties should also not help engaging in tax avoidance or tax evasion.[50] De Broe and Luts argue that this was added to enable national legislators to enact domestic anti-avoidance rules. However, in the event of a conflict between a domestic anti-avoidance rule and a provision of a tax treaty, the contracting state was still obligated to grant the treaty benefit under the principle of *pacta sunt servanda* according to Articles 26 and 27 VCLT as the goal of taking action against tax avoidance and tax evasion was not yet an object and purpose of a tax treaty modelled after the OECD MC.[51] With its 2003 revision, the Commentary listed the prevention of tax avoidance and tax evasion for the first time as a proper purpose of tax treaties, although some authors such as Arnold argue that it was only seen as an ancillary purpose, and the

46. Michael Lang, *Missbrauchsbekämpfung als Ziel und Zweck der DBA?*, in print.
47. Michael Lang, *Verhinderung von Doppel- Und Doppelnichtbesteuerung*, in SWI-Spezial: *Die österreichischen DBA nach BEPS* 45 et seqq. (Linde Verlag 2018).
48. Buffard & Zemanek, *supra* n. 2, at 333.
49. John F. Avery Jones, *Understanding the OECD Model of Tax Convention: The Lesson of History*, 10 Florida Tax Review No. 1, 3 (2009) https://doi.org/10.5744/ftr.2009.1011.
50. OECD Model Commentary 1977, Art. 1, p. 7.
51. Luc De Broe & Joris Luts, *BEPS Action 6: Tax Treaty Abuse*, 43 Intertax 122 et seq. (2015) https://doi.org/10.54648/taxi2015011.

principal purpose still remained the prevention of double taxation.[52] In the 2017 update of the OECD MC, the prevention of tax avoidance and tax evasion was then adopted not only into the title[53] but also into the preamble of the Convention. It now reads as follows:

> (State A) and (State B),
> Desiring to further their economic relationship and to enhance their cooperation in tax matters,
> Intending to conclude a Convention for the elimination of double taxation with respect to taxes on income and on capital without creating opportunities for non-taxation or reduced taxation through tax evasion or avoidance (including through treaty-shopping arrangements aimed at obtaining reliefs provided in this Convention for the indirect benefit of residents of third States),
> Have agreed as follows.[54]

Before delving into the objectives stated in this revised preamble, it must be noted that changes to the existing Model Convention always carry the risk of an *e contrario* conclusion.[55] This means that a change of the title and preamble to include the prevention of tax avoidance and evasion can lead to the assumption that this did not serve as a purpose for tax treaties drafted in accordance with older version of the OECD MC.

In the current version of the preamble, a number of objectives can be identified from its text: The desire to further an economic relationship between two states, to enhance the cooperation in tax matters between two states, the elimination of double taxation or not creating opportunities for non-taxation or reduced taxation through tax evasion or tax avoidance.

According to Engelen, the primary purpose of a tax treaty according to the OECD MC is to avoid international juridical double taxation to advance the international exchange of goods, services, and capital, among other things. They also address other issues such as the prevention of tax evasion or avoidance through exchange of information, assistance in the collection of taxes, and the elimination of discriminatory taxation which can be seen as the secondary purposes.[56] He argues that, since 2003 when the preamble was changed, another objective of the OECD MC is to prevent tax avoidance and evasion. This is supported by the Introduction to the Model Convention which states that the title and preamble not only form part of the context for the

52. *Ibid.*, at 123; Brian J. Arnold, *Tax Treaties and Tax Avoidance: The 2003 Revisions to the Commentary to the OECD Model*, Bulletin for International Taxation 248 (2004).
53. The 2017 updated title now states: Convention between (State A) and (State B) for the elimination of double taxation with respect to taxes on income and on capital and the prevention of tax evasion and avoidance.
54. OECD Model Convention 2017; furthermore, the preamble of the UN Model Convention has been worded identically since its 2021 update.
55. Michael Lang, *BEPS Action 6: Introducing an Antiabuse Rule in Tax Treaties*, 74 Tax Notes International 656 (2014) https://doi.org/10.2139/ssrn.2500827; also regarding the problem of a reverse conclusion after the amendment of Art. 3(2) OECD MC, *see also* Michael Lang, *Tendenzen in Der Rechtsprechung Des Österreichischen Verwaltungsgerichtshofs Zu Den Doppelbesteuerungsabkommen*, IFF Forum für Steuerrecht 32 (2012).
56. Engelen, *supra* n. 14, Chapter 10.3.

Convention but also constitute a general statement of the object and purpose and should therefore be an important factor in its interpretation.[57]

This view is criticized by other authors, such as Lang. When the preamble was changed, it led to the impression that the avoidance of double non-taxation became more important in treaty interpretation. Lang, however, argues that the preamble has no independent normative significance and that it does not introduce a subject-to-tax clause. Therefore, the interpretation depends on a specific provision and not primarily on the preamble.[58] However, as the preambles of the OECD and the UN Model Convention are the same, regardless of what provisions are actually incorporated into the specific tax treaty, that should put an interpretation only using the preamble into perspective.[59]

What is also stated as problematic by Lang and other authors in international tax law is the fact that the preamble is ambiguously worded. First, the avoidance of double taxation itself is not clear as it can refer either to juridical or economic double taxation. As is well known, tax treaties, even though they refer to double taxation in general, try to predominantly eliminate juridical double taxation. While some may argue against a broad object and purpose, others are of the opinion that it is supposed to be broad as it is intended to cover a very broad subject.[60] Second, a tax treaty, according to the preamble, is not intended to create opportunities for non-taxation or reduced taxation. In this regard, Lang states that this objective is subject to the restriction that there should only be disapproval for creating these opportunities if it occurs through tax evasion or avoidance. Therefore, a tax treaty does not generally prevent states from creating opportunities for non-taxation as that would be excessive because tax treaties are still designed in a way to allocate taxing rights without actually obligating states to exercise these taxing rights. Even if one state does not exercise its taxing rights, that does not return the right to tax this income to the other contracting state. Only if that was the case, could non-taxation be avoided. Lang therefore argues that an objective that could be refuted by the treaty provisions themselves would be meaningless.[61] Consequently, that would mean that this object and purpose cannot be used to interpret other provisions. He is also of the opinion that the phrase in the preamble that is in brackets ('including through treaty-shopping arrangements aimed at obtaining reliefs provided in this agreement for the indirect benefit of residents of third jurisdictions') is also problematic due to the Convention's use of them. Their use is almost ambiguous as it is not clear whether the wording in brackets is intended to clarify, restrict, or extend the phrase in front of the brackets. It seems that the treaty-shopping arrangements are not the only ones that can be interpreted as tax avoidance. However, it is unclear if all of these arrangements are to be qualified this way. The significance of this will be further discussed regarding the PPT in Article 29 OECD MC. To

57. *Ibid.*
58. Michael Lang, *Missbrauchsbekämpfung als Ziel und Zweck der DBA?*, in print.
59. *Ibid.*
60. Kaspar Dziurdź, *The Concept of the 'Object and Purpose' in Tax Treaty Law Based on the Vienna Convention (1969) and the Principal Purposes Test Rule*, Bulletin for International Taxation 112 (2024) https://doi.org/10.59403/11fvrdd.
61. Michael Lang, *Missbrauchsbekämpfung als Ziel und Zweck der DBA?*, in print.

summarize, Lang's position is that the amended preamble does not change the content of the individual treaty provisions, therefore, it cannot contribute anything to interpreting them.[62]

The opinion that the treaty's preamble should not be used for interpreting purposes because of its ambiguous wording can be opposed by the following. Ambiguous wording is not only prevailing in the preamble of the Model Conventions but also in every language. Therefore, all language needs interpreting to clarify it. This alone cannot hinder using the preamble for interpretation purposes. The majority of authors in international tax law are of the view that it should be used as a starting point for the interpretation. This is supported by ICJ case law and also by the Introduction to the Model Conventions[63] itself. What is clear, however, is that the preamble is not a subject-to-tax clause but, if there are two interpretations of a tax treaty of which one does while the other does not eliminate double taxation, the preamble (with its stated object and purpose) should be the deciding factor toward adopting the former interpretation.[64]

However, another argument brought forward by De Broe and Luts must be considered. They state that, while the object and purpose of a tax treaty may very well be stated in its preamble, it should be materialized in its operative provisions. As these only allocate taxing rights for certain income to one contracting state without an obligation to said state to actually exercise this right, it cannot be argued that an objective of tax treaties is the prevention of double non-taxation.[65] Even now, years after the introduction of the Base Erosion and Profit Shifting (BEPS) Project, the goal of preventing double non-taxation has not yet materialized more clearly in the operative provisions of the Model Conventions. In light of this, it must be stressed that the preamble of a (tax) treaty is not the only place from where the object and purpose should be extracted. When assumptions can be made from the preamble, they must necessarily be compared against the text of the treaty.

As tax treaties significantly differ and deviate in some way from the models in most cases, it is difficult to make theoretical considerations about the second step of the two-step procedure that Buffard and Zemanek propose. It should be noted, however, that particular attention must be paid to which articles of the Model Conventions have actually been implemented as this influences the possible objects and purposes that a tax treaty can have.[66]

62. Michael Lang, *Missbrauchsbekämpfung als Ziel und Zweck der DBA?*, in print.
63. OECD, *Model Tax Convention on Income and on Capital 2017 (Full Version)* I-7 (OECD 25 April 2019).
64. Engelen, *supra* n. 14, Chapter 10.3.
65. De Broe & Luts, *supra* n. 51, at 143.
66. This statement is, of course, not applicable to older tax treaties that were drafted before the model conventions were even developed.

3.2 Relevance for the PPT

When discussing the object and purpose of a treaty, it is inevitable that the PPT is discussed that was introduced following BEPS Action 6.[67] The PPT according to Article 29(9) Model Convention explicitly states the phrase object and purpose in its paragraph 9. It reads as follows:

> Notwithstanding the other provisions of this Convention, a benefit under this Convention shall not be granted in respect of an item of income or capital if it is reasonable to conclude, having regard to all relevant facts and circumstances, that obtaining that benefit was one of the principal purposes of any arrangement or transaction that resulted directly or indirectly in that benefit, unless it is established that granting that benefit in these circumstances would be in accordance with the object and purpose of the relevant provisions of this Convention.

This test may deny treaty benefits in cases when the benefits are not in accordance with the object and purpose of the relevant provisions. It proposes a two-step process. First, it requires examining the arrangement itself and determining if obtaining a tax benefit through that arrangement was the primary goal. Second, it needs to be tested whether granting that tax benefit would be in accordance with the object and purpose of the treaty provisions. Treaty benefits are denied if obtaining the benefit was one of the principal purposes and it cannot be proven that granting it would be in line with the object and purpose.

While the PPT rule raises a number of questions, for the purpose of this chapter, it is important to consider whether it merely clarifies that the provisions of tax treaties are to be interpreted in all cases according to their object and purpose or whether Article 29(9) OECD MC limits the interpretation according to the object and purpose for cases in which one of the primary reasons for the transaction was the realization of treaty benefits. The former is sometimes referred to as a signalling approach.[68] The reference to the object and purpose would – due to Article 31(1) VCLT – still be applicable to tax treaties with or without the PPT rule which is why the signalling approach would just emphasize the interpretation rule that is already in place. This approach is criticized as it limits the relevance of the PPT rule.[69] However, it can be argued that Article 29(9) OECD MC allows for the interpretation according to the object and purpose to take precedence over the wording of the treaty. Dziurdź states the following:

> Where the taxpayer has no tax motives, he or she can trust the wording of the treaty provisions. Where, in contrast, the taxpayer pursues principal tax motives (the threshold), he or she cannot be sure that the benefits will be granted. Rather, the benefits may be denied under the PPT rule if they violate the object and purpose of the treaty provisions.[70]

67. De Broe & Luts, *supra* n. 51, at 131.
68. Dziurdź, *supra* n. 60, at 120.
69. *Ibid.*
70. *Ibid.*, at 119.

This approach goes too far. International law literature and Article 31(1) VCLT dictate very clearly that the interpretation according to object and purpose finds its limits in the wording of the text. If the PPT, which references exactly this element of treaty interpretation, would then go beyond the wording, it would give precedence to a teleological interpretation that was clearly not intended by the drafters of the treaty. To summarize, the signalling approach would limit the relevance of the PPT rule while the precedence of the object and purpose over the wording of the treaty overreaches the function of the interpretation element that was not intended by the VCLT drafters. Therefore, the approach that would remain is that Article 29(9) OECD MC limits the interpretation according to the object and purpose to cases in which one of the main reasons for the transaction was the realization of treaty benefits. This is also debatable as the aim of the general rule is to interpret a treaty using the four elements of good faith, ordinary meaning, context, and object and purpose. This also applies to tax treaties and, therefore, the interpretation according to one element cannot not be limited. It is hence justifiable that mentioning object and purpose in Article 29(9) OECD MC only serves as a clarification.

Another question that arises from the reference in the PPT rule is the fact that the provision itself refers to the object and purpose of other provisions in the plural form. That implies that there can be multiple purposes in a tax treaty. Article 29(9) OECD therefore confirms the view that the terms 'object and purpose' in Article 31(1) VCLT should be regarded as being plural (*see* section 2.2.1).

Last but not least, it must be mentioned that, while the first step of the PPT is done by the tax administration and only requires that it is reasonable to conclude that obtaining a tax benefit was one of the purposes of a certain arrangement, the burden of proof for the second step falls upon the taxpayer. She has to provide evidence to the contrary and argue that granting the benefit for her tax arrangement is in accordance with the object and purpose of the relevant provisions. This proof is much more difficult to present which is why scholars argue that the burden of proof is effectively shifted to the taxpayer.[71] However, the question arises as to what extent the taxpayer can provide sufficient proof at all if even in tax literature it is still disputed what exactly the object and purpose of a tax treaty is and how it can be determined. With the PPT now being a minimum standard for the signature of the Multilateral Instrument (MLI), in the future, an increasing number of cases will come up, thus, the courts will have to deal with precisely this question.

3.3 Differences Between the OECD and UN Model Conventions

It has to be remarked that the preambles of both the OECD and the UN Model Conventions have the same wording. Both Model Conventions mention object and purpose directly only once in Article 29 OECD MC, the PPT, and in Article 29 UN Model Convention, the Entitlement to Benefits Clause.

71. De Broe & Luts, *supra* n. 51, at 132.

The UN Model Convention states in its Introduction that it generally focuses on giving the source countries more taxing rights under a tax treaty as compared to the residence countries like what is done under the OECD MC. This issue is of much significance for developing countries and was picked up by the UN and resulted in the UN Model Convention.[72] While the wording of the preamble would suggest the same object and purpose for the OECD and UN Model Convention, this Introduction leads to the assumption that the object and purpose differs which would lead to different interpretation results even though the wording of both model conventions are very similar in some points. This view is further stressed through the allocation of taxing rights in the operative provisions of both model conventions. While the OECD MC allocates more taxing rights to the residence state, the UN Model Convention gives more to the source states. As the operative provisions should reflect on the object and purpose of a tax treaty, this leads to the conclusion that the two have a different object and purpose. With that being stated, the problem is somewhat defused as there can be more than one object and purpose in a (tax) treaty which means that while both model conventions differ in this regard, other objects and purposes are still the same.

4 FINAL REMARKS

The element of object and purpose is an important factor when interpreting (tax) treaties even though many aspects of this interpretative method are still very much unclear and disputed in the academic world: The terminology is still not used uniformly, especially by the courts; the methodology to determine object and purpose differs from author to author and from court to court; and the relationship with the other means of interpretation under the VCLT still remains unclear.

While the concept of object and purpose is heavily discussed in literature, it is only an incidental factor in practice. While there are many court cases that reference the object and purpose in some way or another, it rarely seems to be the deciding factor. Therefore, it is often unnecessary to actually determine if Article 31(1) VCLT only describes a singular or plural concept or how it can actually be determined as the courts seem to have little problem doing so for the treaties in question. Still, it can be seen as a missed opportunity that the element of object and purpose was introduced into the VCLT without any real specification on what the drafters actually meant by it, thus leading to the enigma that it is today. Because of this, academia and jurisprudence are still confronted with the circular logic that the object and purpose of a treaty is to be determined in light of its object and purpose.[73]

72. UN, *Model Double Taxation Convention Between Developed and Developing Countries* III et seqq. (UN 2017).
73. Dino Kritsiotis, *The Object and Purpose of a Treaty's Object and Purpose, in Conceptual and Contextual Perspectives on the Modern Law of Treaties* 240 (Michael J. Bowman & Dino Kritsiotis eds, Cambridge University Press 2018).

CHAPTER 6

Subsequent Agreements and Tax Treaty Interpretation

Daniel W. Blum & Dominic Krenn

1 Setting the Scene: General Observations on the Role of Subsequent Agreements and Tax Treaty Interpretation
2 Subsequent Agreements from a General Public International Law Perspective
2.1 The Key Constitutive Elements of Subsequent Agreements Pursuant to Article 31(3)(a) VCLT
2.1.1 Introductory Remarks
2.1.2 'Agreement'
2.1.3 'Between the Parties'
2.1.4 'Regarding the Interpretation of a Tax Treaty'
2.1.5 'Subsequent'
2.2 The Role of Subsequent Agreements Within the VCLT
2.2.1 The Role of Subsequent Agreements and Their Hierarchical Position Within Articles 31 and 33 VCLT
2.2.1.1 General Rule of Interpretation: Article 31(1) to Article 31(4) VCLT
2.2.1.2 The Temporal Element of Subsequent Agreements
2.2.1.3 The Relationship Between Subsequent Agreements and Subsequent Practice in the Sense of Article 31(3)(b) VCLT
2.2.1.4 The Interrelation Between Article 31(3) and Article 32 VCLT

2.2.2 The Distinction Between Interpretation and Modification

3 The Role of Subsequent Agreements in Tax Treaty Interpretation

3.1 General Remarks

3.2 The Commentary to the OECD MC as a Subsequent Agreement?

3.3 Result of MAPs as Subsequent Agreements?

3.4 The MLI as a Subsequent Agreement?

4 Concluding Remarks

1 SETTING THE SCENE: GENERAL OBSERVATIONS ON THE ROLE OF SUBSEQUENT AGREEMENTS AND TAX TREATY INTERPRETATION

Among the generally accepted sources of international law, double taxation conventions (DTCs) are undeniably encompassed within the category of international treaties.[1] Yet another one of these, the Vienna Convention on the Law of Treaties (VCLT), in its Articles 31 to 33 foresees a set of rules that are meant to ensure a uniform interpretation of treaties in public international law.[2] As the judicial and administrative practice of courts and tax authorities around the world shows, the VCLT's interpretation rules are of immense relevance for interpreting DTCs.[3] Even states that have not signed and ratified the VCLT are arguably bound by its content insofar as it is generally considered a mere codification of customary international law.[4] The interpretation process of DTCs thus requires a profound understanding of the interpretation principles under public international law as enshrined in the VCLT.

The VCLT's section 3 dealing with the interpretation of treaties consists of three articles. Article 31 VCLT outlines the general rules of interpretation, Article 32 VCLT considers what is known as 'supplementary means of interpretation', and Article 33 VCLT addresses the situation in which multiple languages are defined as authentic. This chapter discusses one specific element of Article 31 VCLT, specifically paragraph 3, letter a which – as an addition to the general interpretation rule referring to the wording, the object/purpose, and context – requires the interpretation to take into account also subsequent agreements between the parties of the treaty. This chapter aims to examine the meaning of Article 31(3)(a) VCLT and its intra-systematic role in the interpretation process envisaged by the VCLT. The chapter thus first explores the

1. *See* Dietmar Gosch, *Über Die Auslegung von Doppelbesteuerungsabkommen*, 2 I.S.R. 87 (2013).
2. Michael Lang, *Introduction to the Law of Double Taxation Conventions*, No. 62 (Linde Verlag Ges.m.b.H. 3. Auflage ed. 2021).
3. Michael Lang, *Can Law Regulate Its Own Interpretation? Relevance of Articles 31-33 of the Vienna Convention on the Law of Treaties (VCLT) and Article 3 Para. 2 of the Model Convention of the Organisation for Economic Co-operation and Development (OECD MC) for the Interpretation of Double-Taxation Conventions*, in *Research Handbook on International Taxation* 176 et seq. (Yariv Brauner ed., Edward Elgar Publishing 2019).
4. Mark E. Villiger, *The 1969 Vienna Convention on the Law of Treaties: 40 Years after* 132 (BRILL 2009); Oliver Dörr, *Article 31 General Rule of Interpretation, Vienna Convention on the Law of Treaties: A Commentary*, No. 6 (Oliver Dörr & Kirsten Schmalenbach eds, Springer 2d ed. 2018).

key constitutive elements of Article 31 (3)(a) governing the relevance of subsequent agreements from a public international law perspective. The focus then lies on identifying their relevance in treaty interpretation and the interrelation of Article 31(3)(a) VCLT with other means of interpretation foreseen by Article 31, particularly subsequent practice pursuant to paragraph 3, letter b VCLT. Finally, the findings reached in sections 2.1 and 2.2 from a public international law perspective are applied to the realm of DTCs focussing on three particularly relevant aspects in this regard. It is therefore discussed whether the Organisation for Economic Co-operation and Development (OECD) commentary to the Model Convention, the result of mutual agreement procedures (MAPs), or even the Multilateral Instrument (MLI) can be qualified as subsequent agreements within the meaning of Article 31(3)(b) VCLT and hence as a relevant means of interpreting previously concluded DTCs.

2 SUBSEQUENT AGREEMENTS FROM A GENERAL PUBLIC INTERNATIONAL LAW PERSPECTIVE

2.1 The Key Constitutive Elements of Subsequent Agreements Pursuant to Article 31(3)(a) VCLT

2.1.1 Introductory Remarks

The clause defining the role of subsequent agreements in the interpretation of previously concluded international treaties forms part of Article 31 VCLT and hence of the general rule of interpretation. Article 31(3)(a) VCLT reads as follows: 'There shall be taken into account, together with the context any subsequent agreement between the parties regarding the interpretation of the treaty or the application of its provisions.' Thus, according to the wording of the clause, a subsequent agreement in the context of the VCLT requires (i) an 'agreement', (ii) that is concluded 'between the parties', (iii) and regards 'the interpretation of the treaty or the application of its provisions'. Last, such an agreement must be concluded (iv) 'subsequently'. Hence, only those that cumulatively fulfil these requirements fall within the ambit of Article 31(3)(a) VCLT and hence '*shall be*' - together with the context - used as a means of interpreting a treaty.

2.1.2 'Agreement'

In a first step, it hence must be assessed what the VCLT means when indicating an 'agreement'. Reference is made not only in Article 31(3)(a) VCLT but also in Article 31(2)(a) to the term 'agreement' when it is stated that 'any agreement relating to the treaty which was made between all the parties in connection with the conclusion of the treaty' is relevant when interpreting treaties. According to prevailing literature, both the term 'subsequent agreements' used in Article 31(3)(a) VCLT and 'any agreement' used in Article 31(2)(a) VCLT are based on the same understanding of the term 'agreement'.[5] Though the VCLT itself does not explicitly define it, Article 2(1)(a) VCLT uses it to define the term 'treaty'. Accordingly, a treaty for VCLT purposes requires a written agreement between states. The term 'agreement' thus has a wider scope than the term 'treaty'. It appears to be generally accepted in literature that the former term should be interpreted in a broad generic sense.[6] Since Article 31(3)(a) VCLT explicitly uses the term 'agreement' instead of 'treaty' for which the VCLT demands a written form by means of an *argumentum e contrario*, it can be concluded that an agreement does not require a specific degree of formality.[7] Rather, any contractual instruments can be considered agreements irrespective of the fact of whether they are in written or unwritten form.[8] If the provision on subsequent agreements was intended to be limited to those that are written - as some scholars argue - Article 31(3)(a) VCLT could have been easily phrased to require a treaty which is defined by Article 2, letter a VCLT to mean any written agreement.[9]

These considerations find support in statements published by the International Law Commission (ILC) according to which the VCLT does not foresee any particular formal requirements for the term 'agreement'. However, although agreements under Article 31(3)(a) VCLT do not require any specific degree of formality, this does not mean that subsequent agreements are necessarily less official than a 'treaty'. Rather, they can - and often will - be established in written form. The agreement thus qualifies formally as a treaty due to its written form while being treated as a subsequent agreement for purposes of applying Article 31(3)(a) VCLT if it can be derived that the parties intended the treaty to function as a subsequent agreement interpreting the previously concluded treaty. The decisive element is hence not the form but the purpose of the written agreement.[10] As a result, according to the prevailing view, final acts, protocols of signature, understandings, commentaries, or even explanatory

5. Dörr, *supra* n. 4, No. 72; James Crawford, *A Consensualist Interpretation of Article 31(3) of the Vienna Convention on the Law of Treaties, in Treaties and Subsequent Practice* 30 (Georg Nolte ed., Oxford Univ. Press 1st ed., 1. impr. ed. 2013).
6. Katharina Berner, *Subsequent Agreements and Subsequent Practice in Domestic Courts* 104 (Springer 2017); Mark E. Villiger, *Commentary on the 1969 Vienna Convention on the Law of Treaties*, Art. 31, mn 18 (Nijhoff 2009); Dörr, *supra* n. 4, No. 66.
7. Villiger, *Commentary on the 1969 Vienna Convention on the Law of Treaties*, *supra* n. 6, Art. 31, mn 18; Villiger, *The 1969 Vienna Convention on the Law of Treaties: 40 Years after*, *supra* n. 4, at 120; Ulf Linderfalk, *On the Interpretation of Treaties: The Modern International Law as Expressed in the 1969 Vienna Convention on the Law of Treaties* 162 (Springer 2007); Rakhi Agrawal, *Interpretation of International Tax Treaties: Subsequent Agreements and Subsequent Practices*, Asia-Pacific Tax Bulletin 315 (September-October 2014) https://doi.org/10.59403/17yyn88.
8. Dörr, *supra* n. 4, Art. 31, mn 66; Villiger, *Commentary on the 1969 Vienna Convention on the Law of Treaties*, *supra* n. 6, Art. 31, mn 18; Linderfalk, *On the Interpretation of Treaties: The Modern International Law as Expressed in the 1969 Vienna Convention on the Law of Treaties*, *supra* n. 7, at 162.
9. Berner, *supra* n. 6, at 106; however, it should be noted that the degree of formality could be crucial for distinguishing between subsequent agreements and subsequent practice; *see* thereto in more detail under s. 2.2.1.3.
10. *International Law Commission 'Report of the International Law Commission in Its 70th Session' (30 April-1 June and 2 July-10 August 2018) UN Doc A/73/10* 28; *see also*, e.g., Georg Nolte, *'First Report on Subsequent Agreements and Subsequent Practice in Relation to Treaty Interpretation' (19 March 2013) UN Doc A/CN.4/660*, No. 67.

reports may be regarded as such.[11] The finding that the term 'agreement' does not require the same formal pedigree as a treaty is also emphasized in case law. The final award of the *Methanex v. United States* case of the tribunal on jurisdiction and merits states: 'It follows from the wording of Article 31(3)(a) [VCLT] that it is not envisaged that the subsequent agreement need be concluded with the same formal requirements as a treaty; and indeed, were this to be the case, the provision would be otiose.'[12]

Although a subsequent agreement may be informal and need not be legally binding, it nevertheless must be concluded, i.e., has to be based on the mutual consent of the parties to the agreement.[13] Given the lack of any formal requirements established by Article 31(3)(a) VCLT, there is no specific form regarding how the mutual understanding forming the basis for the subsequent agreement between the parties has to be expressed.[14] Of course, the clearest expressions are written manifestations of the parties' mutual will (i.e., supplementary memoranda of understanding).[15] Apart from that, it is also discussed in literature whether silence regarding conduct in a subsequent agreement could be a possible element in expressing implicit consent.[16] Such a view, however, faces severe obstacles and must be dismissed as a result. Subsequent conduct by only one party remaining unknown to the other party cannot establish the basis for a common understanding. However, the crucial question is whether subsequent conduct recognized by the other party can form the basis for a subsequent implicit agreement. The International Court of Justice (ICJ) stated in this regard that a party that did not respond to the finding of a joint commission of technical experts who had been entrusted by both parties to determine the facts of a matter in dispute could not be taken as grounds for concluding that an agreement had been reached on the matter in dispute.[17] Such considerations are also in accordance with the remarks from Nolte who states that a subsequent agreement cannot 'be derived from the mere silence of the parties'.[18]

Another noteworthy element of the discussion concerning the definition of the term 'agreement' for purposes of Article 31(3)(b) VCLT is whether the mutual consent as described above as a necessary prerequisite of an agreement has to establish a binding normative command for both parties. Nolte, for example, argues that any identifiable agreement between the parties would be sufficient to be regarded as an agreement within the meaning of Article 31(3)(a) VCLT irrespective of whether it is

11. Dörr, *supra* n. 4, Art. 31, mn 66.
12. *Methanex v. United States*, Final Award, Part II, Chapter B, para. 20 (NAFTA Chapter 11/UNCITRAL Arb. Trib. 3 August 2005).
13. Georg Nolte, *'Second Report on Subsequent Agreements and Subsequent Practice in Relation to Treaty Interpretation' (26 March 2014) UN Doc A/CN.4/671*, No. 58.
14. Georg Nolte, *Report 1. Jurisprudence of the International Court of Justice, in Treaties and Subsequent Practice* 191 (Georg Nolte ed., Oxford Univ. Press 1st ed., 1. impr. ed. 2013).
15. *Ibid.*
16. Nolte, *'Second Report on Subsequent Agreements and Subsequent Practice in Relation to Treaty Interpretation'*, *supra* n. 13, Nos 58 et seq.
17. *Kasikili/Sedudu Island* case (*Botswana v. Namibia*), I.C.J. Reports 1999, pp. 1089-1091, paras 65-68.
18. Nolte, *'Second Report on Subsequent Agreements and Subsequent Practice in Relation to Treaty Interpretation'*, *supra* n. 13, No. 58; however, *see* in more detail on silence as a possible element with respect to subsequent practice, *ibid.*, paras 59 et seq.

considered binding. In particular, it should not be required that it must be published or registered under Article 102[19] of the Charter of the United Nations.[20] The ILC in this regard states in its Report of the ILC in its 70th Session that a subsequent agreement shall only be taken into account when interpreting treaties. However, it must not necessarily be legally binding.[21] In particular, according to the ILC, an agreement within the meaning of Article 31(3)(a) VCLT requires 'a common understanding regarding the interpretation of a treaty which the parties are aware of an accept. Such agreement may, but need not, be legally binding for it to be taken into account'.[22] Thus, by contrast to other provisions of the VCLT, an agreement pursuant to Article 31(3)(a) VCLT does not need to be legally binding from an international law perspective.[23]

In contrast, Linderfalk argues that an agreement should be understood as an act performed with the purpose of establishing a legal relationship entailing rights and obligations. Therefore, gentlemen's agreements or non-binding agreements should not be considered an agreement for the purposes of Article 31(3)(a) VCLT. Rather, the respective states must have the intention of creating law and a legally binding agreement governed by international law when establishing a subsequent agreement.[24]

Notably, it may happen that even states hold different opinions on whether an agreement concluded between them can be considered a subsequent agreement from a public international law perspective. For example, the 'Calendar of Operation' (it would currently be known as a 'road map') to the Gruber-de Gasperi Agreement (Paris Agreement) was agreed in light of the attack in South Tyrol in the 1960s between Italy and Austria after the General Assembly of the United Nations (UN) requested both states to negotiate in order to settle the dispute.[25] Austria stated that the 'Calendar of Operation' constituted an agreement and can thus be regarded as a subsequent agreement to the Paris Agreement.[26] Italy, however, took the opposite view that it was

19. Article 102(1) of the Charter of the United Nations reads as follows: 'Every treaty and every international agreement entered into by and Member of the United Nations after the present Charter comes into force shall as soon as possible be registered with the Secretariat and published by it.'
20. Nolte, *'Second Report on Subsequent Agreements and Subsequent Practice in Relation to Treaty Interpretation'*, *supra* n. 13, No. 54.
21. *International Law Commission 'Report of the International Law Commission in Its 70th Session' (30 April-1 June and 2 July-10 August 2018) UN Doc A/73/10, supra* n. 10, at 29.
22. *International Law Commission 'Report of the International Law Commission in Its 73rd Session' (18 April-3 June and 4 July-5 August 2022) UN Doc A/77/10* 353; *International Law Commission 'Report of the International Law Commission in Its 70th Session' (30 April-1 June and 2 July-10 August 2018) UN Doc A/73/10, supra* n. 10, at 75.
23. *See* again *International Law Commission 'Report of the International Law Commission in Its 73rd Session' (18 April-3 June and 4 July-5 August 2022) UN Doc A/77/10, supra* n. 22, at 353; however. kindly note that other provisions that use the term 'agreement' require a legally binding instrument.
24. Linderfalk, *On the Interpretation of Treaties: The Modern International Law as Expressed in the 1969 Vienna Convention on the Law of Treaties, supra* n. 7, at 162.
25. *See* thereto Gerhard Hafner, *Subsequent Agreements and Practice: Between Interpretation, Informal Modification, and Formal Amendment, in Treaties and subsequent practice* 110 (Georg Nolte ed., Oxford Univ. Press 1st ed., 1. impr. ed. 2013).
26. *See* thereto Federal Ministry Republic of Austria European and International Affairs: Austria's Neighbours (18 April 2024), https://www.bmeia.gv.at/en/european-foreign-policy/foreign-policy/europe/austrias-neighbours.

not and hence dismissed Austria's position according to which it has to be considered a binding agreement.[27]

Upon closer examination, the above-described discourse appears rather futile. The VCLT's reference to subsequent agreements is meant to ensure the uniform interpretation of a treaty. The term 'agreement' as used in Article 31(3)(a) VCLT indicates that parties have achieved consensus on the interpretation of an existing treaty.[28] At the same time, the mere idea of a subsequent agreement already assumes the existence of a binding obligation (i.e., a treaty) previously concluded between the same parties.[29] In this context, it is clear that only those agreements that are meant by both parties to be binding upon them can be a meaningful factor in the interpretation process. It hence appears reasonable, taking into account the object and purpose of Article 31(3)(a) VCLT, to apply a rather low threshold when identifying agreements as 'subsequent agreements' in the sense of the VCLT. This is because, in any case, only those agreements will be able to inform the interpretation process in a meaningful manner that have the clear intention to bind the parties to the agreement.

Finally, if adhering to a broad understanding of the term 'agreement', the question could be raised as to whether treaties themselves can also be qualified as agreements for the purposes of Article 31(3)(a) VCLT. The answer should clearly be positive. The decisive question then becomes whether the later treaty was meant as a means to settle open questions regarding the interpretation of the previous one or whether the later treaty modifies the previously concluded treaty and/or even leads to a norm conflict that would then have to be resolved by commonly accepted norm conflict resolution mechanisms such as, e.g., the *lex posterior* principle.[30] These two scenarios, however, must be clearly distinguished from each other. Only the former pertains to the question of interpretation by reference to a subsequent agreement.[31] The later treaty would merely supplement the earlier treaty in this case. Thus, both could exist alongside each other.[32]

2.1.3 'Between the Parties'

The respective agreement has to be reached 'between the parties' for it to qualify as a subsequent agreement in the sense of Article 31(3)(a) VCLT. The term 'party' is defined in Article 2(1)(g) VCLT which also applies to Article 31(3)(a) VCLT as follows: 'party means a State which has consented to be bound by the treaty and for which the treaty is in force'.[33] The decisive element is hence that the parties of the previously

27. Hafner, *supra* n. 25, at 110.
28. Berner, *supra* n. 6, at 104.
29. *Ibid.*
30. *Ibid.*, at 105.
31. *See*, in more detail, s. 2.2.2.
32. *Ibid.*; Georg Nolte, *Report 3. Subsequent Agreements and Subsequent Practice of States Outside of Judicial or Quasi-Judicial Proceedings, in Treaties and subsequent practice* 313 (Georg Nolte ed., Oxford Univ. Press 1st ed., 1. impr. ed. 2013).
33. Berner, *supra* n. 6, at 109.

concluded treaty also have to be a party to the subsequent agreement regarding its interpretation.[34]

In principle, the wording of Article 31(3)(a) VCLT only stipulates that a subsequent agreement must be reached 'between the parties'. In the case of a bilateral treaty, both treaty parties therefore have to be parties to the subsequent agreement. It can be disputed, however, whether all parties to a multilateral treaty also have to be a party to the subsequent agreement or whether it suffices that only some parties also enter into the subsequent agreement. According to the prevailing view, one that is concluded only between a subset of the parties to the initial treaty would not be sufficient to be qualified as a subsequent agreement in the context of Article 31(3)(a) VCLT,[35] though this position can be questioned. First, unlike the wording of Article 32(2) VCLT which requires an agreement to be concluded by 'all parties' to the treaty in order for the agreement to form part of the context, Article 31(3)(a) VCLT does not contain such wording. Although a non-uniform interpretation of a multilateral agreement would appear undesirable, Article 31(3)(a) VCLT does not necessarily rule out the possibility that some parties to a multilateral agreement agree on a specific interpretation with a subsequent agreement. This would, however, only bind its parties and would not alter the interpretation of the treaty in circumstances pertaining to states that have not entered into the agreement. Given the high relevance of the parties' intent in the interpretation process, circumstances may arise in which such an outcome would be indicated by a purposive interpretation under Article 31 VCLT. The majority view in literature, however, seems to dismiss this option. This does not render the subsequent agreement between some of the parties to the multilateral treaty completely irrelevant. Instead, such an agreement between a limited number of parties to a multilateral treaty regarding its interpretation or application can be seen as a supplementary means of interpretation under Article 32 VCLT.[36]

A separate but nevertheless highly relevant aspect that pertains to both the definition of the term 'agreement' and the party-related requirement is the question of state representation and the attribution of representative acts. Hence, the relevant question is: Which organs or actors can act on behalf of a state and thus conclude a subsequent agreement between the parties? After all, a state can only act through its organs or other actors that are attributable to it. Under public international law, no universally accepted solution has been found to demarcate acts of representation that can be attributed to a state from legally irrelevant acts. Although academia has produced several approaches (i.e., applying Article 7 or 8 VCLT or the 'Articles on State Responsibility'),[37] none so far have been able to obtain univocal support.

34. Linderfalk, *On the Interpretation of Treaties: The Modern International Law as Expressed in the 1969 Vienna Convention on the Law of Treaties*, *supra* n. 7, at 163.
35. Rahim Moloo, *When Actions Speak Louder Than Words: The Relevance of Subsequent Party Conduct to Treaty Interpretation*, Berkeley Journal of International Law 62 (2013); Linderfalk, *On the Interpretation of Treaties: The Modern International Law as Expressed in the 1969 Vienna Convention on the Law of Treaties*, *supra* n. 7, at 162; Villiger, *Commentary on the 1969 Vienna Convention on the Law of Treaties*, *supra* n. 6, Art. 31, mn 16; Dörr, *supra* n. 4, No. 66.
36. *See* thereto in more detail, Nolte, *'First Report on Subsequent Agreements and Subsequent Practice in Relation to Treaty Interpretation'*, *supra* n. 10, No. 82.
37. *See* in more detail, Berner, *supra* n. 6, at 109 et seq.

One common solution is to apply what is referred to as an internal approach under which every state would independently determine which of its representatives are attributable to it. Under it, a state's internal division of competences would determine the attribution issue under Article 31(3)(a) VCLT.[38] According to Nolte, 'this suggests that only such conduct which is undertaken or deemed to be accepted by those organs of a State party which are internationally regarded as being responsible for the application of the treaty (as a whole, or of a particular provision of a treaty) may be attributed to a State'. This would mean that acts establishing prima facie a subsequent agreement that however leads to a modification of a treaty as opposed to merely regarding its interpretation would not be attributable to a state if performed by organs that are not defined as competent to perform these acts from a domestic constitutional perspective. In contrast, regarding subsequent practice in the sense of Article 31(3)(b) VCLT, which, of course, must, be distinguished from subsequent agreements, Nolte, for example, emphasizes that also the conduct of lower and local authorities should be relevant when interpreting treaties if the higher authorities can be expected to be aware of the practice in question and to accept it as a form of treaty application or interpretation.[39] However, the ICJ indicates in its *Temple of Preah Vihear* case *(Cambodia v. Thailand)* that the mere knowledge of a minor official's conduct should not be sufficient to attribute their knowledge or conduct to the state.[40]

2.1.4 'Regarding the Interpretation of a Tax Treaty'

Even if concluded between the same parties, an agreement will only qualify as subsequent in the context of Article 31(3)(a) VCLT if its object and purpose are to address the interpretation or application of the provisions of the previously concluded treaty. Thus, subsequent agreements are only those 'regarding the interpretation of the treaty or the application of its provisions'. Hence, the purpose has to be to clarify the meaning of a treaty or the application of its provisions.[41]

Arguably, determining the interpretation of a treaty does not have to be the 'sole purpose' and can even be a 'side-effect' as long as the parties were at least aware that the subsequent agreement could have an effect on the interpretation or application of a treaty.[42] The ILC rightfully proceeds one step further and requires that the parties must 'intend, possible among other aims, to clarify the meaning of a treaty or how it is to be applied'.[43] Hence, according to the ILC, a party relying on a subsequent agreement shall provide evidence of the intention; this is the crucial element. It does

38. *Ibid.*
39. Nolte, *'First Report on Subsequent Agreements and Subsequent Practice in Relation to Treaty Interpretation'*, *supra* n. 10, No. 124.
40. *Temple of Preah Vihear* case (*Cambodia v. Thailand*), Merits, Judgment of 15 June 1962, I.C.J. Reports 1962, p. 23.
41. Linderfalk, *On the Interpretation of Treaties: The Modern International Law as Expressed in the 1969 Vienna Convention on the Law of Treaties*, *supra* n. 7, at 164.
42. Berner, *supra* n. 6, at 113 et seq.
43. *International Law Commission 'Report of the International Law Commission in Its 70th Session' (30 April-1 June and 2 July-10 August 2018) UN Doc A/73/10*, *supra* n. 10, at 30 et seq.

not suffice if an agreement contains a passage that could be used for interpreting or application purposes of the treaty if there is no indication whatsoever that clarifying the interpretation of the treaty term was at least deliberately accepted by the parties as a side-effect.[44] Such an indication could be seen in the circumstance that the subsequent agreement contains explicit references to the underlying treaty.[45] For instance, the ICJ decided that a subsequent agreement between the parties cannot be used for interpretation purposes of the previous treaty due to the absence of any reference to it.[46]

As described above, in order to qualify as a subsequent agreement for Article 31(3)(a) VCLT purposes, the agreement's object has to be to regulate the interpretation or the application of an existing treaty. While it appears rather clear what is meant by 'interpretation',[47] the meaning of the wording 'the application of its provisions' is less clear. The VCLT itself does not stipulate a definition for the term 'application'. Arguably there is no meaningful distinction to be made between interpretation and application for the purposes of Article 31(3)(a) VCLT. The ILC itself holds that there is, in principle, no distinct delineation between the two terms. While 'interpretation' refers to a mental process, the term 'application' focuses on an actual conduct (acts and omissions).[48] Linderfalk notes that a typical example of the latter's meaning is when agreements are made for implementing a treaty. Moreover, he emphasizes that there could be a potential overlap between the two terms when an agreement on the treaty's interpretation also includes terms on the application of its provisions or vice versa.[49]

The authors would contend that, within the legal subsumption process, every application first requires an interpretation. The then identified content of the treaty is applied to the facts which subsequently results in identifying the normative command established by the treaty. Hence, at least regarding those treaty rules establishing rights and obligations, any subsequent agreement on the interpretation automatically also entails an agreement on the treaty's application. Since Article 31(3)(a) VCLT covers both (i.e., the interpretation of the treaty and the application of its provisions), a strict distinction not only appears unnecessary but would arguably also be ultimately meaningless since any agreement on the application would also require one on the

44. Linderfalk, *On the Interpretation of Treaties: The Modern International Law as Expressed in the 1969 Vienna Convention on the Law of Treaties, supra* n. 7, at 164.
45. *International Law Commission 'Report of the International Law Commission in Its 70th Session' (30 April-1 June and 2 July-10 August 2018) UN Doc A/73/10, supra* n. 10, at 31.
46. Maritime Delimitation in the Area between Greenland and Jan Mayen, Judgment, I.C.J. Reports 1993, p. 38, at p. 51, para. 28.
47. Berner, *supra* n. 6, at 12 and 114; *International Law Commission 'Report of the International Law Commission in Its 66th Session' (5 May-7 June and 7 July-8 August 2014) UN Doc A/69/10* 26; Dörr, *supra* n. 4, No. 3.
48. *International Law Commission 'Report of the International Law Commission in Its 66th Session' (5 May-7 June and 7 July-8 August 2014) UN Doc A/69/10, supra* n. 47, at 171; *see* as well Berner, *supra* n. 6, at 115; *International Law Commission 'Report of the International Law Commission in Its 70th Session' (30 April-1 June and 2 July-10 August 2018) UN Doc A/73/10, supra* n. 10, at 43.
49. Linderfalk, *On the Interpretation of Treaties: The Modern International Law as Expressed in the 1969 Vienna Convention on the Law of Treaties, supra* n. 7, at 165.

interpretation.[50] The meaning and scope of Article 31(3)(a) VCLT hence arguably would not change if the term 'application' were omitted.

However, it should be noted that a subsequent agreement – according to some voices in literature – plausibly cannot be one 'regarding the interpretation or application' in the event that the respective parties consider the agreement in question to be of lower legal rank than the treaty itself.[51] This position claims to find its basis in the decision of the World Trade Organization (WTO) Panel in its *Chile – Price Band System and Safeguard Measures Relating to Certain Agricultural Products* case on the interpretation of the WTO Agreement on Agriculture. It was found that an Economic Complementarity Agreement between Chile and MERCOSUR could not be regarded as a subsequent agreement under Article 31(3)(a) VCLT due to the fact that the agreement's preamble stipulated that its provisions 'shall adjust' to the WTO Agreements.[52] This position, however, does not appear convincing. The question of whether an agreement qualifies as subsequent in the context of Article 31(3)(a) VCLT is not one of rank or legal pedigree. The term 'agreement' already suggests that also agreements that do not fulfil the formal requirements of a treaty may qualify as a subsequent agreement. If, in fact, also a subsequent agreement would have to have the same legal status as the agreement for which its interpretation is meant to determine the term 'agreement' would have to be read as 'treaty'. This is clearly not intended by the drafters of the VCLT. The decisive question is hence the parties' intent when concluding the subsequent agreement and not the legal pedigree. The WTO panel found the complementarity agreement between Chile and MERCOSUR as not qualifying as a subsequent agreement because the preamble indicated that the complementary agreement could not derogate the primary one but rather 'shall adjust' to it. This, however, should be read as a reference to the interpretative interrelation between the two instruments and not as an indication of legal rank. There was simply no indication that the complementary agreement was meant as a means to determine the interpretation of the previous agreement. Arguably, the key issue was therefore not the different rank but the purpose of the subsequent agreement as derived from its preamble.

2.1.5 'Subsequent'

As the wording of Article 31(3)(a) VCLT requires, the respective agreement must be made 'subsequently' (i.e., after the treaty's conclusion) for it to be encompassed within its scope. The VCLT itself does not provide any definition of this temporal aspect (i.e., the term 'subsequent').[53] However, as previously mentioned above (*see* section 2.1.2), Article 31(2)(a) VCLT refers to agreements that are established 'in connection with the conclusion of the treaty'. Thus, in order to define the term 'subsequent' according to

50. Berner, *supra* n. 6, at 116.
51. Dörr, *supra* n. 4, No. 73.
52. WTO Panel Chile–Price Band System WT/DS207/R, paras 7.83-7.84 (2002).
53. Berner, *supra* n. 6, at 119.

Article 31(3)(a) VCLT, it is helpful to consider Article 31(2)(a) VCLT.[54] Therefore, the time of the 'conclusion of the treaty' can be considered the relevant point in time that constitutes the benchmark against which any temporal posteriority has to be measured. Hence, by contrast to agreements within the meaning of Article 31(2)(a) VCLT, subsequent agreements are those that are established after the treaty's conclusion.[55] Similar to the term 'subsequent', the term 'conclusion of the treaty' is also not defined in the VCLT. According to Nolte, the 'conclusion of the treaty' is not necessarily the moment in which the treaty has entered into force.[56] Rather, according to Nolte and Linderfalk as well as the ILC, the 'conclusion of the treaty' could arguably be defined as the point in time when the interpreted treaty is established as definite.[57] The question of whether the treaty has been ratified or entered into force is not relevant when identifying whether an agreement is subsequent to a previously concluded treaty.

2.2 The Role of Subsequent Agreements Within the VCLT

2.2.1 The Role of Subsequent Agreements and Their Hierarchical Position Within Articles 31 and 33 VCLT

2.2.1.1 General Rule of Interpretation: Article 31(1) to Article 31(4) VCLT

The clause stipulating the relevance of subsequent agreements, Article 31(3) VCLT, forms part of the VCLT's 'general rule of interpretation'. Article 31 VCLT together with Article 32 VCLT that establish 'supplementary means of interpretation' and Article 33 VCLT concerning the 'interpretation of treaties authenticated in two or more languages' form the VCLT's section on treaty interpretation.[58] These articles are considered a codification of customary international law.[59] The customary character is generally accepted and widely shared by many international courts and routinely cited

54. To this end, it should be noted that also Art. 31(2)(b) uses the expression 'in connection with the conclusion of the treaty'.
55. Nolte, *'First Report on Subsequent Agreements and Subsequent Practice in Relation to Treaty Interpretation'*, *supra* n. 10, at 69; Berner, *supra* n. 6, at 119.
56. Nolte, *'First Report on Subsequent Agreements and Subsequent Practice in Relation to Treaty Interpretation'*, *supra* n. 10, at 69 et seq.
57. Linderfalk, *On the Interpretation of Treaties: The Modern International Law as Expressed in the 1969 Vienna Convention on the Law of Treaties*, *supra* n. 7, at 135 and 163; however, *see* other alternatives Berner, *supra* n. 6, at 120; Nolte, *'First Report on Subsequent Agreements and Subsequent Practice in Relation to Treaty Interpretation'*, *supra* n. 10, at 69 et seq.; *International Law Commission 'Report of the International Law Commission in Its 65th Session' (6 May-7 June and 8 July-9 August 2013) UN Doc A/68/10* 28.
58. Alain Pellet, *Canons of Interpretation under the Vienna Convention, in Between the lines of the Vienna Convention?: Canons and Other Principles of Interpretation in Public International Law* 5 (Joseph Klingler et al. eds, Wolters Kluwer 2019).
59. *See*, among others, *ibid.*; Villiger, *The 1969 Vienna Convention on the Law of Treaties: 40 Years after*, *supra* n. 4, at 132 et seq.; Dörr, *supra* n. 4, Nos 6 et seq.; Philip Baker, *Chapter 3: The Localization of Tax Treaty Interpretation, in Building Global International Tax Law: Essays in Honour of Guglielmo Maisto* 47 (Pasquale Pistone ed., IBFD 2022); Paula F. Henin, *In Pari*

by them.[60] Thus, the interpretation rules under the VCLT are viewed as applicable in all states irrespective of whether they have ratified the VCLT.[61] Those stipulated in Articles 31 to 33 VCLT can also be applied to treaties established prior to 1980 and thus before the VCLT entered into force.[62] However, it should also be remembered that the interpretation rules under the VCLT are default rules. Thus, parties are free to include clauses in the treaty on the interpretation that may differ from the rules under the VCLT.[63]

Article 31 VCLT consists of four paragraphs. Paragraph 1 lays down the common interpretation approach according to which the meaning of any treaty shall – in good faith – be determined 'in accordance with the ordinary meaning to be given to the terms of the treaty in their context and in the light of its object and purpose'. Article 31(2) VCLT then specifies the term context to include agreements concluded by 'all parties' to the treaty in connection with its conclusion (letter a) or instruments made by one or more parties in connection with its conclusion and accepted by the other party (letter b). Article 31(3) VCLT requires the interpreter to take into account – together with the context – subsequent agreements (letter a) and subsequent practice (letter b). Last, Article 31(4) VCLT demands that a special meaning shall be given to a term if it is established that the parties so intended.

Among these four paragraphs of Article 31 VCLT, no hierarchy is believed to exist,[64] and all are of equal value. Thus, no particular interpretation method laid down in Article 31 VCLT is understood to supersede the others. Rather, it should be considered in its entirety as one holistic general rule of interpretation comprising various methods that are required to be applied together in order to identify a treaty's meaning.[65] These considerations were confirmed by the ILC in 1966 when stating, 'the article [the general rule of interpretation], when read as a whole, cannot properly be regarded as laying down a legal hierarchy of norms for the interpretation of treaties'.[66] The European Convention on Human Rights (ECHR), for example, consistently applies all means of interpretation of Article 31 VCLT equally when interpreting a treaty.[67] The

Materia Interpretation in Treaty Law, in Between the lines of the Vienna Convention?: Canons and Other Principles of Interpretation in Public International Law 228 (Joseph Klingler et al. eds, Wolters Kluwer 2019).

60. *See*, for instance, ITLOS (Seabed Disputes Chamber) *Responsibilities and Obligations of States Sponsoring Persons and Entities with Respect to Activities in the Area*, 1 February 2011, para. 57; ECHR *Hirsi Jamaa et al v. Italy* (GC) App No. 27765/09, para. 170; Case C-63/09, *Walz*, 6.5.2010, ECLI:EU:C:2010:251, para. 23.
61. Pellet, *supra* n. 58, at 47.
62. Kirsten Schmalenbach, *Article 2 Use of Terms, Vienna Convention on the Law of Treaties: A commentary*, No. 7 (Oliver Dörr & Kirsten Schmalenbach eds, Springer 2d ed. 2018).
63. Steven R. Ratner, *International Rules on Treaty Interpretation*, The Law and Practice of the Northern Ireland Protocol 83 (Cambridge University Press 2022).
64. Villiger, *The 1969 Vienna Convention on the Law of Treaties: 40 Years after*, *supra* n. 4, at 128; Villiger, *Commentary on the 1969 Vienna Convention on the Law of Treaties*, *supra* n. 6, Art. 31, mn 29.
65. *International Law Commission 'Report of the International Law Commission in Its 70th Session' (30 April-1 June and 2 July-10 August 2018) UN Doc A/73/10*, *supra* n. 10, at 17.
66. *ILC Report 1966, International Law Commission 'YBILC 1966 II'* 219, paras 8 and 220, para. 9.
67. ECHR *Golder v. The United Kingdom* App No. 4451/70 para. 30: 'In the way in which it is presented in the "general rule" in Article 31 of the Vienna Convention, the process of

Swiss Federal Administrative Court has also, for instance, emphasized that Article 31(3) VCLT ranks equally with Article 31(2) VCLT,.[68]

Moreover, all interpretation methods established under Article 31 VCLT are of an obligatory character.[69] Hence, when interpreting a treaty, in principle, all means of interpretation as foreseen by Article 31 VCLT must be taken into account. Regarding Article 31(3) VCLT, this is evidenced, for example, by the clause's wording which requires that - together with the context - the therein stated additional means of interpretation '*shall be*' taken into account. If a subsequent agreement fulfilling the criteria of Article 31(3)(a) exists, it thus must be considered. Of course, this does not mean that arguments based on other interpretation methods foreseen by Article 31 cannot outweigh the subsequent agreement, but this finding has to be a result of a careful weighing process taking into account all relevant factors.

Despite their theoretical equality, the thought process encapsulated in Article 31, paragraphs 1 to 4 requires some sort of order. In literature, this process mandated by Article 31 VCLT has been described as following a '*logical*' approach, operating 'from the intrinsic to the extrinsic and from the immediate to the remote'.[70] The commencement of the interpretation process is hence the bare meaning of the text in light of its context as well as object and purpose. The term 'text' in this context includes, for instance, all protocols, annexes, appendices, and footnotes.[71] According to literature[72] and the ILC,[73] it is evident that Article 31(1) VCLT (i.e., the ordinary meaning, object, and purpose) should be the first means applied when interpreting treaties. Subsequently, the conventional view suggests that the instruments comprising the context as defined in Article 31(2) VCLT (e.g., exchange of notes between the parties) should be considered because they are intimately related to the text.[74] Subsequent agreements, subsequent practice, and any relevant rules (i.e., Art 31(3)(c) VCLT) would then follow as a third step within the interpretation process.[75] According to the ILC, subsequent agreements and subsequent practice are 'extrinsic' to the text compared to the ordinary meaning and the context. Article 31(4) VCLT finally stipulates that 'a special meaning shall be given to a term if it is established that the parties so intended'. Thus, Article

interpretation of a treaty is a unity, a single combined operation; this rule, closely integrated, places on the same footing the various elements enumerated in the four paragraphs of the Article.'

68. BVGer, 21.1.2010, BVGE 2010/7 para. 3.5.4.
69. Villiger, *The 1969 Vienna Convention on the Law of Treaties: 40 Years after*, *supra* n. 4, at 129; *ILC Report 1966, International Law Commission 'YBILC 1966 II'*, *supra* n. 66, at 220, para. 9; Moloo, *supra* n. 35, at 44.
70. Villiger, *Commentary on the 1969 Vienna Convention on the Law of Treaties*, *supra* n. 6, Art. 31, mn 31.
71. Ratner, *supra* n. 63, at 84.
72. Villiger, *The 1969 Vienna Convention on the Law of Treaties: 40 Years after*, *supra* n. 4, at 129; Villiger, *Commentary on the 1969 Vienna Convention on the Law of Treaties*, *supra* n. 6, Art. 31, mn 30.
73. *ILC Report 1966, International Law Commission 'YBILC 1966 II'*, *supra* n. 66, at 220, para. 9.
74. *Ibid.*, at 220, para. 9.
75. Moloo, *supra* n. 35, at 44.

31(4) VCLT applies if the parties have agreed to replace the ordinary meaning of a term with a special meaning.[76]

The distinction made by the ILC between interpretation methods within Article 31 VCLT as being either 'intrinsic' or 'extrinsic' to the text, however, does not appear overly meaningful. It seems to emphasize the relevance of the wording (ordinary meaning) instead of the object and purpose. The wording cannot, however, be considered in isolation from its object and purpose. It lies in the nature of language to be imprecise. Hence any treaty term only obtains meaning when it is understood in its context and in light of its object and purpose. Article 31(1) VCLT already indicates the necessity to interpret the wording in light of the context and object/purpose. While paragraph 2 specifies the meaning of the term context, paragraph 3, letter a (regarding letter b, please *see* below) arguably refers to the object and purpose. After all, any subsequent agreement regarding the interpretation must be taken into account together with the context. Article 31(3)(a) VCLT demanding subsequent agreements to be considered 'together with the context' establishes a means to identify the object and purpose of a certain term used by the parties. Hence, the subsequent agreement does not constitute part of the context but – so the authors argue – allows the interpreter to identify the object and purpose. If the parties to a treaty enter into a subsequent agreement concerning the interpretation of that treaty, the meaning thus defined carries interpretative weight because the parties so intended. Thus, if all requirements for a subsequent agreement for Article 31(3)(a) VCLT purposes are met (*see* section 2.1 above), the meaning attributed to a certain term by the parties in it arguably carries a strong weight in the interpretation process. Hence, while the wording may be the starting point of the interpretation process under Article 31(1) VCLT, the context, object, and purpose ultimately determine the process's result. Subsequent agreements obtain their relevance from the fact that they document – even if at a later point in time – the parties' intent for the interpretation of a previously concluded treaty.

2.2.1.2 The Temporal Element of Subsequent Agreements

Arguably, the key element providing interpretative 'weight' to subsequent agreements is their nature as an expression of the parties' intent. However, as the wording already indicates, such agreements regarding the interpretation are 'subsequent', i.e., reached after the treaty's conclusion. The pressing question is hence how a later expressed intention of the treaty can and shall influence the interpretation as opposed to leading to modifying the treaty. After all, according to the ICJ, the terms used in a treaty should be, in principle, interpreted within the meaning which is, by definition, contemporaneous with the treaty's conclusion. Subsequent practice could thus lead to a departure from the original intent based on the meaning at the treaty's conclusion.[77] Such considerations would also apply to subsequent agreements.

76. Dörr, *supra* n. 4, Nos 109 et seq.
77. Case concerning Dispute regarding Navigational and Related Rights (*Costa Rica v. Nicaragua*) Judgment of 13 July 2009, I.C.J. Reports 2009, p. 213 paras 63 et seq.

The ILC itself acknowledges that subsequent agreements 'can support both a contemporaneous and an evolutive interpretation (or, as it is often called, evolutionary interpretation), where appropriate'.[78] From a public international law perspective, it thus has to be, in principle, maintained that the meaning of the respective treaty at the time of the conclusion is decisive.[79] A dynamic approach (i.e., establishing the meaning of a treaty at the time of its interpretation) is acknowledged by public international law only under certain limited conditions, specifically when interpreting generic terms (i.e., if the parties already expect that specific treaty terms could change through time, and they therefore presumably intended to apply the meaning at the time of the interpretation).[80] This is also stressed by the Swiss Federal Court which recently held that a dynamic interpretation of certain generic terms may be acceptable if intended by the parties upon the treaty's conclusion.[81] Hence, again, the parties' intent at the point in time of concluding the treaty is seen as decisive for the permissibility of a dynamic interpretation.

Subsequent agreements, however, are not per se dynamic because they are established after the treaty's conclusion. Rather, they can also be used for applying the static approach (i.e., instituting the meaning of a treaty provision within the object and purpose established at the time of the conclusion).[82] When assessing the relevance of subsequent agreements for the interpretation process, hence, three different scenarios have to be distinguished. First, the interpretative relevance of subsequent agreements will be particularly high if it is a reflection of the initial intent according to the parties, i.e., the intention at the time of the treaty's conclusion. A subsequent agreement that is concluded just a few years after the conclusion of the underlying treaty thus arguably appears more entitled to claim to reflect the original intention of the negotiators at the time of the conclusion than one established many decades after it. However, also a subsequent agreement reached at a vast temporal distance from the treaty's conclusion may be relevant if it establishes a result that is still within the boundaries reached by applying Article 31(1) and 31(2) VCLT and hence a choice is merely made between a variety of different feasible interpretation results. Situations may arise at a later point in time for which no clear intention of the parties can be derived from the original context.[83] In this scenario in which various feasible interpretation results are available (similar to a *non-liquet* situation), the subsequent agreement can arguably be seen as decisive.

---

78. *International Law Commission 'Report of the International Law Commission in Its 70th Session' (30 April-1 June and 2 July-10 August 2018) UN Doc A/73/10, supra* n. 10, at 65.
79. Dörr, *supra* n. 4, No. 22.
80. *Ibid.*, No. 24.; Swiss tribunal federal (Schweizer Bundesgericht) 23.6.2023, 9C-682/2022, para. 9.4.3.
81. Swiss Tribunal Federal Court (Schweizer Bundesgericht) 23.6.2023, 9C-682/2022, paras 9.4.3 et seq. with further domestic and international references.
82. Dörr, *supra* n. 4, No. 27.
83. However, according to Nolte, 'after the Second World War a development set in which moved the emphasis away from the search, in the subsequent conduct, for the original intention of the parties towards determining the meaning of the treaty as it is reflected in the current understanding of the parties' (Nolte, *Report 1. Jurisprudence of the International Court of Justice, in Treaties and subsequent practice, supra* n. 14, at 177).

Of course, in any case, the distinction between a mere interpretation of the treaty and a later modification that exceeds the parameters of the initial content of the treaty must be made. If the subsequent agreement reflects an intention that goes beyond the result reached under applying Article 31(1) and 31(2) VCLT to the previous treaty, the subsequent agreement plausibly leads to a modification and can no longer be considered an interpretation tool (*see* thereto in more detail section 2.2.2). Hence, a later formulated intention of the parties reflected in a subsequent agreement will only become a relevant means of interpretation if it can be established that it still operates within the boundaries set by applying Article 31(1) and (2) VCLT.

In addition, another temporal element arises. The question could be raised as to whether parties can establish subsequent agreements within the meaning of Article 31(3)(a) VCLT that have retroactive effect, i.e., inform the interpretation process even for times that are already past. From a public international law perspective, there should, in principle, be no obstacle to this as long as the limits stipulated by the meaning at the time of the treaty's conclusion are not exceeded (*see* above). From a practical perspective, subsequent agreements will often – within the limits set by domestic constitutional law – have a certain retroactive effect insofar as they will be considered for those periods that are still amenable to an assessment from a domestic procedural perspective.

2.2.1.3 *The Relationship Between Subsequent Agreements and Subsequent Practice in the Sense of Article 31(3)(b) VCLT*

The just-described role of subsequent agreements for Article 31(3)(a) VCLT purposes and the reason for its interpretative relevance requires a distinction to be made within Article 31(3) VCLT.[84] In principle, both letter a (subsequent agreements) and letter b (subsequent practice) are perceived as equally relevant elements of the interpretation process.[85] In academic writing, both are also usually addressed together.[86] Initially, this grouping together of letters a and b seems sensible given that both are characterized by the fact that the relevant process informing the interpretation, i.e., either the conclusion of an agreement or the practice is subsequent, i.e., takes place after the treaty's conclusion (*see* thereto section 2.1.5).[87] Furthermore, both require some form of agreement either 'between the parties regarding the interpretation' (i.e., subsequent agreements) or inferred from a subsequent practice establishing the agreement 'of the parties' (i.e., subsequent practice) relating to the interpretation or application of a treaty. The key difference is that letter b requires a state practice that indicates the

84. Article 31(3)(b) VCLT reads as follows: 'There shall be taken into account, together with the context: any subsequent practice in the application of the treaty which establishes the agreement of the parties regarding its interpretation.'
85. *See* Villiger, *The 1969 Vienna Convention on the Law of Treaties: 40 Years after*, *supra* n. 4, at 128 et seq.
86. For instance, several articles and contributions mention both interpretation principles as subsequent conduct; e.g., Moloo, *supra* n. 35.
87. Berner, *supra* n. 6, at 100.

parties' agreement while letter a directly demands an explicit agreement regarding the interpretation to have been established and not an inference from a practice.[88]

The term 'agreement' within the meaning of Article 31(3)(b) VCLT presupposes, according to academia, the knowledge or awareness of other parties of a certain practice. Thus, it is decisive that one party under a treaty acts based on the belief of a certain meaning of a treaty term and the other party is (or parties are) aware of this assumed underlying understanding and accepts it as what the treaty stipulated.[89] Hence, the agreement has to be inferred from the practice of the two parties. This process, however, is necessarily highly subjective. It can be argued that it is sufficient that both parties to the treaty reach the same understanding individually and thus act accordingly in parallel subsequently without joint conduct being established.[90] The ILC report states thereto that 'subsequent practice at the international level need not necessarily be joint conduct'.

Regarding the term 'practice', in principle, any action or inaction carried out by a party of the treaty can be sufficient to establish a practice for the purposes of Article 31(3)(b) VCLT.[91] However, it must be a sequence of facts or acts and not only one isolated incident.[92]

Thus, the distinction between subsequent agreements in the sense of letter a and subsequent practice for letter b lies in the agreement itself or the way in which the agreement is to be established. While the agreement in the sense of letter a regarding the interpretation or application of a treaty is explicitly established, an agreement within the meaning of Article 31(3)(b) VCLT is inferred from a specific consistently applied practice.[93] The ILC states in this regard:

> Subsequent agreements and subsequent practice under article 31, paragraph 3, are hence distinguished based on whether an agreement of the parties can be identified as such, in a common act or undertaking, or whether it is necessary to identify an agreement through separate acts that in combination demonstrate a common position. A 'subsequent agreement' under article 31, paragraph 3 (a), must therefore be 'reached' and presupposes a deliberate common act or undertaking by the parties, even if it consists of individual acts by which they manifest their common understanding regarding the interpretation of the treaty or the application of its provisions.[94]

At times – so at least some international legal scholars argue – it may be difficult to differentiate between subsequent agreements and subsequent practice.[95] The less

88. *Ibid.*; Villiger, *The 1969 Vienna Convention on the Law of Treaties: 40 Years after*, *supra* n. 4, at 122.
89. Dörr, *supra* n. 4, No. 89.
90. *International Law Commission 'Report of the International Law Commission in Its 70th Session' (30 April-1 June and 2 July-10 August 2018) UN Doc A/73/10*, *supra* n. 10, at 50.
91. Dörr, *supra* n. 4, No. 79.
92. Ian Sinclair, *The Vienna Convention on the Law of Treaties* 137 (Manchester Univ. Press 2., rev.enl. ed. 1984).
93. Berner, *supra* n. 6, at 101.
94. *International Law Commission 'Report of the International Law Commission in Its 70th Session' (30 April-1 June and 2 July-10 August 2018) UN Doc A/73/10*, *supra* n. 10, at 30.
95. *Ibid.*; Agrawal, *supra* n. 7, at 316.

formal the subsequent agreement is, the greater the significance of subsequent practice allegedly is.[96] However, in the authors' opinion, this is a factual/practical issue. If no written agreement exists, the only way to prove its existence may be the inference from actual practice. The distinction between subsequent agreement and subsequent practice, however, in the authors' view, is nevertheless meaningful and should be upheld.

That the identification of an agreement may be difficult if not established in written form and that the interpreter takes recourse to subsequent practice thus coming to subsequent agreement and practice are also identifiable in the ICJ's jurisprudence. In the case *Pulp Mills on the River Uruguay (Argentina v. Uruguay)*, an explicit subsequent verbal agreement between the parties to a treaty was qualified as subsequent practice.[97] This does not change the fact that the agreement fulfils the requirements of Article 31(3)(a) VCLT, however, and should be treated accordingly. Although, in principle, the interpretation methods foreseen by Article 31 VCLT are of equal rank, differences in the persuasiveness of the results reached by means of a certain interpretative method can nevertheless be identified. The arguments derivable from an explicit, ideally written mutual agreement on the interpretation of a previously concluded treaty fulfilling the requirements of Article 31(3)(a) VCLT can be seen as carrying a higher weight than one only inferred from actual practice. After all, such a practice - disregarding all domestic constitutional issues accorded to taking recourse to the practice of the executive branch - may be based on a mere misunderstanding or error or may simply be the result of a pure chance not representing a deliberate choice.

Moreover, acts by state representatives who are also, from a domestic perspective, competent to represent the state internationally at least at the level of international administrative agreements arguably carry a higher argumentative weight than the mere practice of executive organs (e.g., regional tax offices) that are usually not competent to bind the state internationally. Hence, an explicit agreement reached at that level that was already involved in the initial treaty negotiation and which, for example, is mandated in the treaty itself to resolve interpretation conflicts may be seen as carrying a much higher argumentative weight in the interpretation process. In a similar manner, the authors argue that, for example, the practice established by domestic authorities who are competent to represent the state internationally but not to enforce the relevant rules cannot establish subsequent practice in the sense of Article 31(3)(b) VCLT.[98]

The above considerations on the different degrees of persuasiveness arguably accorded to subsequent agreements as opposed to subsequent practice is also emphasized by the position taken by the Swiss Federal Administrative Court which qualifies subsequent practice as a mere supplementary means of interpretation.[99] If subsequent conduct hence is not within the scope of Article 31(3)(a) VCLT because an agreement

96. *See*, for instance, Moloo, *supra* n. 35, at 57 et seq.
97. *Pulp Mills on the River Uruguay (Argentina v. Uruguay)*, Provisional Measures, Order of 13 July 2006, I.C.J. Reports 2006, p. 113, at pp. 127-128, para. 53.
98. Michael Lang, *Art. 3 Abs. 2 OECD-MA Und Die Auslegung von Doppelbesteuerungsabkommen Auslegungsgrundsätze Für DBA*, IWB 284 (2011).
99. BVGer, 21.1.2010, BVGE 2010/7, para. 3.5.4.

was not established in an identifiable way, it could nevertheless be encompassed by Article 32 VCLT.[100]

2.2.1.4 The Interrelation Between Article 31(3) and Article 32 VCLT

The interpretation methods under Article 31 VCLT are, in principle, all considered to be of equal rank. However, the above considerations already indicated that particularly subsequent practice may be perceived rather as a supplementary means of interpretation as foreseen by Article 32 VCLT[101] given their limited persuasiveness in proving the parties' intention and thus the object and purpose of a certain treaty clause. The relationship between Articles 31 VCLT and 32 VCLT on the supplementary means of interpretation is characterized by the subordination of the former under the latter.

In contrast to Article 31 VCLT (e.g., 'shall be interpreted', 'shall comprise', 'shall be taken into account'), Article 32 VCLT merely stipulates an option. Hence, recourse may be taken to supplementary means of interpretation 'in order to confirm the meaning resulting from the application of Art 31, or to determine the meaning when the interpretation according to Art 31(a) leaves the meaning ambiguous or obscure, or leads to a result which is manifestly absurd or unreasonable'. Stated otherwise, Article 32 VCLT has two areas of application. First, it should be used at a second stage within the interpretation process as further evidence when the primary means already provided by Article 31 VCLT have clarified the correct meaning of a treaty provision and have produced a reasonable/valid result. In such a situation, Article 32 VCLT can be used to confirm the meaning resulting from applying Article 31 VCLT.[102] Second, Article 32 VCLT can be used when the correct meaning of the treaty's content cannot be sufficiently clarified by using the interpretation methods foreseen by Article 31 VCLT.[103] Hence, only in the latter case may Article 32 VCLT take precedence over Article 31 VCLT insofar as it may offer the decisive arguments in favour of one of the potential interpretation results.[104] Otherwise, Article 31 VCLT has priority over Article 32 VCLT if the interpretation rules under Article 31 VCLT neither leave the meaning of

100. Moloo, *supra* n. 35, at 76; Georg Ress, *Die Bedeutung der nachfolgenden Praxis für die Vertragsinterpretation nach der Wiener Vertragsrechtskonvention (WVRK), in Die Dynamik des Europäischen Gemeinschaftsrechts: die Auslegung des Europäischen Gemeinschaftsrechts im Lichte nachfolgender Praxis der Mitgliedstaaten und der EG-Organe = The Dynamics of EC-Law* 60 (Roland Bieber & Georg Ress eds, Nomos-Verl.-Ges. 1. Aufl. ed. 1987).
101. *See* in more detail on Art. 32 VCLT Chapter 8 'Supplementary Means of Interpretation and Tax Treaty Interpretation' of Gustavo Weiss de Resende.
102. Villiger, *The 1969 Vienna Convention on the Law of Treaties: 40 Years after, supra* n. 4, at 127; Ulf Linderfalk, *Is the Hierarchical Structure of Articles 31 and 32 of the Vienna Convention Real or Not? Interpreting the Rules of Interpretation*, Netherlands International Law Review 136 (2007) https://doi.org/10.1017/s0165070x07001337.
103. Linderfalk, *supra* n. 102, at 136; Villiger, *The 1969 Vienna Convention on the Law of Treaties: 40 Years after, supra* n. 4, at 127.
104. Ulf Linderfalk, *Is Treaty Interpretation an Art or a Science? International Law and Rational Decision Making*, The European Journal of International Law 184 (Oxford University Press 2015) https://doi.org/10.1093/ejil/chv008.

the treaty ambiguous or obscure nor lead to a result that is manifestly absurd or unreasonable.[105]

Thus, from a theoretical perspective, subsequent agreements as a component of the interpretation mean Article 31 VCLT ranks equally with the interpretation principles under Article 31(1), (2), and (4) VCLT. Further, when subsequent agreements lead to a result that is neither ambiguous nor obscure nor manifestly absurd or unreasonable, they should have priority over supplementary means of interpretation in the sense of Article 32 VCLT. As shown above, other subsequent conduct that does not fulfil the criteria of Article 31(3)(a) VCLT may nevertheless be considered relevant under Article 32 VCLT, e.g., in order to confirm an interpretation result reached by applying Article 31.[106]

2.2.2 *The Distinction Between Interpretation and Modification*

As stated above, every treaty needs to be interpreted even if its scope and meaning seem to be evident and clear. Accordingly, even assuming that this presupposes an interpretation process.[107] Since Article 31(3)(a) VCLT only covers agreements regarding the interpretation of a treaty or the application of its provisions, it is decisive to distinguish between agreements regarding the interpretation (and application) and agreements leading to a modification of a treaty. For the sake of completeness, it should be noted that parties to a treaty can also modify the treaty themselves by reaching another agreement.[108] However, in such a case, the requirements of Article 39 VCLT (general rule regarding amending treaties) and Article 40 VCLT (amending multilateral treaties) must be fulfilled.[109] Hence, the VCLT therefore distinguishes between the mere interpretation of a treaty and changes (amendment and modification)[110] to it.[111] Thus, there are sound reasons that agreements that modify the underlying treaty should not be taken into account when applying Article 31 VCLT for interpretation purposes.[112]

---

105. *Ibid.*
106. Berner, *supra* n. 6, at 150.
107. Dörr, *supra* n. 4, Chapter 14.
108. Sean D. Murphy, *The Relevance of Subsequent Agreement and Subsequent Practice for the Interpretation of Treaties, in Treaties and subsequent practice* 88 (Georg Nolte ed., Oxford Univ. Press 1st ed., 1. impr. ed. 2013).
109. *See* in more detail, Moloo, *supra* n. 35, at 81.
110. For the sake of completeness, it should be noted that modification is an agreement to change the terms of the treaty only between some of the parties. By contrast, amending a treaty is an agreement between all parties involved to the treaty to change the terms of the underlying treaty. However, this distinction is only relevant for multilateral treaties since, for bilateral treaties, any agreement to the change of the treaty terms shall involve all parties; *see* thereto *ibid.*, at 55, n. 70.
111. *International Law Commission 'Report of the International Law Commission in Its 70th Session' (30 April-1 June and 2 July-10 August 2018) UN Doc A/73/10, supra* n. 10, at 58; Berner, *supra* n. 6, at 117.
112. Berner, *supra* n. 6, at 116; however, Dörr states a different view. According to him, the parties are the masters of their treaty. Therefore, they should be not limited to establishing subsequent understandings or agreements. 'If the latter's content would not come within the bounds of an

The distinction between agreements within the meaning of Article 31(3)(a) VCLT and those under Articles 39 et seq. VCLT is a complex issue since it itself entails resolving difficult preliminary questions. In order to delineate interpretation from modification (or amendment), it is to be examined whether the subsequent agreement is targeted at specifying the interpretation of a certain treaty term while maintaining the ordinary meaning of the text, read in good faith, and remaining within the boundaries set by the context and the object and purpose.[113] Hence, a subsequent agreement can only be qualified as interpreting a previously concluded treaty if the result foreseen by it remains within the limits established by applying Article 31(1) and (2) VCLT.

A change in a treaty (i.e., modification or amendment) deliberately aims to transform rights and obligations and generally has no limits.[114] Moreover, modifying a treaty through an agreement must be established on the same legal level as the treaty or as agreed in it.[115] Hence, also from a formal perspective, differences may exist between agreements regarding the interpretation and a change of a treaty.

The first step in making the distinction between an agreement meant to clarify the interpretation of a treaty and an amendment of an existing treaty is to identify the intent of the parties. Only if it can be established that they intended to agree on the interpretation of a previously concluded treaty does Article 31(3)(a) VCLT become a factor. However, it may nevertheless happen that a subsequent agreement that purports to merely interpret a treaty results in a change in it.[116] Hence, it still has to be identified whether the meaning of a treaty term as specified in a subsequent agreement may still be considered falling within the interpretive boundaries set by applying Article 31, paragraphs 1 and 2 VCLT or whether the subsequent agreement essentially modifies the treaty. This may not always lead to clear results. The ILC in this regard seems to take a rather extensive approach granting states broad discretion:

> States and international courts are generally prepared to accord parties a rather wide scope for the interpretation of a treaty by way of a subsequent agreement. This scope may even go beyond the ordinary meaning of the terms of the treaty. The recognition of this scope for the interpretation of a treaty goes hand in hand with the reluctance by States and courts to recognize that an agreement relating to the application of a treaty actually has the effect of amending or modifying the treaty. An agreement to modify a treaty is thus not only excluded but also not to be presumed.[117]

Some authors go as far as to argue that drawing the line between interpretation or changes in a treaty is practically irrelevant. Berner, for example, argues:

ordinary meaning of the terms, they would amount to an amendment of the treaty by implicit agreement'; *see* Dörr, *supra* n. 4, Art. 31, para. 74.

113. Moloo, *supra* n. 35, at 83; Ress, *supra* n. 100, at 62.
114. Ress, *supra* n. 100, at 62.
115. *International Law Commission 'Report of the International Law Commission in Its 70th Session' (30 April-1 June and 2 July-10 August 2018) UN Doc A/73/10, supra* n. 10, at 59; *See* thereto Art. 39 VCLT; and, among others, Hafner, *supra* n. 25, at 115.
116. Moloo, *supra* n. 35, at 80.
117. *International Law Commission 'Report of the International Law Commission in Its 70th Session' (30 April-1 June and 2 July-10 August 2018) UN Doc A/73/10, supra* n. 10, at 59.

> Either, one could first take account of an agreement regarding the modification of the treaty in order to identify the treaty to be interpreted and then interpret the treaty. Or one could start with the original treaty and take account of the agreement regarding the modification of the treaty when interpreting the original treaty.[118]

While the above-quoted statement by the ILC according to which a subsequent agreement in the sense of Article 31(3)(a) VCLT may go beyond the mere wording appears to be a fair assessment. This is because the wording is only one element foreseen by Article 31(1) and (2) VCLT and hence forms only part of the interpretation process establishing the limits for the interpretative relevance of subsequent agreements, the assumed extensive leeway for states to amend treaties by means of subsequent agreements appears questionable. It would appear unsatisfactory to disregard the difference between interpretation and modification given that the VCLT itself makes this distinction that, from a public international law perspective, remains meaningful. First, only those subsequent agreements that regard the interpretation - not the modification - of a treaty qualify as subsequent agreements in the sense of Article 31(3)(a) VCLT and hence have to be taken into account in the interpretation process. Therefore, the demarcation line between interpretation and modification is decisive for assessing an agreement's relevance for interpretation purposes. While defining it will often be burdensome and may not always provide undisputed results, if the subsequent agreement leads to a norm conflict between the initial treaty and its content as foreseen by the subsequent agreement, i.e., that two irreconcilable normative commands applicable to the same facts are established, even the limits of an extensive view of the term 'interpretation' as opposed to modification are reached. The thus-created norm conflict must then be resolved by recourse to the commonly accepted methods for norm confliction resolution.

Second and just as importantly, the distinction between interpretation and modification will be decisive from a state's domestic perspective in many cases which subsequently arguably also has implications for international law. By relying on subsequent agreements to change a treaty, the executive branch of the state could potentially circumvent the restrictions of its competences, i.e., the limits set by the separation of powers. Such circumvention would occur if the constitution requires a treaty to obtain parliamentary approval in order to become binding law within that state's legal system.[119] Thus, some authors in academia argue that changing a treaty can only be made provided that the respective representative of the state in question has the competence to do so.[120] Of course, the legal pedigree and bindingness of an agreement under its internal (constitutional) law is initially irrelevant from a public

118. Berner, *supra* n. 6, at 117.
119. Berner, *supra* n. 6, at 118.
120. Michael Lang, *Doppelbesteuerungsabkommen und innerstaatliches Recht: die Einordnung von Doppelbesteuerungsabkommen in die österreichische Rechtsordnung* 89 (Wirtschaftsverl. Orac 1992); Michael Lang, *Die Besonderheiten der Auslegung des DBA Österreich-USA, in Das neue Doppelbesteuerungsabkommen Österreich-USA* 28 et seq. (Wolfgang Gassner et al. eds, 1997); Michael Thaler, *Enthält das Wiener Übereinkommen über das Recht der Verträge verfassungsändernde Bestimmungen?, in Staatsrecht in Theorie und Praxis: Festschrift Robert Walter zum 60. Geburtstag* 693 et seq. (Heinz Mayer ed., Manz 1991).

international law perspective.[121] Nevertheless, the domestic allocation of competences may be viewed as being relevant for identifying who may actually be considered expressing a state's intention from a public international law perspective. Hence, if adhering to the opinion that only the conduct of those state organs that are declared competent under that state's domestic law may represent a state internationally in a legally relevant manner, it could be argued that an agreement in the sense of Article 31(3)(a) VCLT may only be constituted if established by those organs of a state as foreseen by that state's constitution. Hence, the domestic attribution of competences would also obtain relevance for identifying whether an agreement between the states is at risk.

3 THE ROLE OF SUBSEQUENT AGREEMENTS IN TAX TREATY INTERPRETATION

3.1 General Remarks

Notably, DTCs are treaties under public international law.[122] Thus, courts and tax authorities regularly refer to the interpretation methods established by the VCLT when interpreting DTCs.[123] Hence, also Article 31(3)(a) VCLT becomes a factor when interpreting treaties concerning tax matters (e.g., DTCs, tax information exchange agreements, or multilateral treaties such as the MLI). The following subchapters apply the above theoretical public international law considerations to selected questions from the realm of tax treaty law and discuss whether: (i) the commentary to the Model Convention of the Organisation for Economic Co-operation and Development (OECD MC); (ii) the result of MAPs; or (iii) the MLI may be considered subsequent agreements within the meaning of Article 31(3)(a) VCLT.

3.2 The Commentary to the OECD MC as a Subsequent Agreement?

The exact role of the OECD commentary in tax treaty interpretation is an intensely debated topic and is regularly addressed by courts around the world.[124] Undoubtedly, the OECD commentary has a pivotal function in treaty interpretation, but its exact basis

121. *See* thereto Art. 27 VCLT 'A party may not invoke the provisions of its internal law as justification for its failure to perform a treaty. This rule is without prejudice to article 46'; *see also* Berner, *supra* n. 6, at 118.
122. Kristian Olenik, *Tax Treaties and the Recourse to Historical Interpretation under the Vienna Convention on the Law of Treaties, in History of Tax Treaties: the relevance of the OECD Documents for the Interpretation of Tax Treaties* 63 (Thomas Ecker et al. eds, Linde 2011).
123. *See* Lang, *Can Law Regulate Its Own Interpretation? Relevance of Articles 31-33 of the Vienna Convention on the Law of Treaties (VCLT) and Article 3 Para. 2 of the Model Convention of the Organisation for Economic Co-Operation and Development (OECD MC) for the Interpretation of Double-Taxation Conventions, in Research Handbook on International Taxation, supra* n. 3, at 176 et seq.; Michael Lang, *Einführung in das Recht der Doppelbesteuerungsabkommen* 43 (Linde 2., überarb. Aufl. ed. 2002).
124. *See*, among others, German Federal Fiscal Court (BFH) 25.5.2011, I R 95/10; 9.2.2011, I R 54, 55/10; 8.12.2010 I R 92/09.

within Articles 31 and 32 VCLT remains debated.[125] One particularly controversial issue is the relevance of subsequent OECD commentary versions for interpreting double tax treaties based on previous versions of the OECD MC.[126] This section hence addresses the question of whether a revised, i.e., later, version of the OECD commentary can be qualified as a subsequent agreement; this is a finding that would offer a sound legal basis for its relevance in the interpretation of previously concluded DTCs.[127]

The OECD consistently upholds the view that, when interpreting a double tax treaty, the latest available version of the commentary shall be considered:[128]

> Needless to say, amendments to the Articles of the Model Convention and changes to the Commentaries that are a direct result of these amendments are not relevant to the interpretation or application of previously concluded conventions where the provisions of those conventions are different in substance from the amended Articles. However, other changes or additions to the Commentaries are normally applicable to the interpretation and application of conventions concluded before their adoption, because they reflect the consensus of the OECD member countries as to the proper interpretation of existing provisions and their application to specific situations.[129]

It is hence argued in literature that the OECD MC itself – based on the above-cited wording of the commentary – demands a dynamic approach and thus the application of later commentary versions to previously concluded DTCs.[130] Thus, according to some authors, the subsequent OECD Commentary should be taken into consideration

125. Klaus Vogel, *The Influence of the OECD Commentaries on Treaty Interpretation*, Bulletin – Tax Treaty Monitor 613 et seq. (December 2000).
126. John F. Avery Jones, *The Effect of Changes in the OECD Commentaries after a Treaty is Concluded*, Bulletin for International Taxation 102 et seq. (2002); *§4 Struktur der Besteuerung nach den Doppelbesteuerungsabkommen (Rust), in Internationales Steuerrecht*, Nos 277 et seq. (Gerrit Frotscher & Alexander Rust eds, C.H. Beck 5., völlig überarbeitete Auflage ed. 2020); Steffen Lampert, *Die Dynamische Auslegung von Doppelbesteuerungsabkommen Unter Besonderer Beachtung Des Kommentars Zum OECD-Musterabkommen*, IStR 513 et seq. (2012); Maarten J. Ellis, *The Influence of the OECD Commentaries on Treaty Interpretation: Response to Prof. Dr Klaus Vogel*, Bulletin for International Taxation 617 et seq. (2000); Ulf Linderfalk & Maria Hilling, *The Use of OECD Commentaries as Interpretative Aids: The Static/Ambulatory–Approaches Debate Considered from the Perspective of International Law*, Nordic Tax Journal 34 (2015) https://doi.org/10.1515/ntaxj-2015-0003.
127. Doubtlessly, according to the prevailing opinion, the OECD commentary can be used as an interpretation tool to already existing DTCs; *see* thereto in more detail Michael Lang, *Seminar B, Teil 2: Das OECD-Musterabkommen – 2001 Und Darüber Hinaus: Welche Bedeutungen Haben Die Nach Abschluss Eines Doppelbesteuerungsabkommens Erfolgten Änderungen Des OECD-Kommentars?*, IStR 536 et seq. (2001); Vogel, *supra* n. 125, at 614; Michael Lang, *Wer Hat Das Sagen Im Steuerrecht?*, Österreichische Steuerzeitung 203 et seq. (2006).
128. Ellis, *supra* n. 126, at 618.
129. OECD, *Model Tax Convention on Income and Capital 2017* (Full Version) (2019), para. 35.
130. Helmut Loukota, *Verhandlungen des Dreizehnten Österreichischen Juristentages, in Verhandlungen des Dreizehnten Österreichischen Juristentages* 116 (13 Österreichischer Juristentag 1997, Salzburg Österreichischer Juristentag, 13, 1997 ed., Manz 1997); John F. Avery Jones & Johann Hattingh, *Treaty Interpretation: Global Tax Treaty Commentaries*, s. 3.12.1. (IBFD); Jacques Sasseville, *Temporal Aspects of Tax Treaties, in Tax polymath: A Life in international taxation – essays in honour of John F. Avery Jones* 44 et seq. (Philip Baker ed., IBFD 2010).

when applying a previously concluded DTC provided that the statements of the subsequent commentary are, in principle, covered by its wording.[131]

One potential legal basis for this position could be to qualify the OECD Commentary as a subsequent agreement in the sense of Article 31 (3) (a) VCLT, however, various arguments can be raised against doing so. First, it can be questioned whether the OECD Commentary qualifies as an agreement. After all, it is established by the OECD Council in its capacity as a body of an international organization and thus arguably already as a principle matter cannot be considered a subsequent agreement concluded between the parties within the meaning of Article 31 (3) (a) VCLT.[132] Instead, it would simply be an expression of the OECD's opinion with it acting on its own behalf as an international organization. Given the rather low threshold assumed in public international law literature for identifying an agreement in the context of Article 31(3)(a) VCLT, taking a more extensive view would, however, appear defensible. The key thus lies in the questions of whether: (i) this agreement is reached between the parties; and (ii) whether it actually concerns the interpretation of the respective tax treaty in question. Even if understanding the approval of a new commentary by the delegates of the OECD Member States as constituting an agreement in the sense of Article 31(3)(a) VCLT, it would not be 'between the parties' since the agreement is not strictly limited to the two treaty parties involved. This position has been taken by the German Federal Fiscal Court (German Bundesfinanzhof) in a recent decision that requires the agreement to be reached directly between the two treaty parties in order to qualify as a subsequent agreement. Accordingly, the OECD Commentary could not even be seen as an agreement between the parties even if both parties were also OECD members.[133] The German tax authorities had argued that OECD Member States that have not commented on an amendment of an OECD Commentary are deemed to have agreed to it. Hence, under consideration of the ILC 2018 report, according to the German tax authorities, the interpretation of a DTC should adhere to a dynamic approach.[134]

However, even when applying an extensive view and believing the mediation by the OECD to suffice for establishing an agreement between the parties, an agreement in the sense of Article 31(3)(a) VCLT can never be established when only one of the two parties to the treaty is represented in the OECD.[135] Hence, in such a situation, Article

131. Heinz Jirousek, *Critical Comments on the Interpretation of Tax Treaties*, SWI – Steuer- und Wirtschaft International 117 et seq. (1998); Lampert, *supra* n. 126, at 516 et seq. Notably, as a type of compromise, some scholars consider giving later OECD commentaries in the interpretation process at least the weight of regular literature (*see* thereto Avery Jones, *supra* n. 126, at 103); Brian J. Arnold, *Tax Treaties and Tax Avoidance: The 2003 Revisions to the Commentary to the OECD Model*, Bulletin for International Taxation 260 (2004).

132. *See* thereto in detail s. 2.1.3.

133. German Federal Fiscal Court (BFH) 5.12.2023, I R 42/20, para. 49.

134. German tax authorities statement of 19.4.2023 – IV B 2 – S 1301/22/10002:004, DOK 2022/1218103; *see also* thereto Udo Eversloh, *Bedeutung Des OECD-Musterkommentars Für Die Auslegung von Doppelbesteuerungsabkommen*, RdW – Österreichisches Recht der Wirtschaft 452 (2023).

135. Michael Lang, *Die Bedeutung des Musterabkommens und des Kommentars des OECD-Steuerausschusses für die Auslegung von Doppelbesteuerungsabkommen, in Aktuelle Entwicklungen im internationalen Steuerrecht: das neue Musterabkommen der OECD* 25 (Wolfgang Gassner et al. eds, Linde 1994); Lang, *Seminar B, Teil 2: Das OECD-Musterabkommen – 2001*

31(3)(a) VCLT cannot be used as a meaningful argument in favour of a dynamic interpretation.

Moreover, even if the commentary should be found to establish a common agreement between the parties, this agreement - as the German Bundesfinanzhof correctly points out - is not directed at the individual treaty in question but at the OECD MC. It hence does not regard the interpretation of the previously concluded tax treaty but merely the model on which it was (maybe).[136] From an overall perspective - even when applying an extensive understanding of the term 'agreement between the parties' - the OECD commentary cannot be qualified as a subsequent agreement in the sense of Article 31(3)(a) VCLT. The agreement not only is rather indirect - through the OECD's mediation - but it is also not directed at a specific bilateral tax treaty. In addition, it must be remembered that recourse to subsequent agreements is only one element of the interpretation process and hence can be outweighed by other factors foreseen by the VCLT such as the wording and the provision's systematic role within the treaty. Hence, if the means foreseen by Article 31(1) and (2) VCLT already provide a persuasive result, the subsequent agreement will arguably have a limited function.

As perfectly evidenced by the German Bundesfinanzhof's jurisprudence, another key obstacle to a dynamic approach on the basis of viewing later commentaries as subsequent agreements lies in the separation of powers foreseen by domestic constitutions. This issue contains an international law and a domestic aspect. The court, by reference to German constitutional law, in this regard held that subsequent changes of the OECD Commentary can only be considered a subsequent agreement under Article 31(3)(a) VCLT or subsequent practice within the meaning of Article 31(3)(b) VCLT provided that the change in the subsequent agreement is reflected in an amended DTC or corresponding transformation statutory provisions.[137] Hence, from a German perspective, the German moderate dualist system (i.e., constitutional law) is an obstacle to a dynamic application of a subsequent (revised) OECD Commentary insofar as, for any change at the international level to become binding, it would require the respective transformation into domestic law.[138]

From a mere international law perspective, the question of the separation of powers would appear initially irrelevant since it only pertains to the domestic bindingness of international law. However, at a second glance, the constitutionally envisaged competence could be considered also determining the attribution of state conduct for

Und Darüber Hinaus: Welche Bedeutungen Haben Die Nach Abschluss Eines Doppelbesteuerungsabkommens Erfolgten Änderungen Des OECD-Kommentars?, IStR, *supra* n. 127, at 538; Michael Lang, *Die Bedeutung des OECD-Kommentars und der Reservations, Observations und Positions für die DBA-Auslegung, in Nationale und internationale Unternehmensbesteuerung in der Rechtsordnung: Festschrift für Dietmar Gosch zum Ausscheiden aus dem Richteramt* 238 (Jürgen Lüdicke et al. eds, C.H. Beck 2016).

136. German Federal Fiscal Court (BFH) 5.12.2023, I R 42/20, para. 49.

137. German Federal Fiscal Court (BFH) 11.7.2018, I R 44/16, para. 20; *see* thereto Eversloh, *supra* n. 134, at 451 et seq.; Michael Lang, *Die Auffassung Des BMF Zur Bedeutung Des OECD-Kommentars Für Die Auslegung von DBA*, IStR 549 et seq.

138. Notably, from a mere public international law perspective, the state's internal approach should not be decisive.

international purposes.[139] Hence, a state organ that is not competent to perform the relevant legal act domestically may also not be seen as being able to express a state's intent on the international plain. This view affords opportunities to contend that, already from an international law perspective, the mere consent of the executive branch at the level of an international organization such as the OECD cannot lead to a binding 'agreement between the states' establishing rights and obligations. This is because such an agreement would – under the laws of that state – require legislative consent in order to be attributable to that state. This holds particularly true in cases when the subsequent agreement would, in fact, modify the treaty instead of simply interpreting it.

3.3 Result of MAPs as Subsequent Agreements?

The OECD MC in Article 25(1) and (3) contains a specific provision governing MAPs in the event that diverging views on the interpretation of a treaty in a specific scenario lead to taxation that the taxpayer believes is not in accordance with the convention (MAPs) or in case the states – at a general/abstract level – seek to clarify interpretative issues.[140] From a VCLT standpoint, the question arises as to whether the outcome of a MAP fulfils the requirements established by Article 31(3)(a) VCLT for subsequent agreements and thus has to be referred to as a means of interpretation under the VCLT. All requirements initially seem to be fulfilled. The result of a MAP – in contrast to the OECD Commentary – establishes a written agreement between the parties of the treaty regarding the interpretation of the said treaty. This agreement is reached subsequently, i.e., after the treaty's conclusion. As already the mere wording indicates, the MAP is intended to reach a mutual agreement to avoid diverging interpretations of a DTC concluded between the contracting states. Its intention is thus clearly directed at finding a common interpretation.

However, according to sceptical voices raised in academia, it can be questioned whether tax authorities concluding MAPs can genuinely be considered representing the parties of a treaty within the meaning of Article 31(3)(a) VCLT.[141] This argument was already described above and is based on the view that only the conduct of those state organs that have the competence to set the legal act in question can be attributed to a state that, also for domestic purposes. Two counter arguments can be raised against this proposition with one being specific and one general. First, the parties themselves

139. Lang, *Die Auffassung Des BMF Zur Bedeutung Des OECD-Kommentars Für Die Auslegung von DBA*, *supra* n. 137, at 552.
140. *See* in more detail on the establishment and types of MAPs, Annika Streicher & Heinz Jirousek, *Chapter 7: Mutual Agreement Procedures and the Implementation of Mutual Agreements in Domestic Law*, *in Tax Treaties and Procedural Law* (Georg Kofler et al. eds, IBFD 2020); Frank Pötgens, *Chapter 8: The Resolution of 'Difficulties' or 'Doubts' Related to the Interpretation and Application of a Tax Treaty and Consultation in Cases Not Provided for in the Treaty in Dispute Resolution under Tax Treaties and Beyond* (G. Maisto ed., IBFD 2023), Books IBFD (Accessed 16 May 2024).
141. Lang, *Art. 3 Abs. 2 OECD-MA Und Die Auslegung von Doppelbesteuerungsabkommen Auslegungsgrundsätze Für DBA*, *supra* n. 98, at 284; notably, from a public international law perspective, this should not be an issue.

in Article 25 OECD MC declared the authorities as competent to resolve 'difficulties or doubts arising as to the interpretation or application' of the DTC.[142] Hence, by concluding the tax treaty, the two states have explicitly referred the competence to find an agreement on the interpretation of the treaty to the respective tax authorities. It would be a peculiar result to then argue that they cannot represent the state for international law purposes when their competence to do so is specifically specified in an international treaty. Second, from a general public international law perspective, the mere fact that the mutual agreement is reached between the two competent authorities arguably would not prevent it from qualifying as a subsequent agreement in the sense of Article 31(3)(a) VCLT if adhering to a broader understanding of attributing conduct to a state (*see* section 2.1.3 above). The ILC 2018 report, for example, refers explicitly to MAPs as an example of a subsequent agreement.[143]

From a public international law perspective, it thus seems highly defensible that MAPs can be viewed as fulfilling the requirements of Article 31(3)(a) VCLT and should thus be qualified as subsequent agreements.[144,145] The limits of MAPs qualifying as subsequent agreements and thus as a relevant means of interpretation according to the VCLT will, however, be reached if the authorities, in fact, do not interpret the treaty but modify it.[146] Hence, again, the key demarcation line is established as the border between interpretation and modification. If the result of the MAP does not fit within the boundaries set by applying Article 31(1) and (2) VCLT to the tax treaty, then it must not be taken into account when interpreting the treaty. The authorities competent to lead the MAP are, in principle, not allowed to make a change to a DTC through a MAP. Rather, the first sentence of Article 25(3) OECD MC restricts their competences by stating that MAPs can only be reached upon the 'interpretation or application' of the underlying DTC.[147] Hence, if this line is exceeded, arguably also the competence of the authorities in binding the state would be exceeded.

Additionally, the German Bundesfinanzhof has held that a common understanding (e.g., a MAP) established by the relevant tax authorities of the contracting states can be used as an interpretation tool if the common understanding can be derived from

142. According to Art. 25(3) OECD MC, tax authorities are authorized to resolve difficulties by concluding mutual agreements; *see also* thereto Helmut Loukota, *Das Problem Mit Den 'Öffentlichen Funktionen' Im DBA-Recht*, SWI – Steuer- und Wirtschaft International 52 (2014).
143. *See supra* n. 103, *International Law Commission 'Report of the International Law Commission in Its 70th Session' (30 April-1 June and 2 July-10 August 2018) UN Doc A/73/10*, *supra* n. 10.
144. Christian Gloria, *Das steuerliche Verständigungsverfahren und das Recht auf diplomatischen Schutz: zugleich ein Beitrag zur Lehre von der Auslegung der Doppelbesteuerungsabkommen* 77 (Duncker & Humblot 1988); Helmut Loukota & Heinz Jirousek, *Höchstgerichtliche DBA-Auslegung Und Die Wiener Vertragsrechtskonvention*, Österreichische Steuerzeitung 52 et seq. (2016); Kasper Dziurdź, *Kurzfristige Arbeitnehmerüberlassung Im Internationalen Steuerrecht* 26 (Linde Verlag Ges.m.b.H. 2013); Heinz Jirousek, *Ist Die Verordnung Zu Art 19 DBA Liechtenstein Gesetzwidrig?*, SWI – Steuer- und Wirtschaft International 258 (2015); Pötgens, *supra* n. 140, Chapter 8.3.7.1. with further references.
145. Loukota & Jirousek, *supra* n. 144, at 53.
146. Michael Lang, *Art. 3 Abs. 2 OECD-MA Und Die Auslegung von Doppelbesteuerungsabkommen Auslegungsgrundsätze Für DBA*, *supra* n. 98, at 284; Frank Engelen, *Interpretation of Tax Treaties under International Law*, Books IBFD (accessed 16 May 2024).
147. Pötgens, *supra* n. 140, Chapter 8.3.2.

the wording of the treaty.[148] Hence, the Federal Fiscal Court believes the wording to be the limit within which the result of the MAP must operate. Arguably, this view is too narrow since the wording is only one element of the interpretation process foreseen by Article 31(1) and (2) VCLT.

From a public international law perspective, hence, the stronger arguments favour qualifying MAPs as subsequent agreements as long as they are limited to interpreting a DTC instead of modifying it.[149] The qualification of a mutual agreement pursuant to Article 25 OECD MC as a subsequent agreement under public international law, however, has to be strictly separated from the question of its bindingness under domestic law.[150] In many jurisdictions, the state's domestic legal system will render these mutual agreements non-binding for domestic courts.[151] In this context, domestic courts in many jurisdictions have been rather reluctant to consider MAPs for interpretation purposes.[152] The majority in academia endorses the view that domestic courts should not be bound by those established by the competent authorities based on separation of powers considerations.[153] Nonetheless, is appears a valid point to require them to be at least taken into account by courts in the same manner as courts will consider views expressed in scholarly papers even if they are not legally binding from a domestic perspective.[154]

3.4 The MLI as a Subsequent Agreement?

The relevance of the interpretation methods foreseen by Articles 31 to 33 VCLT is not limited to bilateral treaties but is meant to apply to all treaties within the ambit of Article 2 VCLT.[155] Hence, the VCLT also applies to the MLI itself with the above

148. German Federal Fiscal Court (BFH) 12.10.2011, I R 15/11, para. 16; *see also* on the case, Alexander Rust, *Germany: Interpreting the 183-Day Rule, in Tax Treaty Case Law Around the Globe 2013* (Michael Lang & International Bureau of Fiscal Documentation eds, IBFD Linde 2014).
149. Presumably agreeing, Georg Kofler et al., *Bindungswirkung von Generellen Verständigungsverfahren Aus Deutscher, Österreichischer Und Schweizerischer Sicht*, IStR 955 (2019); Pötgens, *supra* n. 140, Chapter 8.3.7.1. with further references.
150. Hence, according to Streicher and Jirousek, a MAP must at least be 'taken into account' by courts when deciding a case even if domestic courts are not bound by MAPs established by competent tax authorities (e.g., due to constitutional restrictions). Streicher & Jirousek, *supra* n. 140.
151. Kofler et al., *supra* n. 149, at 954 et seq.; *see also* German Federal Fiscal Court (BFH) 10.6.2015, I R 79/13; *see also* thereto Christiane Anger, *Interpretation von Doppelbesteuerungsabkommen Mittels Konsultationsvereinbarungsverordnungen?: Eine Absage Durch Den BFH Am Beispiel Der Konsultationsvereinbarung Zwischen Deutschland Und Der Schweiz Zu Abfindungen*, IStR 57 et seq. (2016); Moris Lehner, *Art. 15 DBA-Schweiz Verbietet Abweichende Konsultationsvereinbarung* 785 et seq. (2015).
152. Pötgens, *supra* n. 140, Chapter 8.3.7.2.
153. Roland Ismer, *DBA-Konkretisierung Durch Die Exekutive? Zur Bindungswirkung von Verständigungsvereinbarungen Nach Art. OECD_MUSTERABK Artikel 25 Abs. OECD_MUSTERABK Artikel 25 Absatz 3 Satz 1 OECD-MA*, IStR 3667 (2009) with further references in n. 13; For a different view, *see* Arvid Aage Skaar, *The Legal Nature of Mutual Agreements under Tax Treaties*, Tax Notes International 1446 (1992).
154. Loukota, *supra* n. 142, at 51; Streicher & Jirousek, *supra* n. 140, Chapter 7.4.1.2.
155. Schmalenbach, *supra* n. 62, No. 15.

considerations being relevant.[156] The key issue discussed here, however, is whether the MLI could be perceived as a subsequent agreement to a respective DTC. In particular, in a scenario in which both contracting states to a DTC opted into the same MLI provision(s), there is obviously an agreement between the same parties.[157] The question hence is whether the parties' intent was to establish a new stand-alone agreement, modify the covered tax agreements, or regulate their interpretation and application. If the latter would be the case, a subsequent agreement may arise.

The relationship between the MLI and covered tax agreements is primarily governed by the compatibility clauses which distinguish four different scenarios.[158] As a principal matter, the compatibility clauses are meant to ensure – in the event of a norm conflict – that the MLI being the *lex posterior* prevails over the covered tax agreement.[159] Whenever the MLI modifies an existing covered tax agreement or supplements it as a stand-alone international agreement, it is quite clear that the MLI is not intended to regulate the covered tax agreement's interpretation. The wording used in it already shows that it primarily aims at modifying existing DTCs in order to implement the relevant measures as developed within the Base Erosion and Profit Shifting (BEPS) process.[160] Thus, although it could be qualified as an agreement within the meaning of Article 31(3)(a) VCLT as subsequently established between the parties provided that both opted into the same provision(s), the necessary purpose of the agreement to pertain to the interpretation or application of a treaty will not be fulfilled. Consequently, whenever the MLI intends to modify DTCs and thus change their content, it exceeds merely interpreting or applying a DTC.[161]

However, the wording used by the explanatory statement regarding Article 6 MLI that foresees a changed preamble could be read in a different way. Interestingly, for the changed preamble pursuant to Article 6 of the MLI, the wording used by the OECD in the explanatory statement could be read as implying that the changed preamble should be understood as a mere clarification and hence could be deemed to constitute a subsequent agreement regarding the DTC's interpretation. Paragraph 76 of the explanatory statement reads as follows: 'While this text is added to the preamble of a Covered Tax Agreement after the original conclusion, the intent of the Contracting Jurisdictions is that the Covered Tax Agreement would be interpreted in line with the purpose of the Covered Tax Agreement described in the preamble text.' Similar language can be found in paragraph 23 which states: 'The inclusion of this statement

156. Michael Lang, *Die Auslegung Des Multilateralen Instrument*, SWI – Steuer- und Wirtschaft International 11 (2017).
157. Daniel Blum & Rita Szudoczky, *Chapter 5: Unveiling the MLI: An Analysis of Its Nature, Relationship to Covered Tax Agreements and Interpretation in Light of the Obligations of Its Parties, in International and EU Tax Multilateralism: Challenges Raised by the MLI*, Chapter 5.3.3.2. (Ana Paula Dourado ed., IBFD 2020).
158. *Ibid.*
159. Blum & Szudoczky, *supra* n. 157, Chapter 5.3.3.2.
160. Svetlana Wakounig, *Interpretation of Terms Used in the Multilateral Instrument, in The OECD Multilateral Instrument for Tax Treaties: Analysis and Effects* 21 (Claus Staringer et al. eds, Wolters Kluwer 2018).
161. *See also* on the question of whether the MLI can be qualified as a subsequent agreement, Blum & Szudoczky, *supra* n. 157, Chapter 5.3.3.2.

in the preamble to the Convention is intended to clarify the intent of the Parties to ensure that Covered Tax Agreements be interpreted in line with the preamble language foreseen in Article 6(1).'[162] Thus, according to the explanatory statement, the OECD seems to believe that the change to the preamble is merely clarifying and assumes that this change under Article 6 of the MLI has a de facto retroactive effect.[163] Initially, all criteria established by Article 31(3)(a) appear to be met. The MLI clearly is an agreement between the parties of the convention, i.e., the covered tax agreement. Admittedly, a rather peculiar situation would arise if a party to the MLI would later not ratify it so that an agreement vis-à-vis the other state was first reached but then, from an international law perspective, was never realized. However, this would not change the nature of the MLI to constitute an agreement.

The key issue is thus whether the change to the preamble is a reflection of the parties' initial intent or whether it goes beyond the scope defined by applying Article 31(1) and (2) VCLT to the treaty. The intention of the parties as reflected in the explanatory statement would initially indicate that Article 6 MLI is intended to interpret the pre-existing treaty while clarifying its object and purpose as established upon its conclusion. At the same time, the wording used by the MLI itself and also its temporal scope would indicate that the MLI is intended to modify covered tax agreements. Article 6(1) MLI foreseeing a change to the preamble indicates a 'modification' of the covered tax agreement. It appears fair to conclude that eliminating double non-taxation was not a general goal of double-tax treaties prior to the BEPS process. If the parties were concerned about the possibility of double non-taxation, they would have been required to envisage a subject-to-tax clause. Hence, arguably in this regard, the changed preamble clearly exceeds the limits set by most existing treaties' wording, context, object, and purpose. Regarding double non-taxation or reduced taxation achieved through evasion or abuse – as the wording of the principal purpose test (PPT) indicates – only a case-by-case analysis of the respective treaty rule in question granting a benefit can show whether it was the parties' intent to grant that benefit. Hence, arguably, the changed preamble does not have any meaning or normative weight.[164] Thus, also the question of whether preventing double non-taxation or reduced taxation in an abuse/avoidance situation can be seen as still operating within the boundaries of interpretation as opposed to modification that can only be assessed on a case-by-case basis. Either way, the changed preamble as foreseen by Article 6 MLI will not inform the interpretative process based on Article 31(3)(a) VCLT in any meaningful way.

162. OECD, *Explanatory Statement to the Multilateral Convention to Implement Tax Treaty Related Measures to Prevent Base Erosion and Profit Shifting*, para. 38 (2016).
163. *See also* on this discussion, Blum & Szudoczky, *supra* n. 157, Chapter 5.3.3.2.
164. Michael Lang, *Verhinderung von Doppel- Und Doppelnichtbesteuerung*, in Die österreichischen DBA nach BEPS, 63 (Stefan Bendlinger ed., Linde 2018).

4 CONCLUDING REMARKS

The interpretation rules under the VCLT are of fundamental importance for interpreting international treaties (such as DTCs). Article 31 VCLT establishes a general rule of interpretation requiring the interpreter to take into account the treaty's wording, its context, and its object and purpose. In addition, Article 31(3)(a) VCLT demands that – together with the context – any subsequent agreement between the parties regarding the interpretation of a previously concluded treaty shall be taken into account. The relevance of subsequent agreements in treaty interpretation pertains thus to a highly controversial topic, specifically the question to which extent treaties can or even have to be interpreted dynamically. In this chapter, the authors argue that subsequent agreements fulfilling the criteria established by Article 31(3)(a) VCLT derive their interpretative weight from their nature of expressing the parties' intent. However, the limits of Article 31(3)(a) VCLT will be reached once the subsequent agreement – albeit claiming to be an interpretation of the treaty – leads to a modification. The interpretative results foreseen by a subsequent agreement hence must remain within the boundaries set by applying Article 31(1) and (2) VCLT, i.e., must not exceed the previously concluded wording interpreted in light of its context, object, and purpose.

Regarding the relevance of subsequent agreements in the realm of tax treaty interpretation, this chapter found that the later version of the OECD Commentary does not qualify as subsequent agreements in the sense of Article 31(3)(a) VLCT. The mediation of the parties' intent through the OECD might not necessarily rule out that the commentary creates an agreement between the parties as long as both treaty parties are also OECD members. However, the fact that the commentary does not regard the interpretation of a concrete bilateral treaty but merely the interpretation of the OECD Model disqualifies the commentary as a subsequent agreement. In contrast, well-founded arguments seem to be available to contend that the result of MAPs constitutes subsequent agreements from an international public law perspective. Their bindingness for courts, however, will depend on the legal pedigree accorded to them by domestic constitutional law. Last, the chapter finds that the change to the preamble as foreseen by Article 6 MLI cannot be considered a subsequent agreement since its normative meaning does not appear highly obscure. Additionally, avoiding double non-taxation cannot be seen as generally falling within the object and purpose of tax treaties based on OECD MC versions predating the BEPS process as reflected in the MLI and the 2017 OECD MC.

CHAPTER 7

Subsequent Practice and Tax Treaty Interpretation

Michael Lang & Eric Coenen

1 Subsequent Practice and the VCLT
2 Subsequent Practice in International Law
  2.1 Distinguishing Between Treaty Interpretation and Modification
  2.2 Relevant Authorities
  2.3 Conduct in the Application of the Treaty
  2.4 Frequency and Uniformity
  2.5 Weight of Subsequent Practice
3 Subsequent Practice in Tax Treaty Law
  3.1 Distinguishing Between Treaty Interpretation and Modification
  3.2 Relevant Authorities
  3.3 Conduct in the Application of the Treaty
  3.4 Frequency and Uniformity
  3.5 Weight of Subsequent Practice
4 Conclusion

1 SUBSEQUENT PRACTICE AND THE VCLT

As the number of bilateral and multilateral treaties increases, so does the importance of interpreting them.[1] The Vienna Convention on the Law of Treaties (VCLT) contains

1. Ulf Linderfalk, *On the Interpretation of Treaties: The Modern International Law as Expressed in the 1969 Vienna Convention on the Law of Treaties* 1 (Springer 2007).

several provisions stipulating the principles on how this is to be accomplished.[2] According to Article 31(3)(b) VCLT 'any subsequent practice in the application of the treaty which establishes the agreement of the parties regarding its interpretation' shall be taken into account for interpreting a treaty. Such subsequent practice aims primarily at evidencing the parties' understanding of the treaty.[3] Whether this means of interpretation shall be of great importance or of less value when interpreting it is answered differently in academic writing. While some argue that '[t]he possibility of influencing the fate of a treaty through the practice of its application should not, however, be overestimated',[4] others contend that subsequent practice may be, 'if used cautiously, a tool for facilitating greater coherence through treaty adaptation to new developments and customary law'.[5] Thus, the relevance and its potential value for interpreting treaties are assessed differently.

The authors will first address subsequent practice in international law in general and then in tax treaty law in particular. Each of these two sections will be structured as follows. First, the distinction between treaty modification and treaty interpretation through subsequent practice is discussed. This will be followed by a consideration of the requirements for establishing it as a means of interpretation, i.e., which authorities are competent to establish subsequent practice, what kind of conduct could be used, and how frequently and uniformly this conduct must be applied. This will lead to an outlook on the weight of such practice when interpreting treaties.

2 SUBSEQUENT PRACTICE IN INTERNATIONAL LAW

2.1 Distinguishing Between Treaty Interpretation and Modification

When dealing with subsequent practice under Article 31(3)(b) VCLT, it is crucial to discuss the differences between the interpretation of a treaty, on the one hand, and its possible modification through a subsequent practice on the other hand. The objective of interpretation is determining the genuine meaning of a provision.[6] Modification, however, leads to a new provision and thus alters the treaty.[7] Nonetheless, it is difficult to determine when interpretation actually becomes modification.[8] In general, it is recognized in the VCLT that an agreement by the parties of a treaty may lead to an

2. Especially Arts 31-33 VCLT.
3. Oliver Dörr, *Vienna Convention on the Law of Treaties: A Commentary*, Art. 31, para. 77 (Oliver Dörr & Kirsten Schmalenbach eds, Springer 2d ed. 2018).
4. Georg Nolte, *Treaties and Their Practice: Symptoms of Their Rise or Decline* 334 (Brill 2018).
5. Irina Buga, *Subsequent Practice and Treaty Modification, in Conceptual and Contextual Perspectives on the Modern Law of Treaties* 390 (Michael Bowman & Dino Kritsiotis eds, Cambridge University Press 2018).
6. Michael Lang, *Can Law Regulate Its Own Interpretation? Relevance and Meaning of Articles 31-33 of the Vienna Convention on the Law of Treaties (VCLT) and Article 3 Para. 2 of the Model Convention of the Organisation for Economic Co-operation and Development (OECD MC) for the Interpretation of Double-Taxation Conventions, in Research Handbook on International Taxation* 180 (Yariv Brauner ed., Edward Elgar Publishing 2020).
7. Irina Buga, *Modification of Treaties by Subsequent Practice* 167 (Oxford University Press 2018).
8. Or even impossible to draw according to Ian Sinclair, *The Vienna Convention on the Law of Treaties* 120 (Manchester Univ. Press 2d ed. 1984).

amendment of it: Article 39 VCLT provides that '[a] treaty may be amended by agreement between the parties'. Thus, the question could be raised as to whether a common subsequent practice under Article 31(3)(b) VCLT by the parties could also do so.

The VCLT's current version does not specifically address the possibility of modifying a treaty through subsequent practice. However, the International Law Commission (ILC) originally proposed to include a provision in the VCLT that would have recognized the modification of a treaty by subsequent practice.[9] Since this did not occur,[10] it is debated in academic writing and case law whether subsequent practice could modify a treaty.[11] The World Trade Organization (WTO) Appellate Body, for instance, denied this possibility since the term 'application' cannot lead to new obligations.[12] Subsequent practice that is beyond mere interpretation has to therefore be considered unlawful. A contrary view is held, for example, by the European Court of Human Rights (ECHR) in the *Öcalan v. Turkey* case in which the ECHR argued that subsequent practice could lead to a modification of a treaty.[13] The International Court of Justice (ICJ), however, neither explicitly allowed this nor denied it[14] which subsequently resulted in differing case law. However, subsequent practice that is

9. The draft Art. 38 read as follows: 'A treaty may be modified by subsequent practice in the application of the treaty establishing the agreement of the parties to modify its provision'; *see* for this draft Art. 38, *Official Records of the United Nations Conference on the Law of Treaties (A/CONF.39/11/Add.2), First and Second Sessions 26 March-24 May 1968 and 9 April-22 May 1969*, paras 342-348.
10. Fifty-three voted against the inclusion of this provision in the VCLT, fifteen voted in favour and twenty-six abstained, *see ILC, Report of the International Law Commission in Its 70th Session (30 April-1 June and 2 July-10 August 2018) UN Doc A/73/10*, para. 26, Conclusion 7.
11. For views in academic writing, *see*: allowing modification by subsequent practice: Buga, *supra* n. 7, at 307 et seq.; Mark Eugen Villiger, *Commentary on the 1969 Vienna Convention on the Law of Treaties* 429 (Nijhoff 2009); denying modification by subsequent practice: Marcelo G. Kohen, *Keeping Subsequent Agreements and Practice in Their Right Limits, in Treaties and Subsequent Practice* 35 et seq. (Georg Nolte ed., Oxford Univ. Press 2013); for views in case law, *see*: denying the modification of a treaty by subsequent practice: *European Communities – Regime for the Importation, Sale and Distribution of Bananas, Second Recourse to Article 21.5 of the DSU by Ecuador (EC – Banans III), WT/DS27/AB/RW2/ECU and Corr. 1, adopted 11 December 2008, WT/DS27/AB/RW/USA and Corr. 1, adopted 22 December 2008*, paras 391-393; leaving it open (this case, however, was before the adoption of the VCLT in 1969): *Temple of Preah Vihear* case *(Cambodia v. Thailand), ICJ Reports 1962*, p. 6, 26; allowing a modification by subsequent practice: *Öcalan v. Turkey [GC], Appl. No. 46221/99, 12 May 2005*, ECHR, para. 163.
12. Appellate Body, *European Communities – Regime for the Importation, Sale and Distribution of Bananas, Second Recourse to Article 21.5 of the DSU by Ecuador (EC – Banans III), WT/DS27/AB/RW2/ECU and Corr. 1, adopted 11 December 2008, WT/DS27/AB/RW/USA and Corr. 1, adopted 22 December 2008*, paras 391-393; this case, however, dealt with a subsequent agreement under Art. 31(3)(a) VCLT. Nonetheless, both provisions, Art. 31(3)(a) and 31(3)(b) VCLT, deal with the term 'application' and, hence, the conclusion of the WTO Appellate Body could also be transferred to subsequent practice; *see also ILC, Report of the International Law Commission in Its 70th Session (30 April-1 June and 2 July-10 August 2018) UN Doc A/73/10, supra* n. 10, para. 32, Conclusion 7; Georg Nolte, *Report 2. Jurisprudence under Special Regimes Relating to Subsequent Agreements and Subsequent Practice, Second Report for the ILC Study Group on Treaties over Time, in Treaties and Subsequent Practice* 223 (Georg Nolte ed., Oxford Univ. Press 2013).
13. *Öcalan v. Turkey [GC], Appl. No. 46221/99, 12 May 2005*, ECHR, para. 163.
14. *ILC, Report of the International Law Commission in Its 70th Session (30 April-1 June and 2 July-10 August 2018) UN Doc A/73/10, supra* n. 10, para. 31, Conclusion 7.

accepted under Article 31(3)(b) VCLT can only contribute to the interpretation of treaties but cannot be used as a tool to modify them.[15] In addition, from a domestic perspective, constitutional concerns could arise if the possibility of modifying a treaty by subsequent practice exists since the consent of domestic parliaments to a treaty change could be circumvented.[16] Therefore, subsequent practice under Article 31(3)(b) VCLT should not result in modifying a treaty as such change requires the approval of the domestic legislature.

According to the ILC, the scope for the interpretation of a treaty may even exceed the parameters of the ordinary meaning of the treaty terms.[17] Nonetheless, there are limits: A manifest misapplication of a treaty no longer falls under the condition 'in the application of the treaty' and therefore cannot establish a subsequent practice.[18]

2.2 Relevant Authorities

It is necessary in the next step to discuss who could be the competent authorities to establish a subsequent practice. Their relevant conduct may be acts of the state 'in the exercise of its executive, legislative, judicial, or other functions'.[19] Article 31(3)(b) VCLT further requires that such conduct must be 'in the application of the treaty'. Treaties are generally applied by the parties to the treaty. Thus, high-ranking government officials and lower authorities could establish a subsequent practice.[20] High-ranking government officials are those who are mentioned in Article 7 VCLT.[21] These include, according to Article 7(2) VCLT:

> Heads of State, Heads of Government and Ministers for Foreign Affairs, for the purpose of performing all acts relating to the conclusion of a treaty; heads of diplomatic missions, for the purpose of adopting the text of a treaty between the accrediting State and the State to which they are accredited; representatives accredited by States to an international conference or to an international organization or one of its organs, for the purpose of adopting the text of a treaty in that conference, organization or organ.

Not included in this list is, for example, the minister of finance.

15. Dörr, *supra* n. 3, para. 77.
16. Stefan Kadelbach, *International Law Commission and Role of Subsequent Practice as a Means of Interpretation under Articles 31 and 32 VCLT*, 46 QIL 15 (2018); *see also ILC, Report of the International Law Commission in Its 70th Session (30 April-1 June and 2 July-10 August 2018) UN Doc A/73/10, supra* n. 10, para. 37, Conclusion 7.
17. *ILC, Report of the International Law Commission in Its 70th Session (30 April-1 June and 2 July-10 August 2018) UN Doc A/73/10, supra* n. 10, para. 24, Conclusion 7.
18. *Ibid.*, para. 19, Conclusion 4.
19. *Ibid.*, para. 2, Conclusion 5; *see also* Richard K. Gardiner, *Treaty Interpretation* 257 (Oxford Univ. Press 2d ed. 2015).
20. *ILC, Report of the International Law Commission in Its 70th Session (30 April-1 June and 2 July-10 August 2018) UN Doc A/73/10, supra* n. 10, paras 6-7, Conclusion 5.
21. In more detail regarding Art. 7 VCLT, *see* Frank Hoffmeister, *Vienna Convention on the Law of Treaties: A Commentary*, Art. 7, paras 22 et seq. (Oliver Dörr & Kirsten Schmalenbach eds, Springer 2d ed. 2018).

However, those officials do not often actually apply treaties,[22] and they are rather generally applied by lower authorities.[23] But their conduct may only establish a subsequent practice under Article 31(3)(b) VCLT if certain requirements are satisfied. The *UNESCO* case[24] can serve as an example to illustrate this. It dealt with the taxing rights of pensions paid to retired former UNESCO officials who were residents of France. The French local tax authorities did not collect taxes on those pensions which was considered a potential subsequent practice by the Arbitral Tribunal deciding in this matter. However, this lower tax authority's practice was not sufficiently unequivocal since the French Government issued contrary pronouncements. Thus, the conduct was not in accordance with the official pronouncements of the higher authority that was considered to be decisive in this matter by the Arbitral Tribunal.[25] In conclusion, it can be stated that both high-ranking government officials and lower authorities could establish subsequent practice under Article 31(3)(b) VCLT. A potential subsequent practice of lower authorities could, however, be prevented by contradictory acts of the government.[26]

This previous view only deals with acts of authorities that are made by organs of the state and are thus attributable to the party. However, there is also a broader concept of relevant authorities for establishing subsequent practice that covers the conduct of states' parties and that of non-state actors such as international bodies or private individuals.[27] The reason for this is that Article 31(3)(b) VCLT only requires conduct 'in the application of the treaty' from which the conclusion can be drawn that also 'conduct by non-state actors which is attributable to one or more States parties and which fall within the scope of what the treaty conceives as forms of its application'.[28] However, the ILC takes a restrictive view of the possible relevance of the conduct of non-state actors for establishing a subsequent practice under Article 31(3)(b) VCLT as their objectives may differ from those of the states' parties: While the ILC recognizes

22. *ILC, Report of the International Law Commission in Its 70th Session (30 April-1 June and 2 July-10 August 2018) UN Doc A/73/10*, *supra* n. 10, para. 6, Conclusion 5.
23. This is also true for tax treaties since they are primarily applied by local tax authorities and not high-ranking government officials; *see* Michael Lang, *Subsequent Practice and Tax Treaties*, *in A Journey Through European and International Taxation: Liber Amicorum in Honour of Peter Essers* 357 (Carla De Pietro et al. eds, Wolters Kluwer 2024); *see also* s. 3.3.
24. *Reports of International Arbitral Awards – Tax Regime Governing Pensions Paid to Retired UNESCO Officials Residing in France (France – UNESCO), 14 January 2003, Volume Xxv*, 257 et seq.
25. *ILC, Report of the International Law Commission in Its 70th Session (30 April-1 June and 2 July-10 August 2018) UN Doc A/73/10*, *supra* n. 10, para. 6, Conclusion 5;
26. *See also* Rahim Moloo, *When Actions Speak Louder Than Words: The Relevance of Subsequent Party Conduct to Treaty Interpretation*, 31 Berkeley J. Int'l L. 69 (2013); Michael Lang, *Die Auffassung des BMF zur Bedeutung des OECD-Kommentars für die Auslegung von DBA*, 32 IStR 554 (2023).
27. Katharina Berner, *Subsequent Agreements and Subsequent Practice in Domestic Courts* 125 (Springer 2017).
28. *ILC, Report of the International Law Commission on the Work of Its Sixty-Sixth Session (5 May-6 June and 7 July-8 August 2014)*, para. 22, Conclusion 6.

some value in such conduct by non-state actors, it also cautions against using it as a subsequent practice and urges critical examination.[29]

2.3 Conduct in the Application of the Treaty

According to the wording of Article 31(3)(b) VCLT, the practice of the parties must be considered 'subsequent'. Therefore, the relevant point in time after which the practice can be considered 'subsequent' must be defined. It may initially appear that the point in time could be the entry into force since only then could conduct be 'in the application of the treaty'. However, this is not considered the relevant moment in time.[30] This results, among other reasons, from an overall consideration of Article 31(2)(a) and Article 31(3) VCLT. According to the former, any agreement relating to the treaty that was made between all the parties in connection with the conclusion of the treaty shall be considered context for the purpose of interpretation.[31] Since all of these agreements – or those in a close relation – [32] thus fall under the context, a practice of the parties can be considered subsequent if it occurs after the treaty's conclusion.[33] This also allows distinguishing agreements within the meaning of the context under Article 31(2)(a) VCLT from subsequent agreements under Article 31(3)(a) VCLT and subsequent practice under Article 31(3)(b) VCLT.[34] The ILC therefore states that 'it is difficult to identify a reason why an agreement or practice that takes place between the moment when the text of a treaty has been established as definitive and the entry into force of that treaty should not be relevant for the purpose of interpretation'.[35]

Next, it is crucial to define what could be considered relevant 'conduct' falling within the scope of Article 31(3)(b) VCLT. Conduct in the context of Article 31(3)(b) VCLT covers both acts and omissions.[36] This conduct must further appear 'in the application of the treaty' in order to establish a subsequent practice under Article 31(3)(b) VCLT. In general, this requirement comprises a wide variety of the parties' acts. Conduct 'in the application of the treaty' includes, for instance, not only official acts but also official statements that the parties issue regarding the interpretation of the

29. *ILC, Report of the International Law Commission in Its 70th Session (30 April-1 June and 2 July-10 August 2018) UN Doc A/73/10, supra* n. 10, para. 17, Conclusion 5.
30. Gardiner, *supra* n. 19, at 261. The treaty's conclusion is often earlier than its entry into force according to Art. 24 VCLT. Regarding its entry into force, *see* Heike Krieger, *Vienna Convention on the Law of Treaties: A Commentary*, Art. 24, paras 7 et seq. (Oliver Dörr & Kirsten Schmalenbach eds, Springer 2d ed. 2018).
31. Georg Nolte, *First Report on Subsequent Agreements and Subsequent Practice in Relation to Treaty Interpretation (19 March 2013) UN Doc A/CN.4/660*, paras 84–87; *see also* Berner, *supra* n. 27, at 119.
32. *ILC, Report of the International Law Commission in Its 70th Session (30 April-1 June and 2 July-10 August 2018) UN Doc A/73/10, supra* n. 10, para. 3, Conclusion 4.
33. The treaty's conclusion is when its text has been established as definite; *see* Frank Hoffmeister, *Vienna Convention on the Law of Treaties: A Commentary*, Art. 10, paras 1 et seq. (Oliver Dörr & Kirsten Schmalenbach eds, Springer 2d ed. 2018).
34. *ILC, Report of the International Law Commission in Its 70th Session (30 April-1 June and 2 July-10 August 2018) UN Doc A/73/10, supra* n. 10, para. 3, Conclusion 4.
35. *Ibid.*, para. 2, Conclusion 4.
36. *Ibid.*, para. 17, Conclusion 4; for the same view in the ICJ's case law, *see*, for instance, *Temple of Preah Vihear* case *(Cambodia v. Thailand), ICJ Reports 1962*, p. 6, at 23.

treaty.[37] What is not considered to be in the application, however, is a manifest misapplication of a treaty.[38] Furthermore, the parties' conduct that is not motivated by a treaty cannot be considered 'in the application of the treaty'.[39] An example used by the ILC for this is in the area of refugee law. The voluntary granting of complementary protection for persons who are denied refugee status by a state under a treaty could not be considered 'in the application of the treaty'. This is because the state does not consider itself actually applying the treaty but rather consisting of a voluntary practice.[40] Therefore, if the state does not consider its conduct to be covered by the treaty, it is not regarded as conduct 'in the application of the treaty'.

Last, the conduct of the parties 'in the application of the treaty' must also establish an agreement. Otherwise, a subsequent practice in accordance with Article 31(3)(b) VCLT cannot be established.[41] In order to understand what is meant by an 'agreement' in the sense of Article 31(3)(b) VCLT, the subsequent agreement according to Article 31(3)(a) VCLT must be distinguished from the agreement that is necessary to establish a subsequent practice under Article 31(3)(b) VCLT. According to the ILC, an agreement under Article 31(3)(a) VCLT must be 'reached' by the parties to the treaty.[42] An agreement for establishing a subsequent practice under Article 31(3)(b) VCLT, however, rather requires a common understanding by them.[43] This view is also shared by the ICJ in the *Kasikili/Sedudu Island (Botswana/Namibia)* case in which it came to the conclusion that the practice of the parties at hand did not establish an agreement. Subsequently, the ICJ stated that it is therefore *a fortiori* not an agreement within the meaning of Article 31(3)(a) VCLT.[44] Hence, it appears that it is applying stricter standards to agreements under Article 31(3)(a) VCLT than those in the context of Article 31(3)(b) VCLT.[45] The ILC thus concludes that the difference between the requirement of an agreement within Article 31(3)(a) and Article 31(3)(b) VCLT 'lies in the manner of establishing the agreement of the parties regarding the interpretation of a treaty, with the difference being in the greater ease with which an agreement is established'.[46]

---

37. *ILC, Report of the International Law Commission in Its 70th Session (30 April-1 June and 2 July-10 August 2018) UN Doc A/73/10, supra* n. 10, at 18, Conclusion 4.
38. The reason for this is that the treaty's application requires an element of good faith; *see Ibid.*, para. 19, Conclusion 4.
39. *Ibid.*, para. 7, Conclusion 6.
40. *Ibid.*, para. 9, Conclusion 6; for another example of conduct that is not motivated by a treaty provision, *see also Maritime Delimitation and Territorial Questions between Qatar and Bahrain* case *(Qatar v. Bahrain), Judgment of 15 February 1995, ICJ Reports 1995*, p. 6, para. 28.
41. Dörr, *supra* n. 3, para. 87.
42. *ILC, Report of the International Law Commission in Its 70th Session (30 April-1 June and 2 July-10 August 2018) UN Doc A/73/10, supra* n. 10, para. 10, Conclusion 4.
43. *Ibid.*, para. 10, Conclusion 3.
44. *Kasikili/Sedudu Island (Botswana/Namibia) case Judgment of 13 December 1999, ICJ Reports 1999*, p. 1045, para. 63.
45. Dörr, *supra* n. 3, para. 88; for the contradictory opinion, *see* James Crawford, *A Consensualist Interpretation of Article 31(3) of the Vienna Convention on the Law of Treaties, in Treaties and Subsequent Practice* 30 (Georg Nolte ed., Oxford Univ. Press 2013); Crawford states that there is no reason for a different meaning of an agreement according to Art. 31(3)(a) and 31(3)(b) VCLT.
46. *ILC, Report of the International Law Commission in Its 70th Session (30 April-1 June and 2 July-10 August 2018) UN Doc A/73/10, supra* n. 10, para. 10, Conclusion 3; the ILC refers in this

Additionally, it is not mandatory that the parties of the treaty are mutually aware of the same understanding of a treaty provision. It rather may be sufficient that each of them achieves the same understanding individually and thus parallel subsequent conduct in both states exists.[47] However, the ICJ's case law states otherwise. In the *Kasikili/Sedudu Island (Botswana/Namibia)* case, it had to deal with an issue regarding an island on the borders between Namibia and Botswana. A treaty between the parties located the dividing line of their territories on the basis of the 'main channel'. However, the treaty did not further clarify whether the north or the south channel was the 'main channel'. It was claimed that a subsequent practice existed as a local tribe showed continued presence on the island since the conclusion of the treaty which led to a subsequent practice. This could be, according to the ICJ, regarded as subsequent practice if both authorities were fully aware of and would accept the occupation of the island in order to determine the line between their territories.[48] Thus, it could also be argued that a practice that is not known by the other party could not establish an agreement under Article 31(3)(b) VCLT.[49] It therefore seems to depend on the circumstances in a specific case whether awareness is mutually necessary or if individually reaching the same understanding could be sufficient. The ILC thus concludes that 'it is sometimes sufficient that the parties reach the same understanding individually, but sometimes necessary that the parties have a mutual awareness of a shared understanding'.[50]

2.4 Frequency and Uniformity

When dealing with subsequent practice under Article 31(3)(b) VCLT, it is often debated whether the practice of the parties must be repeatedly exercised or whether a one-time application of the treaty could be considered sufficient for establishing a subsequent practice. It is regularly stated that it must be 'concordant, common and consistent'.[51] This is also expressly endorsed by the WTO Appellate Body that further stated that one single party's conduct may not be considered sufficient for establishing a subsequent practice under Article 31(3)(b) VCLT.[52] Thus, it could be argued that a

conclusion to the ICJ *Kasikili/Sedudu Island (Botswana/Namibia) case Judgment of 13 December 1999, ICJ Reports 1999*, p. 1045, para. 63.

47. *ILC, Report of the International Law Commission in Its 70th Session (30 April-1 June and 2 July-10 August 2018) UN Doc A/73/10*, *supra* n. 10, para. 8, Conclusion 10 and para. 23, Conclusion 6.
48. *Kasikili/Sedudu Island (Botswana/Namibia) case Judgment of 13 December 1999, ICJ Reports 1999*, p. 1045, para. 74.
49. Dörr, *supra* n. 3, para. 89.
50. *ILC, Report of the International Law Commission in Its 70th Session (30 April-1 June and 2 July-10 August 2018) UN Doc A/73/10*, *supra* n. 10, para. 8, Conclusion 10.
51. Sinclair, *supra* n. 8, at 137.
52. *Japan – Taxes on Alcoholic Beverages AB-1996-2 Report of 4 October 1996 of the World Trade Organization Appellate Body*, at 12-13; *see also* Sinclair, *supra* n. 8, at 137.

subsequent practice that is relevant requires a sequence of acts or omissions by the parties since a 'practice' cannot be established by a single conduct.[53]

However, it is also argued that the number of acts by the parties should not be relevant for the establishment of a subsequent practice. Rather, if a one-time application establishes an agreement, it could be sufficient for a subsequent practice under Article 31(3)(b) VCLT since the emphasis of this provision is not on the word 'practice' but that an agreement is established.[54] This view is also shared by the ILC since the formula 'concordant, common and consistent' regarding the frequency of state conduct cannot be presumed as being 'sufficiently well established to articulate a minimum threshold for the applicability of article 31, paragraph 3 (b) ...'.[55] Rather, the number of repetitions could be used for determining the interpretative weight of subsequent practice but not as a prerequisite for its establishment.[56] Nonetheless, in practice, it would often be unlikely to establish an agreement by a one-time application of a treaty.[57]

Therefore, it could be concluded that a subsequent practice may be established by a one-time application.[58] It thus does not require a sequence of acts in order to be considered for interpretation.[59] However, the number of applications does determine its weight within the process of interpretation.[60] Hence, a subsequent practice that is established by a one-time application may be of less relevance than one that is characterized by several repetitions.[61]

2.5 Weight of Subsequent Practice

The question of the weight to be given to an established subsequent practice under Article 31(3)(b) VCLT should not be confused with the question of whether it should be regarded as such at all.[62] The weight of subsequent practice depends on different factors. First of all, Article 31 VCLT, as the general rule of interpretation, states that a subsequent practice under Article 31(3)(b) VCLT 'shall be taken into account, together with the context'. Therefore, it should not be overestimated in its possible relevance for

---

53. Dörr, *supra* n. 3, para. 80; *see also* Villiger, *Commentary on the 1969 Vienna Convention on the Law of Treaties*, *supra* n. 11, at 431, para. 22; Villiger argues that the 'practice should be consistent rather than haphazard'. However, he also acknowledges the importance of the establishment of an agreement as a requirement for a subsequent practice.
54. Linderfalk, *supra* n. 1, at 166.
55. *ILC, Report of the International Law Commission in Its 70th Session (30 April-1 June and 2 July-10 August 2018) UN Doc A/73/10*, *supra* n. 10, para. 11, Conclusion 9.
56. *Ibid.*, paras 10-11, Conclusion 9; *see also* s. 2.5.
57. *Ibid.*, para. 11, Conclusion 9, n. 393.
58. Linderfalk, *supra* n. 1, at 166.
59. Other opinion: Dörr, *supra* n. 3, para. 80; he argues that a practice 'cannot be established by one isolated incident' and thus a subsequent practice requires a sequence of acts or pronouncements.
60. *ILC, Report of the International Law Commission in Its 70th Session (30 April-1 June and 2 July-10 August 2018) UN Doc A/73/10*, *supra* n. 10, paras 10-11, Conclusion 9.
61. Further on this, *see* s. 2.5.
62. This is also the understanding of the ILC Report, *see ILC, Report of the International Law Commission in Its 70th Session (30 April-1 June and 2 July-10 August 2018) UN Doc A/73/10*, *supra* n. 10, para. 13, Conclusion 9.

the process of interpretation since it is to be seen as 'an integral part of the general rule of interpretation set forth in article 31'.[63] This means that the other means of interpretation must also be considered in the process of interpreting a treaty.[64] The ILC thus states that interpretation can be considered a 'single combined operation' and that various means of interpretation require 'appropriate emphasis'.[65]

It is further often necessary that the nature of the treaty must be considered when discussing whether a subsequent practice of the parties should be regarded as being more or less relevant when interpreting a treaty. The case law on this matter, however, is ambiguous. The WTO Appellate Body,[66] for instance, does not overly emphasize the nature of the treaty but rather the terms of the respective treaty. For the ECHR, however, the nature of the treaty as a human rights treaty is of great relevance when assessing the potential relevance of a means of interpretation.[67] This means that the ECHR, when interpreting a treaty, takes very much into account its inherent nature and, thus, the weight given to a subsequent practice also depends on it. The ILC did not refer to the nature of the treaty to determine the relevance of a subsequent practice for its interpretation in order to 'avoid calling into question the unity of the interpretation process and to avoid any categorization of treaties'.[68] Nevertheless, the relevance of the nature of the treaty may, in any case, be found in its object and purpose since it is difficult to distinguish one from the other.[69] As a result, there are differing views in the case law and academic writing as to the weight to be given to the nature of a treaty when interpreting it.

The question then arises as to how exactly the weight of a subsequent practice in the process of interpretation is to be determined in relation to the other means of interpretation within the VCLT. As already elaborated, establishing subsequent practice under Article 31(3)(b) VCLT does not depend on the number of its applications. Rather, the given weight may be greater or lesser depending on its frequency.[70] If a practice is repeated more often, this subsequent practice should be of greater relevance than one that only appeared once.[71] Furthermore, its weight not only depends on how

63. *Ibid.*, para. 7, Conclusion 2.
64. Specifically, the other means of interpretation stipulated in Arts 31 and 32 VCLT.
65. *ILC, Report of the International Law Commission in Its 70th Session (30 April-1 June and 2 July-10 August 2018) UN Doc A/73/10, supra* n. 10, para. 11, Conclusion 2; *see also* Georg Nolte, *Report 1. Jurisprudence of the International Court of Justice and Arbitral Tribunals of Ad Hoc Jurisdiction Relating to Subsequent Agreements and Subsequent Practice, Introductory Report for the ILC Study Group on Treaties over Time, in Treaties and Subsequent Practice* 177 (Georg Nolte ed., Oxford Univ. Press 2013).
66. Appellate Body, *Brazil – Export Financing Programme for Aircraft, Recourse by Canada to Article 21.5 of the DSU, WT/DS46/AB/RW,* adopted 4 August 2000, para. 45.
67. *Mamatkulov and Askarov v. Turkey [GC], Appl. Nos 46827/99 and 46951/99, 4 February 2005,* ECHR at 111; the ECHR referred, for taking the nature of the treaty into account, to the following case: *Golder v. the United Kingdom*, Judgment of 21 February 1975, Series A No. 18, p. 14.
68. *ILC, Report of the International Law Commission in Its 70th Session (30 April-1 June and 2 July-10 August 2018) UN Doc A/73/10, supra* n. 10, para. 15, Conclusion 2.
69. *Ibid.*
70. *See* s. 2.4.
71. *ILC, Report of the International Law Commission in Its 70th Session (30 April-1 June and 2 July-10 August 2018) UN Doc A/73/10, supra* n. 10, para. 6, Conclusion 9.

and how often it is repeated but also on its consistency and breadth[72] or its clarity and specificity.[73] Regarding the nature of the treaty and its weight in the interpretation, there seem to be different views in case law and academic writing. However, it may also be the case that the subsequent practice is used for the interpretation, but no importance can be attached to it at all because other more convincing means of interpretation suggest a different result.[74]

3 SUBSEQUENT PRACTICE IN TAX TREATY LAW

3.1 Distinguishing Between Treaty Interpretation and Modification

In the area of tax treaties, the fact that subsequent practice can only be of significance in the context of interpretation and not of modification is of significance as not every subsequent practice must therefore be taken into account in the interpretation. In almost all countries, modifying a tax treaty requires legislative approval. A subsequent practice that lies beyond the boundary of interpretation can therefore have no significance within the meaning of Article 31(3)(b) VCLT. Hence, such a practice cannot concretize the content of the tax treaty but instead violates it.

However, it is difficult to answer the question of where interpretation ends and modification begins. The German Federal Tax Court (BFH) uses the wording for this: a subsequent practice is therefore only relevant if it is covered by the wording of the tax treaty. If this is no longer the case, it is also not to be taken into account.[75]

Using the wording as a limit is problematic for several reasons.[76] First, in the area of tax treaties, it does not depend on one language alone in most cases. The national languages of the two contracting states are often stipulated as authentic languages in the tax treaty. Some states have more than one national language and often ensure that all of them are listed as authentic in their tax treaties. In addition, English or another 'neutral' language is often also included among the authentic languages. In the case of provisions that are modelled on the Model Convention of the Organisation for Economic Co-operation and Development (OECD MC), it must also be taken into account that the Model Convention is written in English and French. Even if these two languages or one of them is not one of the authentic languages of a bilateral tax treaty,

---

72. *Ibid.*, para. 12, Conclusion 9; the breadth of a practice, however, is more relevant in multilateral treaties since not all of the parties engaging in the practice is a prerequisite for establishing a subsequent practice, *see* Dörr, *supra* n. 3, para. 84; therefore, in the case of bilateral treaties such as tax treaties, breadth is not as relevant to the interpretative weight given to a subsequent practice as, for instance, the elements of consistency or the number of repetitions.
73. *See*, for instance, Appellate Body, *United State – Subsidies on Upland Cotton (US – Upland Cotton), WT/DS627/AB/R, adopted 21 March 2005*, para. 625; *see also ILC, Report of the International Law Commission in Its 70th Session (30 April-1 June and 2 July-10 August 2018) UN Doc A/73/10*, *supra* n. 10, para. 2, Conclusion 9.
74. Moloo, *supra* n. 26, at 76.
75. For an overview of the case law, *see* Michael Lang, *Auslegung und Anwendung von DBA, in 100 Jahre Steuerrechtsprechung in Deutschland 1918-2018: Festschrift für den Bundesfinanzhof* 986 et seq. (Klaus-Dieter Drüen et al. eds, Ottoschmidt 2018).
76. *Ibid.*

the version in these languages must also be used when interpreting such provisions.[77] If a provision of the United Nations Model Convention (UN MC) was the inspiration, this means that even the version of this provision in the six UN languages is relevant.[78] All of this demonstrates that the wording is not a genuine limit. A subsequent practice could still be covered by the wording in one language but not in another.

Article 33(4) VCLT addresses how to proceed in such constellations: '[...] when a comparison of the authentic texts discloses a difference of meaning which the application of articles 31 and 32 does not remove, the meaning which best reconciles the texts, having regard to the object and purpose of the treaty, shall be adopted'. This also expresses the fact that the wording of a provision of a tax treaty cannot be examined in isolation. The other aspects relevant under Articles 31 and 32 VCLT must always be taken into account, and particularly the 'object and purpose of the treaty' must also be observed. The wording in a single language should certainly not be singled out and regarded as the limit of interpretation. Efforts to reconcile the texts may result in the meaning of an expression being either much narrower or much broader than it initially appears when viewed in a single language.

The ILC Report from 2018 sees the limit for the consideration of subsequent practice in a manifest misapplication:[79] 'A manifest misapplication of a treaty, as opposed to a bona fide application (even if erroneous), is therefore not an "application of the treaty" in the sense of articles 31 and 32.' This means that there are limits to the consideration of subsequent practice, however, they are relatively broad. The phrase 'even if erroneous' in the sentence quoted from the ILC Report also reminds us that the consideration of subsequent practice does not necessarily mean that the interpretation expressed in it must ultimately be authoritative. Other aspects that must also be taken into account in the interpretation may be more convincing and ultimately lead to a different view prevailing than that expressed in the subsequent practice.

3.2 Relevant Authorities

The ILC Report first mentions that the 'subsequent practice of States in the application of a treaty may certainly be performed by the high-ranking government officials mentioned in Article 7 of the 1969 Vienna Convention'.[80] According to Article 7(2) VCLT, this includes in any case:

> (a) Heads of State, Heads of Government and Ministers for Foreign Affairs, for the purpose of performing all acts relating to the conclusion of a treaty; (b) heads of diplomatic missions, for the purpose of adopting the text of a treaty between the accrediting State and the State to which they are accredited; (c) representatives

77. Michael Lang, *Auslegung von Doppelbesteuerungsabkommen und authentische Vertragssprachen*, 20 IStR 406 et seq. (2011).
78. *Ibid.*, at 409.
79. *ILC, Report of the International Law Commission in Its 70th Session (30 April-1 June and 2 July-10 August 2018) UN Doc A/73/10, supra* n. 10, para. 19, Conclusion 4.
80. *Ibid.*, para. 6, Conclusion 5.

> accredited by States to an international conference or to an international organization or one of its organs, for the purpose of adopting the text of a treaty in that conference, organization or organ.

Finance ministers or their representatives are not explicitly mentioned. However, the ILC Report limits this anyway:[81] 'Yet, since most treaties typically are not applied by such high officials, international courts and tribunals have recognized that the conduct of lower authorities may also, under certain conditions, constitute relevant subsequent practice in the application of a treaty.' The ILC Report also mentions an example from the field of tax law:[82]

> And in the case of Tax regime governing pensions paid to retired UNESCO officials residing in France, the Arbitral Tribunal accepted, in principle, the practice of the French tax administration of not collecting taxes on the pensions of retired UNESCO employees as being relevant subsequent practice. Ultimately, however, the Arbitral Tribunal considered some contrary official pronouncements by a higher authority, the French Government, to be decisive.

From this, the ILC Report draws the following conclusion:[83] 'The practice of lower and local officials may thus be subsequent practice "of a party in the application of a treaty" if this practice is sufficiently unequivocal and if the Government can be expected to be aware of this practice and has not contradicted it within a reasonable time.'

The Austrian Constitutional Court went in a similar direction in a decision on tax treaty law in 2015:[84]

> One can only speak of a subsequent practice within the meaning of Article 31 (3) (b) VCLT to be taken into account in the interpretation of the treaty if the authorities entrusted with the application of the law represent a uniform view that has remained undisputed, i.e. has not been challenged before the courts or confirmed by the appellate court.[85]

This view was endorsed by the Swiss Federal Court in 2023:[86]

> In academic writing, it was rightly pointed out that the OECD Commentary itself does not yet embody a consistent application practice and that the local tax authorities and courts – and not the representatives of the Member States in the

---

81. *Ibid.*
82. *Ibid.*
83. *Ibid.*, para. 7, Conclusion 5.
84. Verfassungsgerichtshof 25.9.2015, V 41/2015; *see also* Michael Lang, *Wer hat das Sagen im Steuerrecht? Die Bedeutung des OECD-Steuerausschusses und seiner Working Parties*, 59 Österreichische Steuerzeitung 208 et seq. (2006).
85. Free translation by the authors.
86. No. 9C_682/2022, 9C_683/2022, para. 9.4.4. (Schweizerisches Bundesgericht 23 June 2023); the court referred to the following literature, among others, Michael Lang, *Die Bedeutung des OECD-Kommentars und der Reservations, Observations und Positions für die DBA-Auslegung, in Nationale und internationale Unternehmensbesteuerung in der Rechtsordnung: Festschrift für Dietmar Gosch zum Ausscheiden aus dem Richteramt* 239 (Jürgen Lüdicke et al. eds, C.H.Beck 2016); *ILC, Report of the International Law Commission in Its 70th Session (30 April-1 June and 2 July-10 August 2018) UN Doc A/73/10, supra* n. 10, paras 6 and 9, Conclusion 5.

OECD Fiscal Affairs Committee or the supreme tax authority of the Member States – are typically entrusted with the application of the tax treaties.[87]

Only in exceptional cases is the application of tax treaties not in the hands of the local tax authorities. This is always the case when a 'competent authority' is mentioned in a provision of a tax treaty.[88] Article 3(1) OECD MC provides a definition for this which is then to be filled in during the bilateral treaty negotiations and where ministries of finance or other supreme tax authorities are often mentioned. The 'competent authorities' are responsible for applying Articles 4(3), 26, 27, 29(6), and 29(8) OECD MC. The interpretations of these treaty provisions that are expressed in their application can therefore also have significance as 'subsequent practice'.

The application of Article 25 OECD MC is also required by the 'competent authorities'. However, a distinction must be made here: For the interpretation of this provision itself, the competent authorities can justify a subsequent practice to be taken into account.[89] This may, for example, concern the questions of how the competent authorities can communicate with each other on the basis of Article 25 OECD MC and how, for example, a mutual agreement can be reached. It could make a difference here whether the competent authorities conduct mutual agreement procedures only in person or also by email or even by telephone and whether it must be signed by the representatives of both delegations, whether documented email correspondence is also sufficient, or whether this agreement can also be concluded merely in a telephone conversation of which a record is then kept by each of the competent persons.

On the basis of Article 25 OECD MC, the competent authorities can also establish subsequent practice if they conclude a mutual agreement in an individual case. In such cases, it cannot be ruled out that interpreting the other provisions of a tax treaty by the competent authorities in a procedure under Article 25 OECD MC could also be taken into account for their interpretation. However, the reason for the necessity of such an individual mutual agreement procedure is that the local tax authorities often previously held different views and, therefore, there was no consistent subsequent practice. The conclusion of one or more individual mutual agreements to resolve a previously existing conflict of interpretation will hence not be sufficient to establish a subsequent practice. This is because applying a tax treaty in the vast majority of cases is not carried out by the competent authorities but by the local tax authorities. It is therefore crucial whether the view expressed by the former in an individual mutual agreement is also followed at the local level, at least subsequently. Ultimately, the subsequent practice of the local tax authorities is thus also important here.

According to Article 25(3), sentence 1 OECD MC, however, the competent authorities may also carry out mutual agreement procedures that do not concern one or more specific cases and whose aim is to resolve cases that are of a general nature. In

87. Free translation by the authors.
88. Michael Lang, *Missbrauchsbekämpfung als Ziel und Zweck der DBA?, in Aktuelle Praxis- und Grundsatzfragen des internationalen Steuerrechts* (Lars Hummel & Bert Kaminski eds, forthcoming).
89. *See* Lang, *Subsequent Practice and Tax Treaties, in A Journey Through European and International Taxation: Liber Amicorum in Honour of Peter Essers, supra* n. 23, at 357 et seq.

this case – with the exception of Article 25(3), sentence 1 OECD MC – the competent authorities do not apply the treaty but merely comment on the interpretation of individual tax treaty provisions. Therefore, the conclusion of such a mutual agreement cannot establish a subsequent practice for the tax treaty provision for which the interpretation is at issue in the mutual agreement. The decisive factor is again what the practice of the local tax authorities is in this regard. However, a distinction will also have to be made as to whether they actually apply the tax treaty itself in their practice or whether they are, under their domestic law, actually obligated or feel required to take the content of the mutual agreement into account irrespective of how they understand the content of the actually relevant tax treaty provision. In the latter case, it is doubtful that the local tax authorities can actually establish a subsequent practice on that.

3.3 Conduct in the Application of the Treaty

The latter constellation already shows that it is decisive whether a practice is actually attributable to a tax treaty provision and has its reason in a particular interpretation of it. The ILC Report properly states:[90] 'Subsequent conduct that is not motivated by a treaty obligation is not "in the application of the treaty" or "regarding" its interpretation, within the meaning of article 31.'

If the practice adheres to a changed view of the OECD Commentary, this will therefore not necessarily be relevant under Article 31(3)(b) VCLT. This is because, if the practitioners merely feel bound by the respective version of the OECD Commentary without there being a specific provision in the tax treaty itself that declares the current version of the OECD Commentary to be relevant for interpreting it, it cannot be assumed that the practice that has arisen is motivated by the tax treaty.

A distinction must also be made as to whether a certain practice is motivated by the domestic tax law of the state or by the tax treaty. If certain income is therefore not taxed in a state under domestic law, this cannot be seen as an indication that a tax treaty provision has been applied that excludes taxation in this state.[91] This is because the tax treaty was not applied in this case.

This also applies in the case of a treaty override. If a provision of domestic tax law requires taxation, irrespective of whether this would even be permissible under a tax treaty, it is motivated by domestic tax law and not by the tax treaty. In this case, taxation is therefore not considered a subsequent practice since it is not motivated by the tax treaty.

A subsequent practice also does not arise from the fact that tax authorities provide legal opinions on the interpretation of individual tax treaty provisions that are not binding as such. Then, the authority providing the opinion does not constitute an 'application' of the treaty. The situation is different if an authority is authorized to issue

90. *ILC, Report of the International Law Commission in Its 70th Session (30 April-1 June and 2 July-10 August 2018) UN Doc A/73/10, supra* n. 10, para. 7, Conclusion 6.
91. Michael Lang, *Hinterbliebenenpensionen und Art 19 Abs 2 OECD-MA*, 34 Steuer- und Wirtschaft International 98 et seq. (2024).

binding rulings on the interpretation of tax treaty provisions. In this case, this authority applies these in this respect and can thus contribute to the emergence of a 'subsequent practice'.

However, the participation of a government's representatives in a resolution on the amendment of the OECD Commentary cannot be regarded as 'subsequent practice': An amendment of the OECD Commentary is not considered conduct in the application of a tax treaty. The representatives of the states in the OECD function as members of an OECD body and apply the OECD statute but do not apply a tax treaty.[92]

Finally, there are also situations in which tax treaty provisions are primarily applied by the taxpayers and no tax authority takes any action at all. Taxpayers in many tax systems have to declare and pay their taxes, and the tax administration only intervenes in cases of a tax audit, when they are requested to do so or are suspicious that a specific taxpayer is not complying with the law. In this case, the conduct established by the taxpayers – as non-state actors – pursuant to Article 31(3)(b) VCLT may also become relevant. However, this can only be the case if the tax authorities are aware of this practice, and it is clear that it is tolerated by the tax authorities.[93] The conduct of non-state actors is only insofar relevant as it informs about the subsequent practice of the state actors and therefore has to be taken into account with caution.

3.4 Frequency and Uniformity

The value of subsequent practice depends on the extent to which it is 'concordant, common, and consistent'.[94] When applying a treaty that – as may be the case with a tax treaty – is applied thousands or even hundreds of thousands of times, it will not be sufficient to simply provide evidence of a *single* case of application if subsequent practice with weight is to be established. It must also be taken into account that there are often different regional authorities in many countries. Therefore, if a consistent practice is to be established in a state, the practice in different regions must be assessed.

The decisive factor is that this practice is either not disputed or has been confirmed by the courts. If it is questioned by the local authorities and their decisions are challenged in the courts, this initially evidences that a consistent practice does not exist. Only if the courts confirm the local tax authorities' opinion can a subsequent practice be assumed. However, if that is rejected by the courts, there can be no question again of subsequent practice. In this case, it is yet uncertain whether a subsequent practice will later develop on the basis of the opinion expressed by the courts.

For a subsequent practice to arise in accordance with Article 31(3)(b) VCLT, it must be consistent in both states, and it is sufficient for it to be verifiable in parallel in both of them.[95] It is not a prerequisite that the authorities are aware of the practice in

---

92. Lang, *Die Auffassung des BMF zur Bedeutung des OECD-Kommentars für die Auslegung von DBA*, 32 IStR, *supra* n. 26, at 554.
93. *See* *ILC, Report of the International Law Commission in Its 70th Session (30 April-1 June and 2 July-10 August 2018) UN Doc A/73/10*, *supra* n. 10, para. 1, Conclusion 10.
94. *Ibid.*, para. 10, Conclusion 9.
95. *Ibid.*, para. 23, Conclusion 6.

the respective other contracting state. However, it must be motivated by the tax treaty itself in both states.[96]

If a practice can only be proven in one country, then this practice is at least relevant under Article 32 VCLT according to the ILC Report.[97] It is then only of secondary relevance but must also be taken into account in the interpretation. This applies in any case if no practice can be proven in the other contracting state. If this is contrary to that of the first state, its relevance will also have to be relativized for the purposes of Article 32 VCLT.

3.5 Weight of Subsequent Practice

In cases when subsequent practice can be proven, Article 31(3)(b) VCLT requires that this practice 'shall be taken into account'. However, this does not mean that it is of paramount or even special importance. It must be taken into account in the same way as all other aspects relevant to the interpretation, and it can easily be the case that other arguments make another interpretation appear more obvious and that this interpretation has the more convincing arguments in its favour.[98]

The fact that tax treaties are not among the international treaties that not only entitle and obligate the contracting states but also have a considerable impact on third parties – specifically the taxpayers covered by them – also advocates for particular caution with regard to subsequent practice.[99] Tax treaties intervene intensively in the tax laws of the respective contracting states by restricting existing tax obligations when necessary.[100] Regardless of a specific constitutional situation, legal certainty becomes majorly relevant in the area of tax law. Taxpayers expect to be able to derive their rights and obligations from the provisions that affect them. However, if their content was only to be substantiated in practice following the tax treaty's conclusion and its legislative approval, this legal certainty would suffer. Therefore, according to the object and purpose of the tax treaties, the significance of 'subsequent practice' must be assumed to be limited at most.

In addition, tax treaties are predominantly based on the OECD MC or the UN MC. Model conventions have the advantage that they save the delegations negotiating a tax treaty from having to waste a significant amount of time or effort to create one each time and can rely on tried and tested provisions. However, this is also closely linked to the effect that, by adopting the provisions of one of the model conventions, the content of these provisions is already established. They are already explained in the OECD or

96. *Ibid.*, para. 7, Conclusion 6.
97. *Ibid.*, para. 35, Conclusion 4.
98. Michael Lang, *Die Bedeutung von Verständigungsvereinbarungen nach Art. 3 Abs 2 OECD-Musterabkommen 2017, in Territorialität und Personalität: Festschrift für Moris Lehner zum 70. Geburtstag* 210 (Roland Ismer et al. eds, ottoschmidt 2019).
99. Michael Lang, *Doppelbesteuerungsabkommen und innerstaatliches Recht: Die Einordnung von Doppelbesteuerungsabkommen in die österreichische Rechtsordnung* 86 et seq. (Wirtschaftsverlag Orac 1992).
100. Klaus Vogel & Rainer Prokisch, *General Report, in Interpretation of Double Taxation Conventions* 57 (IFA ed., 1993).

UN Commentaries, and it is often possible to refer to case law from other countries that have already concluded tax treaties with identical provisions. However, this advantage is forfeited or would at least be relativized if subsequent practice was to be a significant factor in the interpretation of tax treaties. This is because they are usually bilateral treaties and, in such a context, subsequent practice can only be determined at a bilateral level and could therefore develop differently for each tax treaty for that reason. The greater the significance of subsequent practice for the interpretation, the greater the risk that the content of identical provisions in different tax treaties will diverge. Therefore, adopting provisions of one of the Model Conventions is a clear indication that the contracting states intended to give minimal or no importance to the necessarily bilateral subsequent practice concerning the interpretation of those provisions.

For tax treaties, it must also be taken into account that those modelled on the OECD MC or the UN MC have their own interpretation provision. Although Article 3(2) OECD MC is controversial, according to the view expressed here, it emphasizes the interpretation from the 'context' of the tax treaty.[101] Only in the rare cases in which this interpretation fails is it necessary to rely on the domestic law of the state of application. It is clear that 'context' does not merely refer to the eponymous expression in Article 31 VCLT as it also covers other aspects of interpretation addressed in Articles 31 and 32 VCLT. However, this does not mean that it refers to them in their entirety. It is conceivable that the mention of 'context' in Article 3(2) OECD MC is to be understood as meaning that neither 'subsequent agreements' nor 'subsequent practice' have little or no significance in the interpretation of tax treaties.[102] This is supported by the arguments mentioned above that suggest that subsequent practice should only be included in the interpretation with great restraint, if at all.

This view is confirmed by the amendments made to Article 3(2) OECD MC in 2017. This is because, according to its new wording, mutual agreements are subordinate to the 'context' in terms of interpretation. Their special mention in Article 3(2) OECD MC also makes it clear that they do not fall under the 'context' at all.[103] Insofar as the 'mutual agreements' correspond to the 'subsequent agreements' according to Article 31(3)(a) VCLT, this means that the latter are only of subordinate importance. In view of the fact that there is often a fluid transition between 'subsequent agreements' and 'subsequent practice' and the consideration of both aspects is regulated in parallel, at least in the VCLT, there is some evidence to suggest that the revised provision of Article 3(2) OECD MC should be interpreted as an additional indication that subsequent practice is only of subordinate importance.

Finally, there are also significant practical arguments as to why 'subsequent practice' can only be of minor importance when interpreting tax treaties. First and foremost, it concerns the practice of the local tax authorities which may have

101. *See* Chapter 11 in this book.
102. Lang, *Can Law Regulate Its Own Interpretation? Relevance and Meaning of Articles 31-33 of the Vienna Convention on the Law of Treaties (VCLT) and Article 3 Para. 2 of the Model Convention of the Organisation for Economic Co-operation and Development (OECD MC) for the Interpretation of Double-Taxation Conventions*, in *Research Handbook on International Taxation*, *supra* n. 6, at 179.
103. *Ibid.*, at 188.

significance for the 'subsequent practice' relevant under Article 31(3)(b) VCLT. However, how the local tax authorities decide in – other – individual cases is generally beyond the knowledge of those taxpayers who have to interpret the provisions of a tax treaty when fulfilling their tax obligations. Although the tax administration has access to this information, it is generally unable to disclose it in individual tax procedures as this is prevented by tax secrecy in many countries. As a result, it is usually not possible to justify its own decisions with a uniform practice nor to provide evidence of this in court proceedings. The tax authorities' unverifiable assertion of a certain practice, however, will not generally satisfy the requirements of a state governed by the rule of law. This is only different in cases when decisions are published as often occurs with court judgments or, in some countries, with certain rulings. However, even in these cases, it is probably not always possible to conclude from published decisions that there is consistent practice everywhere. If a ruling has been granted in individual cases in which a certain interpretation of a tax treaty provision is advocated, this does not mean that the same legal issue will be assessed in the same way by the competent local authorities in all other comparable cases. Even in decisions by a court, it cannot always be assumed as certain that the tax authorities will follow a decision issued in an individual case in the future. In many countries, it is common for tax authorities that disagree with the decision to disregard it in other cases in order to provoke further court decisions on the same legal issue. The tax authorities then want to take the opportunity to convince the same or another court of the administration's opinion.

4 CONCLUSION

The considerations have shown that, in the area of the VCLT, subsequent practice must be taken into account for interpreting international public law treaties but that the significance can be very different. The VCLT affords sufficient opportunities to differentiate according to the various contexts in which the treaty provisions are located and according to the object and purpose of the specific treaty.

This is particularly important for interpreting tax treaties as, within the scope of their application, it is already very difficult to identify any relevant subsequent practice at all. A subsequent practice that would mean a modification of a tax treaty has no significance for the interpretation but simply proves to be unlawful. The relevant authorities are usually the local tax authorities and only rarely are the 'competent authorities' under the tax treaties. However, their practice is often unknown or cannot be used to resolve other tax cases for reasons of tax confidentiality. Furthermore, it must be a matter of conduct in applying a treaty. The authorities' involvement in the amendment of the OECD Commentary is therefore not relevant. The practice must be motivated by the fact that the tax authorities want to comply with the requirements of a tax treaty. Finally, especially in the area of tax law when tax treaty provisions often have to be applied in thousands of cases, it must be ensured that this is not a singular practice but a consistent one that is not limited to just one region.

If a subsequent practice can be identified at all, there are a number of reasons to assume that its significance for interpreting tax treaties is particularly low. This can be deduced from the requirement of legal certainty which is decisive in almost all states and underpins tax provisions and thus also tax treaty provisions. The interpretation of these treaties therefore requires substantial restraint in terms of their object and purpose when later using practice, i.e., after their conclusion and entry into force, for interpreting these provisions. Tax treaty provisions that are modelled on the OECD MC are also designed to be uniformly understood in all countries that use the same model provision. This also suggests that the significance of the necessarily bilateral subsequent practice should be considered low. The fact that tax treaties generally have their own interpretation clause with the provision modelled on Article 3(2) OECD MC makes it easier to treat subsequent practice differently from other treaties when interpreting them. According to the interpretation of Article 3(2) OECD MC favoured here, this provision emphasizes an interpretation from the 'context' of the tax treaty. The term 'context' certainly has a broader meaning than simply referring to the 'context' of Article 31 VCLT. However, this provision also makes it possible to see the subsequent practice of Article 31(3)(b) VCLT as not covered or only covered to a very limited extent by the 'context' of Article 3(2) OECD MC.

CHAPTER 8

Supplementary Means of Interpretation and Tax Treaty Interpretation

Gustavo Weiss de Resende

1 Introduction and Relationship to Article 31 VCLT
2 Significance of Supplementary Means of Interpretation and the Open-Ended List of Article 32 VCLT
 2.1 Explicitly Foreseen Supplementary Means
  2.1.1 *Travaux Préparatoires*
  2.1.2 Circumstances of Conclusion
 2.2 Other Possible Supplementary Means of Interpretation
 2.3 Giving Meaning Through Article 32 VCLT: Confirmation and Determination
3 Applicability of Article 32 VCLT for the Interpretation of Tax Treaties
 3.1 Traditional Supplementary Means of Interpretation in the Context of Double Tax Treaties
  3.1.1 *Travaux Préparatoires* as By-Products of International Negotiations on Tax Treaties
  3.1.2 Circumstances of Conclusion on Tax Treaty Negotiations
 3.2 Other Possible Supplementary Means in Tax Treaty Interpretation
 3.3 The Legal Status of the OECD Model Convention Commentaries
 3.4 Giving Meaning to Tax Treaties Through Article 32 VCLT
4 Conclusion

1 INTRODUCTION AND RELATIONSHIP TO ARTICLE 31 VCLT

'There are few aspects of international law more important than the interpretation of treaties.'[1] The now more than 50-year-old statement by Jennings is applicable today more than ever in an era of globalization and complexity. In contemporary (public) international law, disagreements over the interpretation of particular treaty clauses continue to be a common phenomenon, and conflicts brought before international adjudication typically revolve around issues of treaty interpretation.[2] The same applies to tax treaties[3] of which their interpretation produces effects that not only go beyond the mere relationship between the contracting states but also directly affect the taxpayer and the way that tax administrations operate internally.

As discussed in other chapters of this book, the correctness of an interpretation outcome is assessed by consulting the interpretation guidelines outlined in international law as articulated in the 1969 Vienna Convention on the Law of Treaties (VCLT), specifically in Articles 31-33.[4] Thus, the outcome of an interpretation process is deemed to be accurate when it can be effectively justified as aligning with the stipulations of these articles of the Vienna Convention.[5] This chapter thus concerns itself specifically with what is referred to as the supplementary means of interpretation contained within Article 32 VCLT and its use for tax treaty interpretation as opposed to the primary[6] means of interpretation discussed thus far in Article 31 VCLT.

This will be done by first dissecting Article 32 VCLT from an exclusively public international law perspective in section 2 where not only the explicitly foreseen supplementary means will be discussed but also other possible methods of supplementary interpretation and, in particular, the way in which they may be employed. Following this analysis, section 3 will delve deeper into the implications of the supplementary means for tax treaty interpretation in a manner that mirrors the investigation conducted in the previous section. Furthermore, this section will deal with the longstanding question of the legal status and use of the Organisation for Economic Co-operation and Development (OECD) Model Convention Commentaries within the framework of the Vienna Convention.

First and foremost, however, it is essential to understand the dynamics between those two articles so as to clarify the interplay between what could be called primary

---

1. Robert Jennings, *General Course on Principles of International Law* (Vol. 121 ed., A.W. Sijthoff 1967), p. 544.
2. Jeremy Hill, *Aust's Modern Treaty Law and Practice* (Cambridge 4th ed. 2023), p. 238.
3. *See* Frank Engelen, *Interpretation of Tax Treaties under International Law* (2004), Chapter 10.
4. As, according to the prevailing opinion, the VCLT's interpretation rules are part of international customary law. *See* Michael Lang, *Introduction to the Law of Double Taxation Conventions* (Linde 3d ed. 2021), p. 14.
5. *See also* Ulf Linderfalk, *Is the Hierarchical Structure of Articles 31 and 32 of the Vienna Convention Real or Not? Interpreting the Rules of Interpretation*, Netherlands International Law Review (2007), p. 134 https://doi.org/10.1017/s0165070x07001337.
6. While the Vienna Convention does not use this term itself, it is often adopted by international law commentators. *See, e.g.*, Humphrey Waldock, *Third Report on the Law of Treaties*, Yearbook of the International Law Commission (Document A/CN.4/167 and Add.1-3 ed. 1964), p. 99; Mark E. Villiger, *Commentary on the 1969 Vienna Convention on the Law of Treaties* (Martinus Nijhoff Publishers 2009), p. 444.

and mere supplementary means of interpretation. These terms can nonetheless be misleading as their relative importance might be even greater than assumed by this denomination as will be demonstrated further on in this chapter.[7] Whereas Article 31 is titled 'General rule of interpretation', indicating its broad nature, Article 32 is labelled as a mere 'Supplementary means of interpretation' alongside the general rule. The juxtaposition of 'rule' and 'means' in the headings implies that Article 32 serves as a supplement to Article 31 which assumes a primary role in the interpretative process.[8] Based on this language found in Articles 31 and 32 VCLT, the relationship between primary and supplementary means of interpretation appears prima facie hierarchical.[9] Their respective values are not subject to case-specific determination but rather governed by the broadly formulated articles and, accordingly, whenever interpretation is necessary to ascertain the correct meaning of a treaty provision, the primary means of interpretation should be the initial recourse.[10]

The supplementary means would thus become a factor during a subsequent stage of the interpretation process after the general means of interpretation based on Article 31 VCLT have been proven to be insufficient for elucidating the meaning by themselves. According to the wording of the Vienna Convention, supplementary means of interpretation are employed when the interpretation under Article 31 results in ambiguity, obscurity, or a manifestly absurd or unreasonable outcome. Conversely, if the primary means have effectively clarified the correct meaning of a treaty provision, supplementary means seem to be possibly utilized solely for the purpose of confirming that meaning.[11]

In this context, Article 32 aligns especially with paragraphs 2 and 3 of the general rules contained in Article 31 VCLT that similarly incorporate extrinsic materials into the interpretation process to contextualize the treaty.[12] However, in this case, the identified material is assigned a lower significance as it is considered merely supplementary. The differentiation between the primary interpretative means contained in Article 31 VCLT and the supplementary ones in Article 32 thus rests on their connection to the (presumed) intentions of the parties and, more precisely, their 'agreement'. The text is assumed to authentically represent their consent with extrinsic means such as subsequent agreements and practice included among the primary means only when they

7. Refer to ss 2.3 and 3.4.
8. Michael Reisman, *Opinion with Respect to Selected International Legal Problems in LCIA Case No. 7941* (2009), para. 8.
9. Even though the preparatory works of the Vienna Conference that occurred in 1968 show that some states were not willing to accept this relationship as can be seen in United Nations Conference on the Law of Treaties, *Official Records of the United Nations Conference on the Law of Treaties, First Session (Summary Records of the Plenary Meetings and of the Meetings of the Committee of the Whole)* (1968), Document A/CONF.39/C.1/SR.33, paras 27 and 75.
10. Ulf Linderfalk, *Is the Hierarchical Structure of Articles 31 and 32 of the Vienna Convention Real or Not? Interpreting the Rules of Interpretation*, Netherlands International Law Review (2007), p. 136.
11. *Ibid.* This is not necessarily how Art. 32 VCLT is employed in practice, however, as will be discussed further on in this chapter.
12. Oliver Dörr, *Supplementary Means of Interpretation, in Vienna Convention on the Law of Treaties. A Commentary* (Oliver Dörr & Kirsten Schmalenbach eds, Springer 2d ed. 2018), p. 617.

signify 'agreement' among the parties.[13] In contrast, Article 32 does not necessitate such an agreement thereby leading to the interpretation means gathered there being regarded as considerably less reliable[14] and thus working as a secondary layer of interpretation to (tax) treaties. The connection between the authentic interpretation under Article 31 and the supplementary interpretation under Article 32 is forged by the confirmatory role ascribed to the latter.

2 SIGNIFICANCE OF SUPPLEMENTARY MEANS OF INTERPRETATION AND THE OPEN-ENDED LIST OF ARTICLE 32 VCLT

2.1 Explicitly Foreseen Supplementary Means

Prior to delving into the function of Article 32 VCLT within the interpretative framework of the Vienna Convention, it is beneficial to initially recognize and elucidate which 'supplementary means of interpretation' it addresses. The wording of the article is as follows:

> Article 32: Recourse may be had to supplementary means of interpretation, including the preparatory work of the treaty and the circumstances of its conclusion, in order to confirm the meaning resulting from the application of article 31, or to determine the meaning when the interpretation according to article 31:
>
> (a) leaves the meaning ambiguous or obscure; or
> (b) leads to a result which is manifestly absurd or unreasonable.

It is important to note from the outset that this article specifically mentions the preparatory work of the treaty – commonly known as *travaux préparatoires* – and the circumstances of its conclusion. However, its language, by comprising the term 'including', does not prevent the interpreter from considering other forms of supplementary means of interpretation.[15] This section will nevertheless attend to the explicitly foreseen supplementary means of interpretation, their meaning, contours, and usability in practice.

2.1.1 Travaux Préparatoires

The term '*travaux préparatoires*' – also known as 'preparatory work' – while being widely recognized as the most important supplementary means of interpretation,[16] lacks a specific definition within Article 32 and the Vienna Convention as a whole. As a matter of fact, the International Law Commission (ILC), responsible for formulating

13. *Ibid.* As discussed in other chapters of this book in relation to Art. 31, para. 3, for example.
14. *Ibid.*, p. 618.
15. *See* Jeremy Hill, *Aust's Modern Treaty Law and Practice* (Cambridge 4th ed. 2023), p. 258.
16. Refer to the widely cited Mark E. Villiger, *Commentary on the 1969 Vienna Convention on the Law of Treaties* (Martinus Nijhoff Publishers 2009), p. 445.

the VCLT, believed that attempting to define it would not only yield little benefit but might also risk excluding pertinent evidence from an analysis.[17] In this context, there are two main challenges linked to using *travaux*: identifying what would they be and drawing inferences from them.[18]

If interpreted literally, the *travaux* should encompass any and all documents generated throughout the stages of preparing, debating, drafting, and negotiating a treaty[19] as they would contain potential evidence of what the drafters of the treaty might have had intended.[20] This definition would encompass a very broad range of documents with the main requirements being that they are developed during and in connection with the negotiations. In this sense, the aim of employing preparatory work in the first place is to discern the genuine meaning of the agreement between the parties contained in a particular treaty. Therefore, authors commonly agree on three main conditions that must be met before the relevant material can be deemed *travaux préparatoires*:[21]

(1) Only materials and processes that can be objectively evaluated by an interpreter qualify as preparatory work. They must be elements of the external world so that individuals can become aware of them.
(2) The materials under consideration must be capable of elucidating a shared understanding among the negotiating parties regarding the meaning of the treaty provisions. Therefore, these materials can only be regarded as authentic preparatory work if they were, at least at one stage, part of the negotiating process and accessible to all of the negotiators.[22]
(3) To be pertinent as *travaux*, the material must directly relate to the treaty under consideration, be part of its negotiation process, and aim to clarify its substance.[23]

---

17. International Law Commission, *Documents of the Second Part of the Seventeenth Session and of the Eighteenth Session Including the Reports of the Commission to the General Assembly*, Yearbook of the International Law Commission (Vol. II ed. 1966), p. 223.
18. Esmé Shirlow & Michael Waibel, *A Sliding Scale Approach to Travaux in Treaty Interpretation: The Case of Investment Treaties*, The British Yearbook of International Law (2021), p. 7f. https://doi.org/10.1093/bybil/brab001.
19. Chang-fa Lo, *Treaty Interpretation under the Vienna Convention on the Law of Treaties* (Springer Singapore 1st ed. 2017), p. 229.
20. Arnold Duncan McNair, *The Law of Treaties* (Clarendon Press 1961), p. 411f.
21. *See* Oliver Dörr, *Supplementary Means of Interpretation, in Vienna Convention on the Law of Treaties. A Commentary* (Oliver Dörr & Kirsten Schmalenbach eds, Springer 2d ed. 2018), p. 621.
22. This is particularly pertinent regarding documents from a single source such as statements from individual governments or state representatives outside treaty negotiations, national legislative documents, and explanations provided to a legislative body as part of a national ratification process. These can only be considered if, at some stage, they were incorporated into the negotiation process, made known to other participants, and did not merely remain unilateral aspirations, inclinations, or opinions. *Ibid.*
23. However, the ICJ has, on occasion, cited material related to an identical predecessor treaty and even similar ones, applying that material as if it was preparatory work for the treaty under consideration. *Ibid.*, p. 623. *See also* LaGrand (*Germany v. United States of America*), Judgment, I.C.J. Reports 2001, p. 466, paras 105ff. While these materials should not be considered *travaux*, they definitely can be deemed to be other supplementary means. Refer to s. 2.2 and especially s. 3.2.

Thus, if the abovementioned requirements are fulfilled, this category of preparatory documents may include, e.g., the successive drafts of the treaty, negotiation records, minutes of commission and plenary proceedings, memoranda and statements from governments and their representatives, diplomatic exchanges between the parties, and interpretative statements made by the chairman of a drafting committee.[24] Many of these have been used by the International Court of Justice (ICJ) in the past,[25] including others less related to the negotiation process such as intergovernmental documents that were prepared previous to the negotiations.[26]

As can be determined from the above, the materials that can be deemed to be *travaux préparatoires* will inevitably be diverse depending on the type of treaty and how the negotiations were conducted. The primary issue that arises with this is what should be the interpretative value given to this amalgamation of distinct documents[27] as it is essential to differentiate between identifying the elements that constitute the *travaux préparatoires* of a treaty and determining the significance assigned to each element in the interpretative process.[28] This means that the concern regarding extraneous material lies not in its permissibility but in the delicate equilibrium required when deriving the meaning of the final text from such materials.[29] Mainly, the relative importance of the *travaux* will hinge on its clarity, accessibility, direct relevance to the treaty terms in question and consistency with the other means of interpretation or, to clarify, its cogency depends on the extent to which it represents a common understanding of the parties as to the meaning of treaty terms.[30]

Travaux préparatoires, concisely stated, encompass materials that document the negotiations and other circumstances leading to the formal conclusion of a treaty. Due to this broad definition encompassing (also) the inclusion of outdated negotiation positions, these preparatory documents can potentially mislead an interpreter regarding the signatories' intentions at the time of signing the treaty.[31] Furthermore, it is vital to remember that, in many cases, critical discussions can take place in private and,

24. For instance, in Yves Le Bouthillier, *Article 32, in Les conventions de Vienne sur le droit des traités. Commentaire article par article* (Olivier Corten ed., Bruylant 2006), p. 1354f.
25. Martin Ris, *Treaty Interpretation and ICJ Recourse to Travaux Preparatoires: Towards a Proposed Amendment of Articles 31 and 32 of the Vienna Convention on the Law of Treaties*, XIV Boston College International & Comparative Law Review (1991), p. 133f.
26. Refer, for instance, to Aegean Sea Continental Shelf, Judgment, I.C.J. Reports 1978, pp. 26ff.
27. Jeremy Hill, *Aust's Modern Treaty Law and Practice* (Cambridge 4th ed. 2023), p. 256.
28. *See* Makane Moïse Mbengue, *Rules of Interpretation (Article 32 of the Vienna Convention on the Law of Treaties)*, 31 ICSID Review (2016), p. 390 https://doi.org/10.1093/icsidreview/siw004.
29. Refer to Daniel Patrick O'Connell, *International Law* (Stevens 2d ed. 1970), p. 263.
30. *See* Humphrey Waldock, *Third Report on the Law of Treaties*, Yearbook of the International Law Commission (Document A/CN.4/167 and Add.1-3 ed. 1964), para. 48.
31. In its commentary on the Final Draft, the ILC provides two distinct explanations for why *travaux préparatoires* should have a less prominent role in treaty interpretation: one tied to the lack of an authentic character of these documents as an element of interpretation when compared to Art. 31 VCLT; and the other tied to the incompleteness or misleading character of treaty negotiations. Refer to ILC, *Draft Articles on the Law of Treaties with Commentaries.* (1966), pp. 219ff. *See also* Bishnu N. Mehrish, *Travaux Preparatoires as an Element in the Interpretation of Treaties*, 11 Indian Journal of International Law (1971), pp. 39ff.

consequently, may not be documented in the negotiation records[32] which could further undermine – or mislead the interpreter – as to the importance of the preparatory works. This implies that, while the *travaux préparatoires* can contain crucial information for interpreting a treaty, it can also be faulty and misleading in many cases and must thus be approached cautiously as the supplementary means of interpretation that it represents.

Furthermore, it becomes apparent from the organization of Articles 31 and 32 that preparatory work must be discerned from the context of a treaty; this is addressed in Article 31(2) VCLT and in Chapter 4 of this book.[33] However, delineating this distinction is challenging, and it is perhaps most effectively made based on whether the material in question was pertinent in formulating the text of the treaty for which it would most likely be defined as *travaux préparatoires* or in emphasizing the consensus existing at the time of its conclusion where it would most likely be deemed to be part of the context of the treaty.[34]

Hence the – at least apparent[35] – supporting role of the *travaux* is made clear, and the restrictive use of preparatory works can be seen in multiple instances of older case law[36] and in the ILC's work on the law of treaties.[37] Accordingly, caution must always be exercised when using *travaux préparatoires* as supplementary means of interpretation.[38] Nevertheless, experience has demonstrated that courts and tribunals tend to seize any sort of document that might seem helpful in deciding the matter at hand,[39]

32. Ian Sinclair, *The Vienna Convention on the Law of Treaties* (Manchester Univ. Press 1984), p. 142f.
33. It might be argued that such distinctions can be irrelevant in some cases as the interpretation process should be a 'single, combined operation' as seen in the ILC Report of 2018. However, the ILC Report also indicates that appropriate emphasis should be placed on the various means of interpretation that the author believes is made easier and more precise by (attempting) to classify each means under a specific provision as will be discussed further on. *See* the ILC's opinion in International Law Commission, *Chapter IV: Subsequent Agreements and Subsequent Practices in Relation to the Interpretation of the Treaties*, p. 24.
34. Oliver Dörr, *Supplementary Means of Interpretation, in Vienna Convention on the Law of Treaties. A Commentary* (Oliver Dörr & Kirsten Schmalenbach eds, Springer 2d ed. 2018), p. 624.
35. *See* the opposing opinion of Stephen Schwebel, *May Preparatory Work Be Used to Correct Rather Than Confirm the 'Clear' Meaning of a Treaty Provision?, in Theory of International Law at the Threshold of the 21st Century. Essays in honour of Krzysztof Skubiszewski* (Jerzy Makarczyk ed., Martinus Nijhoff/Kluwer Law International 1996), pp. 542ff. This will be further discussed in s. 2.3.
36. Such as S.S. Lotus (*Fr. v. Turk.*), 1927 P.C.I.J. (ser. A) No. 10 (September 7), para. 37; Admission of a State to the United Nations (Charter, Art. 4), Advisory Opinion: I.C.J. Reports 1948, p. 10; and Constitution of the Maritime Safety Committee of the Inter-Governmental Maritime Consultative Organization, Advisory Opinion of 8 June 1960: I.C.J. Reports 1960, p. 13f. Even between different courts, there is a tendency to reproduce past decisions when it comes to interpretation. *See* the opinion on this 'cocktail party' of Katharina Berner, *Judicial Dialogue and Treaty Interpretation: Revisiting the 'Cocktail Party' of International Law*, 54 Archiv des Völkerrechts (2016), p. 87f. https://doi.org/10.1628/000389216x14610487055677.
37. *See* Humphrey Waldock, *Third Report on the Law of Treaties*, Yearbook of the International Law Commission (Document A/CN.4/167 and Add.1-3 ed. 1964), pp. 57ff.
38. James Crawford & Ian Brownlie, *Brownlie's Principles of Public International Law* (Oxford University Press 8th ed. 2012), p. 383f.
39. Richard K. Gardiner, *Treaty Interpretation* (Oxford University Press 2010), p. 99f.

and parties will commonly resort[40] to the *travaux préparatoires* in an attempt to strengthen their argument irrespective of the 'supplementary' nature of the documents. In fact, the only viable means by which preparatory work can be purposefully overlooked is if the idea that a treaty is significantly connected to the intentions of its drafters is somehow disregarded which is an implausible concept, to say the least.[41] This indicates that the *travaux* might have greater importance than initially assumed for these preparatory works.

2.1.2 Circumstances of Conclusion

Next to the preparatory work of a treaty, Article 32 VCLT foresees what is known as the circumstances of conclusion as further supplementary means of interpretation. According to the ILC's work on the subject, this formula is intended to encompass both the contemporary circumstances and the historical context in which the treaty was concluded.[42] Nonetheless, some ambiguity exists concerning the differentiation between *travaux préparatoires* and the circumstances of conclusion of a specific treaty that are both mentioned expressly in the Convention. In essence, if a material or document is generated concurrently with the treaty negotiation, it should be considered part of the *travaux préparatoires*. Conversely, if a material or document predates the commencement of negotiations but nevertheless bears an influence on them, it would fall within the purview of the circumstances of conclusion.[43] This does not indicate, however, that there would be any type of hierarchy between these supplementary means – even though the preparatory works are used more frequently[44] – and one would not necessarily prevail over the other.

This means that, in truth, there is an overlap between the circumstances of conclusion and the preparatory work of a treaty much like how they extend alongside and interact with the elements of Article 31 VCLT, such as the object and purpose of a treaty.[45] The main difference between them will be a *timing* one and, as such, it is likely that both will be used for interpreting a treaty provision. Considering this timing

40. Ulf Linderfalk, *Is the Hierarchical Structure of Articles 31 and 32 of the Vienna Convention Real or Not? Interpreting the Rules of Interpretation*, Netherlands International Law Review (2007), p. 137f.
41. *See* Jan Klabbers, *International Legal Histories: The Declining Importance of Travaux Préparatoires in Treaty Interpretation?*, Netherlands International Law Review (2003), p. 279.
42. Humphrey Waldock, *Third Report on the Law of Treaties*, Yearbook of the International Law Commission (Document A/CN.4/167 and Add.1-3 ed. 1964), p. 59.
43. Chang-fa Lo, *Treaty Interpretation Under the Vienna Convention on the Law of Treaties* (Springer Singapore 1st ed. 2017), p. 230. The International Centre for Settlement of Investment Disputes (ICSID) took a different stance, however, in *Kiliç v. Turkmenistan* in which it held that the circumstances surrounding a treaty's conclusion include the processes related to its negotiation, conclusion, and signing as well as the events leading up to its ratification, mixing up concepts. *Kiliç İnşaat İthalat İhracat Sanayi Ve Ticaret Anonim Şirketi v. Turkmenistan*, ICSID Case No. ARB/10/1, Decision on Art. VII.2 of the Turkey-Turkmenistan Bilateral Investment Treaty, p. 48.
44. Luigi Sbolci, *Supplementary Means of Interpretation, in The Law of Treaties Beyond the Vienna Convention: [Essays in Honour of Professor Giorgio Gaja]* (Enzo Cannizzaro ed., Oxford Univ. Press 1st publ ed. 2011), p. 156f.
45. *See* Richard K. Gardiner, *Treaty Interpretation* (Oxford University Press 2010), p. 343f.

difference, the substance of the circumstances of conclusion can be somewhat distinct from the *travaux*, including, for instance, the political, social, historical,[46] and cultural factors, that is, the *extrinsic circumstances* encompassing a treaty's conclusion.[47] In ICJ and World Trade Organization (WTO) jurisprudence, historical materials and backgrounds as well as provisions in the predecessor agreements alongside unilateral acts and materials have all been regarded as circumstances surrounding this.[48]

In addition, in contrast to the preparatory works that are documents developed and made available during the negotiation process, there may be cases in which, in order to understand the circumstances of conclusion, it is necessary for the interpreter to look for documents and information entirely extrinsic to the negotiations but may have influenced or have the power to indicate the reality of the situation that the parties wished to regulate by means of the treaty.[49] As such, external factors corresponding to the economic, political, and social conditions of the parties, their affiliation with specific groupings, or their status such as being importing or exporting countries may also be considered circumstances of a treaty's conclusion.[50]

Moreover, legislative acts and court judgments of certain negotiating states can form part of the historical background of a treaty and consequently contribute to the circumstances surrounding its conclusion.[51] This highlights the fact that not only multilateral sources of a treaty can be considered circumstances of conclusion but also

46. In the WTO case of *US-Stainless Steel* (Mexico), the United States contended that specific historical materials constituted circumstances of the conclusion. Despite this assertion, the Appellate Body deemed it unnecessary to resort to such supplementary means. Nevertheless, it engaged in a comprehensive analysis of the supplementary means and did not dismiss the possibility that historical materials could be considered circumstances of the conclusion of the WTO's Anti-Dumping Agreement. *See* Report of the Appellate Body. United States – Final Anti-Dumping Measures on Stainless Steel from Mexico. WT/DS344/AB/R, paras 129ff.
47. Mark E. Villiger, *Commentary on the 1969 Vienna Convention on the Law of Treaties* (Martinus Nijhoff Publishers 2009), p. 445.
48. For instance, in the *Asylum* case, the ICJ invoked, in the interpretation of the Havana Convention of 1928, 'one of the most firmly established traditions of Latin America, namely, non-intervention'. The court dismissed a particular proposed interpretation as it would contradict that tradition. Colombian-Peruvian asylum case, Judgment of 20 November 1950: I.C.J. Reports, p. 285. In the *EC- Chicken Cuts* case, the Appellate Body of the WTO provided an expansive interpretation of the term, asserting, 'An event, act, or instrument may be relevant [...] not only if it has actually influenced a specific aspect of the treaty text in the sense of a relationship of cause and effect; it may also qualify as a "circumstance of the conclusion" when it helps to discern what the common intentions of the parties were at the time of the conclusion with respect to the treaty or specific provision.' European Communities – Customs Classification of Frozen Boneless Chicken Cuts. WT/DS269/AB/R, p. 113. *See also* Chang-fa Lo, *Treaty Interpretation under the Vienna Convention on the Law of Treaties* (Springer Singapore 1st ed. 2017), p. 231.
49. Ian Sinclair, *The Vienna Convention on the Law of Treaties* (Manchester Univ. Press 1984), p. 141.
50. Mustafa Kamil Yasseen, *L'interprétation Des Traités d'après La Convention de Vienne Sur Le Droit Des Traités (Volume 151)*, Collected Courses of the Hague Academy of International Law (1976), p. 90f.
51. Refer once more to case European Communities – Customs Classification of Frozen Boneless Chicken Cuts. WT/DS269/AB/R; and Oliver Dörr, *Supplementary Means of Interpretation, in Vienna Convention on the Law of Treaties. A Commentary* (Oliver Dörr & Kirsten Schmalenbach eds, Springer 2d ed. 2018), p. 626.

unilateral ones provided that they are pertinent to the interpreted treaty's conclusion.[52] This clarification was provided by the WTO Appellate Body[53] emphasizing that a 'direct link' to the treaty text or a 'direct influence' on the common intentions of the parties is not a prerequisite for an event, act, or instrument to be considered a 'circumstance of conclusion' for a treaty under Article 32 VCLT.

Finally, much like the *travaux préparatoires*, the circumstances of the conclusion of a treaty must be distinguished from the treaty's context referred to in the general rule of interpretation under Article 31(1) VCLT. As discussed in other chapters of this book, this article confines the definition of the treaty's context to the treaty text – including its preamble and annexes; any agreement among all of the parties related to the treaty's conclusion; and any instrument made by one or more parties in connection with the latter – that is accepted by the other parties as a related instrument to the treaty. The context of a treaty encompasses elements that are intrinsic to the treaty's text or closely linked to it whereas the circumstances of conclusion carry a more extrinsic dimension,[54] meaning rather the factual situation at the time of conclusion not taking into consideration the substance of the treaty or consensus between the parties.[55]

2.2 Other Possible Supplementary Means of Interpretation

As mentioned previously, the initial clause of Article 32 VCLT stipulates that 'recourse may be had to supplementary means of interpretation, *including* the preparatory work of the treaty and the circumstances of its conclusion'. This implies that the means discussed earlier serve as illustrations and do not preclude the consideration of additional supplementary means of interpretation.[56] The fact that the listing in Article 32 is non-exhaustive is deliberate thereby ensuring, through a broad scope of possible means of interpretation,[57] that the interpreter cannot preclude any sort of documents or

52. *See* Chang-fa Lo, *Treaty Interpretation Under the Vienna Convention on the Law of Treaties* (Springer Singapore 1st ed. 2017), p. 232.
53. In EC – Computer Equipment, the Appellate Body considers that 'the classification practice in the European Communities during the Uruguay Round is part of "the circumstances of conclusion" of the WTO Agreement and may be used as a supplementary means of interpretation within the meaning of Article 32 of the Vienna Convention'. *See* European Communities – Customs Classification of Certain Computer Equipment – AB-1998-2, p. 35. It was also confirmed in *EC–Chicken Cuts* that not only multilateral sources but also unilateral acts, instruments, or statements of individual negotiating parties can aid in understanding the reality the parties intended to regulate through the treaty. European Communities – Customs Classification of Frozen Boneless Chicken Cuts. WT/DS269/AB/R, p. 113.
54. Makane Moïse Mbengue, *Rules of Interpretation (Article 32 of the Vienna Convention on the Law of Treaties)*, 31 ICSID Review (2016), p. 391f. https://doi.org/10.1093/icsidreview/siw004.
55. Oliver Dörr, *Supplementary Means of Interpretation, in Vienna Convention on the Law of Treaties. A Commentary* (Oliver Dörr & Kirsten Schmalenbach eds, Springer 2d ed. 2018), p. 626.
56. *See,* for instance, the decision once again in *EC– Chicken Cuts,* European Communities – Customs Classification of Frozen Boneless Chicken Cuts. WT/DS269/AB/R, p. 110; and Jeremy Hill, *Aust's Modern Treaty Law and Practice* (Cambridge 4th ed. 2023), p. 258.
57. Mustafa Kamil Yasseen, *L'interprétation Des Traités d'après La Convention de Vienne Sur Le Droit Des Traités (Volume 151),* Collected Courses of the Hague Academy of International Law. (1976) (Enzo Cannizzaro ed., Oxford Univ. Press 1st publ ed. 2011), p. 78f.

materials that might cover the substance of the treaty and thus be relevant to the process of interpretation.

Considering this non-exhaustiveness, any material that is not strictly part of the negotiating process but is a factor due to its coverage of the treaty's substance and/or reference by the negotiators should be incorporated into the interpretative process as 'other supplementary means'.[58] It is imperative to underscore that the interpreter is devoid of discretion regarding the utilization of a specific document irrespective of its classification as a 'mere' supplementary means under Article 32 VCLT. An intrinsic obligation exists within the interpretative process to diligently examine and consider all available materials. The interpreter's role is thus to perform a reasoned and objective evaluation of the significance of these materials.

When taking into account this broadness of possible other supplementary means, some authors consider that the rational techniques of interpretation[59] would be included in this plethora of available instruments.[60] While not necessarily incorrect, as there is little to no restriction on what these other means might be, they seem to pertain rather to substantive matters for consideration instead of general interpretative principles or techniques.[61] Consequently, when Article 32 permits including additional means of interpretation and restricts them from the outset to a supplementary role, it should not be presumed to encompass principles beyond the general rule of interpretation.[62] For instance, this category of preparatory works could include an earlier version of the treaty under interpretation; interpretative declarations made by treaty parties that do not qualify as reservations; agreements and practices among a subgroup of parties to a treaty that fall outside the scope of authentic interpretation in Article 31(2) and (3); and non-authentic translations of the authenticated text and thus not falling under Articles 33, etc.[63]

Additionally, the unilateral behaviour of parties subsequent to a treaty's conclusion should be considered. While not constituting a practice that establishes the agreement of the parties regarding interpretation under Article 31 VCLT, such behaviour can be valuable for indicating a party's intent at the time the treaty was

58. *See* Oliver Dörr, *Supplementary Means of Interpretation, in Vienna Convention on the Law of Treaties. A Commentary* (Oliver Dörr & Kirsten Schmalenbach eds, Springer 2d ed. 2018), p. 627.
59. Principles of interpretation used in a 'statutory' interpretation such as *per analogiam, e contrario, contra proferentem, eiusdem generis, expressio unius est exclusio alterius, lex posterior derogat legi priori*, etc.
60. *See* Lassa Oppenheim, *International Law* (Longmans, Green and Co. 1912), pp. 759ff.; Mark E. Villiger, *Commentary on the 1969 Vienna Convention on the Law of Treaties* (Martinus Nijhoff Publishers 2009), p. 445; and Chang-fa Lo, *Treaty Interpretation under the Vienna Convention on the Law of Treaties* (Springer Singapore 1st ed. 2017), p. 228. Opposing opinion in Richard K. Gardiner, *Treaty Interpretation* (Oxford University Press 2010), p. 349f.
61. Also on this opinion, *see* Oliver Dörr, *Supplementary Means of Interpretation, in Vienna Convention on the Law of Treaties. A Commentary* (Oliver Dörr & Kirsten Schmalenbach eds, Springer 2d ed. 2018), p. 626f.
62. *Ibid.*
63. *See* Mark E. Villiger, *Commentary on the 1969 Vienna Convention on the Law of Treaties* (Martinus Nijhoff Publishers 2009), p. 445f.

concluded.[64] This is recognized by the ILC regarding a party's conduct when exercising its executive, legislative, and judicial functions[65] when a subsequent practice as a supplementary means of interpretation under Article 32 VCLT will consist of conduct by one or more parties in applying the treaty after its conclusion.[66] The interpretative weight of subsequent practice in relation to other means of interpretation often depends on their clarity and specificity in relation to the treaty concerned.[67] This is confirmed, for example, by ICJ decisions as well as arbitral awards and reports of the WTO panels and Appellate Body.[68]

Considering the possibility of using subsequent practice as a supplementary means of interpretation, it is finally worth noting that there is, in principle, no time requirement for these such as that stipulated for the preparatory works or circumstances of conclusion. There is, nevertheless, an argument to be made that, since both explicitly mentioned supplementary means have a timing factor imbued into them, this restriction would also apply to other supplementary means of interpretation. However, as there is no restriction mentioned in Article 32 VCLT whatsoever, the author sees no issue with classifying posterior documents that cover the treaty's substance within this category as they will, due to this, already have a reduced interpretative value based rather on the cogency of their arguments. This is tied to the fact that the interpreter has an obligation to always make an honest effort to locate and consider any and all materials that might help to find the correct interpretation result even if these materials might come into existence after a treaty's conclusion.[69] Therefore, even materials subsequent to the treaty can theoretically be used as other supplementary means as long as they are related to its content. Their interpretative relevance thus derives not from their classification within Article 31 or 32, which ultimately is of little relevance - if at all - but rather from how strong the arguments contained within them are for the interpretation of a specific provision.[70] It is important to remember that their use, even

64. Luigi Sbolci, *Supplementary Means of Interpretation*, in *The Law of Treaties Beyond the Vienna Convention: [Essays in Honour of Professor Giorgio Gaja]* (Enzo Cannizzaro ed., Oxford Univ. Press 1st publ ed. 2011), p. 158f.
65. Furthermore, the practice of lower and local officials may also be subsequent practice 'of a party in the application of a treaty' if this practice is sufficiently unequivocal and if the government can be expected to be aware of this practice and has not contradicted it within a reasonable time. Refer to International Law Commission, *Chapter IV: Subsequent Agreements and Subsequent Practices in Relation to the Interpretation of the Treaties*, pp. 24 and 40.
66. *Ibid.* According to the ILC, additional behaviour, including that of non-state actors, does not qualify as subsequent practice under Art. 32. Nevertheless, such conduct may be pertinent when evaluating the subsequent practice of the parties to a treaty. For a discussion on the classification on subsequent practice for interpretation, *see* Yilin Wang, *The Fight Between Interpretation and Modification: A Critique of Sanum v Laos*, 35 ICSID Review (2020), pp. 239ff. https://doi.org/10.1093/icsidreview/siaa024.
67. *Ibid.*, p. 60.
68. Refer to the work of Georg Nolte, *Subsequent Practice as a Means of Interpretation in the Jurisprudence of the WTO Appellate Body, in The Law of Treaties Beyond the Vienna Convention: [Essays in Honour of Professor Giorgio Gaja]* (Enzo Cannizzaro ed., Oxford Univ. Press 1st publ ed. 2011), pp. 138ff.
69. For more on this opinion, refer to s. 3.3.
70. As per European Communities - Customs Classification of Frozen Boneless Chicken Cuts. WT/DS269/AB/R, p. 119.

after the treaty's conclusion, is not outright excluded as long as all involved parties become aware of these means for their consideration.

2.3 Giving Meaning Through Article 32 VCLT: Confirmation and Determination

As discussed previously, the supplementary means of interpretation contained within Article 32 VCLT, while encompassing many different - and important - types of documents and circumstances, are not really autonomous in relation to Article 31 VCLT and the general rules of interpretation operating as supplements in direct correlation to the latter. Nonetheless, the supplementary means outlined in Article 32 are not solely subordinate in the interpretative process that is developed as a single unit. Some authors argue that their function is discretionary and dependent,[71] that is, that the provision might offer the interpreter a choice by articulating that 'recourse *may* be had to supplementary means'. However, this possibility is directly contrary to the fundamental idea of interpretation that an interpreter makes all efforts to ascertain the meaning of a certain provision, which includes the supplementary means of interpretation. The option for a distinction between Articles 31 and 32 using the terms 'shall' and 'may', respectively, is founded on the fact that *travaux préparatoires*, circumstances of conclusion, or other supplementary means might not be available to the interpreter during the process of interpretation.[72] If these materials do exist, however, they mandatorily have to be regarded by the interpreter even if lesser weight is granted to them.

With this in mind, some questions arise regarding supplementary means of interpretation. How can these means then be used if they are apparently relegated to a mere subsidiary function? Following the wording of Article 32 VCLT, there are two scenarios in which a treaty interpreter may resort to supplementary means. The first is when it is necessary to *confirm* the meaning resulting from the application of Article 31, and the second is when it is required to *determine* the meaning when the interpretation according to Article 31 leaves the meaning ambiguous or obscure or leads to a manifestly absurd or unreasonable result. Stated differently, supplementary means can have two primary functions according to the Convention: the confirming function and the determining function.[73]

The confirming function is to be utilized to corroborate the meaning derived from applying the general rules of interpretation in Article 31 VCLT. Therefore, if Article 31 has yielded a result, its validity may be affirmed by resorting to the supplementary

71. Makane Moïse Mbengue, *Rules of Interpretation (Article 32 of the Vienna Convention on the Law of Treaties)*, 31 ICSID Review (2016), p. 399 https://doi.org/10.1093/icsidreview/siw004.
72. The alleged possibility contained within Art. 32 VCLT is further discussed in s. 3.4.
73. *See*, for instance, Chang-fa Lo, *Treaty Interpretation under the Vienna Convention on the Law of Treaties* (Springer Singapore 1st ed. 2017), p. 224.

means outlined in Article 32[74] which is a use that has been widely accepted and employed throughout the ages in international case law.[75]

Furthermore, confirming a meaning through supplementary means can occur in a couple of different ways. First, they can be considered confirming an interpretation derived from applying the general rule because they furnish the interpreter with elements that directly and explicitly substantiate the interpretation in question.[76] In some instances, rather than specifically 'confirming', they are considered 'supporting', 'explaining', or 'bolstering' a specific interpretation.[77] Furthermore, the supplementary means can also be regarded as confirming a particular meaning if their content, at the least, does not contradict the one derived from applying the general rules of interpretation.[78] This is pertinent as it indicates that supplementary means are not required to offer direct and explicit evidence to confirm a particular meaning as this confirmation may also be inferred from the absence of conclusive evidence or the non-decisive nature of the supplementary means being employed. Finally, the confirmation role can be used simply to refute the argument of a specific party even if initially deemed unnecessary by the interpreter.[79]

However, scrutinizing the supplementary means, particularly the *travaux préparatoires*, to determine if it does indeed 'confirm' a specific meaning derived from Article 31 VCLT carries an implicit risk that it may not do so. Consequently, the confirmatory function may possibly not fulfil its purpose and potentially convert the exercise into one in which the supplementary means necessitate a re-evaluation of the application of the general rule to identify an acceptable interpretation that is then confirmed.[80] In such instances, the interpreter must reassess its stance given that

74. Some authors consider this to represent a logical flaw since whether any supplementary means of interpretation confirms a particular interpretation can hardly be determined unless there is recourse to it in the first place. Thus, it is questionable why an interpreter would ever wish to resort to supplementary means of interpretation if the meaning is already clear through Art. 31 VCLT. *See* David W. Greig, *International Law* (Butterworth 2d ed., 2. repr ed. 1980), pp. 481ff.
75. For instance, Territorial Dispute (Libyan Arab Jamahiriya/Chad) (Judgment) [1994] ICJ Rep 6; China – Measures affecting Trading Rights and Distribution Services for Certain Publications and Audiovisual Entertainment Products–Report of the Appellate Body (2009) WT/DS363/AB/R; *Togo Electricité et GDF-Suez Energie Services v. La Republique Togolaise*, ICSID Case No ARB/06/07, paras 45f.; and *Philip Morris Brands SARL and others v. Oriental Republic of Uruguay*, ICSID Case No. ARB/10/7, para. 34.
76. Makane Moïse Mbengue, *Rules of Interpretation (Article 32 of the Vienna Convention on the Law of Treaties)*, 31 ICSID Review (2016), p. 406 https://doi.org/10.1093/icsidreview/siw004.
77. *See*, for example, *Burlington Resources Inc and Others v. Republic of Ecuador*, ICSID Case No ARB/08/5, para. 62; *Yukos v. Russian Federation; Hulley Enterprises Limited (Cyprus) v. Russian Federation*, PCA Case No. AA, para. 226.
78. As was the case in *Camuzzi International SA v. Argentine Republic*, ICSID Case No. ARB/03/02, Decision on Objection to Jurisdiction (11 May 2005) paras 133ff. For more information on this non-preclusion of a meaning, refer to Sienho Yee, *Notes on the International Court of Justice (Part 6): The Fourth Use of Travaux Préparatoires in the LaGrand Case: To Prove the Nonpreclusion of an Interpretation*, 16 Chinese Journal of International Law (2017), pp. 353ff. https://doi.org/10.1093/chinesejil/jmx022.
79. *See* the case in Report of the Appellate Body. United States – Final Anti-Dumping Measures on Stainless Steel from Mexico. WT/DS344/AB/R, para. 128.
80. Oliver Dörr, *Supplementary Means of Interpretation, in Vienna Convention on the Law of Treaties. A Commentary* (Oliver Dörr & Kirsten Schmalenbach eds, Springer 2d ed. 2018), p. 629.

supplementary means are equally indicative of the parties' intention whether they confirm or contradict the purportedly clear[81] meaning of the treaty text.[82]

It can be argued that in the (rare) instances when supplementary means distinctly oppose the ordinary meaning of a provision within its context, precedence must be accorded to the latter.[83] In reality, however, what is occurring is that the 'confirming' function is elucidating a previously overlooked ambiguity or obscurity in the interpretation stemming from Article 31 VCLT. The confirmatory process of interpretation may, from this perspective, unveil a vagueness that had previously gone unnoticed. As a result, the examination of the preparatory work will actually transition from a prima facie confirming role to a determining one.

Thus, Article 32 VCLT allows the interpreter to employ these means in basically any situation without imposing significant restrictions on their application.[84] Consequently, there will be few situations for which the supplementary means of interpretation cannot *possibly* be used as their sole true limitation is that they cannot be invoked from the outset of interpretation. This is a reasonable proposition considering the inherent pitfalls associated with using materials lacking the authentic element found in the general rules of interpretation.[85] Additionally, it is evident that the

81. It is important to highlight, however, that courts in most cases view treaty terms as being 'clear' in light of the ordinary meaning of the rule not necessarily considering the term for further interpretation. *See* the study from Mark E. Villiger, *The Rules on Interpretation: Misgivings, Misunderstandings, Miscarriage? The 'Crucible' Intended by the International Law Commission, in The Law of Treaties Beyond the Vienna Convention: [Essays in Honour of Professor Giorgio Gaja]* (Enzo Cannizzaro ed., Oxford Univ. Press 1st publ ed. 2011), p. 117.
82. In this sense, *see* the (dissenting) opinion of Stephen Schwebel, *May Preparatory Work Be Used to Correct Rather Than Confirm the 'Clear' Meaning of a Treaty Provision?, in Theory of International Law at the Threshold of the 21st Century. Essays in honour of Krzysztof Skubiszewski* (Jerzy Makarczyk ed.), pp. 543ff.; and Richard K. Gardiner, *Treaty Interpretation* (Oxford University Press 2010), pp. 316ff. Opposing opinion in Makane Moïse Mbengue, *Rules of Interpretation (Article 32 of the Vienna Convention on the Law of Treaties)*, 31 ICSID Review (2016), p. 407 https://doi.org/10.1093/icsidreview/siw004; and Ulf Linderfalk, *Is the Hierarchical Structure of Articles 31 and 32 of the Vienna Convention Real or Not? Interpreting the Rules of Interpretation*, Netherlands International Law Review (2007), p. 138f.
83. Especially considering that the ILC meticulously deliberated on the term 'confirm' while the possibility of employing the term 'verify' was also proposed. The latter term would have nearly incorporated preparatory work into the initial stages of interpretation. However, the commission ultimately opted for 'confirm'. *See* United Nations Conference on the Law of Treaties, *Official Records of the United Nations Conference on the Law of Treaties, First Session (Summary Records of the Plenary Meetings and of the Meetings of the Committee of the Whole)* (1968), Document A/CONF.39/C.1/SR.33. Dissenting opinion advocating for the verifying effect of Art. 32 VCLT: Esmé Shirlow & Michael Waibel, *A Sliding Scale Approach to Travaux in Treaty Interpretation: The Case of Investment Treaties*, 0 The British Yearbook of International Law (2021), p. 33f. https://doi.org/10.1093/bybil/brab001.
84. *See* Donald H. Regan, *Understanding What the Vienna Convention Says About Identifying and Using 'Sources for Treaty Interpretation', in The Oxford Handbook on the Sources of International Law* (Samantha Besson & Jean D'Aspremont eds, Oxford University Press 1st ed. 2017), p. 12; and Mark E. Villiger, *Commentary on the 1969 Vienna Convention on the Law of Treaties* (Martinus Nijhoff Publishers 2009), p. 447. The ICJ has had recourse in many instances to the supplementary means even when it deemed the interpretation deriving from Art. 31 VCLT to already be 'clear'. Refer also once more to Territorial Dispute (Libyan Arab Jamahiriya/Chad) (Judgment) [1994] ICJ Rep 6.
85. As was discussed in s. 1. *Ibid.*

confirmatory mode of utilizing supplementary means of interpretation holds a significance in the system of the Vienna rules comparable to that of the general rule of interpretation.[86] This is because the supplementary means have the potential to lead the result of the interpretative process in a completely different direction than initially expected.

As foreseen in Article 32 VCLT, there are apparently only two situations in which an interpreter is permitted to disregard – or deviate from – the interpretation based on the general rules of interpretation due to a supplementary means, i.e., when there is ambiguity or obscurity in Article 32(a) or a manifestly absurd or unreasonable meaning in Article 32(b) VCLT. Nevertheless, in practice and considering the duty that the interpreter has to strive for the correct interpretation using all materials available when an interpreter is unable to ascertain the meaning of a treaty provision by applying Article 31 VCLT, recourse to supplementary means of interpretation becomes inevitable. This leads to situations where resorting to Article 32 becomes a practical imperative.[87] The prevailing understanding of this provision suggests that it is only in restricted instances that supplementary means can exert a definitive influence on treaty interpretation[88] as they are used to *determine* the meaning of a specific treaty provision. However, the importance that the supplementary means seem to have goes much further in practice since, as was demonstrated previously, it is also possible to reach this determining function through the confirmatory function of a supplementary means in case this first analysis leads, for instance, to an ambiguity.[89]

In instances when an interpretation pursuant to Article 31 still results in ambiguity or obscurity, it is important to recognize varying degrees of uncertainty in the interpreted term, giving rise to two distinct scenarios. The first arises when the level of ambiguity or obscurity is minimal characterized by a general and broad meaning that requires the interpreter to select from a specific range of meanings. Conversely, a second scenario emerges when the level of ambiguity and obscurity is considerably higher thereby rendering the meaning significantly unclear. In such cases, the interpreter lacks a reasonable understanding of the potential range of meanings and must primarily rely on the supplementary means to determine it.[90] The spectrum of ordinary meanings associated with a particular term in a treaty is typically broad, and the nature of the issue prompting an exploration of potential interpretations may suggest the existence of varied meanings.[91]

Naturally, irrespective of the level of ambiguity, the interpreter is to have recourse to the supplementary means for assisting in the interpretation process. As long as the ambiguity or obscurity persists to any degree – according to the interpreter

86. Oliver Dörr, *Supplementary Means of Interpretation, in Vienna Convention on the Law of Treaties. A Commentary* (Oliver Dörr & Kirsten Schmalenbach eds, Springer 2d ed. 2018), p. 629.
87. *See* Yves Le Bouthillier, *Article 32, in Les conventions de Vienne sur le droit des traités. Commentaire article par article* (Olivier Corten ed., Bruylant 2006), p. 1351f.
88. *Ibid.*, p. 630.
89. Refer also, for instance, to *HICEE B.V. v. The Slovak Republic*, UNCITRAL, PCA Case No. 2009-11, Partial Award, para. 138.
90. On this opinion, *see* Chang-fa Lo, *Treaty Interpretation Under the Vienna Convention on the Law of Treaties* (Springer Singapore 1st ed. 2017), p. 226.
91. Richard K. Gardiner, *Treaty Interpretation* (Oxford University Press 2010), p. 328f.

conducting the analysis based on objective criteria – after applying the general rules of interpretation, the relevance and utilization of supplementary means are easily foreseeable.[92] This leads to a relatively low threshold when applying Article 32(a) VCLT, which implies that it is comparatively simple to objectively justify recourse to this specific provision. The sole obligation incumbent upon the interpreter is to elucidate this step by delineating the inadequate outcomes stemming from the application of the general rule, and then establish the importance of this supplementary mean for the interpretation of the provision under discussion. Fundamentally, the expansive concept of ambiguity and obscurity evidently surpasses the purportedly supplementary nature of the supplementary means of interpretation.[93]

Furthermore, even if the words of a treaty are deemed to be clear if their application would hypothetically lead to a specific result that would be manifestly absurd or unreasonable, the interpreter must seek another interpretation through Article 32(b) VCLT.[94] The outcome of applying this 'absurdity' principle outlined in Article 32(b) VCLT would entail a complete reversal of the interpretation derived from the general means of interpretation thereby positioning this provision as a genuine exception to the general rules of interpretation.[95]

Ostensibly, this confers significant authority upon the treaty interpreter to diverge from the outcome of the interpretation concluded under Article 31. However, this purportedly yields minimal practical utility[96] as it is essential to underscore that a 'manifestly absurd' or 'unreasonable' result has an exceptionally high threshold to be employed.[97]

In contrast to the requirements for an ambiguous or obscure meaning, the standard for satisfying the criterion of manifest absurdity or unreasonableness stipulated in Article 32(b) is unmistakably considerably elevated even when compared to an absolutely unclear ambiguity deriving from Article 32(a) VCLT. The absurdity or unreasonableness must be glaringly evident which means that it must be unmistakably apparent from all perspectives. One of the few potential scenarios of an unreasonable outcome could arise when applying the general rule leads to an interpretation of a

92. *See*, for instance, the WTO case on US–Measures Affecting Gambling where the Appellate Body found that, due to a persistent ambiguity in treaty terms due not to dictionary definitions but after investigating the context of the treaty, that recourse to supplementary means was required. United States – Measures Affecting the Cross-Border Supply of Gambling and Betting Services, WT/DS285/AB/R, para. 195.
93. *Ibid.*, p. 631.
94. Jeremy Hill, *Aust's Modern Treaty Law and Practice* (Cambridge 4th ed. 2023), p. 260.
95. Chang-fa Lo, *Treaty Interpretation Under the Vienna Convention on the Law of Treaties* (Springer Singapore 1st ed. 2017), p. 227.
96. The events for using this article are deemed very unlikely by some authors, and there is very little (correct) applicability of this provision in case law. *See* Mark E. Villiger, *Commentary on the 1969 Vienna Convention on the Law of Treaties* (Martinus Nijhoff Publishers 2009), p. 447; and the decision in *Champion Trading Company v. Arab Republic of Egypt*, ICSID Case No. ARB/02/9, Decision on Jurisdiction, para. 288. Here, the ICSID decided to invoke Art. 32(b) VCLT merely to exclude a specific meaning from the general rules of interpretation.
97. Makane Moïse Mbengue, *Rules of Interpretation (Article 32 of the Vienna Convention on the Law of Treaties)*, 31 ICSID Review (2016), p. 411 https://doi.org/10.1093/icsidreview/siw004.

treaty provision that conflicts with another rule enshrined in the same treaty or otherwise agreed upon by the parties involved.[98]

3 APPLICABILITY OF ARTICLE 32 VCLT FOR THE INTERPRETATION OF TAX TREATIES

The question that arises is thus what the utility of the provisions discussed so far – and of Article 32 VCLT as a whole – is or can be for the interpretation of *tax treaties* as the previous section has occupied itself strictly with the public international aspect of their interpretation. As can be determined from the previous section, the question to be answered here is not whether using these extraneous materials is permissible when interpreting (tax) treaties but rather what is the relative value of these materials when doing so. This section will hence delve more comprehensively into the importance of the supplementary means for the interpretation of double tax treaties with special attention to case law involving these means.

3.1 Traditional Supplementary Means of Interpretation in the Context of Double Tax Treaties

3.1.1 Travaux Préparatoires *as By-Products of International Negotiations on Tax Treaties*

The supplementary means of interpretation contained in Article 32 VCLT and particularly the expressly mentioned preparatory works were drafted especially with multilateral conventions in mind, commonly the end result of long, difficult, and protracted negotiations.[99] However, in contrast to broader treaties often involving multiple contracting parties, double tax treaties typically possess limited *travaux préparatoires*. The bilateral and often relatively secretive nature of tax treaty negotiations contributes to the unavailability of *travaux préparatoires* in this field where many of the discussions are conducted privately and, despite the common exchange of preliminary drafts,[100] evolve in a highly oral manner. Hence, the negotiating history of double tax treaties is generally inadequately or sparsely documented, if at all.[101]

98. *See* Yves Le Bouthillier, *Article 32, in Les conventions de Vienne sur le droit des traités. Commentaire article par article* (Olivier Corten ed., Bruylant 2006), pp. 1351ff.
99. Klaus Vogel & Alexander Rust, *Introduction, in Klaus Vogel on Double Taxation Conventions* (Ekkehart Reimer & Alexander Rust eds), p. 40.
100. In a few instances, such as in Austria, the ministry of finance shares some of these drafts with specific institutions such as the Chamber of Commerce and the Chamber of Tax Advisers. However, these documents bear a mere semi-publicity and can thus not really be used as *travaux* based on the requirements discussed in s. 2.1.1.
101. Such is also the case with bilateral investment treaties (BIT). Refer to Makane Moïse Mbengue, *Rules of Interpretation (Article 32 of the Vienna Convention on the Law of Treaties)*, 31 ICSID Review (2016), p. 402 https://doi.org/10.1093/icsidreview/siw004. However, some authors believe that, in the specific case of BITs, there is an overt reliance on *travaux*. *See* Pratyush Panjwani, *The Role of Travaux in Interpreting BIT Provisions: Are Tribunals Over-Prepared to*

A further notable issue with double tax treaties (DTTs) is that the preparatory materials, unilateral negotiation minutes, and explanatory memoranda are furthermore commonly inaccessible to the public[102] due to the often-confidential nature between two states and the possible economic impacts of these negotiations.[103] Consequently, there is a debate concerning the appropriateness and extent of utilizing these materials against taxpayers that tax administrations might certainly do.[104] In some instances, even when the taxpayer has sought access to the preparatory work related to the treaty, tax authorities have been known to deny this access,[105] making it nearly impossible for taxpayers to use *travaux* as a supplementary means of interpretation. It is reasonable to assume, however, that it would be possible for them to use it advantageously should the taxpayer obtain the preparatory works of a tax treaty.[106]

Due to the reasons above, there are not all that many instances where *travaux préparatoires* are used as a supplementary means of interpretation in tax treaty case law.[107] Furthermore, when mentioned at all, it is oftentimes done in a rather questionable and roundabout way: in the *Irish Bank Resolution Corporation*, for instance, the UK Upper Tribunal considered in 2019 that both the OECD Model Convention and the commentaries were *travaux préparatoires*.[108] While their actual legal status is very debatable,[109] it seems questionable at best, in this case, to consider without further explanation that the convention and commentaries fulfil the requirements of being

Resort to Preparatory Works?, 20 Journal of World Investment & Trade (2019), pp. 490ff. https://doi.org/10.1163/22119000-12340140.

102. Some authors consider that a distinction could thus be made between using *travaux* on an international and a domestic level. While, in the relationship between the states as contracting parties with an international perspective, using any materials and drafts can easily be taken into account, from a domestic perspective, their relevance and possibility and their use can become indistinct since the negotiations that lead up to the treaty are oftentimes not made public and thus cannot bind the taxpayer. *See* Michael Edwardes-Ker, *Tax Treaty Interpretation: The International Tax Treaties Service* (In-Depth 1994), Chapter 22.03, pp. 1ff.
103. In some cases, they are stored in an archive and made public after a set time period. After this time, there would theoretically be no problem using these documents even if they were not immediately available and were unilaterally developed as long as they express an agreement between the parties.
104. This brings about the issue that the taxpayer might only have access to these materials when the tax administration decides to use them against the taxpayer or otherwise possibly omitting the materials in their entirety. From this perspective, materials handed out by the tax administration on a selective basis should not be allowed as they should be available not only to all parties to the treaty but also the taxpayers affected by them.
105. *See*, for instance, *Steinar Klaboe v. Her Majesty the Queen*. Tax Court of Canada. 2006 TCC 239.
106. Antun Belamarik, *Specialities in Interpretation of Tax Treaties, in Fundamental Issues and Practical Problems in Tax Treaty Interpretation* (Michael Schilcher & Patrick Weninger eds, Wien: Linde 2008), p. 84.
107. And, when used, this is done with the utmost care. Refer, for instance, to Dalton Luiz Dallazem, *Tax Treaty Interpretation in the U.S. and the Vienna Convention on The Law of Treaties: Is There Room for Compromise?*, 40 Journal of Law and Commerce (2021), pp. 18ff. https://doi.org/10.5195/jlc.2021.229.
108. *Irish Bank Resolution Corporation and Irish Nationwide Building Society v. HMRC. United Kingdom Upper Tribunal* [2019] UKUT 0277 (TCC) & [2017] UKFTT 702 (TC). *See also* case A-6306/2015 of the Swiss Bundesverwaltungsgericht/Tribunal administratif fédéral of 15 May 2017.
109. To be further discussed in s. 3.3.

considered *travaux*[110] as they might not even have been an actual part of the negotiations.[111]

In *Cudd Pressure Control* of Canada's Federal Court of Appeals, the judges go even further and consider the preparatory work of the deliberations of the Fiscal Committee of the League of Nations in the 1930s and 1940s alongside the commentaries to be *travaux préparatoires* of the actual treaty under discussion from 1942.[112] This seems to deviate even further from the definition of *travaux préparatoires* and, while the importance of external sources such as the OECD Commentaries is undeniable, attempts at classifying these sources 'correctly' seem to be inconsistent at the very least.[113] Nevertheless, while there might be differences more prominent between the contents in Article 31 VCLT when compared to Article 32 that might assist in evaluating the relative value a specific document will have in interpreting a tax treaty,[114] within Article 32 itself, the distinction between *travaux* and circumstances is rather of a formal nature tied to technical rigour bearing no relevant impact in practice. Thus, even if the aforementioned decisions might have lacked precision when attempting to define what the preparatory works were, the final result should have been the same. From a technical standpoint and considering the proximity between these two concepts, it is interesting to examine how the circumstances of conclusion can be employed in tax treaty interpretation considering their relationship with the preparatory work.

3.1.2 Circumstances of Conclusion on Tax Treaty Negotiations

Interestingly, there are very few decisions in which circumstances of conclusion are explicitly mentioned at all in relation to tax treaties. A possible explanation for this would be that, since the fine line – and possible overlap – between *travaux* and circumstances is not always clear,[115] there are instances when *travaux* is mentioned when perhaps the more 'correct' classification would have been a circumstance of conclusion.[116] The *travaux* are an integral part of the negotiation process through the existence of documents corroborating their meaning. However, the circumstances of

110. As discussed in s. 2.1.1.
111. In which case, they should much rather be considered a circumstance of conclusion, as will be discussed in the following section. Naturally, the argument could be made that, if a treaty in accordance with the OECD MC is negotiated, the negotiators more likely than not used the Model Convention and the Commentary for the discussions.
112. *Cudd Pressure Control Inc. v. Her Majesty the Queen*. Canadian Federal Court of Appeal. A-369-95, para. 20.
113. While, in some cases, the judges prefer to adopt an (understandably so) neutral stance and mention the commentaries without attempting to classify them alongside the *travaux*. *See*, for example, cases *RMM Enterprises Inc. and Equilease Corporation v. Her Majesty the Queen. Tax Court of Canada. 94-1732(IT)G*; and *Commissioner of Inland Revenue v. JFP Energy Inc. New Zealand Court of Appeal. CA260/89*.
114. Even though there are naturally overlaps between these two. Refer also to the discussion in s. 3.3.
115. Refer to s. 2.1.2.
116. *See* once more *Irish Bank Resolution Corporation and Irish Nationwide Building Society v. HMRC. United Kingdom Upper Tribunal.* [2019] UKUT 0277 (TCC) & [2017] UKFTT 702 (TC).

conclusion reveal themselves in the form of historical materials, backgrounds, provisions in predecessor agreements, and unilateral acts and materials that can also have a similar significance when interpreting double tax treaties. However, the author had difficulty encountering decisions that specifically address the circumstances of conclusion in this context.

Nevertheless, even if not explicitly mentioned, the circumstances of conclusion could possibly include, for instance, comparisons with provisions of other treaties when these form part of a line of treaties that bear a logical connection with the treaty in question such as is the case with (previous) double tax treaties.[117] Naturally, each of these treaties has a logic by themselves, but they can be quite useful as circumstances of conclusion in certain situations, especially if they are between the parties involved.[118] After all, the objective of examining supplementary means is to ascertain whether these materials exerted a significant influence on the ultimate version of a treaty and could illuminate the common goals and intentions of the parties as reflected in the text.[119]

Apart from the analysis of past treaties between both parties involved in the treaty being interpreted, treaties between one of the parties with third states will have a reduced importance in any case but can also have relevance when interpreting a newer treaty with comparable provisions.[120] Furthermore, judicial decisions by tax courts and legislative materials previous[121] to the negotiations could also be used as circumstances of conclusion[122] as they address the content of the double tax treaty in many cases while clarifying what the national position was on the matter prior to its conclusion.

3.2 Other Possible Supplementary Means in Tax Treaty Interpretation

As mentioned in section 2.2, the open-ended list within Article 32 VCLT indicates that the previously discussed means are intended to serve as illustrative examples, demonstrating their applicability in various contexts while not precluding the possibility of considering other, additional supplementary methods of interpretation. For tax treaties, this could mean, for instance, preparatory works of previous double tax treaties or

117. Refer, for instance, to cases *W.C.M. International Ltd. v. Ministero delle Finanze*. Italian Corte Suprema di Cassazione. Case 14202; and *The Estate of the Late Frederick J. Haas v. Her Majesty the Queen. Tax Court of Canada. 98-1768-IT-G*. This could also be the case for Art. 31(2) VCLT.
118. Should an international treaty serve as a predecessor treaty, it fundamentally contributes to the circumstances surrounding the conclusion of another, subsequent treaty. *See* the non-tax decision in United States – Definitive Anti-Dumping and Countervailing Duties on Certain Products from China, WT/DS379/AB/R, para. 579.
119. Daniel Patrick O'Connell, *International Law* (Stevens 2d ed. 1970), p. 262f.
120. The German Federal Fiscal Court has been known to do this, for instance, in BFH-Judgment from 9 December 1985 (I R 128/80) BFH BStBl. II (1988), pp. 810ff. *See also* the opinion of Ekkehart Reimer, *Interpretation of Tax Treaties*, European Taxation (1999), p. 467. The same applies to cases of double tax treaties between third parties with even lower usability but not necessarily non-existent.
121. If they are posterior, they might still be considered 'other supplementary means'.
122. Petrus Johann Hattingh, *The Interpretation of Bilateral Tax Treaties: Changing Tax Law – Unchanging Treaty Obligations?* (University of Cambridge 2021), p. 153.

even legislation implementing the treaty into national law. This is the case in *Société N*,[123] a Belgian case for which the *travaux préparatoires* of the Luxemburgish law[124] implementing the Belgium-Luxembourg double tax treaty was taken into consideration as a supplementary means of interpretation.

In this sense, the other supplementary means could particularly encompass materials that succeed the treaty itself. While those could naturally not have been used by the parties in preparing the materials and are thus not an integral part of the treaty in and of itself, they can present relative value based on the cogency of the arguments presented for these subsequent materials. Here, it would be worth mentioning (foreign) court decisions and academic writings[125] depending on how convincing their reasoning is. Since they do not precede the treaty, the parties could not have taken them into account when agreeing on the text, but the strength of the arguments and the relative importance and knowledge of the interpreter could definitely have an impact on the relevance of such posterior documents. This was the case in *Fothergill*[126] where it was argued that, for instance, the decision rendered by a Supreme Court or the opinion issued by a court of cassation holds significant authority while a ruling from a lower court typically lacks such weight. The eminence, experience, and reputation of a jurist, for instance, can be a crucial factor for assessing whether and to what degree the court should consider their opinion, naturally depending on the legal system in question.[127]

When dealing with subsequent 'materials', once again, what is known as (unilateral) subsequent practice as clarified in the ILC report is noteworthy.[128] Usually, case law on subsequent practice rather deals with Article 31(3) VCLT,[129] and there were no cases found that deal with *unilateral* subsequent practice as a supplementary means of interpretation, albeit their use is theoretically possible. It could happen, for instance, through the practice of local tax administrations in an initial step and then at a later stage in the case of that decision being contested and confirmed through judicial decisions.[130] Depending on the cogency of the arguments, it could serve as a strong indication of the intention of that specific contracting state on how to interpret a provision of the tax treaty in light of common domestic practice.

123. *Société anonyme de droit luxembourgeois N. v. L'État Belge. Hof van Beroep* (Court of Appeal) Brussels. Case 2011/AR/2950.
124. Projet de loi portant approbation de la Convention entre le Grand-Duché de Luxembourg et la Belgique en vue d'éviter les doubles impositions, n° 1470, 991.
125. *See* Tolley's International Series Ned Shelton, *Interpretation and Application of Tax Treaties* (London: LexisNexis UK 2004), p. 182.
126. *Fothergill v. Monarch Airlines Ltd (1981) AC 251;* 2 All ER 696; (1980) 3 WLR 209; (1980).
127. *Ibid.*, opinion of Lord Scarman, para. 134. This is rather a characteristic of interpretation within the context of Anglo-American systems.
128. International Law Commission, *Chapter IV: Subsequent Agreements and Subsequent Practices in Relation to the Interpretation of the Treaties*.
129. *See*, for instance, *Finanzamt v. I. German Federal Fiscal Court*. Case I R 81/04.
130. Some courts highlight the importance for this subsequent practice to have a legally binding nature, otherwise, it should not be expected of taxpayers to monitor and respect these practices. Refer to the decision in *AAA v. Financial Directoratej*. Supreme Administrative Court of the Czech Republic. 2Afs 108/2004 - 106.

As previously discussed, the WTO Appellate Body asserts that a singular act typically fails to suffice for establishing subsequent practice;[131] instead, it is a series of actions signifying the parties' consensus on a particular aspect that holds relevance. Nonetheless, this notion, as delineated by the ILC, is primarily confined to Article 31(3) VCLT whereas, under Article 32 unilateral practices, even if not thoroughly established, could be taken into consideration, albeit with diminished interpretative significance.[132] Although the threshold for acceptance is lower, the overall interpretative value attributed to such practices is also diminished.

A prime candidate for inclusion as an 'other supplementary means' is once again the OECD Commentary. Given that these means encompass essentially anything outside the preceding categories, they function as an expansive list and a container for documents potentially pertinent to interpretation. Consequently, commentaries issued by the OECD subsequent to the treaty's signing, albeit with limited applicability, may serve under Article 32 VCLT. This again incites the question of how to classify the legal status of the commentaries within the Vienna Convention – if at all.

3.3 The Legal Status of the OECD Model Convention Commentaries

The issue of the legal status of model conventions and their commentaries is a longstanding one. It is noteworthy that the commentaries to the model convention that were directly or indirectly part of the negotiations of a given tax treaty can significantly influence and sometimes decisively shape the choice among potential interpretations of legal provisions given the inherent possibility of defending more than one interpretation. This happens even though the commentaries commonly have absolutely no legal authority in domestic law.[133]

While the importance and use by courts and interpreters of the commentaries is undeniable,[134] even if not being a part of the agreement itself, it is quite controversial whether this practice is in accordance with Articles 31 and 32 of the Vienna Convention.[135] This has been intensely debated by academia[136] with many different positions on the topic and no definitive answer. While the author does not intend to present an

131. Refer to s. 2.2.
132. *See* International Law Commission, *Chapter IV: Subsequent Agreements and Subsequent Practices in Relation to the Interpretation of the Treaties*, pp. 40ff.
133. *See* the discussion in Maryna Glukh et al., *The OECD Model Tax Convention and Its Commentaries as a Source of Interpretation of Double Taxation Treaties in Ukraine*, 11 Juridical Tribune (2021), pp. 263ff. https://doi.org/10.24818/tbj/2021/11/2.08.
134. Refer, for example, to *Thiel v. FCT, High Court of Australia*, 21 ATR 531, 537 (1990).
135. Klaus Vogel & Alexander Rust, *Introduction, in Klaus Vogel on Double Taxation Conventions* (Ekkehart Reimer & Alexander Rust eds, 2022), p. 46.
136. *See*, for instance, Xaver Ditz & Carolin Seibert, *Die Bedeutung Des OECD-Musterkommentars Für Die Auslegung von Doppelbesteuerungsabkommen*, Internationale Steuer-Rundschau (2023), pp. 155ff.; Monica Erasmus-Koen & Sjoerd Douma, *Legal Status of the OECD Commentaries: In Search of the Holy Grail of International Tax Law*, 61 Bulletin for International Taxation (2007), pp. 339ff.; and Frank Engelen, *Some Observations on the Legal Status of the Commentaries on the OECD Model*, 60 Bulletin for International Taxation (2006), pp. 105ff.

absolute solution to this decade-long feud,[137] there are some considerations to be made that might provide a structured way to approach this discussion. The relevance of addressing this problem in the first place lies in the relevance of the commentaries themselves for tax treaty interpretation,[138] and it can actually be divided into two primary questions surrounding it: (I) where exactly are the commentaries to the OECD model convention – or any model convention, for that matter – to be classified under the VCLT, if at all; and (II) what is the relative importance of the commentaries for (tax) treaty interpretation and is this in any way influenced by the classification of the commentaries?

The first question is of a more objective nature and can furthermore be divided based on a question of *timing*. It will greatly affect how to classify the commentaries if they exist (a) prior to the treaty under discussion or if they (b) supersede it. If the commentaries under analysis have been developed and published *before* the treaty, there is an actual possibility that they were directly or indirectly part of the negotiations themselves. Therefore, there are a couple of options on how to classify the commentaries. As seen in the other chapters of this book, there are academics advocating for possible allocations under Article 31(1) VCLT,[139] Article 31(2) VCLT,[140] Article 31(3) VCLT,[141] and Article 31(4) VCLT.[142] They all have their merits and weaknesses, however, the object exceeds the parameters of the goal of this chapter. Since the main focus of this work is on Article 32 VCLT, the analysis will be directed at situations where the commentaries might fall within its scope.

Naturally, interpretation is an indivisible operation where one step of the process flows into another. Thus, in many cases, and as was seen previously with *travaux préparatoires* and the circumstances of conclusion, there will not be such a clear or sharp distinction between the paragraphs of an article. Nevertheless, especially concerning the relationship between Article 31 and Article 32 VCLT and considering their content, a differentiation between them might bring some insight as to the relative importance the commentaries should have for the interpreter. This logic would follow the same classification process discussed previously,[143] and the commentaries could be considered to be *travaux préparatoires* if they were part of the negotiations leading up

137. It is furthermore recognized that, of the answers provided so far, none really perfectly fit into the scope of the article chosen. *See* Philip Baker, *Double Taxation Conventions* (Sweet & Maxwell 2001), p. E-14f.
138. Since they are commonly seen as a foundation, i.e., a non-binding guide with extensive practical effects. Refer to Klaus Vogel & Ranier Prokisch, *Interpretations of Double Taxation Conventions*, Cahiers de Droit Fiscal International (International Fiscal Association 1993), pp. 64ff.
139. *See*, for instance, Guglielmo Maisto et al., *The Interpretation of Income Tax Treaties with Particular Reference to the Commentaries on the OECD Model* (2005), p. 32f.
140. *See*, for instance, Katharina Perrou, *Tax Treaty Interpretation in Greece, in Tax Treaty Interpretation* (Michael Lang ed., Linde 2001), p. 163.
141. Commonly as a relevant form of 'international law' as discussed in Maria Teresa Soler Roch & Ribes Aurora Ribes, *Tax Treaty Interpretation in Spain, in Tax Treaty Interpretation* (Michael Lang ed., Linde 2001), p. 310f.
142. *See* David Ward, *The Role of the Commentaries on the OECD Model in the Tax Treaty Interpretation Process*, 60 Bulletin for International Taxation (2006), p. 98f. Refer also to the discussion conducted in the previous chapters.
143. Refer to ss 2.1 and 2.2.

to signing the tax treaty.[144] Otherwise, and considering the practical importance of the commentaries, it is safe to assume that they could, in the least, be considered circumstances of conclusion being part of the contemporary background involving these treaty negotiations.[145] Considering, however, that the differentiation between the preparatory work and circumstances of conclusion is not always clear and easy to make,[146] the practical difference of classifying the commentaries under one or the other is rather of a formal nature bearing no practical relevance for the overall importance of the commentary.

What is important to remember is that the commentaries are not a homogeneous document and, depending on which provision of a treaty is being discussed; whether this specific provision in the treaty is identical to the OECD Model Convention; and whether the contracting parties are OECD Member States - and if they made any reservations relating to that specific provision - are all factors that must be taken into account not only for classifying the commentaries within the Vienna Convention[147] but also - and this relates to question (II) mentioned *supra* - for determining the relative value of the commentaries for tax treaty interpretation. One of the main points of critique when classifying the commentaries under Article 32 is that they are *far too important* to be deemed to be 'mere' supplementary means.[148] However, as has been demonstrated previously,[149] the means actually hold a significance that is comparable to the general rule of interpretation contained in Article 31 VCLT[150] and ultimately, where it is classified only has a marginal impact serving rather as an indication of the relative value attached to the means of interpretation, in this case, the commentary. In this context, answering the questions posed previously regarding commentaries existing contemporaneously to the treaty as to (I) the classification and (II) the relative value of these documents can be described visually as such.

144. It is debatable whether an explicit mention is necessary as the language of the OECD Model Convention commonly serves as a default language in treaty negotiations as discussed in Yariv Brauner, *Tax Treaty Negotiations: Myth and Reality*, 4(8) International Tax Studies (2021), p. 62f.

145. *See*, for instance, the decision in *Eagle Distribuidora de Bebidas SA v. Second Group of the Revenue Department in Brasilia*. First Council of Taxpayers (First Chamber). Appeal number 148.709. (2006) 9 ITLR, paras 657ff. For an opinion on this, refer to Petrus Johann Hattingh, *The Interpretation of Bilateral Tax Treaties: Changing Tax Law – Unchanging Treaty Obligations?* (University of Cambridge 2021), p. 214f.

146. Refer to s. 2.1.2.

147. It is also important to remember that the commentaries do not have to be forcibly subsumed in the VCLT. *See* Maarten Ellis, *The Role of the Commentaries on the OECD Model in the Tax Treaty Interpretation Process: Response to David Ward*, 60 Bulletin for International Taxation (2006), pp. 103ff.

148. *See* John Avery Jones, *The Binding Nature of the OECD Commentaries from the UK Point of View, in The Legal Status of the OECD Commentaries* (Frank Engelen & Sjoerd Douma eds, 2008), p. 162f; and Klaus Vogel & Alexander Rust, *Introduction, in Klaus Vogel on Double Taxation Conventions* (Ekkehart Reimer & Alexander Rust eds, 2022), p. 46.

149. Refer to s. 2.3.

150. *See* once more, Oliver Dörr, *Supplementary Means of Interpretation, in Vienna Convention on the Law of Treaties. A Commentary* (Oliver Dörr & Kirsten Schmalenbach eds, Springer 2d ed. 2018), p. 629.

Figure 8.1 Classification and Importance of OECD Commentaries

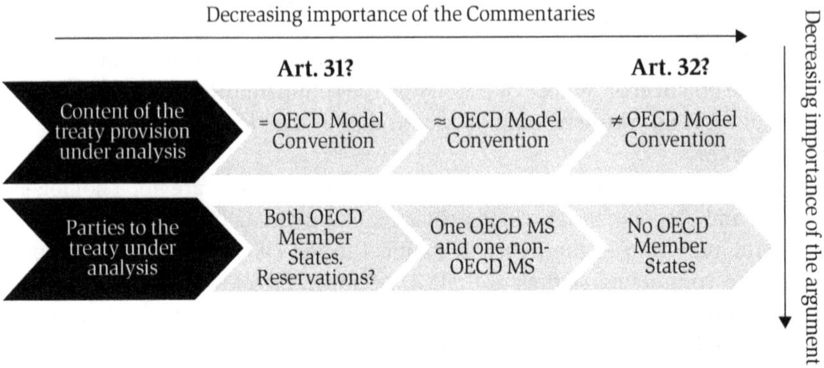

Source: Developed by the Author.

Accordingly, if the treaty content is identical to the provision contained in the OECD Model Convention, the likelihood of this specific section of the commentary to be analysed under Article 31 VCLT as meaning 'as intended by the parties', for example, through Article 31(4) VCLT or any of its other paragraphs as well as their relative importance for interpreting a treaty provision is higher.[151] Conversely, the further away the provision under analysis is from the OECD Model,[152] the lower the value the commentaries will have[153] and the likelihood they will be deemed to be 'mere' supplementary means increases classified either as *travaux* or circumstances of conclusion. The same applies, to a lesser degree, regarding the parties to the treaty under analysis. When both are OECD Member States – especially without reservations on that specific provision[154] – the relative importance of the commentaries is greater,

151. They can nevertheless still be analysed as a supplementary means depending on the situation as decided by the court in Administration Fédérale des Contributions. Swiss Bundesverwaltungsgericht/Tribunal administratif federal. Case A-6306/2015 (2017), where the court noted that OECD documents do not serve as binding international standards in a strict sense and instead act as supplementary means of interpretation. Nevertheless, given that Art. 25bis of the Treaty with Spain aligns with the OECD's standard for information exchange outlined in Art. 26 of the OECD Model, it would be appropriate to interpret the provision's requirements through the lens of the OECD Commentary. On this same opinion, *see See* Klaus Vogel, *The Influence of the OECD Commentaries on Treaty Interpretation*, 54 Bulletin for International Taxation (2000), p. 614f.
152. A difference in wording, by and of itself, does not signify the irrelevance of the OECD Model Convention and its commentaries but merely require reasons to be given as to why they should be taken into account. *See* the opinion in Michael Lang & Florian Brugger, *The Role of the OECD Commentary in Tax Treaty Interpretation*, 95 Australian Tax Forum (2008), p. 100f.
153. This was also affirmed recently by the German Federal Fiscal Court in its judgment I R 42/20, from 5 December 2023, para. 44.
154. When a member country lodges a reservation, it signals its intention to deviate from a specific provision of the OECD Model. For more on reservations and observations, refer to Guglielmo Maisto, *The Observations on the OECD Commentaries in the Interpretation of Tax Treaties*, Bulletin – Tax Treaty Monitor (2005), pp. 15ff.; and Ines Hofbauer, *Tax Treaty Interpretation in Austria, in Tax Treaty Interpretation* (Michael Lang ed., Linde 2001), p. 26.

and they have a greater chance of being considered under one of the aspects of Article 31 VCLT by demonstrating a more cohesive connection to the (presumed) intentions of the parties.[155] Contrarily, if both parties are non-OECD Member States, the likelihood of the commentaries being relevant decreases, and they might rather represent a supplementary means of interpretation. As can be derived from the above, both their classification and the relative importance existing before the treaty are going to be variable as it is not possible to reach a general classification that would be appropriate for the commentaries in every situation.[156]

Another issue entirely is regarding later commentaries, that is, those that have been implemented *after* the negotiations of a specific tax treaty ended, initiating the debate on a static or ambulatory interpretation approach.[157] Regarding their classification, they cannot, in any case, fall under the scope of Article 31 VCLT.[158] Furthermore, they cannot be *travaux* or circumstances of conclusion since those also necessarily predate the treaty's conclusion.[159] Nevertheless, there are no interpretative constraints to these commentaries falling into the scope of 'other' supplementary means of interpretation in Article 32 VCLT[160] as this article contains an open-ended list.[161] This is, in truth, the only possibility for later commentaries to be taken into consideration[162] within the scope of the Vienna Convention as, considering it does not fulfil the

155. Refer to the relationship between Arts 31 and 32 in s. 1.
156. On this same opinion, Rodrigo Gómez-Ballina, *The Relevance of the Commentaries to the OECD-MC for the Interpretation of Bilateral Tax Treaties, in Fundamental Issues and Practical Problems in Tax Treaty Interpretation* (Michael Schilcher & Patrick Weninger eds, Wien: Linde 2008), p. 107f.
157. *See* the discussion in Ulf Linderfalk & Maria Hilling, *The Use of OECD Commentaries as Interpretative Aids: The Static/Ambulatory–Approaches Debate Considered from the Perspective of International Law*, Nordic Tax Law Journal (2015), pp. 34ff. https://doi.org/10.1515/ntaxj-2015-0003.
158. As explained by Lang, they cannot be classified as 'context' under Art. 31(1) and (2) VCLT as only the Commentary existing at the time of a treaty's conclusion is deemed context. Such revisions also fail to meet the criteria for 'subsequent agreements' as outlined in Art. 31(3)(a) VCLT, lacking parliamentary ratification. Moreover, they do not qualify as 'subsequent practice' under lit. 'b' of the same provision without evidence proving both contracting states have adopted the practices indicated by the Commentary revisions. Furthermore, alterations to the Commentary post-treaty conclusion do not provide a 'special meaning' under Art. 31(4) VCLT given the parties could not have anticipated interpretations that emerged after their agreement. *See* Michael Lang, *Introduction to the Law of Double Taxation Conventions* (Linde 3d ed. 2021), p. 22f. For a different view on the interpretation of 'context' within the VCLT, refer to Edwin van der Bruggen, *Unless the Vienna Convention Otherwise Requires: Notes on the Relationship between Article 3(2) of the OECD Model Tax Convention and Articles 31 and 32 of the Vienna Convention on the Law of Treaties*, 43 European Taxation (2003), pp. 142ff.
159. Refer to ss 3.1 and 3.2. *See also* John Avery Jones, *The Effect of Changes in the OECD Commentaries after a Treaty Is Concluded*, 56 Bulletin for International Fiscal Documentation (2002), p. 102f.
160. *See* the opinion of Peter Wattel & Otto Marres, *The Legal Status of the OECD Commentary and Static or Ambulatory Interpretation of Tax Treaties*, European Taxation (2003), pp. 222ff.
161. Refer to s. 2.2 and the discussion on whether posterior documents can be included at all within the context of Art. 32 VCLT.
162. This is also the case if the double tax treaty was renegotiated at a later time than the updated commentaries to the model convention as recently discussed by the German Federal Fiscal Court. This court ruled that the mere fact that a double taxation agreement was amended shortly after the revision of the OECD Commentaries does not justify interpreting the DTT in accordance with this amended document. *See BFH v. 25.5.2011* – I R 95/10, FR 2011, 1175; and

requirements for any of the previous articles, it is the all-encompassing 'umbrella' provision that can encompass these documents.

Concerning their relative value, however, later amendments to the OECD Commentary will naturally have very restricted use considering how far they deviate from the will and intention of the parties especially when compared with other documents and indicators.[163] The OECD attempts to determine the interpretative value of the OECD commentary itself by introducing the commentaries[164] which is an absurd proposition for a group of individuals aiming to determine how relevant their own work shall be.[165] Nevertheless, that is not to say that these posterior comments should have no relevance at all. Some authors divide their importance based on the type of posterior comment that is under analysis, making a distinction between mere clarifying amendments and actual changes.[166]

This concept, however, should be approached with the utmost care as practice shows that authorities will always tend to attempt to classify any and all changes as simple clarifications in order to be able to apply changes, oftentimes with a retroactive result.[167] Furthermore, in order to determine whether a specific amendment is merely clarifying in nature, the provision's content must be interpreted without the amendment in the first place and, only when this content before and after the clarification are identical is the amendment clarifying. However, in this case, the clarification was unnecessary from the outset.

Consequently, it seems reasonable to acknowledge that subsequent OECD commentaries can inform the interpretation process as 'other supplementary means of interpretation' under Article 32 VCLT if dealing with the substance of the treaty under discussion. Their influence and relative value are contingent upon the argumentative strength they bring to the understanding of treaty provisions.[168] These later versions

the discussion in Xaver Ditz & Carolin Seibert, *Die Bedeutung Des OECD-Musterkommentars Für Die Auslegung von Doppelbesteuerungsabkommen*, Internationale Steuer-Rundschau (2023), p. 156f.

163. In some cases, courts refuse to use them resulting in a fragmentation of laws. *See* Austrian Supreme Administrative Court. Decision 92/13/0172 (1996) and the commentary on Michael Lang, *Later Commentaries of the OECD Committee on Fiscal Affairs, Not to Affect the Interpretation of Previously Concluded Tax Treaties*, 25 Intertax (1997), p. 8f. https://doi.org/10.54648/taxi1997003.

164. OECD, *Model Tax Convention on Income and on Capital*, Commentary (2017), p. 20.

165. *See* the opinion of Maarten Ellis, *The Influence of the OECD Commentaries on Treaty Interpretation: Response to Prof. Dr Klaus Vogel*, 54 Bulletin for International Fiscal Documentation (2000), p. 618f.

166. *See* Helmut Loukota, *Die Bedeutung Der Änderungen Des OECD-Musterabkommens Für Österreich*, Steuer und Wirtschaft International (1995), pp. 450ff.; and Mike Waters, *The Relevance of the OECD Commentaries in the Interpretation of Tax Treaties, in Praxis des Internationalen Steuerrechts. Festschrift für Helmut Loukota zum 65. Geburtstag* (Michael Lang & Heinz Jirousek eds), pp. 679ff. For other views, refer also to Marcus Schmitt, *The Relevance of Amendments to the OECD-Commentary for the Interpretation of Tax Treaties (Static or Dynamic Approach), in Fundamental Issues and Practical Problems in Tax Treaty Interpretation* (Michael Schilcher & Patrick Weninger eds, Wien: Linde 2008), pp. 122ff.

167. Michael Lang, *Wer Hat Das Sagen Im Steuerrecht?*, Österreichische Steuerzeitung (2006), p. 203f.

168. Refer to the opinion of the Swiss Federal Court on the interpretation of a case involving a professional athlete residing in Switzerland who had been active in the United Arab Emirates

could be considered similar to other scholarly works and judicial decisions, drawing persuasive power solely from the cogency of their arguments. This approach underscores a cautious openness to integrating newer commentaries through Article 32 provided they present compelling legal reasoning, albeit within a framework that largely respects the interpretations established at the time of the treaty's conclusion. Such a view has seen confirmation through case law as was the context of *Taise Fire*.[169] Here, the court was persuaded that the later commentary reflected the original intention of the older version and, convinced by the cogency of the arguments contained within it,[170] used the later commentary as a supplementary means of interpretation – albeit not explicitly recognized as such.

Most of the literature surrounding tax treaty interpretation, particularly Article 32 VCLT, focuses on the role of the OECD Model Convention and its commentaries.[171] While these elements are important, they do not exclude other documents and tools for interpretation as their significance varies with each case. In essence, regardless of their formal classification, the commentaries can be valuable for offering insights into the potential interpretation of tax treaties, possibly elucidating the parties' intentions if predating a treaty or at least through the cogency of its arguments when amended after the treaty and covering its substance. The final question then becomes how these commentaries, along with other supplementary means, can be effectively utilized in interpreting tax treaties and giving meaning to them.

3.4 Giving Meaning to Tax Treaties Through Article 32 VCLT

Considering that the possibilities of giving meaning by supplementary means have already been thoroughly discussed in section 2.3 of this chapter, the part related to the interpretation of tax treaties will be restricted to an evaluation of the practical use of these supplementary means in the context of case law where they exist.

One of the main discussions regarding the confirming meaning within (tax) treaties is, as discussed *supra*,[172] whether there is the possibility to 'confirm' the meaning in tax treaties even if the meaning is 'clear' from the general rules of interpretation. In *Commonwealth Development Corporation*,[173] the OECD commentaries are deemed to be preparatory works but nevertheless unnecessary for interpreting

in Case 9C_682/2022. Swiss Federal Court (2023); and the analysis by Michael Lang, *Schweizer Bundesgericht Zur Bedeutung Des OECD-Kommentars*, Steuer und Wirtschaft (2023), pp. 418ff.

169. *Taisei Fire and Marine Insurance Co., Ltd. v. Commissioner of Internal Revenue*. United States Tax Court. 104 T.C. 535 (1995).
170. For more information, *see* Sonika Dutta, *The Interpretation of Treaty Law under Special Consideration of the Vienna Convention on the Law of Treaties (VCLT), in Fundamental Issues and Practical Problems in Tax Treaty Interpretation* (Michael Schilcher & Patrick Weninger eds, Wien: Linde 2008), p. 39f.
171. Even considering their questionable democratic legitimacy. *See* the opinion of Maarten Ellis, *The Role of the Commentaries on the OECD Model in the Tax Treaty Interpretation Process: Response to David Ward*, 60 Bulletin for International Taxation (2006), pp. 103ff.
172. Refer to s. 2.3.
173. *Commonwealth Development Corporation v. The Commissioner of Inland Revenue*. The Fiji Court of Appeal. Civil Appeal No. ABU0022 (1994).

an already clear provision of the treaty based on the general rule of interpretation of Article 31 VCLT. There is, however, robust case law to be found for which courts rely on preparatory work or the circumstances of a treaty's conclusion as a means of confirming meanings already deemed clear from applying the general rule such as, for instance, in *Territorial Dispute (Libya/Chad)*[174] and *Kasikili/Sedudu Island* case.[175] Furthermore, there is also tax case law for which the OECD commentaries are deemed to be too important to be used only when there is an obscure or ambiguous meaning[176] and are employed even without a proper technical justification funded by the Vienna Convention as can be seen in *Société Générale Valeurs Mobilières Inc.*[177]

Consequently, based on the case law seen thus far and considering the previously discussed categorization of the OECD Model Tax Convention's Commentaries within Article 31 or 32 of the VCLT, this classification appears to be of limited consequence much like other means of interpretation. This is due to the fact that, regardless of it, interpreters always retain the obligation to refer to a supplementary means when pertinent when the commentaries continue taking centre stage in the decisions and discussions revolving around tax treaty interpretation. It is thus the relative weight that is to be given to the supplementary means that will vary based on specific and objective criteria. For the commentaries, for example, these include the treaty's alignment with the OECD Model, membership status of the parties within the OECD, and any reservations they may have articulated thereby ensuring a balanced and informed approach to treaty interpretation.

In this sense, engaging with supplementary means – regardless of how they are defined – is not just an option for the interpreter but an essential aspect of the process of establishing the meaning of a tax treaty. When a case arises for which the supplementary means are used to confirm the meaning of a tax treaty and this does not occur, this attempt at confirmation in truth serves the purpose of revealing a previously unknown obscurity.[178] This reaffirms their importance in tax treaty interpretation, leading the interpretative process of a tax treaty back and into a different direction than before.

Finally, based on the public international law analysis developed in section 2.3, it can be inferred that there are mainly three situations in which an interpreter will (be able to) use the supplementary means with the determining function: (i) a *low* level of ambiguity or obscurity where the interpreter must choose within a range of possible meanings; (ii) a *high* level of ambiguity or obscurity where there is no discernible range of meanings for the interpreter to choose from – both (i) and (ii) contained within

174. Case Concerning the Territorial Dispute *(Libyan Arab Jamahiriy/Chad)*, Judgment, ICJ Report 1994, note 8, 27-28, para. 5.
175. Kasikili/Sedudu Island (Botswana/Namibia), Judgment, ICJ Report 1999, para. 46.
176. Some authors even consider that, considering the extensive effort invested in the commentary, it raises questions about whether states truly intend for it to merely possess a secondary status, as discussed previously. Refer to John Avery Jones, *The Binding Nature of the OECD Commentaries from the UK Point of View, in The Legal Status of the OECD Commentaries* (Frank Engelen & Sjoerd Douma eds, 2008).
177. *Société Générale Valeurs Mobilières Inc. v. Her Majesty the Queen*, Canada Tax Court. 2013-4035(IT)G (2016).
178. As discussed in s. 2.3.

Article 32(a) VCLT; and (iii) a manifestly absurd or unreasonable meaning contained within Article 32(b) VCLT.

However, in the realm of double tax treaties, the cumulative expertise and practices associated with the sheer number of existing treaties as well as the different model conventions generate a significant number of cases due for interpretation being discussed with regards to tax treaties on a daily basis, creating many unresolved issues of interpretation. Furthermore, tax case law seldom explicitly mentions Article 32 VCLT at all in its reasoning making it virtually impossible to evaluate whether – if at all – there is a distinction in using supplementary means between public international law and tax treaty interpretation. The threshold for doing so in cases of a high degree of ambiguity, and especially in the case of a manifestly absurd meaning, is simply too great.[179] It is reasonable to assume that, in both public international law and double tax treaties, Article 32(a) and (b) VCLT will be used primarily in cases when there is a low level of ambiguity or obscurity, presenting itself with a range of possible meanings.

An attempt to corroborate this observation with case law did not yield any findings where a high level of obscurity or a manifestly absurd conclusion was present.[180] This unfortunately does not allow drawing any conclusive evidence as to if and how the determining function within the context of double tax treaties might be used differently than for public international law.

4 CONCLUSION

The supplementary means of interpretation of Article 32 of the Vienna Convention, although prima facie relegated to a secondary role in interpreting (tax) treaties, actually fulfil a role almost as important as that of the general rules of interpretation contained in Article 31 VCLT. The principle articulated in Article 32 VCLT, including preparatory work and the circumstances surrounding a treaty's conclusion, inherently offers a wide array of documents available for treaty interpretation. This provision's non-exclusive listing encourages interpreters to utilize any and all materials that, while not a direct by-product of the (presumed) will of the parties, can offer significant insights into the treaty's intent and substance. This open-ended list given to interpreters obligates them to consider any relevant material that aids in clarifying the treaty's meaning thereby granting them a substantially broad scope as to which documents may be used as long as the substance of the treaty is concerned.

This approach underscores the importance of a holistic approach to tax treaty interpretation where the interpreter's objective justifications play a crucial role in

179. The lack of use of the argument of a 'manifestly absurd meaning' in Art. 32(b) VCLT might also be explained through a non-legal facet: due to a matter of politeness and the lack of need to use such a recourse considering all of the others already available, interpreters might find themselves resistant to the idea of using this provision at all in the first place.

180. That is not to say, however, that there are no tax decisions dealing with absurd conclusions, but those issues are commonly resolved through other means and not Art. 32 VCLT. *See*, for instance, Michael Lang, *DBA Malta: Wechsel von Der Freistellungs- Zur Anrechnungsmethode Auf Grundlage Einer EAS-Rechtsauskunft Des BMF?*, 34 Steuer und Wirtschaft International (2024), pp. 10ff.

determining the relevance and weight of supplementary materials in establishing the treaty's intended meaning, especially in complex scenarios. Accordingly, the confirmative role of the supplementary means of interpretation as well as the concepts of ambiguity and obscurity of the determining function extend beyond the ostensibly supportive role of supplementary means, potentially broadening the scope of interpretation beyond initial expectations and ensuring that these supplementary means are, in truth, not merely 'supplementary' as in 'with less importance'.

Beyond discussing the mere permissibility of utilizing extraneous materials for treaty interpretation, it is also essential to venture into the domain of assessing their availability and relative value. The challenges associated with the traditional supplementary means, such as *travaux préparatoires*, in the realm of double tax treaties are notably accentuated due to the often limited and confidential nature of tax treaty negotiations. This scarcity of documentation inherently complicates the application of these materials, fostering a debate on their appropriateness and the extent to which they can be employed against taxpayers.

Moreover, the legal ambiguity surrounding the status of OECD Model Conventions and their commentaries, as highlighted through case law, suggest that, while they may not hold a uniform status across all instances, they can hold undeniable – but variable – value depending on a number of factors. These include the alignment of the treaty under analysis with the OECD Model, membership status of the parties within the OECD, and any reservations that might have been articulated regarding the provision to be interpreted. Fundamentally, the commentaries, irrespective of their categorization, serve as a significant resource for providing insights into interpreting tax treaties. They can offer a window into the original intentions behind the treaty provisions if they predate the treaty's conclusion and, even when amended post-treaty, their argumentative strength can still illuminate the substantive aspects of the treaty. Classifying these commentaries under Article 31 or 32 VCLT or even as different categories of supplementary means, while possible, can ultimately only aid in determining the relative value that these documents will have for tax treaty interpretation.

Finally, the role of Article 32 VCLT in interpreting tax treaties, although discussed with special attention in the literature in relation to the OECD commentaries, allows a plethora of other documents including judicial decisions by tax courts, legislative materials, and unilateral practices of countries to be taken into account. This allows a holistic approach to the interpretative process in which all possibly relevant documents dealing with the substance of a given treaty can be considered – even if, when more detached from the presumed will of the parties, they may contain a reduced interpretative value when compared to those derived from the general rules of interpretation.

CHAPTER 9

Authentic Languages and Tax Treaty Interpretation

Yasmin Lawson[*]

1 Setting the Scene: Multilingual Tax Treaties
2 Applicability of Article 33 VCLT to Tax Treaties
3 Article 33 VCLT
3.1 Object of Interpretation (Article 33(1) & (2) VCLT)
3.2 Equal Authority (Article 33(1) VCLT)
3.3 Presumption of Same Meaning (Article 33(3) VCLT)
4 Difference of Meaning (Article 33(4) VCLT)
5 Conclusion

1 SETTING THE SCENE: MULTILINGUAL TAX TREATIES

More than three thousand years ago, pharaoh Ramses II and Hittite king Hattusilis II concluded the Egyptian-Hittite peace treaty ('eternal treaty') promising peace and brotherhood for all time. Two independent versions of this treaty were composed: the Egyptian one that was formulated in Egyptian and then translated to Akkadian and sent engraved into a silver plate to Hittite and the Hittite version that was drafted in Hittitan inscribed into another silver plate in an Akkadian translation and then sent to Egypt. There, it was again translated into Egyptian.[1] While the process of concluding this treaty may differ from the current day procedures - no longer are treaty texts engraved into silver plates - overall, this is not at all an unfamiliar situation. Today, it is common

* The author thanks Prof. Dr DDr h.c. Michael Lang, Prof. Dr Pasquale Pistone and Dr Gustavo Weiss de Resende, LLM for their insight and invaluable help in preparing this chapter.

1. Trevor Bryce, *The 'Eternal Treaty' from the Hittite perspective*, 6 BMSAES 1 (2006).

practice for bilateral treaties to be concluded in the official languages of the contracting states with the additional use of a common language.[2]

For tax treaties, this is often but not always the case and, in fact, heavily depends on individual state practice.[3] Both Switzerland and Belgium, for example, have multiple domestic official languages (four and three, respectively). While Switzerland concludes tax treaties with German-speaking countries in only German,[4] with France only in French,[5] and with Italy in only Italian,[6] Belgium will usually require authentic treaty texts in every one of its domestic official languages.[7] Similarly, the text of the India-UK Treaty is authentic both in English and Hindi.[8] Contrarily, the tax treaty between Zimbabwe and South Africa was concluded solely in English despite both countries having a multiplicity of domestic authentic languages.[9]

Other times, the contracting states will use not only their respective official languages but will also prepare an additional version in a common language[10] – as was done by Egypt and Hittite via the translation into Akkadian. Today, this common language is frequently, though not necessarily, English[11] or French.[12] Some treaties are even exclusively concluded in a common language even if it is not an official language in either of the contracting states.[13]

2. *See* for a review of the historical developments in the use of languages in treaty practice, e.g., Meinhard Hilf, *Die Auslegung mehrsprachiger Verträge* 5 et seq. (Springer Verlag 1973).
3. As well as presumably, domestic constitutional law. This chapter will solely relate to international law aspects.
4. E.g., 30 January 1974, Abkommen zwischen der Republik Österreich und der Schweizerischen Eidgenossenschaft zur Vermeidung der Doppelbesteuerung auf dem Gebiete der Steuern vom Einkommen und vom Vermögen.
5. Most recently 25 June 2014, *Accord modifiant le protocole additionnel à la Convention entre la Suisse et la France du 9 septembre 1966 modifiée, en vue d'éliminer les doubles impositions en matière d'impôts sur le revenu et sur la fortune et de prévenir la fraude et l'évasion fiscales* (12 April 2024), https://www.fedlex.admin.ch/eli/oc/2016/228/fr.
6. Most recently 23 February 2015, *Protocollo che modifica la Convenzione tra la Confederazione Svizzera e la Repubblica Italiana per evitare le doppie imposizioni e per regolare talune altre questioni in materia di imposte sul reddito e sul patrimonio, con Protocollo aggiuntivo, conclusa a Roma il 9 marzo 1976, così come modificata dal Protocollo del 28 aprile 1978* (12 April 2024), https://www.fedlex.admin.ch/eli/oc/2016/451/it.
7. *See* (6 June 2024), https://www.minfin.fgov.be/myminfin-web/pages/public/fisconet/compare/27c5818d-7978-4749-a1ee-4f4816d3306d/52de8acf-d427-47bc-b098-904ded84dd2b/52de8acf-d427-47bc-b098-904ded84dd2b.
8. UK-India Double Taxation Convention signed 25 January 1993.
9. Agreement lor the avoidance of double taxation and the prevention of fiscal evasion with respect to taxes on Income, 4 August 2015.
10. Dinah Shelton, *Reconcilable Differences: The Interpretation of Multilingual Treaties*, 3 Hastings International and Comparative Law Review 615 (1997).
11. As is the case, for example, in an overwhelming number of Austrian treaties: Albania, Armenia, Azerbaijan, Bahrain, Belarus, Bosnia and Herzegovina, Bulgaria, Chile, China, Cyprus, Estonia, Georgia, Iceland, Israel, Kazakhstan, Qatar, Kyrgyzstan, Kosovo, Croatia, Kuba, Kuwait, Latvia, Lithuania, Malaysia, Macedonia, Mexico, Moldavia, Mongolia, Montenegro, Norway, Poland, Romania, Russia, San Marino, Saudi Arabia, Serbia, Slovenia, Tadzhikistan, Taiwan, Turkey, Turkmenistan, Uzbekistan, Venezuela, United Arab Emirates, and Vietnam.
12. To remain with the Austrian example, *see*, e.g., the tax treaty between Austria and Algeria or Morocco.
13. E.g., the Austrian treaties with Argentina, the Czech Republic, Egypt, Korea, Nepal, Pakistan, and Thailand.

However, a perfect translation from one language to another is practically impossible as they have grown over centuries developing specific terms of phrases or subtexts that simply cannot be transposed. This necessarily leads to situations, where despite the best intentions of the parties to a treaty, the different language texts deviate from one another. This presents issues for the interpreter as the normative content of such a provision must initially seem unclear even though the parties came to an agreement. In other cases, the parties might in effect not have reached a consensus regarding a provision and conscientiously used terms that do not correspond with one another. Here, the questions posed to the interpreter are vastly different, and it might even be challenged whether any norm has come into existence.

This uncertainty stemming from multilingual treaties may be one of the reasons why states choose to use particularly English and French as a common language in the conclusion of tax treaties: The Model Convention of the Organisation for Economic Co-operation and Development (OECD MC) on which many current tax treaties are based was published by the Organisation for Economic Co-operation and Development (OECD) in two official versions of English and French. This might afford parties to a treaty some security in the negotiations as to the content of the treaty to which they are agreeing even if they cannot be certain about the treaty text in the official language of the other contracting state. Nonetheless, the use of such a model convention that is authentic in English and French might create additional questions for the interpreter of any bilateral tax treaty, e.g., regarding the weight and importance of a treaty text in a language corresponding to the underlying model as opposed to the other authentic texts. Even more acutely, the Multilateral Instrument (MLI) which is a multilateral tax treaty amending covered bilateral tax treaties was only authenticated in English and French.[14] As a consequence, some treaties may have paragraphs that have authentic versions in a different language than the remainder of the treaty.[15]

Overall, international tax treaty practice presents a unique plethora of different linguistic approaches and influences, raising issues of conformity and consistency across the texts and of stronger or weaker relevance of the authentic languages. Some aspects of this were addressed by the International Law Commission (ILC) already in 1966: 'Few plurilingual treaties containing more than one or two articles are without some discrepancy between the texts. The different genius of the languages, the absence of a complete consensus ad idem, or lack of sufficient time to co-ordinate the texts may result in minor or even major discrepancies in the meaning of the texts.'[16] The ILC's discussions finally resulted in the drafting of Article 33 Vienna Convention on the Law of Treaties (VCLT) which aims to guide the interpretation of multilingual treaties. This chapter will analyse this provision and its content as it relates to tax treaties. A central question will certainly be the influence of the OECD MC and/or the UN Model Convention (UN MC) on the relative weight of the authentic language versions.

14. *See* (12 April 2024), https://www.oecd.org/tax/treaties/multilateral-convention-to-implement-tax-treaty-related-measures-to-prevent-beps.htm.
15. Josef Schuch & Jean-Philippe Van West, *Authentic Languages and Official Translations of the Multilateral Instrument and Covered Tax Agreements*, in Lang et al. (eds), *The OECD Multilateral Instrument for Tax Treaties: Analysis and Effects* 68 (Kluwer Law International 2018).
16. ILC, Final Draft, Commentary to Art. 29, para. 6.

2 APPLICABILITY OF ARTICLE 33 VCLT TO TAX TREATIES

Section 3 of the VCLT contains a catalogue of rules pertaining to the interpretation of treaties. Article 31 sets out the general rule of interpretation according to which a 'treaty shall be interpreted in good faith in accordance with the ordinary meaning[17] to be given to the terms of the treaty in their context and in the light of its object and purpose'.[18] Following Article 32, certain supplementary means of interpretation are also open to the interpreter.[19] While these rules are of a general scope and applicable to all treaties, Article 33 VCLT relates to the very specific issue of multiple authentic language versions and interpreting such multilingual treaties.

Before analysing the content of this rule in the concrete case of tax treaties, it must first be determined whether tax treaties may fall within the scope of Article 33 VCLT.

According to Article 1 in connection with Article 2(1)(a), the VCLT can apply to treaties in written form that are governed by international law.[20] This criterion first delimits international law from national law and, second, requires that the parties to the treaties have the intention of establishing a legal relationship, i.e., to be bound in some way by the treaty.[21] The scope of the VCLT therefore will generally cover tax treaties as they fulfil the criteria of Article 2. Furthermore, because this provision does not limit the number of parties to a treaty,[22] not only bilateral tax treaties but also multilateral tax conventions such as the MLI[23] are within the scope of the convention.

For the VCLT and its Article 33 to be relevant for interpreting any individual multilingual tax treaty, however, it is necessary that all parties to the treaty are also parties to the VCLT. The VCLT is itself just an international treaty and thus only binding for states that have agreed to it. However, even if not all contracting parties are members of the VCLT, it might be argued that the interpretational rule of Article 33 should nonetheless apply in and of itself as customary international law. The VCLT was codified in 1969 with the intention of preparing written documentation of established customary international law. The character of Articles 31 and 32 as

17. *See* on this issue, Georg Kofler & Bence Péter Komár, *The 'Ordinary Meaning', the 'Special Meaning', and Tax Treaty Interpretation*, in this book.
18. Article 31, para. 1 VCLT; *see* on this rule in relationship to tax treaties, the other chapters of this book.
19. The provision limits this use to: (1) confirming the meaning resulting from the application of Art. 31; or (2) determining the meaning when the interpretation according to Art. 31 leaves the meaning ambiguous or obscure or leads to a manifestly absurd or unreasonable result. *See* for a discussion of this provision Gustavo Weiss de Resende, *Supplementary Means of Interpretation (Art 32 VCLT) and Tax Treaty Interpretation*, in this book.
20. Kristen Schmalenbach, *Art 2, in Vienna Convention on the Law of Treaties: A Commentary*, para. 23 (Dörr & Schmalenbach eds, Springer 2018); Art. 1 VCLT further requires that the treaty is concluded between states. As this is not a relevant issue in the context of this chapter, this requirement will not be addressed. For a fundamental exploration including further references, *see, e.g.*, Kristen Schmalenbach, *Art 1, in Vienna Convention on the Law of Treaties: A Commentary*, paras 8 et seq. (Dörr & Schmalenbach eds, Springer 2018).
21. Schmalenbach, *supra* n. 20, Art. 2, para. 30.
22. Though unilateral declarations are excluded; *see* Schmalenbach, *supra* n. 20, Art. 2, para. 15.
23. Michael Lang, *Die Auslegung des multilateralen Instruments*, 1 SWI 11 (2017).

customary international law is generally undisputed,[24] and these provisions may therefore be relevant in the interpretative process even if (some of the) contracting states have not signed the VCLT[25] or it was not in force when entering into the treaty.[26] This is less certain for Article 33 VCLT. In particular, the ILC explicitly excluded this discussion from its findings on customary international law in its 2018 report.[27] Though it should be the case that such provisions that were not customary international law at the time of the VCLT's codification have become part of that canon,[28] the legal character of Article 33 still remains unclear.[29] Ultimately, however, the precise delimitation of this legal character might be of little importance as the interpretative rule of Article 33 may guide an interpreter simply as part of any holistic interpretative process as will be more comprehensively depicted in the following chapters.

Furthermore, as tax treaties are of the same legal status as the VCLT (or customary international law), states have the discretion to deviate from the rules set out in the VCLT by including special interpretative rules in their treaties.[30] In fact, tax treaties usually contain precisely such rules governing their interpretation and even indications on how to interpret those that are authenticated in multiple languages. The latter can be found in most cases in the treaty's final provision where the parties stipulate which language texts are 'authentic' (more on this in Chapter 3(3.1)) and, in some cases, which of these should prevail in the event of conflict (*see* Chapter 3(3.2)). A provision governing the interpretation of tax treaties in general is contained in Article 3(2) of the respective treaty in most cases. This rule requires that:

> as regards the application of the Convention at any time by a Contracting State, any term not defined therein shall, unless the context otherwise requires or the competent authorities agree to a different meaning pursuant to the provisions of Article 25, have the meaning that it has at that time under the law of that State for

24. *See* with further references, e.g., J. Bossuyt, *Chapter 8: Principles of Tax Treaty Interpretation in The Legal Status of Extrinsic Instruments for the Interpretation of Tax Treaties* (IBFD 2022), Books IBFD (accessed 11 April 2024), 8.1.1.
25. Stefan Bendlinger & Georg Kofler, *Auslegung von Doppelbesteuerungsabkommen*, in *Internationales Steuerrecht*, para. 1 (Bendlinger et al eds, LexisNexis 2018); Georg Kofler, *Vor Art. 1*, in *DBA*, para. 60 (Aigner et al. eds, Linde 2019).
26. In relation to Art. 33, *see* explicitly Oliver Dörr, *Art 33, in Vienna Convention on the Law of Treaties: A Commentary*, para. 5 (Dörr & Schmalenbach eds, Springer 2018).
27. ILC, *Report on the work of the seventieth session*, p. 19 (2018): 'The Commission nevertheless decided not to address such questions, including the question of how far article 33 reflects customary international law.'
28. Bendlinger & Kofler, *supra* n. 25, at para. 1; Michael Lang, *Wer hat das Sagen im Steuerrecht?*, 10 ÖStZ 205 (2006).
29. Though parts of the literature do consider it to be part of customary international law, *see* Schuch & van West, *supra* n. 15, at 76; Liliana E. Popa, *The Holistic Interpretation of Treaties at the International Court of Justice*, 87 Nordic J. Int'l L. 307 et seq. (2018) https://doi.org/10.1163/15718107-08703002; this also seems to be supported by the consistency of the International Court of Justice (ICJ) case law before and after adopting the VCLT, *ibid.*, at p. 302.
30. Even if the rules apply as customary international law; *see* Michael Lang, *Can Law Regulate Its Own Interpretation? Relevance of Articles 31-33 of the Vienna Convention on the Law of Treaties (VCLT) and Article 3 Para. 2 of the Model Convention of the Organisation for Economic Co-operation and Development (OECD MC) for the Interpretation of Double-Taxation Conventions*, in *Research Handbook on International Taxation* 176 (Yariv Brauner ed., Edward Elgar Publishing 2019); Kofler, *supra* n. 25, para. 60.

> the purposes of the taxes to which the Convention applies, any meaning under the applicable tax laws of that State prevailing over a meaning given to the term under other laws of that State.[31]

The relationship between this rule and the VCLT in general is one of the most fundamental questions in interpreting tax treaties[32] and, as such, cannot be discussed thoroughly within the confines of this chapter.

Under the conditions that the contracting parties of a tax treaty are VCLT members and specific rules within the tax treaty do not disallow it, Article 33 VCLT may consulted when interpreting a multilingual tax treaty (if the material conditions laid out below are met). As noted above, in the context of international tax law, individual bilateral or multilateral treaties are not the only basis for linguistic uncertainty. The basis for negotiating treaties or individual treaty provisions is usually either the OECD MC or the UN MC. These model conventions were published by the respective organizations in multiple official languages; for the OECD MC, these are French and English, and the UN MC has six official language texts.[33] In the situation of discrepancies between these texts, might the rules of Article 33 VCLT be used to derive a '"common" meaning'? An example of such a discrepancy can be found in Article 16 OECD MC where the English text refers to a 'member of the board of directors' as opposed to the French 'membre du conseil d'administration ou de surveillance'.[34]

The scope of the VCLT is limited by Article 2(1)(a) VCLT to treaties when the parties have the intention to be bound in some way by the treaty.[35] Non-legally binding agreements therefore do not fulfil this requirement and are thus not treaties within the sense of Articles 1 and 2 VCLT. The VCLT cannot apply to such agreements. This author opines that the rules contained in Article 33 VCLT also cannot be applied as part of the canon of customary international law as it would be difficult to establish the needed international consensus or practice. As will be set out in the further analysis of the content of Article 33 VCLT below, this provision serves two primary goals. First, it imposes an obligation on the interpreter to consider all language texts and not disregard any one of them based on any mechanical *ex ante* priority rules. Second, it requires a thorough interpretation of all of them considering historical, teleological, and systematic arguments. Such an analysis, if applied to a bilateral treaty, will result

31. OECD, *Model Tax Convention on Income and on Capital* (2017).
32. Fundamentally, Lang, *Can Law Regulate Its Own Interpretation? Relevance of Articles 31-33 of the Vienna Convention on the Law of Treaties (VCLT) and Article 3 Para. 2 of the Model Convention of the Organisation for Economic Co-operation and Development (OECD MC) for the Interpretation of Double-Taxation Conventions*, *supra* n. 30; Michael Lang & Benjamin Beer in this book.
33. Arab, Chinese, English, French, Russian, and Spanish.
34. The texts also deviate in terms of defining the covered income: 'fees and other similar payments' as opposed to 'tantièmes, jetons de présence et autres rétributions similaires'; *see*, for a detailed discussion of the historical background of this provision, e.g., Elisabeth Pamperl, *Article 16 of the OECD Model Convention: History, Scope and Future* 25 et seq. (IBFD 2015); Pasquale Pistone, *Article 16: Directors' Fees/Directors' Fees and Remuneration of Top-Level Management Officials: Global Tax Treaty Commentaries* (Global Topics IBFD), Chapter 1.2. (accessed 12 April 2024); Pasquale Pistone, *The Impact of Conceptual and Linguistic Diversity on the Interpretation and Application of Article 16 of the OECD Model Convention*, in *Tax Treaties after the BEPS Project: A Tribute to Jacques Sasseville* 256 (Brian J. Arnold ed., CTF 2018).
35. Schmalenbach, *supra* n. 20, at Art. 2, para. 30.

in the meaning of the norm as expressed through the different language texts. The two central rules can certainly also be applied to an OECD or UN MC analysis and will provide valuable guidance to the interpreter in determining the norm as contained in any bilateral treaty based on either model. When interpreting a bilateral treaty all official language versions of the MC may be considered in this process for which one might be of more relevance than the other depending on the case at hand.[36] Even further, when a thorough interpretation of the model, having taken account of the guidance as contained in Article 33 VCLT, has led to a common meaning of that underlying model, such meaning will also inform that of the norm as contained in the treaty.

3 ARTICLE 33 VCLT

3.1 Object of Interpretation (Article 33(1) & (2) VCLT)

Article 33 VCLT first delimitates the object of interpretation in paragraph 1, first half-sentence and paragraph 2:

1. When a treaty has been authenticated in two or more languages, ...
2. A version of the treaty in a language other than one of those in which the text was authenticated shall be considered an authentic text only if the treaty so provides or the parties so agree.

These provisions therefore provide for the application of the interpretation rules of Articles 33(1) et seq. VCLT only when there are at least two authenticated language texts or at least one authenticated language text and an additional version that is also an authentic text based on the consensus of the parties[37] (as expressed either within the treaty text or otherwise). A text is 'authenticated' when it is designated by the parties as such, most commonly in the final clauses of a treaty testimonium.[38] Without a specific clause, the fact that a treaty was concluded in a language implies the authority of that language version.[39]

Accordingly, if there is only one authenticated or authentic text, Article 33 VCLT cannot apply.[40] Such is the case for several Swiss tax treaties[41] or the Australia-US treaty:[42] Here, as there are no multiple language versions, applying Article 33 VCLT would be futile in any case unless, of course, such a monolingual treaty is subject to the

36. If, e.g., historical considerations tend to give more weight to either language version; similarly, Kofler *supra* n. 25, para. 70; *see also* Pistone, *supra* n. 34, at 258 et seq.
37. E.g., later translations for accession of additional parties; a well-known example of this is, e.g., the EU treaties.
38. Dörr, *supra* n. 26, at para. 14.
39. Jean Hardy, *The Interpretation of Plurilingual Treaties by International Courts and Tribunals*, 37 Brit. Y. B. Int'l L. 74 (1961).
40. Dörr, *supra* n. 26, at para. 14.
41. *See supra* nn 4, 5 and 6.
42. Convention between the Government of the United States of America and the Government of Australia for the Avoidance of Double Taxation and the Prevention of Fiscal Evasion with Respect to Taxes on Income, 6 August 1982.

MLI in which case at least some provisions or some words will be authentic in English and French. When interpreting these specific provisions, Article 33 VCLT may be relevant even regarding a 'monolingual' treaty.

Determining the scope clarifies the role of texts in other languages in the interpretative process as follows:

- If the contracting states held their negotiations and prepared a draft of the treaty text in a language that is later not authenticated, such language versions are not the object of interpretation according to Articles 33(1) et seq. VCLT as they are not authenticated texts. Certainly, these preparatory documents must be taken into account during the interpretation process, most commonly under Article 32 VCLT (though they might certainly also contain indications of the purpose of the treaty under Article 31 VCLT and possibly be relevant for deviations under Article 33(4) VCLT; *see* below on this). The weight of these texts in the interpretation process must therefore significantly reduced vis a vis the authenticated texts.
- Other translations of the concluded treaty, whether official or unofficial, will usually have no or only a minor role in the interpretation process. Official texts are those that were signed by the contracting parties but are not accepted as authentic.[43] These again may serve as additional tools in the interpretation process but will usually be of limited relevance.[44] That unofficial translations, such as solely unilateral translations, may be of relevance when interpreting a treaty seems improbable as no consensus at all with the other contracting party/parties was reached. An example of this might be the current Italian state practice of providing an Italian translation of tax treaties on the government website. In this case, the parties to the treaties did not consent to this translation and thus cannot be bound or affected by it in any way.[45]
- Similarly, the OECD MC is also not an authenticated text even though it formed the basis of the negotiations: Independent of whether any of the authenticated texts correspond to the OECD MC's official languages, this convention itself is just another interpretative tool available to the interpreter.[46]

The MLI is itself a treaty authenticated in two languages and is thus the object of interpretation in the sense of Article 33(1) and (2) VCLT. Accordingly, if a treaty is subject to the amendments as contained in the MLI, it must be read together with the relevant sections of the MLI. Irrespective of the authentic languages of the treaty per se, it is relevant in both English and French. Accordingly, a treaty may be authentic only

43. Dörr, *supra* n. 26, at para. 19; ILC, *Final Draft, Commentary to Article 29*, 224, paras 1 and 3.
44. Hardy, *supra* n. 39, at 74; though the situation might be different in domestic law; *see id.*, 136 et seq.
45. Whether the taxpayer can rely on these translations is a question of domestic constitutional law and does not impact the relationship between the contracting parties.
46. *See* on this discussion also Michael Lang, *Auslegung von Doppelbesteuerungsabkommen und authentische Vertragssprachen*, IStR 407 (2011).

in Chinese, but the sections as derogated by the MLI will be authentic only in English and French.[47]

Article 33 VCLT is therefore relevant when interpreting treaties that are authentic in more than one language, including tax treaties that were derogated by the MLI.

3.2 Equal Authority (Article 33(1) VCLT)

Article 33 VCLT contains several indications on how such multiple authentic texts should be approached by the interpreter. Fundamentally, Article 33(1) VCLT states that all authenticated versions have equal authority: '1. When a treaty has been authenticated in two or more languages, *the text is equally authoritative in each language*, unless the treaty provides or the parties agree that, in case of divergence, a particular text shall prevail' (emphasis added).

The normative content of this rule seems to be somewhat ambiguous; the ILC Commentary on this provision makes no additional remarks, and the literature frequently just states this sentence and then proceeds to a discussion on paragraph 3.[48] This author posits that the rule serves more as a negation of any *ex ante* priority rule for any one version of the text. Before drafting the VCLT, parts of the literature seemed to argue for general presumptions of greater authority of either the drafting language,[49] the narrower text[50] or the 'clearer' text.[51] Such general presumptions could lead the courts to disregard translated texts *ex ante* or fail to consider additional arguments against the prevailing value of the narrower text or one that initially seems clearer. Article 33(1) now makes it explicitly clear that the starting point for interpreting a multilingual treaty should be to regard all treaty texts as being of equal authority. In this author's opinion, this should define the starting point for interpretation as considering every treaty text and, on this basis, conducting a thorough interpretation.

However, equal authority must not be confused with equal weight.[52] There can be a plethora of arguments to award one language version greater weight during the interpretation process than another. One example of this is certainly the original drafting language of which the importance is, in fact, frequently critically discussed in the literature under the heading of Article 33 VCLT.[53] However, this author intimates that this discussion is actually separate from Article 33 VCLT. Just because this article does not provide for any primacy of the drafting language (which it quite clearly does not) does not mean that under another method of interpretation – usually the historical method – the drafting language cannot be of particular relevance. It sometimes seems

47. *See* Lang, *Die Auslegung des multilateralen Instruments, supra* n. 23, at 22.
48. Or suggests that para. 1 does not include any material interpretative rule but just defines the object of interpretation; *see, e.g.*, Peter Germer, *Interpretation of Plurilingual Treaties: A Study of Article 33 of the Vienna Convention on the Law of Treaties*, 2 Harvard International Law Journal 401 (1970).
49. *See* on this issue below.
50. Germer, *supra* n. 48, at 412.
51. Hardy, *supra* n. 39, at 87 et seq.; on this also below.
52. Dörr, *supra* n. 26, at para. 22.
53. For many, e.g., Paolo Arginelli, *Multilingual Tax Treaties: Interpretation, Semantic Analysis and Legal Theory* 120 et seq. (IBFD 2015); Dörr, *supra* n. 26, at para. 8.

that authors look at one interpretation rule in isolation and require it to provide the one true outcome. Such an expectation, however, simply will not be fulfilled in all cases. This is why the canon of interpretational rules is one where different interpretational arguments can be taken into account and weighed to find the 'correct' meaning of a norm. Article 33(4) VCLT references Articles 31 and 32 VCLT as being relevant for establishing the common meaning of all language texts. Thus, though Article 33 VCLT itself contains no explicit rule, it stresses the relevance of conducting a full interpretation for which such additional arguments may be included in the interpretation process.[54] Article 33 VCLT does not disallow this in any way. It just requires the interpreter to fairly consider every authentic language text which, in fact, ensures that no relevant and convincing arguments are disregarded because of any strict *ex ante* preference. This serves to underline interpretation as a holistic process for which one argument cannot be considered in isolation from all other possible arguments.

Article 33(1) VCLT itself contains one exception to this general rule of equal authority that mainly serves to express the dispositive nature of Article 33 VCLT:[55] Parties to a treaty are free to determine that one language version prevails in the event of conflict.[56] Article 33(3) VCLT also indicates at what point this prevailing version should be consulted which is only after the interpretation of all language versions has led to the result that there is no common meaning (more on this below). It should not be the case that the interpreter only considers the prevailing version.[57]

It is not necessary that this prevailing version is determined in the treaty text itself; unwritten agreements can also be encompassed by this phrase.[58] From this, some authors derive a prevailing force of authenticated French or English language versions (as these are the OECD MC's official languages) – even if not provided for explicitly in the treaty.[59] As the contracting states used the OECD MC as a basis for their treaty negotiations, they implicitly intended to have the meaning as expressed in it prevail in their bilateral relations. Though this author is unsure whether such a treaty

54. The cases as cited in these discussions also do not insinuate that, in terms of authority, the drafting language should prevail in all cases. In *Mavrommatis*, the drafting language was but one argument brought forth and could just be part of the historical interpretation; *Mavrommatis Palestine Concessions* (*Greece v. U.K.*), 1924 P.C.I.J. (ser. B) No. 3 (30 August) para. 41; also ICJ, Exchange of Greek and Turkish Populations, Advisory Opinion, 1925 P.C.I.J. (ser. B) No. 10 (21 February) para. 44; with regards to *Mavrommatis*, the Draft Commentary to Art. 33 (then Art. 29) actually already made it clear that the court did not formulate a rule of general precedence as is now sometimes argued (ILC, Final Draft, Commentary to Art. 29, para. 8); *see also* Hardy, *supra* n. 39, at 80.
55. Dörr, *supra* n. 26, at para. 23.
56. For the Austrian treaties, this is usually English (Belarus, Cyprus, Israel, Kazakhstan, Kyrgyzstan, Kosovo, Croatia, Cuba, Kuwait, Latvia, Lithuania, Malaysia, Macedonia, Mexico, Moldavia, Mongolia, Montenegro, Norway, Poland, Qatar, Romania, Russia, San Marino, Saudi Arabia, Serbia, Slovenia, Tadzhikistan, Taiwan, Turkey, Turkmenistan, Uzbekistan, Venezuela, United Arab Emirates, and Vietnam) and, in rare cases, French (only in the treaties with Algeria and Marocco).
57. Not as clearly expressed in the Commentary: ILC, *Final Draft, Commentary to Article 29*, para. 4 as 'master text'.
58. Dörr, *supra* n. 26, at para. 25.
59. *See* Lang, *Auslegung von Doppelbesteuerungsabkommen und authentische Vertragssprachen*, *supra* n. 46, at 406 et seq.

version in the language of the underlying MC prevails in the sense of Article 33(1) VCLT or due to Article 32(1) VCLT, this question is ultimately of only minimal importance. The interpretative process is holistic for which the individual arguments and aspects contribute to one another and cannot (and need not) in all cases be clearly delimited.[60] If English (or French) is an authenticated language and the treaty text in English (or French) is the same as that of the OECD MC, this indicates that the parties wanted to remain true to the OECD MC's content and interpretation. It is possible to reach this interpretational result by granting greater weight to this text in the sense of Article 33(1) VCLT. However, such increased weight could also be argued as part of the historical, teleological, and systematic interpretation of the texts. For example, a treaty has authentic language versions in Arab, English, and German. The English version adheres verbatim to the OECD MC. When now interpreting this treaty, all three language versions must be considered. When interpreting the German (or Arab) text, the Arab (or German text) and the English text form part of the context: If now the English text follows verbatim the OECD MC, this is a relevant indication of the telos of the provision. In most cases, it seems probable that, by conducting a thorough interpretation of the treaty texts in their respective languages, a common meaning would be reached. Should this not be the case and the differences in the translation are too severe, Article 33(4) VCLT can apply. At this stage, the object and purpose of the treaty must be used to consolidate the meaning (in more detail on this later). Here, the English text might be a central factor leading effectively to the same result as considering the English text as a prevailing text under Article 33(1) VCLT. This point also serves to underline the usefulness of the interpretative rule contained in Article 33 VCLT even in situations when the parties to the tax treaty are not VCLT members. This provision also only codifies aspects of the interpretational process of which many are also reflected in arguments that could be derived from a teleological or historical standpoint.

Generally, when the English text of the OECD MC forms the basis of a negotiation, this implies a greater weight of the English text during the interpretation process. Similarly, Belgium insists on having authentic language versions of their tax treaties in Dutch and French. If the French OECD MC influenced the formulation of the treaty, the French text will have greater weight in the interpretation than the Dutch one - despite both texts being equally authentic. The same also holds true for Indian treaties authenticated in Hindi and English relating to the English text.[61]

However, such an increased value of English or French stemming from the negotiation of the bilateral treaty cannot automatically extend to such articles or sections that were amended by the MLI. Certainly, the English or French MLI text may be of increased value (e.g., because this language formed the basis of the MLI negotiation), but this enquiry must be kept separate from considerations stemming

60. Popa, *supra* n. 29, at 331; Richard Xenophon Resch, *Tax Treaty Interpretation and Authentic Languages: Lessons from Polish Case Law*, 5 Intertax 471 (2020) https://doi.org/10.54648/taxi 2020044.
61. *See* on this, e.g., Pistone, *supra* n. 34, at 5.1.3.1.2.3.

from any individual bilateral treaty. Fundamentally, the only authentic languages of the MLI are English and French.

A second situation in which the increased relevance of English or French fails to apply is when the bilateral treaty deviates from the underlying model convention. This can be the case either when the model foresees that the countries amend the treaty text according to the specific bilateral situation (e.g., under Article 2(3) or 3(1)(f) OECD MC) or when the parties want to regulate a set of circumstances different to the rule as contained in the model convention (e.g., to encourage certain economic activity or scholarly exchange between the contracting states). To extend any prevailing value of the language text that corresponds to the MC also to such provisions would no longer be in accordance with the parties' intent. Here, other arguments for additional or reduced weight of either language text must be considered - such might lie in the language used over the course of the negotiations, for example. The interpreter thus cannot apply a broad-brush approach for interpreting an entire treaty but must carefully examine whether considerations of prevailing weight may apply to any individual provision.

3.3 Presumption of Same Meaning (Article 33(3) VCLT)

Article 33(3) VCLT contains the general approach to interpreting the authenticated texts: '3. The terms of the treaty are *presumed* to have the *same meaning* in each authentic text' (emphasis added).

This provision requires, first and foremost, that 'every effort should be made to find a common meaning for the texts before preferring one to another'.[62] As a first step, the interpreter should therefore review all authenticated texts and determine the meaning of the norm considering every interpretational method foreseen in Articles 31 et seq. VCLT. This already includes the context, the legal history, and the purpose of a provision; it therefore allows the use of the OECD or UN MC and Commentaries as a resource. As mentioned above, other authenticated texts also form part of the context and can be used for interpretative purposes.[63] It is to be expected that, in many cases, supposed discrepancies between the different texts can be resolved by conducting such a thorough interpretation - for example, if they were due to a translation error or if historical documents lead to a clear harmonious result, etc. Article 33(1) VCLT serves to underline this importance of an exhaustive interpretation of the norm. It does not require that the texts have to be consolidated forcibly, but it requires the applicant to first thoroughly examine whether the interpretative process may lead to a common reading and thus the meaning of the norm.[64]

Parts of the literature infer from Article 33(3) VCLT that domestic courts can rely solely on the authenticated text in the domestic official language.[65] The reasoning is the following: If all texts are of the same authority and if all of them are presumed to have

62. ILC, *Final Draft, Commentary to Article 29*, para. 7.
63. Arginelli, *supra* n. 53, at 120; Pistone, *supra* n. 34, at 5.1.3.1.2.1.
64. Arginelli, *supra* n. 53, at 119.
65. E.g., Germer, *supra* n. 48, at 412; Schuch & van West, *supra* n. 15, at 76.

the same meaning, it should be sufficient to examine only one of them.[66] However, this essentially shifts the obligation of finding discrepancies to the taxpayer and also fails to realize that of a state to act in accordance with the treaty entered into as the obligations can, according to Article 33(1) VCLT, only be gathered from an examination of all authentic texts. Accordingly, the prevailing opinion has moved away from this approach and requires courts to consider every language version.[67]

Article 33(3) VCLT instead serves to guide the interpreter in the course of the grammatical interpretation of a provision:[68] Language is the tool that the contracting states use (and, in most cases, must use) to communicate with one another and to finalize the result of the negotiation process, i.e., a conglomerate of words or phrases together making up the text of the norm. Language, however, is imperfect.[69] It must be as language is used to describe anything and everything from highly nuanced and technical concepts to feelings and factual conditions up to and including legal norms. Words may have one meaning in one context and a different meaning in another one. A grammatical structure might permit one or two or a plethora of different meanings to be inferred from a text. The meaning of a sentence might change based on the time or the place where it is read or even depending on the person reading it.

The wording of a norm must therefore be understood as being only the medium through which its normative content is communicated to its addressee or applicant;[70] nothing more and nothing less. At least for now, it remains mostly impossible to detach norms from the natural human language.[71] This clear delimitation between the wording of a norm and the norm itself is necessary to understand the purpose of the grammatical interpretation and thus also of Article 33 VCLT: It aims only at inferring the meaning of the words as they are written. The grammatical interpretation is therefore the necessary *starting point* for any interpretation and serves as the basis for the further interpretative process.

There certainly is no one natural meaning of a word that holds true in every context. To reference a 'natural' or 'clear' meaning is to begin with the end result of the interpretation thereby disregarding any other interpretative issues or questions that might arise.[72] It is necessary to approach the legal text from an objective position[73]

66. *See* for an example of the issue of different language texts before a monolingual court, e.g., Jonathan Schwarz, *What is in a Language? Parlez-vous français?*, kluwertaxblog 31 March 2022 (26 April 2024), https://kluwertaxblog.com/2022/03/31/what-is-in-a-language-parlez-vous-francais/.
67. For a thorough analysis on tax treaties, *see* Lang, *Auslegung von Doppelbesteuerungsabkommen und authentische Vertragssprachen*, *supra* n. 46, at 405.
68. Dörr, *supra* n. 26, at para. 32.
69. Arginelli, *supra* n. 53, at 116; Karl Larenz & Claus-Wilhelm Canaris, *Methodenlehre der Rechtswissenschaft* 141 (Springer 1995).
70. Ernst A. Kramer, *Juristische Methodenlehre* 57 (Stämpfli 2010); Friedrich Müller & Ralph Christensen, *Juristische Methodik I*, para. 308 (Duncker & Humblot 2013); Klaus Röhl & Hans Röhl, *Allgemeine Rechtslehre* 19 (Carl Heymanns 2008).
71. Whether this will ever be the situation remains uncertain; *see* already Helmut Coing, *Juristische Methodenlehre* 4 (de Gruyter 1972); though a diversification of used media is certainly even currently taking place; Röhl & Röhl. *supra* n. 70 at 19. Additionally, there are some examples of norms being communicated not via language but, e.g., through signs or symbols. However, such has not yet been of great significance in the area of (international) tax law.
72. *See* Kramer, *supra* n. 70, at 82.

without reading the desired result into it from the beginning. The ambiguity from which this difficulty in determining the grammatical meaning of any word is often described with the three-area model (Drei-Bereiche-Modell)[74] that serves as a visualization of the difficulties of requiring a purely literal meaning or placing too much emphasis on the text as it is written:

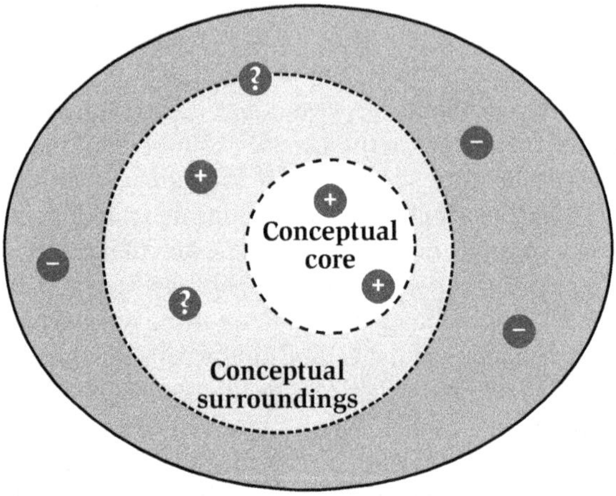

This model considers a word to consist of a conceptual core within which lie the 'positive candidates', its conceptual surroundings (or 'halo')[75] containing 'neutral candidates' and, finally, the area that certainly will no longer be covered by the word 'negative candidates'. An example of this might be the term 'student' contained in Article 20 OECD MC. Within its conceptual core, a student is someone who is learning at college or university. In the United States, the term is also used to describe pupils, i.e., someone who is learning in school. Depending on the cultural background, this meaning might fall within the conceptual core or the conceptual halo. The term 'student' can further be used to describe someone who knows about a subject and is interested in it but may not have studied it formally. Certainly not covered by the term 'student' would be a teacher or professor. The borders between the three areas are fluid (when, for example, should a university assistant who not only teaches but also pursues a doctorate degree be categorized?). The French 'étudiant' (as used in the French OECD MC) might furthermore be an adjective that covers the term 'collegiate' (as in collegiate activities) but might also denominate something as being for or by students. By considering the (grammatical) context, it is clear that this meaning is not covered by that of the norm – further showcasing that a grammatical analysis cannot stop at an individual word and must also take into account the context. It also shows that some discrepancies between the meaning of words between the different authentic languages – even if the meaning is a negative candidate for one language – do not

73. *See* Coing, *supra* n. 71, at 25.
74. *See, e.g.*, Röhl & Röhl, *supra* n. 70, at 35.
75. Möllers, *Legal Methods* (Beck 2020).

automatically lead to a conflict or any issue in finding a common meaning. This very nature of the language being vague implies that the grammatical interpretation cannot be the be-all and end-all of interpretative methods but that there must be other aspects also relevant in determining the normative content of a legal provision.[76] It further implies that delimitating interpretative from non-interpretative activity is also not as clear-cut as often argued.

With multilingual texts, this issue is, of course, exacerbated due to the additional step of translating (or agreeing on the wording in two or more different languages). This is fundamentally due to the fact that there is no perfect translation from one language to another either because there is no expression in the other language at all (e.g., the German 'doch', for which there is no corresponding expression in English)[77] or because the translation encapsulates further[78] or fewer[79] meanings.[80] In the English-French example above, this divergence could be consolidated simply by taking into account the (linguistic) context. Nonetheless, not all divergences between languages may be so easily resolved.

4 DIFFERENCE OF MEANING (ARTICLE 33(4) VCLT)

This exploration brings us directly to Article 33(4) VCLT: '4. Except where a particular text prevails in accordance with paragraph 1, when a comparison of the authentic texts discloses a *difference of meaning* which the application of articles 31 and 32 does not remove, *the meaning which best reconciles the texts, having regard to the object and purpose of the treaty, shall be adopted*' (emphasis added).

This paragraph concerns situations in which the different language texts cannot be consolidated through the interpretative methods of Articles 31 et seq. VCLT. For example, in the tax treaty between Poland and Sweden, the Polish text of Article 11 was missing the requirement of beneficial ownership that was required in both the Swedish and the English versions of the treaty. All three texts are authentic.[81] Recently, the tax authorities in Austria had to analyse the method article of the tax treaty between Austria and Malta that is authentic in both English and German. The English provision adheres to the OECD MC while the German text contains an additional caveat in the formulation of the exemption method: It should apply in cases when *only* the source state has a taxing right – i.e., not in those of open distributive rules – as opposed to

---

76. Kramer, *supra* n. 70, at 57; Karl Engisch, *Einführung in das juristische Denken* 73 (Beck 2018).
77. Somewhat similar is 'nevertheless/however' or 'yes' depending on the context.
78. As, e.g., the French 'tantièmes et jetons de presence' as opposed to the English 'directors' fees' in Art. 16 OECD MC; *see* on this Pistone, *supra* n. 34, at 5.1.1.1. et seq.
79. E.g., the English 'facts' as a translation for the German 'Tatbestandsmerkmale' where 'facts' is a much broader term encompassing not only the factual elements as required by a norm for its legal consequence to apply but also real-life facts in the sense of information or something that is known to be true.
80. On this extensively, *see* Umberto Eco, *Quasi dasselbe mit anderen Worten: Über das Übersetzen* (Carl Hanser Verlag 2009).
81. Resch, *supra* n. 60, at 471; though, in this case, the English text was connotated as the prevailing version.

cases when *also* the source state has a taxing right.[82] For situations such as these when the different authentic texts cannot be read in such a way as to contain the same meaning, Article 33(4) VCLT may become a factor. At what point this is the case, i.e., when Article 33(3) ceases to apply and precedence is given to Article 33 VCLT, of course leaves room for discussion. In the treaty between Austria and Malta, it could well be argued that the consideration of systematic, historical, and teleological arguments would have sufficed to correct the German wording. Unfortunately, the Austrian tax administration did not follow this view. In what is referred to as an 'Express-Antwort-Service' (EAS), it published the view that according to the German wording of the provision and taking into account the telos of Double tax conventions (DTCs) according to the new preamble after the MLI, the exemption method should in fact not be applicable in cases when both states have a taxing right. It is clear that this view is highly unconvincing. However, the Polish court confronted with the three diverging language texts in fact considered all three and finally decided that the omission of the beneficial ownership criterion in the Polish text was an error, and it should have been included. Whether these two results stem from applying Article 33(4) VCLT, i.e., a conflict between the texts arose and was solved, or whether a common meaning could be found already under Article 33(3) VCLT is difficult to say. However, as Michael Lang convincingly presents, the interpretative process cannot be clearly split into completely separate steps. On the contrary, it is a holistic process for which the different arguments available to the interpreter must be considered and weighed.[83] A clear border is thus not necessary.

Some authors argue that multiple authentic or official versions of a legal text will lead to a broadened grammatical meaning ('Wortlautgrenze').[84] This would be due to the fact that the conceptual surroundings overall are broader when there are multiple language versions. For example, Article 16 of the France-Mauritius treaty adheres to the French OECD MC in its French text and the English OECD MC in its English text. While the English version covers 'fees and other similar payments', the French texts use the broader term of 'tantièmes et jetons de présence'.[85] It might therefore be argued that the France-Mauritius treaty encapsulates both thereby effectively increasing the items of income falling under this provision. However, the opposite might be true. Only such items of income that may be subsumed under both language texts are in fact within the scope of Article 16 of the France-Mauritius Treaty. This would even lead to some clearly positive candidates falling out of scope because they could not be considered even as neutral candidates in the other language. However, to automatically exclude these items that are only negative candidates for one of the items would effectively lend priority to the narrower of the terms. As already discussed above, this is not in accordance with Article 33(1) VCLT that requires giving each text equal

82. For a detailed analysis of this provision and the response of the Austrian tax administration, *see* Michael Lang, *DBA Malta: Wechsel von der Freistellungs- zur Anrechnungsmethode auf Grundlage einer EAS-Rechtsauskunft des BMF?*, 1 SWI 10 et seq. (2024)
83. Compare *ibid.*, at p. 16.
84. Hilf, *supra* n. 2 at 33; relating to EU law Karl Riesenhuber, *Interpretation of EU Secondary Law, in European Legal Methodology*, 231, para. 18 (Riesenhuber eds, intersentia 2017).
85. Pistone, *supra* n. 34, at 5.1.1.1 et seq.

authority.[86] Furthermore, in the case of the tax treaty between Austria and Malta, there is no such 'common core' because the two texts are mutually exclusive. This author therefore finds this view as expressed in the literature convincing: If there is more than one authenticated language version of a text, the possible grammatical meaning of a norm is in fact broadened and covers all items that fall under either of the language versions even if they would be negative candidates under another language text. Furthermore, Article 33(4) VCLT does not require the interpreter to decide for or against any language text. Instead, he is to find the meaning that best represents the underlying object and purpose – which may be closer to one of the language texts, but it could just as well be the case that all language versions fail to accurately capture the content of the norm.

When reading Article 33(4) VCLT, it might seem as though the sentence implies a reduced relevance of the object and purpose by only employing the interpreter to 'have regard' to such arguments. However, such a reading would lead to Article 33(4) VCLT granting a grammatical argument, i.e., the wording, additional weight. This provision only becomes necessary when the interpretation of the language texts has failed to clearly indicate the normative content of a provision due to irreconcilable differences in the wording. To then award it with additional weight in the interpretation would be counterintuitive. Instead, Article 33(4) VCLT provides (albeit vague) guidance as to relevant arguments to solve issues of discrepancies.

A consolidated meaning should be found based on the 'object and purpose of the treaty', i.e., teleological considerations. Article 33(4) VCLT does not include a reference to either the historical or the systematic method as provided for in Articles 31 and 32 VCLT. The original draft as presented by the ILC did not, in fact, contain any limitation as to how the meaning should be found.[87] Only later did the Vienna Conference add this section to the text of the provision. The background for the addition of the reference to 'object and purpose' of the treaty was to better guide the interpreter: Without it, the compromise solution as envisaged by Article 33(4) would grant full discretion to the interpreter.[88] According to the materials available, the apparent inspiration was the decision by the Permanent Court of International Justice in *Mavrommatis*.[89] This would imply that the reference to 'object and purpose' can be read much more extensively and also include in particular historical arguments – as the reasoning of the court in *Mavrommatis* pertained in particular to the 'intent of the

86. Just imagine an extreme case in which there is a multilateral treaty in several authenticated language versions. Of these, most use an expansive term. However, one translator chose to employ an extremely narrow term covering only one aspect of the term used in the other authenticated versions. Even in such a case, only the extremely narrow meaning could be followed if adhering to the approach laid out above. It is clear that this will not reflect the intent of the parties in most cases. *See* in detail on this discussion in particular, Hilf, *supra* n. 2, at 95 et seq.; Hardy, *supra* n. 39, at 88 et seq.
87. ILC, *Final Draft*, Art. 29.
88. UN conference on the law of treaties official records, A/CONF.39/C.1/8, plenary meeting 34, paras 39-70.
89. *Id.*, para. 40.

parties'.[90] It must also be stressed that, historically, a more objective approach to interpretation was prevalent in the context of international law which might have further influenced the wording of Article 33(4) VCLT.[91] That this addition truly narrows the discretion of the interpreter seems doubtful. Just as a general rule, the teleological method is the one lending the broadest discretion as determining an (implicit) meaning of a text is a subjective operation.[92] The phrasing of Article 33(4) VCLT further softens its guiding force by using the word 'best' – this can only be determined by the interpreter and is not based on any objective criteria.[93] This sentence, however, could also be read as requiring the interpreter to present a valid and convincing argument for the reached interpretative result thus enabling a critical examination. This author would therefore consider Article 33(4) to once again effectively require the interpreter to use all of the interpretative methods to ascertain the meaning of a treaty provision and to thoroughly present all relevant arguments.[94] Overall, it might be considered to amend the wording of Article 33(4) VCLT to include a reference to all interpretative methods.

In the context of tax treaties, this final provision of Article 33 VCLT directly permits the reference to the OECD or UN MC and Commentaries as part of the interpretative rule specific to multilingual treaties. When there is a discrepancy between the authenticated language texts, the interpreter must find a consolidated meaning on the basis of the telos, the context, and the history of the norm. Certainly, the OECD and UN MC may form the basis for particularly teleological and historical arguments. In particular, it might be that the relevant MC can provide arguments for special relevance to be given to one language text over another. Several situations may be considered. A treaty was negotiated on the basis of a model convention, and the parties agreed to an authentic text in the language of this model convention – such as, for example, the treaty between Austria and Malta where the English text follows the English OECD MC. Here, historical arguments imply that the English text must have greater weight in the interpretative process. Accordingly, the English version of the OECD or UN MC also must be of greater importance than the others as this was the one the parties considered.[95] This still does not imply any general presumption for an English or French authenticated text; the result also must not be 'for' one language version and 'against' the other. As stated above, the wording of a norm is just the medium through which it is expressed, and the grammatical interpretation is but one of the interpretative methods. The goal as expressed in Article 33(4) VCLT is to find the overall meaning of the norm to which the parties agreed that may have found a more appropriate expression in one text or the other or even in neither.

90. ICJ, *Mavrommatis Palestine Concessions* (*Greece v. U.K.*), 1924 P.C.I.J. (ser. B) No. 3 (30 August), para. 19.
91. *See* Dinah Shelton, *Reconcilable Differences-The Interpretation of Multilingual Treaties*, 3 Hastings International and Comparative Law Review 627 (1997).
92. *See* Oliver Dörr, *Art 31, in Vienna Convention on the Law of Treaties: A Commentary*, paras 55 et seq. (Dörr & Schmalenbach eds, Springer 2018).
93. Dörr, *supra* n. 26, at para. 37.
94. Similarly, already Germer, *supra* n. 48, at 426 et seq.; Popa, *supra* n. 29, at 331.
95. Pistone, *supra* n. 34, at 258 et seq.

If there is no authentic text in the language of a model convention used as a basis for negotiation, the model convention can nonetheless be taken into account under Article 33(4) VCLT – as from the model convention arguments regarding the general telos of a provision may be gathered. Finally, there are cases – such as the Mauritius-France treaty mentioned above – where the parties agreed to authentic texts in multiple official languages of the model conventions. This presents special issues in which the model conventions themselves deviate from one another (as is the case, e.g., for Article 16 OECD MC) – which, again, cannot be solved by Article 33 on its own.[96] However, they do not need to be. As perfectly stated by Germer: 'The search for a single criterion for the solution of all problems concerning plurilingual treaties has ... been definitely called off' and will not be ignited again in this chapter.

5 CONCLUSION

Tax treaties are usually concluded in multiple languages and are thus presented to the interpreter in multiple different texts that need to be consolidated to find the meaning of the actual norms hidden behind this linguistic cover. Multilingualism in tax treaties presents the interpreter with certain unique issues. Article 33 VCLT contains a general rule for interpreting multilingual tax treaties that this chapter has endeavoured to more comprehensively analyse, reaching the following central conclusions:

(1) First, the scope of Article 33 VCLT is limited by its paragraphs 1 and 2 to 'authenticated texts'. It therefore initially seems that Article 33 VCLT is not the correct method for introducing the OECD or UN MC or Commentaries into the interpretational process. Article 33(1) and (2) VCLT in connection with Articles 1 and 2 VCLT quite clearly delimitate the object of interpretation under this provision to authenticated treaty texts. The OECD and UN MC are neither a treaty – as countries do not agree to be bound by it – nor an authenticated text. Nonetheless, such texts may be a significant factor in the interpretative process and be valuable sources. Article 33 VCLT may furthermore be of relevance for analysing the underlying model conventions themselves as they are also authenticated in multiple languages.

(2) Second, Article 33(1) VCLT makes it clear that all authenticated texts have the same authority. This clearly implies that an English or French treaty text, just because it corresponds to the OECD MC, does not *automatically* overrule the others – though, of course, the implication that the parties wanted to include the norm as suggested by the underlying model will, in most cases, lead to a de facto prevailing force of such language version as this will most closely

96. *See* Pistone, *supra* n. 34, at 258 for a discussion of the different situations that may arise for Art. 16 OECD MC and the respective weight of the different language texts.

correspond to the parties' intent. Nonetheless, there might be a situation in which historical documents show that the parties actively deviated in the other language version in order to reach a certain outcome but overlooked the need to also amend the English or French text.

(3) Accordingly, Article 33(3) VCLT requires that the interpreter first analyses all treaty texts taking into account every methodological consideration available to him under Articles 31 and 32 VCLT. At this stage, the OECD, UN MC, and Commentaries will already be valuable tools to possibly consolidate different language texts that initially do not seem to align with one another. At this stage, other authenticated texts can also add to the interpretation considering they are part of the context. However, this must not lead to an interpreter only regarding the English or French text simply because this text aligns with the underlying model convention, though these language texts will certainly have significant weight for purposes of the interpretation.

(4) All of this is not to say that the English or French versions of a treaty based on the OECD MC may not carry greater weight than the other language versions. In the course of interpreting the individual language versions according to Articles 31 and 32 VCLT, the other authenticated language versions do form part of the context and a treaty text in English that corresponds to (or deviates from) the OECD MC in English may also lead the interpreter to historical or teleological arguments that can be taken into account. Just because all texts must have the same authority, they do not necessarily have to have the same weight in the interpretative process.

(5) Due to adopting the MLI in two authentic languages, even treaties that were only authenticated in a singular language will now have to be analysed taking into account Article 33 VCLT. A prevailing weight of either of the two authenticated texts of the MLI can further only stem from the MLI itself (e.g., if it could be reconstructed that the debate on a certain article was conducted only in English, the English text would have increased relevance in the interpretation process) Any rules on a prevailing language within a bilateral treaty do not extend to the MLI.

(6) Finally, should a discrepancy arise between the different authenticated texts, the interpreter must find a consolidated meaning based on the object and purpose of the treaty. Though the wording of Article 33(4) VCLT only references the telos, a historical analysis of this provision indicates that also other (such as systematic and historical) arguments may be considered. Thus, at the latest, at this point of divergence, the OECD or UN MC and Commentaries must be a significant factor also within the bounds of Article 33 VCLT.

Overall, interpreting multilingual treaties mirrors the generally adopted canon of interpretative rules. Discrepancies between different language texts must always be consolidated through historical, teleological, and systematic arguments which either lead to a common meaning simply according to applying Articles 31 et seq. VCLT or Article 33(4) VCLT. While differing texts, mistranslations, and covert disagreements may pose difficult questions, 'the questions of language only relate to the text of a treaty. The text of a treaty is, however, nothing more than the starting point for interpretation'.[97]

97. Lang, *Die Auslegung des multilateralen Instruments, supra* n. 23, at 22 et seq.; translated by the author.

CHAPTER 10

Customary International Law and Tax Treaty Interpretation

Claus Staringer & Timoleon Angelos Christodoulopoulos

1 Introduction
2 CIL as a Source of International Law
2.1 Sources of International Law
2.1.1 Introduction
2.1.2 International Custom
2.1.3 International Conventions
2.2 Hierarchy of Sources of International Law
3 Is There CITL?
3.1 Potential Candidate Norms
3.2 OECD Models and Commentaries as CIL?
3.2.1 Existence of General and Consistent State Practice
3.2.2 Existence of *Opinio Juris*
3.3 Principal Purpose Test
3.3.1 General Overview
3.3.2 Existence of General and Consistent State Practice
3.3.3 Existence of *Opinio Juris*
3.4 CFC Rules
3.5 Permanent Establishment
3.6 Arm's Length Principle
4 The Role of Article 31(3)(c) VCLT in the Tax Treaty Interpretation Process
4.1 The Concept of Article 31(3)(c) VCLT

4.2 The Relevance of Article 31(3)(c) VCLT for Interpreting Tax Treaties
5 Concluding Remarks

1 INTRODUCTION

The area of international taxation has traditionally been regulated through double tax treaties (DTTs). The existing international tax regime is the result of the work undertaken in the context of the League of Nations and led to the first bilateral model convention in 1928, i.e., the Mexico and London Model Tax Conventions (1943 and 1946, respectively), its establishment culminating after the Organisation for Economic Co-operation and Development (OECD) published its Model Tax Convention in 1963.[1]

Since the 1920s and up until the 2010s, the allocation of taxing rights between different states had been achieved through an ever-expanding network of bilateral DTTs,[2] with few exceptions to this rule.[3] It is illustrative that there are currently between 3,000 to 4,000 bilateral DTTs that show a high degree of standardization as to their content and structure (estimated at more than 75%).[4] A major development in the international tax landscape was the introduction of the Multilateral Instrument (MLI) in 2016 which constitutes the first major multilateral double tax agreement with wide representativeness.[5]

Given the prevalence of a system based on an immense number of DTTs, the existence (or non-existence) of tax rules of a customary international law (CIL) nature is a matter that has not been dealt with much in literature. Nevertheless, certain aspects of this system have been examined to a certain extent in academia. The usual starting point for such analyses is whether the existence of a wide network of DTTs comprising common terms and concepts can lead to the formation of customary international tax

1. *See* OECD, *Model Tax Convention on Income and on Capital: Condensed Version 2017* 9-10 (OECD 18 December 2017).
2. The international tax regime that was established through the work of the League of Nations has been described as the '1920s compromise'. *See* Michael J. Graetz & Michael M. O'Hear, *The 'Original Intent' of U. S. International Taxation*, 46 Duke L.J. 1033-1034 (1997) https://doi.org/10.2307/1372916; Craig Elliffe, *The Brave (and Uncertain) New World of International Taxation under the 2020s Compromise*, 14 World Tax J. 241-243 (2022) https://doi.org/10.59403/1h6s7gc.
3. *See*, for example, *Denmark – Faroe Islands – Finland – Iceland – Norway – Sweden Income and Capital Tax Treaty (Nordic Convention)*, 23 September 1996.
4. *See* Elliott Ash & Omri Marian, *The Making of International Tax Law: Empirical Evidence from Tax Treaties Text*, 24 Fla. Tax Rev. 153 (2020); Reuven S. Avi-Yonah, *Double Tax Treaties: An Introduction, in The Effect of Treaties on Foreign Direct Investment: Bilateral Investment Treaties, Double Taxation Treaties, and Investment Flows* 99 (Karl P. Sauvant & Lisa E. Sachs eds, Oxford Univ. Press 2009); Rita Szudoczky, *Principles in International Taxation: Their Role in the Consolidation, Control and Disintegration of the International Tax Regime* 136 (Habilitation thesis WU (Vienna Univ. of Econ. and Bus.) 2021).
5. *Multilateral Convention to Implement Tax Treaty Related Measures to Prevent Base Erosion and Profit Shifting*, 7 June 2017. As of 22 February 2024, the MLI has been signed by 102 jurisdictions and has been ratified and entered into force in 87 jurisdictions. *See* OECD, *BEPS Actions: Base Erosion and Profit Shifting (BEPS)*, https://www.oecd.org/tax/beps/beps-actions/ (last visited 15 July 2024).

law (CITL).[6] This matter has become even more topical in view of the emergence of the significant body of the OECD's work in the field of international tax going beyond the conventional scope of DTTs such as the Base Erosion and Profit Shifting (BEPS) Project[7] and, more recently, not only the work on Pillar 1 and Pillar 2[8] but also the corresponding work of the United Nations (UN).

In an era when the development of international taxation norms is furthered by standard setting at the level of international organizations such as the OECD and the UN, it is being argued that, under certain conditions, introducing common rules in the domestic legal order of a large number of States could lead to the formation of CITL.[9] Similar to the case with DTT rules, should a CITL rule come into existence, States would then be bound by it even if they have not enacted such an explicit rule in their DTTs or their domestic legal order. If rules similar to such CITL would pre-exist, e.g., in a bilateral DTT, the question would arise whether such CITL would govern the interpretation of DTTs.

In view of the above considerations, the purpose of this chapter is to examine under which conditions CITL can indeed exist. To accomplish this, the authors will first refer to the sources of international law, the constituent elements of CIL and what leads to the creation of custom, as well as the hierarchy between CIL and treaties. Second, certain rules of international tax law (based on DTTs) will be explored that have been brought forward in literature as potential 'candidates' to become CITL. Last, it will be examined the importance of Article 31(3)(c) of the Vienna Convention on the Law of Treaties (VCLT) in the context of this discussion.[10]

There is one important caveat as to the scope of this chapter. In accordance with the overall topic of the present book (which is on tax treaty interpretation), the issue of CIL is only addressed in relation to tax treaties but not to the contracting States' domestic laws. For this reason, it will not be investigated whether CIL could establish limits to national tax policy, e.g., whether it could create jurisdictional limits for domestic tax legislation.[11]

6. International Law Association, Committee on Formation of Customary (General) International Law, *Final Report of the Committee: Statement of Principles Applicable to the Formation of General Customary International Law* 46 et seq. (2000), https://www.law.umich.edu/facultyhome/drwcasebook/Documents/Documents/ILA%20Report%20on%20Formation%20of%20Customary%20International%20Law.pdf (last visited 15 July 2024).
7. OECD, *BEPS Actions: Base Erosion and Profit Shifting (BEPS)*, *supra* n. 5.
8. *See* OECD, *Multilateral Convention to Implement Amount A of Pillar One*, available at https://www.oecd.org/en/topics/sub-issues/reallocation-of-taxing-rights-to-market-jurisdictions/multilateral-convention-to-implement-amount-a-of-pillar-one.html (visited 15 July 2024); OECD, *Pillar One: Amount B – Inclusive Framework on BEPS* (2024); OECD, *Global Anti-base Erosion Model Rules (Pillar Two)*, https://www.oecd.org/en/topics/sub-issues/global-minimum-tax/global-anti-base-erosion-model-rules-pillar-two.html (last visited 15 July 2024).
9. *See*, for example, Reuven S. Avi-Yonah, *UTPR's Dynamic Connection to Customary International Tax Law*, 108 Tax Notes Int'l 951-952 (2022).
10. *Vienna Convention on the Law of Treaties*, 23 May 1969.
11. This issue, which has been traditionally labelled as 'extraterritorial taxation', has gained recent attention in the debate on the OECD's Global Minimum Tax Project (also known as 'Pillar 2'). Pillar 2 imposes significant economic pressure on low-tax countries to levy a minimum tax of 15% on large multinationals because such tax will otherwise be levied on entities resident in high-tax countries who are either in control of a low-taxed group entity (known as the 'income

2 CIL AS A SOURCE OF INTERNATIONAL LAW

2.1 Sources of International Law

2.1.1 Introduction

The 'doctrine of sources of international law' is generally seen to be enshrined in Article 38 of the Statute of the International Court of Justice (ICJ) that was derived from Article 38 of the Statute of the Permanent Court of International Justice (PCIJ).[12] Although, at its inception, this provision was merely intended to provide a list of the sources of international law that the ICJ must apply, it soon acquired broad importance beyond the one initially anticipated. Thus, it is generally perceived to enumerate the sources of international law.[13] The reason for this conclusion is that the ICJ's function is to decide disputes submitted to it 'in accordance with international law', and all UN Member States are ipso facto parties to the ICJ Statute pursuant to Article 93 of the UN Charter.[14]

Article 38(1) of the ICJ Statute provides that:

> The Court, whose function is to decide in accordance with international law such disputes as are submitted to it, shall apply:
>
> a. international conventions, whether general or particular, establishing rules expressly recognized by the contesting states;
> b. international custom, as evidence of a general practice accepted as law;
> c. the general principles of law recognized by civilized nations;
> d. subject to the provisions of Article 59, judicial decisions and the teachings of the most highly qualified publicists of the various nations, as subsidiary means for the determination of rules of law.

Certain conclusions may be drawn from analysing this provision. Going from bottom to top of the list included in Article 38(1) ICJ Statute, it is clear that judicial decisions and teachings of academic writers constitute a subsidiary means for the determination of rules of law. At the same time, while the general principles of law typically rank the same with international conventions and international custom, their role is to accompany these two sources of international law. In practice, this places

---

inclusion rule' (IIR)) or who are controlled by such a low-taxed group entity (known as the 'undertaxed profits rule' (UTPR)). For the current debate on whether specifically the UTPR could violate CIL, *see* Jefferson VanderWolk, *Much Ado about Pillar 2*, 108 Tax Notes Int'l 822-823 (2022); Avi-Yonah, *UTPR's Dynamic Connection to Customary International Tax Law*, *supra* n. 9, at 951-952; Jefferson VanderWolk, *The UTPR Is Far from Becoming Part of Customary International Tax Law*, 108 Tax Notes Int'l 1069-1070 (2022).

12. Given the dissolution of the PCIJ in 1946 and its replacement by the ICJ, reference will hereinafter be made only to the ICJ.
13. *See* Malgosia Fitzmaurice, *The History of Article 38 of the Statute of the International Court of Justice: The Journey from the Past to the Present*, in *The Oxford Handbook of the Sources of International Law* 182 (Samantha Besson & Jean d'Aspremont eds, Oxford Univ. Press 2017).
14. *See* Malcolm N. Shaw, *International Law* 59 (Cambridge Univ. Press 9th ed. 2021).

them in third place after international conventions and CIL.[15] The relationship between the two remaining sources of international law, specifically international conventions and CIL, however, is not explicitly addressed in Article 38(1) of the ICJ Statute given that it does not contain any indications as to the superiority of either one.

The examination of the general principles of law recognized by civilized nations, the judicial decisions, and the teachings of academic writers are beyond the scope of this chapter and will not be referred to any further herein. Only international conventions and international custom will be further investigated in this chapter with the focus being on CIL.

2.1.2 International Custom

Article 38 ICJ Statute refers to international custom as 'evidence of a general practice accepted as law'.[16] In *Fisheries (UK v. Norway)*, CIL was described as 'the generalization of the practice of States' in Judge Read's dissenting opinion.[17] Custom is regarded as an 'authentic expression of the needs and values of the community at any given time' and constitutes a 'dynamic' source of law given the nature of the international law system that is characterized by a lack of centralized legislature, executive, and judicial systems.[18]

Having a close look at the wording of Article 38(1)(b) ICJ Statute, two basic elements can be discerned: first, the actual conduct of States ('evidence of a general practice') and, second, a subjective belief that this conduct is required by law ('accepted as law'). It can be deduced that the existence and content of CIL are determined by reference to the actual behaviour of States and to the requirement that they recognize a legal obligation or a right to act in that way.[19] This methodology, commonly known as 'the two-element approach', was first applied in *Lotus*[20] and was confirmed in *North Sea Continental Shelf* in which the ICJ stressed that 'not only must the acts concerned amount to a settled practice, but they must also be such, or be carried out in such a way, as to be evidence of a belief that the practice is rendered obligatory by the existence of a rule of law requiring it'.[21] The two-element approach was also followed in subsequent cases before the ICJ.[22] Given this body of case law, the

15. Alain Pellet & Daniel Müller, *Article 38, in The Statute of the International Court of Justice: A Commentary* 850 (Andreas Zimmermann et al. eds, Oxford Univ. Press 2d ed. 2012).
16. James R. Crawford, *Brownlie's Principles of Public International Law* 23 (Oxford Univ. Press 8th ed. 2012).
17. *Fisheries (UK v. Norway)* [1951] I.C.J., at 191.
18. Shaw, *supra* n. 14, at 61.
19. Commentary on Conclusion 2, para. 1, United Nations, *Report of the International Law Commission: Seventieth Session (30 April-1 June and 2 July-10 August 2018)*, A/73/10, 93 (2018), https://legal.un.org/ilc/reports/2018/english/a_73_10_advance.pdf (last visited 15 July 2024).
20. *The Case of the S.S. 'Lotus' (France v. Turkey) Judgment* [1927] P.C.I.J. (ser. A) No. 10, at 38.
21. *North Sea Continental Shelf (Federal Republic of Germany v. Denmark; Federal Republic of Germany v. Netherlands) (Judgment)* [1969] I.C.J. Rep 3, at 44, para. 77.
22. *See Continental Shelf (Libyan Arab Jamahirya v. Malta) (Judgment)* [1985] I.C.J. Rep 13, at 29, para. 47; *Military and Paramilitary Activities in and against Nicaragua (Nicaragua v. United States) (Merits)* [1986] I.C.J. Rep 14, at 97, para. 183 and at 110, para. 211; *Legality of the Threat*

existence of CIL as part of the international law order will be, as such, beyond doubt; the difficulty is more in determining in which situations and as to which content concrete CIL norms actually arise.

In 2018, the International Law Commission (ILC) of the UN published its report on the work of the seventieth session (the '2018 ILC Report').[23] Chapter V of the 2018 ILC Report deals with the identification of CIL and, based its conclusions, among other sources, on an updated bibliography, comments, and observations received from governments, and ICJ case law, among other sources. Thus, it constitutes a valuable source for a systematic understanding of the concept of CIL, for identifying its existence, and the evidence for the presence of its constituent elements.

Its first constituent element, i.e., the existence of State practice, from which the formation or expression of CIL rules can be deduced, may include physical and verbal acts as well as inaction. Conclusion 6(2) of the 2018 ILC Report contains a non-exclusive list of forms of State practice. It may thus be evidenced through diplomatic acts and correspondence; conduct in connection with resolutions adopted by an international organization or at an intergovernmental conference; conduct in connection with treaties; executive conduct, including operational conduct 'on the ground'; legislative and administrative acts; and national court decisions.[24] Thus, the ICJ has established in its case law the existence of CIL from different sources such as from practice,[25] resolutions of the United Nations General Assembly,[26] and a Nuremberg Tribunal decision.[27,28] It must be clarified, however, that there is no hierarchical relationship among the various forms of State practice. Thus, all of its different forms typically have the same probative value with their weight being determined on an ad hoc basis with regard to the context of each case.[29]

---

or Use of Nuclear Weapons (Advisory Opinion) [1996] I.C.J. Rep 226, at 253-255, paras 65-73; *Jurisdictional Immunities of the State (Germany v. Italy: Greece intervening) (Judgment)* [2012] I.C.J. Rep 99, at 122, para. 55.

23. United Nations, *Report of the International Law Commission: Seventieth Session (30 April-1 June and 2 July-10 August 2018)*, *supra* n. 19.
24. Conclusion 6(2), United Nations, *Report of the International Law Commission: Seventieth Session (30 April-1 June and 2 July-10 August 2018)*, *supra* n. 19, at 90; For more information, *see* Crawford, *Brownlie's Principles of Public International Law*, *supra* n. 16, at 24. Shaw, *supra* n. 14, at 68.
25. *Delimitation of the Marine Boundary in the Gulf of Maine Area (Canada v. United States of America) (Judgment)* [1984] I.C.J. Rep 246, at 269, para. 111.
26. *Legality of the Threat or Use of Nuclear Weapons (Advisory Opinion)*, *supra* n. 22, at 254-255, para. 70.
27. *Legal Consequences of the Construction of a Wall in the Occupied Palestinian Territory (Advisory Opinion)* [2006] I.C.J. Rep 136, at 172, para. 89, referring to Judgment of the International Military Tribunal of Nuremberg, 30 September and 1 October 1946, at 65.
28. *See* James R. Crawford, *The Identification and Development of Customary International Law: Keynote Speech, Spring Conference of the British Branch of the International Law Association* 8-9 (London: International Law Association 2014).
29. Conclusion 6(3), United Nations, *Report of the International Law Commission: Seventieth Session (30 April-1 June and 2 July-10 August 2018)*, *supra* n. 19, at 90; *See* Commentary on Conclusion 6, para. 8, United Nations, *Report of the International Law Commission: Seventieth Session (30 April-1 June and 2 July-10 August 2018)*, *supra* n. 19, at 99.

For State practice to lead to CIL formation, it must be 'general'.[30] The concept of generality comprises two different aspects. First, the State practice under examination must be 'sufficiently wide and representative'. In this respect, the number of members of the international community that engage in the practice cannot merely be identified in the abstract but may even vary to a large extent from one case to another depending on the frequency of the circumstances under which the States should act. In any event, it is not required that all States participate in the practice at issue.[31] However, the fewer the instances where the practice at hand is observed, the more difficult it would be to demonstrate the existence of a CIL rule.[32] Second, a practice must be 'representative', also having regard to the circumstances of each case. Therefore, the interests at stake, the geographical regions involved, or whether specially affected States have participated in the practice examined should be taken into account.[33]

Apart from 'general', State practice must also be 'consistent' which requires that a pattern of behaviour can be identified.[34] Stated differently, when the facts surrounding the examination of practice present blatant uncertainty, contradiction, fluctuation, or discrepancy to the extent that no constant or uniform usages can be deduced, no CIL rule can be said to exist.[35] Nevertheless, small inconsistencies or contradictions do not necessarily render the finding of general practice impossible as absolute consistency is not required.[36] A perfect application of the rules forming part of the practice is not expected nor is rigorous conformity therewith necessary.[37]

The second constituent element of CIL is the existence of a subjective element, specifically the acceptance of the relevant practice as law (*opinio juris sive necessitatis* or, more simply, *opinio juris*). Pursuant to the 2018 ILC Report, forms of evidence of *opinio juris* may include public statements made on behalf of States, official publications, government legal opinions, diplomatic correspondence, national court decisions, treaty provisions, and conduct in connection with resolutions adopted by an international organization or at an intergovernmental conference.[38] Thus, it can be noticed that one can notice that the forms of evidence of the two constituent elements of CIL,

30. Conclusion 8, United Nations, *Report of the International Law Commission: Seventieth Session (30 April-1 June and 2 July-10 August 2018)*, *supra* n. 19, at 91.
31. Conclusion 6(3), United Nations, *Report of the International Law Commission: Seventieth Session (30 April-1 June and 2 July-10 August 2018)*, *supra* n. 19, at 91; *See* Commentary on Conclusion 8, para. 3, United Nations, *Report of the International Law Commission: Seventieth Session (30 April-1 June and 2 July-10 August 2018)*, *supra* n. 19, at 100-101.
32. *Ure v. The Commonwealth of Australia* [2016] FCAFC 8, para. 37.
33. *See* Commentary on Conclusion 8, para. 4, United Nations, *Report of the International Law Commission: Seventieth Session (30 April-1 June and 2 July-10 August 2018)*, *supra* n. 19, at 101.
34. Conclusion 8, United Nations, *Report of the International Law Commission: Seventieth Session (30 April-1 June and 2 July-10 August 2018)*, *supra* n. 19, at 91.
35. *Colombian-Peruvian asylum case* [1950] I.C.J. Rep 266, at 277; *See also* Commentary on Conclusion 8, para. 5, United Nations, *Report of the International Law Commission: Seventieth Session (30 April-1 June and 2 July-10 August 2018)*, *supra* n. 19, at 101.
36. *See also* Commentary on Conclusion 8, para. 7, United Nations, *Report of the International Law Commission: Seventieth Session (30 April-1 June and 2 July-10 August 2018)*, *supra* n. 19, at 101.
37. *Military and Paramilitary Activities in and against Nicaragua (Nicaragua v. United States of America) (Merits)*, *supra* n. 22, at 98, para. 186.
38. Conclusion 10, United Nations, *Report of the International Law Commission: Seventieth Session (30 April-1 June and 2 July-10 August 2018)*, *supra* n. 19, at 103.

i.e., State practice and *opinio juris* may overlap, as evidence regarding the existence of both may be present in the same material. In any event, though, their identification should be made through a separate assessment for each element.[39]

The meaning of *opinio juris* is that State practice must be undertaken with a sense of legal right or legal obligation.[40] In other words, it must be accompanied by the belief that it is permitted, required, or prohibited by CIL, and the States must feel that they conform to a legal obligation.[41] Therefore, it must be established that States' conduct was based on the conviction that they were legally compelled or entitled to act in this was by reason of the rule of CIL.[42] Being itself law, CIL is the outcome of an 'act of willing or positing', and *opinio juris* can be characterized as a collective act of will.[43]

Importantly, *opinio juris* is not the only motive that can explain certain State behaviour. Having said this, it must be distinguished from other motives such as comity, political expediency, or convenience in which cases, no CIL rule can be discerned.[44] In addition to this, examining *opinio juris* should occur both with respect to the States that manifest the behaviour in question and those that are in a position to react to it. Therefore, it must be proved that both categories of States have perceived the practice as obligatory by the existence of a rule requiring it.[45] The finding of *opinio juris* is thus not very likely in cases where States are 'profoundly divided'.[46]

It has been seen as an important characteristic of CIL that it has inherent flexibility as it does not have to be formally 'agreed on' by states but is manifested in its application by the ICJ.[47] This flexible application of CIL by the ICJ contributes to the

39. *See* Commentary on Conclusion 10, para. 3, United Nations, *Report of the International Law Commission: Seventieth Session (30 April-1 June and 2 July-10 August 2018)*, *supra* n. 19, at 103.
40. Conclusion 9, United Nations, *Report of the International Law Commission: Seventieth Session (30 April-1 June and 2 July-10 August 2018)*, *supra* n. 19, at 91.
41. *North Sea Continental Shelf*, *supra* n. 21, at 44, para. 77.
42. *See* Commentary on Conclusion 9, para. 2, United Nations, *Report of the International Law Commission: Seventieth Session (30 April-1 June and 2 July-10 August 2018)*, *supra* n. 19, at 102.
43. David Lefkowitz, *Sources in Legal-Positivist Theories: Law as Necessarily Posited and the Challenge of Customary Law Creation* 337 (Samantha Besson & D' Aspremont, Jean eds, Oxford Univ. Press 2017).
44. Commentary on Conclusion 9, para. 3, United Nations, *Report of the International Law Commission: Seventieth Session (30 April-1 June and 2 July-10 August 2018)*, *supra* n. 19, at 102; *Colombian-Peruvian asylum case* [1950] I.C.J. Rep 266, at 277 and 286.
45. ICJ: *Military and Paramilitary Activities in and against Nicaragua (Nicaragua v. United States of America) (Merits)*, *supra* n. 22, at 109, para. 207; Commentary on Conclusion 9, para. 5, United Nations, *Report of the International Law Commission: Seventieth Session (30 April-1 June and 2 July-10 August 2018)*, *supra* n. 19, at 102-103.
46. ICJ: *Legality of the Threat or Use of Nuclear Weapons (Advisory Opinion)*, *supra* n. 22, at 254, para. 67.
47. International Law Commission United Nations General Assembly, *First Report on Formation and Evidence of Customary International Law, by Michael Wood, Special Rapporteur*, A/CN.4/663, para. 101 (17 May 2013), https://legal.un.org/ilc/documentation/english/a_cn4_663.pdf (last visited 15 July 2024); Peter Tomka, *Custom and the International Court of Justice*, 12 Law & Prac. Int'l Cts. 7 Trib. 197 (2013) https://doi.org/10.1163/15718034-12341253; Fitzmaurice, *supra* n. 13, at 185.

progressive development of international law, particularly in the absence of international conventions.[48] Thus, CIL may be seen to endorse effectiveness and efficiency in addressing international law issues.[49]

At the same time, the ICJ has often been criticized for its case law on the formation of CIL.[50] In part, such criticism may derive from the difficulties in collating the necessary evidence for its identification or from the relative weight given by the ICJ in individual cases to the elements of *opinio juris* and that of practice.[51] A more fundamental point of concern is that the flexibility in identifying CIL (which necessarily grants the ICJ a fair amount of judicial discretion) can often result in legal uncertainty.[52] The two lines of criticism, though logically separate,[53] are intrinsically linked: The potential existence of a CIL rule crucially depends on finding evidence that it genuinely exists. No different from any other court of law, the ICJ also has to evaluate the evidence presented to it which is never a mechanical exercise but requires qualitative judgment. Finding such judgment for the existence of CIL has the inherent risk that the line between *lex lata* (i.e., how international law currently stands) and *lex ferenda* (i.e., how it may be desired) becomes blurred.[54] Overall, the value of custom in today's international law system has become a matter of debate. Certain scholars consider CIL an obsolete or less significant source of international law or contend that it is 'slow-moving' and cannot progress at the same rate of development in relations among States in modern times. Hence, they argue that CIL has begun losing its relevance.[55] On the contrary, others posit that it is a dynamic process and its role is not diminishing or that it is even more important than treaties since, unlike the latter, it has universal application.[56] It is indeed a fact that the ICJ has still relied on the concept of

48. Eduardo Jiménez de Aréchaga, *Custom, in Change and Stability in International Law-Making* 3 (Antonio Cassese & Joseph H. H. Weiler eds, Walter de Gruyter 2010).
49. Eyal Benvenisti, *Customary International Law as a Judicial Tool for Promoting Efficiency, in The Impact of International Law on International Cooperation: Theoretical Perspectives* 98 (Eyal Benvenisti & Moshe Hirsch eds, Cambridge Univ. Press 2004).
50. Birgit Schlütter, *Developments in Customary International Law: Theory and the Practice of the International Court of Justice and the International Ad Hoc Criminal Tribunals for Rwanda and Yugoslavia* 170 (Martinus Nijhoff Publishers 2010). Another author argues that the ICJ has blurred the distinction between State practice and *opinio juris, see* Onuma Yashuaki, *Is the International Court of Justice an Emperor Without Clothes?*, 8 Int'l Legal Theory 16 (2002).
51. Theodor Meron, *War Crimes Law Comes of Age: Essays* 157 (Clarendon 1998); Jonathan I. Charney, *Customary International Law in the Nicaragua Case Judgment on the Merits*, 1 Hague Y.B. of Int'l Law 22 (1988).
52. Shaw, *supra* n. 14, at 62.
53. Crawford, *Brownlie's Principles of Public International Law, supra* n. 16, at 23.
54. Not surprisingly, the ICJ was criticized for its recognition of CIL, for instance, by virtue of the mere fact that the relevant rules were found in a widely adopted treaty or in UN resolutions or regional organizations, while State practice based on a contrary rule was simply absent. *See* Charney, *supra* n. 51, at 22; Fitzmaurice, *supra* n. 13, at 185-186.
55. *See* indicatively Wolfgang Gaston Friedmann, *The Changing Structure of International Law* 121-123 (Columbia Univ. Press 2d ed. 1966); Ingrid Detter Delupis, *The Concept of International Law* 115-116 (Norstedts Förl. 1987); Joel P. Trachtman, *The Growing Obsolescence of Customary International Law*, in *Custom's Future: International Law in a Changing World* 172-204 (Curtis A. Bradley ed., Cambridge Univ. Press 2016).
56. Brian D. Lepard, *Customary International Law as a Dynamic Process*, in *Custom's Future: International Law in a Changing World* 62-94 (Curtis A. Bradley ed., Cambridge Univ. 2016); Anthony A. D'Amato, *The Concept of Custom in International Law* 12 (Cornell Univ. Press 1971);

CIL in some recent cases.[57] A more balanced view therefore acknowledges that, while it is not always the most ideal instrument to regulate the complexities of modern world affairs, it may still be appropriate to do this in certain cases.[58] It will be examined in more detail below whether international tax law is such an appropriate territory for reverting to CIL.[59]

2.1.3 International Conventions

A treaty is defined in Article 2(1) of the VCLT as 'an international agreement concluded between states in written form and governed by international law, whether embodied in a single instrument or in two or more related instruments and whatever its particular designation'.[60] An international convention resembles a contract, which stipulates a number of propositions that are considered binding upon the contracting parties.

Article 38 ICJ Statute refers to international conventions that establish rules that are expressly recognized by the States that are parties thereto. Through treaties, which can be either general or particular,[61] States bind themselves to certain conduct or behaviour or assume rights and obligations that they undertake to carry out. The obligatory character of international conventions is based on the *pacta sunt servanda* principle as stipulated in the Vienna Convention, arguably constituting CIL in itself.[62] Notably, creating conventional obligations under a treaty is a different matter from the establishment of sources of general international law. According to J. Crawford, 'treaties as such should be regarded as a source of obligation and not a source of rules of general application'.[63]

In today's world, treaties are considered the most important source of obligations in the field of international law.[64] It is held that they are a 'more modern and more deliberate method' of creating law than custom.[65] As treaties clearly express the contracting parties' consent, many scholars consider them the most significant source of international law. As opposed to custom, they constitute an explicit agreement

Omri Sender & Michael Wood, *Custom's Bright Future: The Continuing Importance of Customary International Law*, in *Custom's Future: International Law in a Changing World* 360-370 (Curtis A. Bradley ed., Cambridge Univ. Press 2016).

57. *Ahmadou Sadio Diallo (Republic of Guinea v. Democratic Republic of the Congo)* (Preliminary Objections) [2007] I.C.J. Rep 582, at 614-616, paras 87-93; *Jurisdictional Immunities of the State (Germany v. Italy: Greece intervening) (Judgment), supra* n. 22, at 122-145, paras 54-107; *See also* Sender & Wood, *supra* n. 56, at 365; Fitzmaurice, *supra* n. 13, at 184.
58. Shaw *supra* n. 14, at 62.
59. *See* s. 3 below.
60. United Nations, Vienna Convention on the Law of Treaties, 23 May 1969.
61. Article 38 ICJ Statute.
62. Article 26 VCLT stipulates that 'every treaty in force is binding upon the parties to it and must be performed by them in good faith'.
63. Crawford, *Brownlie's Principles of Public International Law, supra* n. 16, at 21.
64. Crawford, *The Identification and Development of Customary International Law: Keynote Speech, Spring Conference of the British Branch of the International Law Association, supra* n. 28.
65. Shaw, *supra* n. 14, at 78.

among the parties involved and, hence, they are regarded as practically superior.[66] Thus, it is not a surprise that, over the decades, relations among States have been increasingly regulated through international agreements rather than by CIL. For areas governed by conventions, it is obvious that there is not much room left for CIL.

However, this does not exclude that custom and treaties may interact with each other. Where a CIL rule allegedly exists, treaties may constitute evidence for its identification as they may arguably reflect customary law (i.e., so that treaties are only of a declaratory nature). In such cases, treaties 'may have an important role to play in recording and defining rules deriving from custom or indeed in developing them'.[67] In this regard, treaties can potentially reflect CIL in several ways. First, a treaty may purposely incorporate an already established CIL rule, in which case the treaty may include an express statement to this effect. When no such statement is found in the treaty text, regard may be had to its *travaux préparatoires*. Second, a treaty may contribute to the crystallization of an emerging CIL rule around a treaty rule if sufficient State practice and *opinio juris* for it are given. Third, a widely adopted treaty may immediately give rise to a general practice that is accepted as law (*opinio juris*) from thereon thereby generating a new CIL rule.[68] In any event, all such cases require fulfilling the two constituent elements of CIL, i.e., State practice and *opinio juris*. These are significant obstacles to overcome before CIL can come into existence. Even the ILC points out that establishing that a treaty has generated a CIL rule is a process that is 'not lightly to be regarded as having occurred'.[69] A general practice accepted as law 'in the sense of the provision invoked' must be observed in order to evidence that the behaviour of the contracting States is not attributed to fulfilling a treaty obligation but rather to the acceptance of the rule as binding under CIL.[70] All in all, the inclusion of a rule in a number of treaties may indicate that the rule in question reflects a CIL rule, but this is not necessarily certain.[71]

Further guidance on the likelihood of creating CIL through international conventions can be drawn from a categorization of such conventions that were made in

66. Grigory I. Tunkin, *Theory of International Law* 91-113 (Harvard Univ. Press, 1974); Pellet, *supra* n. 15, at 850; Friedmann, *supra* n. 55, at 123-124; Hugh W.A. Thirlway, *International Customary Law and Codification: An Examination of the Continuing Role of Custom in the Present Period of Codification of International Law* 35 (A.W. Sijthoff 1972); Shaw, *supra* n. 14, at 79.
67. *Continental Shelf (Libyan Arab Jamahiriya/Malta) (Judgment)*, *supra* n. 22, at 13, at 29-30, para. 27; *See also* Commentary on Conclusion 11, para. 2, United Nations, *Report of the International Law Commission: Seventieth Session (30 April-1 June and 2 July-10 August 2018)*, *supra* n. 19, at 105.
68. Conclusion 11 of United Nations, *Report of the International Law Commission: Seventieth Session (30 April-1 June and 2 July-10 August 2018)*, *supra* n. 19, at 91.
69. Commentary on Conclusion 11, para. 7, United Nations, *Report of the International Law Commission: Seventieth Session (30 April-1 June and 2 July-10 August 2018)*, *supra* n. 19, at 107.
70. *North Sea Continental Shelf*, *supra* n. 21, at 44, paras 72 and 74; *See also* Commentary on Conclusion 11, para. 7, United Nations, *Report of the International Law Commission: Seventieth Session (30 April-1 June and 2 July-10 August 2018)*, *supra* n. 19, at 107.
71. Conclusion 11 of United Nations, *Report of the International Law Commission: Seventieth Session (30 April-1 June and 2 July-10 August 2018)*, *supra* n. 19, at 91.

international law doctrine distinguishing two categories of conventions, i.e., 'law-making treaties' and 'treaty-contracts'.[72] While the purpose of the former is to have universal or general relevance and therefore create 'general' norms of international law (e.g., through a widely adopted multilateral convention),[73] the objective of the latter is to function as a contract between a limited number of States thereby creating 'individual' norms (e.g., in a bilateral treaty governing the situation of only two contracting States).[74] It is obvious that 'law-making treaties' have much more potential to confirm or create CIL as States express through them how they either perceive the status quo of international law on a given topic or that they want to introduce rules that will guide future conduct on a matter of international law.[75] Even if non-signatories accepted the position of such 'law-making treaty' with *opinio juris*, CIL may arise.[76] On the contrary, 'treaty-contracts' are not likely to have a significant impact on creating CIL given their limited scope and relevance.[77]

In some areas of international law, there may be a practice that 'treaty-contracts' (e.g., bilateral agreements) are concluded by States in many bilateral situations with a standardized content. As an example, DTTs may fall into the category of such standardized groups of bilateral treaties as their content and structure frequently adhere to the design offered by model conventions endorsed by international organizations, most prominently the Model Tax Convention on Income and on Capital of the Organisation for Economic Co-operation and Development (OECD MC) (or the United Nations Model Double Taxation Convention between Developed and Developing Countries (UN MC)). Assuming that such model-driven DTTs are indeed standardized (which is more an experiment of thought than reality given the significant degree of variation that even such tax treaty models allow), the question may arise of whether such a broad network of (allegedly identical) bilateral double tax conventions could indicate the existence of CIL on such DTTs' content. However, as always with CIL, caution should be practised as it will only exist if States enter into such standardized bilateral treaties not just as a matter of political fact but with *opinio juris*.[78] Stated differently, States would have to feel bound by law (i.e., by CIL) to adopt the standardized content in their bilateral treaties thereby making bilateral negotiations redundant. States' actual practice which invariably consists in a negotiation process

72. For an analysis of the concepts 'law-making' treaties and 'treaty-contracts', refer to Tunkin, *supra* n. 66, at 91 et seq.
73. *See also* Commentary on Conclusion 11, para. 3, United Nations, *Report of the International Law Commission: Seventieth Session (30 April-1 June and 2 July-10 August 2018)*, *supra* n. 19, at 105.
74. Shaw, *supra* n. 14, at 79; Hans Kelsen, *Principles of International Law* 457 (Holt, Rinehart & Winston 2d ed. 1967).
75. Shaw, *supra* n. 14, at 80.
76. Commentary on Conclusion 9, para. 4, United Nations, *Report of the International Law Commission: Seventieth Session (30 April-1 June and 2 July-10 August 2018)*, *supra* n. 19, at 102.
77. Although they may, as stated above, nevertheless potentially provide evidence to its existence. *See* Crawford, *Brownlie's Principles of Public International Law*, *supra* n. 16, at 30-31.
78. Roberto Codorniz Leite Pereira, *The Emergence of Transparency and Exchange of Information for Tax Purposes on Request as an International Tax Custom*, 48 Intertax 628 and 633 (2020) https://doi.org/10.54648/taxi2020057; Chantal Thomas, *Customary International Law and State Taxation of Corporate Income: The Case for the Separate Accounting Method*, 14 Berkeley J. Int'l Law 130 (1996).

proves otherwise. Thus, there is no conviction of *opinio juris* in negotiating tax treaties. Its absence is paradoxically shown by the existence of the broad treaty network itself: If CIL existed in this area, it would not have been even necessary to enter into bilateral treaties as they would only be of a declaratory nature. Put differently, the more bilateral treaties are concluded (even if largely standardized), the less this demonstrates the existence of CIL.[79]

2.2 Hierarchy of Sources of International Law

The hierarchy of sources of international law is a discussion surrounded by inherent complexity due to the absence of a 'constitutional document' in this area which would explicitly clarify such hierarchy. For this reason, it could arguably be believed that the hierarchy of international law rules is not itself based on law.[80] Thus, a structural analysis of the international legal order such as that offered by the Stufenbau theory of hierarchy of norms could be beneficial. This conceptual framework could first provide a theoretical background to explain why the sources of international law can be considered law themselves. Second, it can elucidate the issue of hierarchy.

Based on this theory, legal norms of international law, such as rules of CIL or treaties, constitute (sets of) claims and prescriptions that exist because they are posited pursuant to a norm of a higher order that governs the lawmaking of these lower-order norms. The process of this higher-order norm coming into existence is itself based on a norm of an even higher order until this hierarchy reaches a rule whereof the creation does not depend on a higher-order norm ('Grundnorm'). This norm would constitute the foundation of the legal system at issue and the presumption of the latter's existence. The legal claim enshrined in this highest-order norm would then be impossible to justify by reference to another positive norm of a higher order.[81] The highest-order norm and all of the norms below it would form a normative order. Stated in a different manner, higher-order norms constitute the source of validity of lower-order norms.[82] Accordingly, sources of international law themselves are part of the law and not external to it. In fact, they are a variant of norms that authorize humans to create them ('empowerment norms').[83]

In light of the above theory, accepting that international law is a distinct normative order would mean that its sources are also law. Thus, the sources of international law and how they are derived would have to be identified. Put differently, it must be established what norms of international law (the 'source law') authorize the

79. *See* Céline Braumann, *Taxes and Custom: Tax Treaties as Evidence for Customary International Law*, 23 J. Int'l Econ. L. 755 (10 November 2020) https://doi.org/10.1093/jiel/jgaa019; Szudoczky, *supra* n. 4, at 151.
80. Jörg Kammerhofer, *Sources in Legal-Positivist Theories: The Pure Theory's Structural Analysis of the Law*, *in The Oxford Handbook of the Sources of International Law* 352 (Samantha Besson & Jean D' Aspremont eds, Oxford Univ. Press 2017).
81. Lefkowitz, *supra* n. 43, at 328.
82. Hans Kelsen, *Reine Rechtslehre* 228 (Deuticke 2d ed. 1960).
83. Hans Kelsen, *Allgemeine Theorie Der Normen* 82-84 (Manz 1979). *See also* Kammerhofer, *supra* n. 80, at 347.

creation of the rules that govern the creation of substantive international law rules. The positive norms forming part of the 'source law', which would necessarily be those linked to the basic norm (Grundnorm) are the 'constitution' of international law.[84] Accordingly, among other constellations, one could be imagined in which a positive norm empowers the creation of all sources of international law (i.e., a positive constitution beyond the sources of international law) or another one where a complex basic norm (Grundnorm) *itself* comprises the different highest positive norms that govern the creation of these sources.[85] In either constellation discussed herein, it could not be argued that CIL takes precedence over treaty law or vice versa.

There are different approaches in international law literature on Article 38(1) ICJ Statute. Some first argued that the order of appearance of the sources of international law in the text of Article 38(1)(a) and (b) ICJ Statute implicitly assumes a hierarchy among the sources of international law. However, the existence of a formal hierarchy among the different sources cannot be deduced from the wording of the provision nor is it endorsed by prominent scholars who indeed argue that there is no formal hierarchy between CIL and treaties.[86] Proponents of this opinion posit that conflicts between CIL and treaty obligations are to be resolved through traditional conflict rules such as *lex specialis derogat legi generali* and *lex posterior derogat legi priori*. In this way, conflict rules do not stipulate any hierarchy between the different sources of international law, but they rather provide ad hoc solutions to normative conflicts having regard to the facts and circumstances of the case at hand.[87] The strength of this approach is that it focuses on the specific rules in question and makes the issue of hierarchy a matter of legal interpretation rather than giving superiority to either CIL or international treaties as a matter of category (or principle).[88] From a more practical perspective, it is widely accepted that international conventions are the most important source of international law in modern times.[89] At least for areas of law where dense treaty networks exist among States, this will lead to an operational primacy of international conventions if they provide concrete and detailed rules that regulate the specific relations between the contracting States. Given the usual granularity of conventions, it is only natural to look

84. Kammerhofer, *supra* n. 80, at 354-355.
85. Kammerhofer, *supra* n. 80, at 356-359.
86. Crawford, *Brownlie's Principles of Public International Law, supra* n. 16, at 22; Shaw, *supra* n. 14, at 104-105; Erica de Wet, *Sources and the Hierarchy of International Law: The Place of Peremptory Norms and Article 103 of the UN Charter Within the Sources of International Law*, in *The Oxford Handbook of the Sources of International Law* 626-627 (Samantha Besson & Jean D' Aspremont eds, Oxford University Press 2017). This, of course, assumes that the relevant rule of both types of international law, either in CIL or in treaties, is not to be seen as *jus cogens*.
87. de Wet, *supra* n. 86, at 628; Shaw, *supra* n. 14, at 104-105.
88. *See* for an overview of various positions, Mario Prost, *Sources and the Hierarchy of International Law: Source Preferences and Scales of Values, in The Oxford Handbook of the Sources of International Law* 645-646 (Samantha Besson & Jean D' Aspremont eds, Oxford University Press 2017).
89. Crawford, *Brownlie's Principles of Public International Law, supra* n. 16, at 30; Jan Klabbers, *International Law* 25 (Cambridge Univ. Press 4th ed. 2024); Duncan B. Hollis, *The Oxford Guide to Treaties* 7 (Duncan B. Hollis ed., Oxford Univ. Press 2d ed. 2020). For additional relevant sources, refer to Prost, *supra* n. 88, at 645-646.

at them in the first place while recourse to (allegedly existing) CIL may be contemplated exceptionally when conventions are silent on the specific issue. At the same time, it is practically unlikely that a CIL norm would supersede an existing specific norm of a convention as the mere existence of such a conventional norm would question either the presence of States practice or of *opinio juris* on the issue at hand. Concisely stated, there would have been a good reason why States regulated their international relations by a convention thereby avoiding the uncertainties that would come with relying on (or hoping for) CIL.

3 IS THERE CITL?

3.1 Potential Candidate Norms

The previous sections discussed the sources of international law, particularly international custom and international conventions. The focus was on the constituent elements of CIL and the hierarchy of sources of international law. The following ones will now turn to the CIL's role in the context of international tax treaties which may be, in theory, twofold. On the one hand, if a certain norm of international tax law should become CITL, it would also be applicable in the relations between States where no DTT between them contains such a norm or where no DTT exists altogether. On the other hand, allegedly existing CITL norms could influence States in making (i.e., negotiating) DTTs as they would be under a legal obligation to follow such CITL in their bilateral tax treaty which would then be of a declaratory nature only.

For this experiment of thought, the following section shall investigate whether certain norms that belong to the area of international tax law are or at least may have the potential to become CITL. The analysis will cover the OECD MC and its Commentary as well as norms such as the permanent establishment (PE) rules, the arm's length principle (ALP), the principal purpose test (PPT), and the controlled foreign company (CFC) rules.[90] None of the below is pure fantasy as all of the candidate norms dealt with have been proposed (or at least discussed) in literature for their suitability as CITL. For ease of reference, the norms that will be examined are taken from the OECD MC as explained by its Commentary.

3.2 OECD Models and Commentaries as CIL?

Several norms belonging to the area of international tax law that were discussed as having the potential for constituting CITL may relate to the interpretation of DTTs.

90. Other potential candidate norms are not examined in this chapter, although other proposals have been made in literature. Indicatively, for non-discrimination, *see* Reuven S. Avi-Yonah, *Does Customary International Tax Law Exist?*, *in Research Handbook on International Taxation* 8-9 (Yariv Brauner ed., Elgar 2020); for transparency and exchange of information, *see* Leite Pereira, *supra* n. 78; for the separate accounting method, *see* Thomas, *supra* n. 78; for the primacy of source taxation, *see* Braumann, *supra* n. 79, at 756 et seq.; for the single tax principle, *see* Szudoczky, *supra* n. 4, at 154-158.

Such norms, for example, are those found in the OECD MC and its Commentary as well as in other Model Conventions and Commentaries thereon that were based on their OECD equivalents, notably the UN MC and its Commentary.[91]

In the event that any norms found in these instruments constituted CITL, this would mean that subject to any indications to the contrary, any provisions of DTTs drafted after these Model Conventions and their Commentaries would have to be interpreted in conformity with these alleged rules of CITL. As always with CIL, the examination of whether the OECD MC and the Commentary thereon can evolve into CITL would require the existence of State practice and *opinio juris*. This would consist of a (slow) process in which a non-binding practice would gradually transform into a CIL rule after its adoption by different States out of non-legal motives (e.g., practicality). Insofar as this practice was consistently applied by these States, other States might rely on this conduct with the former ones becoming bound by the legitimate expectations of the latter.[92]

3.2.1 Existence of General and Consistent State Practice

Initially, certain remarks should be made about the nature of the OECD MC and its Commentary before delving into the analysis of the two constituent elements of CIL. It is important to note that the legal basis for their adoption by the OECD Council was not Article 5(a) ('binding decisions') but rather Article 5(b) of the OECD Convention ('recommendations to Members').[93] When the OECD Council relies on Article 5(b) OECD Convention to issue a recommendation, such recommendation is 'submitted to the Members for consideration in order that they *may, if they consider it opportune*, provide for their implementation' (emphasis added).[94] It follows that implementing recommendations, such as the OECD MC and its Commentary, is at the discretion of each OECD member. Thus, despite the OECD MC's significant practical influence,[95]

91. Given that the majority of norms of the other Model Conventions, notably the UN MC, and their Commentaries are based on those drafted by the OECD, reference will hereinafter be made only to the latter ones. However, the argumentation followed in this chapter is applicable *mutatis mutandis* to all other Model Conventions and Commentaries unless otherwise stated.
92. Martti Nieminen, *Dual Role of the OECD Commentaries: Part 1*, 43 Intertax 638 (2015) https://doi.org/10.54648/taxi2015062; *See also* Mark E. Villiger, *Customary International Law and Treaties: A Manual on the Theory and Practice of the Interrelation of Sources* 53 et seq. (Kluwer Law International 2d fully rev. ed. 1997); International Law Association, *supra* n. 6, at 8.
93. OECD, *Convention on the OECD* (14 December 1960), https://web-archive.oecd.org/temp/2024-06-24/68345-oecd-convention.htm#Text (last visited 15 July 2024); OECD, *Recommendation of the OECD Council Concerning the Model Tax Convention on Income and on Capital*, C(97)195/FINAL (23 October 1997), https://one.oecd.org/document/C(97)195/FINAL/en/pdf (last visited 15 July 2024); OECD, *Model Tax Convention on Income and on Capital: Condensed Version 2017*, *supra* n. 1, para. 3.
94. *See* Rule 18(b) OECD, *Rules of Procedure of the Organisation* (October 2013).
95. Philipp Genschel & Thomas Rixen, *Settling and Unsettling the Transnational Legal Order of International Taxation, in Transnational Legal Orders* 161-162 (Terence C. Halliday & Gregory Schaffer eds, Cambridge Univ. Press 2015).

OECD member countries are free to consult or completely disregard it in the context of the negotiation and conclusion of bilateral DTTs.[96]

From the analysis of the legal nature of the OECD MC and its Commentary, an important conclusion can be drawn that is relevant to the assessment of whether these instruments are or have the potential to become CIL. Neither the OECD MC nor its Commentary are binding legal instruments of international law, particularly an international convention within the meaning of Article 38(1)(a) ICJ Statute. Having this in mind, it is clear that the OECD MC *as such* does not constitute State practice. In fact, all States that apply and interpret the international tax law norms contained in the OECD MC do not technically apply and interpret the norms contained therein but those included in the DTTs entered into among them (even if these were based on the OECD MC itself). In attempting to identify CITL rules, it is the DTTs signed between the states that must be examined and not the OECD MC itself.

The above conclusion is further corroborated by the fact that the OECD MC itself does not lead to the creation of any *legal obligation* for any State. In other words, it does not have *itself* any legal effect on subjects of international law (i.e., States). Hence, Model Conventions do not provide evidence of State practice as they simply do not produce any *legal* result.[97] Moreover, the OECD MC *as a whole* does not have the required *precision* to constitute 'law'[98] as it leaves 'a certain degree of flexibility' and 'latitude' while, in many cases, 'alternative or additional provisions' are mentioned in the Commentaries.[99] Thus, it has been correctly pointed out that the potential identification of CITL cannot extend to 'the' OECD MC and its Commentary as a whole. Rather, an examination would have to be made of each norm on a case-by-case basis.[100] Accordingly, the existing DTTs (i.e., over 3,000 DTTs that are currently in force) would have to be examined in order to identify the existence of State practice for each different rule in isolation. The finding of State practice would have to be substantiated by identifying a 'general' (i.e., sufficiently wide and representative) and consistent use of these norms by a large number of States.[101]

Regarding the OECD Commentaries, their legal status is a topic that has been examined by many scholars. The nature of the OECD Commentaries has been dealt with from the perspective of their qualification as a means of interpretation under Article 31(2) or (3) VCLT or as supplementary means of interpretation under Article 32

96. Nieminen, *supra* n. 92, at 638.
97. For the opposing view, *see* Leite Pereira, *supra* n. 78, at 637.
98. *See* Kenneth W. Abbott & Duncan Snidal, *Hard and Soft Law in International Governance*, 54 Int'l Org. (2000) https://doi.org/10.1162/002081800551280; Craig West, *References to the OECD Commentaries in Tax Treaties: A Steady March from 'Soft' Law to 'Hard' Law?*, 9 World Tax J. 149 (2017) https://doi.org/10.59403/3n2nstx, who discuss the three characteristics of 'hard law', specifically 'obligation', 'precision', and 'delegation'.
99. Introduction, OECD, *Model Tax Convention on Income and on Capital: Condensed Version 2017*, *supra* n. 1, at 29.
100. Jan Wouters & Maarten Vidal, *The OECD Model Tax Convention Commentaries and the European Court of Justice: Law, Guidance, Inspiration?*, *in The Legal Status of the OECD Commentaries*, s. 3 (Sjoerd Douma & Frank Engelen eds, IBFD 2008).
101. The materials evidencing the existence of State practice may also evidence the existence of *opinio juris*. *See* s. 2.1.2. above and s. 3.2.2. below.

VCLT,[102] their nature as 'soft law' or 'hard law'[103] and, finally, their potential to constitute CIL.[104]

Similar to the OECD MC, the Commentaries that accompany it are non-binding recommendations. Although they are not designed to be annexed to the DTTs signed by OECD member countries, 'they can be of great assistance in the application and interpretation of the conventions'.[105] This in itself does not altogether exclude the possibility that the norms contained therein could transform into CIL. Indeed, what matters is whether a large number of States interpret the provisions of their DTTs in line with the guidance found in the OECD Commentary (general and consistent practice) based on a sense of legal obligation (*opinio juris*). If this is the case, the norms of the Commentaries that are used for DTT interpretation may acquire the status of CIL.

Just like the OECD MC, the Commentaries are approved with unanimity by the nearly forty OECD member countries. In addition to this, many non-member countries participate in the drafting while the interpretation guidance given in the Commentaries is also used as the basis for drafting the Commentary on the UN MC, which also has broad acceptance around the world. Thus, it has been argued that many norms found in the Commentary on the OECD MC have virtually universal acceptance through the Commentaries adopted by these two international organizations and can support the creation of CIL rules.[106] Nevertheless, a general and consistent State practice cannot be identified indirectly through participation alone in international organizations that draft non-binding recommendations. Although their wide endorsement in the context of international organizations is an indication of the existence of CIL, in the authors' view, these recommendations must also be applied in practice in order to give rise to a custom. Stated otherwise, State practice would also have to be externalized through *actual conduct* by State organs (e.g., either application of the same norm by States in their bilateral relations or application by one State and acceptance by the other State). In this regard, conduct capable of supporting the creation of CIL rules based on norms found in the Commentary would be, for example, the practice of tax administrations or national courts to 'routinely' resort to the same norm of the Commentary to interpret the same norm of the DTT signed between them, a practice which, as per the OECD Commentary, is increasingly becoming common.[107] This entails that identifying State practice would have to be made for each norm in isolation and not be deduced *in*

102. *See* indicatively Nieminen, *supra* n. 92, at 636-659; Jonathan Schwarz, *Schwarz on Tax Treaties* 132 et seq. (Wolters Kluwer 6th ed. 2021); Michael Lang & Florian Brugger, *The Role of the OECD Commentary in Tax Treaty Interpretation*, 23 Austl. Tax F. 95-108 (2008); Hans Pijl, *The OECD Commentary as a Source of International Law and the Role of the Judiciary*, 46 Eur. Taxn. 216-224 (2006); Ekkehart Reimer, *Interpretation of Tax Treaties*, 39 Eur. Taxn. 458-474 (1999).
103. West, *supra* n. 98, at 117-159.
104. *See* indicatively Wouters & Vidal, *supra* n. 100, s. 3; David A. Ward, *The Role of the Commentaries on the OECD Model in the Tax Treaty Interpretation Process*, 60 Bull. for Int'l Taxn. 99-100 (2006); Nieminen, *supra* n. 92, at 638-639.
105. Introduction, OECD, *Model Tax Convention on Income and on Capital: Condensed Version 2017*, *supra* n. 1, para. 29.
106. Nieminen, *supra* n. 92, at 639.
107. Introduction, OECD, *Model Tax Convention on Income and on Capital: Condensed Version 2017*, *supra* n. 1, paras 29.1 and 29.3.

abstracto for the entirety of the Commentary due to the membership of a country in the international organization that has issued the Models and the Commentaries.[108]

This exercise would require the assessment of the entire State practice including, for example, the administrative application of the DTT with reference to the relevant Commentary, the reference to Commentaries by the national courts, the exchange of letters between ministries of finance, etc. Finding 'general' and 'consistent' practice would require a uniform application of a norm by the State organs. However, there seems to be, for example, frequent inconsistency in the Commentaries' use by the executive and the judicial arms of States.[109] The absence of a uniform application not only within individual States but also by different States around the world therefore speaks against the existence of State practice.

3.2.2 Existence of **Opinio Juris**

Not every State practice is adequate for leading to the creation of CIL. State practice, apart from being 'general' and 'consistent', must be accompanied by *opinio juris*.[110] In the case of the OECD MC, it seems clear that the necessary sense of legal obligation is not present.

First, there is no indication that any state whatsoever recognizes the (norms found in the) OECD MC as binding. Moreover, the fact that the OECD MC is not a binding legal instrument of international law, particularly an international convention within the meaning of Article 38(1)(a) ICJ Statute, shows that it can neither have the same capacity as a treaty to codify CIL rules nor to result in the crystallization of a current or generate a new CIL rule as per Conclusion 11 of the 2018 ILC Report. Nor does it constitute a resolution of an international organization within the meaning of Conclusion 12 of the 2018 ILC Report, which is another source of material that bears some significance for identifying CIL.[111] All of this decreases the chances of proving the existence of 'general' and 'consistent' State practice accompanied by *opinio juris*.

Second, the absence of a sense of legal obligation is evident as, in the absence of a DTT, States do not normally apply the OECD MC norms. Rather, they apply their domestic law, which departs from these norms in many (if not most) cases. For example, in cases where no DTT is in force, many States levy a higher withholding tax (WHT) on dividend distributions or interest payments than the limit stipulated in the OECD MC. This is not only evidence of the absence of State practice but also of the inexistence of *opinio juris*. States do not feel that they have to comply with a

108. For a contrary view, *see* Ward, *supra* n. 104, at 100. That author argues that, due to the constant changes in Commentaries and, most notably, the observations thereto, the reservations to the OECD MC articles and the disagreement therewith by non-OECD member countries suggest that Commentaries are not widely followed in practice and, for this reason, there is no State practice.
109. West, *supra* n. 98, at 124.
110. Similar to the identification of State practice, the presence of *opinio juris* could not be attributed to the OECD Commentary as a whole but only to individual norm found therein on a case-by-case basis.
111. *See* by analogy, West, *supra* n. 98, at 125, where this analysis is made for the OECD Commentary.

(hypothetical) rule of international law to apply a reduced WHT rate. Instead, they only apply such reduced WHT rates when they have entered into a DTT with another State, that is, they apply lower WHT rates only when there is an explicit contractual obligation. Therefore, it cannot be argued that the OECD MC itself has the potential to form CITL.

Concerning the OECD Commentary, there does not appear to be sufficient evidence that the States, through their organs, adopt a certain practice (i.e., interpretation of provisions of their DTTs by reference to the OECD Commentary) having a sense of legal obligation or having the intention to contribute to the creation of such an obligation.[112] First, there are typically no individual declarations by States that they consider the reference to Commentaries binding as law. Membership to an international organization such as the OECD cannot alone be regarded as a State declaration, taking also into account the non-binding nature of the Commentary. Second, national courts, while quoting and analysing the OECD Commentary,[113] consider it merely guidance for interpretation (whether under Article 31 or 32 VCLT) and not a set of rules to which the reference is binding.[114]

At the same time, it has been illustrated that multiple DTTs directly refer to Commentaries or parts thereof as mandatory or non-mandatory sources of interpretation.[115] Irrespective of whether these references have the potential to constitute 'general' State practice (which the authors opine is not the case due to the limited number of such instances), bilateral DTTs are closer to the concept of 'treaty-contracts' of which the purpose is to regulate the relations between the contracting states only. When the contracting states include a reference to the Commentaries in their DTT, their intention is not to 'elaborate their perception of international law upon any given topic or establish new rules which are to guide them for the future in their international conduct'.[116] They merely intend to undertake a contractual obligation with a single counterparty to interpret the DTT between them in a specific way having regard to their individual interests.[117] Including references to the OECD Commentaries in isolated instances may be contrasted with a (hypothetical) multilateral 'law-making' treaty in which the states would clarify their perception as to whether the OECD Commentaries are binding. As opposed to the latter case, which would have more potential for

112. *See also* Ward, *supra* n. 104, at 100; Nieminen, *supra* n. 92, at 639.
113. Introduction, OECD, *Model Tax Convention on Income and on Capital: Condensed Version 2017*, *supra* n. 1, para. 29.3.
114. West, *supra* n. 98, at 159.
115. West has identified 131 instances in which DTTs (or their protocols) make reference to the OECD Commentaries. That author divided these into five different categories, specifically: (1) full reference, (2) full reference (combined), (3) partial reference, (4) clarification reference, and (5) confirmation reference, each of which may have different variations. The wording of some of these variations implies that the contracting States intended to render the interpretation based on the OECD Commentaries binding whereas other variations do not mandatorily require the interpretation to take account of the Commentaries. *See* West, *supra* n. 98, at 127 et seq.
116. Shaw, *supra* n. 14, at 80.
117. *See also* Dirk Broekhuijsen & Irma Mosquera Valderrama, *Revisiting the Case of Customary International Tax Law*, 23 Int'l Comm. Law Rev. 89 (31 March 2021) https://doi.org/10.1163/18719732-12341459.

forming CIL, isolated references to the OECD Commentaries in bilateral 'treaty-contracts' are too weak to establish the necessary evidence for the existence of CIL.[118]

From the above, it can be concluded that the reasons behind the use by States of the Commentaries for DTT interpretation purposes are other than the existence of *opinio juris*. Arguably, the Commentaries are referred to by States for the purposes of practicality and simplicity as they provide a coordinated way to interpret DTTs in a multitude of different instances.[119]

In the absence of adequate evidence as to the existence of State practice and particularly *opinio* juris, OECD MC and Commentaries (as well as other Model Conventions and Commentaries) do not meet the requirements for becoming CIL.

3.3 Principal Purpose Test

3.3.1 General Overview

Article 7(1) of the OECD Multilateral Convention to Implement Tax Treaty Related Measures to Prevent BEPS (MLI) was part of the output of BEPS Action 6.[120] The latter's objective was to prevent access to treaty benefits in inappropriate circumstances. This provision introduced a general anti-abuse rule (GAAR), i.e., the famous PPT, at the level of tax treaties.[121] The PPT is one of the minimum standards of the BEPS Project and needs to be accompanied by another minimum standard, specifically the inclusion in a DTT's Preamble of the goal to prevent treaty abuse, stipulated in Article 6 MLI. With the 2017 update, the PPT found its way into Article 29(9) of the OECD MC.

At its core, the PPT comprises two different elements. The first one is a 'motive test' asking whether it can be reasonably concluded that obtaining a tax benefit was 'one of the principal purposes of any arrangement or transaction'. The second element, however, declares such a tax-related motive, if existing, irrelevant if it can be demonstrated that 'obtaining the benefit would be in accordance with the object and purpose of the tax convention'. A comprehensive examination of the two elements of the PPT is beyond the scope of this chapter.[122]

118. Nieminen, *supra* n. 92, at 639; Shaw, *supra* n. 14, at 80.
119. *See also* Nieminen, *supra* n. 92, at 639.
120. *See* OECD, *OECD/G20 Base Erosion and Profit Shifting Project, Preventing the Granting of Treaty Benefits in Inappropriate Circumstances, Action 6: 2015 Final Report* (2015).
121. OECD, *Multilateral Convention to Implement Tax Treaty Related Measures to Prevent Base Erosion and Profit Shifting* (22 September 2017), available at https://www.oecd.org/content/dam/oecd/en/topics/policy-sub-issues/beps-mli/multilateral-convention-to-implement-tax-treaty-related-measures-to-prevent-beps.pdf (last visited 15 July 2024).
122. Many scholars and commentators have expressed their opinion on the PPT's content and function. *See* indicatively, Michael Lang, *The Signalling Function of Article 29(9) of the OECD Model: The 'Principal Purpose Test'*, 74 Bull. for Int'l Taxn. (2020) https://doi.org/10.59403/3ndvejx; Luc De Broe & Joris Luts, *BEPS Action 6: Tax Treaty Abuse*, 43 Intertax (2015) https://doi.org/10.54648/taxi2015011; Vikram Chand, *The Principal Purpose Test in the Multilateral Convention: An In-Depth Analysis*, 46 Intertax (2018) https://doi.org/10.54648/taxi2018004; Blazej Kuźniacki, *The Principal Purpose Test (PPT) in BEPS Action 6 and the MLI: Exploring Challenges Arising from Its Legal Implementation and Practical Application*, 10 World Tax J. (2018) https://doi.org/10.59403/3vnt53r; Andrés Báez Moreno, *GAARs and Treaties:*

It must be noted that BEPS Action 6 and Article 7 MLI offered states certain alternatives to the mere introduction of the PPT in order to meet the minimum standard. Instead, Article 7(15) and 7(16) of the MLI allow for the introduction of a combination of either the PPT and a simplified or detailed limitation on benefits (LoB) clause or, alternatively, a detailed LoB clause together with rules to tackle conduit financing structures. Thus, the introduction of the PPT is not a *conditio sine qua non* for compliance with the minimum standard.

3.3.2 Existence of General and Consistent State Practice

Some very beneficial information for assessing the first of the two elements of State practice, i.e., the generality of the State practice, is contained in the Peer Review Reports on Treaty Shopping published by the OECD Inclusive Framework (IF) on an annual basis. A review of these reports can provide valuable information as to whether the *adoption* of the Action 6 minimum standards (in this case, the PPT) is *sufficiently wide and representative*.

According to the Sixth Peer Review Report published on 21 March 2024, over 1,270 DTTs and two MTTs between members of the IF complied with the minimum standard as of 31 May 2023. Interestingly, eighty-five agreements not subject to Peer Review by the OECD IF as they constitute agreements entered into between IF members and non-members also complied with the minimum standard. Thus, the total number of agreements concluded by members of the IF that complied with the minimum standard amounted to approximately 1,360. All of these treaties included the preamble statement and the PPT. In fifty-two of them, the PPT was supplemented with an LoB clause. It follows that there has been an exponential increase in the number of DTTs that complied with the minimum standard (from only 13 agreements in 2018 to about 1,360 in 2023).[123] Moreover, for the agreements listed under the MLI, all ninety-six IF members that are parties and signatories thereto are implementing the preamble statement and the PPT. At the same time, thirteen countries have opted to accompany their PPT with a simplified LoB clause while seven countries have agreed to accept simplified LoB clauses in treaties with counterparties that have opted for it.[124] Could it be concluded, based on this information, that the introduction by ninety-six countries of the PPT in about 1,360 treaties as well as the commitment of about fifty

From the Guiding Principle to the Principal Purpose Test. What Have We Gained from BEPS Action 6?, 45 Intertax (2017) https://doi.org/10.54648/taxi2017036; Ameya Mithe, *Critical Analysis of the Principal Purpose Test and the Limitation on Benefits Rule: A World Divided but It Takes Two to Tango*, 12 World Tax J. (2020) https://doi.org/10.59403/1vs36t8; Konstantinos Taramountas, *The PPT: The Introduction of a Uniform Standard with an Uncertain Application*, 47 Intertax (2019) https://doi.org/10.54648/taxi2019094; Michael Lang & Oleksandr Nesterov -Surmenko, *The Principal Purpose Test of Article 29(9) OECD Model (2017)*, in *Anti-abuse Rules and Tax Treaties* 211-222 (Georg Kofler et al. eds, Kluwer 2024).

123. OECD, *Prevention of Tax Treaty Abuse: Sixth Peer Review Report on Treaty Shopping – Inclusive Framework on BEPS: Action 6*, paras 24-26 (20 March 2024), https://doi.org/10.1787/36cebf8 e-en (last visited 22 March 2024).

124. OECD, *Prevention of Tax Treaty Abuse: Sixth Peer Review Report on Treaty Shopping – Inclusive Framework on BEPS: Action 6*, *supra* n. 123, para. 30.

more jurisdictions (i.e., more than 140 in total) to do the same is general State practice?[125]

Having regard to the aforementioned figures, it must be examined whether the adoption by ninety-five countries of the PPT in approximately 1,360 treaties can be regarded as *sufficiently* wide and representative practice. In this respect, it must be clarified that absolute numbers alone cannot have a decisive influence on the formation of a CIL rule. In addition, the number and distribution of States participating in the relevant practice as well as the number of instances of this practice cannot be identified in the abstract.[126] The figures presented above represent about 50% of existing States (nearly 75% of existing states if those that committed to introducing the PPT are also taken into account) and about 2/5 of the DTTs in force. Although absolute numbers alone cannot by themselves have a decisive influence on the formation of a CIL rule,[127] it may be concluded that, as of today, no general practice is present. The existence of 25%-30% of States that have not yet agreed on adhering to the PPT is an indication that there is no general State practice on the PPT and even more as the 'PPT willing' States were only able to implement it thus far into in no more than two-fifths of all existing DTTs (whether through the MLI or otherwise). Nonetheless, it cannot be denied that the inclusion of the PPT in DTTs is certainly 'on the rise' given that this test was developed in the MLI and incorporated into the OECD MC only a few years ago. Therefore, even if current State practice is not sufficiently wide yet, this cannot be entirely ruled out for the (longer-term) future.[128]

Beyond pure statistics, there are, nevertheless, further considerations concerning identifying the existence of State practice. The fact that a significant number of States have introduced the PPT in their DTTs or have committed to do so does not by itself provide adequate evidence for the identification of a CIL norm formation. What really matters is the *actual* conduct of States, that is, how the PPT is applied *in practice* and how the obligations flowing therefrom are fulfilled by the State organs (notably by the tax administrations and the national courts). Only when States *apply* the PPT in a general (i.e., sufficiently wide and representative) and consistent manner can a CIL rule come into existence. However, as will be seen immediately below, arguing for such a consistent application is not an easy task.

The PPT is a treaty GAAR, and its role is therefore to tackle tax avoidance resulting from abusive arrangements and transactions performed by taxpayers. The idea of GAARs, either in domestic laws or in tax treaties, is not new. However, the real value of the PPT is that it aims to unify the fight against tax avoidance by establishing

---

125. *See*, for example, Irma J. Mosquera Valderrama, *BEPS Principal Purpose Test and Customary International Law*, 33 Leiden J. Int'l Law 759 (2020) https://doi.org/10.1017/s0922156520000278.
126. *See* Commentary on Conclusion 8, para. 3, United Nations, *Report of the International Law Commission: Seventieth Session (30 April-1 June and 2 July-10 August 2018)*, *supra* n. 19, at 101.
127. Tarcissio Gazzini, *The Role of Customary International Law in the Protection of Foreign Investment*, 8 J. World Inv. & Trade 704 (2007); *see also* Alexis Galán & Ricardo García Antón, *Principal Purpose Test and Customary International Law: A Note of Caution*, 14 World Tax J. 632 (2022) https://doi.org/10.59403/3s5jc0d.
128. Avi-Yonah, *Does Customary International Tax Law Exist?*, *supra* n. 90, at 11.

the *same* GAAR in *any* treaty that adopts the PPT following Article 29(9) of the OECD MC. Thereby, it requires all States that implement the PPT in their treaty network to *uniformly* combat abusive structures, i.e., through interpreting treaty rules by their object and purpose, which is the superior goal of the PPT. Nonetheless, looking at the volume of literature that has been written about the PPT thus far, it is reasonable to state that this unification effect of the PPT has not (yet) been achieved. As a matter of fact, there is significant scholarly dispute around the PPT concept,[129] and it can be expected that it will, at best, take a long time until courts clarify the real meaning of the PPT enough so that there will be a globally consistent understanding. The core of the issue is that the PPT was not introduced on a greenfield but rather within the background of many different anti-abuse regimes, doctrines, etc., that were in practical use by States (either based on their domestic law or treaties). Despite certain similarities, many countries have their own legal traditions and apply rules that comprise different concepts of abuse with different scopes. The various abuse doctrines were summarized as 'sham, legally ineffective transactions, substance over form, abuse of law, *fraus legis*, or simply as the general anti-avoidance rule (GAAR)'.[130] Each of these doctrines may approach the same event from another perspective. For instance, the doctrines of sham and substance over form entail determining the true nature of legal transactions in cases where the parties have either simulated or have not entered into a transaction or entered into one that is different from what is stipulated in the contract. In this respect, the relevant rule of tax law will not apply to the sham but rather to the 'true' legal relationship. Conversely, abuse of law and *fraus legis* doctrines may lead to the substitution of the valid legal facts and circumstances by different ones with the latter triggering the tax liability that would have otherwise prevailed.[131] The variety of anti-abuse doctrines is notorious, and it will very likely continue when it comes to the PPT's interpretation because it is difficult to abandon deeply rooted anti-abuse concepts (that continue to exist outside tax treaty law) overnight in tax treaty cases.[132] In a CIL context, the resulting variety of views on the PPT obviously undermines the second element of 'generality', i.e., *consistency*.[133]

3.3.3 *Existence of* Opinio Juris

For *opinio juris* to exist, it would be necessary that State practice be accompanied by acceptance of the PPT as law. In this respect, it has been argued that States develop a sense of compliance out of legal obligation due to the effect of Peer Review Reports on

129. *See* the recent analysis of Lang & Nesterov-Surmenko, *supra* n. 122, at 211 et seq.
130. Stef van Weeghel, *General Report*, in *Tax Treaties and Tax Avoidance: Application of Anti-Avoidance Provisions* 22 (IFA Cahiers Vol. 95a, IBFD 2010). *See also* Jörg M. Mössner, *Tax Avoidance Concepts and European Tax Education*, 39 Eur. Taxn. (1999); Xavier Oberson, *Tax Avoidance Concepts and European Tax Education*, 39 Eur. Taxn. (1999).
131. van Weeghel, *supra* n. 130, at 22.
132. Similarly, there is little appetite within the EU Member States to accept that Art. 6 of the ATAD did introduce a common, and for the individual Member States therefore new, concept of combating abuse in corporate tax matters (which is conceptually very similar if not identical to the PPT).
133. Galán & García Antón, *supra* n. 127, at 633.

Treaty Shopping published by the OECD on an annual basis.[134] Although, based on that argument, countries are free to implement the minimum standard either through the MLI or on a bilateral basis, 'a jurisdiction is required to implement the minimum standard when requested to do so by another member of the Inclusive Framework'.[135] Stated differently, the requirement to comply with the PPT suggests that States do so because they accept it as law, otherwise risking being found as non-compliant by other countries. This position has been criticized by other scholars as being circular, i.e., assuming what needs to be shown.[136]

From a close inspection of the BEPS Action 6 Final Report, it appears that there is no indication of whether the members of the OECD IF had the intention that the PPT would develop into a CIL norm. On the contrary, there is an indication of why the PPT was not accepted as law by the OECD IF members. On the one hand, it is stressed that countries 'commit to adopt in their bilateral treaties measures that implement the minimum standard described in the preceding paragraph if requested to do so by other countries that have made the same commitment and that will request the inclusion of these measures'.[137] On the other hand, this requirement is not rigid. First, the OECD recognizes that this commitment is not tantamount to committing to conclude new or amend existing DTTs within a specified period of time as doing so depends on the overall balance of a DTT's provisions. Second and most importantly, 'if a country is not itself concerned by the effect of treaty-shopping on its own taxation rights as a State of source, it will not be obliged to apply provisions such as the LoB or the PPT as long as it agrees to include in a treaty provisions that its treaty partner will be able to use for that purpose'.[138]

The above statements carry some importance. In all three cases, reference is made to the inclusion of the PPT at a *treaty* level. First, the minimum standard must be implemented in a DTT if required by the other contracting party. Second, States are not bound to conclude new or amend existing DTTs in order to implement the PPT. Thus, insofar as there is no DTT between the States concerned, the PPT will not apply. Last, States are *not* under the obligation to apply the LoB or the PPT if they are not concerned about the impact of treaty-shopping on their own taxation rights, insofar as they agree on the inclusion of the PPT in the DTT and its application (where necessary) by their treaty partners. The discretion granted to States about when and under what circumstances to apply the PPT (if at all) clearly suggests that compliance with it is not accompanied by acceptance as law. This is obviously also confirmed by the MLI which is clearly *not* assuming a legal obligation to adopt the PPT but rather allowing an alternative thereto, specifically the LoB clause.

134. Mosquera Valderrama, *supra* n. 125, at 762.
135. *See* para. 15, OECD, *Prevention of Treaty Abuse: Peer Review Report on Treaty Shopping – Inclusive Framework on BEPS: Action 6*, 16 (2019), https://doi.org/10.1787/9789264312388-en (last visited 15 July 2024).
136. Galán & García Antón, *supra* n. 127, at 646.
137. OECD, *OECD/G20 Base Erosion and Profit Shifting Project, Preventing the Granting of Treaty Benefits in Inappropriate Circumstances, Action 6: 2015 Final Report*, *supra* n. 120, para. 23.
138. OECD, *OECD/G20 Base Erosion and Profit Shifting Project, Preventing the Granting of Treaty Benefits in Inappropriate Circumstances, Action 6: 2015 Final Report*, *supra* n. 120, para. 23.

Apart from the above, the nature of the MLI itself would also have to be examined.[139] Some scholars argue that the MLI has a twofold nature. On the one hand, it presents characteristics pertaining to multilateralism and thus represents a wide consensus of States towards the adoption of common international tax law rules (which could potentially lead to the creation of CIL). On the other hand, it has strong bilateral characteristics as its purpose was to provide the necessary flexibility that would lead to the rapid and simultaneous amendment of hundreds of DTTs.[140] In this regard, it has been properly explained that the MLI's bilateral nature prevails over the multilateral one and, thus, the MLI enhances bilateralism in the area of international tax law.[141] Accordingly, it primarily presents the features of a 'treaty-contract' rather than those of a 'law-making treaty'. Irrespective of being a significant and innovative step towards global alignment, its main purpose was to constitute 'an effective mechanism to implement agreed changes in a synchronized and efficient manner across the network of existing agreements for the avoidance of double taxation on income without the need to bilaterally renegotiate each such agreement'. Hence, the parties to the MLI did not have any intention of introducing universally binding tax law but rather needed an efficient and effective mechanism to amend their treaties and implement the changes to which they committed without having to renegotiate each DTT separately. This is rather clearly demonstrated by the fact that the signatory States of the MLI were responsible for specifically nominating the 'Covered Tax Agreements' that they wanted to be covered by the MLI (while other bilateral tax treaties could be excluded from the MLI's scope).

The previous point is supported by another argument coming from an examination of the wording of the PPT. In this respect, for identifying CIL, it is necessary that 'the provision concerned should, at all events potentially, be of a *fundamentally norm-creating character such as could be regarded as forming the basis of a general rule of law*' (emphasis added).[142] Nevertheless, the PPT does not provide evidence of general recognition by the international community that a rule of law or a legal obligation exists. This is clear from the wording of the rule which states that 'notwithstanding the other provisions of *this Convention*, a benefit under *this Convention* shall not be granted [...], unless it is established that granting that benefit in these circumstances would be in accordance with the object and purpose of the relevant provisions of *this Convention*' (emphasis added).[143] On the contrary, the wording of treaties that reflect CIL contain '*general* norms, framed as legal propositions, to govern

139. Although the MLI is merely a means of implementation of the PPT while the commitment to it was done through the BEPS Final Reports, it would also have to be assessed whether the inclusion of the PPT in the MLI signals the acceptance of this norm as law.

140. Ricardo García Antón, *Multilateral Dynamics in Bilateral Settings: Back to Realpolitik*, Bri Tax Rev. 477 et seq. (2019); Yariv Brauner, *McBEPS: The MLI – The First Multilateral Tax Treaty That Has Never Been*, 46 Intertax (2018) https://doi.org/10.54648/taxi2018003.

141. Brauner, *supra* n. 140.

142. *North Sea Continental Shelf*, *supra* n. 21, at 43, para. 72; *See also* Commentary on Conclusion 11, para. 7, United Nations, *Report of the International Law Commission: Seventieth Session (30 April-1 June and 2 July-10 August 2018)*, *supra* n. 19, at 107.

143. Article 29(9) OECD, *Model Tax Convention on Income and on Capital: Condensed Version 2017*, *supra* n. 1.

the conduct of parties'.[144] An example is the provisions of the Genocide Convention of 1948 which creates rules for which the wording is drafted in such a way as to express a universal obligation for all States.[145] Contrary to the wording of treaty provisions that actually reflect CIL rules, the PPT seems to be clearly designed to be limited to the conduct between the parties to a specific DTT inter se. Thus, it follows from the wording of the PPT that it merely aims at creating a contractual obligation between the contracting States rather than a universal obligation for all States.[146]

3.4 CFC Rules

CFC rules are special anti-avoidance rules (SAARs) of which the objective is to tackle the practice where taxpayers resident in one jurisdiction shift income to companies based in low-tax jurisdictions and in this way achieve the 'deferral' of taxation until the moment of repatriation (which may occur much later or never).

The above practice was a corollary of the principles forming part of the international consensus of the 1920s on the allocation of taxing rights between source and residence States (i.e., the jurisdiction to tax). In this regard, States have the right to tax based on two nexus criteria, that is, first, based on the source of income and, second, based on the taxpayer's residence. Source States may, for instance, impose tax on certain types of passive income (through a WHT on gross amounts) while residence States may tax the residual income based on the principle of worldwide taxation, however, granting relief from double taxation. Importantly, resident companies and their foreign subsidiaries are to be treated as separate entities for tax purposes. The obvious consequence of this is that a state cannot regard the foreign subsidiary of a resident company as forming part of the latter in order to tax it.[147] At the same time, the existence of a two-tiered system of taxation results in the residence state taxing shareholders for income earned through foreign companies only when it is actually distributed. This implies that the residence state cannot tax unless a distribution of profits takes place, if at all.[148] CFC rules depart from the principles on the jurisdiction to tax as they enable a state to tax the profits of a foreign company even though it is an entity separate from its shareholder(s). Admittedly, CFC rules are typically a feature of domestic law and therefore do not perfectly fit into the scope of this chapter which is focusing its search for CITL candidates on elements of tax treaties.[149] There are, however, two reasons to deal with CFC rules in the present context. First, much of the early discussion on the existence of CITL was held precisely on this topic, particularly

144. Crawford, *Brownlie's Principles of Public International Law*, *supra* n. 16, at 31.
145. *See*, for example, Arts II, III, IV, VI and VII of the UN Convention on the Prevention and Punishment of the Crime of Genocide, 9 December 1948.
146. Crawford, *Brownlie's Principles of Public International Law*, *supra* n. 16, at 31.
147. Brain J. Arnold, *The Evolution of Controlled Foreign Corporation Rules and Beyond*, 73 Bull. for Int'l Taxn. 632 (2019) https://doi.org/10.59403/1qh2n7n.
148. Daniel W. Blum, *Controlled Foreign Companies: Selected Policy Issues – or the Missing Elements of BEPS Action 3 and the Anti-tax Avoidance Directive*, 46 Intertax 298-300 (2018) https://doi.org/10.54648/taxi2018031.
149. As explained in s. 3.1. above.

among United States (US) scholars.[150] Second, although CFC rules are mainly introduced in domestic laws, it is still a technical option to have them included in bilateral tax treaties. Such a bilateral agreement on (then likely reciprocal) CFC rules could avoid the discussion of whether they violate the Contracting States' obligations under tax treaties.[151]

The first country that decided to address the issue of deferral was the US which introduced the Subpart F Rules in 1962.[152] Thereafter, a number of major economies, particularly Canada, France, Germany, Japan, and the United Kingdom introduced CFC rules up until the mid-1980s.[153] As of 1996, fourteen OECD member countries had introduced CFC rules[154] while the number of States that had done so upon the issuance of the OECD's report on Harmful Tax Competition had risen to nineteen, including Korea and Mexico.[155] In 2015, when the OECD issued its Final Report on BEPS Action 3, thirty countries that participated in the BEPS Project had introduced CFC rules.[156] This number increased further in the aftermath of the BEPS Project as the European Union (EU) adopted the EU Anti-tax Avoidance Directive (ATAD) due to which several EU Member States had to introduce CFC rules as of 2019 at the latest.[157] In spite of these growing numbers, it follows that the number of countries that had adopted CFC rules up until 2019 is still not enough for the existing State practice to be characterized as *sufficiently* wide and representative. In fact, it seems that most countries in the world have not adopted CFC rules yet and, for this reason, it cannot be argued that they constitute *general* State practice.

There is even more evidence against the existence of State practice of CFC rules. Concerning their practical application, the CFC rules of each country present different characteristics from those of other countries. This is a strong challenge to the idea of *consistency* of State practice. While CFC rules have the same ultimate goal and may operate in a somehow similar manner in the various tax systems (i.e., they entail the inclusion of certain types of foreign passive income in the tax base of a resident shareholder), they nonetheless present different characteristics. Notably, there may be variations in the definition of a CFC, the level of foreign tax of CFCs, or the definition of CFC income of which the examination is beyond the scope of this chapter.[158] To illustrate, one notable difference is the way of inclusion of CFC income in the income

150. *See* Avi-Yonah, *Does Customary International Tax Law Exist?*, *supra* n. 90, at 4-5.
151. For this discussion recently, *see* Claus Staringer & Ruth Mirembe, *Impact of Domestic SAARs on Tax Treaties*, *in Anti-abuse Rules and Tax Treaties* 36 et seq. (Georg Kofler et al. eds, Kluwer 2024).
152. United States, Internal Revenue Code, §§951-960.
153. Avi-Yonah, *Does Customary International Tax Law Exist?*, *supra* n. 90, at 4.
154. *See* OECD, *Controlled Foreign Company Legislation, Studies in Foreign Source Income* (1996); OECD, *Harmful Tax Competition: An Emerging Global Issue* 41 and 63 (1998), https://www.ustaxcourt.gov/opinions/2017/148_TC_No_10_transparency.pdf (last visited 15 July 2024).
155. Arnold, *supra* n. 147, at 638.
156. *See* Executive Summary, OECD, *OECD/G20 Base Erosion and Profit Shifting Project, Designing Effective Controlled Foreign Company Rules, Action 3: 2015 Final Report* 9 (2015).
157. Articles 7 and 8, Council Directive (EU) 2016/1164 of 12 July 2016 laying down rules against tax avoidance practices that directly affect the functioning of the internal market, OJ L 193/1, 19.7.2016.
158. In this respect, *see* Arnold, *supra* n. 147, at 634-638.

of resident taxpayers. This result can be reached through different approaches depending on the legal framework applicable at each instance but, practically, only two of these approaches are common. First, the inclusion of income at the level of the shareholder could be achieved by means of 'piercing the corporate veil', i.e., by disregarding the CFC and attributing its income directly to the shareholder. Second, this could be achieved through the concept of a 'deemed dividend' which is economically equivalent to taxing the foreign subsidiary.[159] In this approach, the CFC is deemed to distribute its profits without its nature as a separate taxable entity being challenged. The legal consequences vary depending on the approach that is applied.[160]

In light of the above, it can be understood that, when enacting its CFC rules, each country takes into account its legal framework and, most importantly, its policy objectives.[161] The existence of a common goal, that is, tackling deferral of taxation through the inclusion in the shareholder's tax base of the CFC's income (even disregarding the different approaches in defining this income) cannot overcome the differences in the technical aspects of the rules and hence does not constitute adequate evidence for the existence of consistent State practice.

Equally, there is also no indication of the existence of *opinio juris* when States do actually introduce CFC rules. Rather, there is significant evidence to the contrary: When the OECD issued its BEPS Report on CFCs in 2015, it was very clear that it outlined nothing more than a policy recommendation for States. By no means did the OECD assume that there would be a pre-existing international law obligation that could legally require States to implement CFC rules. Additionally, until the adoption, shortly after the OECD BEPS Reports, of the ATAD, which imposed an implementing obligation on EU Member States in 2016 (to be fulfilled by 2018) based on European law, EU Member States were free to employ a CFC regime (in fact, some Member States did while others did not). Ultimately, the introduction of CFC rules by States (or the EU, thereby binding its Member States) is not adhering to a legal obligation but is a policy choice with no *opinio juris*.

3.5 Permanent Establishment

'PE' is a very old concept in the area of tax law. Its first use can be traced back to the late 19th century, and its first appearance in a DTT was in the 1899 DTT between Austria/Hungary and Prussia.[162] It has been characterized as the most important threshold for the taxation of business profits by the source state.[163] The DTT definition of PE has influenced the domestic legislation of countries. In some of them, the

159. Avi-Yonah, *supra* n. 90, at 4.
160. Blum, *supra* n. 148, at 307.
161. Daniel Gutmann et al., *The Impact of the ATAD on Domestic Systems: A Comparative Survey*, 57 Eur. Taxn. 12 et seq. (2016) https://doi.org/10.59403/34ah6ye.
162. John F. Avery Jones et al., *The Origins of Concepts and Expressions Used in the OECD Model and Their Adoption by States*, 60 Bull. for Int'l Taxn. 233-234 (2006).
163. Brian J. Arnold, *Threshold Requirements for Taxing Business Profits under Tax Treaties*, 57 Bull. for Int'l Taxn. 478 (2003); Jeffrey Owens, *The Taxation of Multinational Enterprises: An Elusive Balance*, 67 Bull. for Int'l Taxn., s. 4 (2013) https://doi.org/10.59403/1kr44wj.

legislature has aligned the domestic law definition to that of the OECD MC while others interpret the PE definition in their domestic law in light of the DTT definition. Some countries may include a direct reference in their legislation to the OECD MC definition.[164] Thus, it would be reasonable to examine whether there can be identified State practice in the application of the PE concept.

In assessing the existence of state practice in the case of the PE threshold, the term's content would first need to be circumscribed. A PE is defined in Article 5(1) OECD MC as 'a fixed place of business through which the business of the enterprise is wholly or partly carried on'.[165] The wording of the definition ('fixed place of business') implies a taxpayer's physical presence in the source state.[166] The physical presence requirement is linked to the concept of 'economic allegiance', which relates to a taxpayer's economic ties with a particular country and was used in the preparatory work of the model tax conventions prepared by the League of Nations.[167,168] Thus, taxing rights were allocated having regard to a taxpayer's participation in the economic life of a state (in the case of a PE, this would be the source state) and the place where the income was produced being considered which, in the case of business activities, is the most important factor.[169]

It is noteworthy that, at that time, the largest part of economic activity outside the residence State was carried out through the physical presence of the taxpayer in the source state, e.g., through 'Mines and Oil Wells', 'Industrial Establishments' or 'Factories', and 'Commercial Establishments'.[170] As a corollary, the nexus between business profits and the various physical places contributing to the production of these profits was a rather significant factor in the allocation of taxing rights in respect of this

164. Jacques Sasseville & Arvid A. Skaar, *General Report, in Is There a Permanent Establishment?* 61-62 (IFA Cahiers 2009, Vol. 94A).
165. Article 5(1) OECD, *Model Tax Convention on Income and on Capital: Condensed Version 2017, supra* n. 1.
166. Paragraph 6, Commentary on Art. 5, OECD, *Model Tax Convention on Income and on Capital: Condensed Version 2017, supra* n. 1.
167. Stjepan Gadžo, *Legal Fundamentals of Income Tax Jurisdiction, in Nexus Requirements for Taxation of Non-residents' Business Income: A Normative Evaluation in the Context of the Global Economy*, s. 2.2.6.2.1. (IBFD 2018).
168. The concept was used in the Report of the Four Economists in 1923 in order to formulate general principles that would constitute the basis of an international tax framework. Four factors demonstrating economic allegiance were identified: (a) the origin of wealth or income, (b) the situs of wealth or income, (c) the enforcement of the rights to wealth or income, and (d) the place of residence of domicile of the person entitled to dispose of the wealth or income. The first and fourth of these factors were considered the most important ones for the allocation of taxing rights. *See* OECD, *OECD/G20 Base Erosion and Profit Shifting Project, Addressing the Tax Challenges of the Digital Economy, Action 1: 2015 Final Report*, paras 28-29 (2015), https://www.oecd-ilibrary.org/taxation/addressing-the-tax-challenges-of-the-digital-economy-action-1-2015-final-report_9789264241046-en (last visited 15 July 2024) https://doi.org/10.1787/9789264241046-en.
169. 'Of preponderant weight'. *See* OECD, *OECD/G20 Base Erosion and Profit Shifting Project, Addressing the Tax Challenges of the Digital Economy, Action 1: 2015 Final Report, supra* n. 168, para. 30.
170. OECD, *OECD/G20 Base Erosion and Profit Shifting Project, Addressing the Tax Challenges of the Digital Economy, Action 1: 2015 Final Report, supra* n. 168, para. 30.

type of income.[171] Given that the PE threshold was conceived in an era when businesses operated in the traditional manner and their physical presence could arguably not be disputed, the PE concept was quite effective for allocating taxing rights between residence and source States and eliminating juridical double taxation.[172]

The PE definition does not, however, consist of only one test. The basic rule stipulated in the basic rule of Article 5(1) OECD MC is further complemented and clarified by Article 5(2) OECD MC and broadened or narrowed (as applicable) by Article 5(3)-(6) OECD MC, which will be analysed below. Thus, the PE concept not only consists of the basic rule enshrined in Article 5(1) OECD MC but also of the rules contained in Article 5(2)-(6).[173] It can be argued that all of these provisions *together* constitute the PE threshold, specifically the norm that has to be examined in order to identify State practice. Furthermore, the existence of *general* and *consistent* State practice would require, in the authors' view, that the combination of the different rules of the equivalent of Article 5 OECD MC (whether in DTTs or in domestic law) would result in the application of the same norm.[174] Stated otherwise, the application of the PE threshold (as circumscribed above) by the different countries should arguably be sufficiently representative.

The acceptance of the same PE threshold *norm* throughout the States would theoretically result in the absence of any disputes regarding the (non-)recognition of a PE. Stated in a different way, there would not be any disagreement about the existence of a PE in cross-border transactions. However, the reality is that countries neither interpret nor apply even the basic PE definition in the same manner. In a myriad of cases, the countries involved may take a different view about the existence of a PE. One of many illustrative examples is the recent *McDonald's* case where a company resident in Luxembourg allocated certain franchise rights to its US branch which qualified as a PE from a Luxembourg tax perspective but was not a PE for US tax purposes.[175] One further example is the fact that the EU's ATAD 2 Directive covers hybrid mismatches arising in the case of 'disregarded PEs', specifically arrangements that are treated as giving rise to a PE under the laws of the head office jurisdiction and not treated as doing so under the laws of the source jurisdiction.[176] This constitutes clear evidence that

171. OECD, *OECD/G20 Base Erosion and Profit Shifting Project, Addressing the Tax Challenges of the Digital Economy, Action 1: 2015 Final Report, supra* n. 168, para. 30.
172. Vishesh Dhuldhoya, *The Future of the Permanent Establishment Concept*, 72 Bull. for Int'l Taxn., s. 3.1. (2018) https://doi.org/10.59403/q53pbj.
173. Owens, *supra* n. 163, s. 4.
174. However, it has also been argued that Art. 5 OECD MC does not have a 'fundamentally norm creating character' as it is a specific and detailed rule. Thus, the existence of general and consistent state practice can be assessed only in the case of the PE threshold's core content, i.e., the element of 'physical presence'. *See* Szudoczky, *supra* n. 4, at 161.
175. The result was that royalties received by the taxpayer were not taxable anywhere. *See* Commission Decision (EU) 2019/1252 of 19 September 2018 on tax rulings SA.38945 (2015/C) (ex 2015/NN) (ex 2014/CP) granted by Luxembourg in favour of McDonald's Europe, OJ L/195/20; However, *see* Fadi Shaheen, *Tax Treaty Aspects of the McDonald's State Aid Investigation*, Tax Notes Int'l, Special Reports 337-338 (24 April 2017).That author argues that the US branch constituted a PE even for US tax purposes.
176. Council Directive (EU) 2017/952 of 29 May 2017 amending Directive (EU) 2016/1164 as regards hybrid mismatches with third countries, OJ L 144/1, 7.6.2017; *See also* Elizabeth Gil

applying the basic rule of Article 5(1) OECD MC does not amount to *general* and *consistent* State practice. The evidence is rather to the contrary.

Equally, there is evidence that the PE threshold norm does not amount to *general* and *consistent* practice as do the other provisions of Article 5 OECD MC (and its predecessors) that broaden or narrow the PE threshold. One example is Article 5(2) OECD MC which contains a positive list of examples of places of business that may constitute a PE. On the one hand, many (perhaps the majority of) countries take the view that that provision is not a deeming provision, that is, the conditions of the basic rule need to be met for one of the places of business in that provision to constitute a PE. On the other hand, there may be countries that have a different view regarding this matter (e.g., countries that follow the UN MC)[177] which means that the rule of Article 5(1) OECD MC may be extended in certain cases through the equivalent of Article 5(2) OECD MC.

In addition to the differences in interpreting and applying the rules of Article 5(1) and (2) OECD MC, there have been amendments to the wording and/or the interpretation of other provisions of Article OECD MC.[178] In the aftermath of the BEPS Project, the scope of Article 5(5) OECD MC (and hence the scope of the PE threshold norm) was amended so as to cover a wider range of transactions beyond those pertaining to the habitual exercise of the authority to conclude contracts in the name of the enterprise, which was previously the only case.[179] At the same time, the independent agent exception of Article 5(6) OECD MC became narrower after the 2017 amendments to the OECD MC Commentary. Moreover, the scope of Article 5(4) OECD MC (specific activity exemptions) became broader with the 2017 amendments as the 'preparatory and auxiliary' requirement became a general requirement for all of the specific activities

García, *Addressing Hybrid PE Mismatches: The Guidance of the Code of Conduct Group*, 57 Eur. Taxn. 94-98 (2017) https://doi.org/10.59403/3wm10ak.

177. Sasseville & Skaar, *supra* n. 164, at 31-32.
178. The developments of the last two decades in the information and communication technologies as well as the digitalization of the economy resulted in the obsolescence of certain traditional business models and, further, in the emergence of new business models. The latter rely to a very large extent on intangible assets, the massive use of data, and multi-sided business models that derive their value from externalities that are generated by products that are free to the consumers. The new business models posed significant challenges to the international tax system, including regarding the application of the PE concept. As opposed to 'brick and mortar' industries, the new business models have the capability to generate profits in source states with reduced or even without any physical presence therein. In this context, determining whether source states have the right to tax profits realized through the new business models became much more difficult, not least concerning the application of the PE concept. In certain cases, the traditional PE concept may not guarantee any taxing rights to source states and, hence, one of the issues that the BEPS Project had to address was how to apply the PE rules to the digital economy. *See* OECD, *Addressing Base Erosion and Profit Shifting* (OECD 2013); Owens, *supra* n. 163, s. 4; Daniel W. Blum, *Permanent Establishments and Action 1 on the Digital Economy of the OECD Base Erosion and Profit Shifting Initiative: The Nexus Criterion Redefined?*, 69 Bull. for Int'l Taxn., s. 3.1. (2015) https://doi.org/10.59403/2dbvjz3.
179. The objective of the amendment of Art. 5(5) OECD MC was to prevent abuses of the rule of Art. 5(1) OECD MC through the appointment by taxpayers of representatives that act on their behalf in the source state. In this respect, *see* David Feuerstein, *The Agency Permanent Establishment, in Series on International Tax Law: Permanent Establishments in International and EU Tax Law* 107 (Michael Lang et al. eds, Linde 2011); Dhuldhoya, *supra* n. 172, s. 2.2.2.

mentioned in that article whereas, in the past, that requirement applied only to the activities in (e) and (f). Last, the anti-fragmentation rule of Article 5(4.1) OECD MC was inserted in 2017 with the purpose of excluding the application of Article 5(4) OECD MC to arrangements that resulted in the artificial split of business activities in different places within the source state.[180] All of these amendments resulted in rendering the PE threshold norm broader than it was before 2017 thereby granting more taxing rights to source states.[181] Anticipating that several countries will adopt these amendments (or some of them) in (some of) their DTTs or in their domestic law while others will not, would call into question the existence of State practice even in the future.[182,183] Last but not least, as has been correctly pointed out by Szudoczky, more evidence against the generality of practice is the inclusion of technical services provisions in several DTTs. These provide for the taxation of service providers in the source state irrespective of any physical presence and, consequently, they constitute a departure from the PE threshold's core characteristic.[184]

As to the *opinio juris* requirement, the amendments to Article 5 OECD MC and the concomitant widening of its scope are a clear indication that the PE threshold was not perceived as CIL by the jurisdictions that participated in the OECD IF when developing such amendments. There is no evidence that, when discussing the potential amendments to the PE threshold, jurisdictions participating in the IF believed that the implementation of such amendments would result in the violation of a pre-existing CIL rule (i.e., a general and consistent state practice that is accompanied by *opinio juris*). Nor is there any evidence indicating that they perceived that their potential future conduct (i.e., the application of the amendments) would be carried out with a sense of legal obligation. The same argument applies *mutatis mutandis* to the concept of 'significant economic presence' elaborated by the OECD in BEPS Action 1 and the subsequent work on Amount A under Pillar 1 which constitutes a deviation from the most important element of the PE concept, i.e., the physical presence requirement.[185]

---

180. Most interestingly, this rule covers not only the artificial splitting of business activities carried on by the same foreign enterprise but also of those carried on by closely related enterprises.
181. Dhuldhoya, *supra* n. 172, s. 3.1.
182. While some countries follow the PE definition of the OECD MC, not all of them do so. For example, the wording of Luxembourg's domestic PE definition found in Art. 16(1) of the Luxembourgish Tax Adaptation Law differs from the definition given in Art. 5(1) OECD MC. Another example is Greece which has not adopted the 2017 amendments of Art. 5 OECD MC in the domestic law definition of Art. 6 of the Greek Income Tax Law. This leads to the application of different PE thresholds depending on whether these countries apply a DTT or their domestic law.
183. It must be stressed that the argumentation elaborated on in this paragraph can apply *mutatis mutandis* in respect of amendments to the OECD MC Commentary as these have influenced (or are likely to influence in the future) the interpretation and application of the PE threshold norm by some countries but not *all* countries. Indicatively, the Commentary was amended so as to include text on electronic commerce (*see* paras 122-131 Commentary on Art. 5 OECD MC). Chile, Greece, Mexico, Portugal, and Turkey have made Observations to the Commentary regarding electronic commerce.
184. Szudoczky, *supra* n. 4, at 161.
185. OECD, *OECD/G20 Base Erosion and Profit Shifting Project, Addressing the Tax Challenges of the Digital Economy, Action 1: 2015 Final Report*, *supra* n. 168, paras 277 et seq. Influenced by the work carried out in the context of BEPS Action 1, countries such as India and Italy introduced a significant economic presence test in their domestic legislation in 2018. Through this concept,

In addition, the fact that several countries want to tax the income derived by non-residents from their territory based on approaches fundamentally different from the physical presence concept is another indication of the absence of *opinio juris* in the case of the PE threshold.[186]

It follows from the analysis in this section that there is an abundance of arguments evidencing the absence of the first constituent element of CIL, i.e., general and consistent State practice. This is largely due to the fact that, while a PE provision is found in virtually all DTTs and domestic laws of countries, there are numerous differences in the rules that form the PE threshold norm. Besides, there also is no evidence of *opinio juris* in the case of PE as inferred from the fact that the PE threshold has been amended several times and from the discussion about abandoning and/or replacing it altogether. Thus, the authors posit that it cannot be supported that the PE threshold constitutes a CIL rule.

3.6 Arm's Length Principle

A frequently mentioned CIL candidate concept is the ALP. The ALP was proposed in the 1930s by Mitchell B. Carroll and, through the League of Nations 1946 London and Mexico Model Conventions,[187] it made its way into the 1963 OECD MC[188] and all subsequent OECD MCs. Throughout the decades, it has been widely adopted in the DTT practice of virtually all States and, hence, it can be argued that it is an internationally recognized standard for the allocation of income between associated enterprises.[189] Moreover, the ALP has been adopted at the level of domestic legislation in most countries around the world and, in this sense, it forms part of a set of rules that constitute the 'income allocation system' for domestic tax purposes.[190]

---

they expanded their taxing rights over income of non-resident digital businesses without traditional PEs. With respect to India, *see* I.T.A. 1961, s. 9; for Italy, *see* I.T.C. 1986, Art. 162; *See* Raffaele Petruzzi & Abhishek Padwalkar, *Pillar One, Pillar Two, Transfer Pricing and the Arm's Length Principle: A Tangled Web of New and Old Taxing Rules*, 77 Bull. for Int'l Taxn. 449 (2023) https://doi.org/10.59403/1v4xcrm; Daniel W. Blum, *Normativity and Its Source in International Tax Law: International Tax Discourse between Positivism*, in *Normativity in International Tax Law*, s. 4.2.3.4.5.2. (IBFD 2023).

186. Szudoczky, *supra* n. 4, at 161; Stjepan Gadžo, *Nexus Requirements for Taxation of Non-residents' Business Income: A Normative Evaluation in the Context of the Global Economy*, s. 3.4. (IBFD 2018) https://doi.org/10.59403/emy4w5.
187. *See* Leage of Nations Fiscal Committee, *London and Mexico Model Tax Conventions*: Commentary and Text, C.88.M.88.1946.II.A., Art. VI(1)(B) Model Bilateral Convention for the Prevention of the Double Taxation of Income (Mexico Draft) and Art. VI(1)(B) Model Bilateral Convention for the Prevention of the Double Taxation of Income (London Draft).
188. OECD, *Draft Double Taxation Convention on Income and Capital 1963* (1963).
189. Jens Wittendorff, *Consistency: Domestic vs. International Transfer Pricing Law*, Tax Notes Int'l 1127 (18 June 2012); Petruzzi & Padwalkar, *supra* n. 185, at 448.
190. The ALP's wide adoption can be verified by the TP Country Profiles at the OECD's website. From a list of seventy-six countries, only Brazil has stated that its domestic legislation or regulation does not refer to the ALP. *See* OECD, *Transfer Pricing Country Profiles*, https://web-archive.oecd.org/temp/2023-08-02/72854-transfer-pricing-country-profiles.htm#tpcountryprofiles (last visited 15 July 2024).

Article 9(1) OECD MC is the 'authoritative statement' of the ALP for tax treaty purposes.[191] It stipulates that the tax authorities of a Contracting State may, for calculating enterprises' tax liabilities, make adjustments to the accounts of such enterprises if the latter do not depict the 'true' taxable profits arising in that State due to the 'special relations' between the associated enterprises concerned. The purpose of this provision is to restore the conditions that would have prevailed if the transactions between the involved enterprises had taken place 'on normal open market commercial terms (on an arm's length basis)'.[192] In this respect, the OECD Transfer Pricing (TP) Guidelines provide internationally agreed guidelines for the application of the ALP in practice.[193] The ALP is also recognized by the UN as it is enshrined in Article 9 UN MC[194] with the UN TP Manual elaborating on the UN's approach to how the ALP is to be applied in practice.[195] The rationale behind the ALP, both under the OECD and the UN Models, is to reach an approximation of a market-based outcome for intra-group transactions.

The ALP's success and wide adoption by nearly all States around the world is indeed the result of the fact that this principle has been endorsed both by the OECD and the UN. Nevertheless, although (primarily) Article 9(1) OECD MC and (secondarily) Article 9(1) UN MC have played a fundamental role in the acceptance the ALP enjoys in the international tax community, the interpretation and application thereof have proved to be challenging in practice primarily due to significant inconsistencies in interpretation of this principle.[196] Thus, the fact that the ALP has been adopted by the vast majority of States does not in itself mean that it can be elevated to CIL. To determine whether or not the ALP forms part of CIL, both *usus* and *opinio juris* must be present.

The first issue for determining the existence of *general* and *consistent* State practice in the sense of actual *usus* is whether countries share the same concept of 'arm's length'. Stated otherwise, it would have to be established that there is generality and consistency in the adherence by States to the core integral components of the ALP. In this respect, the quintessential element inherent in the ALP concept is the treatment of associated enterprises as if they were unrelated parties. While this may seem to initially be clear, it is not; there is significant inconsistency among States' practice on whether the ALP is to be applied to separate legal entities only or whether it should be relevant also between headquarters and PEs. The latter is the claim of what is referred

191. *See* Commentary on Art. 9, para. 1, OECD, *Model Tax Convention on Income and on Capital: Condensed Version 2017*, *supra* n. 1.
192. *See* Commentary on Art. 9, para. 2, OECD, *Model Tax Convention on Income and on Capital: Condensed Version 2017*, *supra* n. 1.
193. OECD, *OECD Transfer Pricing Guidelines for Multinational Enterprises and Tax Administrations 2022* (2022).
194. UN, *United Nations Model Double Taxation Convention between Developed and Developing Countries 2021* (2021).
195. UN, *United Nations Practical Manual on Transfer Pricing for Developing Countries (2021)* (2021).
196. Abhishek Padwalkar & Camilo C. Rodriguez Peña, *Normative Conflicts When Applying the Arm's Length Principle: When Soft Law Developments Meet Hard Law Realities of National Legislation*, 15 World Tax J. 208 (2023) https://doi.org/10.59403/3pa7nrb.

to as the OECD Authorized Approach (AOA), which is far from being universally accepted, however, even among OECD member countries.[197] Thus, even if the third-party fiction of the ALP as such may be understood consistently, its actual scope is not. Examining the details of what it actually means, there is even much less consistency among States. This is due to the fact that the ALP's separate entity approach is notoriously complex and rich in details.[198] The breadth (or, perhaps, vagueness) of the concept, for example, its reliance on facts (i.e., accurate delineation of the transaction) or the testing of a transaction's commercial rationality (i.e., recognition of the transaction), allows significant room to subjectivity. Simply stated, there is no common understanding of what 'arm's length' actually means in its details. This is above all evidenced by the never-ending disputes on TP among taxpayers, tax authorities, and courts when attempting to reach a market-based outcome, both domestically and cross-border. Indicatively, based on the OECD statistics, there has been a substantial (and ever-increasing) number of international TP disputes that have been submitted to mutual agreement procedure (MAP). Within 2022, there were 1,167 MAP TP cases initiated while the end inventory of the same year amounted to 2,853 such cases.[199] This tremendous number of MAP cases and the resultant tax uncertainty is a very strong indication against the existence of general and consistent State practice.[200] This susceptibility of the ALP to disputes may be traced back to the OECD's (and others') reliance on soft law instruments that aim to clarify the ALP, notably the OECD TP Guidelines.[201] As the number of disputes in this area shows, this attempt to 'unify' the ALP through soft law has failed. By contrast, such a soft law approach has led to the ALP developing in different directions and has created inconsistencies in its application under different domestic laws.[202] Therefore, in honesty, there is still no harmonized approach.[203] Taking this into account, there is no uniform State practice to establish CIL.[204] Furthermore, the candidacy of the ALP for forming part of CIL suffers

197. *See also* Szudoczky, *supra* n. 4, at 164-165. Not only less fundamental but also noticeable is the inconsistency in the ALP's scope under the OECD's own TP guidance. This is the case, for instance, with hard-to-value intangibles (HTVIs) for which ex-post information is used for determining the arm's length nature of past transactions involving intangibles, although unrelated parties under market conditions would only have regard to the information available at that time in order to assess the circumstances upon executing the transaction.
198. *See also* Szudoczky, *supra* n. 4, at 164-165.
199. OECD, *2022 Mutual Agreement Procedure Statistics*, https://web-archive.oecd.org/temp/2023-11-14/417871-mutual-agreement-procedure-statistics.htm (last visited 15 July 2024); European Commission, *Overview of Numbers Submitted for Statistics on Pending Mutual Agreement Procedures (MAPs) under the Arbitration Convention (AC) at the End of 2022*, https://taxation-customs.ec.europa.eu/document/download/955bc56e-f316-4823-b62e-e564fa3a5d76_en?filename=AC%20MAP_2022_Final.pdf (last visited 15 July 2024).
200. For a thorough review concerning the timing aspects of dispute resolution through MAPs, *see* Michelle Markham, *The Timely Resolution of Mutual Agreement Procedure Disputes: Secrets of Success?*, 77 Bull. for Int'l Taxn. (2023) https://doi.org/10.59403/3mds71d.
201. Padwalkar & Rodriguez Peña, *supra* n. 196, at 212.
202. Wittendorff, *supra* n. 189, at 1127; Richard S. Collier & Ian F. Dykes, *On the Apparent Widespread Misapplication of the OECD Transfer Pricing Guidelines*, 76 Bull. for Int'l Taxn., s. 2 (2022) https://doi.org/10.59403/3c7s063.
203. Padwalkar & Rodriguez Peña, *supra* n. 196, at 212.
204. The ALP is not only applied between different enterprises belonging to the same group but also for the attribution of profits to PEs as per Art. 7(2) OECD MC. In this regard, Hongler has argued

not only from inconsistency in State practice but also from the absence of *opinio juris*. A prominent indication against the existence of *opinio juris* comes from the OECD IF work on Pillar 1. One of the key outcomes of Pillar 1 is 'Amount A' which involves a predetermined formula based on which a portion of profits is redistributed to market jurisdictions. Thus, the approach endorsed through Amount A comprises strong elements of formulary apportionment (i.e., ALP's rival concept). This arguably constitutes a major departure from the ALP and the 'traditional' TP rules as those are interpreted by the OECD TP Guidelines[205] even though the application of these rules is reserved for Multinational Enterprise (MNE) groups with (adjusted) pre-tax revenues of more than EUR 20 billion (revenue test) and a pre-tax profit margin exceeding 10% (profitability test). The conclusion that Pillar 1 deviates from the ALP is also obvious in the case of the other major outcomes of Pillar 1, i.e., Amount B, which applies to *all* MNE entities falling within the ambit of the TP rules of the jurisdictions where they are based. Amount B, which seeks to 'simplify and streamline the application of the arm's length principle to in-country baseline marketing and distribution activities', sets forth a pricing framework that includes a three-step process to determine a fixed return on sales for distributors covered by its scope.[206] The fact that nearly 150 countries discussed (and many accepted) adopting Pillar 1 rules, some of which may not result in non-arm's length outcomes,[207] is a strong indication that none of the countries involved in the OECD IF felt bound by a CIL rule. Thus, even if arguing that there is general and consistent practice in applying the ALP, the reality is that formulary apportionment has always been[208] and still remains a legitimate alternative thereto.[209]

4 THE ROLE OF ARTICLE 31(3)(C) VCLT IN THE TAX TREATY INTERPRETATION PROCESS

4.1 The Concept of Article 31(3)(c) VCLT

Article 31(3)(c) VCLT is the part of the general rule of interpretation pursuant to which the treaty interpreter can identify the circumstances under which rules of international law *outside* the treaty concerned may be considered in the interpretation process. The purpose of including this matter in the present chapter is that, as will be seen more analytically below, the objective of this provision is to enable the use, among other

that many states follow a worldwide taxation system not providing unilateral relief in respect of foreign PE profits which is evidence of an absence of general and consistent state practice. *See* Peter Hongler, *Justice in International Tax Law: A Normative Review of the International Tax Regime*, s. 4.3.2.8.5.2. (IBFD 2019).

205. Petruzzi & Padwalkar, *supra* n. 185, at 449.

206. OECD, *Pillar One: Amount B – Inclusive Framework on BEPS*, *supra* n. 8, at 6-7.

207. Petruzzi & Padwalkar, *supra* n. 185, at 448-449.

208. *See*, for example, European Commission, *Proposal for a Council Directive on a Common Consolidated Corporate Tax Base (CCCTB)*, 25 October 2016, COM/2016/0683 final – 2016/0336 (CNS).

209. Further evidence to this conclusion is the discussion on the BEFIT Proposal in the EU. *See* European Commission, *Proposal for a Council Directive on Business in Europe: Framework for Income Taxation (BEFIT)*, 12 September 2023, COM/2023/532 final.

sources of international law, of CIL as well as other treaties for identifying or clarifying the meaning of a treaty provision that is subject to interpretation. Thus, this section completes the discussion about the relevance of CIL to tax treaty interpretation.

The text of Article 31(3)(c) VCLT reads as follows: 'There shall be taken into account, together with the context: (...) (c) any relevant rules of international law applicable in the relations between the parties.' This provision embodies the principle of systemic integration according to which treaties, no matter their subject matter, constitute a creation of international law and, consequently, their existence and operation are governed by the latter.[210] Hence, as regards issues not expressly addressed by it, an international convention must be interpreted and applied having regard to the general principles of international law.[211] Nevertheless, Article 31(3)(c) VCLT cannot lead to a situation in which the provisions of the applicable treaty are displaced or replaced by those of another treaty. The purpose of this provision is purely to contribute to the furthering of the interpretation process.[212]

Although the order of the rules of art. Article 31 VCLT is not hierarchical, the process to be followed is arguably clear. It should begin with the ordinary meaning of the terms, the context, and the treaty's object and purpose and then proceed to agreements made upon the treaty's conclusion as well as instruments produced thereupon by the contracting parties and, last, to subsequent agreements, subsequent practice and, thereafter, to relevant rules of international law.[213] However, like all other parts of Article 31 VCLT, the rule of Article 31(3)(c) VCLT may not be of relevance in every single case, but when it is, it must be utilized.[214] This means that the rule of Article 31(3)(c) VCLT forms part of the interpretation process enshrined in Article 31 VCLT and, as a corollary, it does not constitute by itself a panacea nor should its use undermine the application of the other interpretation rules contained in that article. It should be used carefully in the interpretation process and only when this is required.[215]

210. United Nations, *Yearbook of the International Law Commission 2006, Vol. 2, Part 2, Report of the Commission to the General Assembly on the Work of Its Fifty-Eighth Session*, A/CN.4/SER.A/2006/Add.l (Part 2) 180 (2018), https://www.un-ilibrary.org/content/books/9789210556583/read (last visited 15 July 2024); Campbell McLachlan, *The Principle of Systemic Integration and Article 31(3)(C) of the Vienna Convention*, 54 Int'l & Comp. L.Q. 280 (2005) https://doi.org/10.1093/iclq/lei001.
211. McLachlan, *supra* n. 210, at 280; Arnold D. McNair, *The Law of Treaties* 466 (Clarendon Press 1961); *See also Georges Pinson (France) v. United Mexican States* [1928] Reports of International Arbitral Awards 327, at 422, para. 50.
212. Richard Gardiner, *Treaty Interpretation* 291 (Oxford Univ. Press 2d ed. 2015); Duncan French, *Treaty Interpretation and the Incorporation of Extraneous Legal Rules*, 55 Int'l & Comp. L.Q. 283 (2006) https://doi.org/10.1093/iclq/lei082; Sumith S. Bhat, *A Study of the Issue of 'Relevant Rules' of International Law for the Purposes of Interpretation of Treaties under Article 31(3)(c) of the Vienna Convention on the Law of Treaties*, 21 Int'l Comm. Law Rev. 217 (2019) https://doi.org/10.1163/18719732-12341398.
213. *See also* Gardiner, *supra* n. 212, at 290.
214. French, *supra* n. 212, at 301.
215. Bhat, *supra* n. 212, at 215.

The initial reason for the conception of the predecessor of Article 31(3)(c) VCLT was to deal with the issue of intertemporal law.[216] In practical terms, the intention of its drafters was to stipulate a rule to determine whether the interpretation of the treaty terms would be carried out taking into account the '*general rules of international law in force at the time of its conclusion*' (emphasis added) or the rules applicable at some other time (e.g., the time of its application).[217] In view of the continuous development and changes in international law, whether through CIL or international conventions, complexities in the interpretation of treaty rules were likely to arise and even more so when the concepts used in a treaty are open or evolving.[218] In this regard, an appropriate approach would be required to address the dynamism of international law in the context of a treaty interpretation exercise in a particular instance after its conclusion.[219] Indeed, the purpose of this article was to identify whether and under what circumstances an 'evolutionary interpretation' could be performed having regard to developments in international law extraneous to a given treaty.[220]

Despite the above, the final version of the rule that was submitted to the 1969 Vienna conference made no reference to the matter of intertemporal law. Nevertheless, the issue is implicitly covered by Article 31(3)(c) VCLT and in the reference to good faith in Article 31(1) VCLT.[221] As opposed to the version that contained an explicit reference, the final version of the rule was considered more appropriate to accommodate all different circumstances pertaining to intertemporal law.[222] Therefore, the reference to general rules of international law in force at the time of the conclusion of a treaty was omitted. This did not, however, render the scope of Article 31(3)(c) VCLT narrower. On the contrary, the provision covers all relevant obligations of international law nature that are applicable in the relations among the parties to the treaty under interpretation. These obligations may derive from other treaties, CIL rules, or general principles of law.[223]

---

216. *See* Ulf Linderfalk, *Doing the Right Thing for the Right Reason: Why Dynamic or Static Approaches Should Be Taken in the Interpretation of Treaties,* 10 Int'l Comm. Law Rev. 111 et seq. (2008) https://doi.org/10.1163/187197308x311272; Gardiner, *supra* n. 212, at 290.
217. Paragraph 16, United Nations, *Yearbook of the International Law Commission 2006, Vol. 2, Part 2, Report of the Commission to the General Assembly on the Work of Its Fifty-Eighth Session, supra* n. 210, at 293; Panos Merkouris, *Debating the Ouroboros of International Law: The Drafting History of Article 31(3)(c)*, 9 Int'l Comm. Law Rev. 15 (2007) https://doi.org/10.1163/187197407x196721.
218. Paragraph 23, United Nations, *Yearbook of the International Law Commission 2006, Vol. 2, Part 2, Report of the Commission to the General Assembly on the Work of Its Fifty-Eighth Session, supra* n. 210, at 181.
219. McLachlan, *supra* n. 210, at 282.
220. Gardiner, *supra* n. 212, at 291.
221. Gardiner, *supra* n. 212, at 297.
222. Paragraph 16, United Nations, *Yearbook of the International Law Commission 2006, Vol. 2, Part 2, Report of the Commission to the General Assembly on the Work of Its Fifty-Eighth Session, supra* n. 210, at 222.
223. Paragraphs 18, 20 and 21, United Nations, *Yearbook of the International Law Commission 2006, Vol. 2, Part 2, Report of the Commission to the General Assembly on the Work of Its Fifty-Eighth Session, supra* n. 210, at 180; *See also Oil Platforms (Islamic Republic of Iran v. United States of America) (Merits)* [2003] I.C.J. Rep 160, at 182, para. 41.

Having a close look at the wording of Article 31(3)(c) VCLT, four distinct elements that merit examination can be discerned: 'rules of international law', 'relevant', 'applicable in the relations between the parties', and 'parties'. Regarding the first term, to determine which rules of international law are covered, reference could be made to Article 38(1) ICJ Statute which is regarded as listing the sources of international law.[224] In this respect, most authors contend that the rules of international law to be taken into account are other treaties, CIL, and general principles of law for interpretation purposes.[225] Thus, subsidiary means (i.e., judicial decisions and teachings of the most highly qualified publicists) should be excluded as they do not constitute formal sources for the purposes of Article 31(3)(c) VCLT.[226] Other authors suggest that the subsidiary means referred to in that provision (i.e., judicial decisions and teachings of the most highly qualified publicists) could also be considered insofar as they contribute to identifying the 'rules of international law'.[227] Second, the rules of international law may be considered 'relevant' when they either deal with the same subject matter as the treaty provision undergoing interpretation or may indirectly affect the interpretation thereof (which, for example, might be the case with general principles).[228] Third, based on a textual analysis of the wording of Article 31(3)(c) VCLT ('rules'), the matter of applicability in the relations between the parties should be perceived as referring to all rules of international law that are *legally* binding to the parties.[229] The last element, specifically the term 'parties', has sparked vibrant debate among scholars.[230]

The two main interpretations of 'parties' suggest that: (1) either all parties *to the interpreted treaty* must be parties to the treaty being used for interpretation under Article 31(3)(c) VCLT; or (2) all parties *to the specific dispute* must be parties to that

224. *See* s. 2.1.1 above; *See also Arbitration under Chapter Eleven of NAFTA, Pope & Talbot v. Canada (Award in respect of Damages)* [2002] UNCITRAL, para. 46; *See also Golder v. the United Kingdom (Application No. 4451/70)* [1975] E.Ct.H.R., para. 35; *Demir and Baykara v. Turkey (Application No. 34503/97)* [2008] E.Ct.H.R., paras 69-73.
225. McLachlan, *supra* n. 210, at 290; Gabrielle Marceau, *Conflicts of Norms and Conflicts of Jurisdictions The Relationship Between the WTO Agreement and MEAs and Other Treaties*, 35 J. World Trade 1087 (2001) https://doi.org/10.54648/384808.
226. Georg Schwarzenberger, *International Law, Vol 1, International Law as Applied by International Courts and Tribunals* 28 (Stevens 3rd ed. 1957); Bhat, *supra* n. 212, at 195.
227. *See* indicatively Gardiner, *supra* n. 212, at 307.
228. For an overview of the concept of 'relevance', *see* Francesco Avella, *Using EU Law to Interpret Undefined Tax Treaty Terms: Article 31(3)(c) of the Vienna Convention on the Law of Treaties and Article 3(2) of the OECD Model Convention*, 4 World Tax J. 99 (2012) https://doi.org/10.59403/zdy7sz; Merkouris, *supra* n. 217; Bhat, *supra* n. 212, at 196.
229. McLachlan, *supra* n. 210, at 290. However, the ECtHR has pointed out that, pursuant to Art. 31(3)(c) VCLT, it may take into account, along with binding rules of international law, also non-binding instruments; *See also Golder v. the United Kingdom*, *supra* n. 224, paras 67, 68, 78, 85 and 86; Gardiner, *supra* n. 212, at 307; Avella, *supra* n. 228, at 99.
230. *See* Ulf Linderfalk, *Who Are 'The Parties'? Article 31, Paragraph 3(C) of the 1969 Vienna Convention and the 'Principle of Systemic Integration' Revisited*, 55 Neth. Int'l L. Rev. (2008) https://doi.org/10.1017/s0165070x08003434; Gardiner, *supra* n. 212, at 310-317; French, *supra* n. 212, at 305-307; Benn McGrady, *Fragmentation of International Law or 'Systemic Integration' of Treaty Regimes: EC-Biotech Products and the Proper Interpretation of Article 31(3)(c) of the Vienna Convention on the Law of Treaties*, 42 J. World Trade 594 et seq. (2008) https://doi.org/10.54648/trad2008025.

other treaty.[231] Assuming that the treaty interpreter would resort to Article 31(3)(c) VCLT in order to interpret a tax treaty term, no controversy would arise in the case of bilateral DTTs as *all* Contracting States would also be parties to another international agreement. The situation might be more complicated in the case of multilateral tax treaties (MTTs) such as the Nordic Convention.[232] In such a case, adopting one or the other view would make a difference. Adopting the first approach, no other treaty could be used in the context of a dispute between two Contracting States of an MTT for the interpretation thereof unless *all* States were parties to both treaties. Conversely, if the second view was followed in the context of a dispute between only two Contracting States of an MTT, using another treaty for the interpretation of a term of that MTT in a case where *only these two contracting states* are parties to another international agreement would be feasible. While the second view would provide more flexibility in terms of allowing the use of a large number of treaties for interpreting MTT terms, it could lead to inconsistent interpretations depending on the Contracting States in dispute each particular time.[233] This would not be the case under the first view which suggests that all parties to an MTT would need to be parties to another treaty for the latter to fall within the ambit of Article 31(3)(c) VCLT. Although the wording of the provision ('the parties') seems to afford discretion for adopting either interpretation, the context of Article 31(3)(c), the object and purpose of the treaty, and the preparatory work of the VCLT point towards this stricter approach.[234]

4.2 The Relevance of Article 31(3)(c) VCLT for Interpreting Tax Treaties

The question, however, is whether Article 31(3)(c) VCLT is likely to play a fundamental role in tax treaty interpretation. The additional value that this rule can offer to the interpretation process seems to be low due to the States' tendency to regulate their bilateral relations in tax matters comprehensively in one single DTT. Parallel tax treaties among the same two States are rather unusual and, when they exist, they are typically different in scope (e.g., covering taxes on income or inheritance tax) so that the rules of one treaty are not necessarily 'relevant' (as required by Article 31(3)(c) VCLT) for the other.[235] Setting such 'parallel' tax treaties aside, Article 31(3)(c) VCLT may theoretically allow CIL (as another potentially 'relevant' source of international law) to influence tax treaty interpretation. However, CIL's existence would have to be confirmed before, which is, as detailed above, not an easy task.

Outside the conventional sources of international law, Avella has identified an interaction between Article 31(3)(c) VCLT and EU law.[236] He suggests that, under certain conditions, rules of EU law can be taken into account in the context of the

231. Linderfalk, *supra* n. 230, at 345; French, *supra* n. 212, at 305-307.
232. *Denmark – Faroe Islands – Finland – Iceland – Norway – Sweden Income and Capital Tax Treaty (Nordic Convention)*, 23 September 1996, *supra* n. 3.
233. Gardiner, *supra* n. 212, at 314.
234. Linderfalk, *supra* n. 230, at 358.
235. *See* in general, French, *supra* n. 212, at 302.
236. Avella, *supra* n. 228.

interpretation of DTT provisions. This is essentially premised on the technical nature of EU law as part of international law as the EU is, after all, an international organization. Avella argues that rules of both primary and secondary EU law that concern the taxes covered by DTTs must be used for interpreting terms of DTTs entered into between EU Member States (but not between EU Member States and third States as the latter are not 'parties' to the EU as required by Article 31(3)(c) VCLT).[237] However, Avella also recognizes that Article 31(3)(c) VCLT forms part of a broader interpretation process and, therefore, the appropriateness of its use must be assessed on a case-by-case basis.[238]

The recourse to EU law as a source of interpreting DTTs is interesting due to the EU's (or at least the Commission's) increased activity in tax areas that were traditionally seen as strongholds of DTT regulation. A recent example is the Commission's draft for an EU TP Directive that attempts to establish a 'European arm's length principle' to be applied among EU Member States.[239] Other examples include the infamous 'Danish holding cases' decided by the Court of Justice of the European Union (CJEU) on the entitlement of low-substance entities for benefits under the EU Parent/Subsidiary Directive and the EU Interest/Royalties Directive which can be translated into the DTT world as 'beneficial ownership' issues. Additionally, the GAAR introduced in the EU by Article 6 ATAD is very similar to the PPT under Article 29(9) of the OECD MC. In all such cases of (potential) EU law 'in parallel to tax treaties', for purposes of Article 31(3)(c) VCLT, it must be ensured, however, that the individual element of EU law actually addresses the same issue as a DTT. Only then could EU law be 'relevant' for DTT interpretation as required by Article 31(3)(c) VCLT. Accordingly, a thorough analysis of both instruments, the DTT in question and EU law, is needed to avoid 'comparing apples with oranges'. This risk, which is not exclusive to DTTs, may be the reason why the practical importance of Article 31(3)(c) for interpreting international law conventions is seen as minimal.[240]

One example in which EU law and a DTT rule might be indeed comparable is the current draft of the EU TP Directive. In fact, this draft intends to align its 'European arm's length principle' with the DTT ALP of Article 9 OECD MC and further explored by the OECD TP Guidelines. There is even a reference in the draft to the OECD's existing body of work in this area.[241] Therefore, although not necessarily identical, the

237. Avella, *supra* n. 228, at 108. For the interaction between EU law and tax treaties between EU Member States and non-EU Member States, *see* Ilaria Panzeri, *Tax Treaties Versus EU Law: Which Should Prevail?*, 61 Eur. Taxn. 147 et seq. (2021) https://doi.org/10.59403/10jtd78.

238. Avella, *supra* n. 228, at 109.

239. European Commission, *Proposal for a Council Directive on Transfer Pricing*, 12 September 2023, COM(2023) 529 final.

240. Even outside the area of tax treaties, an author has argued that, generally, there has been reluctance in referring to Art. 31(3)(C) VCLT. *See* Philippe Sands, *Sustainable Development: Treaty, Custom, and the Cross-Fertilization of International Law*, *in International Law and Sustainable Development: Past Achievements and Future Challenges* 49-50 (Alan Boyle & David Freestone eds, Oxford Univ. Press 1999); United Nations, *Report of the International Law Commission, Fifty-Sixth Session (3 May-4 June and 5 July-6 August 2004)*, A/59/10, 301 (2004).

241. Articles 3(18) and 14(1), European Commission, *Proposal for a Council Directive on Transfer Pricing*, *supra* n. 239. According to the Directive Proposal, EU Member States must interpret the

two instruments will at least significantly overlap. This may well end up in a case for Article 31(3)(c) VCLT so that the 'European arm's length principle' (as it will ultimately be defined by the CJEU when interpreting the Directive) can influence the interpretation of bilateral intra-EU DTTs. This result could, however, be achieved even without recourse to Article 31(3)(c) VCLT: Under EU law principles, an EU Directive (like the TP Directive, if adopted) will always have supremacy over intra-EU DTTs concluded among EU Member States. Thus, the difference is primarily on methodology, i.e., whether EU law prevails by its legal supremacy or as an element of interpretation.

5 CONCLUDING REMARKS

This chapter explored whether using common terms and concepts within DTTs can lead to the formation of CIL rules (referred to as CITL). The hypothesis of CITL would entail that States would be bound by rules elevated to this level even in the absence of explicit corresponding rules in a DTT. Equally, States would be under an international law obligation to respect such CITL rules when applying their existing DTT network or negotiating new DTTs. Such effects may be seen as far-reaching (or even far-fetched). Nonetheless, there is a fair amount of recent literature on the idea of CITL. The reason for this is certainly the noticeable trend to more standardization in the international tax arena, in particular, pushed by the work of international organizations such as the OECD (beyond the boundaries of its membership through the IF) and the UN.

The present chapter analysed several 'usual suspects' among DTT norms (as proposed by literature) on their potential to evolve into CITL. The result was that none of those attempts was successful. Overall, the reason for this outcome is the enormous obstacles that would have to be eliminated in order for these rules to constitute CIL. These hurdles are no different for tax treaty law from any other area of law: the existence of 'general' and 'consistent' State practice, and *opinio juris*, as recently laid down again in the 2018 ILC Report.

The first element, State practice, needs to be sufficiently wide and representative without significant uncertainty or contradiction. Importantly, such State practice would require more than States simply employing an instrument in their DTT network a truly consistent application by authorities and courts is required. In a technical area like tax law that is naturally full of details (and disputes over them), this is almost impossible to achieve.

The second element, *opinio juris*, did prove itself to be even more unrealistic. For it to exist, States must not only just follow a certain international tax concept in their DTT network but also do it with a sense of legal obligation. States must feel that they *must* employ such concepts as a matter of law and not as a policy choice. In current States' practice (even if it was seen as 'general' and 'consistent'), there was no evidence found for *opinio juris*. In contrast, the high degree of standardization in the

ALP in accordance with the 2022 version of the OECD TP Guidelines and any further amendments thereto that the EU approved in the context of the OECD Committee on Fiscal Affairs.

world of DTTs is the result of sovereign policy decisions made by the States, which feel it is practical (but not legally binding) to follow certain standards in their treaty negotiations. From this perspective, also the sheer number of mostly similar bilateral DTTs does not support but rather contradicts the existence of CITL; if it really existed, it would not have been necessary to conclude all these DTTs.

CHAPTER 11

The Relation Between Article 3(2) OECD MC and the Interpretation Rules of the Vienna Convention on the Law of Treaties

Michael Lang & Benjamin Beer

1 Article 3(2) OECD MC and the Vienna Convention on the Law of Treaties
2 Historic Development of Article 3(2) OECD MC
3 The Role of Definitions
4 When Does the Context *Require* an Autonomous Interpretation?
5 The Meaning of the Term 'Context' in Article 3(2) OECD MC
6 The Relation Between the Context and Competent Authority Agreements
7 Application of the Treaty
8 The Recourse to Domestic Law
9 Concluding Remarks

1 ARTICLE 3(2) OECD MC AND THE VIENNA CONVENTION ON THE LAW OF TREATIES

The interpretation rules contained in Articles 31-33 of the Vienna Convention on the Law of Treaties (VCLT) are often used by courts and tax authorities for interpreting double taxation conventions (DTCs).[1] However, it must be acknowledged that DTCs

1. For example, in the recent jurisprudence by the German Federal Tax Court (BFH) BFH, 5 December 2023 – I R 42/20, para. 36. *See, also*, Michael Lang, *Can Law Regulate Its Own Interpretation? Relevance of Articles 31-33 of the Vienna Convention on the Law of Treaties (VCLT) and Article 3 Para. 2 of the Model Convention of the Organisation for Economic Co-operation and*

are treaties under international law – just like the VCLT itself.[2] Therefore, they are not hierarchically related to each other but are instead of equal rank, notwithstanding the multilateral nature of the VCLT.[3] The fact that the VCLT is considered to be part of customary international law[4] does not change the equal status between a DTC and the VCLT[5] either because customary international law also does not have a higher rank than an international treaty.[6]

States can either explicitly or implicitly decide on the interpretation of the treaties they conclude. Therefore, it cannot be assumed that the VCLT's interpretation rules are necessarily applicable for interpreting DTCs,[7] including those concluded after the VCLT's entry into force in 1980.[8] Rather, whether those VCLT rules apply to tax treaties depends on their suitability for this specific field of application which means that not all of those rules disclosed in it necessarily have the same relevance for tax treaty interpretation.[9] States that conclude international treaties may create their own rules for interpretation as part of such a treaty.[10]

Development (OECD MC) for the Interpretation of Double-Taxation Conventions, in Research Handbook on International Taxation 176 et seq. (Yariv Brauner ed., Edward Elgar Publishing 2019).

2. *See* Franz Wassermeyer & Klaus-Dieter Drüen, *OECD-MA 2017 Art. 3, in Doppelbesteuerung: Kommentar zu allen Doppelbesteuerungsabkommen*, para. 76 (Franz Wassermeyer et al. eds, Verlag C.H. Beck oHG 2018).
3. *See* Michael Lang, *Introduction to the Law of Double Taxation Conventions* 13 (Linde Verlag Ges. m. b. H. 3d ed. 2021); Lang, *Can Law Regulate Its Own Interpretation? Relevance of Articles 31-33 of the Vienna Convention on the Law of Treaties (VCLT) and Article 3 Para. 2 of the Model Convention of the Organisation for Economic Co-operation and Development (OECD MC) for the Interpretation of Double-Taxation Conventions, supra* n. 1, at 176 et seq.
4. *See* Philip Baker, *Chapter 3: The Localization of Tax Treaty Interpretation, in Building Global International Tax Law: Essays in Honour of Guglielmo Maisto* 47 (IBFD 2022); Christian Gloria, *Die Doppelbesteuerungsabkommen der Bundesrepublik Deutschland und die Bedeutung der Lex-Fori-Klausel für ihre Auslegung: Ein Plädoyer für die Auslegung der DBA nach den Regeln der WVK*, 33 R.I.W. 972 et seq. (1986).
5. *See* Bernhard Kempen et al., *Völkerrecht* 53 et seq. (Verlag Franz Vahlen, Helbing Lichtenhahn, MANZ'sche Verlags- und Universitätsbuchhandlung GmbH 3d ed. 2021); Michael Potacs, *Rechtstheorie* 70 et seq. (UTB, Facultas 2d ed. 2019); Klaus Vogel & Rainer Prokisch, *General Report, in Interpretation of Double Taxation Conventions* 66 et seq. (IFA ed., 1993).
6. *See* Lang, *Introduction to the Law of Double Taxation Conventions, supra* n. 3, at 13; Peter Hongler, *International Law of Taxation* 29 (Oxford University Press 2021).
7. *See* Lang, *Can Law Regulate Its Own Interpretation? Relevance of Articles 31-33 of the Vienna Convention on the Law of Treaties (VCLT) and Article 3 Para. 2 of the Model Convention of the Organisation for Economic Co-operation and Development (OECD MC) for the Interpretation of Double-Taxation Conventions, supra* n. 1, at 176 et seq. *See also* Gloria, *supra* n. 4, at 972 et seq. who elaborates on the question of whether DTCs are to be interpreted in accordance with the VCLT which he confirms unless there would be a diverging customary international law for DTCs.
8. Article 4 VCLT. *See* Kempen et al., *supra* n. 5, at 53; Christina Binder & Karl Zemanek, *II. Abschnitt: Die Völkerrechtsquellen: 2. Kapitel: Das Völkervertragsrecht, in Österreichisches Handbuch des Völkerrechts* 57 (August Reinisch ed., MANZ'sche Verlags- und Universitätsbuchhandlung GmbH 6th ed. 2021); Michael Lang, *DBA-Auslegung nach der Wiener Vertragsrechtskonvention versus nach Art. 3 Abs. 2 OECD-MA?, in Globalisiertes Steuerrecht: Anspruch und Verantwortung – Festschrift für Heinz-Klaus Kroppen* 668 et seq. (Roman Seer & Stephan Rasch eds, Verlag Dr Otto Schmidt KG 2020); Ian Sinclair, *The Vienna Convention on the Law of Treaties* 1 (Manchester University Press 2d ed. 1984).
9. *See* Lang, *Introduction to the Law of Double Taxation Conventions, supra* n. 3, at 13.
10. *See* Lang, *Can Law Regulate Its Own Interpretation? Relevance of Articles 31-33 of the Vienna Convention on the Law of Treaties (VCLT) and Article 3 Para. 2 of the Model Convention of the*

In the event that there would be no codified rules of interpretation or they could not apply to a specific case, the canon of legal interpretation methods would be considered for the interpretation of the treaty itself. Also, in such a situation, an interpretation would begin with the wording of a term, proceed by regarding it within its own context and determining its object and purpose. Further, based on its historic development,[11] content would be attributed to the term establishing what the legislator must accept as having been actually stated by him.[12] The interpretation provisions of the VCLT therefore essentially codify what would also be done without them.[13] This is especially the case due to the fact that Articles 31-33 VCLT do not establish a rigid hierarchy between the different means of interpretation and, in each individual case, all aspects that may qualify as relevant for the interpretation need to be considered.[14] The situation is different, however, with the existence of interpretation provisions in such a way as then the interpretation provisions need to be interpreted themselves in detail.

In the case of DTCs, states usually incorporate[15] the interpretation rule that is currently stated in Article 3(2) Model Convention of the Organisation for Economic Co-operation and Development (OECD MC) 2017[16] and reads as follows:

> As regards the application of the Convention at any time by a Contracting State, any term not defined therein shall, unless the context otherwise requires or the competent authorities agree to a different meaning pursuant to the provisions of Article 25, have the meaning that it has at that time under the law of that State for the purposes of the taxes to which the Convention applies, any meaning under the applicable tax laws of that State prevailing over a meaning given to the term under other laws of that State.

It is crucial to consider how such an interpretation clause in an international treaty aligns with the VCLT's interpretation provisions. Additionally, if an international treaty lacks rules for its own interpretation, it raises the question of how it should then be interpreted and, if it does have them, they may have priority over the general rules of interpretation codified in the VCLT, as has been argued in literature.[17] However,

---

Organisation for Economic Co-operation and Development (OECD MC) for the Interpretation of Double-Taxation Conventions, supra n. 1, at 176 et seq.

11. *See ibid.*, at 174.
12. *See* Heinz Peter Rill, *Juristische Methodenlehre und Rechtsbegriff*, 10 Z.f.V. 465 et seq. (1985).
13. *See* Lang, *Can Law Regulate Its Own Interpretation? Relevance of Articles 31-33 of the Vienna Convention on the Law of Treaties (VCLT) and Article 3 Para. 2 of the Model Convention of the Organisation for Economic Co-operation and Development (OECD MC) for the Interpretation of Double-Taxation Conventions, supra* n. 1, at 183.
14. *See*, with further references, Michael Lang & Florian Brugger, *The Role of the OECD Commentary in Tax Treaty Interpretation*, 23 Australian Tax Forum 100 (2008). *See also* in detail Chapter 1 in this book.
15. *See* Klaus Vogel, *Problems of the Interpretation of Tax Treaties*, 10 S.W.I. 111 (2000).
16. OECD, *Model Tax Convention on Income and on Capital* (2017).
17. *See*, for example, what has been stated in the case of Cf. *Fowler v. Revenue & Customs Commissioners* (UKFTT 234 (TC), 12 April 2016), paras 99-100: 'Article 3(2) of the Treaty is a special rule of interpretation within Article 31(4) of the Vienna Convention, as opposed to the general rules of interpretation contained in Articles 31(1)-(3) of the Vienna Convention. [...] As a special rule of interpretation Article 3(2) has priority over such general rules.' Regarding the Fowler, case *see* Michael Lang, *Chapter 22: Fowler v. Commissioners for Her Majesty's Revenue*

under the interpretation provision of Article 3(2) OECD MC, a deviation from the VCLT due to possibly construing the principle of the authoritativeness of domestic law can only occur[18] when a term is not defined in the tax treaty,[19] the context does not require otherwise, and the competent authorities do not agree to a different meaning following a mutual agreement procedure (MAP).

2 HISTORIC DEVELOPMENT OF ARTICLE 3(2) OECD MC

In the area of DTCs, the interpretation clause now codified in Article 3(2) OECD MC[20] was first[21] used as a treaty provision in the 1945 DTC between the United States and the United Kingdom[22] breaking the trend of a continuous increase of definitions in earlier treaties.[23] Article II(3) of the 1945 DTC between the United States and the United Kingdom states:

> In the application of the provisions of the present Convention by one of the Contracting Parties any term not otherwise defined shall, unless the context otherwise requires, have the meaning which it has under the laws of that

and Customs: Some Thoughts on Tax Treaty Interpretation, in Thinker, Teacher, Traveler: Reimagining International Tax: Essays in Honor of H. David Rosenbloom 22 (Georg Kofler et al. eds, IBFD 2021) who argues that the case can be regarded as a missed opportunity for an autonomous interpretation because the UK Supreme Court did not elaborate on the context but looked directly to the UK domestic law. *See*, for further disclosure on the case, Jonathan Schwarz, *Article 3(2) of the OECD and UN Models: An International View*, 76 Bull. Intl. Taxn. (2021) https://doi.org/10.59403/2qhxx6b.

18. Such would be the case if Art. 3(2) OECD MC would indeed construe the principle of the authoritativeness of domestic law. *See* in detail, Michael Lang, *Die Bedeutung des Musterabkommens und des Kommentars des OECD-Steuerausschusses für die Auslegung von Doppelbesteuerungsabkommen, in Aktuelle Entwicklungen im Internationalen Steuerrecht: Das neue Musterabkommen der OECD* 33 et seq. (Wolfgang Gassner et al. eds, 1994).
19. *See* Michael Lang, *Art. 3 Abs. 2 OECD-MA und die Auslegung von Doppelbesteuerungsabkommen*, 58 I.W.B. 287 (2011); Gloria, *supra* n. 4, at 975. *See also* Bernhard Gröhs & Christopher Herbst, *Die Interpretation von Doppelbesteuerungsabkommen als Problem der Auslegung von völkerrechtlichen Verträgen im nationalen Recht*, 11 Z.f.V. 22 (1986).
20. In the 1945 DTC between the United States and the United Kingdom, it has been codified in Art. II(3).
21. Apparently, it did not appear in the League of Nations Model Convention. *See* for further information, Kees van Raad, *1992 Additions to Articles 3(2) (Interpretation) and 24 (Non-discrimination) of the 1992 OECD Model and Commentary*, 20 Intertax 672 (1992) https://doi.org/10.54648/taxi1992095.
22. The National Archives, FO 93/8/206: Convention. Double Taxation: Deceased persons. (16 April 1945). Convention and Protocol. Double Taxation: Taxes on Income. (16 April 1945-6 June 1946). *See* John F. Avery Jones, *The United Kingdom's Influence on the OECD Model Tax Convention*, 56 B.T.R. 662 (2011); John F. Avery Jones, *Article 3(2) of the OECD Model Convention and the Commentary to It: Treaty Interpretation*, 33 E.T. 252 (1993). Before that, a similar provision was used in a domestic US regulation from 1940 relating to the tax treaty with Sweden from 1939 (US Regs. TD4975, 1940-2 Cum. Bull. 43.). It stated: 'Any word or term used in these Regulations which is not defined in the Convention but is defined in the Internal Revenue Code shall be given the definition therein.' *See also* John F. Avery Jones & Johann Hattingh, *Treaty Interpretation, in Global Tax Treaty Commentaries*, s. 1.2.2. and 1.2.3. (2021) who consider the modern Art. 3(2) OECD MC 'a natural progression from these'. However, it needs to be remembered that this US domestic rule does not contain the *context-requirement*.
23. John F. Avery Jones, *Chapter 6: The Interaction Between Tax Treaty Provisions and Domestic Law, in Tax Treaties and Domestic Law* 124 (Guglielmo Maisto ed., IBFD 2006).

Contracting Party relating to the taxes which are the subject of the present Convention.[24]

It has been argued that the United Kingdom had played a significant role in negotiating this provision; at least it is likely to have requested the phrase 'unless the context otherwise requires'.[25] Indeed, provisions similar to Article 3(2) OECD MC are deeply rooted in common law,[26] where they apparently are being used as a safeguard in contracts or statutes.[27] The phrase 'unless the context otherwise requires' was deemed necessary because of the strict interpretation of the wording of provisions by judges in common law countries.[28]

The historical documents relating to the 1945 DTC between the United Kingdom and the United States, however, do not reveal a detailed disclosure of its interpretation provision. It has not been mentioned in the Memorandum by the Chancellor of the Exchequer and its annex from 1 January 1945 which summarizes the discussions preceding the first formal draft of the treaty and primarily focuses on the occurrence of double taxation and the ways to resolve it based on the different types of income.[29] Therefore, it can be assumed that it has not been a central aspect of the negotiation process thus far. A draft was been prepared until 15 January 1945 by representatives of the contracting states[30] which most likely already included the interpretation provision of Article II(3) in its final form.[31] The comments from the United Kingdom on the draft

24. The same provision has been included in Art. II(2) of the 1945 DTC between the United States and the United Kingdom relating to taxes on the estates of deceased persons. It is argued that these provisions are modelled after Art. XIII of the 1944 DTC between the United States and Canada. *See* The National Archives, *Double Taxation Treaty Between United States and United Kingdom*, FO 44586, Nos 60 and 87 (first session) and FO 51679, No. 175 (second session). Article XIII of the 1944 DTC between the United States and Canada, however, did not mention a recourse on domestic law. This historic circumstance further stresses that the parties did not intend for an interpretation of treaty terms generally based on domestic law. The general resemblance of previous DTCs seems also to be the attitude of Mitchell B. Carroll towards the 1945 DTC between the United States and the United Kingdom. *See* The National Archives, *Hearing Before A Subcommittee of the United States Senate Seventy-Ninth Congress*, FO 44586, No. 129.
25. *See* John F. Avery Jones, *The Benefits of Article 3(2) of the OECD Model, in Essays on Tax Treaties: A Tribute to David A. Ward* 6 (Guglielmo Maisto et al. eds, IBFD 2014); Avery Jones, *The United Kingdom's Influence on the OECD Model Tax Convention*, *supra* n. 22, at 662.
26. *See* Rafael Tena Castro, *When Does 'the Context Otherwise Require' in Article 3 of the OECD Model Convention?*, 42 Intertax 714 (2014) https://doi.org/10.54648/taxi2014064.
27. *See* Michael Lang, *Tax Treaty Interpretation and Art 3 (2) OECD Model Convention, in Tax Treaty Interpretation in Light of the Vienna Convention on the Law of Treaties*, s. III. 1 (Robert Danon et al. eds, IBFD) forthcoming; Michael Lang, *Tax Treaty Interpretation: A Response to John Avery Jones*, 75 Bull. Intl. Taxn. 665 et seq. (2020) https://doi.org/10.59403/826m30.
28. *See* John F. Avery Jones et al., *The Origins of Concepts and Expressions Used in the OECD Model and Their Adoption by States*, 61 Bull. Intl. Taxn. 221 (2006); Klaus Vogel, *Klaus Vogel on Double Taxation Conventions* 169 (3d ed. 1996).
29. *See* The National Archives, *Double Taxation Discussions with United States: Communicates Copy of Cabinet Print W.P.(45) 1 of 1st January, 1945, Being a Memorandum by the Chancellor of the Exchequer Summarizing the Results of Discussions with the United States on Double Taxation*, FO 44585 Nos 6-8.
30. *See* The National Archives, *Negotiations for a Double Taxation Treaty with the United States, Message for Sir C. Gregg (BIR) from Mr. Willis*, FO 44585 No. 15.
31. Article II(3) of the draft from 16 March 1945 is most likely not altered by the numerous previous telegrams given that it is not being mentioned and resembles Art. II(3) of the final version of the

articles also do not mention the interpretation provision[32] nor the further amendments that had been requested during the negotiation process. There are also no handwritten remarks regarding the interpretation provision on the printed version of the treaty, which is different for several other treaty provisions.[33] In the Foreign Relations Committee's reports on the Death Duties Convention which provides extensive guidelines on the treaty provisions, only the following is stated regarding Article II(2) of the Convention between the USA and the UK With Respect to Taxes on Estates of Deceased Persons which is the same provision as Article II(3) in the corresponding income tax treaty: 'This article defines the terms "United States", "United Kingdom", "territory", and "tax", and provides that terms not defined in the convention shall have the meaning assigned to them in the laws of the respective countries unless the context of the convention otherwise requires.'[34] The Foreign Relations Committee's reports on the corresponding income tax treaty do not provide any disclosure on the interpretation provision of its Article II(3).[35] No information can further be found in the minutes of the first session of the Hearing Before a Subcommittee on Foreign Relations United States Senate for which the US negotiators and external experts were questioned by the US Senate on 23 May 1945 and 13 June 1945.[36] The same applies to the explanations and minutes of the second session of the Hearing Before a Subcommittee on Foreign Relations United States Senate from 17 April 1946.[37] Apparently, the contracting states did not focus on the treaty's interpretation provision and left the historic circumstances that led to its insertion vague.

Since its version of 1963,[38] the interpretation clause of Article 3(2) OECD MC has been contained in the Model Convention in which it stated at that time: 'As regards the application of the Convention by a Contracting State any term not otherwise defined shall, unless the context otherwise requires, have the meaning which it has under the laws of that Contracting State relating to the taxes which are subject of the Convention.' The reasons that led the Organisation for Economic Co-operation and Development

1945 DTC between the United States and the United Kingdom. *See* the National Archives, *Double Taxation Treaty Between United States and United Kingdom: Encloses Copy of Retyping of the Draft Convention Relating to the Avoidance of Double Taxation, with Respect to Taxes on Income, Being the Edition Numbered U.K./30/1/45 as Amended by Agreement Reached Through Exchange of Telegrams (numbers given)*, FO 44585, Nos 125-145.

32. *See* The National Archives, *Cypher From Foreign Office To Washington, February 16th, 1945*, FO 44585 Nos 46-48.
33. *See* The National Archives, *Double Taxation Treaties Between United Kingdom and the United States: Encloses Copy of the Agreement for the Printer*, FO 44586 Nos 8-38.
34. *See* The National Archives, *Technical Memorandum of the Treasury Department on the Convention with Respect to Taxes on Estates*, FO 44586, No. 97 (first session) and FO 51679 No.169 (second session).
35. *See* The National Archives, *Technical Memorandum of the Treasury Department on the Convention with Respect to Taxes on Income*, FO 44586, No. 80 (first session) and FO 51679 No.151 (second session).
36. *See* The National Archives, *Hearing Before a Subcommittee of the United States Senate Seventy-Ninth Congress*, FO 44586, Nos 108-150.
37. *See* The *National Archives, Hearing Before a Subcommittee of the United States Senate Seventy-Ninth Congress*, FO 51679, Nos 122-142.
38. OECD, *Model Tax Convention on Income and on Capital* (1963).

(OECD) to insert Article 3(2) into the Model Tax Convention in 1963 are also vague.[39] What is known is that there were no issues with inserting the provision into the OECD MC 1963.[40] It would have most likely been intensively discussed, however, if it was intended to fundamentally shape the interpretation of DTCs by confirming the authoritativeness of domestic law. Therefore, the present authors opine that it cannot be understood as departing from an autonomous interpretation of international treaties.[41] This fact is further supported by the vague circumstances regarding the insertion of its predecessor in the 1945 DTC between the United States and the United Kingdom. Additionally, its interpretation provision would have been thoroughly analysed if it was intended to state the authoritativeness of domestic law for treaty interpretation.

The wording has been subject to change twice.[42] In 1995,[43] it was changed to:

> As regards the application of the convention at any time by a contracting state, any term not defined therein shall, unless the context otherwise requires, have the meaning it has at that time under the law of that State for the purposes of the taxes to which the Convention applies, any meaning under the applicable tax laws of that State prevailing over a meaning given to the term under other laws of that State.

It can consequently be seen that the focus of the amendment involved timing issues regarding the application of domestic law. Moreover, a distinction between the domestic tax laws and the other domestic laws was added.

---

39. Only the following has been stated in the OECD Commentary from 1963: 'The rule of interpretation laid down in paragraph 2 corresponds to similar provisions normally appearing in double taxation Conventions. The rule of interpretation in paragraph 2 of Article 6 on the taxation of income from immovable property, which has to be regarded as "lex specialis" is in no way affected by the present general rule of interpretation.' This was also the proposition by Working Party 14 of the fiscal committee consisting of Austria and Sweden [FC/WP14(59)1]. The 1977 version of the OECD Commentary stated: 'This paragraph provides a general rule of interpretation in respect of terms used in the Convention but not defined therein.' Since its 1992 version, the Commentary provides guidelines on Art. 3(2) OECD MC that are more detailed.
40. Apparently, Art. 3(2) OECD started to gain international attention in the late 1970s. *See*, for that, van Raad, *supra* n. 21, at 672 who provides further references. *See also* Helmut Debatin, *Auslegungsmaximen zum Internationalen Steuerrecht*, 15 A.W.D. (1969). *See also* Lang, *DBA-Auslegung nach der Wiener Vertragsrechtskonvention versus nach Art. 3 Abs. 2 OECD-MA?, in Globalisiertes Steuerrecht: Anspruch und Verantwortung: Festschrift für Heinz-Klaus Kroppen*, *supra* n. 8, at 681.
41. *See* Lang, *Tax Treaty Interpretation and Art 3 (2) OECD Model Convention, in Tax Treaty Interpretation in Light of the Vienna Convention on the Law of Treaties*, *supra* n. 27, s. III. 1 forthcoming; Lang, *Chapter 22: Fowler v. Commissioners for Her Majesty's Revenue and Customs: Some Thoughts on Tax Treaty Interpretation*, *supra* n. 17, at 316; Lang, *Tax Treaty Interpretation: A Response to John Avery Jones*, *supra* n. 27, at 666; Lang, *Art. 3 Abs. 2 OECD-MA und die Auslegung von Doppelbesteuerungsabkommen*, *supra* n. 19, at 289; Michael Lang, *Die Bedeutung des originär innerstaatlichen Rechts für die Auslegung von Doppelbesteuerungsabkommen (Art. 3 Abs. 2 OECD-MA), in Aussensteuerrecht Doppelbesteuerungsabkommen und EU-Recht im Spannungsverhältnis: Festschrift für Helmut Debatin zum 70. Geburtstag* 289 (Gabriele Burmester & Dieter Endres eds, 1997).
42. *See*, for a detailed analysis of the changes in the 1992 OECD Commentary, van Raad, *supra* n. 21, at 6723 et seq. These changes have been crucial in implementing the ambulatory approach when referring to domestic law under Art. 3(2) OECD MC.
43. OECD, *Model Tax Convention on Income and on Capital* (1995).

Despite no changes in the wording of Article 3(2) OECD MC, the OECD Partnership Report from 1999[44] has been crucial to its understanding. In the corresponding changes to the OECD Model Commentary proposed by the OECD, what is referred to as the 'new approach' has been implemented by stating in the commentary regarding the method articles that the qualification of the source state should be regarded as decisive when it comes to a qualification conflict.[45]

The second change in the wording of Article 3(2) OECD MC occurred with the OECD MC 2017 which is also the most recent version. Due to this change, the phrase 'or the competent authorities agree to a different meaning pursuant to the provisions of Article 25' has been added after the phrase 'unless the context otherwise requires'. Apparently, recourse to domestic law should therefore not only not be taken when the context otherwise requires but rather also when the treaty parties establish a competent authority agreement by concluding a MAP.

Article 3(2) OECD MC is the object of controversial discussion in academia. Questions are being raised and discussed in particular regarding how Article 3(2) OECD MC relates to definitions in the treaty, what is meant by *context* and when it does otherwise require, and how the context exception relates to competent authority agreements. Further questions are which types of competent authority agreements are being covered, which states are actually applying the treaty, which areas of domestic law can be taken into account, and whether a static or an ambulatory approach is to be pursued when applying domestic law?[46]

3 THE ROLE OF DEFINITIONS

It can be deduced from the wording of Article 3(2) OECD MC that the recourse to domestic law is only relevant in cases where there is no definition of a term[47] in the

44. OECD, *The Application of the OECD Model Tax Convention to Partnerships* (1999).
45. The term 'qualification conflict' has been borrowed from international private law with certain modifications by Edgar Herzfeld, *Probleme des Internationalen Steuerrechts unter besonderer Berücksichtigung des Territorialitätsproblems und des Qualifikationsproblems*, 6 Vierteljahresschrift für Steuer und Finanzrecht 456 et seq. (Carl Heymanns Verlag) and refers to issues of interpretation regarding allocation rules in DTCs. *See* Michael Lang, *Qualification Conflicts, in Global Tax Treaty Commentaries*, s. 1.1 and 1.2 (2020). The OECD, in the development of the 'new approach', strongly differs between conflicts of interpretation and conflicts of qualification. *See*, in detail, s. 7 in this chapter.
46. *See* Frank A. Engelen, *Interpretation of Tax Treaties under International Law* 475 et seq. (IBFD 2004) who recapitulates some of the most eminent questions relating to Art. 3(2) OECD MC.
47. *See* John F. Avery Jones, *Chapter 3: Tax Treaties – The Perspective of Common Law Countries, in Courts and Tax Treaty Law* 73 et seq. (Guglielmo Maisto ed., IBFD 2007) who discusses what is meant by *term*. It is not to be understood as only referring to single words but also groups of words as has been elaborated on by Jasper Bossuyt, *The Legal Status of Extrinsic Instruments for the Interpretation of Tax Treaties* 1288 (IBFD 2021). *See also*, for the question whether the term under domestic law must be identical to the treaty term, Porus Kaka, *Judicial Evolution of the Relevance of Domestic Law and Article 3(2) in International Tax Jurisprudence, in Building Global International Tax Law: Essays in Honour of Guglielmo Maisto* 349 et seq. (Pasquale Pistone ed., IBFD 2022).

treaty itself.[48] It is also accepted in literature that recourse to domestic law does not occur if such a definition exists.[49]

However, DTCs contain different types of definitions.[50] The majority of those contained in the OECD MC are exhaustive definitions[51] indicating that they assign a certain meaning to a term,[52] and they can be identified as they contain the term 'mean'.[53] Such is the case for the terms 'company' (letter b), 'enterprise of a Contracting State' and 'enterprise of the other Contracting State' (letter d), 'international traffic' (letter e), 'competent authority' (letter f), 'national' (letter g), and 'recognised pension fund' (letter i) of Article 3(1). These terms should be considered to be defined in any case meaning that, whenever one of them applies, recourse to domestic law in accordance with Article 3(2) OECD MC may not be taken.[54] This applies even if a definition is not satisfactory itself[55] as is the case for the term 'enterprise'.[56]

According to Article 3(1) OECD MC, the term 'person' includes an individual, a company, and any other body of persons (letter a) and the term 'business' includes the performance of professional services and of other activities of an independent character (letter h). Evidently, 'include' is of a less definitive nature than 'mean' since it affords opportunities, for example, for the term 'person' to be construed as something other than an individual, for instance, a company and any other body of persons.[57] The term 'business' is based on the former Article 14 of previous Model Conventions dealing with independent personal services.[58] The intent behind it is to ensure that all income that was previously qualified under Article 14 is now to be done so under Article 7 OECD MC.[59] However, given that both the 'mean' and the 'include' definitions are elements of Article 3 OECD MC that are referred to as 'general definitions', the authors posit that it should, following a systematic interpretation, be prohibited to have recourse to domestic law whenever dealing with a term referred to in Article 3(1) OECD

48. *See* Lang, *Art. 3 Abs. 2 OECD-MA und die Auslegung von Doppelbesteuerungsabkommen, supra* n. 19, at 287. *See*, however, John F. Avery Jones, *Some Thoughts on Article 3(2), in Liber Amicorum Luc Hinnekens* 1 et seq. (Emile Bruylant, S.A. 2002) who advocates for expanding the role of domestic law in relation to treaty definitions.
49. *See* Helmut Debatin, *System und Auslegung der Doppelbesteuerungsabkommen*, 38 Der Betrieb, Beilage Nr. 23/85 5 (1985). *See* however Avery Jones, *The Benefits of Article 3(2) of the OECD Model, supra* n. 25, at 12 et seq. who states that some definitions should be eliminated in order to enhance the scope of Art. 3(2) OECD MC.
50. *See* Debatin, *Auslegungsmaximen zum Internationalen Steuerrecht, supra* n. 40, at 479 et seq.
51. Contra Richard X. Resch, *Tax Treaty Interpretation: A Response to Michael Lang*, 66 B.T.R. 608 et seq. (2021).
52. *See* Lang, *Tax Treaty Interpretation and Art 3 (2) OECD Model Convention, in Tax Treaty Interpretation in Light of the Vienna Convention on the Law of Treaties, supra* n. 27, s. III. 4.
53. *Ibid.*
54. *Ibid.*
55. *See* Michael Lang, *DBA und Personengesellschaften: Grundfragen der Abkommensauslegung*, 16 IStR 609 (2007).
56. *See* Daniel Dürrschmidt, *Zu Art. 3 Abs. 1 Buchst. c und d, in DBA: Doppelbesteuerungsabkommen*, para. 40 (Klaus Vogel & Moris Lehner eds, Verlag C.H. Beck oHG 7th ed.).
57. *See* John F. Avery Jones et al., *The Interpretation of Tax Treaties with Particular Reference to Article 3(2) of the OECD Model: I*, 29 B.T.R. 21 (1984).
58. *See* Lang, *Tax Treaty Interpretation and Art 3 (2) OECD Model Convention, supra* n. 27, s. III. 4.
59. *See* Lang, *Tax Treaty Interpretation: A Response to John Avery Jones, supra* n. 27, at 661.

MC.[60] Both types of definitions are within the meaning of Article 3(2) OECD MC which means that the existence of a non-exhaustive definition would also prevent having recourse to domestic law.[61] The same should apply to exhaustive definitions in other parts of the DTC as they are contained in Articles 5, 11(3), and 12(2) OECD MC.[62]

Since all of the abovementioned definitions rely on other terms, the question arises as to how those should be interpreted; at some level, any definition relies on terms not being defined themselves.[63] Given the fact that they are defined in a DTC-autonomous manner, it can be concluded that also the defining terms are to be interpreted in the same manner. This is the case because only if the defining terms are also interpreted this way, without recourse to domestic law, a uniform meaning of the DTC not depending on domestic law can be ensured.[64] A non-uniform meaning of a defined term would be in direct conflict with the purpose of the definitions which is to ensure such a uniform and autonomous meaning.

In several cases, elements of the general definitions in Article 3(1) OECD MC are also found in the distributive rules. For example, the terms 'ship' and 'aircraft' are used to define 'international traffic' in Article 3(1)(e) OECD MC, however, they are also being used in Articles 6(2), 8(1), 13(3), 15(3), and 22(3) OECD MC. Considering that terms defined in Article 3(1) OECD MC or in other definitions or used in those definitions do not permit a recourse to domestic law, this must also apply to the terms used in other parts of the DTC.[65] Otherwise, the interpretation would be inconsistent within it.

Somewhat special cases are Article 6(2) and Article 10(3) OECD MC since they are tied to a qualification in domestic law.[66] Particularly striking is the definition in Article 6(2) OECD MC in which a distinction is even made between the first and the

60. Another opinion is favoured by Avery Jones et al., *The Interpretation of Tax Treaties with Particular Reference to Article 3(2) of the OECD Model: I*, *supra* n. 57, at 21, who state that domestic law can be used to complete the definition.
61. This is also argued by Wassermeyer & Drüen, *supra* n. 2, para. 74. Arguing differently is Dirk Pohl, *Artikel 3 Allgemeine Begriffsbestimmungen, in DBA Kommentar*, para. 69 (Jens Schönfeld & Xaver Ditz eds, Verlag Dr Otto Schmidt KG 2d ed. 2019). *See also* Avery Jones & Hattingh, *supra* n. 22, s. 4.3.2.2. who contend that such an interpretation would be too literal, and it needs to be distinguished between exhaustive definitions and non-exhaustive definitions.
62. Article 11(3) OECD MC 1963 contained a definition tied to a domestic law qualification. Since the OECD MC 1977, however, the term 'interest' is defined autonomously. *See* Michael Lang, *Hybride Finanzierungen im Internationalen Steuerrecht* 91 et seq. (Wirtschaftsverlag Dr. Anton Orac 1991).
63. *See* Debatin, *System und Auslegung der Doppelbesteuerungsabkommen*, *supra* n. 49, at 5 et seq.; Debatin, *Auslegungsmaximen zum Internationalen Steuerrecht*, *supra* n. 40, at 480 et seq.
64. *See* Lang, *Tax Treaty Interpretation and Art 3 (2) OECD Model Convention, in Tax Treaty Interpretation in Light of the Vienna Convention on the Law of Treaties*, *supra* n. 27, s. III. 4; Lang, *Tax Treaty Interpretation: A Response to John Avery Jones*, *supra* n. 27, at 661.
65. *See* Lang, *Tax Treaty Interpretation and Art 3 (2) OECD Model Convention*, *supra* n. 27, s. III. 4; Lang, *Tax Treaty Interpretation: A Response to John Avery Jones*, *supra* n. 27, at 661.
66. *See* Debatin, *Auslegungsmaximen zum Internationalen Steuerrecht*, *supra* n. 40, at 481; Debatin, *System und Auslegung der Doppelbesteuerungsabkommen*, *supra* n. 49, at 5 discusses this type of definitions in detail. *See also* Lang, *Tax Treaty Interpretation and Art 3 (2) OECD Model Convention*, *supra* n. 27, s. III.4 forthcoming; Lang, *Die Bedeutung des originär innerstaatlichen Rechts für die Auslegung von Doppelbesteuerungsabkommen (Art. 3 Abs. 2 OECD-MA)*, *supra* n. 41, at 298 et seq.

second sentence.[67] The first sentence states that domestic law is prevailing and also binds the other state when defining immovable property.[68] However, it is indicated in the second sentence that, notwithstanding the first sentence, there is immovable property in some situations even if the qualification under domestic law would differ.[69] The key difference between a definition that refers to domestic law and the interpretation of an undefined term based on domestic law is that a definition that refers to the domestic law of one state is binding to both states.[70] The fact that the OECD decided to specifically reference domestic law in these cases may indicate that this reference should generally not be taken in other cases since, otherwise, those in the abovementioned cases would be superfluous.[71]

4 WHEN DOES THE CONTEXT *REQUIRE* AN AUTONOMOUS INTERPRETATION?

In the event that a term is not defined in a tax treaty, it does not mean that there is no possible interpretation binding for both contracting states.[72] According to Article 3(2) OECD MC, recourse to domestic law for interpreting that term can only be taken unless the context otherwise requires.[73] What the context requires is therefore crucial when determining whether recourse to domestic law may be taken. This question is subject to a controversial debate and is deeply connected to the question of which states can be considered to apply the treaty.[74] On the one hand, it is argued that the term should be read narrowly, almost as if it did not exist, and the domestic law meaning should be applied to treaty terms.[75] On the other hand, it is argued that the term should be read

67. *See* for a detailed analysis of Art. 6(2) OECD MC Michael Lang, *The Relation Between Tax Treaty Law and National Law in the Definition of Immovable Property under Article 6(2) of the OECD Model, in Immovable Property under Domestic Law, EU Law and Tax Treaties*, s. 5.3 (Guglielmo Maisto ed., IBFD 2015).
68. *See* Debatin, *Auslegungsmaximen zum Internationalen Steuerrecht, supra* n. 40, at 481.
69. For further examples, *see* Lang, *Die Bedeutung des originär innerstaatlichen Rechts für die Auslegung von Doppelbesteuerungsabkommen (Art. 3 Abs. 2 OECD-MA), supra* n. 41, at 298 et seq.
70. *See* Debatin, *Auslegungsmaximen zum Internationalen Steuerrecht, supra* n. 40, at 481 et seq.; Debatin, *System und Auslegung der Doppelbesteuerungsabkommen, supra* n. 49, at 5.
71. *See* Dürrschmidt, *Zu Art. 3 Abs. 1 Buchst. c und d, in DBA: Doppelbesteuerungsabkommen, supra* n. 56, para. 125b, who however rejects this argument in the end; Lang, *DBA-Auslegung nach der Wiener Vertragsrechtskonvention versus nach Art. 3 Abs. 2 OECD-MA?, in Globalisiertes Steuerrecht: Anspruch und Verantwortung: Festschrift für Heinz-Klaus Kroppen, supra* n. 8, at 680 et seq.; Lang, *Tax Treaty Interpretation: A Response to John Avery Jones, supra* n. 27, at 667; Lang, *Art. 3 Abs. 2 OECD-MA und die Auslegung von Doppelbesteuerungsabkommen, supra* n. 19, at 289; Wolfgang Gassner & Michael Lang, *Double Non-Taxation of a Belgian Tax Law Professor Lecturing in Vienna, in Liber Amicorum Luc Hinnekens* 227 (Emile Bruylant, S.A. 2002).
72. *See* Debatin, *Auslegungsmaximen zum Internationalen Steuerrecht, supra* n. 40, at 482 et seq.
73. 'Otherwise' means an autonomous interpretation. *See* Dürrschmidt, *Zu Art. 3 Abs. 1 Buchst. c und d, in DBA: Doppelbesteuerungsabkommen, supra* n. 56, para. 116b.
74. *See*, for the latter question, s. 7 in this chapter.
75. *See* John F. Avery Jones et al., *The Interpretation of Tax Treaties with Particular Reference to Article 3(2) of the OECD Model: II*, 29 B.T.R. 106 (1984) who appear to adhere to that approach.

as indicating an autonomous interpretation.[76] It is even argued that the meaning of the term 'context' cannot be determined at all and that it should only be based on whether 'something else is required'.[77]

Historical reasons, precisely the common law tradition as mentioned above, could be used as an advocate for not leaning towards the autonomous interpretation at first sight.[78] However, given the vague historical circumstances of how the interpretation clause was adopted into the OECD MC and how its predecessor became part of the 1945 DTC between the United States and the United Kingdom, it is to be assumed that no paradigm shift was intended for the interpretation of tax treaties.[79] Its insertion into the respective treaty and the OECD MC would have been a much more significant factor during the negotiations if such a fundamental change was intended for tax treaty interpretation.[80] Reading the phrase as generally not leaning towards an autonomous interpretation would also lead to domestic law being referred to frequently in the interpretation of DTCs which could also lead to qualification conflicts.

Additionally, it needs to be considered that the phrase 'unless the context otherwise requires' is also found in Article 3(1) OECD MC stating general definitions which could also indicate that the phrase might be only of insignificant relevance.[81] It is indeed difficult to imagine that a definition would be disregarded because the context would require such.[82] However, it must be acknowledged that the phrase is not part of the definitions in Articles 6(2)[83] and 10(3) OECD MC. Furthermore, the 'context' in Article 3(2) has a different function than the one in Article 3(1) OECD MC because the former is the gatekeeper of preventing double taxation or double non-taxation whereas this would not be a problem in the latter.[84] It could also be argued that the reference to

Ottmar Bühler, *Prinzipien des Internationalen Steuerrechts* 60 et seq. (Internationales Steuerdokumentationsbüro Amsterdam, C.H. Beck'sche Verlagsbuchhandlung 2d ed. 1965) argues that each of the two contracting states should interpret terms based on its domestic law.

76. Recently Lang, *Tax Treaty Interpretation and Art 3 (2) OECD Model Convention, in Tax Treaty Interpretation in Light of the Vienna Convention on the Law of Treaties, supra* n. 27.
77. *See* Gloria, *supra* n. 4, at 978.
78. *See* Lang, *Tax Treaty Interpretation and Art 3 (2) OECD Model Convention, supra* n. 27, s. III. 1 forthcoming; Lang, *Tax Treaty Interpretation: A Response to John Avery Jones, supra* n. 27, at 665; Avery Jones et al., *The Interpretation of Tax Treaties with Particular Reference to Article 3(2) of the OECD Model: II, supra* n. 75, at 90 et seq.
79. *See* Lang, *Art. 3 Abs. 2 OECD-MA und die Auslegung von Doppelbesteuerungsabkommen, supra* n. 19, at 289; Lang, *Die Bedeutung des Musterabkommens und des Kommentars des OECD-Steuerausschusses für die Auslegung von Doppelbesteuerungsabkommen, supra* n. 18, at 35 et seq.
80. *See also* s. 2 in this chapter.
81. *See* Bossuyt, *supra* n. 47, at 1316 et seq.
82. *See* Lang, *Tax Treaty Interpretation: A Response to John Avery Jones, supra* n. 27, at 666. *See*, for example, when the context requires definitions of Art. 3(1) OECD MC to not be referred to Avery Jones & Hattingh, *supra* n. 22, s. 5.1.2.3.
83. *See*, for the relation between Art. 6(2) OECD MC and Art. 3(2) OECD MC, Working Party N°14 of the Fiscal Committee (Austria and Sweden), *Report on General Provisions to Be Inserted in Conventions for the Avoidance of Double Taxation*, Received 25 February 1959, FC/WP14(59)1 10 (3 March 1959); Working Party N°14 of the Fiscal Committee (Austria and Sweden); *Report on the Article on Definitions*, FC/WP14(61)1 2 (9 January 1961).
84. *See* Lang, *Tax Treaty Interpretation: A Response to John Avery Jones, supra* n. 27, at 666.

the 'context' in Article 3(1) OECD MC indicates a high importance of the context since it could even take precedence over a definition.[85]

It is further being argued that requiring the context to indicate an autonomous interpretation only in rare cases combined with a frequent recourse to domestic law would facilitate administrative practice. This would allow tax authorities to be able to work primarily with their own domestic law of which they have the most knowledge.[86]

Reading Article 3(2) OECD MC to confirm the importance of the context of the treaty leads to the predominance of autonomous interpretations. This is because recourse to domestic law is taken only in the rare cases when the context of the tax treaty does not provide an interpretation[87] and therefore places substantial emphasis on the context[88] that should be primarily regarded.[89] This view considers Article 3(2) OECD MC as a confirmation of the general rules of legal interpretation that have been codified in the VCLT for international conventions.[90]

In general, however, an interpretation based on the context of the tax treaty will make it possible to determine the meaning of a treaty provision.[91] It is pointed out in literature that in both tax treaty law and domestic law, the interpretation of unclear provisions based on their wording, systematic considerations, object, and purpose as well as their historic development is the everyday work of a lawyer who is usually successful when employing all of these interpretation methods.[92]

The object and purpose of tax treaties, i.e., the allocation of taxing rights between the contracting states eventually leading to preventing double taxation and, in some cases, unintended double non-taxation,[93] endorse a broad interpretation of the term

85. *See* Lang, *Die Bedeutung des originär innerstaatlichen Rechts für die Auslegung von Doppelbesteuerungsabkommen (Art. 3 Abs. 2 OECD-MA)*, *supra* n. 41, at 289 et seq.
86. *See* Helmut Loukota, *Der Ministerialentwurf für ein DBA-Durchführungsgesetz*, 7 S.W.I. 285 et seq. (1997); Helmut Loukota, *Internationale Steuerfälle* 187 et seq. (Verlag Orac Ges. m. b. H. & Co KG 1989); Helmut Loukota, *Über das Verhältnis zwischen internationalem und nationalem Recht*, 16 F.J. 107 (1976).
87. *See* Lang, *Die Bedeutung des Musterabkommens und des Kommentars des OECD-Steuerausschusses für die Auslegung von Doppelbesteuerungsabkommen*, *supra* n. 18, at 34.
88. *See* Gröhs & Herbst, *supra* n. 19, at 23 et seq.
89. *See, inter alia*, Lang, *Art. 3 Abs. 2 OECD-MA und die Auslegung von Doppelbesteuerungsabkommen*, *supra* n. 19, at 287; Michael Lang, *Doppelbesteuerungsabkommen und Innerstaatliches Recht* 108 et seq. (Wirtschaftsverlag Dr. Anton Orac 1992); Michael Lang, *Die Einwirkungen der Doppelbesteuerungsabkommen auf das innerstaatliche Recht*, 28 F.J. 72 et seq. (1988); Debatin, *System und Auslegung der Doppelbesteuerungsabkommen*, *supra* n. 49, at 5.
90. *See* Lang, *Tax Treaty Interpretation: A Response to John Avery Jones*, *supra* n. 27, at 668; Lang, *Art. 3 Abs. 2 OECD-MA und die Auslegung von Doppelbesteuerungsabkommen*, *supra* n. 19, at 287.
91. *See* Lang, *Tax Treaty Interpretation and Art 3 (2) OECD Model Convention, in Tax Treaty Interpretation in Light of the Vienna Convention on the Law of Treaties*, *supra* n. 27, s. III.2; Lang, *Tax Treaty Interpretation: A Response to John Avery Jones*, *supra* n. 27, at 668.
92. *See* Lang, *Tax Treaty Interpretation: A Response to John Avery Jones*, *supra* n. 27, at 668; Lang, *Art. 3 Abs. 2 OECD-MA und die Auslegung von Doppelbesteuerungsabkommen*, *supra* n. 19, at 287 et seq.; Vogel, *Problems of the Interpretation of Tax Treaties*, *supra* n. 15, at 111; Lang, *Die Bedeutung des originär innerstaatlichen Rechts für die Auslegung von Doppelbesteuerungsabkommen (Art. 3 Abs. 2 OECD-MA)*, *supra* n. 41, at 303 et seq.
93. *See* Lang, *Introduction to the Law of Double Taxation Conventions*, *supra* n. 3, at 1 et seq.; Klaus Vogel, *Das oberste österreichische Steuergericht erklärt Verluste bei DBA-Freistellung für abzugsfähig*, 11 IStR 93 (2002).

'context' leading to an autonomous interpretation.[94] Tax treaties can only prevent double taxation or double non-taxation when the source state and the residence state apply them identically.[95] If, however, both states recur to their domestic law, these situations may occur[96] indicating that a way needs to be determined to prevent both states from simultaneously applying their domestic law. The present authors opine that the simplest way this could be achieved is by forwarding an autonomous interpretation that can only be concluded in the majority of the cases if the context is understood broadly.

Even if there was a desire to take recourse to domestic law, an autonomous interpretation needs to be conducted at the first level.[97] What is meant by a term in a treaty must be understood in order to enable finding a comparable concept in domestic law.[98] At that point, the interpretation can be kept entirely autonomous, and there are sound reasons to do so.[99] This is especially the case when a treaty is concluded in a language that is different from the language of the domestic law.[100] J.F. Avery Jones and J. Hattingh explain how to proceed in such a case on the example of interpreting 'term': 'As domestic law will not be written in the third (or sole other) language, there

94. *See* Lang, *Art. 3 Abs. 2 OECD-MA und die Auslegung von Doppelbesteuerungsabkommen, supra* n. 19, at 287; Lang, *Die Bedeutung des Musterabkommens und des Kommentars des OECD-Steuerausschusses für die Auslegung von Doppelbesteuerungsabkommen, supra* n. 18, at 34; Lang, *Die Bedeutung des originär innerstaatlichen Rechts für die Auslegung von Doppelbesteuerungsabkommen (Art. 3 Abs. 2 OECD-MA), supra* n. 41, at 301 et seq.; *See* Debatin, *System und Auslegung der Doppelbesteuerungsabkommen, supra* n. 49, at 6 f.; Michael Lang, *Die Auslegung von Doppelbesteuerungsabkommen als Problem der Planungssicherheit bei grenzüberschreitenden Sachverhalten, in Handbuch der internationalen Steuerplanung* 1873 et seq. (Siegfried Grotherr ed., 3d ed. 2011). The latter states that an autonomous interpretation following a broad understanding of the term 'context' would enhance planning certainty. *See also* Lang, *DBA-Auslegung nach der Wiener Vertragsrechtskonvention versus nach Art. 3 Abs. 2 OECD-MA?, in Globalisiertes Steuerrecht: Anspruch und Verantwortung: Festschrift für Heinz-Klaus Kroppen, supra* n. 8, at 680. This is also already the conclusion by Herzfeld, *supra* n. 45, at 470 who has introduced the term 'qualification conflict' to international tax law: 'A particular problem construes the problem here in discussion [i.e. conflicts of qualification] in the law of international treaties, especially Double Taxation Conventions, also with regard to tax law concepts; it would be in accordance with the object and purpose of the treaty to determine uniform connecting concepts wherever possible; the principles established for unilateral domestic rules must be taken into account alternatively.'

95. *See* Lang, *DBA und Personengesellschaften: Grundfragen der Abkommensauslegung, supra* n. 55, at 609; *See* Lang, *Die Bedeutung des originär innerstaatlichen Rechts für die Auslegung von Doppelbesteuerungsabkommen (Art. 3 Abs. 2 OECD-MA), supra* n. 41, at 285 et seq. Arguing in this context is also Michael Beusch, ... *Wenn Der Zusammenhang nichts Anderes erfordert: Art. 3 Abs. 2 OECD MA in der jüngeren Rechtsprechung der Schweizer Gerichte, in Panoptikum des Steuerrechts: Festschrift für Madeleine Simonek* 226 (Peter Hongler & Marc Vogelsang eds, Stämpfli Verlag 2024).

96. *See* Jörg Manfred Mössner, *Klaus Vogel Lecture 2009: Comments*, 65 Bull. Intl. Taxn. 19 (2010) https://doi.org/10.59403/3504fbv.

97. *See* Lang, *Tax Treaty Interpretation and Art 3 (2) OECD Model Convention, in Tax Treaty Interpretation in Light of the Vienna Convention on the Law of Treaties, supra* n. 27, s. III. 2.

98. *Ibid.*

99. *See* Lang, *Tax Treaty Interpretation: A Response to John Avery Jones, supra* n. 27, at 661 et seq.

100. This issue can be portrayed based on the DTC between Austria and Tunisia (Convention between the Republic of Austria and the Republic of Tunisia for the Avoidance of Double Taxation with Respect to Taxes on Income and Capital [23 June 1977], Treaties & Models IBFD). The only official language is French. *See* for further elaboration *ibid.*, at 662.

will never be an identical word in domestic law and it is essential to give meaning to 'term' that conveys the equivalent concept.'[101] However, to find an equivalent concept in the other language, any term first needs to be interpreted autonomously.[102] This may also occur in situations when the relevant languages are English or French, however, domestic law just does not use the same wording as the treaty.[103]

It has been argued against this that would it not be required to find a comparable construct of an autonomous interpretation in domestic law because '[treaty] negotiators choose the terms they use for a reason, namely, because they hint at the essential characteristics of what is to be implied'.[104] The present authors submit that this may be the case when the contracting states include terms in the tax treaty that are not part of the OECD Model Convention but are recognizable constructs of the legal systems of only one of the two states. In such a situation, the domestic law background is taken into account when interpreting the term. This is not the case, however, because the context does not require otherwise. Instead, in such a situation, the context rather does require taking recourse to domestic law which then forms part of the context.[105] An example would be what is known as the 'silent partnership' (stille Gesellschaft) that is familiar to the German and Austrian legal system.[106] For example, in the United Kingdom and the United States, there is no equivalent concept.[107] However, this can only apply when the contracting states have referred to a recognizable construct of their domestic law deliberately and thereby *hint* at it and not when they have done it without planning to do so. Whether they have done so deliberately is again the matter of interpretation.[108] However, when the treaty negotiators decide to adhere to the wording of the OECD MC for certain parts of the treaty, they intentionally do not refer to specific domestic terminology. Thereby, they *hint* at an autonomous interpretation.

In the case of *Thiel*, the High Court of Australia accordingly ruled that recourse to domestic Australian law could not be taken in accordance with a treaty provision modelled after Article 3(2) OECD MC regarding the terms 'enterprise' and 'profits' 'because these words had no established meaning under the laws relating to Australian income tax'.[109] Therefore, the terms had to be interpreted autonomously which

101. *See* Avery Jones & Hattingh, *supra* n. 22, s. 4.3.2.1.
102. *See* Gloria, *supra* n. 4, at 975 et seq.
103. *See* Lang, *Tax Treaty Interpretation and Art 3 (2) OECD Model Convention, supra* n. 27, s. III. 2.
104. *See* Resch, *Tax Treaty Interpretation: A Response to Michael Lang, supra* n. 51, at 615.
105. Lang, *Tax Treaty Interpretation and Art 3 (2) OECD Model Convention, supra* n. 27, s. III. 2; Lang, *Art. 3 Abs. 2 OECD-MA und die Auslegung von Doppelbesteuerungsabkommen, supra* n. 19, at 289 et seq.
106. *See* Lang, *Tax Treaty Interpretation and Art 3 (2) OECD Model Convention, supra* n. 27, s. III. 2; Michael Lang & Veronika Daurer, *Doppelbesteuerungsabkommen Österreich-Slowenien: Kommentar* 28 et seq. (Linde Verlag Ges. m.b.H. 2015); Michael Lang & Karin Simader, *Doppelbesteuerungsabkommen Österreich-Kroatien* 47 et seq. (Linde Verlag Ges. m.b.H. 2013).
107. *See*, for a detailed analysis of the occurrence of silent partnerships in different legal systems, Peter Jung, *§3 Wurzeln der stillen Gesellschaft und Stellung im ausländischen Recht, in Handbuch Stille Gesellschaft* 31 et seq. (Peter Blaurock ed., 8th ed. 2016).
108. Other examples would be profit-sharing loans (partiarische Darlehen) and profit-sharing bonds (partiarische Anleihen). *See*, for that, Daniela Hohenwarter, *Chapter 7: Austria, in Tax Treaties and Domestic Law* 177 et seq. (Guglielmo Maisto ed., IBFD 2006).
109. *Thiel v. Federal Commissioner of Taxation*, No. 171 CLR 338 (High Court 22 August 1990).

indicates that this is possible after all since an interpretation must always be found, and domestic law is apparently not always of assistance even if when referred to. Therefore, if an autonomous interpretation is always possible and even if arguing in favour of the authoritativeness of domestic law inevitable in some cases (when the context requires such), there would be no criticism if conducting an autonomous interpretation in any case.[110] This argument is stressed further by examining what would happen if changes were made to domestic law. If a term once had a comparable concept in domestic law that is, however, changed during time, it would mean that the previous interpretation based on domestic law would have to be disregarded if Article 3(2) OECD MC was to be regarded as referring to domestic law at the time the treaty was being applied.[111]

When following the autonomous interpretation, domestic law is still of relevance; however, not due to the fact that it would be not possible but rather because the context indeed required recourse to domestic law as part of the autonomous interpretation.[112] It is the role of domestic law to create taxing rights and the role of a tax treaty to restrict the taxing rights under domestic law to prevent double taxation or attribute taxing rights to prevent an unintended form of double non-taxation.[113] Therefore, only a person liable to tax under domestic law can be the beneficiary of a tax treaty in the first place meaning that there is a nexus between domestic tax law and tax treaty law.[114] This is the case, however, because the context of the treaty requires such a nexus.[115]

It is sometimes argued in academic writing that an interpretation of Article 3(2) OECD MC, that indicates the autonomous interpretation of treaty terms, would violate the principle of effectiveness[116] according to which 'treaties are to be interpreted with reference to their declared or apparent objects and purposes'.[117] The autonomous

110. Lang, *Tax Treaty Interpretation and Art 3 (2) OECD Model Convention, supra* n. 27, s. III. 2.
111. *See* s. 8 in this chapter.
112. *See* Lang, *Art. 3 Abs. 2 OECD-MA und die Auslegung von Doppelbesteuerungsabkommen, supra* n. 19, at 287 et seq.; Michael Lang, *The Significance of National Tax Law in Interpreting and Applying Double Taxation Treaties*, 9 S.W.I. 67 et seq. (1999); Lang, *Die Bedeutung des originär innerstaatlichen Rechts für die Auslegung von Doppelbesteuerungsabkommen (Art. 3 Abs. 2 OECD-MA), supra* n. 41, at 301 et seq.; *See* Debatin, *Auslegungsmaximen zum Internationalen Steuerrecht, supra* n. 40, at 481 et seq.
113. *See* Lang, *Die Bedeutung des originär innerstaatlichen Rechts für die Auslegung von Doppelbesteuerungsabkommen (Art. 3 Abs. 2 OECD-MA), supra* n. 41, at 296 et seq.; Debatin, *Auslegungsmaximen zum Internationalen Steuerrecht, supra* n. 40, at 483 et seq.; Lang, *The Significance of National Tax Law in Interpreting and Applying Double Taxation Treaties, supra* n. 112, at 67 et seq.
114. *See* Lang, *The Significance of National Tax Law in Interpreting and Applying Double Taxation Treaties, supra* n. 112, at 67 et seq.; Lang, *Die Bedeutung des originär innerstaatlichen Rechts für die Auslegung von Doppelbesteuerungsabkommen (Art. 3 Abs. 2 OECD-MA), supra* n. 41; *See* Debatin, *Auslegungsmaximen zum Internationalen Steuerrecht, supra* n. 40, at 483 et seq.
115. *See* Lang, *Art. 3 Abs. 2 OECD-MA und die Auslegung von Doppelbesteuerungsabkommen, supra* n. 19, at 287 et seq.; Lang, *The Significance of National Tax Law in Interpreting and Applying Double Taxation Treaties, supra* n. 112, at 67 et seq.
116. *See* Bossuyt, *supra* n. 47, at 1316; Resch, *Tax Treaty Interpretation: A Response to Michael Lang, supra* n. 51, at 608.
117. Oliver Dörr, *Part III Observance, Application and Interpretation of Treaties, Section 1 Interpretation of Treaties, Article 31. General Rule of Interpretation, in Vienna Convention on the Law of Treaties: A Commentary* 565 (Oliver Dörr & Kirsten Schmalenbach eds, Springer 2d ed. 2020); the author also provides examples from ICJ-jurisprudence.

interpretation aligns with the overall object and purpose of a tax treaty as double taxation is prevented by it. This interpretation in fact confirms the principle of effectiveness instead of neglecting it. The interpretation presented here is also in accordance with the second dimension of the principle of effectiveness according to which provisions should not be interpreted in a way that would render them meaningless[118] but rather to have significance.[119] With this approach, Article 3(2) OECD MC can be considered a genuine link between a tax treaty and the VCLT and therefore has a function in such a way as to confirm that the interpretation principles codified in the VCLT are applicable for interpreting DTCs that would not necessarily be the case otherwise. This means that the approach for interpreting Article 3(2) OECD MC presented here does not render Article 3(2) OECD MC ineffective and therefore aligns with the principle of effectiveness.

Between the two positions presented above, a mediatory approach exists that has been developed by K. Vogel[120] and relies on the wording of the provision of Article 3(2) OECD MC and particularly the term 'require'.[121] According to this approach, not every possible interpretation based on the context of the treaty should take precedence over one based on domestic law. Only if strong and convincing arguments, therefore not any arguments, would advocate for an interpretation based on the context of the treaty and against one based on domestic law should the context be regarded as to 'require' otherwise.[122] The term 'require' is differentiated from the term 'indicate'.[123] However, since the latter is not used in the OECD MC, such a comparison is not necessarily valid.[124] The wording 'require' would also allow an interpretation under which the

118. *See* Bossuyt, *supra* n. 47, at 1316; Resch, *Tax Treaty Interpretation: A Response to Michael Lang, supra* n. 51, at 608.
119. *See also* with further references for the two dimensions of the principle of effectiveness, Edwin van der Bruggen, *Unless the Vienna Convention Otherwise Requires: Notes on the Relationship Between Article 3(2) of the OECD Model Tax Convention and Articles 31 and 32 of the Vienna Convention on the Law of Treaties*, 43 E.T. 146 (2003).
120. *See* Klaus Vogel, *Doppelbesteuerungsabkommen und ihre Auslegung (II)*, 61 StuW 297 et seq. (1982); Vogel & Prokisch, *supra* n. 5, at 81. *See also* Avery Jones et al., *The Interpretation of Tax Treaties with Particular Reference to Article 3(2) of the OECD Model: II, supra* n. 75, at 108. This mediatory approach is also favoured by Jörg Manfred Mössner, *Zur Auslegung von Dopelbesteuerungsabkommen, in Law of Nations Law of International Organizations World's Economic Law: Liber amicorum honouring Ignaz Seidl-Hohenveldern* 426 (Karl-Heinz Böckstiegel et al. eds, Carl Heymanns Verlag KG 1988) with slight modifications.
121. *See* Dürrschmidt, *Zu Art. 3 Abs. 1 Buchst. c und d, in DBA: Doppelbesteuerungsabkommen, supra* n. 56, para. 71; Vogel & Prokisch, *supra* n. 5, at 81.
122. *See* Vogel, *Doppelbesteuerungsabkommen und ihre Auslegung (II), supra* n. 120, at 297. *See also* Resch, *Tax Treaty Interpretation: A Response to Michael Lang, supra* n. 51, at 630 who even argues that an autonomous interpretation would need to be *absolutely necessary* for the context to require such. *See also* Wassermeyer & Drüen, *supra* n. 2, para. 82 who argue in a similar direction. As Harry A. Shannon, *United States Income Tax Treaties: Reference to Domestic Law for the Meaning of Undefined Terms*, 17 Intertax 461 (1989) https://doi.org/10.54648/taxi198 9089 points out, Art. 3(2) does not state 'unless the context yields no other, or absolutely no other, interpretation'.
123. *See* Vogel, *Doppelbesteuerungsabkommen und ihre Auslegung (II), supra* n. 120, at 297.
124. *See* Lang, *Tax Treaty Interpretation and Art 3 (2) OECD Model Convention, in Tax Treaty Interpretation in Light of the Vienna Convention on the Law of Treaties, supra* n. 27, s. III. 3; Lang, *Die Bedeutung des Musterabkommens und des Kommentars des OECD-Steuerausschusses für die Auslegung von Doppelbesteuerungsabkommen, supra* n. 18, at 35 et seq.; Lang, *Die*

states are 'required' to perform an autonomous interpretation whenever it is possible.[125] In general, it is at least questionable which significance can be attributed to 'require',[126] especially when giving preference to an autonomous interpretation.[127] The wording can therefore be considered inconclusive.[128]

Even if attempting to derive from the wording of Article 3(2) OECD MC that the reference to domestic law was the rule and taking into account the context was the exception, it would not necessarily lead to the conclusion that the general rule should be interpreted broadly and the exception should be interpreted only restrictively.[129] Rather, they constitute two separate rules that could either be interpreted narrowly or broadly.[130] This fact therefore also does not prohibit an extensive interpretation of the term 'context' according to the present authors as it just states that both rules may have a different scope of application.

Some authors mention the 'unless' condition that they distinguish from the German translation 'wenn der Zusammenhang nichts anderes erfordert'.[131] It is argued that 'unless' has a different meaning than 'wenn … nicht' that is proverbially translated as 'if … not' with the former indicating a priority of the general rule over the exception and the latter not doing so.[132] The present authors posit that this linguistic subtlety cannot lead to the fundamentally different results in interpretation especially given the

Bedeutung des originär innerstaatlichen Rechts für die Auslegung von Doppelbesteuerungsabkommen (Art. 3 Abs. 2 OECD-MA), *supra* n. 41, at 288 et seq.

125. *See* Lang, *Tax Treaty Interpretation and Art 3 (2) OECD Model Convention*, *supra* n. 27, s. III. 3.
126. *See* Lang, *Die Auslegung von Doppelbesteuerungsabkommen als Problem der Planungssicherheit bei grenzüberschreitenden Sachverhalten*, *supra* n. 94, at 1876; Maarten J. Ellis, *The Influence of the OECD Commentaries on Treaty Interpretation: Response to Prof. Dr Klaus Vogel*, 55 Bull. Intl. Taxn. 617 (2000).
127. *See* Gloria, *supra* n. 4, at 971 et seq.
128. In this respect, the common law tradition of Art. 3(2) OECD MC and especially 'unless the context otherwise requires' need to be considered: The latter phrase appears to have been used interchangeably with phrases such as 'unless the contrary intention appears' (*see*, for that, Avery Jones et al., *The Origins of Concepts and Expressions USED in the OECD Model and Their Adoption by States*, *supra* n. 28, at 221) and, therefore, the same normative substance can be attributed to both of them. Therefore, the term 'require' cannot be considered changing the interpretation of DTCs in the way that the mediatory approach would suggest.
129. Lang, *Tax Treaty Interpretation and Art 3 (2) OECD Model Convention*, *supra* n. 27, s. III. 3. A diverging view is represented by John F. Avery Jones, *Article 3(2) and Conflicts of Qualification: A View from the Other End of the Spectrum*, *in Tax Treaty Interpretation in Light of the Vienna Convention on the Law of Treaties* (Robert Danon et al. eds, Wolters Kluwer 2024) forthcoming who states that considering the rule and the exception as equal or putting even further emphasis on the rule would mean to 'put the cart before the horse'.
130. *See* Lang, *Tax Treaty Interpretation and Art 3 (2) OECD Model Convention*, *supra* n. 27, s. III. 3.
131. BMF, *OECD-Musterabkommen 2003 zur Vermeidung der Doppelbesteuerung auf dem Gebiet der Steuern vom Einkommen und vom Vermögen*, BMF-Schreiben vom 18 February 2004 – IV B 6 S 1315 – 8/04 (Berlin: BMF, 2004), Art. 3(2). *See also* Richard X Resch, *Tax Treaty Interpretation: The Meaning and Application of Article 3(2)* 103 et seq. (tredition 2020).
132. *See* Avery Jones, *Article 3(2) and Conflicts of Qualification: A View from the Other End of the Spectrum*, *supra* n. 129 forthcoming; Resch, *Tax Treaty Interpretation: A Response to Michael Lang*, *supra* n. 51, at 629.

fact that the OECD apparently seems to use 'unless' and 'if ... not' interchangeably.[133] The Commentary states, 'the domestic law meaning of an undefined term applies only if the context does not require an alternative interpretation'.[134] Therefore, 'unless' and 'if ... not' cannot be understood as having a different meaning, at least in the given context. Another interpretation would not be in accordance with the approach followed by the OECD itself.

Interpreting the 'context' restrictively and the portrayed mediatory approach come with the danger of enhancing instead of preventing situations of double taxation and should therefore be disregarded.

5 THE MEANING OF THE TERM 'CONTEXT' IN ARTICLE 3(2) OECD MC

Now that it has been established that the phrase 'unless the context otherwise requires' should be understood as giving preference to an interpretation based on the context of the treaty, the question then arises as to what 'the context' actually means.

The concept of context is a means of interpretation that is also known to the VCLT. Article 31(1) and (2) of the VCLT state the following:

> 1. A treaty shall be interpreted in good faith in accordance with the ordinary meaning to be given to the terms of the treaty in their context and in the light of its object and purpose.
> 2. The context for the purpose of the interpretation of a treaty shall comprise, in addition to the text, including its preamble and annexes:
>   (a) any agreement relating to the treaty which was made between all the parties in connection with the conclusion of the treaty;
>   (b) any instrument which was made by one or more parties in connection with the conclusion of the treaty and accepted by the other parties as an instrument related to the treaty.

Given the same wording, it is sometimes being argued that the context in Article 3(2) OECD MC should be equated with that in Article 31 VCLT.[135] However, such an equation is not convincing: Article 3(2) OECD MC does not explicitly refer to the VCLT in any case[136] which means that the two 'contexts' can also be distinguished from each other, and there are favourable reasons for doing so.[137] J.F. Avery Jones et al. state:

---

133. This has been stressed by Avery Jones, *Article 3(2) and Conflicts of Qualification: A View from the Other End of the Spectrum*, *supra* n. 129.
134. OECD, *Commentary on Article 3 Concerning General Definitions*, Model Tax Convention on Income and on Capital, para. 11 (2017).
135. Gröhs & Herbst, *supra* n. 19, at 24 argue that the two 'contexts' should be considered the same. *See also* Vogel, *Doppelbesteuerungsabkommen und ihre Auslegung (II)*, *supra* n. 120, at 297 who argues (own translation): 'The "context" includes, in particular, the relevant provisions of both national legal systems, the MC and the MC Commentary, in addition to the contractual deed and any additional documents, but within the framework of the principles on the interpretative significance of the MC.'
136. This has been stressed by Gloria, *supra* n. 4, at 976.
137. *See* Vogel, *Doppelbesteuerungsabkommen und ihre Auslegung (II)*, *supra* n. 120, at 297; Manfred Mössner, *Zur Auslegung von Dopelbesteuerungsabkommen*, *supra* n. 120, at 425. *See also* Lang, *Tax Treaty Interpretation: A Response to John Avery Jones*, *supra* n. 27, at 667.

> Applying the Vienna context definition to the expression 'unless the context otherwise requires' would make no sense because the Vienna context was not meant to be used in isolation from these other factors.[138]

E. van der Bruggen even points out that some may argue that the phrase unless the context otherwise requires 'may lead to an absurd result if "context" is taken to have the same meaning as in Art. 31 of the VCLT, because Art. 3(2) is part of what international law considers "context" (to the term in dispute) in the first place'.[139] He further states:

> It is highly unlikely that Art. 3(2) can be understood in a way that would exclude all other rules of interpretation, now codified in the VCLT. To see the domestic renvoi as a *lex specialis* which displaces the Vienna rules would not only be highly irregular (and thus a suspect interpretation), but it would also lead to inconsistencies in the treaty text itself. In addition, it would mean that such fundamental notions as 'good faith', the principle of effectiveness and the general principles of international law must be deemed to have been 'contracted out' of the tax treaty. It would also mean that the tax treaties may apparently not be explained with reference to supplementary means of interpretation. Within the text of the provision, all this can only be avoided if 'context' in Art. 3(2) is given such a wide meaning that it would include all the elements and instruments of Art. 31 and 32 of the VCLT.[140]

'Context' within the meaning of Article 3(2) OECD MC should therefore be understood as referring to all interpretation methods applicable under international law, precisely Articles 31 to 33 of the VCLT, and not – as it is sometimes argued – only the 'context' in the VCLT.[141] Otherwise, DTCs would not be able to fulfil their object and purpose.[142]

Regarding the equation of the context in Article 3(2) OECD MC with all of the interpretation methods in the VCLT, a restriction must be made: In the case of tax law, which is more invasive into the legal sphere of individuals than in other fields of law,[143] caution needs to be exercised when dealing with subsequent agreements and practices disclosed in Article 31(3) VCLT.[144] In many jurisdictions, the rule of law is particularly

138. *See* Avery Jones et al., *The Interpretation of Tax Treaties with Particular Reference to Article 3(2) of the OECD Model: II*, *supra* n. 75, at 104.
139. *See* van der Bruggen, *supra* n. 119, at 144.
140. *Ibid.*, at 154 et seq.
141. *See* Lang, *Die Bedeutung des originär innerstaatlichen Rechts für die Auslegung von Doppelbesteuerungsabkommen (Art. 3 Abs. 2 OECD-MA)*, *supra* n. 41, at 288. *See also* with further references Lang, *Die Bedeutung des Musterabkommens und des Kommentars des OECD-Steuerausschusses für die Auslegung von Doppelbesteuerungsabkommen*, *supra* n. 18, at 34 et seq. *See also* Lang, *Tax Treaty Interpretation: A Response to John Avery Jones*, *supra* n. 27, at 667; Lang, *Die Auslegung von Doppelbesteuerungsabkommen als Problem der Planungssicherheit bei grenzüberschreitenden Sachverhalten*, *supra* n. 94, at 1876.
142. *See* Lang, *Die Bedeutung des Musterabkommens und des Kommentars des OECD-Steuerausschusses für die Auslegung von Doppelbesteuerungsabkommen*, *supra* n. 18, at 34 et seq.; Vogel & Prokisch, *supra* n. 5, at 82 et seq.
143. *See* Vogel & Prokisch, *supra* n. 5, at 57.
144. *See* Michael Lang, *Aussagen des VfGH zur Auslegung von Doppelbesteuerungsabkommen*, 25 S.W.I. 569 et seq. (2015); Lang, *Die Auslegung von Doppelbesteuerungsabkommen als Problem der Planungssicherheit bei grenzüberschreitenden Sachverhalten*, *supra* n. 94, at 1870 et seq.;

important in tax law stressing the importance of being able to predict legal consequences which may be even higher in tax law than in other legal areas.[145] This needs to be considered when interpreting tax treaties because it would counteract the requirement of a high degree of determination if the content of norms could be altered relatively easily by subsequent agreements and practice. Therefore, subsequent agreements and practice should only be applied restrictively when interpreting tax treaties and therefore only be a minor factor as part of the context in Article 3(2) OECD MC.

6 THE RELATION BETWEEN THE CONTEXT AND COMPETENT AUTHORITY AGREEMENTS

Under this broad understanding of the term 'context', the question arises whether competent authority agreements resulting from MAPs could be part of the context. For the older Model Conventions, this might be the case.[146] Beginning with the OECD MC 2017, however, the wording has changed as MAPs are mentioned separately thereby indicating a paradigm shift in the understanding of the 'context' in Article 3(2) OECD MC.[147]

As has been stated above while paraphrasing the historic development of Article 3(2) OECD MC, the OECD MC 2017 introduced the possibility of competent authority agreements preventing recourse to domestic law under Article 3(2) OECD MC. This stipulation originated with the US tax treaty policy.[148] According to the OECD Commentary, the reason for this change was the following:

Michael Lang, *Wer hat das Sagen im Steuerrecht? Die Bedeutung des OECD-Steuerausschusses und seiner Working Parties*, 59 ÖStZ 208 et seq. (2006); Lang, *Die Bedeutung des Musterabkommens und des Kommentars des OECD-Steuerausschusses für die Auslegung von Doppelbesteuerungsabkommen*, *supra* n. 18, at 25 et seq. *See also* Franz & Drüen, *supra* n. 2, para. 79 who even argue that subsequent agreements and practices cannot be taken into account for interpreting DTCs because it would otherwise violate the (German) constitution.

145. *See*, for the legal situation in Austria, Heinz Peter Rill & Benjamin Kneihs, *Art 18 Abs 1-2 B-VG, in Rill-Schäfer-Kommentar Bundesverfassungsrecht*, paras 51 et seq. (Benjamin Kneihs & Georg Lienbacher eds, 31st ed. 2023); Michael Potacs, *'Wirtschaftliche Betrachtungsweise' als steuerrechtliches Interpretationsprinzip, in Steuerwissenschaften und betriebliches Rechnungswesen: Strukturen – Prinzipien: Neuerungen: Festschrift für Herbert Kofler zum 60. Geburtstag* 150 et seq. (Sabine Urnik et al. eds, Linde Verlag Ges. m.b.H. 2009); Lang, *Doppelbesteuerungsabkommen und innerstaatliches Recht*, *supra* n. 89, at 86 et seq.; Hans Georg Ruppe, *Legalitätsprinzip und Abgabenrecht, in Steuerbilanzreform und Verfassungsrecht* 43 et seq. (Wolfgang Gassner & Eduard Lechner eds, Wirtschaftsverlag Dr Anton Orac 1991st ed.). In Germany, arguments have been brought forward in a similar direction by Diana Beck, *Qualifikationskonflikte im Internationalen Steuerrecht: Ursachenanalyse, Systematisierung und Lösungskonzepte* 134 (SpringerGabler 2016).
146. This is Alexander Rust's opinion as has been stated by Jacques Sasseville, *The 2017 Change to Article 3(2) of the OECD Model: Comments on Professor Alexander Rust's Presentation*, 75 Bull. Intl. Taxn. 282 (2020) https://doi.org/10.59403/3crn35f.
147. *See* Michael Lang, *Die Bedeutung von Verständigungsvereinbarungen Nach Art. 3 Abs 2 OECD Musterabkommen 2017, in Territorialität und Personalität: Festschrift für Moris Lehner* 220 (Roland Ismer et al. eds, Verlag C.H. Beck oHG 2019).
148. *See* in detail Johann Hattingh, *Dangerous Transplantation: Importing Big Government into Article 3(2) of the OECD Model Tax Convention, in Dispute Resolution under Tax Treaties and Beyond* 206 et seq. (Guglielmo Maisto ed., IBFD 2023).

> In 2017, the wording of paragraph 2 was amended to remove any doubt that in case where a mutual agreement reached under Art 25 indicates that the competent authorities have agreed on a common meaning of an undefined term, the domestic law meaning of that term would not be applicable, as is the case when a term is defined in the Convention or when the context requires a meaning that is different from the domestic law meaning.[149]

Apparently, it is meant to clarify that MAPs have always been an option. The OECD Commentary has stated since 1995: 'States that are able to enter into mutual agreements (under the provisions of Article 25, and, in particular paragraph 3 thereof), that establish the meanings of terms not defined in the Convention should take those agreements into account in interpreting those terms.'[150]

However, prior to the amendment in 2017, there was no legal basis for considering competent authority agreements as results of MAPs for interpreting DTCs. Therefore, they could, at best, only have been regarded as subsequent agreements under Article 31(3)(a) VCLT with only a minor role for interpretation.[151] Whether such a qualification could be possible is questionable.[152] In any case, however, the context requirement takes precedence.

The competent authorities are also not allowed under the new legislation to disregard an interpretation based on the context.[153] Therefore, only if there is no definition contained in the treaty and its context, thus every interpretation method of the VCLT with the abovementioned limitations fails to provide an interpretation, competent authority agreements resulting from MAPs can be decisive, especially in court.[154]

Another question arises regarding the reference to competent authority agreements, i.e., under which type of MAP of Article 25 OECD MC the agreement needs to be reached.[155] Article 25(3) OECD MC states: 'The competent authorities of the Contracting States shall endeavour to resolve by mutual agreement any difficulties or

149. OECD, *Commentary on Article 3 Concerning General Definitions*, *supra* n. 134, para. 13.2.
150. *Ibid.*, s. 13.2.
151. *See* Jürgen Romstorfer, *Besteuerung Schweizer AHV-Renten aus einer früheren öffentlich-rechtlichen Beschäftigung nach dem DBA Schweiz*, 33 S.W.I. 576 et seq. (2023); Lang, *Art. 3 Abs. 2 OECD-MA und die Auslegung von Doppelbesteuerungsabkommen*, *supra* n. 19, at 283 et seq.
152. *See* in detail Ch. 6 in this book.
153. *See* Lang, *Die Bedeutung von Verständigungsvereinbarungen nach Art. 3 Abs 2 OECD Musterabkommen 2017*, *in Territorialität und Personalität: Festschrift für Moris Lehner*, *supra* n. 147, at 221.
154. Compare Debatin, *Das neue Doppelbesteuerungsabkommen mit den USA (Teil 1)*, 43 D.B. 603 (1990); Lang, *Die Bedeutung von Verständigungsvereinbarungen Nach Art. 3 Abs 2 OECD Musterabkommen 2017*, *supra* n. 147, at 221.
155. There are three types of MAPs under Art. 25 OECD MC: Agreement procedures understood in a narrower sense concluded to prevent double taxation or double non-taxation in singular cases under Art. 25(1) and (2) OECD MC; consultation procedures for the amicable resolution of difficulties and doubts arising in the interpretation of DTCs under Art. 25(3), first sentence OECD MC; and supplementary procedures to avoid cases of double taxation not addressed by the treaty per se. *See* for an overview, Klaus-Dieter Drüen et al., *OECD-MA 2017 Art. 25*, *in Doppelbesteuerung: Kommentar zu allen Doppelbesteuerungsabkommen*, paras 4 et seq. (Franz Wassermeyer et al. eds, Verlag C.H. Beck oHG 2020); *see also* Romstorfer, *supra* n. 151, at 571 et seq.

doubts arising as to the interpretation or application of the Convention. They may also consult together for the elimination of double taxation in cases not provided for in the Convention.' J.F. Avery Jones concluded in 2018 that the MAP under Article 25(3) first sentence OECD MC is the only type that is being referenced in Article 3(2) OECD MC: 'Since this paragraph contains the only reference to interpretation in article 25, it is difficult to see that any other part of this article could be relevant.'[156] While this is certainly correct insofar as this is the most likely scenario in which a MAP is concluded for resolving an interpretation issue,[157] regard also needs to be taken to the fact that Article 3(2) OECD MC references Article 25 OECD MC in general and not only its paragraph 3. Therefore, MAPs according to Article 25(1) and (2) OECD MC could also be covered by the reference in Article 3(2) OECD MC.[158] This is supported by the OECD Commentary: 'Some states, however, consider that this exception should only be applicable in mutual agreements reached under paragraph 3 of Article 25; these states are free to replace the phrase "pursuant to the provisions of Article 25" by "pursuant to the provisions of paragraph 3 of Article 25".' Accordingly, if states have not changed the default reference to Article 25 OECD MC in Article 3(2) OECD MC, they acknowledge that MAPs that have been concluded for singular cases on the basis of Article 25(1) and (2) OECD MC are to be taken into consideration for interpreting a DTC.[159]

MAPs that have been concluded for singular cases do not have to be extended for the purpose of Article 3(2) OECD MC.[160] States are free to decide on an extension but are not obligated to do so.[161] In the event that states have decided not to do so, the reference of Article 3(2) OECD MC would still cover it. This can be deduced from the abovementioned phrase of the commentary that states are allowed to restrict the reference in Article 3(2) OECD MC to MAPs conducted under Article 25(3) OECD MC. This solution has a disadvantage insofar as equal cases may be treated differently only based on the fact that a MAP under Article 25(1) and (2) OECD MC has been conducted in one case but not in the other.[162] However, taxpayers can avoid such a situation by requesting another MAP that may lead to the same solution[163] or they can achieve their equal treatment in an arbitration procedure under Article 25(5) OECD MC. Despite not being explicitly mentioned in Article 3(2) OECD MC, arbitration decisions under Article

156. John F. Avery Jones, *Tax Treaty Interpretation*, Global Tax Treaty Commentaries, s. 4.3.3. (2018) as quoted in Lang, *Die Bedeutung von Verständigungsvereinbarungen nach Art. 3 Abs 2 OECD Musterabkommen 2017*, *supra* n. 147, at 222. However, this is no longer stated in the most recent version of the GTTC. *See* Avery Jones & Hattingh, *supra* n. 22, s. 4.3.3.
157. *See* Dietmar Gosch, *Über die Auslegung von Doppelbesteuerungsabkommen*, 2 I.S.R. 92 (2013).
158. *See* Daniel Dürrschmidt, *Zu Art. 3 Abs. 2, in DBA: Doppelbesteuerungsabkommen*, para. 122a (Klaus Vogel & Moris Lehner eds, Verlag C.H. Beck oHG 7th ed.).
159. *See* Lang, *Die Bedeutung von Verständigungsvereinbarungen nach Art. 3 Abs 2 OECD Musterabkommen 2017*, *supra* n. 147, at 222.
160. Another opinion has been presented for Art. 3 para. 2 US MC 1981 similar to Art. 3(2) OECD MC in its 2017 version by Shannon, *supra* n. 122, at 461.
161. *See* Lang, *Die Bedeutung von Verständigungsvereinbarungen nach Art. 3 Abs 2 OECD Musterabkommen 2017*, *supra* n. 147, at 223 et seq.
162. *Ibid.*
163. *Ibid.*

25(5) OECD MC are also covered by the reference. This results from the fact that arbitration under Article 25(5) OECD MC has to be implemented through a MAP.[164]

MAPs based on singular cases under Article 25 (1) and (2) OECD MC come with a lack of transparency since other taxpayers, possibly in similar situations, probably are not aware that one has been concluded and are therefore not able to rely on its results. The competent authorities should therefore consider conducting a MAP under Article 25(3) OECD MC in order to provide clarity exceeding the singular case.[165] These MAPs should also be published in order to ensure the clarity necessary to be regarded under Article 3(2) OECD MC.[166]

In summary, the amendment is only of little significance because if, as the present authors suggest, the term 'context' is interpreted broadly, the cases in which recourse needs to be taken to domestic law are already extremely rare. Therefore, only in extraordinary cases will competent authority agreements be relevant. However, they will form another barrier[167] before recourse can be taken to domestic law.[168]

7 APPLICATION OF THE TREATY

The highly controversial question at issue lies in the inconspicuously seeming first part of Article 3(2) OECD MC that reads as follows: 'As regards the application of the Convention at any time by a Contracting State'. Of key importance is the word 'application'. When both the source state and the residence state are considered applying the treaty, they are both allowed to take recourse to their domestic law and define terms according to it.[169] Inevitably, this would lead to possible qualification conflicts, meaning that both states treat a term differently when considering taxation, eventually leading to double taxation (positive qualification conflict) or double non-taxation (negative qualification conflict).[170] Both of these situations should be avoided by DTCs. As a result, several approaches have been developed in academic writing attempting to do so.

For instance, it is argued that only the source state should be considered to apply a DTC[171] which would evidently prevent qualification conflicts. If only the source state

164. *See ibid.*, at 223.
165. *See ibid.*, at 224.
166. *See* Frank P. G. Pötgens & Elene M.L. Kool, *The Status of Mutual Agreement Between the Netherlands and Germany on the Allocation of Severance Payments*, 58 E.T. 530 (2018).
167. *See* Dürrschmidt, *Zu Art. 3 Abs. 2, in DBA: Doppelbesteuerungsabkommen*, *supra* n. 158, para. 122.
168. *See* Lang, *DBA-Auslegung nach der Wiener Vertragsrechtskonvention versus nach Art. 3 Abs. 2 OECD-MA?, in Globalisiertes Steuerrecht: Anspruch und Verantwortung: Festschrift für Heinz-Klaus Kroppen*, *supra* n. 8, at 682.
169. This issue was identified in literature long ago. *See*, for example, Helmut Debatin, *Qualifikationsprobleme im Doppelbesteuerungsrecht*, 35 (62) F.R. (1979); *See also* Gloria, *supra* n. 4.
170. *See* Gloria, *supra* n. 4, at 971.
171. *See* Avery Jones, *Article 3(2) of the OECD Model Convention and the Commentary to It: Tretay Interpretation*, *supra* n. 22, at 255 who has argued there that the differences in interpretation

is considered to apply a DTC, it may subsequently take recourse to its domestic law. If, however, only one state can apply its domestic law, qualification conflicts cannot occur because there are no different qualifications that could possibly impose one. It is – at least initially – being argued by J.F. Avery Jones that two steps are performed by the residence state:

> first, checking whether the source state has taxed the income in accordance with the treaty, which merely involves the residence state reading, not applying the treaty; and secondly, granting credit or exemption, which involves the residence state doing something which it would not have done apart from the treaty. There is little doubt that, on any basis, in the second step, by granting credit or exemption, the residence state does apply the treaty, but the categorization of the income is not relevant to this stage. [...] [The] residence state is not applying the treaty when making this check on whether the taxation in the source state is in accordance with the treaty. It is not doing anything as a result of the treaty; it is merely reading the treaty to see if someone else, the source state, has applied the treaty correctly.[172]

It is further stated that the object and purpose of tax treaties may forward this approach given the abovementioned possible situations of double taxation and double non-taxation when considering both states as applying the treaty.[173]

According to E. van der Bruggen, the wording might support this view: 'The strongest argument is, however, found in the fact that Art. 3(2) refers to "application by a contracting state" and not by both contracting states.'[174] However, even J.F. Avery Jones admits that a 'literal reading is that both states apply their own domestic law in relation to an undefined type of income'.[175] The wording therefore does not suggest a clear interpretation. It is even controversial among scholars with English as their native language.[176]

Regarding the wording, it needs to be taken into account that Article 3(2) OECD MC refers not only to the application of the (entire) treaty but also the distributive rules which means that, even though the source state is addressed by the distributive rules

may have arisen due to differences between the English 'to apply' and the German 'anwenden'. The present authors opine that the issue is not caused by this distinction.

See also John F. Avery Jones, *Qualification Conflicts: The Meaning of Application in Art 3 (2) of the OECD Model, in Festschrift für Karl Beusch zum 68. Geburtstag am 31. Oktober 1993*, 47 et seq. (Heinrich Beisse et al. eds, Walter De Gruyter & Co 1993).

172. Avery Jones, *Article 3(2) of the OECD Model Convention and the Commentary to It: Tretay Interpretation, supra* n. 22, at 255; Avery Jones et al., *The Interpretation of Tax Treaties with Particular Reference to Article 3(2) of the OECD Model: I, supra* n. 57, at 50 et seq. According to Resch, *Tax Treaty Interpretation: A Response to Michael Lang, supra* n. 51, at 615 this position is no longer adhered to by J.F. Avery Jones 'because his overall position has been reformulated several times over the decades'.
173. *See* John F. Avery Jones, *A Fresh Look at Article 3(2) of the OECD Model*, 75 Bull. Intl. Taxn. 657 (2020) https://doi.org/10.59403/xgw0x3.
174. *See* van der Bruggen, *supra* n. 119, at 144.
175. *See* Avery Jones, *A Fresh Look at Article 3(2) of the OECD Model, supra* n. 173, at 657.
176. *See* Philip Baker, *The Interpretation of Double Taxation Conventions, in Double Taxation Conventions*, para. E.21 (Sweet & Maxwell 3d ed. 2001).

and may be regarded as the only state applying them, it not necessarily is the only state applying the treaty as such.[177] Whenever the residence state grants a credit or exemption under the method article, it must take recourse to the distributive rules and thereby also apply them.[178] Therefore, also the residence state needs to be considered applying the treaty. The division of the DTC into distributive rules and the method article indicates that there are indeed two addressees (source state and residence state) and, consequently, also two states applying the treaty.[179]

Another argument that has been developed and proposed by R. Resch is the fact that the contracting states apply the treaty in different roles and at different points in time (known as the 'temporal logic of tax treaties').[180] The source state is the first state to qualify the income and therefore the first applicant of the treaty which means that the term is already defined at the time the residence state applies the method article.[181] It will therefore apply the treaty according to the qualification of the source state unless the context otherwise requires.[182] Nevertheless, it is clear that, even when employing the credit method, taxes may still be computed separately in each state. There is no chronological order. The tax authorities of the residence state are not at all required to wait with their assessment until the tax in the source state is levied. If the latter is determined or imposed at a later time, the assessment in the residence state must be modified accordingly. With the exemption method, the priority of the source state is not taken into account as both states operate independently thereby allowing them to calculate and assess taxes autonomously.[183]

Therefore, the present authors suggest that both states be considered applying the treaty, which is also argued in academic writing.[184] Accordingly, K. Vogel defines application as 'any decision by a tax authority or a court on a tax issue for which the treaty is (or should be) applied. The exemption of income under the treaty is also its "application", as is the decision that the treaty in a particular case is not to be

177. *See* Jörg Manfred Mössner, *Auslegung von Doppelbesteuerungsabkommen: Auf Ein Neues!, in Festschrift für Jürgen Lüdicke* 487 et seq. (Dietmar Gosch et al. eds, Verlag C.H. Beck oHG 2019).
178. *See* Dürrschmidt, *Zu Art. 3 Abs. 2, in DBA: Doppelbesteuerungsabkommen, supra* n. 158, paras 65 et seq. who argues that exempting income from taxation in accordance with the exemption method also construes the application of a treaty; Klaus Vogel, *Doppelbesteuerungsabkommen als Anwendungsgebiet des Allgemeinen Völkervertragsrecht, in Recht zwischen Umbruch und Bewahrung* 1155 et seq. (Ulrich Beyerlin et al. eds, Springer 1995).
179. *See* Gosch, *supra* n. 157, at 93.
180. *See* Resch, *Tax Treaty Interpretation: A Response to Michael Lang, supra* n. 51, at 620 et seq.
181. *Ibid.*, at 622.
182. *Ibid.*
183. *See* Lang, *Tax Treaty Interpretation: A Response to John Avery Jones*, Taxn., *supra* n. 27, at 663.
184. *See* Debatin, *Auslegungsmaximen zum Internationalen Steuerrecht, supra* n. 40. *See also* for an overview Resch, *Tax Treaty Interpretation: The Meaning and Application of Article 3(2), supra* n. 131, at 29 et seq. and 91 et seq. who considers the assumption to be wrong.

applied'.[185] Therefore, in this perspective, it is not differentiated whether 'a treaty confirms or restricts the contracting state's rights to impose a tax'.[186]

The OECD has recognized this issue and dealt with it by implementing the 'new approach'[187] based on the assumption that the contracting states have to frequently take recourse to domestic law.[188] It relies on the method article (Article 23A and 23B OECD MC). The corresponding provisions in the Commentary state that the residence state should, when applying the method article, be obligated to grant relief for a qualification conflict and exempt the income or capital from taxation or credit it accordingly.[189] Apparently, the qualification of the source state is considered to be decisive under the method article and not under Article 3(2) OECD MC.[190]

Considering only one qualification as relevant under Article 23(1) OECD MC has the logical prerequisite that two qualifications exist. This also means that the OECD's 'new approach' regards both states as applying the DTC which is the key difference to considering only the source state as applying the treaty as has been the view in literature as presented above: 'If the OECD assumes that a conflict to be solved by article 23 of the OECD Model is at hand, it must also assume that article 3(2) also regards each of the two states as a state that applies the treaty.'[191]

However, it should be mentioned that the 'new approach' is also not convincing. First and foremost, it is unclear how the Commentary deduces the conclusion that 'the two Articles [Articles 23A and 23B OECD MC] require that relief from double taxation be granted by the State of residence notwithstanding the conflict of qualification resulting from these differences in domestic law'[192] from the wording 'income […] which may be taxed in the other Contracting State in accordance with the provisions of the Convention' in Article 23A(1) and Article 23B(1) OECD MC as it is not further

185. *See* Vogel, *Doppelbesteuerungsabkommen und Ihre Auslegung (II)*, *supra* n. 120, at 296. A similar definition is presented by Wassermeyer & Drüen, *supra* n. 2, para. 72 who state that the applying person does not matter and may include the taxpayer, his tax advisor, financial authorities, or courts. It is always applied when its wording is interpreted which can also happen as part of an academic work.
186. Vera Hellebrandt, *Chapter 4: Conflicts of Qualification under Article 23A(4)*, *in Exemption Method and Credit Method: The Application of Article 23 of the OECD Model* 111 (Georg Kofler et al. eds, IBFD 2022).
187. *See*, in detail, François Barreau & Rita Julien, *Conflicts of Qualification under Articles 23A(1) and 23B(1)*, *in Exemption Method and Credit Method: The Application of Article 23 of the OECD Model* 54 et seq. (Georg Kofler et al. eds, IBFD 2022).
188. *See* Lang, *Introduction to the Law of Double Taxation Conventions*, *supra* n. 3, at 30; Lang, *Art. 3 Abs. 2 OECD-MA und Die Auslegung von Doppelbesteuerungsabkommen*, *supra* n. 19, at 292; Michael Lang, *Qualifikationskonflikte im Recht der Doppelbesteuerungsabkommen*, *in Staaten und Steuern: Festschrift für Klaus Vogel zum 70. Geburtstag* 909 et seq. (C.F. Müller Verlag, Hüthig GmbH 2000). It has been proven that the cases mentioned in the Partnership Report could also be resolved by an autonomous interpretation. *See*, in detail, Michael Lang, *Application of the OECD Model Tax Convention to Partnerships: A Critical Analysis of the Report Prepared by the OECD Committee on Fiscal Affairs* (Linde Verlag Ges. m.b.H. 2000).
189. *See* OECD, *Commentary on Articles 23A and 23B Concerning the Methods for Elimination of Double Taxation*, Model Tax Convention on Income and on Capital, para. 32.3 (2017).
190. *See* Lang, *Tax Treaty Interpretation and Art 3 (2) OECD Model Convention*, *in Tax Treaty Interpretation in Light of the Vienna Convention on the Law of Treaties*, *supra* n. 27, s. II. 2.
191. *See* Lang, *Tax Treaty Interpretation: A Response to John Avery Jones*, *supra* n. 27, at 664.
192. *See* OECD, *Commentary on Articles 23A and 23B Concerning the Methods for Elimination of Double Taxation*, Model Tax Convention on Income and on Capital, *supra* n. 189, para. 32.3.

explained within the Commentary[193] and not stipulated by any linguistic reason.[194] Further, the 'new approach' distinguishes between cases in which the qualification of the source state is to be followed under the context of the treaty (conflict of interpretation that is not solved by the 'new approach')[195] and the cases in which the source state is required to refer to its domestic law (conflict of qualification that is solved by the 'new approach').[196] The distinction between these cases, however, is unclear because whether the context of the treaty requires a certain result can be raised in every case and will not be solved in most of them.[197] The 'new approach' also has its limits when dealing with closed distributive rules such as Article 19 OECD MC because, in such cases, no recourse is taken to the method article as only one state has an exclusive taxing right.[198] The present authors thus submit that the 'new approach' should therefore only be followed insofar as regarding both contracting states as applying the treaty.

193. *See* Gassner & Lang, *supra* n. 71, at 227; also Lang, *Art. 3 Abs. 2 OECD-MA und die Auslegung von Doppelbesteuerungsabkommen, supra* n. 19, at 292.
194. *See* Lang, *Tax Treaty Interpretation: A Response to John Avery Jones, supra* n. 27, at 664.
195. *See* OECD, *Commentary on Articles 23A and 23B Concerning the Methods for Elimination of Double Taxation*, Model Tax Convention on Income and on Capital, *supra* n. 189, para. 32.5. For these situations, Art. 23A(4) OECD MC has been introduced which applies in cases of double non-taxation as the result of a different interpretation or a different appreciation of facts.
196. *See ibid.*, para. 32.3. *See* Lang, *DBA und Personengesellschaften: Grundfragen der Abkommensauslegung, supra* n. 55, at 608; Lang, *Qualifikationskonflikte im Recht der Doppelbesteuerungsabkommen, in Staaten und Steuern: Festschrift für Klaus Vogel zum 70. Geburtstag, supra* n. 188, at 918 et seq.; *See also* Bossuyt, *supra* n. 47, at 1287.
197. *See* Lang, *Art. 3 Abs. 2 OECD-MA und die Auslegung von Doppelbesteuerungsabkommen, supra* n. 19, at 292; Lang, *DBA und Personengesellschaften: Grundfragen der Abkommensauslegung, supra* n. 55, at 608; Lang, *Qualifikationskonflikte im Recht der Doppelbesteuerungsabkommen, supra* n. 188, at 918 et seq. *See also* Michael Lang, *Zurechnungskonflikt bei Durchgriff durch eine Schweizer Gesellschaft*, 32 S.W.I. 119 et seq. (2022). Accordingly, a differentiation between conflicts of interpretation and conflicts of qualification should therefore not be drawn. This is especially the case because the term 'qualification conflict' is usually not being used as a legal term which means that there is no need for defining it exactly and distinguishing it from the other similar concepts. *See* Lang, *Qualification Conflicts, in Global Tax Treaty Commentaries, supra* n. 45, s. 1.2.
198. *See* Klaus Vogel, *Conflicts of Qualification: The Discussion Is Not Finished*, 58 Bull. Intl. Taxn. 43 (2003); van Raad, *supra* n. 21, at 672. This critique of the 'new approach' has been adapted by Alexander Rust, *The New Approach to Qualification Conflicts Has Its Limits*, 58 Bull. Intl. Taxn. 49 (2003). The latter references Vogel, *Klaus Vogel on Double Taxation Conventions, supra* n. 28, at 1259. He reasons from the proviso safeguarding progression contained in Art. 23A(3) and Art. 23B(2) that the OECD Model does not rule out the simultaneous application of complete distributive rules and Art. 23. *See also* John F. Avery Jones, *Conflicts of Qualification: Comment on Prof. Vogel's and Alexander Rust's Articles*, 58 Bull. Intl. Taxn. 184 et seq. (2003). The latter proposes amending Art. 23A(4) OECD MC in such a way that it should provide that neither Art. 23 nor Art. 18 or 19 require exemption by the residence state for exemption countries if the source state has exempted the income in question. For credit countries, he suggests including a new provision relieving the residence state of its obligation to grant an exemption under Art. 18 or 19 instead of a credit under Art. 23A in the case that the source state does not tax. *See*, for a detailed overview, Richard X. Resch, *May Be Taxed for Whatever Reason: Conflicts of Qualification: The Discussion Is Finished*, 48 Intertax (2020) https://doi.org/10.54648/taxi2020016 who argues that the 'new approach' is indeed suitable for also dealing with closed distributive rules.

8 THE RECOURSE TO DOMESTIC LAW

Based on the views presented by the present authors, recourse to domestic law in the interpretation of DTCs is only relevant if a term is not defined in the treaty itself, all methods of interpretation of the VCLT fail to provide an interpretation and the contracting states cannot agree on a common interpretation through a MAP. Domestic law therefore is only a minor factor for interpreting DTCs.[199] However, if recourse to domestic law does need to be taken in such a rare case, further questions arise, specifically which domestic laws could be taken into account and which timing is relevant, so a static or an ambulatory[200] approach.

Since 1995,[201] it has been explicitly mentioned in the OECD MC that the meaning of a term in domestic tax law should supersede a meaning in the other laws of that state that, however, should be considered when the term has no particular meaning in domestic tax laws.[202] Before that, however, the legal situation was the same so the explicit reference in the OECD MC can be considered superfluous.[203] It can be deduced from the system and the objective of tax treaties that tax laws should first be considered and other laws only after that.[204]

Despite all of the controversies surrounding Article 3(2) OECD MC, there was widespread agreement that domestic law, if applied after all, had to be applied following an ambulatory approach.[205] The current domestic legal situation applicable

199. *See* Lang, *Art. 3 Abs. 2 OECD-MA und die Auslegung von Doppelbesteuerungsabkommen, supra* n. 19, at 287; Michael Lang & Ursula Zieseritsch, *Der Begriff der unselbständigen Arbeit nach Art 15 OECD-MA, in Arbeitnehmer im Recht der Doppelbesteuerungsabkommen* 44 et seq. (Wolfgang Gassner et al. eds, Linde Verlag Ges. m.b.H. 2003); Lang, *Die Einwirkungen der Doppelbesteuerungsabkommen auf das innerstaatliche Recht, supra* n. 89, at 72 et seq.; Gröhs & Herbst, *supra* n. 19, at 24 et seq.
200. Or evolutionary approach as has been suggested by Bossuyt, *supra* n. 47, at 1297.
201. The amendment was part of the report *The 1995 Update to the Model Tax Convention* that was adopted by the OECD Council on 21 September 1995.
202. *See* Michael Lang, *Die Bedeutung der 1995 erfolgten Änderung des OECD-Musterabkommens und des Kommentars des OECD-Steuerausschusses für die Doppelbesteuerungsabkommen, in Die Weiterentwicklung des OECD-Musterabkommens* 34 (Michael Lang ed., Linde Verlag Ges. m.b.H.).
203. However, *see* Vogel, *Doppelbesteuerungsabkommen und ihre Auslegung (II), supra* n. 120, at 293 who states that only domestic laws about the precise tax to which the DTC can be considered.
204. *See* Lang, *Art. 3 Abs. 2 OECD-MA und die Auslegung von Doppelbesteuerungsabkommen, supra* n. 19, at 292.
205. *See* Lang, *Introduction to the Law of Double Taxation Conventions, supra* n. 3, at 29; Lang, *Art. 3 Abs. 2 OECD-MA und die Auslegung von Doppelbesteuerungsabkommen, supra* n. 19, at 287; Avery Jones, *Article 3(2) of the OECD Model Convention and the Commentary to It: Tretay Interpretation, supra* n. 22, at 253 et seq.; Michael Lang, *Verfassungsrechtliche Bedenken gegen die Verweisungsnormen in Doppelbesteuerungsabkommen*, 42 ÖStZ 13 (1989); Vogel, *Doppelbesteuerungsabkommen und ihre Auslegung (II), supra* n. 120, at 296; Avery Jones et al., *The Interpretation of Tax Treaties with Particular Reference to Article 3(2) of the OECD Model: I, supra* n. 57, at 25 et seq.; *see*, for a differentiating view, Gröhs & Herbst, *supra* n. 19, at 24 et seq. It is held that this approach enhances the functionality of the treaty and is not in violation of democratic principles as an ambulatory approach for referring to the commentary would be. *See* Hongler, *supra* n. 6, at 35.

to a certain case was therefore decisive but not the legal situation at the time of concluding the tax treaty.[206]

In a decision from 1982, known as the *Melford* case, the Canadian Supreme Court, however, followed a static approach.[207] Despite being swiftly 'rectified' by the Canadian authorities due to the Income Tax Conventions Interpretation Act (ITCIA),[208] the OECD has taken the opportunity to add the phrase 'at the time the treaty is being applied' into the treaty text of Article 3(2) OECD MC thereby making the ambulatory approach official. Apparently, stating the dynamic approach when applying domestic law explicitly in the 1992 version of the Commentary[209] and in Article 3(2) OECD MC 1995 has therefore only been a clarification following the *Melford* decision.

The present authors assert that clarifying provisions should generally be met with a healthy degree of scepticism. It is common practice in some states to describe provisions as clarifying in order to make it easier for this meaning to apply to facts that lie in the past.[210] However, this is only compatible to a limited extent with a prohibition of retroactivity known in many legal systems.[211] Whether the wording of an amendment is really only clarifying or whether it has a normative content can therefore only be determined by comparing the old with the new legal situation.[212] In the given situation, the Austrian Supreme Administrative Court has, regarding this change in the OECD MC, decided to only apply an ambulatory approach in the treaties including an explicit reference. The other treaties were considered following a static approach.[213] Here, the risk of clarifying amendments can be seen as it may lead courts to draw the conclusion that a clarifying amendment leads to a material change even though that was never intended.

206. *See*, for an exhaustive elaboration on this question, Bossuyt, *supra* n. 47, at 1297 et seq. who, however, after due consideration of the arguments that have been brought up in literature, favours the static approach: 'As a consequence, a change in domestic law [...] cannot resort any effect for the purposes of interpreting an undefined treaty term.'
207. Supreme Court of Canada, *The Queen v. Melford Developments, Inc.*, 1982 DTC 6281, 6285. *See*, for an overview, Manfred Mössner, *Zur Auslegung von Dopelbesteuerungsabkommen*, *supra* n. 120, at 407 et seq. *See also* Vogel, *Doppelbesteuerungsabkommen und ihre Auslegung (II)*, *supra* n. 120, at 296.
208. *See* Jean-Marc Déry & David A. Ward, *National Report: Canada, in Interpretation of Double Taxation Conventions* 264 et seq. (IFA ed., 1993).
209. *See* Lang, *Die Bedeutung des originär innerstaatlichen Rechts für die Auslegung von Doppelbesteuerungsabkommen (Art. 3 Abs. 2 OECD-MA)*, *supra* n. 41, at 290 et seq.
210. *See* Lang, *DBA und Personengesellschaften: Grundfragen der Abkommensauslegung*, 16 IStR, *supra* n. 55, at 606 et seq. who discusses the similar situation of changes in the OECD Commentary that are labelled as being merely clarifying.
211. *See ibid.*
212. *See ibid.*
213. Verwaltungsgerichtshof 19 December 2006, 2005/15/0158. *See*, for an overview on the case, Michael Lang, *Die Maßgeblichkeit des innerstaatlichen Rechts für die DBA-Auslegung in der jüngsten Rechtsprechung des VwGH*, 17 S.W.I. 202 et seq. (2007). *See also* Lang, *Art. 3 Abs. 2 OECD-MA und die Auslegung von Doppelbesteuerungsabkommen*, *supra* n. 19, at 291 et seq.

9 CONCLUDING REMARKS

The preceding remarks have highlighted several problems arising from the possibility of recourse to domestic law under Article 3(2) OECD MC. One question remains: What would be the consequences if it were simply deleted? As has been shown, Article 3(2) OECD MC serves a purpose insofar as confirming that an interpretation based on the context means one based on the VCLT and, therefore, it is one based on the general interpretation principles that have been codified in its Articles 31-33. The provision also allows placing less emphasis or even excluding subsequent agreements and practice. However, in light of all the interpretation issues caused by Article 3(2) OECD MC, it would be better to delete this provision from the OECD MC.[214] The legal situation would not really be different as all of the means of interpretation would still have to be taken into account, the meaning of a provision would have to be determined in an autonomous way, not being unnecessarily influenced by domestic law, and being cautious about taking subsequent agreements and subsequent practice into consideration.

214. This was already suggested by Vogel & Prokisch, *supra* n. 5, at 84.

www.ingramcontent.com/pod-product-compliance
Lightning Source LLC
Chambersburg PA
CBHW071240230926
51849CB00001B/166
9789403544885